A *Variorum* *Commentary* *on*

the *Poems* *of* *John* *Milton*

MERRITT Y. HUGHES

General Editor

THE COMPLETE SERIES

Volume I

The Latin and Greek Poems
    Douglas Bush

The Italian Poems
    J. E. Shaw and A. Bartlett Giamatti

Volume II

The Minor English Poems
    A. S. P. Woodhouse and Douglas Bush

Volume III

Paradise Lost
    Merritt Y. Hughes

Volume IV

Paradise Regained
    Walter MacKellar

Volume V

Samson Agonistes
    William R. Parker and John M. Steadman

Volume VI

The Prosody of the English Poems
    Edward R. Weismiller

A Variorum Commentary on

The Poems of John Milton

Volume Two

THE MINOR ENGLISH POEMS

A. S. P. WOODHOUSE *and* DOUGLAS BUSH

Part Three

With a review of Studies of Verse Form by
EDWARD R. WEISMILLER

London
ROUTLEDGE & KEGAN PAUL

First published 1972
by Routledge & Kegan Paul Ltd
Broadway House, 68–74 Carter Lane
London, E.C.4
Printed in Great Britain
at the University Printing House, Cambridge
(Brooke Crutchley, University Printer)
© Columbia University Press 1972
ISBN 0 7100 7193 0

Publication of this VARIORUM COMMENTARY
ON THE POEMS OF JOHN MILTON was made possible by funds granted by the Carnegie Corporation
of New York. That Corporation is not, however,
the author, owner, publisher, or proprietor of this
publication, and is not to be understood as
approving by virtue of its grant any of the statements made or views expressed therein.

Contents

ABBREVIATIONS FOR THE TITLES
OF MILTON'S WRITINGS

Variorum *Commentary*		Columbia *Works*
Acced	Accedence Commenc't Grammar	G
AddCM	Additional Correspondence and Marginalia	ACM
AddCorr	Additional Correspondence	AC
Animad	Animadversions upon the Remonstrants Defence	A
Apol	An Apology against a Pamphlet	AP
Arc	Arcades	ARC
Areop	Areopagitica	AR
Asclep	'Asclepiads' (called 'Choriambics,' *Works* 1, 327)	
BrNotes	Brief Notes upon a late Sermon	BN or N
Bucer	The Judgement of Martin Bucer, concerning Divorce	M
CarEl	Carmina Elegiaca	CE
Carrier 1, 2	On the University Carrier; Another on the same	UC
CharLP	Milton's Character of the Long Parliament	TC
Circum	Upon the Circumcision	CI
CivP	A Treatise of Civil power	CP
Colas	Colasterion	C
ComBk	Commonplace Book	CB
Comus	Comus	CO
DDD	The Doctrine and Discipline of Divorce	*D. and D.*

Abbreviations: Titles of Milton's Writings

Variorum Commentary		Columbia Works
DecDut	Declaration against the Dutch	DEC
Def 1	Pro Populo Anglicano Defensio (First Defence of the English People)	1D
Def 2	Pro Populo Anglicano Defensio Secunda (Second Defence)	2D
Defpro Se	Pro Se Defensio	SD
DocCh	De Doctrina Christiana	CD
EC	English Correspondence	EC
Educ	Of Education	E
EffSc	In Effigiei Eius Sculptorem	IEE
Eikon	Eikonoklastes	K
El 1, &c.	Elegia 1, &c.	EL
Eli	In obitum Praesulis Eliensis	PE
EpDam	Epitaphium Damonis	ED
Epistol	Familiar Letters of Milton	FE
EProl	Early Prolusion by Milton	EP
EpWin	Epitaph on the Marchioness of Winchester	EM
FInf	On the Death of a fair Infant	I
Hirelings	Considerations touching The likeliest means to remove Hirelings out of the church	H
HistBr	History of Britain	B
HistMosc	Brief History of Moscovia	HM
Hor	Fifth Ode of Horace	HOR
Idea	De Idea Platonica	IPA
IlPen	Il Penseroso	IP

Abbreviations: Titles of Milton's Writings

Variorum Commentary		Columbia Works
InvBom	In inventorem Bombardae	IB
L'All	L'Allegro	L'A
Leon 1, &c.	Ad Leonoram Romae canentem	LR
LetFr	Letter to a Friend	LF
LetMonk	Letter to General Monk	LM
LetPat	A Declaration or Letters Patents of the Election of this Present King of Poland	LP
Log	Art of Logic	LO
Lyc	Lycidas	L
Mansus	Mansus	MA
Mar	Marginalia	MAR
May	Song. On May Morning	MM
MC	Miscellaneous Correspondence	MC
Nat	On the Morning of Christ's Nativity	N
Naturam	Naturam non pati senium	NS
NewF	On the new forcers of Conscience	FC
OAP	Observations on the Articles of Peace	O
Passion	The Passion	PA
Patrem	Ad Patrem	ADP
PE	Of Prelatical Episcopacy	P
PhilReg	Philosophus ad Regem	PAR
PL	Paradise Lost	PL
PR	Paradise Regain'd	PR
Procan	In obitum Procancellarii medici	PM
ProdBom 1, &c.	In Proditionem Bombardicam 1, &c.	PB

Abbreviations: Titles of Milton's Writings

Variorum Commentary		Columbia Works
Prol 1, &c.	Prolusions 1, &c.	PO
Propos	Proposalls of Certaine Expedients for the Preventing of a Civill War Now Feard	PRO
Ps 1, &c.	Psalms 1, &c.	PS
QNov	In quintum Novembris	QN
RCG	The Reason of Church-governement Urg'd against Prelaty	CG
Ref	Of Reformation Touching Church-Discipline in England	R
REW	The Readie & Easie Way to Establish a Free Commonwealth	W
Rous	Ad Joannem Rousium	JR
RH	Apologus de Rustico et Hero	RH
SA	Samson Agonistes	SA
Salmas 1, &c.	On Salmasius 1, &c.	
Sals	Ad Salsillum poetam Romanum	AS
Shak	On Shakespear. 1630	SH
SolMus	At a solemn Musick	SM
Sonn 1, &c.	Sonnet 1, &c.	S
Tetr	Tetrachordon	T
Time	On Time	TI
TKM	The Tenure of Kings and Magistrates	TE
TR	Of True Religion, Haeresie, Schism, Toleration	TR
Vac	At a Vacation Exercise in the Colledge	V

ABBREVIATIONS FOR TITLES OF
PERIODICALS, ETC.

AJP	*American Journal of Philology*
AN&Q	*American Notes and Queries*
CL	*Comparative Literature*
ELH	*Journal of English Literary History*
ELN	*English Language Notes*
ES	*English Studies*
Essays and Studies	*Essays and Studies by Members of the English Association*
Explic.	*The Explicator*
Facs.	Vol. I of H. F. Fletcher's facsimile ed. (see Index, under Milton)
HLQ	*Huntington Library Quarterly*
JEGP	*Journal of English and Germanic Philology*
JHI	*Journal of the History of Ideas*
JWCI	*Journal of the Warburg and Courtauld Institutes*
MiltonN	*Milton Newsletter* (1970 f., *Milton Quarterly*)
MLN	*Modern Language Notes*
MLQ	*Modern Language Quarterly*
MLR	*Modern Language Review*
MP	*Modern Philology*
N&Q	*Notes and Queries*
PBSA	*Papers of the Bibliographical Society of America*
PMLA	*Publications of the Modern Language Association of America*
PQ	*Philological Quarterly*
RES	*Review of English Studies*
SCN	*Seventeenth-Century News*
SEL	*Studies in English Literature*
SB	*Studies in Bibliography*
SP	*Studies in Philology*
TLS	[London] *Times Literary Supplement*
TSLL	*Texas Studies in Literature and Language*
UTQ	*University of Toronto Quarterly*
V.C.	*Variorum Commentary*

A Mask Presented At Ludlow-Castle, 1634 [Comus]

I. DATE, CIRCUMSTANCES, AND TEXT [D.B.]

While the date of *Arcades* remains conjectural, we have the solid fact that *A Mask* was acted on 29 September 1634, at Ludlow Castle in Shropshire. The performance was a part of the inaugural festivities for the Earl of Bridgewater, the new Lord President of Wales. The Earl was both the stepson and the son-in-law of the Countess Dowager of Derby, and it was presumably the success of *Arcades*, which had been written for her, that led to Milton's second and larger commission; and the main agent would again be Henry Lawes, who produced *A Mask*, composed music for the songs, played the role of the Attendant Spirit, and in 1637-8 published the text. Although such an occasion would bring in a much larger audience than *Arcades*, the later masque was still in some sense a family affair. The parts of the Lady and the two Brothers were taken by the Earl's children, Lady Alice Egerton, Viscount Brackley, and Thomas Egerton, aged fifteen, eleven, and nine respectively; all three had already had experience in court masques. Milton's plot concerned the family, since the children were supposedly on their way to Ludlow to join their parents and share in the celebration—a reminder that characters in a masque might have a dual role, as characters in a fable and as themselves. We do not know who played Sabrina and Comus —perhaps paid professionals (for suggestions about Sabrina see below,

889–900 n.). Parker (142) finds it 'difficult to avoid the conjecture that Milton may have played Comus himself'—a conjecture others may find it difficult to entertain. He argues, logically, that the actor could not have been of noble birth, since such a person would not have been omitted from the list of names in the editions of 1637 and 1645. If he were a fellow musician of Lawes, 'at least one song would have been written for him'—though he does have a virtual song (below, 93–144 n.). The employment of a professional actor, Parker thinks, would have contravened the spirit of a family occasion.

The performance of the masque on 'Michaelmasse night' (title page of 1637) leads J. G. Taaffe (*ELN* 6, 1968–9, 257–62) to point out more than one kind of significance attached to the Feast of St Michael and All Angels. It was a day for paying rent and—a fact of more public importance—it was the day for civic elections and for officials to take office for the coming year. The Anglican Collect for the day 'celebrates that hierarchy which exists among earthly and heavenly guardians.' Michaelmas had also a related but very different tradition, a brief interlude of 'misrule' between the outgoing officials' resignation of authority and their successors' assumption of it—what at Kidderminster, less than thirty miles away, was celebrated as the 'lawless hour.' Such traditions suggest a familiar and appropriate background for Milton's depiction of both order and disorder.

The script, as given in the Bridgewater MS., was 115 lines shorter than the text we read (Darbishire, 2, 336–7; Parker, 793, n. 48), and the epilogue, in briefer form, served as a prologue: details are recorded below in the notes, e.g., on '1st Direction' and lines 194–224, 736–54, 778–805, 987, 996, 999–1010. Some conjectures about stage settings and business are also given at significant points. Milton—now, we may remember, aged 25—would no doubt have spent much of the summer and perhaps spring in writing so elaborate a work, and composition would have entailed some adapting of his ideas to suit the experienced Lawes. We may remember also that the wholly illogical title *Comus* was not Milton's; it was used by John Toland in 1698 and Elijah Fenton in 1725, and soon became established for theatrical convenience (see the end of II below, and Parker, 789, n. 2); it was then carried over into literary usage.

Some further particulars about the MSS. and early editions are given at the beginning of the Notes in v below.

J. T. Shawcross ('Certain Relationships of the Manuscripts of *Comus*,' *PBSA* 54, 1960, 38–56, 293–4) makes a 'fresh examination of the alterations and variants in the text' which 'suggests (1) that the Bridgewater MS was derived from a copy of the Trinity MS text during its development into the version which we now know; (2) that the manuscripts of the songs written by Henry Lawes which are extant do not proceed from the Bridgewater MS; (3) that the 1637 edition was set from a revised intermediate copy with some corrections and revisions from the Trinity MS; and (4) that the copy used for 1645 derived from the 1637 edition with changes.' Thus 'at least parts of the present version of *Comus* were composed in autumn–winter, 1637–38; the Bridgewater MS was not transcribed until then; the manuscripts of the songs may date before or after that time; and the 1637 edition may actually have been published in 1638, before 15 March.'

Shawcross's evidence is much too minute and complex to be outlined, but some summaries of facts and inferences may be quoted:

The printed editions offer a text which includes lines 357–65 and 779–806 (neither group is actually found in the manuscripts) and the final revisions and augmentations of lines 384–85, of lines 672–705 as recorded on the pasted leaf of the Trinity MS, and of lines 976–1023 on p. 29 of that manuscript [all MS. and printed texts are given in Fletcher, *Facs.* 1]. The Bridgewater MS contains the first version of lines 384–85; lines 672–78, 688–96, 701–5 of the pasted leaf (without a few emendations); the first version of lines 976–1023 as recorded in the Trinity MS on p. 28; and a number of lines of Milton's basic transcription in the Trinity MS which were omitted in the published editions (those after line 409) or deleted before publication (those after 356, 429, 678, and 995). Lines 679–87, added later than lines 672–78, 688–705 to the pasted leaf, are not included in the Bridgewater MS; but the line after 678, 'poore ladie,' which was deleted when lines 679–87 were added, does appear. In addition this version omits lines 188–90, 195–225, 632–37 (636–37 were added after 632–35 and 638 in the Trinity MS), 697–700, 737–55, and 847. The basic form of the poem in the Trinity MS includes the first version of lines 384–85; omitted or deleted material after lines 356, 409, 429, 678, and 995; unrevised material on p. 24; and the ending on p. 28; and does not include lines 357–65, the pasted leaf and the inserted lines 662–66 on p. 23 (first versions of both appear on p. 24), lines 779–806, and the new material on p. 29. (39)

Shawcross's general conclusions are these (52–3):

This new dating (both of the Bridgewater MS and of at least parts of the transcription in the Trinity MS) points to renewed poetic activity in the latter part of 1637, at which time (23 Nov. 1637) Milton wrote to Charles Diodati: 'Do you ask what I am meditating? By the help of Heaven, an immortality of fame. But what am I doing? I am letting my wings grow and preparing to fly; but my Pegasus has not yet feathers enough to soar aloft in the fields of air' (translation by Hanford). Soon afterwards *Lycidas*, which elaborates upon his situation, was completed. Around this same time *Comus* was revised in an attempt to sublimate what Tillyard calls the high and solemn themes of an otherwise academic dispute ['The Action of *Comus*': see below, IV, under 1943]. What may have happened is that Milton, again becoming creatively active in the early fall of 1637, made revisions to *Comus*, allowed the intermediate copy to be made, made additional revisions to *Lycidas* and to *Comus*, and allowed publication of both. Because of the shortness of time involved in this new dating, I suggest, as Miss Darbishire already has in her remarks for the 1953 Milton Society meeting, that *Comus* was published in 1638, possibly between February and 15 Mar. 1637/8. This later publication date may explain why Milton thought that Sir Henry Wotton had not seen his poem before 6 Apr. 1638.

While Shawcross's acute argument may be wholly correct, part of it rests on evidence somewhat less than certain. One may not be quite so confident that (48) 'The evidence of handwriting is conclusive in re-dating parts of the Trinity MS of *Comus* and therefore successive versions based upon those parts. Dated by the change from Greek "ε" to Italian "e," Milton's autograph places certain sections of *Comus* and the Bridgewater MS, which incorporates these sections, around the end of 1637, for the Italian "e" is found frequently in revisions of the Trinity MS of *Comus*. Helen Darbishire has pointed out that Milton was beginning to use the Italian "e" in autograph before the Italian trip, as it appears in *Lycidas*. It is used there only six times, four being in reworked material....'A supposed exception to his normal early practice, 'the existence of one early example of Italian "e" in Milton's signature, as Bachelor of Arts, in the University Subscriptions Book...January 1629,' Shawcross later (293-4) found to have been Sotheby's erroneous reading of a Greek 'ε'—a discovery which, he says, 'further validates' his 'conclusions about the manuscripts of *Comus*.' If Milton had taken up the Italian 'e' before 1637, 'it should be observable in the entries from the Commonplace Book where only the Greek "ε" is found, in more words from *Lycidas*, and in other manuscript materials definitely dated before 1638. The evidence is strong on the side of the conclusion that Milton began to use the Italian "e" in 1637 and that he increased that usage during the early months of 1638.' The 'basic transcription' of *Comus* 'reveals at least two instances of Italian "e"'; but 'in his reworkings of *Comus*, Milton exhibits rather extensive use' of it. 'This increased but inconsistent use would suggest that these revisions were made in late 1637 or early 1638' (49-50).

The words and music of the five songs in *Comus* are reproduced in these works:

(1) *The Mask of Comus: The Poem, Originally called 'A Mask Presented at Ludlow Castle, 1634, &c.,' edited by E. H. Visiak. The Airs of the five Songs reprinted from the Composer's autograph manuscript edited by Hubert J. Foss...* Bloomsbury: The Nonesuch Press, 1937.

(2) *The Masque of Comus*, with a preface by Mark Van Doren (in place of Visiak) and the same preface and musical material from Hubert Foss (New York: The Heritage Press, [1955]). In both these editions, 1937 and 1955, Foss's version of words and music embodies collation of Lawes' manuscript with the version in British Museum Add. MSS. 11518.

(3) Fletcher's Facsimile edition of Milton, the work continually cited in this commentary (1, 340 f.). This version is taken from the British Museum MS. only, the autograph not having been available in war-time.

(4) J. S. Diekhoff, ed., *A Maske at Ludlow: Essays on Milton's Comus* (Cleveland, 1968), 241 f. This version is the one prepared by Foss.

A few remarks may be quoted from Foss's preface. 'Lawes was hardly an innovator, but he made a progressive contribution to music in adapting the free rhythms of the madrigalists to the more set and barred rhythms of the operatic style which was then coming in. He wanted to set "words with just note and accent", and in this he succeeded.' Foss thinks the first song, *Sweet Echo* (229–42), 'a very beautiful work, and separated from the other four songs by a great gulf,' the other four being 'of more conventional and historic interest.'[1] There is general discussion of Lawes as a composer in the commentary above on *Sonnet* 13.

II. *Comus* AND THE MASQUE[1]

The common judgment that *Comus* is not a true masque may be represented by a few witnesses from the list below. H. A. Evans remarks that a 'comparison with any one of Jonson's masques...makes this clear at a glance' (*English Masques*, xxxiii, n. 2). Sir W. W. Greg finds that its elaborate action places *Comus* rather in the category of drama (*Pastoral*

---

[1] The music for the songs in *Comus* is minutely examined by J. T. Shawcross ('Henry Lawes's Settings of Songs for Milton's "Comus,"' *Journal of the Rutgers University Library* 28, 1964–5, 22–8). He concludes 'that the extant music, at best, only approximates the earliest songs and is probably incomplete....Perhaps most directly significant...is the underscoring of Milton's frequent changing of text and apparent lack of satisfaction with his earlier work. When he goes so far as to alter that which had been set to music, music being an integral part of a mask, we may be assured that his approach to this mask (now really poem rather than dramatic work) and its thesis had altered in some way.'

[1] [Some accounts of the masque, and some of Jonson's work, are these: Herbert A. Evans, ed., *English Masques* (London, 1897; repr. 1906); W. W. Greg, *Pastoral Poetry & Pastoral Drama* (London, 1906); Paul Reyher, *Les Masques Anglais* (Paris, 1909); Mary Sullivan, *Court Masques of James I* (New York, 1913); E. K. Chambers, 'The Mask,' *The Elizabethan Stage* (Oxford, 1923), I, 149–212; C. H. Herford and P. and E. M. Simpson, eds., *Ben Jonson* (11 v., Oxford, 1925–52); Enid Welsford, *The Court Masque* (Cambridge, 1927); Edward J. Dent, *Foundations of English Opera: A Study of Musical Drama in England during the Seventeenth Century* (Cambridge, 1928); A. Nicoll, *Stuart Masques and the Renaissance Stage* (London, 1937); Gerald E. Bentley, *The Jacobean and Caroline Stage* (7 v., Oxford, 1941–68); Allan H. Gilbert, *The Symbolic Persons in the Masques of Ben Jonson* (Durham, N.C., 1948); W. T. Furniss, 'Ben Jonson's Masques,' pp. 89–179 in Richard B. Young et al., *Three Studies in the Renaissance* (New Haven, 1958); Stephen Orgel, *The Jonsonian Masque* (Cambridge, Mass., 1965), and the introduction to his edition, *Ben Jonson: The Complete Masques* (New Haven and London, 1969); John C. Meagher, *Method and Meaning in Jonson's Masques* (Notre Dame, Ind., 1966); T. J. B. Spencer et al., *A Book of Masques* (Cambridge, 1967: cited hereafter as Spencer); John G. Demaray, *Milton and the Masque Tradition* (Cambridge, Mass., 1968: cited hereafter as *Masque Tradition*).]

Poetry, 399). C. H. Herford affirms that 'The noble poetry of *Comus* only accentuates the perishable quality of the Masque-form which it transgresses or ignores' (*Ben Jonson* 2, 250). Enid Welsford (*The Court Masque*) objects to the doctrine and whole overt tendency of *Comus* as running counter to the spirit and tradition of the masque (according to her own highly metaphysical conception of the genre). E. J. Dent asserts that *Comus*, 'the most celebrated of the masques,' 'entirely disregards the conventional masque form, and has no bearing on the development of English opera' (*Foundations of English Opera*, 38). Partly similar objections have been lodged by a few more recent critics. For the moment, it is enough to recall that in the editions for which they were respectively responsible Lawes and Milton entitled the work *A Maske* (or *Mask*), which seems to determine conclusively that in intention and, as was then thought in result, *Comus* was indeed a masque; and that view is not qualified by the fact that Lawes in his dedication (1637) spoke of 'This Poem,' and that Sir Henry Wotton called it 'a dainty peece of entertainment.'[2] In short, while the reader's judgment may or may not agree with Milton's, there is no escaping the obligation to read *Comus* in relation to the masque form. All that is relevant for that purpose may be discerned in the Stuart masques and above all in the practice of Ben Jonson. Certain facts are of paramount importance: the masque was the peculiar possession of the court and aristocracy; it was a dramatic form, but the element of drama was subordinated at once to the purpose of social entertainment, culminating in the dance, and to the purpose of elaborate compliment. To these facts all the features of the genre may be directly or indirectly traced.

The structural principle of the masque is found in the necessity of getting the dancers into position and bringing the complimenters to the complimented. It is therefore essentially processional: witness James Shirley's elaborate *Triumph of Peace* (1634), in which the procession actually starts at Ely and Hatton Houses and proceeds to the Banqueting House at Whitehall, where the masque is to be performed. This general

---

[2] In the MS. Milton himself at first described *Arcades* as 'Part of a maske' and changed the phrase later to 'Part of an Entertainment' (*Works* 1, 452; *Facs.* 384).

fact Milton clearly grasped, since in the rudimentary *Arcades* dialogue and songs occur on the way to complimenting the Dowager Countess of Derby; and in *Comus* the action occurs on—one might almost say, is— a journey to Ludlow, a journey which is made to bear its symbolic significance. Yet if the masque is to fulfil its purpose of social entertainment and provide occasion for the various features to be noted below, it cannot be a simple procession. (In *The Triumph of Peace* it ceases to be that as soon as Whitehall is reached.) It is best defined, then, as an artistically retarded procession, culminating in elaborate compliment and ceremonial dance, which in turn may usher in an evening of dancing.

Miss Welsford (*Court Masque*, 320–1, 397 f.) has read deep significance into the central place of the dance. Hymen, she declares, is the patron deity of the masque, and the marriage masque, in which he often figures (cf. *L'All* 125 and n.), she tacitly accepts as the controlling norm of the genre. Thus the masque expresses the spontaneous forces of life and love, youth and spring, but these forces are brought into order and harmony by Hymen, the god of marriage, and of more than marriage, of the social bond in all its forms; it is these forces, thus reduced to order and harmony, that are symbolized in the dance. Hence the only moral the true masque can convey, the one that consciously or unconsciously it always does convey, is the identification of goodness 'with harmony, order, and at bottom with self-expressive love,' a moral in which 'there is no real contradiction between Hymen as the leader of the Dance of Youth, and Hymen as the Good Principle of the Universe, the vanquisher of all the forces of unreason and unrest' (320). That Hymen is the patron of the genre, and that the marriage masque (instead of being merely one rather common subdivision) is the controlling norm, remain unverifiable assumptions; and the profundities of Miss Welsford's interpretation seem oddly at variance with the superficial and sophisticated tone of most of the Stuart masques except *Comus*. Milton's moral (as she understands it) Miss Welsford utterly repudiates as the very antithesis of all that the masque should mean. We return to the prosaic fact that the dance is central to the masque as social entertainment, and that in one way or another the action must culminate in the ceremonial dance.

Miss Welsford is not alone in finding that in *Comus* the dance receives little emphasis and can scarcely be regarded as the culmination of the action, although Milton, we remember, is at pains to present it as a dance of triumph 'O're sensual Folly, and Intemperance' (973–4).

In the court masques dances were also interspersed. They were of two kinds: 'stately figure dances performed by the masquers alone...and commonly distinguished as the Entry, the Main, and the Going-out'; and the livelier Revels, 'danced by the masquers with partners of the opposite sex chosen from the audience,' which 'took place after the Main, and were doubtless often kept up for a considerable time' (Evans, xxxiv). In such interspersed dances *Comus* is entirely lacking, except for the entry of Comus and his rout of monsters, and that belongs rather to the tradition of the antimasque. For the rest, what dances there are are concentrated at the end. In comparison with most printed masques, *Comus* is niggardly of directions or descriptions, and we have no way of telling whether the final dance—call it the Main or the Going-out—was danced by the Attendant Spirit and the Lady and the two Brothers (a small and ill-balanced group compared with the usual eight, twelve, or sixteen), or whether, as seems more likely, the number was augmented and balance attained.

Considered as compliment, the masque fulfilled its function in two ways: first, by being presented in honour of some person or persons (in marriage masques, the newly united pair; in the court masques, most commonly the sovereign and his consort; in *Comus*, the Earl and Countess of Bridgewater); and, secondly, by including speeches of high-flown compliment, not to say fulsome flattery (see the gibes in Beaumont and Fletcher, *The Maid's Tragedy* I. I. 6–11). This Milton omits, relying on the virtue of the children as the best testimony to that of the parents. Somewhat earlier Ben Jonson had shown rare skill in combining compliment to the sovereign with enforcement of his moral theme, as in *Pleasure reconcild to Vertue* (1618), where the happy union of the two under the presiding rule of Virtue is presented as characteristic of James's reign.

Compliment and formal dance alike mark the masque as the possession of the court and the nobility; and with this fact may be associated the courtly tone of the genre, which in Stuart times isolated it from the more popular forms of literature and entertainment and from the surging currents of the nation's life. In Shirley's *Triumph of Peace* the isolation is underlined in the comic antimasque of the artisans and wives who invade the scene to stare and wonder at the entertainment of the privileged, which they have helped to prepare. This isolation is only revealed in another form in Davenant's more serious concern with the state of the nation in *Salmacida Spolia* (1640), so suggestive of the opening chapters of Clarendon's *History*. *Comus*, of course, was not written for the court and does not manifest this isolation. Indeed, remembering the Lady's comment on 'lewdly-pamper'd Luxury' (767–72) and her assertion (rendered ironical by the event) that 'courtiesie...oft is sooner found in lowly sheds...then in...Courts of Princes' (321–4), we may be disposed to deny its courtly and aristocratic tone; but, in view of the identity of the chief actors, who appear in their own persons, of the gallant and chivalrous bearing of the Brothers, and the high-bred fortitude of the Lady, this would clearly be a mistake. *Comus* is evidently, if unobtrusively, aristocratic poetry; and this is important because the aristocratic and chivalric note makes its contribution to the romanticism of the masque.

As a dramatic form, the masque presents persons and a thread of action, however tenuous. Sometimes the story comes from classic myth, as in William Browne's *Inner Temple Masque* (1615), which utilizes the Homeric episode of Ulysses and Circe. More often the fiction is invented to suit the occasion, the theme to be developed, and the compliment to be paid. In his various inventions Ben Jonson shows much ingenuity; for example, in *Pleasure* (the masque most interesting for comparison with *Comus*) the action, though slight, bears steadily on his theme. Still more ingenious, though directed wholly to compliment and entertainment, is Carew's *Coelum Britannicum* (1634), in which Jove, impressed by the marital fidelity and felicity of Charles and Henrietta Maria, determines to reform, and to this end despatches Mercury as his ambassador to the happy pair. Often, however, the desire for spectacle and variety reduces the masque to a series of disconnected scenes, notably in *The Triumph of Peace*. In *Comus* the action is fuller and more highly

744

unified than in almost any other example, and it is this that has led to the opinion that the piece approximates rather to allegorical drama than to the masque proper.

We should remember, though, that the masque was in its own age less sharply defined than we are sometimes prone to imagine, as E. Haun reminds us ('An Inquiry into the Genre of *Comus*,' *Essays in Honor of Walter Clyde Curry*, Nashville, 1954, 221–39); and Evans finds three by Jonson 'to which the application of the word is not warranted by their contents' (xxxiii–iv, n. 2). The border line between masque and romantic comedy was vague, and no one can tell the precise degree of attenuation necessary to turn *A Midsummer Night's Dream* or *The Tempest* into a masque, or at least a masque-like entertainment. Further, the masque was the forerunner of light opera, the form in which it was to re-emerge after the Restoration, and already in Milton's day this development had begun in Italy (see G. L. Finney in III below).

Returning to the masque proper, we may briefly note its other features and ask how far they are represented in *Comus*. In the number of his masquers and the role assigned to them Milton departs radically from current practice. Normally the masquers, from eight to sixteen in number, were seen and not heard, and the speeches and songs were assigned to paid actors. If we regard the persons playing the Attendant Spirit (that is, Lawes) and Comus [and Sabrina?] as belonging to the latter category, and the Lady and her two Brothers as the masquers, Milton's departure immediately becomes apparent, even if we suppose the number to have been increased for the final dance.

In *Comus* the claims of music and song are met, and the common opinion that 'the musical element throughout is entirely subordinate' (Evans, *Masques*, xxxiii, n. 2) can only be referred to the preponderance of the dramatic element: dialogue and debate, while recognized features of the masque, are nowhere else so fully exploited and with such steady purpose.[3] To music and song was added what may be called 'contained'

---

[3] W. M. Evans (*Henry Lawes*, 1941, 79) suggests that for the large role given to the speeches Milton and Lawes had a precedent in *Coelum Britannicum*, in which Lawes was associated with Carew [this last point is questionable: see below, III. 3].

poetry, an element in which *Comus* is obviously rich enough to furnish forth dozens of court masques. In them the poetry is largely confined to the lyrics; in *Comus* it extends to monologues, dialogue, and debate, and incidentally makes good whatever deficiency (by contemporary standards) there may have been in scenic effects. *Comus* appeals to the imagination by the ear more than by the eye; and the persistent impression that it was designed for open-air presentation is testimony to the power of poetry to call up a scene, much in the manner of Shakespeare.

Spectacle was a legitimate but, in Jonson's view, an encroaching element in the court masques: we remember his *Expostulation with Inigo Jones* and its ironic 'Painting & Carpentry are yᵉ Soule of Masque' (*Ben Jonson* 8, 404). It is not clear how elaborate the settings were for *Comus*, since, as we have observed, the 'directions' are much more meagre than is common in printed masques, or how much the apparent simplicity was due to the wishes of Milton and Lawes, and how much to the impossibility, in Shropshire, of elaborate staging. But it is at least evident that there are none of those surprising effects wrought by machinery which are commented on in such masques as *Coelum Britannicum* and Townshend's *Tempe Restord*. There were, however, three settings: 'The first Scene discovers a wilde Wood'; 'The Scene changes to a stately Palace, set out with all manner of deliciousness: soft Musick, Tables spred with all dainties'; 'The Scene changes, presenting Ludlow Town and the Presidents Castle....' None of these would present very much difficulty.[4] And each of them is closely related to the action and has its own symbolic value.

[4] From the word 'discovers' Allardyce Nicoll (*Stuart Masques*, 104–5) infers the presence of a curtain and suggests that for the rest 'back-shutters' would suffice, with or without the addition of 'side-wings,' while the final scene would be a perspective, inspired by those at Whitehall of London houses. We may add that the words 'descends or enters' suggest some doubt whether the requisite 'machine' would be available (see v below, n. on first Direction). The only problem connected with the rising of Sabrina and her nymphs lies in the fact that no indication is given of a change of scene from the Palace of Comus: one may reasonably infer that the Palace is open to view and that the debate of Comus and the Lady is conducted before it. Then the hollow from which Sabrina rises could be without and forward and on one side of the Palace.

[The probable manner in which *Comus* was staged—presumably in the Great Hall of Ludlow Castle—is discussed, e.g. by W. M. Evans (*Henry Lawes*, 100–6), M. Nicolson

Against another developing feature of the masque, the antimasque, Jonson manifested no such hostility and he eagerly advanced it by his experiments.[5] In the *Masque of Queenes* (1609) he provided twelve hags, marshalled by their dame, as 'a foyle, or false-Masque' to contrast with the twelve queens whose virtues are celebrated by Fame. Contrast is the note of the antimasque: its figures are often ugly or grotesque, drawn from low life, and presented with a degree of realism, as a foil to the solemnity, beauty, and aristocratic idealism of the main masque. In the *Masque of Queenes* the antimasque, after its fantastic dance, disappears at the approach of Heroic Virtue ushering in the main masque; but in later examples the antimasque is sometimes expanded into a scene of low comedy, as in *For the Honour of Wales*, provided as an additional anti-masque to introduce the revived *Pleasure* (which already has its anti-masque centred on the figure of Comus), or as in the antimasques of *Oberon* (1611) or *The Masque of Augures* (1622); and *The Triumph of Peace* provided a whole series of antimasques. In *Comus* the antimasque is represented by the rout of monsters and their leader, but Milton characteristically integrates it in his theme and action. So complete indeed is the integration, and so far does Comus transcend the role of leader of the antimasque, that the poet provides a second example in the 'Countrey-Dancers' whose antics precede the final dance of 'Court guise' and are cut short by the Attendant Spirit.

Something must be said about what was referred to above as the romanticism of the masque. The masque belongs to a gracious world of make-believe, and stands at a far remove from common life, which intrudes, if at all, only in the antimasque and as a foil, usually with comic

(*John Milton*, 69–73), and most fully by J. G. Demaray (*Masque Tradition*, 74 f., 97–121), who takes account of Miss Evans' views and of some pages in James Arnold's unpublished thesis on *Comus* (Princeton, 1951). Demaray suggests (101, etc.) that antimasque costumes, beast heads, and other accessories 'may have been borrowed from Sir Henry Herbert's revels storeroom' in London, as properties had been in 1602 for 'The Entertainment of Queen Elizabeth at Harefield.']

[5] ['*Hymenaei* (1606) established the pattern for Jonson's later works by introducing a grotesque dance balanced against a final figured dance. Jonson repeated this experiment in *The Haddington Masque* (1608) and then became fully aware of the aesthetic implications of this arrangement of dances in *The Masque of Queenes*.' (Demaray, *Masque Tradition*, 18)]

effect. The elements that go to produce this world of make-believe are diverse, and not all of them, of course, are found in every masque; but a representative selection can be readily made. Most important perhaps is the ideal code of manners—and, wherever morality obtrudes, of morals—which pervades the masque: a code which descended from medieval chivalry through the Renaissance ideal of the courtier. Sometimes the chivalric note is specific, as in Jonson's *Speeches at Prince Henries Barriers* (1610) and *Oberon* (1611); more often the note of chivalry is merely suggested. Combined with it is a marked infusion of the idyllic. Although, as Greg observed (378), the English masque offers surprisingly few examples of strictly pastoral subjects, a subdued pastoral strain is sometimes present, as it clearly is in *Comus*, and the suggestions of natural setting, which are frequent in the masques, are predominantly Arcadian. Other forms of the idyllic, and notably the idea of the Golden Age Restored (to use the title of Jonson's masque of 1615) also appear. Nor is the suggestion of the idyllic confined to Pan and the shepherds or to the myth of the Golden Age; it colours much of the moralized allusion to classic myth in which the masques abound, and such allusion merges rapidly with allegory and the train of personified qualities. In *Comus* we observe, in addition to the characteristic Miltonic wealth of allusion, a free adaptation of classic myth—really a making of new myth—more suggestive of Spenser than of any contemporary writer of masques; this is indeed one of the distinctive achievements of *Comus*. Milton's natural affinity with Spenser was recognized by his publisher Humphrey Moseley in 1645 and by Milton himself when, much later, he said to Dryden that he was Spenser's poetic son, and this affinity received some support from the form he was here using. For the world of the masque was in one view an inheritance from Spenser's land of Faerie: or rather, some of the rich and diverse elements of his poem may be recognized in the fragile and artificial structure of the masque. In the *Faerie Queene* the genius of the poet can induce a willing suspension of disbelief in his romance. Only by *Comus* perhaps is this effect achieved in the masque, or even aimed at. For the effect is foreign to a genre whose note is the sophisticated, if less intense, pleasure of a self-conscious romanticism that holds reality at arm's length. [On Spenser and *Comus* see III. 4 below.]

In *Comus* the theme at least is intended to be taken with entire seriousness, and that theme, if modern criticism is on the right track, is less simple than the obtrusive moral found by the older critics. The question naturally arises as to what precedent existed for embodying in the masque ethical doctrine of any kind. Even the literature of pure entertainment was more or less subject to the all but universal principle that the end of poetry was delightful teaching. In introducing the *Masque of Queenes* Jonson reiterated the principle, 'observing that rule of the best Artist [Horace], to suffer no object of delight to passe w'thout his mixture of profit, & example' (*Ben Jonson* 7, 282). And in the preface to *Hymenaei* he contrasted the permanent value of the inner meaning with the temporary delight of the outward spectacle (ibid. 7, 209):

It is a noble and just advantage, that the things subjected to understanding have of those which are objected to sense, that the one sort are but momentarie, and meerely taking; the other impressing, and lasting: Else the glorie of all these solemnities had perish'd like a blaze, and gone out, in the beholders eyes. So short-liv'd are the bodies of all things, in comparison of their soules.... This it is hath made the most royall Princes, and greatest persons (who are commonly the personaters of these actions) not onely studious of riches, and magnificence in the outward celebration, or shew; (which rightly becomes them) but curious after the most high, and heartie inventions, to furnish the inward parts: (and those grounded upon antiquitie, and solide learnings) which, though their voyce be taught to sound to present occasions, their sense, or doth, or should alwayes lay hold on more remov'd mysteries.

Jonson showed no little skill in combining doctrine not only with entertainment but with compliment; that is, in making his compliment the attribution of the virtue the piece expounded. But doctrine had always to be accommodated to entertainment and compliment; and in other poets, in whom the courtier predominated over the moralist, the theme was completely subordinated, as in Carew's light-hearted *Coelum Britannicum*. Or austere morality might be gently and elegantly flouted, as in Browne's charming *Inner Temple Masque*, which altogether divests the myth of

Circe of the cautionary quality that allegorical tradition had imposed upon it (*Poems*, ed. Goodwin, 2, 175; Spencer, *Masques*, 190):

> What sing the sweet birds in each grove?
> Nought but love.
> What sound our echoes day and night?
> All delight.
> What doth each wind breathe as it fleets?
> Endless sweets.

There is no hint of Stoic severity, such as Comus—and some critics—condemn in the Lady: the enchantment of beauty, love, and pleasure is freely allowed,

> Here where delight
> Might well allure
> A very Stoic from this night
> To turn an Epicure. (Goodwin, 2, 190; Spencer, 199)

But this sentiment is not to be taken seriously; the moral is attuned to the entertainment, not the entertainment to the moral.

Compliment and entertainment often conceal the affinity of the masque with the moral interlude, an affinity which comes into late evidence in Thomas Nabbes's *Microcosmus. A Morall Maske* (acted and printed, 1637), where the epithet 'Morall' is significant. The title page states that it was 'presented with generall liking, at the private house in Salisbury Court, and heere Set down according to the intention of the Authour.' The masque opens with a macrocosmic setting, in which, on Nature's appeal to Janus, 'The figure of eternall providence,' the warring elements are reduced to order by Love, and then proceeds to the story of Physander, the Microcosmus of the title. Betrothed to Bellanima, he is enticed from her by Malus Genius (with help from the four Humours and the five Senses), delivered over to Sensuality, abandoned by her when his health and fortune are gone, healed by Temperance and Bonus Genius, and, after acquittal before the Court of Conscience, is restored to Bellanima; Love and the Virtues smile upon the union and the Dwellers in Elysium perform their ceremonial dance. This is of

course exceptional, but it reveals a potentiality in the moral masque
which Milton also developed.

We must recognize the occasional presence of ideas of some interest
in masques that do not assert their moral purpose in the title. In *Tempe
Restord* (presented at court and printed in 1632) Aurelian Townshend
handled the myth of Circe in a spirit very different from Browne's.
Circe has usurped the vale of Tempe; one of her victims, restored to
human form, flees to Virtue for protection; smitten by Cupid with love
for her victim, Circe enters in pursuit, attended by a train of Nymphs,
and by her followers, barbarians and others half-transformed to beasts
(who furnish the antimasque); rebuked by Jupiter, and under Cupid's
sway, Circe renounces her evil ways and surrenders her usurped
domain—to the pure and beneficent rule of Heroic Virtue and Beauty,
that is, of Charles and his queen, and thus is Tempe restored. The
'Allegory' is thus explained: the escaped victim is an incontinent man
who, struggling with his affections, is at last persuaded by reason to
fly from those sensual desires which had corrupted his judgment; Circe
signifies desire in general, which sways all living creatures and, being a
mixture of the divine and the sensible, may lead some to virtue, others
to vice. The Nymphs denote the virtues, the beasts the vices. Circe's
beauty and the aspect of her palace show that desire cannot be moved
without the appearance of beauty, true or false. The Nymphs, good spirits
diffused throughout the universe, serve Circe and live with her in all
liberty and pleasure; the flowers they gather for her signify virtues and
sciences by which men are prepared and disposed to good. The beasts
who, contrary to their nature, make her sport, show how sensual desire
causes men to lose virtue and valour and become slaves to their brutish
affections. They invade Tempe, the happy retreat of the Muses and their
followers, and seek to drive out the only true possessors, the lovers of
science and virtue. Rescue is effected by a union of Beauty and Heroic
Virtue, figuring a 'Harmony of the Irascible and concupiscible parts
obedient to the rationall and highest part of the soule,' but not without
'a divine Beame comming from above.' 'In Heiroicke vertue is figured
the Kings Majestie' and in corporeal Beauty the Queen's majesty, which

'may draw us to the contemplation of the Beauty of the soule, unto which it hath Analogy.' (*Aurelian Townshend's Poems and Masks*, ed. E. K. Chambers, Oxford, 1912, 96–9.) [J. G. Demaray (*Masque Tradition*, 78–85) sees *Tempe Restord* as possibly a strong influence on *Comus*: below, III. 3.]

Perhaps more illuminating for comparison and contrast with *Comus* is another embodiment of a humanistic ethic in the main current of the court masque, Jonson's *Pleasure reconcild to Vertue* (1618); it was not well received by its audience. [Here Comus is a belly-god who haunts a grove at the foot of Mount Atlas, the hill of knowledge. He and his followers (the first antimasque) are routed by Hercules; under the eyes of Pleasure and Virtue the hero is invited to rest. After a second anti-masque (of Pigmies), Mercury heralds the arrival of twelve princes who have been bred 'in this rough Mountaine, & neere Atlas head,' and 'are now to profit by the reconciliation of Virtue with Pleasure, and be admitted into the garden of the Hesperides' (*Ben Jonson 2*, 305). The mountain opens and the twelve princes descend to execute the dances and songs that form the main masque. They are led by Daedalus, whose songs expound the union of virtue and pleasure, the toils and rewards of discipline.]

Although *Pleasure* was not printed until 1640, Herford, like some other critics, can say that 'Milton had clearly studied' it. Resemblances cited are few and general.[6] [No doubt the young Milton, when called upon for a masque, would study the available masques by the chief and scholarly practitioner, and the theme of *Pleasure* might have especially attracted him, but it is surely misleading to speak of the masque as Jonson's '*Comus*' (*Ben Jonson 2*, 309).] There is nothing in common between Milton's magician and Jonson's Comus, the gross patron of meat and drink, who disappears with the antimasque; it is in their moral theme that the masques are comparable, for Jonson also confronts 'Vertue, &

---

[6] *Ben Jonson 2*, 307–9 [and E. Welsford, *Court Masque*, 314–23, and Tillyard, 'The Action of *Comus*,' *Studies in Milton* (London, 1951), 95–6]. Herford and Simpson suggest that Milton procured a copy from the Egertons or someone else about the court (*Ben Jonson 10*, 574–5). [See the full analysis of *Pleasure* in S. Orgel, *The Jonsonian Masque* (1965), 150–85; see also G. W. Whiting below (*Comus* III. 3 and IV, under 1958) and Demaray, 87–8.]

hir noted opposite, / Pleasure.' By a skilful use of the idyllic motif, the golden age restored, Jonson combines the enforcement of his moral with compliment to James. Long at odds, Virtue and Pleasure are reconciled in the new golden age; but idyllicism is not allowed to obscure morality. The reconciliation, it is made abundantly clear, is possible only in minds that willingly acquiesce in the primacy of virtue (lines 208-13: *Ben Jonson* 7, 486):

> Theis now she trusts wth Pleasure, & to theis
> She gives an entraunce to the Hesperides,
> Faire Beuties garden[s]: Neither can she feare
> they should grow soft, or wax effeminat here,
> Since in hir sight, & by hir charge all's don,
> Pleasure ye Servant, Vertue looking on.

The votaries of Virtue (who are the masquers) inhabit her sacred mountain, Atlas, from which they descend, 'To walke wth Pleasure, not to dwell'; for 'Theis, theis are howres, by Vertue spar'd' (328-9)—the very thought of Milton, not in *Comus* but in the sonnet to Lawrence. It is upon this note that Jonson introduces the dance. For all the reconciliation achieved, he is not forgetful of the potential and recurrent conflict of 'Vertue, & hir noted opposite, Pleasure,' or of the vigilance required. Thus the masque ends not with compliment but with exhortation:

> She, she it is, in darknes shines,
> 'tis she y^t still hir-self refines,
>   by hir owne light, to everie eye,
> more seene, more knowne, when Vice stands by.
> And though a stranger here on earth,
>   in heaven she hath hir right of birth.
>   There, there is Vertues seat.
> Strive to keepe hir your owne,
>   'tis only she, can make you great,
>   though place, here, make you knowne.

While the ethical theme of *Comus* moves on or to another level, Jonson's simpler moral is no less emphatically presented than Milton's.

Whether it is properly classified as a masque or a masque-like entertainment, *Comus* clearly draws upon all the chief elements of the form and recombines them to advance its own poetic and ethical purpose. It is more heavily freighted with a more complex body of doctrine than any other masque, and to present this Milton resorts to a weightier and more unified action and to more substantial characters than are met with elsewhere. But the comparison of *Comus* to stage drama is, taken by itself, misleading. There is, to repeat an earlier comment, another tradition that goes to its making: Milton recognized and developed the inheritance of the masque from Spenser, and it is to the handling of action, character, and moral in the *Faerie Queene* that *Comus* most closely approximates. Thus the action is, on the literal level, romance and remote from reality, though with its own coherence, but its force and meaning are allegorical; and the characters also are allegorical in the Spenserian mode, which permits a significant if limited degree of individuation. Not that *Comus* exhibits these qualities as fully or successfully as the *Faerie Queene*, but that these are the terms in which it is desirable to read what Lawes was after all right in calling 'This Poem'—the terms in which most of the difficulties that have troubled critics disappear. In addition, then—not contradiction—to its relation to the masque, *Comus* is Spenserian poetry: literal romance, a world of make-believe, embodies a meaning that is real and not remote from life; and the Lady (to take the most crucial example) is, like Una, at once a figure of romance, a personified virtue, and (within the limits imposed by these considerations) a human character.

[It is not a concern of this Commentary to give an account of the fortunes of *Comus* on the stage. In various adaptations it was especially popular during the period 1738–1843; indeed it was through the theatre that the masque acquired in the early 18th century the totally illogical title of *Comus*. Those who want information about this rather odd chapter of Miltonic and theatrical history may find it in Alwin Thaler's 'Milton in the Theatre' (*Shakspere's Silences*, Cambridge, Mass., 1929, 232–56; enlarged from an article in *SP* 17, 1920). Thaler's account has been supplemented by E. C. Peple, 'Notes on Some Productions of *Comus*,' *SP* 36 (1939), 235–42; in regard to quotations drawn in 1761 from Dalton's version of 1738, by Ann Gossman and G. W. Whiting, *RES*

11 (1960), 56–60; and by C. H. Shattuck, 'Macready's *Comus*: A Prompt-Book Study,' *JEGP* 60 (1961), 731–48. Some performances in Edinburgh in 1748–51 are noted by J. McKenzie (*N&Q* 198, 1953, 158–9, and 1, 1954, 199).]

III. SOURCES AND ANALOGUES

The tradition that Milton found his starting point for *Comus* in an actual incident, the separation of Lady Alice from her brothers when overtaken by night in Haywood forest on their way to Ludlow, was sensibly rejected by Masson and others, on the ground that the story of such an adventure is more likely to have been derived from the masque than the masque from the story [cf. Parker, 791, n. 37].

Comus appears to have no single literary source [apart from the basic myth of Circe, given by Homer, Ovid, and others, and variously adapted by Renaissance writers (see M. Y. Hughes, 'Spenser's Acrasia and the Circe of the Renaissance,' *JHI* 4, 1943, 381–99)]. Arguments and suggestions in regard to sources and analogues vary widely in plausibility and importance. These materials are discussed under the following headings: (1) Peele, *The Old Wives' Tale*; (2) Fletcher, *The Faithful Shepherdess*; (3) Masques of Jonson, Browne, Townshend, and Carew; (4) Spenser, *Faerie Queene*; (5) Shakespeare; (6) Italian plays; (7) The figure of Comus; (8) Myths of Circe and Bacchus; (9) Traditional arguments in Comus's plea to the Lady; (10) Traditional arguments in the Lady's reply; (11) Plato, Platonism, and Platonic Love; (12) Christian Elements. A number of these topics of course come up in the criticism summarized in IV below and some of them in the Notes in V.

(1) George Peele, *The Old Wives' Tale* (1595: *Works*, ed. Bullen, 1, 303–47) and related material. Points of similarity in the action were first put forth by Isaac Reed (*Biographia Dramatica*, 1782, 2, 441; cf. Warton and Todd) and somewhat elaborated by Bertha Badt (*Archiv für das Studium der neueren Sprachen* 123, 1909, 305–9). Isolation of such points is bound to exaggerate the impression of similarity, which can be fully corrected only by the reading of Peele's rambling folk-play, but a summary may serve to set the matter in focus.

(1) The first scene is in a dark wood, whence three characters, Antic, Frolic, and Fantastic, are rescued by a rustic, Clunch the Smith, and taken to his cottage to be welcomed by Madge, the old wife who is to tell the tale. No sooner is it begun than action—the play proper—replaces narration. (2) Two Brothers (the time is now day) enter in quest of their sister Delia, and meet an old man, Erestus, who gives them encouraging advice and identifies himself as 'the white bear of England's wood.' He tells them that the 'cursèd sorcerer' Sacrapant has put on him a spell which nightly transforms him to a white bear—this in order to steal from him his wife, Venelia, who, now insane, crosses the scene. Lampriscus enters, to complain of his two daughters, one a handsome shrew, the other so ill-favoured as to make marriage impossible, and is directed to send them to the well for the water of life. (3) Now enter Huanebango 'with his two-hand sword' and Booby (later named Corebus) the Clown, both in quest of the conjurer and in absurd discourse about winning a lady who is in his power. (4) 'Enter Sacrapant in his study.' He tells in soliloquy how he learned from his witch-mother, Meroe, to transform men's shapes, and how, changing himself into a dragon, he stole away the king's daughter Delia to revive himself, since, though young in appearance through his magic, he was really 'aged, crookèd, weak, and numb.' (His acts were done in Thessaly, though the scene is now in England.) Delia enters and demands of the magician 'the best meat from the King of England's table, and the best wine in all France, brought in by the veriest knave in all Spain,' and a Friar brings the required food and drink. (5) The Two Brothers enter (and the magician hurries Delia away). They inquire of her whereabouts and are answered by Echo, whereupon they recall the white bear's counsel, draw swords, and advance. But Sacrapant returns, amid thunder and lightning, and the Brothers are borne away by two Furies to his cell, while the magician soliloquizes for the audience's information: he has given Delia a potion and by his art has 'made her to forget herself'; he is to live and do what he will so long as he preserves a light in a glass (which he exhibits). It can be extinguished only by one who is neither wife, widow, nor maid, and he is 'Never to die but by a dead man's

hand.' He withdraws. (6) Enter, in quest of Delia, 'the Wandering Knight,' Eumenides, with Erestus, who counsels him to give all he has till dead men's bones come at his call; whereupon Erestus leaves, and Eumenides lies down and sleeps. (7) Enter Wiggen, Corebus (see above, 3), Churchwarden, and Sexton, Wiggen demanding the burial of Jack, the others refusing till the fee is paid, which Eumenides, awaking, pays with all he has. (8) Enter Huanebango, followed by Corebus: both are disposed of by Sacrapant, the former carried off by Furies, the latter struck blind. (9) Sacrapant has caused Delia to forget herself and answer to the new name of Berecynthia, and also to forget her Brothers and to ply them with a goad as they dig at his orders in the enchanted ground. They uncover the magic glass, but Delia covers it again. Sacrapant, reentering, bears Delia away. (10) The two daughters of Lampriscus (above, 2) reach the Well of Life, quarrelling and breaking their pitchers. Two Furies carry in the unconscious Huanebango. A Head speaks from the Well. The shrewish sister breaks her second pitcher on the Head. Thunder and lightning follow. Huanebango rises and courts the shrew but, being deaf, cannot hear her rude replies. (11) Enter Eumenides, followed by the Ghost of Jack (above, 7), who in recompense for his burial enters the knight's service and at once provides him with food and money, on condition that they share equally all the knight wins on his journey. (12) Corebus and the ugly daughter come to the Well, and, gently treated, the Head, and a second Head, yield them corn and gold. (13) Approaching the cell of Sacrapant, Eumenides asks whether it were not well to say one's prayers backwards. The Ghost of Jack reassures him and stops his ears with wool against the magician's enchanting speeches. (14) Sacrapant enters, but his wreath is plucked off by the invisible Ghost, who takes his sword and bids Eumenides dig with it till he finds the glass with the light (above, 5). When it is found, the Ghost bids the knight 'wind this horn,' whereupon Venelia, the stolen wife of Erestus (above, 2), who is neither wife, widow, nor maid, appears, breaks the glass, and blows out the light. (15) The Ghost draws a curtain and shows Delia asleep. Eumenides makes his suit and is accepted by Delia. (16) The Ghost of Jack returns bearing the head of Sacrapant, no longer young in appearance but in its true form (above, 4); Jack is the dead man who alone could slay him (above, 5). Again the horn is sounded, and Venelia, Delia's Two Brothers, and Erestus enter; the Brothers bless Delia's union with Eumenides. General rejoicing is interrupted by the Ghost's demand for half of the knight's gain (above, 11). Eumenides honourably prepares to sacrifice Delia. Satisfied with such evidence of constancy, the Ghost descends again to the grave Eumenides' generosity has procured for him (above, 7); and the others resolve: 'We will to Thessaly with joyful hearts.'

Some resemblances are merely coincidental, such as the opening scene in a wood at night (since the main action in Peele is by day), and Peele's conventional use of Echo, which Milton avoids. Erestus is a figure very remote from the Attendant Spirit; Sacrapant and Delia and their relations are quite unlike Comus and the Lady and theirs. Sacrapant has, to be sure, learned his arts from his mother; but Delia has drunk of, not refused, his potion, and that she is discovered seated and asleep gives slight basis for the Lady imprisoned by Comus' magic chair. Peele's Two Brothers have nothing in common with Milton's except that they are in quest of their sister, and they have no part in her rescue. The Ghost of Jack, even if combined with the Well of Life (with which he has no connection), could hardly have suggested Sabrina. The case for Peele as a source seems to be less convincing than Arthos (5, 9, 12: see end of this section) finds it. The most perhaps that can be said is that Peele makes use of certain folk motifs—basically that of the damsel stolen away by the evil magician and her brothers' attempted rescue—with which Milton may also have been familiar. There is likewise no good case for William Drury's *Alvredus sive Alfredus* (1620), which E. A. Hall notices as dependent upon Peele and advances as a more probable source (*Manly Anniversary Studies in Language and Literature*, Chicago, 1923, 140-4).

The same basic motif, but with the King of Elfland replacing the magician, is found in the folk-tale of Childe Rowland, known to Shakespeare and possibly to Milton, as J. Jacobs argued ('Childe Rowland,' *Folk-Lore* 2, 1891, 182-97). Since no version is known to have been in print in Milton's day, the argument has to rely on the oral dissemination of the story, whose details can be gathered only from versions recorded much later. Most of these details are quite remote from *Comus*. Three brothers come in succession to rescue their sister, but only the last and youngest succeeds in freeing her and them. Two points only can be urged: Childe Rowland's obedience to the injunction to taste nothing offered to him in Elfland [and that is a common item in myth and folklore], and the king's releasing of the two older brothers (under Rowland's compulsion) by means of a bright red liquor, kept in a crystal phial, with which he touches their lips, nostrils, eyelids, ears, and finger-tips (which seems to bear the same relation to extreme unction as Sabrina's release of the Lady bears to baptism). For further criticism of Jacobs see F. Brie, 'Das Märchen von Childe Rowland und sein Nachleben,' *Palaestra* 148 (1925), 118–43. The latest discussion of folk motifs in *Comus* (and of other sources) is in John Arthos, *On A Mask Presented at Ludlow-Castle* (Ann Arbor, 1954), ch. 1, 'On the Power of the Sources.'

(2) John Fletcher, *The Faithful Shepherdess* (*c.* 1609, 1629, 1634) is briefly noticed as an influence on *Comus* by Warton (135) and Todd [and often cited in their notes], and was treated in some detail by W. E. A. Axon ('Milton's "Comus" and Fletcher's "Faithful Shepherdess" Compared,' *Manchester Quarterly* 1, 1882, 285–95). A recent discussion is that of Arthos (9–14). While it also embodies folk motifs, Fletcher's play, unlike Peele's, offers no parallels, however remote, with the action of *Comus*, although Warton [on line 78] declares: 'The Spirit in *Comus* is the Satyre in Fletcher's *Faithful Shepherdess*. He is sent by Pan to guide shepherds passing through a forest by moonlight, and to protect innocence in distress' (3. 1. 181 f.); [and Arthos, 11, notes 'the appearance of the River God with his likeness to Sabrina']. It is thus unnecessary to summarize the plot in detail. 'The central action,' according to Arthos (9–10), '...derives from the plot of Amarillis to separate Perigot and Amoret,' which for a time she succeeds in doing, with the help of the Sullen Shepherd and by her own transformation into the likeness of Amoret, effected by the magic well. But this is an undue simplification. There are in fact two faithful shepherdesses. One is the chaste Amoret, who is faithful to Perigot even when he, deluded by the

unchaste approaches of Amarillis in her guise, attempts to slay her. The other is Clorin, vowed to virginity and perpetual mourning for her dead lover. Arthos finds her attitude sometimes morbid, sometimes ridiculous, but it seems doubtful whether audiences that could appreciate Shakespeare's Isabella or Milton's Lady would do so. Hers is the opening scene and at the end she is the *dea ex machina*. Skilled in medicinal herbs, she cures all wounds, and, wise in moral counsel, reforms all sinners, except only the lustful and cynical Sullen Shepherd, who is irreclaimable. In her beneficent actions she is seconded by the good Satyr, servant to Pan; and pious counsel is also given and the moral drawn by the priest of Pan. The theme of the play is chastity, but the chaste characters (Clorin, Amoret, Perigot; the bashful Daphnis, who may strike us as an artificial prig but is surprisingly dismissed with praise, and Thenot, whose love for Clorin is inspired by her chaste devotion to her dead lover and cannot be requited) are set against the unchaste group, Amarillis, Cloe, Alexis, and the Sullen Shepherd, who introduce into the central scenes a predominant note of lust and violence and create an atmosphere very unlike that of *Comus*. [Arthos (9–14) finds more general and particular resemblances, though he acknowledges that Fletcher's account of chastity was in need of Miltonic elevation.] It seems certain, however, that Milton knew the play and drew upon it for some of his images (v: Notes, *passim*) and lyric measures. The poetry is indeed the best part of *The Faithful Shepherdess*, and Warton (135) was perhaps right in attributing to its influence some part of the 'Dorique delicacy' Sir Henry Wotton admired.

(3) Masques of Jonson, Browne, Townshend, and Carew

[Jonson's *Pleasure reconcild to Vertue* (1618), often accepted as a source (although not yet in print), is discussed above, toward the end of II: *Comus* and the Masque. For G. W. Whiting's theory of *Comus* as a sort of reply to Jonson's *Hymenaei*, see below, IV: Criticism, under 1958. Demaray (*Masque Tradition*, 21–30), who seems to ignore Whiting, sees *Hymenaei* as fixing the pattern of later masques, those of Jonson, Townshend, Carew, and Milton, and (24–5) lists structural similarities between it and *Comus*; he also discusses Jonson on pp. 59–65, etc.

William Browne's *Inner Temple Masque* (1615) is sometimes named among Milton's sources, but—apart from the fact that it was not printed until 1772—there is no likeness at all in their treatment of the story of Circe (see comments above, in II), and the story itself was of course common property. See R. F. Hill's edition in *A Book of Masques*, ed. T. J. B. Spencer (1967). Demaray (85–7) sees enough parallels between Browne and *Comus* to admit 'possible derivation.'

Aurelian Townshend's *Tempe Restord* (1632) is discussed, as an analogue, by Woodhouse (II, above). J. G. Demaray ('Milton's *Comus*: The Sequel to a Masque of Circe,' *HLQ* 29, 1965–6, 245–54) shifts the focus from the young poet to his elder, the experienced actor-producer, Henry Lawes. From Townshend's two masques of 1632, *Albions Triumph* and *Tempe Restord*, 'Lawes could have obtained ideas for the three scenic backgrounds in *Comus*: the wild wood, Comus' stately palace, and Ludlow town and castle.' 'With the exception of *Coelum Britannicum*, ... no other masques of the 1630's had settings so closely resembling those in *Comus*.' As for the theme and action of *Tempe Restord* (outlined in II by Woodhouse), Demaray notes in it, as in *Comus*, 'the strange herbs, the enchanted cup, the magic wand, the transformed prisoners, and the divine beam from above—all in a masque which is based upon the contrast between excessive pleasure and praiseworthy virtue. In *Tempe Restored* one discovers Henry Lawes, perhaps in the role of a Sphere, singing in the celestial heavens. And in the same masque one finds Ladies Alice and Catherine Egerton, together with other ladies representing Influences and Stars, dancing in harmonious movement in imitation of the "starry quire"' (251–2). Demaray imagines how Lawes, commissioned to produce a masque for the Earl of Bridgewater, might have brought his recent experience to bear on the planning of *Comus*.

In his book of 1968 (67–8, 78–82, 88–96) Demaray enlarges this account. He recognizes (81) that Townshend's Circe 'voluntarily surrenders her wand in the main masque and so becomes reconciled to the virtuous main figures' (cf. Woodhouse, II above). However, in spite of this and Townshend's structural looseness, he thinks that, of the masques performed at court shortly before *Comus*, *Tempe Restord* 'most closely' resembles it (82).

Willa M. Evans (*Henry Lawes*, 1941, 79, 96) has put among influences on *Comus* Thomas Carew's *Coelum Britannicum* (performed on 18 February 1634, and printed in the same year). One reason is the large portion given to speeches. Another is a 'framework. . .so nearly identical' with that of *Comus* that 'one might suspect that Lawes urged the younger collaborator to follow the pattern devised by the older.' But this structural identity does not seem so readily apparent; Demaray (71–3) finds Miss Evans' 'highly selective comparison. . .misleading.' And it is a question if Lawes collaborated in Carew's masque (*Poems of Thomas Carew*, ed. R. Dunlap, 276–7; G. E. Bentley, *Jacobean and Caroline Stage*, 3, 109–10).]

(4) The Influence of Spenser

As has been suggested above (II), *Comus*, whatever its precise relation to the masque, is clearly allegorical poetry in the general tradition of Spenser. Hanford ('Youth,' 139–42) emphasizes a direct debt to the *Faerie Queene*: 'The myth of Circe had long been established as a Platonic symbol of the degradation of the soul through sensuality. . . .It had received imaginative transformation and adaptation to the Christian ideal of sexual purity at the hands of Spenser in the second book of the *Faerie Queene*. . . .It is. . .to Spenser that *Comus* is most deeply indebted in its poetic essence. In his elaboration of the fiction, as in the quality of his emotion, Milton has been influenced by his master's romantic allegory of chastity in the third book. . . .This is clearest. . .in the parallel between the rescue of Amoret in Book III and the freeing of the Lady. . . . In both works the enchanter is surprised as he stands before his enthralled victim endeavoring to subdue her will to his lust. In Spenser the rescuer (Britomart). . .is told that only he can undo the spell which he has worked. In Milton the brothers. . .are informed. . .that they should have secured him [Comus]. . ."Without his rod reversed / And backward mutters of dissevering power / We cannot free the Lady" [But see below, v, 814–17 n., on Ovid]. . . .The relationship. . .extends to the fundamental philosophy and poetic method. . . .Britomart. . .is Spenser's symbol of what Milton calls the sun-clad power of chastity. The martial conception underlies such passages as *Comus*, 440 ff. The idea that chastity draws down Heaven to its defense, which is the dominant motive in the whole of *Comus*, is set forth in the episode of Proteus's rescue of Florimel ⟨*F.Q.* 3. 8. 29 f.⟩....A more specific suggestion came ...from...the Garden of Adonis ⟨3. 6⟩....The immediate pattern of Milton's description ⟨in the Epilogue⟩ is Spenser, who introduces as symbols of the Platonic creative principle first Venus and Adonis, then Cupid and Psyche, endowing the last ⟨after Apuleius⟩ with a daughter, Pleasure.' Hanford identifies 'Meliboeus old' with Spenser ⟨see below, v, 821 n.⟩.

It might be argued (as it is in Woodhouse, *UTQ* 11, 1941–2, 59–60) that the principal debt of *Comus* to Spenser is to *F.Q.* 2. 12, where Acrasia is as evidently Spenser's adaptation of the Circe theme as Comus is Milton's, and not to *F.Q.* 3, where the character of Britomart has singularly little in common with that of the Lady and where the motive of chastity and the outcome are entirely different. It is also possible to see in the symbolism of water in Sabrina's release of the Lady a further debt to *F.Q.* 1. 11. 29–30 and 2. 10. 45–6 (Woodhouse, *UTQ* 19, 1949–50, 221–2, and below, v, 821 n.; see also IV). But with Hanford's final judgment one may certainly concur: '...*Comus* was written under the dominating poetic influence of Spenser....Imitative, on the other hand, *Comus* certainly is not, for the unique personality of Milton is stamped upon the whole composition and the accent of his poetic idiom is heard everywhere' (142). This is a reservation to be heeded by proponents of influences far less pervasive than Spenser's. [See Robert Hoopes, *Right Reason in the English Renaissance* (Cambridge, Mass., 1962), on Spenser and Milton, and his forthcoming book on these two poets.]

[The fullest study of this question (with much reference to recent scholarship) is by Joan L. Klein ('Some Spenserian Influences on Milton's *Comus*,' *Annuale Mediaevale*, Duquesne University, 5, 1964, 27–47). Mrs Klein begins with Milton's Spenserian conception of the role of the Christian poet and poetry (including pagan myth and its allegorical potentialities). This conception of the poet is embodied in the Attendant Spirit (512–18, etc.), who is also a virtual guardian angel. Milton carries through the masque a thread of pagan images that adumbrate Christian ideas; it starts in the first line with the suggestion of the Christian heaven. Mrs Klein links Comus especially with the 'magicians and Circe figures described in the *Faerie Queene*,' namely, Archimago, Phaedria, Acrasia, Busirane, and Mammon (35–8); the forces of hell are opposed by those of heaven. The primary source of Comus's dark wood is Spenser's wood of Error. The Spenserian theme of 'the pilgrimage and its attendant trials' is of course central in *Comus*. Milton's Lady is less like Spenser's heroine of Chastity, Britomart, than like Una, in that the Lady and Una both represent 'the very real power of virtue to know and achieve good' (41); and such virtue, which on earth needs rational and intellectual discipline, has its heavenly goal and sanctions. Mrs Klein favours Steadman's interpretation of haemony as *Christian* knowledge (see below, v, 635–6 n.), since Milton's plant is superior in power to moly (43–6). She follows Woodhouse in taking Sabrina and water as the symbols of divine grace, a symbolism already employed by Spenser.

A. K. Hieatt ('Milton's Comus and Spenser's False Genius,' *UTQ* 38, 1968–9, 313–18) sees Spenser's false Genius (*F.Q.* 2. 12. 46–9) as 'the chief constitutive figure' for Comus: he is 'The foe of life,' the servant of the sensual Acrasia; he carries a staff and offers wine to visitors. Comus enters 'with a Charming Rod in one hand, his Glass in the other' [the rod has a precedent in Circe's wand, though in *Comus* wine only is the agent of transformation]. The Lady's brothers throw the glass to the ground as [Warton noted] Guyon threw down the false Genius' bowl and the goblet of Excess. The presentation of the false Genius is 'silently emblematic,' while 'Comus speaks to us through a varied and subtle (if disordered) register of rhetoric.' But there is a rhetorical relation in the traditional motif of the rose (*F.Q.* 2. 12. 74–5; *Comus* 742–3); [see 742–3 n. and F. Bruser in III. 9 below].

The 'complementary tradition of the true Genius' (*F.Q.* 2. 12. 47–8, 3. 6. 31 f.), the porter of the Garden of Adonis, the servant of Venus and Nature, also colours Milton's conception. In his epilogue Spenser's Venus and Adonis represent the process of physical generation, far below 'Celestiall Cupid' and Psyche [see below, 1001 n., 1002–10 n.]. But Spenser's true Genius is also a 'celestiall powre' (*F.Q.* 2. 12. 47) and a personal guardian and may have contributed to the Attendant Spirit. The 'most significant' thing is that Milton at no point defends 'a merely passive virginity'; he associates the Lady 'with that Spenserian principle whose main embodiment' is Britomart [but see the comment on Hanford earlier in this section]. *Comus* shows a surprising dominance of Spenser's 'mythic formulations': the chaining of Amoret and the 'backward mutters of dissevering power' (*F.Q.* 3. 12. 19 f.; *Comus* 816) [though Ovid is behind both (see comment on Hanford above and 814–17 n.)]; Sabrina's liberation of the Lady and Cymoent's rescue of Marinell; etc.

On the general subject of style Carey remarks (171): 'Surprisingly Spenser contributes only one or two phrases, but his effect on the vocabulary is considerable'; he lists examples.]

(5) Shakespeare and Minor Poets

[The texture of *Comus*—like that of most of Milton's verse—suggests that his memory was stored not only with the ancient classics but with much English and foreign poetry of the Renaissance; and, as we might expect, his language and imagery often took similar form. The large gatherings of Warton and Todd have been augmented by later editors and commentators. In one area of prime interest, Alwin Thaler assembled possible Shakespearian echoes noted already and added to them ('The Shaksperian Element in Milton,' *PMLA* 40, 1925, 645–91; enlarged in *Shakspere's Silences*, Cambridge, Mass., 1929, 139–208). Thaler had nearly forty items from *Comus*, the largest groups of parallels being with *A Midsummer Night's Dream*, *The Tempest*, and *Hamlet*; he added some in *SAMLA Studies in Milton* (ed. J. Max Patrick, Gainesville, 1953), 80–99. All this material has been collected and augmented in Thaler's *Shakespeare and Our World* (Knoxville, 1966), 139–227. In '*Comus* and Shakespeare' (*Essays and Studies* 31, 1946, 68–80) Ethel Seaton found echoes of the *Dream* and *The Tempest* but stressed the influence of *Romeo and Juliet* (see also IV below, under 1946). In '*Comus* and *The Tempest*' (*Shakespeare Quarterly* 10, 1959, 177–83) John M. Major was concerned with the larger elements of form and theme. He noted the partly dramatic character of *Comus* and the partly masque-like character of *The Tempest*, and the lyrical strain of both. Both works embody the opposition of good and evil in contrasted groups of persons, the one side being aided by Providence. Both—*The Tempest* less centrally—oppose chastity to lust. The Attendant Spirit is a more exalted and more specifically Christian counterpart of Ariel (whom he clearly echoes in the epilogue). The bad Comus and the good Prospero are both magicians. Miranda and the more self-reliant Lady have some qualities in common. And above all there is a likeness in the general atmosphere of strangeness and wonder, grotesqueness and beauty. Carey (who does not cite Thaler) says (171), with more specific assurance than one may share, that Shakespeare yields 'thirty-two indisputable echoes, coming from fourteen of the plays and from *Lucrece*. The plays most drawn on are *Midsummer Night's Dream* (5 echoes), *Measure for Measure* and *Tempest* (4), and *Hamlet* and *Macbeth* (3).'

Minor poets whose names turn up with special frequency in the notes are Sylvester, Phineas and Giles Fletcher, Edward Fairfax (the Spenserian translator of Tasso), and Jonson (who of course is not minor). Carey (171) finds ten echoes of Sylvester and seven of Jonson, 'the other notable English influences.' Drayton and others come up in connection with Sabrina (below, 823–31 n., etc.).

It may be repeated, in regard to phrases and passages cited from these and other writers, that they are given mainly as illustrative parallels in idea, image, diction, and idiom, and that only a limited number can be taken—according to readers' varying critical judgments—as probable 'sources' for Milton.]

(6) Italian Plays

(i) Mario Praz ('Milton and Poussin,' *Seventeenth Century Studies Presented to Sir Herbert Grierson*, Oxford, 1938, 192–210) expressed surprise because, while we have 'heard much about the Spenserian character of *Comus*,...nobody seems to have been aware that Tasso's *Aminta* is the real model. Comus's arguments to persuade the Lady to forsake her virginity are a development of those Dafne uses with Silvia...; Comus himself acts the part of Tasso's Satyr. *Comus* is a spiritualized *Aminta*; the Satyr binds Silvia naked to a tree and tries to violate her, but Comus' fetters are the invisible work of a spell. Thus sensuality has been carried away from the senses. Tasso's pastoral, with its tender atmosphere, its passions, and its despairs...has been transformed almost beyond recognition into a morality in antique garb' (202). Suggestive as is the brief characterization of *Comus* (introduced to support the thesis that Milton, like Poussin, marks the transition from a free Renaissance to a confined neoclassical style), one must dismiss as wholly untenable Praz's suggestion of Tasso as source. It is evident even from his own short summary, which omits the attempted suicide of Aminta on the false news of Silvia's death, his lucky (if somewhat ludicrous) escape, and her final relenting. There is not a single similarity in plot; the suggested division of Comus' role between Dafne, the friend of Silvia, and the Satyr convicts itself; and the theme and tendency of the two pieces are, as nearly as may be, diametrically opposed.

(ii) More serious attention is due to Gretchen L. Finney's claim for *La Catena d'Adone* (1626), adapted from Marino's *L'Adone* by Ottavio Tronsarelli (*SP* 37, 1940, 482–500; *Musical Backgrounds*, 1962, 175–94). There are certainly a number of points of resemblance, which, however, create a somewhat false impression when isolated. The action turns on the vain attempt of the sorceress Falsirena to win Adonis away from Venus; he proves faithful despite her magic and her wiles, and is finally rescued by Love and restored to his goddess. The piece opens with an expository prologue by Apollo, then a chorus of the Cyclops. Falsirena learns of Adonis from Idonia (who represents Concupiscence). Adonis, fleeing from the wrath of Mars, is lost in the wood, experiences imagined fears not unlike those mentioned by the Lady, and appeals to Echo (who comforts him), and he falls asleep, to be awakened by Falsirena, who promises him shelter and refreshment. Like the Lady, he follows his guide, in the hope of finding his way back to Venus. The act closes with a chorus of Nymphs, followers of Falsirena, singing the pleasures of love. Oraspe arrives with invisible chains forged by Vulcan. Arsete (reason) tries vainly to prevent the binding of Adonis. The scene changes to a palace of gold in which Adonis is held captive by the chains. He resists the advances of Falsirena, who faints and falls into a mad despair, presented by a dance of Nymphs. She decides to withdraw and appeal to

Pluto, and her frenzied rites are described by Idonia. Learning from Pluto of Adonis' love for Venus, Falsirena disguises herself as the goddess; but Venus and Love appear in time to rescue the faithful Adonis, and Love restores him to Venus. Amid some common elements, there is much in each Italian piece that is absent from the other; and despite an allegorical element in both, their themes are far from identical. Adonis, like Aminta, stands not for chastity but for fidelity in love.

For some things in *Comus* that are not in *La Catena d'Adone*, Mrs Finney finds suggestions in the crowded pages of Marino's epic, *L'Adone*. Some of Falsirena's followers are there transformed to beasts (a common derivation from the Circe myth). Failing to subdue Adonis by argument, Falsirena resorts to enchantment; she is equipped with wand and cup (though the wand is put to different use, and Adonis drinks the cup and thus loses the ring Venus had given him to protect him against evil); there is a distant resemblance to the Attendant Spirit in the intervention of Mercury, Jove's messenger, who gives Adonis a magic herb potent against enchantment (for this of course Marino and Milton have a common source in Homer). Mercury is unable completely to free Adonis, who is now transformed to a bird, but must return to the garden, there to bathe in the fountain, dipping his wings seven times in the water, before he is wholly freed. This done, he hastens to find the magic ring and escapes. The poem continues after the death of Adonis. It was accompanied by an allegorical interpretation by Lorenzo Scoto. This does not in general serve much to draw together the meanings of Milton and Marino; but it is interesting to find Scoto taking the bird's bathing in the fountain as representing salvation by grace, since Adonis had been powerless to save himself. The episode is perhaps too remote to have suggested the freeing of the Lady by Sabrina's 'Drops...of pretious cure,' but as analogue it confirms the symbolic use of water to represent an infusion of grace (see below: IV, Woodhouse, under 1941–50). [Demaray (*Masque Tradition*, 145–6) and Carey (171) are sceptical about the *Catena* as an influence.]

(7) The Figure of Comus

Comus came into being as a person through the writings of Philostratus, Erycius Puteanus, Ben Jonson, and others. Puteanus was treated at some length by Todd, who elaborated material in Richard Hole's *Remarks on the Arabian Nights' Entertainments* (1797, 232–9), and minutely by R. H. Singleton ('Milton's *Comus* and the *Comus* of Erycius Puteanus,' *PMLA* 58, 1943, 949–57). The fullest discussion of Philostratus is in Arthos (7–8, 42, 53–6, 65).

Comus as the name of a god of feast and revelry did not occur until late in classical antiquity. The common noun *komos* meant revels or a band of revellers or, less often, the ode sung at a festal procession (Liddell and Scott). The first authentic reference to Comus seems to be that in the *Imagines* (1. 2) of Philostratus the elder (*c.* 170 to *c.* 245 A.D.). It describes in detail a shrouded scene of midnight revelry at a wedding feast, with a suggestion of riot and dissipation. Comus is not represented as the leader of the revels but as a youth, delicate and not yet full-grown, who has come, flushed with wine and crowned with roses, to join the other revellers at the feast. (This fact suggested to Edgar Wind the possibility that 'Comus in antiquity may have been an aspect of Hymen made into a separate god':[1] Arthos, 53.) He stands at the entrance, half asleep, as it seems, with his torch ready to fall from his hand. Philostratus dwells on the excellence of the painting, especially the 'dewy look of the roses.' He is referred to, and in part followed by, Vincenzo Cartari, who notes the resemblance of Comus to Bacchus and describes him as the 'god of Feasts, Banquets, and mirth-ministring conventicles'; his head is wreathed with 'a garland of sweet-smelling flowers' and beside him is 'a great goblet of wine, and hard by that a musicall instrument like to a Cymball.' The flowers Cartari takes as signifying 'joy, mirth, and pleasance, and the instrument the lightnesse of heart, and contempt of sadnesse and melancholike cogitations: his pleasant, fresh, and lively countenance shewes, that by the operation and stirring vertue of wine, mens spirits are awaked and made joyfull, as without doubt a moderat and temperate receit thereof, quickeneth... drooping sences, infusing... a more loftie and aspiring thought' (*Le*

---

[1] Burton couples the two, though rather casually: '...Comus and Hymen love masks and all such merriments above measure' (*Anat.* 3. 2. 3: 3, 178).

2-2

Imagini de gli Dei, in R. Linche, *The Fountaine of Ancient Fiction*, 1599, sig. xiii^v-[xiv^v], quoted by Arthos, 54). [See the picture of Comus (from Cartari, Lyons, 1581, 347) reproduced in S. Orgel, *The Jonsonian Masque*, and one of Comus and revellers (from Philostratus, *Les Images*, Paris, 1614, 9), and Orgel's comments on these and on the figure of Comus in general (153 f.).]

Philostratus (the Aldine edition of whose *Imagines* had appeared in 1503) inspired Mantegna's unfinished painting known as *The Realm of Comus* (but referred to by the artist as *istoria de Como* and *tabula de lo dio Como*) which was completed by Lorenzo Costa (Arthos, 54–5). Philostratus calls Comus a *daimon* and is followed by the earliest Latin translators, who also call him a god (Arthos, 42, 68, n. 33). In both suggestions Milton seems to acquiesce, in view of the genealogy he invents for Comus: his mother Circe is [as in the original myth] a daughter of the sun, and Comus shares with her something of the demonic character and is a spirit connected with nature, while his father Bacchus is a god. Though Philostratus makes no direct connection between Comus and Bacchus, his description invites the idea, and Lilius Giraldus says: *Comus...deus fuit conviviorum & comessationum. quidam ex Graecis scriptoribus cum Dionysio coniungunt* (*Historiae Deorum, Opera*, Basle, 1580, 1, 45). There would seem to be nothing demonic or divine in Philostratus' Comus, and no suggestion of any struggle between vice and virtue; it is only in his personal attractiveness and in the air of licence in his surroundings that he at all anticipates Milton's character and his setting. But the youthful Bacchic figure, though not under the specific name of Comus, lent himself to the well-worn theme of the choice and can be found representing Vice, or rather, perhaps, Pleasure, in paintings of the sixteenth century. Speaking of Correggio's companion paintings of Virtue and Pleasure, Edgar Wind (*Bellini's Feast of the Gods*, Cambridge, Mass., 1948, 52) remarks that the latter figure 'was made to convey the notion of demoniac possession, thus moving away from Philostratus' towards Milton's idea of Comus' (Arthos, 55–6).

Philostratus was the ultimate source of the much elaborated Comus of the Dutch Erycius Puteanus, whose *Comus, sive Phagesiposia Cim-meria: Somnium* (Louvain, 1608; Oxford, 1634) has been carefully ana-lysed by Singleton. Here Comus is a youthful and effeminate figure, curled, perfumed, and rose-crowned, bearing the marks of over-indulgence in food and wine. He is the leader of a band of revellers who presents himself as the son of Mercury and Venus and as the god of revelry, the patron of all sensual delights. He is attended by Luxury and Wantonness, and his train includes Love, Laughter, Sensual Joy, Satiety, and Drunkenness. In his palace is the very picture that Philo-stratus had described, and Puteanus supplies a Latin version of the des-cription; but he greatly elaborates the original, heavily emphasizing the erotic and presenting Comus for the first time not as reveller merely but as seducer, and as the proponent of a thoroughgoing philosophy of sensual pleasure. The action (as summarized by Singleton, 950–3) has little or nothing in common with Milton's. It is cast in the form of a dream.

At the entrance to a dark wood Puteanus encounters Comus with his attendants and worshippers. The leader announces his descent and sets forth his philosophy of sensual pleasure. Puteanus longs to flee, but a cloud envelops him and carries him to the sunless home of the Cim-merians, where he sees in a secluded vale the palace of Comus. Here he is joined by a friend, Aderba. Declaring that virtue has nothing to fear from the terrors of darkness, Puteanus, accompanied by Aderba, ap-proaches the palace, safely passing Lycus (brother of Cerberus), who rushes out at them from a cave. Then a crowd of devotees emerges from the palace to greet Comus and his train, many of whom are monsters concealing their brutal features behind a mask. Puteanus comments on Comus' false philosophy; but, impelled by curiosity, the pair mingle with the throng and do not refuse the wine proffered at their entry. They first find themselves in a bridal chamber with statues of Venus, Cupid, Bacchus, and Ceres ⟨cf. above, Wind's suggestion of Comus as an aspect of Hymen, and, for the attendant gods, Milton, *El* 6. 51–2⟩ and witness a series of symbolic rites. They proceed to a torchlit portico and here see the picture of Comus described by Philostratus; then on to the banquet hall, where, amid luxury and uproar, men and women are gorging on food and wine. They meet another friend, Tabutius, who was in youth a follower of Comus but now observes the rites only to condemn them. His moralizing is interrupted by Comus, who quiets the tumult and sings an Anacreontic ode in praise of wine, the dance, and wanton love. The song is greeted with wild applause. When this subsides, Tabutius resumes his moralizing. Then the suit of two revellers to a serving maid called Circe gives rise to such commotion that Comus is unable to quell it, and, attended by Luxury and Wantonness, he retires. Puteanus awakes, welcoming the light of day.

There are a few incidental parallels, chief among them the shift from a dark wood to Comus' palace and the presentation of a cup to those entering the palace; but the cup is not a magic potion and Comus does not figure as a magician. It is in his role as seducer from virtue and in his philosophy of sensual pleasure that he seems to anticipate Milton's enchanter. Between the Anacreontic ode and Comus's lyric address in Milton (93–144) Singleton points out some similarities: the invitation first to drink, then to beat the ground in dance and bind the head with a garland of roses; the banishment of every serious thought, the invoking of Venus, and the idea that darkness will conceal what is evil. These, with Puteanus' faith in virtue as a sufficient guard against nocturnal terrors, exhaust the points of resemblance. Whether or not Puteanus is to be regarded as one of Milton's sources, he develops the conception of Comus in various directions and, among others, some of those taken by Milton.

Meanwhile another strain in Philostratus, quite remote from Milton, was being developed. Todd (58 n.) quoted Dekker's *Gull's Hornbook* (1609: ed. R. B. McKerrow, London, 1904, 4; *Thomas Dekker*, ed. E. D. Pendry, 75), where, after invocations to Sylvanus and the 'noblest drunkard Bacchus,' Dekker proceeds: 'Thirdly...Comus, thou clerk of Gluttony's kitchen,...let me not rise from table, till I am perfect in all the general rules of epicures and cormorants.' This is the type of figure, patron of food and wine, adopted by Jonson in *Pleasure reconcild to Vertue* (performed 1618; published 1640): 'Comus, ye god of cheere, or yᵉ belly, riding in tryumph, his head crownd with roses..., his haire curld'; he is a comic centre of the first antimasque, which is danced by men in the shape of bottles and tuns (*Ben Jonson* 7, 479). It is doubtless Jonson's Comus—as Elton (*Comus*, Oxford, 1894) observes—that Massinger refers to as 'the god of pleasure,...our Comus' (*The City Madam* 4. 2). But (as Warton noted) Jonson took a kindlier view of Comus in the same capacity when he addressed Sir Robert Wroth (*Ben Jonson* 8, 98): 'Thus Pan, and Sylvane, having had their rites, / Comus puts in, for new delights; / And fills thy open hall with mirth, and cheere, / As if in Saturnes raigne it were.' [R. C. Fox (*N&Q* 9, 1962, 52–3) noted that Comus is mentioned along with Bacchus and Priapus in *The Poetaster* 3. 4. 114–16 (*Ben Jonson* 4, 249).]

Milton, it is clear, takes his own line with Comus, playing down the *bon vivant*, retaining something of god and demon, but emphasizing both the seducer and the magician (the latter role, like the demonic, derived from his mother Circe), and plainly identifying Comus with vice in the contest between vice and virtue.

(8) The Myths of Circe and Bacchus

Critics since Newton have recognized Milton's use of the story of Circe, as he himself indicated in the parentage he assigned to Comus. Since the myths of both Circe and Bacchus need to be treated in close relation to Milton's text, the evidence is assembled in v below, notes on 46–57.

(9) Traditional Arguments in Comus' Plea to the Lady (705–54)

Todd in his edition of *Comus* (Canterbury, 1798, 710 n.) cited a speech in Thomas Randolph's *The Muses Looking-Glasse* (2. 3), a play acted in 1630 f. and published in *Poems* (1638). The suggestion was revived by C. B. Cooper (*MLN* 32, 1917, 436) and by G. C. Moore Smith (*TLS*, 19 Jan. 1922, 44). The passage is this (*Poems*, ed. Oxford, 1640, 29; *Works*, ed. Hazlitt, 1, 208–9):

> Nature has been bountifull
> To provide pleasures, and shall we be niggards
> At plenteous boards? He's a discourteous guest
> That will observe a diet at a feast.

When nature thought the earth alone too little
To find us meat, and therefore stor'd the ayre
With winged creatures, not contented yet
Shee made the water fruitfull to delight us.
Nay I believe the other Element too
Doth nurse some curious dainty for mans food;
If we would use the skill to catch the Salamander:
Did she doe this to have us eat with temperance?
Or when she gave so many different Odors
Of spices, unguents, and all sorts of flowers,
She cry'd not—stop your noses: would she give us
So sweet a quire of wing'd Musitians
To have us deafe? or when she plac'd us here,
Here in a Paradice, where such pleasing prospects,
So many ravishing colours entice the eye,
Was it to have us wink? when she bestow'd
So powerfull faces, such commanding beauties
On many glorious Nymphs, was it to say
Be chast and continent? Not to enjoy
All pleasures, and at full, were to make nature
Guilty of that she ner'e was guilty of,
A vanity in her works.

The case for some influence on Milton from Randolph is convincing
(see also the notes on *Comus* III and *L'All* 24). Randolph (1605–35)
attended Westminster School and Trinity College, Cambridge (B.A.,
1628; M.A., 1631). The fact that his residence [perhaps not continuous
in 1628–31] covered the whole period of Milton's increases the probability
of their acquaintance. Randolph's talent developed early and in his short
life he wrote a great deal (see above, *Sonn* 7. 4–8 n.). J. S. Smart (reported
by Smith, *TLS*, above) suggested that 'our common Friend Mr. R.' who
sent to Sir Henry Wotton 'the late R's Poems, Printed at Oxford,
wherunto it ⟨*Comus*⟩ was added' (Wotton to Milton, *Works* I, 476) was
not John Rouse, as Warton and Masson thought, but Robert Randolph,
the brother and literary executor of Thomas. [See, however, Parker,
816–17, n. 96.] If this were so, Milton might well have seen the poems in
MS. (they were first printed in 1638); and, as Smith suggested, *The*

Muses Looking-Glasse may, like *Aristippus,* have been acted at Cambridge while Milton was there. Citing in corroboration *Upon Love fondly refused for Conscience' sake* (Randolph, *Works* 2, 631–3), Smart asserts that the thought and style of the lines quoted above are so characteristic of Randolph as to rule out the idea of his having borrowed from the unpublished *Comus,* and he adds: 'It is possible that when Milton wrote *Comus* he had Randolph and his favourite doctrines and practice in view, and intended an answer or criticism—in other words, that Randolph is Comus, and the Lady is Milton replying to him.' [This, and Hanford's similar opinion (below, *Comus* IV, under 1925) are surely exaggerated.

The appeal to nature, put in various ways, was a commonplace of Renaissance naturalism and libertinism; English writers usually set forth the arguments with a view to providing the answers of orthodox morality, but some—such as Marlowe and the young Donne—could expound them with more or less unqualified sympathy. A number of examples were given by D. Bush, *Mythol.* (1932, 135, n. 27, and elsewhere; 1963, 133, n. 26, and elsewhere): Tasso, *Aminta*; Guarini, *Pastor Fido*; G. Pettie, *Petite Pallace* ('Germanicus and Agrippina'); Lyly, the opening pages of *Euphues*; Sidney, *Arcadia, Works* 1, 402–10; Warner, *Albion's England* 5. 24; Spenser, *F.Q.* 2. 6. 15, 2. 12. 74–5; Daniel, *Complaint of Rosamond*; Marlowe, *Hero and Leander*; Shakespeare, *Venus and Adonis*; Drayton, *England's Heroical Epistles* (King John to Matilda); various early poems of Donne; P. Fletcher, *Venus and Anchises*; etc.]

H. Schaus hardly allowed for the commonness of the traditional arguments in making a more specific case for 'The Relationship of *Comus* to *Hero and Leander* and *Venus and Adonis*' (University of Texas *Studies in English* 25, 1945–6, 129–41).

F. Bruser ('*Comus* and the Rose Song,' *SP* 44, 1947, 625–44) outlined the tradition of the *carpe diem* motif as it lies behind Comus' plea and relates to the theme of the masque. Beginning with the pagan sense of life as fleeting, it developed two opposing currents. The more obvious line continued the exhortation to pleasure. In the other, when the idea is set in Christian thought against the background of eternity, it becomes temptation to be resisted, and the very brevity of life means that time is short in which to pursue virtue and seek salvation. Thus there are two senses in which one may 'seize the day.' The first strain is illustrated in Anacreon, Catullus, Horace, and, with the specific image of plucking the rose, in Ausonius (*De Rosis Nascentibus* 49–50: L.C.L., 2, 280), an image which becomes, in the *Roman de la Rose*, 'a natural symbol for the loss of virginity.' The theme was revived in the late Renaissance and was widely diffused in the two contexts of exhortation and temptation. In England the most famous examples are the rose song in the *F.Q.* 2. 12. 74–5, Fairfax's *Jerusalem* 16. 15, Herrick's *To the Virgins, to make much of Time*, and Marvell's *To his Coy Mistress*. The Christian interpretation appears, e.g., in the verse of Drummond and in Jeremy Taylor's *Holy Dying*. While Spenser is wholeheartedly on the Christian side, he is aware of the complexity of the problem and seeks a reconciliation of the claims of chastity and love in the story of Britomart. But his disciples, the Fletchers, exemplify simple and stark opposition: the invitation to pleasure in Phineas' *Venus and Anchises* (not that that sober cleric would have really endorsed the sensual creed) and the temptation to vice in Giles's *C.V.* 2. 46–60. Spenser 'opposes to license the ideal of married love'; in *Comus* the Lady's 'denial must be viewed...in the light of the Epilogue,' of which the author adopts Woodhouse's interpretation. When *Comus* is placed in the whole tradition, we see that 'Milton takes the thorny path of virtue, but the roses grow along the way.'

(10) Traditional Arguments in the Lady's Reply (755–98)

[George Sandys' moral and religious allegorization of the story of Circe and Ulysses (*Ovid*, 1632, 475, 480–1) was partly quoted by D. Bush (*Mythol.*, 1932, 267–8; 1963, 280), and bits of it are quoted below, v, 56–7, 635–6 nn.

When the Lady rebuts Comus' inferences from nature's prodigality by asserting that nature 'Means her provision only to the good / That live according to her sober laws' (764–5), she is appealing to a long tradition, Platonic, Stoic, and Christian. That tradition is outlined by W. G. Madsen, 'The Idea of Nature in Milton's Poetry' (*Three Studies in the*

Renaissance, by Richard B. Young et al., New Haven, 1958); see also R. Hoopes, III. 4 above). It will be enough to quote here from Richard Hooker (*Eccles. Pol.* I. 8. 9, *Works*, 1888, I, 233; Madsen, 203):

Laws of Reason have these marks to be known by. Such as keep them resemble most lively in their voluntary actions that very manner of working which Nature herself doth necessarily observe in the course of the whole world. The works of Nature are all behoveful, beautiful, without superfluity or defect; even so theirs, if they be framed according to that which the Law of Reason teacheth.... Law rational therefore, which men commonly use to call the Law of Nature, meaning thereby the Law which human Nature knoweth itself in reason universally bound unto, which also for that cause may be termed most fitly the Law of Reason; this Law, I say, comprehendeth all those things which men by the light of their natural understanding evidently know, or at leastwise may know, to be beseeming or unbeseeming, virtuous or vicious, good or evil for them to do.

Though the Lady does not carry the argument on to the higher ground of 'the sage / And serious doctrine of Virginity' (785–6), the doctrine is nevertheless central to her position. And there is again implied a tradition of Platonic and Christian thought which can be followed through treatments of the subject in the Fathers: Clement of Alexandria, Gregory of Nyssa, St Augustine, St Ambrose (Madsen, 206–8).] See notes on the passage in v below.

(11) Plato, Platonism, and Platonic Love

[The shortest and most valuable introduction to or comment upon *Comus* is the passage in the *Apology* (1642: *Works* 3, 302–6) in which Milton recalled the growth of his youthful ideal of chastity and love and some of the reading that nourished it. However familiar the passage is to all students of Milton, it would seem to demand formal recognition here. At first, he tells us, he was captivated by, and delighted to imitate, 'the smooth Elegiack Poets,' that is, the Roman poets of love, Ovid, Propertius, and Tibullus. He continued to admire their art, though he came to recoil from their sensual view of love and found more complete satisfaction in the Christian idealism of 'the two famous renowners of Beatrice and Laura,' Dante and Petrarch. 'And long it was not after, when I was confirm'd in this opinion, that he who would not be frustrate

777

of his hope to write well hereafter in laudable things, ought him selfe to bee a true Poem, that is, a composition, and patterne of the best and honourablest things. . . .' Then came 'those lofty Fables and Romances' of knighthood, and Milton's instincts transposed the chivalric code into a higher key, 'So that even those books which to many others have bin the fuell of wantonnesse and loose living,. . .prov'd to me so many incitements. . .to the love and stedfast observation of that vertue which abhorres the society of Bordello's.'

Thus from the Laureat fraternity of Poets, riper yeares, and the ceaselesse round of study and reading led me to the shady spaces of philosophy, but chiefly to the divine volumes of Plato, and his equall [i.e. contemporary] Xenophon. Where if I should tell ye what I learnt, of chastity and love, I meane that which is truly so, whose charming cup is only vertue which she bears in her hand to those who are worthy. The rest are cheated with a thick intoxicating potion which a certaine Sorceresse the abuser of loves name carries about; and how the first and chiefest office of love, begins and ends in the soule, producing those happy twins of her divine generation knowledge and vertue. . . .

Last of all not in time, but as perfection is last, that care was ever had of me, with my earliest capacity not to be negligently train'd in the precepts of Christian Religion: This that I have hitherto related, hath bin to shew, that though Christianity had bin but slightly taught me, yet a certain reserv'dnesse of naturall disposition, and morall discipline learnt out of the noblest Philosophy was anough to keep me in disdain of farre less incontinences then this of the Burdello. But having had the doctrine of holy Scripture unfolding those chaste and high mysteries with timeliest care infus'd, that *the body is for the Lord and the Lord for the body*, thus also I argu'd to my selfe; that if unchastity in a woman whom Saint Paul termes the glory of man, be such a scandall and dishonour, then certainly in a man who is both the image and glory of God, it must, though commonly not so thought, be much more deflouring and dishonourable. In that he sins both against his owne body which is the perfeter sex, and his own glory which is in the woman, and that which is worst, against the image and glory of God which is in himselfe. Nor did I slumber over that place [Rev. 14. 3-4] expressing such high rewards of ever accompanying the Lambe, with those celestiall songs to others inapprehensible, but not to those who were not defil'd with women, which doubtlesse meanes fornication: For mariage must not be call'd a defilement.]

While the usually unphilosophical Warton recognized Plato's presence in *Comus* (below, v, 462–74 n.), the analysis of Milton's Platonism has been modern. J. S. Harrison (*Platonism in English Poetry of the Sixteenth and Seventeenth Centuries*, New York, 1903, 48, 50) wrote: 'The fundamental idea of Plato on which Milton built his doctrine of chastity is the one taught in the "Phaedo," that every experience of the soul gained through the medium of the senses tends to degrade the soul's pure essence into the grosser, corporeal form of the body.' 'In Plato the fundamental idea is somewhat different from Milton's; for Plato is concerned with the problem of the attainment by the soul of pure knowledge, and he means by sense knowledge not sensuality in the restricted moral signification of that word, but in the broader signification of all experience gained through all the senses.' This important reservation seems not to have been heeded by later critics; but it gives additional impetus to the quest for supplementary sources.

J. H. Hanford ('Youth,' 1925, 138–9) emphasized Milton's debt to Plato in the period of *Comus* and in the work itself, and noted that the 'myth of Circe had been long established as a Platonic symbol of the degradation of the soul through sensuality and as such had attracted Milton as early as the first Latin elegy.' Hanford pointed out that, combined with his Platonic ethics and couched in his Platonic phrasing, there is a distinctively Christian meaning, which Milton was to link closely, in the *Apology*, not with Plato alone but with the poets. 'That a poet should be a poet's guide to emotional Platonism is very natural. That Spenser should have been the guide of Milton is particularly so.' In Spenser Milton found 'not only his own serious love of virtue combined with a fine responsiveness to sensuous beauty, but the embodiment of the Platonic philosophy with which he was already acquainted, touched after the fashion of the Renaissance with the romantic charm of sex. The two influences are henceforth one. They combine in *Comus* to give a quality of poetic inspiration wholly new in Milton's work, a fusion of the ecstacies of sense and spirit which the poet has hitherto been unable to obtain.'

Herbert Agar (*Milton and Plato*, Princeton, 1928, 38–42) contented himself with pointing to passages which seem to depend directly or indirectly on Plato: 18–21, 111–16, 380–4, 419–79, 458–62, 462–75 (see notes on these lines in v below).

[In his introduction and notes Hughes (1937) summed up Milton's harmonious fusion of Platonism, Spenser, and Christianity.] Wright (1938) insisted on the Platonic (rather than Christian) character of *Comus* (see v, notes on 1–4, 6, 975).

G. F. Sensabaugh ('The Milieu of *Comus*,' *SP* 41, 1944, 238–49) attempted to show that Milton was writing with an awareness of the revived cult of Platonic love as it was introduced into the English court by Henrietta Maria. He assumed moral corruption at court, ignoring the admission to the contrary of so strong a Puritan as Mrs Hutchinson, and gave no satisfactory evidence that the Platonic cult was a cloak for licence. His citations from contemporary plays represent, not licentious inferences from Platonic love, but (if anything) reactions against its rarified idealism; and his citations from sermons do not bear at all directly on the subject but are formulations of the Puritan ideal of marriage (which has no place in *Comus*); nor are the passages cited from *Comus* more cogent. The reason offered for Milton's interest in the subject (which the article does not establish) is that, having decided (in defiance of Puritan rule) not to marry, he must make clear that he did not share the artificial and insincere idealism of the court. [The article does at least make clear the gulf between the fervour of *Comus* and the courtly fad; and Mrs Hutchinson may not have been acquainted with the creed and apparent practice of Carew, Suckling, and other Cavalier poets.]

Irene Samuel (*Plato and Milton*, Ithaca, 1947) used Hanford's suggestion to support her thesis that the Platonism of the early poems is not 'exactly Platonic,' but is of the modified kind common and indeed conventional in the Renaissance, whereas Plato's influence became progressively purer and stronger throughout the rest of Milton's life and work. That the Platonism of *Comus* is from Plato and his tradition in the Renaissance rather than from Plato alone is no doubt true.

Arthos (*A Mask*, 1954) has, like Wright, insisted on the Platonic rather than Christian character of *Comus*, though he assembles much material from other sources. He is cited above and below. In a later study, 'Milton, Ficino, and the *Charmides*' (*Studies in the Renaissance* 6, 1959, 261–74), Arthos argued that chastity, which is evidently a comprehensive virtue including temperance and continence and sometimes to be equated with virtue itself, is Milton's equivalent for the *sophrosyne* of Plato's *Charmides* as interpreted by Ficino (who renders it as *temperantia*) in the summary and explanation prefaced to his translation. Common to *sophrosyne* and chastity are the control of bodily desires in the interest of the soul, the apparent inclusiveness of the virtue and its implying of other virtues, and (in the Elder Brother's speeches) their association with philosophical wisdom. But the evidence adduced is suggestive rather than conclusive.

The same year brought another study of the influence of Renaissance Platonism and Ficino in particular, Sears Jayne's 'The Subject of Milton's Ludlow *Mask*' (*PMLA* 74, 1959, 533–43). In *Comus*, Jayne contends, the 'Platonism is not classical Platonism, but Renaissance Platonism, and Milton's principal authority is not Plato, but Ficino'; for there he found 'Platonism, mythology, and Christianity...already synthesized.' This important article, however, depends on a particular and suggestive interpretation of *Comus*, so that it has been summarized below in IV: Criticism.

(12) Christian Elements

[Of prime importance here also is the passage summarized and quoted from Milton's *Apology* in (11) above.

R. L. Ramsay ('Morality Themes,' *SP* 15, 1918, 147–8) found in *Comus*, alone among Milton's early works, the unmistakable presence of the most important of 'the four morality plots, the Conflict of Vices and Virtues....The plot is roughly that of the old morality; but how far transformed! In place of the personified Mankind is the Lady; the Good Angel is quite recognizable in the Attendant Spirit; the two brothers are the Virtues; Comus and his crew are the Vices; and Sabrina is the Grace who regularly entered at the last stage to deliver Mankind from the entanglement of sin.' Ramsay thought it a dramatic weakness that the Lady, unlike Mankind, was impregnable. 'But with this important restriction, all the stages of the typical morality plot are easily discernible: the opening scene of Innocence and Security, the great Temptation scene, the Life-in-Sin replaced here by the merely external magic spell that falls upon the Lady, and lastly the Deliverance thru Sabrina's aid.... And yet, altho the characters of *Comus* cannot hide their descent from the personified abstraction, either in name or nature, they have at least advanced farther on the road to personality than any other members of their class.... *Comus* is thus half a morality, half a parable.']

It is not surprising that the Christian strain in *Comus* admits of no such precise documentation of sources as even the Platonic does; Milton's whole environment and sensibility were Christian. Further, the mode is not that of scriptural poetry (of the freer sort exemplified in the *Nativity*, much less of the stricter as in the two epics and *Samson*) but of moral and religious allegory. Christian reference becomes specific only at the end, indeed in the final couplet with its affirmation about 'Heav'n it self'; it is the culmination of a steady progression from 'nature' to 'grace.' [But Christian reference may seem hardly less specific, or is at least transparent, in, e.g., 9–14, 17, 212 f., 328, 416–18, 452–62, 488, 599, 664, 776–8, 937—as some of Woodhouse's notes indicate.] Up to the advent of Sabrina Christian conceptions appear only in embryo and as premonitions, and Sabrina herself is recognized as Christian only when her symbolic value is apprehended. The briefest discussion of the subject of course implies a degree of interpretation, and some critics deny or slight the Christian elements in the poem [or question Woodhouse's particular interpretative scheme: see IV below, under and after 1941].

But it is easy to define the Christian ideas: (1) the conception of Providence dominates the whole action, is recognized and confidently asserted by the Elder Brother, and is symbolized by the Attendant Spirit; (2) the high value set, not upon chastity alone, but upon virginity (which qualifies it to become the symbol of chastity on the level of grace), goes back to St Paul and receives heavy emphasis in patristic and medieval Christianity; (3) the image of life as a journey, a pilgrimage, is recurrent in Christian tradition, as in Book I of the *Faerie Queene* before

Milton and *Pilgrim's Progress* after him, and in *Comus* is symbolized in the journey to Ludlow; (4) the conviction that, while man may and must struggle against evil, he cannot win the victory of his own strength but only by God's grace, is of the essence of Christian (and not least of Reformation) theology; and saving grace is symbolized by the necessary intervention of Sabrina; (5) water, the specific symbol chosen, is that used in the sacrament of baptism, but extended to signify any infusion of saving grace (in accordance with Protestant emphasis on the immediacy of God's operation on mind and heart, which is not necessarily channelled through the sacraments); (6) one effect of the working of grace was liberation, the entering into Christian liberty, an idea which received renewed emphasis in Protestantism and was to become central in Milton's thinking: it meant the identification of liberty with obedience to God and hence with virtue ('Love vertue, she alone is free'); and it made possible a new outlook upon the whole order of nature, a vision in which everything fell into place in a hierarchy of values and was for the good a good: this is the vision embodied in the Epilogue; (7) the specifically Christian conception of God's mercy and condescension finds at last direct and not merely symbolic expression in the concluding couplet.

[Suggested sources for a Christian interpretation of 'Haemony' are discussed below, v, 628–37 and notes.]

[Our last entry is in a rather special category, since the 'source' here is Milton himself. G. Williamson ('The Context of *Comus*,' *Milton & Others*, London and Chicago, 1965, 26–41) traces Milton's growing awareness of the opposed worlds of sense and virtue as it appears in his early poems. After recalling Milton's account, in the *Apology* (1642), of his youthful idealism, his movement from the merely aesthetic to the Platonic and Christian love of the good, Williamson goes back to the Latin elegies, 'the scene of Milton's ethical development.' The young poet had revealed his strong sensuous instincts in *Elegies* 1, 7, and 5; but in *Elegy* 6 the inspiration of wine and love had been ranked well below the heroic themes of the ascetic poet-priest. A similar dichotomy, however mild, had been set up between Mirth and Melancholy. Thus the basic ingredients of *Comus* had already appeared—even Platonism, in *Il Penseroso*. But now L'Allegro took a licentious form and evoked real opposition. The 'myth of Circe offered a basic myth or trial' for Milton's moral hero. Williamson notes how those early embryonic ideas and issues are in *Comus* fully and forcefully defined and set in conflict. (He follows Hanford in linking *Comus* with Spenser's third book, and Sabrina with Britomart; for Woodhouse's comment see III. 5 above.) The same conflict was to reappear in *Lycidas* with Amaryllis and Neaera—and finally in *Samson*.]

IV. CRITICISM [A.S.P.W. AND D.B.]

[The following survey of modern criticism provides a degree of perspective by beginning with Dr Johnson (whom modern critics do not forget) and citing a few spokesmen for the period 1779–1900. For recent decades the survey is much more than representative but somewhat less than complete. The order is as usual chronological. In the list of critics those whose names have an asterisk were summarized by Woodhouse: Johnson*; Warton*; Hazlitt; Macaulay*; Bagehot; Masson; M. Pattison; O. Elton; W. V. Moody*; Sir W. Raleigh; Sir W. W. Greg*; C. H. Herford; J. H. Hanford*; D. Saurat; E. Welsford*; W. Lewis; Sir II. J. C. Grierson; E. M. W. Tillyard*; C. S. Lewis; R. Macaulay; H. Belloc; F. R. Leavis; M. Y. Hughes; W. Haller; B. A. Wright; G. W. Knight; P. P. Morand; C. Williams; A. S. P. Woodhouse*; Tillyard*; K. Muir*; Haller; E. Seaton; J. C. Maxwell*; M. M. Ross; M. Miller; J. Blondel; D. C. Allen*; C. Clarke*; M. Macklem*; M. Mack; C. Brooks and J. E. Hardy; R. M. Adams*; R. H. Bowers; N. E. Enkvist; J. Arthos; F. T. Prince; D. Taylor; A. E. Dyson; K. Muir; J. W. Saunders; M. Van Doren; W. B. C. Watkins; D. Daiches; R. Tuve*; G. and M. Bullough; W. G. Madsen*; G. W. Whiting*; S. Jayne*; E. Saillens; D. Wilkinson (and G. Rans); J. B. Broadbent; E. Sirluck; T. Wheeler; R. Daniells; M. Nicolson; M.-S. Røstvig; Blondel; T. A. Riese; J. I. Ades; A. Arai; C. L. Barber; G. H. Carrithers; E. LaGuardia; I. G. MacCaffrey; R. B. Wilkenfeld; R. Neuse; B. Rajan; P. Brockbank; J. G. Demaray; W. J. Grace; J. S. Lawry; J. Reesing; J. Carey; J. B. Leishman; D. M. Rosenberg; P. E. Boyette.

Comus

A Maske at Ludlow, ed. J. S. Diekhoff (Cleveland, 1968), contains the articles and essays of Woodhouse, Allen, Adams, Dyson, R. Tuve, Jayne, Barber; an introduction by the editor, emphasizing the family character of the production, and his article on the text (*PMLA* 52, 1937, 705–28); the Bridgewater text of *Comus*; and Lawes' version of the songs with his music.]

Samuel Johnson (*Lives*, ed. Hill, 1905, 1, 167–9) set the fashion for a number of later critics in praising the poetry of *Comus*, but also in treating it as drama and finding it deficient as such. *Comus* 'exhibits his [Milton's] power of description and his vigour of sentiment, employed in the praise and defence of virtue. A work more truly poetical is rarely found; allusions, images and descriptive epithets embellish almost every period with lavish decoration. As a series of lines, therefore, it may be considered worthy of all the admiration with which the votaries have received it.' To the masque form as such Johnson barely refers—perhaps because his point of view is insensibly governed by seeing versions of *Comus* on the stage. 'As a drama it is deficient. The action is not probable. A Masque, in those parts where supernatural intervention is admitted, must indeed be given up to all the freaks of imagination; but, so far as the action is merely human it ought to be reasonable...,' as the Brothers' leaving the Lady alone and unguarded is not, though here the defect is 'over-balanced by its convenience.' The 'prologue spoken in the wild wood by the attendant Spirit is addressed to the audience; a mode of communication...contrary to the nature of dramatick representation....' The speeches 'have not the spriteliness of a dialogue animated by reciprocal contention, but seem rather declamations deliberately composed and formally repeated on a moral question. The auditor therefore listens as to a lecture, without passion, without anxiety.' 'The song of Comus has airiness and jollity.... The following soliloquies of Comus and the Lady are elegant, but tedious.' 'At last the Brothers enter, with too much tranquillity; and when they have feared lest their sister should be in danger, and hoped that she is not in danger, the Elder makes a speech in praise of chastity, and the Younger finds how fine it is to be a philosopher.' Similar criticism of the dialogue with the Attendant Spirit follows, and his 'long narration' is declared 'of no use because it is false, and therefore unsuitable to a good Being.' 'In all these parts the language is poetical and the sentiments are generous, but there is something wanting to allure attention.' 'The dispute between the Lady and Comus is the most animated and affecting scene of the drama, and wants nothing but a brisker reciprocation of objections and replies, to invite attention and detain it.' But in the work as a whole 'the figures are too bold and the language too luxuriant for dialogue: it is a drama in the epick style, inelegantly splendid, and tediously instructive.'

From Johnson onward, a good deal of criticism has turned on the respective importance of masque, drama, and poetry, in the effect of *Comus*.

Against Johnson's treatment of *Comus* as an unsuccessful drama Thomas Warton protested (*Poems...by John Milton*, 1785; revised and enlarged, 1791, 262–3; in Todd, 4, 177–8): 'We must not read *Comus* with an eye to the stage, or with the expectation of dramatic propriety ....*Comus* is a suite of Speeches, not interesting by discrimination of character; not conveying a variety of incidents, nor gradually exciting curiosity; but perpetually attracting attention by sublime sentiment, by fanciful imagery of the richest vein, by an exuberance of picturesque description, poetical allusion, and ornamental expression. While it widely departs from the grotesque anomalies of the Mask now in fashion, it does not nearly approach to the natural constitution of a regular play.... This is the first time the old English Mask was in some degree reduced to the principles and form of rational composition; yet still it could not but retain some of its arbitrary peculiarities.' Then, after some defence of *Comus* against Johnson's objections: 'But we must not too scrupulously attend to the exigencies of situation, nor suffer ourselves to suppose that we are reading a play, which Milton did not mean to write. These splendid insertions ⟨of whose dramatic impropriety Johnson had complained⟩ will please, independently of the story, from which however they result; and their elegance and sublimity will overbalance their want of place. In Greek tragedy, such sentimental harangues, arising from the subject, would have been given to a chorus. On the whole, whether

Comus, be or be not, deficient as a drama, whether it is considered as an Epic drama, a series of lines, a Mask, or a poem, I am of opinion, that our author is here only inferiour to his own *Paradise Lost.*'

[Hazlitt, reviewing a performance of *Comus* (11 June 1815: *Works*, ed. Howe, 5, 230-3), contrasted Shakespeare's dramatic with Milton's undramatic genius: Milton's characters are only a vehicle for his own sentiments. 'Comus is a didactic poem, or a dialogue in verse, on the advantages or disadvantages of virtue and vice. It is merely a discussion of general topics, but with a beauty of language and richness of illustration, that in the perusal leave no feeling of the want of any more powerful interest.' But 'These kind of allegorical compositions are necessarily unfit for actual representation,' because the imagination is limited by the immediate response of the senses. *Comus* is a 'most delightful poem,' but it lacks the interest and passion of *Lycidas* and *Samson.*]

In his essay on Milton (*Edinburgh Review* 42, 1825, 314-15; *Miscellaneous Works*, ed. Lady Trevelyan, 5 v., New York and London, n.d., 1, 26-7) the young Macaulay wrote in the vein of Warton (and of Sir Henry Wotton's letter, which he quoted). *Comus*, 'framed on the model of the Italian Masque,' 'is certainly the noblest performance of the kind...in any language,' far above the pastoral dramas of Fletcher, Tasso, and Guarini. Milton made *Comus* 'what it ought to be, essentially lyrical, and dramatic only in semblance.... The speeches must be read as majestic soliloquies; and he who so reads them will be enraptured with their eloquence, their sublimity, and their music. The interruptions of ⟨i.e. occasioned by⟩ the dialogue, however, impose a constraint upon the writer, and break the illusion of the reader. The finest passages are those which are lyric in form as well as in spirit.' [Macaulay anticipates some later criticism in feeling a dichotomy: 'It is when Milton escapes from the shackles of the dialogue, when he is discharged from the labour of uniting two incongruous styles, when he is at liberty to indulge his choral raptures without reserve, that he rises even above himself.']

[At the end of his long review (1859) of Masson's first volume, Walter Bagehot ('John Milton,' *Literary Studies*, London, 1932, 1, 195-6;

787

Works, ed. N. St John-Stevas, London and Cambridge, Mass., 1965, 2, 148) gave his second-last paragraph to *Comus*. Although Bagehot was a cultivated and highly intelligent man, he was disposed to save Milton the artist by throwing his beliefs and convictions overboard—like other men of his century up through Sir Walter Raleigh. This is part of his comment: '*Comus* has no longer the peculiar exceptional popularity which it used to have. We can talk without general odium of its defects. Its characters are nothing, its sentiments are tedious, its story is not interesting. But it is only when we have realised the magnitude of its deficiencies that we comprehend the peculiarity of its greatness. Its power is in its style. A grave and firm music pervades it: it is soft, without a thought of weakness; harmonious and yet strong; impressive, as few such poems are, yet covered with a bloom of beauty and a complexity of charm that few poems have either. We have, perhaps, light literature in itself better, that we read oftener and more easily, that lingers more in our memories; but we have not any, we question if there ever will be any, which gives so true a conception of the capacity and the dignity of the mind by which it was produced. The breath of solemnity which hovers round the music attaches us to the writer. Every line, here as elsewhere in Milton, excites the idea of indefinite power.']

[Several of the older modern commentators may be grouped together. In Masson's edition of the poems (London, 1874; 2nd ed., 1890), which was standard for several decades, the introduction to and commentary on *Comus* were more biographical and historical than interpretative. Masson's mixture of light and darkness is illustrated by quotations and comments in notes on lines 1001 and 1002–10.

Mark Pattison (*Milton*, 1879) quoted once from *Comus*, described the circumstances of its production, and used two or three highly and vaguely laudatory phrases.

Oliver Elton, in his small edition of *Comus* (1894; repr. 1928), found the songs inferior to many contemporary lyrics, in being less simple, sensuous, and passionate. 'The true superiority of *Comus* lies...in its "more exercised and self-conscious art."' Milton kept and enhanced the mythological and pastoral elements, and still more the allegorical purpose, 'and these two points...take us away at once from the associations of the usual masque. Here he is original; here he quits a factitious form of writing, and shews his real self.' 'The theme of the poem is Virtue,—Chastity,—its praise and victory.' The words on Platonic love of the good in Milton's *Apology for Smectymnuus* 'are the text of *Comus*.' But while the Greek emphasizes the philosophic vision of truth, the Protestant Milton emphasizes cleanness of life and soul. Milton's stern sense of the need for discipline 'made him take for praise the narrowest form of purity, and denounce the contrary as the worst fault of all, with the zest of his party. We cannot imagine Dante thus restricting himself, or laying all the emphasis here.']

W. V. Moody (*Poetical Works*, 1899, 32–8) recognized developments in masque, drama, and lyric verse as preparing the way for *Comus*: 'Jonson's example ⟨in refusing to subordinate his work to musician and producer⟩ led other poets to give the masque a much more conscientious treatment than it had hitherto received. His work had only to be supplemented by the exquisite lyrical sense of John Fletcher, in his *Faithful Shepherdess*, and by the magic fancy of Shakespeare, in such masque-like creations as *Midsummer Night's Dream* and the *Tempest*, to prepare the instrument wholly for Milton's hand.' 'In *Comus* Milton pushed much further...the supremacy of the poet over the musician and the stage carpenter.... The bulk of the masque is dignified blank verse, unhurried by the necessity for spectacular effect, and with its serious mood unrelieved by lyrical episodes'—a departure which has led some critics to deny *Comus* the title of masque.

Further, 'adoption of a simple human story for the central motive instead of a more artificial and fantastic theme, marks off *Comus* from the ordinary masque, and brings it nearer to the romantic drama of the Shakespeare or Fletcher type.' But upon this simple human story 'is imposed a mythological element which is entirely in the masque spirit, though it is made to subserve ends of moral teaching essentially alien to the ordinary masque-writer's aim.' The Circean Comus and his transformed followers are 'an allegory of that Platonic doctrine of idealism' expressed by the Elder Brother ⟨452–68⟩. The followers have put themselves in the magician's power. 'So long as the heart is sound and the will firm there is nothing to fear from malice, sorcery, or evil chance' ⟨588–98⟩. This doctrine is verified in 'the famous dialogue' of the Lady and Comus ⟨658–812⟩, 'in which the moral meaning of the masque is fully developed.' Here Comus, 'no vulgar incarnation of sensuality,' 'seeks to melt her resolution by all the devices of sophistry and beguiling suggestion,' while into her replies (as 'into the speeches of the Elder Brother') 'Milton has put a profound moral conviction, a conviction which gave to his whole life...a singular crystalline glow.' 'It is easy for us to underestimate the beauty and value of this "sage and serious doctrine of virginity" as it is set forth in the pages of *Comus*,' if we fail to make allowance for 'a nineteenth century moral sense, mellowed by a larger humanism than seventeenth century England knew,' or to remember that Milton 'achieved this ideal only by severe struggle, and in the face of a nature uncommonly exposed to passion.' Compared with earlier figures bearing the name ⟨see above, III. 7⟩, the 'character of Comus may fairly be regarded as an authentic creation of Milton's....To oppose the promptings of the lady's chaste heart, he creates a nature as poignant in its way as the mightier incarnation of evil in the Lucifer of *Paradise Lost*, and as far removed as that from the imagery of popular moral terrorism.' On Comus and his crew 'Milton chiefly depended for that spectacular interest and that remoteness from actuality which is proper to the masque.' But he added two figures deftly calculated to the same end, and to enrich the lyric quality and deepen the philosophic symbolism of the poem: the Attendant Spirit and Sabrina. More consistently and effectively than his Renaissance predecessors, Milton combines classic myth and pseudomyth with Christian truth. In his epilogue the Attendant Spirit 'is manifestly akin to the Ariel of the *Tempest*....Yet this very song is a description, under a thin classic veil, of the bliss of the redeemed spirits in Heaven, and an exposition of Milton's mystic doctrine of paradisaic Love. In the magic herb Hæmony...there is a recollection of the herb Moly....Yet there can be little doubt that the plant symbolizes Christian grace.' 'Sabrina,...called up from her watery depths by the Attendant Spirit to release the lady..., is conceived more purely in the masque spirit' and 'is perhaps a recollection from...*The Faithful Shepherdess.*' ⟨In her Moody apparently sees no religious or moral significance.⟩

In *Comus*, more than any other work except *Samson*, Milton 'shows his power as an artist...; over its diverse and seemingly irreconcilable elements has gone the cool hand of the master, to build and subdue.' 'On the moral side...there is to many minds something not quite persuasive in *Comus*; its high doctrine comes at times a little priggishly and with a flavor of unripeness from a young man's lips. But its art is wholly admirable.' There 'presides over the poem from the first line to the last the fine economy of a mind that compels everything into the service of a dominant idea. Milton never demonstrated his character, both as artist and as man, more signally than when he made the quaint vehicle of the masque...bear the burden of a profound personal philosophy, and bear it, not as a burden, but as an essence.'

[It may be observed that Moody shows more sympathetic understanding of Milton's moral and religious theme and of his art than a good many later critics.]

[Sir Walter Raleigh (*Milton*, London, 1900) reserved most of his anti-Puritanism for Milton's later works, and his remarks on *Comus* are few and incidental. The chief one (28) leaves us with the impression that Comus is Youth, Beauty, Love, and Merry England: 'Comus, we are told, stands for a whole array of ugly vices—riot, intemperance, gluttony, and luxury. But what a delicate monster he is, and what a ravishing lyric strain he is master of! The pleasure that Milton forswore was a young god, the companion of Love and Youth, not an aged Silenus among the wine-skins. He viewed and described one whole realm of pagan loveliness, and then he turned his face the other way, and never looked back. Love is of the valley, and he lifted his eyes to the hills. His guiding star was not Christianity, which in its most characteristic and beautiful aspects had no fascination for him, but rather that severe and self-centred ideal of life and character which is called Puritanism.']

Sir W. W. Greg, in his large historical survey, *Pastoral Poetry & Pastoral Drama* (1906, 390–404), treated *Comus* mainly on its formal side. After paying tribute to the beauty of the poetry, he turned to consider the work as a masque. He deplored the tendency to declare it 'not a masque at all but a play' and to treat it as such. 'It is no more a regular play than it is a strict masque, but a dramatic composition containing elements of both in almost equal proportions.' Giving ample occasion for the variety and beauty of setting and other qualities expected of a masque, it added yet other features of which one may ask whether, instead of heightening, they do not 'diminish its merits as a work of literature and art': (i) 'a philosophical and moral intention, which, however veiled in fanciful imagery and clothed in limpid verse,...obtrudes itself directly in the length of some of the speeches; refuses, that is, to subserve the aesthetic purpose, and endeavours to divert the poetic beauty to its own non-aesthetic ends'; (ii) 'somewhat of dramatic emotion, of incident which depended for its value upon its effect on the characters involved'—a feature ill served by the machinery of the masque and interfering with the traditional effects of the form. Superior to Jonson's and to every other masque in its poetry, *Comus* seems inferior in its ability to produce these effects: 'the interest is that of the drama... while the medium adopted is that of the masque...'; 'the dramatic interest is a clog on the scenic elaboration of the form, while the form is necessarily inadequate to the rendering of the content.' 'The action is too much abstracted, the characters too allegorical, to satisfy in us the dramatic expectations which they nevertheless call forth; while, on the other hand, they remain too concrete and individual to be adequately rendered by purely spectacular means.' Nor can the 'philosophical and moral intention' (i above) be thus rendered, but requires the long speeches inimical at once to dramatic treatment and masque-like effects. Not necessarily connected with such objections, but rather with Milton's own temper and defective taste (as Greg avers), is the disagreeable fact that the Lady is presented, not as 'innocent,' but as too well aware of the ways of the world, and as self-consciously virtuous in their presence: Una, confronted by the Lion, did not immediately protest her chastity. The Lady, on the contrary, '"doth protest too much."' Finally, with all his praise of the poetry, Greg decides that it too has lapses and is less varied, and less certain in its touch, than that of *Lycidas*, or of *L'Allegro* and *Il Penseroso* (which on grounds of style he would put later than the 'prentice work' of Comus).

[Greg's moral censure was repeated by C. H. Herford ('Dante and Milton,' *Bulletin of the John Rylands Library*, 8, 1924; repr. in *The Post-War Mind of Germany and Other European Studies*, Oxford, 1927), who was quoted by Grierson (see below, under 1929).]

Apart from his consideration of Spenser as a literary source (III above), J. H. Hanford ('Youth,' 1925, 143) treats *Comus* mainly as a record of Milton's personal preoccupation with the subject of chastity: 'The intensity with which he seized upon this virtue as the center and test of his ethical idealism is explained by the strength of his own romantic passion.... Occasional passages give direct and moving expression to Milton's wider ethical convictions, but it is "the sage and serious doctrine of virginity" that holds the center of his thought and the mood of the poem contrasts strikingly with the glowing but mature enthusiasm of *Paradise Lost*. As a matter of fact *Comus* appears to reflect a partial suppression of the poet's sensuous excitement rather than its supersedence or complete conversion. For Milton this could be no resting-place, however happy the immediate poetic product.' The point of view did not change in Hanford's *John Milton, Englishman* (New York, 1949, 63–4): 'The theme of chastity was near his heart and he yearned to preach it.' 'The Lady is an ideal embodiment of the informed and fastidious innocence which had won him his academic nickname. Her brothers are protective males, already principled in virtue's book. Thyrsis...is divine guidance....All the experience and conviction of Milton's youth are here. He has known and weighed the arguments of the enchanter. The Lady's eloquent answer is ready to his lips. It is... no fanciful idea that...*Comus* was written as a more or less official reply to the libertine philosophy of his fellow student, Thomas Randolph.' Milton's philosophy is 'a Christianized Platonism. The pattern of true love is laid up in Heaven and earthly virtue is a discipline preparatory to its enjoyment.' [Much the same view is outlined in *Poems*, ed. Hanford (1953).]

[D. Saurat (*Milton: Man and Thinker*, New York, 1925) found in *Comus* no artificial choice of theme but an expression of one of the young poet's 'deepest needs... : the need to triumph over sensuality, which in itself implies sensuality' (19); 'like the great ascetics of primitive magic, Milton was chaste in order to acquire supernatural powers.... *Comus* was to be the glorification of the magic powers of chastity' (9). Saurat further saw in the masque attitudes to nature, to passion and reason, destined to reappear in Milton's mature synthesis.]

Enid Welsford (*The Court Masque*, 1927, 320–1, etc.) does not dispute the dependence of *Comus* on the formal conventions of the masque, but sees its ethic (as she interprets it) as utterly alien to the spirit of the form. In her view (which is partly summarized in II above) the norm for the genre is the marriage masque and Hymen is its patron deity, the symbol of harmonious youth, love, and order. 'But the golden world ruled by Hymen is emphatically not the right symbol for Milton's harsh creed, in which goodness is identified with power rather than with love, and evil is identified with sensuality rather than with cruelty and selfishness, and in which the Universe rests not upon self-expressive love but upon an everlasting antagonism, an ultimately insoluble dualism.' There remains, however, the poetry of *Comus* to be accounted for. 'Fortunately, Milton's poetic morality was a wider, richer thing than his religious ethic. Though the idea of the golden world was a symbol fitted for a philosophy larger and sweeter than his own, he yet allows it to colour his imagination and soften the asperity of his judgments.' He 'tells us again and again that Comus was evil, but there is very little in his presentment of him to suggest it. ...' Miss Welsford finds much in common between Comus and the Attendant Spirit in their response to natural beauty, quoting from the former's entering words (111 f.) and the latter's epilogue (975 f.).

[Anti-Puritan prejudice—though *Comus* can hardly be called Puritan —may be said to have reached its crudest level in Wyndham Lewis (*The Lion and the Fox*, London and New York, 1927, 233): 'Milton has succeeded in making of what he calls *chastity* something obscene. That is one of his principal achievements. It actually is calculated to *repel* by its stupidity and coldness as effectively as an over-hot sticky and strong-smelling obscenity could ever do.'

To return to the temperate and scholarly line, anti-Puritanism had a distinguished representative in Sir Herbert Grierson (*Cross Currents in English Literature of the XVIIth Century*, 1929, 244–5). Most of what he says about *Comus* is quoted from Herford (whose essay of 1924 was cited above), though Grierson's better self rebelled and made some amends: '"*Comus*", says Professor Herford, "is a Puritan hymn to Chastity," but Professor Herford goes on to point out an essential difference between Milton's celebration of that high virtue in *Comus* and Dante's in the *Vita Nuova*. Beatrice in the latter inspires purity because she kindles in the hearts of her beholders a love that casts out baseness. Purity is the aura which surrounds the burning flame of love. It is not by the love which she awakens that Milton's Lady in *Comus* repels impurity. "Milton's Chastity, sublime and exalted as it is, is at bottom a *self-regarding* virtue; his warrior maiden is concerned to disable her foes, not to ennoble them; and if a momentary suggestion of the creative and transforming glance of Beatrice has come into Milton's picture, if the Gorgon shield of her rigid look does not only freeze base thoughts, but awakens wonder and reverence, the change is important, not because her enemy is a "nobil cosa", but because he is no longer formidable.... Great and noble as both are, Dante's spirit is the richer and more human for it knows not only purity but love, a purity that is rooted in love...; whereas Milton describes a virtue which with all its dazzling and soaring splendour only repels and repudiates the humanity below it." "A self-regarding virtue"—that is what all Puritan virtues are apt to prove. But to be fair to Milton, remember that *Comus* was written before he had known love as a serious, transforming experience; and in every young man at that stage purity will be to some extent—it may have also a religious sanction—a self-regarding virtue, a protection of the citadel of man's soul against "The expense of spirit in a waste of shame," a guarding of the soul for an experience that is yet to come. Moreover, Milton and his Puritan friends set a higher value on marriage as the final sanction of love than perhaps Dante himself did, for whom the love of Beatrice and his marriage with Gemma were of a different order of things: "Hail, wedded Love,...."']

E. M. W. Tillyard (*Milton*, 1930, 66–75) objects alike to Johnson's treatment of *Comus* as if it were drama and Warton's defence of it as if it were not drama at all. He asserts, with telling examples, that Milton is at times writing dramatically, at others with no regard for probability. 'The fact is that Milton is not always certain whether or not he is in Arcadia,' and the uncertainty communicates itself to the style, in which he appears to be experimenting in different modes. The result is that *Comus* is much inferior in unity of tone to the *Nativity*, *L'Allegro* and *Il Penseroso*, and *Lycidas*; and to this Tillyard attributes Milton's reluctance to publish it as evinced by the Virgilian motto. Intent on seeing *Comus* as a literary experiment, Tillyard questions Hanford's and Saurat's insistence (from different points of view) on Milton's deep preoccupation with the subject of chastity; but he admits its temporary importance to him and discusses the matter in an appendix (374–83). [Here Tillyard, in part following Saurat, argues 'that at the time of writing *Comus* Milton did hold' some sort of belief in the magical powers attainable through chastity; 'that the belief was imposed and discordant with his real nature; and that this imposition partly accounts for *Comus* not being a completely sound whole' (374). None of these three propositions seems to have found much favour. Tillyard's later discussion of *Comus* is noticed below, under 1943.]

[Excerpts from C. S. Lewis' 'A Note on *Comus*' (*RES* 8, 1932, 170–6; repr. in his *Studies in Medieval and Renaissance Literature*, Cambridge, 1966) are given in various notes in v below, e.g. on line 4. This is his general conclusion: 'It may seem rash, on the strength of a few alterations, and those minute ones, to speak of a general characteristic in Milton's revision. Yet it is just on such apparent *minutiæ* that the total effect of a poem depends; and that there is a common tendency in the alterations I have discussed, few readers will probably dispute.... The poet cuts away technical terms and colloquialisms; he will have nothing ebullient; he increases the gnomic element at the expense of the dramatic. In general, he *subdues*; and he does so in the interests of unity in tone. The process is one of conventionalisation, in this sense only—that the poet, having determined on what plane of convention (at what distance from real life and violent emotion) he is to work, brings everything on to that plane; how many individual beauties he must thereby lose is to him a matter of indifference. As a result we have that dearly bought singleness of quality—

> smooth and full as if one gush
> Of life had washed it—

which sets *Comus*, for all its lack of human interest, in a place apart and unapproachable.

'Whether Milton's aim was a good one—whether he paid too high a price for it and sacrificed better things for its sake—these are questions that each will answer according to his philosophy. But if we blame *Comus* for its lack of dramatic quality, it is, at least, relevant to remember that Milton could have made it—nay, originally had made it—more lively than it is; that he laboured to produce the quality we condemn and knowingly jettisoned something of that whose absence we deplore. It is arguable that he chose wrongly; but the example of what may be called poetic chastity—an example "set the first in English"—deserves attention.'

One might add, from Lewis' essay on Tasso (*Studies*, 117): 'Asceticism is far more characteristic of Catholicism than of the Puritans. Celibacy and the praise of virginity are Catholic: the honour of the marriage bed is Puritan. Milton was being typically Puritan when he wrote, something too excessively, of the loves of Adam and Eve. *Comus* is his least Puritan poem.']

[Two more anti-Puritan witnesses may be added. Rose Macaulay, the novelist and seventeenth-century amateur, expressed the conventional sentiments with more vivacity than her predecessors (*Milton*, London, 1934; rev. 1957; pp. 37–9). Hilaire Belloc (*Milton*, London and Philadelphia, 1935, 101–11) found the manner of *Comus* unsatisfactory (though it included great beauties), and complained of Milton's excessive self-consciousness and especially of 'the Manichæan taint' of his false Puritan morals and 'horror of sex.']

[Since F. R. Leavis seems averse to being anthologized, one prudently and regretfully resorts to inadequate outline and paraphrase. In 'Milton's Verse' (*Revaluation*, 1936; 1963 ed., 47–57, on *Comus*) he remarks on 'a certain sensuous poverty' in the texture of *Paradise Lost* and, for contrast, quotes Comus' speech on Nature's bounties (709–35), a passage 'very unlike anything in *Paradise Lost*' and indeed unlike most of *Comus*. He feels here 'the momentary predominance in Milton of Shakespeare' because this speech has more sensuous richness, subtlety, and sensitivity than anything in Milton's three later long works. He then points out the tactual and visual immediacy and vitality of the varied crowding images and the essential part played by sound and rhythm in the total effect. In these lines we are not conscious of words and style; we directly experience 'feelings and perceptions.' All this actuality and movement 'would be quite impossible in the Grand Style; the tyrannical stylization forbids.' Leavis nowhere touches the function of this kind of writing in revealing the character of the speaker and contributing to the development of Milton's theme. He remarks further on the exquisite quality of the songs, which are designed 'to produce in words effects analogous to those of music.']

[In the introduction to his richly annotated and widely used edition of the minor poems (1937: xxxix–xlvii), M. Y. Hughes gave a balanced exposition of *Comus*, placing it in its formal and ideological setting and finding 'Milton's Puritanism...at one with his Platonism.' In his *Complete Poems and Major Prose* (1957) the shorter and more detached introduction to *Comus* surveyed the diversity of critical interpretations that had been multiplying in later years.]

[William Haller (*The Rise of Puritanism*, 1938, 1957, 317–21) is concerned with the Puritan moulding of Milton's artistic powers and poetic aims. The 'startling intensity' of *Comus* owed much to the spirit and pervasive influence of Puritan preachers. 'They too cast the lessons of their inner experience into the image of the pilgrim, seemingly lost, but not abandoned by God, encountering temptation and danger but journeying steadfastly toward heaven, led by the light within.' '*Comus*, with all its lovely reminiscence of the high poetry of the Renaissance, is the poet's version of that sermon of spiritual wayfaring which it would have been his part to preach if he had ever in fact mounted the pulpit.

'The theme of Milton's sermon, like that of many another Puritan sermon, is temptation, or rather the sense of freedom from moral danger which is enjoyed by the good who know their own minds and are assured of their own election.' 'To the young and high-hearted as well as to the saints of God, evil has no terrors, and Milton was both a young man and a Puritan saint when he wrote this poem.' He 'gives us, not wisdom concerning the problem of moral choice, but the exultation of a most extraordinary and very vital young person upon having chosen,' 'the exultation he felt in the realization of his powers and the choice of his career.'

'The invective of *Lycidas* and of the antiprelatical tracts against the blind mouths of the church are both anticipated when the Lady says that nature's blessings are meant to be dispensed in even proportion to just men, not crammed by swinish gluttons.' See Haller also under 1946.]

[B. A. Wright's edition of the *Shorter Poems* (1938; repr., 1944 f.) is abundantly quoted in Woodhouse's notes below. Wright holds to an exclusively Platonic interpretation.]

[G. Wilson Knight (*Burning Oracle*, 1939, 64–70): 'In *Comus* Milton attempts a complex work, with a central opposition of sensuous temptation and religious abstinence. It repeats former essences with a more spontaneous up-gushing of pure Elizabethanism, which does not blend any too easily with the poem's ethical nature. *A Midsummer Night's Dream* has been a helpful, and understood, influence. The setting continues Milton's love of nature architectural, and the prevailing darkness his feeling for subdued light' (65). Knight sees Comus as 'far too attractive' [for the unconscious irony of Comus' self-revealed perversion, see below, notes on 93–144, 112–14, etc.]. The central debate between Comus and the Lady dramatizes a conflict in Milton's own mind, 'to be made even more explicit in *Lycidas*' (66). Knight follows Leavis in praising the active poetry of Comus' speech on the bounties of nature ('Indeed, Milton never in all his work shows so convincing a cosmic apprehension') and in missing the point of the speech. But he recognizes, as not all critics have done, 'that the Lady's answer...is equally fine';

it 'has fire and vigour; and indeed enjoys an Elizabethan and dramatic force unique in Milton' (67). 'The statement that nature itself demands continence and that virtue is the only true freedom, we need not deny; but "virtue" is finally as undefined as the evil of Comus, except by the poetry, which upsets the ethical balance' (67).

'Music and sounds play a heavy part; indeed, they are in this darkened wood our main terms of reference.'

The 'conflict' in *Comus* is 'narrower' than that in *The Tempest*, but 'similarly universal' (69). 'Milton starts his life-work with the grave manner and "solemn music" of Shakespeare's close'—although, if we put *Samson* beside *Hamlet*, 'we find Milton ending where Shakespeare's greater work begins.']

[Paul Phelps Morand (*De Comus A Satan*, Paris, 1939) undertook to show in Milton an opposition between thinker and poet and also between confident youth and embittered age. His view of *Comus* (57–65) is mainly in the line of opinions cited already. Milton turned from the heaven of his earlier poems to earth, but only an artificial Arcadia, the unreal, perfect world of Spenser, with characters less attractive than Spenser's. Milton's interest is really in masculine chastity; the circumstances of the production require the Lady. She is the cold creation of a self-sufficient young man who has no knowledge of sin, repentance, humility, or the need of grace. Since the Lady cannot be tempted, there is no drama, only an unpleasant external event. The plot is an occasion for Milton to set forth two theories: the all-sufficient moral power of chastity and the possibility that matter may be transformed by moral causes (*Comus* 413–62; *PL* 5. 413 f.). Only in *Comus* does Milton attribute magical power to virginity (later he accepts chastity within marriage). He is himself a strongly sensual innocent; 'Il aime son Comus' (62).]

[Charles Williams' introduction to *The English Poems of John Milton* (1940)—the only piece of writing, T. S. Eliot said emphatically in 1947, that had won him toward Milton—was the product of a Christian (and poetic) faith that, in essentials, he shared with his subject. He recognized that 'The peculiar opposition to high speculations on the nature of chastity felt in both academic and unacademic circles had prevented any serious appreciation of that great miracle of the transmutation of the flesh proposed in *Comus'* (ix). To quote his appreciation in full (x–xi):

'*Comus* is a kind of philosophical ballet. Comus himself is, no doubt, a black enchanter, but he talks the most beautiful poetry, and he does not seriously interrupt the dance of the three young creatures opposed to him, with their heavenly attendant: there is a particular evasion of violence (when Comus is "driven in"). But what is this ritual ballet about? It is about an attempted outrage on a Mystery. The mystery which Comus desires to profane is the Mystery of Chastity. It is no use trying to deal with *Comus* and omitting chastity...Chastity (not only, though perhaps chiefly, that particular form of it which is Virginity...) is the means, in *Comus*, by which all evils are defeated, the flesh is transmuted, and a very high and particular Joy ensured. It may be true that we ourselves do not believe that to be so, but our disbelief is largely as habitual as our admiration of *Comus*. That is why it has been possible to admire *Comus* without any serious realization of the mystery of chastity, in spite of John Milton.

> To him that dares
> Arm his profane tongue with contemptuous words
> Against the Sun-clad power of Chastity,
> Fain would I something say, yet to what end?...

And that, as one may say, is that. Comus is a fool in these matters, and

> worthy that thou should'st not know
> More happiness than is thy present lot.

But the Lady and her brothers and the Attendant Spirit and Sabrina do know. They know that Chastity is the guardian and protector of fruitfulness, that Temperance is the means of intense Joy. In their eyes Comus, by refusing to admit the general principle of things and to be obedient to it, is foolishly and sinfully limiting the nature of Joy. He prefers drunkenness to the taste of wine and promiscuousness to sensitiveness. He knows nothing about that other power which can make the flesh itself immortal; he prefers to sit about in sepulchres. Let him, cries the whole lovely dance.

Obedience then and Joy are the knowledge, in their degree, of those three Youths of *Comus*. And *Paradise Lost*, following long after, did not forget its prelude.']

A. S. P. Woodhouse ('The Argument of Milton's *Comus*,' *UTQ* 11, 1941–2, 46–71) is credited by Brooks and Hardy, Adams, Madsen, et al. (below) with having given a new direction to the study of the poem and initiated the debate which has centred on its meaning. This, if true, is a serious charge; but it seems to demand a somewhat fuller summary of the article, with its sequel ('*Comus* Once More,' ibid. 19, 1949–50, 218–23), than modesty would otherwise allow, as well as the recognition that the first article especially was pioneer work, leaving some things unaccounted for and others perhaps overemphasized. The concern was with meaning and structure alone, and the work was read not as masque only, but as allegorical poetry in the tradition of Spenser, 'Where more is meant then meets the ear.'

The poem assumes an 'intellectual frame of reference,' repeatedly met as late as Milton's day, namely, the recognition of two orders or levels of experience, the one pertaining to man as man and called the order of nature, the other to man as Christian and called the order of grace. Abstractly stated, the movement in the poem is from nature to grace. Concretely this movement is presented in three scenes in the Lady's journey to Ludlow: (i) the Wild Wood, a symbol of the world in which good and evil grow up together and have to be discriminated: if Comus is present in the wood, so also is the Attendant Spirit, the symbol of God's providential intervention in the order of nature, to guide and protect the aspirants after virtue; (ii) the palace of Comus, which represents a concentration of evil in the world, and hence a condition of special temptation and testing; and (iii) Ludlow, the goal of the journey, literally home, and symbolically heaven. In the preparatory discourse of the two Brothers (330–608), with its insistence on the self-protective and self-illuminating power of virtue, the argument moves from the natural (through the teaching of Plato) to the verge of a Christian conception of virtue (and specifically of chastity) and to a recognition that virtue grounded within the individual is also supported by God's providence from without—a conviction ratified by the appearance of the Attendant Spirit (489). (The view here taken is not that the attitude and reasoning of the Elder Brother are defective, as some critics say, but adequate *so far as they go*, and a foundation for what is to follow.)

In the debate between Comus and the Lady (658–812) two views of nature are presented: Comus sees only nature the abundant, the profuse, marked by 'waste fertility' (728), and the lesson he draws is one of incontinence; the Lady does not deny this aspect of nature, but only its completeness and the correctness of Comus' inference; her emphasis falls on nature as a rational order, and the lesson she draws is that of temperance in the use of nature's gifts. (In this twofold view of nature we have a premonition of the view maintained in *PL* 7, in the account of creation. In respect of natural beauty the contention that Comus and the 'good' characters respond equally to it is utterly misleading unless one recognizes that Comus perverts this beauty in the very act of responding to it (93–144), while the others know that nature 'Means her provision only to the good' (764), a position to be cleared and fortified when in the Epilogue the whole of existence is looked at from the vantage point of grace.) So far in the debate, the argument has proceeded on the level of nature and the point at issue has been the natural virtues of continence and temperance. Comus, as the Lady well knows, can follow her to no higher ground; so she speaks but briefly of 'the Sun-clad power of Chastity,' trusting to the reader to remember the Elder Brother's exposition, and 'the sage / And serious doctrine of Virginity' (785–6) she refuses to do more than mention.

Here, confessedly, there is some problem, crystallized in comments of later critics. Is this doctrine of virginity differentiated from simple chastity, or is it a synonym therefor? The contention here is that in *Comus* and in the later autobiographical passage in the *Apology for Smectymnuus* (*Works* 3, 302–6), which refers to the period that includes the composition of the masque, three stages with their appropriate virtues are recognized: (i) that of nature or natural law (temperance and continence); (ii) that of Platonic idealism, which raises the issue to the verge of Christian revelation (chastity); and (iii) that of grace (with virginity, not as conterminous with Christian virtue, but employed as an appropriate symbol for it—that is, of a state higher and more dynamic than a merely self-dependent pursuit of Platonic idealism can afford). In his temptation of the Lady, Comus is foiled by her virtue. But this is neither the triumph of virtue nor the resolution of the action which all previous critics were content to see in it. For, if Comus is foiled, the Lady is immobilized; and if indeed the action is a journey to Ludlow, then the Lady must be freed to pursue that journey, and it is precisely this freeing that neither the Brothers (natural virtue including Platonic idealism) nor the Attendant Spirit (in his character of providential agent in the natural order) but only Sabrina's intervention can effect. Here, then, is the decisive resolution of the action. Sabrina frees the Lady and removes the retarding power of the enchanter's spell; she restores the good and destroys the evil by the symbolic sprinkling of victim and imprisoning seat with water, those 'Drops...of pretious cure' (911–12). The symbolism is most familiar to us in the sacrament of baptism; but here it represents, not baptism of course, but an infusion of divine grace which sets the believer free. The best gloss on Milton comes from Spenser: when the Redcross Knight is hard beset by the Dragon (Sin or Satan), he falls into a stream of living water and comes forth restored for the conflict (*F.Q.* 1. 11. 29–30); and when Prince Arthur would destroy the monster Maleger (Original Sin), he has no resource left but to submerge him in the waters of the nearby lake (ibid. 2. 11. 46). By grace, thus symbolized, the power of the enchanter is destroyed and the Lady is freed to resume her progress to Ludlow (home and heaven); and, lest we should miss the point, the Attendant Spirit says: 'Com Lady while Heaven lends us grace, / Let us fly this cursed place, / ...And not many furlongs thence / Is your Fathers residence' (937–46). The episode not only provides the resolution of the action; it raises the issue to the level of grace. And it is from this level that the Epilogue looks back on the whole progression and suggests, in the language of image and symbol, that for the Christian everything in God's creation has its due place in an ascending scale: the whole realm of natural beauty (975–95), the reproductive power (996–1001), intellectual love (1002–10), and, as the culmination of it all, and the secret of this retrospective vision, those two marks of the Gospel: Christian liberty and Heaven's condescension to erring man (1017–22).

[After Woodhouse's first article (1941), and perhaps especially after his second (1950), most critics reacted to his interpretation in one way or another, and such reactions are partly indicated in pages that follow. While accepting much of his general view, probably many readers demur at the triple equation set forth in the middle of the summary above, an equation which may seem more schematic than the text warrants. This equation is not stated in Woodhouse's later and shorter interpretation (*The Poet and his Faith*, 1965, 96–100); an extract from this is given below, in the note on 975–1022.]

In 'The Action of *Comus*' (*Essays and Studies* 28, 1943; revised in his *Studies in Milton*, 1951, 82–99), E. M. W. Tillyard re-examined *Comus* with special attention to two additions to the original text of 1634 (MS.) made in the first printed text (1637), namely: (i) in the Lady's reply to Comus ('Shall I go on?...thy false head,' with Comus' aside admitting her power, 778 f.), and (ii) the passage in the Epilogue referring to Venus and Adonis and Cupid and Psyche (995 f.). The former carries the defence on from temperance to 'the Sun-clad power of Chastity' and thence to 'the sage / And serious doctrine of Virginity'; and this by its mystical and ascetic emphasis accentuates the contrast of her position to the epicurean naturalism of Comus, but it merely accentuates and does not alter the Lady's negative position. The addition to the Epilogue, on the other hand, introduces a new element in the echo of Spenser's Garden of Adonis with its inhabitants, Venus and Adonis and Cupid and Psyche (*F.Q.* 3. 6: a relation first noticed by Warton). Here Tillyard (later than but independently of Woodhouse) sees a contrast to both the licence of Comus and the negative and ascetic position of the Lady, the idea of marriage as the solvent. The union of Cupid and Psyche (despite the fact that they are 'far above' the garden, not in it, and that Cupid is described as 'Celestial') figures human marriage, and the addition does not confirm but changes the whole direction of the preceding movement. Moreover, Spenser's Garden of Adonis emphasizes, as Comus does, the prolific fertility of nature, but without his perverse inferences. In the first version, while the Lady is assumed to be victorious, neither she nor Comus (whose argument is the more powerfully presented) is right: each sees a half-truth. This Milton came to recognize (perhaps also reflecting that in her social position and environment, and by virtue of her beauty, the Lady Alice was destined for marriage, not celibacy), and thus made the Attendant Spirit present the medial and correct position between Comus and the Lady; he was enabled to do so by the traditional recognition of two types of chastity, the virginal and the marital, represented, for example, by Phineas Fletcher's Parthenia and Agnia respectively (*P.I.* 10. 24–40). It is the position of Parthenia that Milton celebrates in the first version, and indeed intensifies in the first addition; it is towards the position of Agnia that the Attendant Spirit redirects the movement in the lines added to the Epilogue.

K. Muir ('Three Hundred Years of Milton's Poems,' *Penguin New Writing* 24, 1945, 128–46) defends *Comus* against such critics as Greg, Herford, and Wyndham Lewis. He rejects Tillyard's view that the additions of 1637 redirect the meaning: they merely make more explicit what has been clear from the beginning, that the convictions attributed to the Lady are one-sided and exaggerated. It is significant that she substitutes chastity for Charity as the companion of Faith and Hope, 'and nothing could better indicate the limitations of her virtue' (143). For the rest, 'Milton chose neither side in the debate; the licence of Comus is contrasted with the limitations of the Lady.' [See also Muir under 1955 below.]

[In '"Hail Wedded Love"' (*ELH* 13, 1946, 79–97) William Haller, discussing Puritan and Miltonic ideals of love and marriage, questions the psychologizing of Saurat, Hanford, Tillyard, and Woodhouse in regard to *Comus*. The exaltation of virginity seen by these critics would be 'contrary to the whole tenor of the religious and moral training to which he [Milton] had been subjected and to the ideas which he himself began to set forth so unequivocally in 1642' (88). Obviously he could not make the Lady a Britomart seeking her husband. Besides, Milton was a very self-conscious artist and not disposed to relieve supposed private emotions by putting them into a masque designed for a special occasion and for the young Lady Alice Egerton. In giving her 'the rôle of maiden chastity, assailed but never hurt,' Milton was doing what was 'entirely proper, conventional, and expected'; and he naturally filled her speeches with Platonic and Spenserian ideas of virtue.]

[Ethel Seaton ('*Comus* and Shakespeare,' *Essays and Studies* 31, 1946; cf. III. 5 above) found *Romeo and Juliet* the strongest Shakespearian influence on *Comus*. However that may be, Miss Seaton wound up with a brief comparison of Juliet and the Lady, and, since the Lady has had her detractors, some sentences may be quoted. 'Is not the under-current of *Romeo and Juliet* throughout *Comus* a proof of Milton's firm hold on normal thought and feeling? Both girls are normal in their swift responses: Juliet in a youthful and innocent passion, the Lady in a clear-sighted discernment of evil once she has experienced falsity.... She is no abstraction, but a high-spirited girl. Juliet is young, passionate, "an impatient child" on the night before some festival. The Lady's youth is manifested in her blunt outspokenness.... The mystic gardens are symbolic of the renewal of life and Psyche's offspring are Youth and Joy. This is no contradiction of the theme, but its complement; not a denial of life, but acceptance of another approach to life,...another kind of flowering, the expansion into the fuller and initiated life, the "sublime notion and high mystery", through that liberating passion of chastity which "does not destroy but express and enlarge the spirit"; "Thou canst not touch the freedom of my mind."']

Reacting against what he considers over-reading of the work, J. C. Maxwell ('The Pseudo-Problem of *Comus*,' *Cambridge Journal* 1, 1947–8, 376–80) upholds three propositions: (i) 'The doctrine that virginity is, or is symbolic of, a uniquely blessed state,... is not central to the poem' (against Woodhouse, some part of whose analysis he accepts); (ii) 'There is no suggestion that the Lady's virtue is narrow or one-sided' (against Tillyard and Muir); (iii) 'There is no contradiction between either the 1634 version as a whole, or the Lady's speeches in particular, and the doctrine of the Epilogue' (against Tillyard). Maxwell argues (i) that, while virtue in the particular context inevitably implies chastity, it is virtue and not chastity for which the Lady and, through her,

Milton assert a special power of self-protection and divine guidance and aid (210–12, 588, 969–74, 1018–22). (ii) Except for the introduction of Chastity as the companion of Faith and Hope and supported by Conscience (210–12), which is perfectly natural in the Lady's circumstances, there is no 'particular textual argument for the view that the Lady is presented as narrow and limited.' (iii) Virtue in general is the theme, though in the context it takes the form of chastity. If this particular virtue 'is never...viewed in connection with...wedded love' (Woodhouse), neither is it contrasted therewith. Nor is it readily conceivable that a masque should either preach a 'purely restrictive virtue' (Tillyard) or display 'in action the limitations of such virtue' (Muir).

[Malcolm M. Ross ('Milton and the Protestant Aesthetic: The Early Poems,' *UTQ* 17, 1947–8, 346–60; *Poetry & Dogma*, 1954, 183–204), writing from a strongly Anglo-Catholic standpoint, finds the religious symbolism of *Comus* merely ethical, external, and shrivelled. The Nun of *Il Penseroso* 'makes Contemplation visible....In her, purity is for the sake of devotion and achieves the rapt soul sitting in the eyes....' But the Lady, 'the ethical symbol of *Comus*,' 'has no capacity for ecstasy, except in the contemplation of her own virtue and the means for its defence.' 'Faith, Hope, and *Chastity*. And the greatest of these is chastity! The substitution of chastity for charity is the reduction of the highest supernatural grace to a secondary practical virtue....The Lady is wholly self-regarding' (196). In the Sabrina scene 'Virginity turns out to be nothing, after all, but virginity—in the utterly physical sense.' 'The great doctrine towards which time and the will of heaven have been leading us is nothing more than practical sexual prudence' (199–200). Although Ross quotes Woodhouse with approval, in his own vehement misreading he seems—following Milton's outrageous substitution of Chastity for Charity—to have exchanged the text of *Comus* for *Pamela*.]

[Milton Miller ('Milton's Imagination and the Idyllic Solution,' *Western Review* 13, 1948, 35–43), starting from opposition to Middleton Murry et al., sees Milton's 'idyllic imagination...certainly tied up with the strength and certainty of his faith.' It shows itself very early in his English poetry. 'Its tone is set forever after in the general idyll of man's redemption,' as in the *Nativity*. 'Then it takes a multitude of forms.' In *Comus* as elsewhere, 'neither the world nor man is idyllic—*it is the solution that is idyllic*'—witness *Comus* 5–11—'*and the idyllic solution is the Christian solution.*' 'Milton does not deny the lady in *Comus* the reality of the temptation,...but neither does he deny the reality of the "unblemish't form of Chastity." And the idyllic solution lies in the perhaps too great reliance upon the unassailability of human virtue....But it is in such passages, where the free mind rejects evil, that Milton rises to a sublimity found only in the very greatest poetry.' In *Comus*, 'and again in paradise, the touchstone of his idyllic imagination is the way in which the optimism plays between a real and an imagined world without however losing its hold on the reality of this "darksome House of mortal Clay." The main preoccupation of Milton's theme is not...the tragic flaw in the nature of things, but rather that there is a way out through faith and virtue and, above all, through the high gracious act of him who bled "to give us ease." Milton does not forget that decay is the lot of everything, but it is not original sin which is the motivating force of his imagination—his impetus is the redemption and the way out of the closed circle.' Going on to *Paradise Lost*, which treats the theme on a grand scale, Miller remarks that there is 'no poet whom Plato would more readily have received into his Republic, at least if his Republic were at the same time a Christian state; for Milton's idyll is the idyll of the good and the triumph of man's will over evil in the figure of a redeeming Christ.' His poetry does not, like Shakespeare or Homer, 'have the tragic tension which questions man's relation to the gods or their final wisdom and goodness....In Milton the good always overcomes the evil, and there Plato would have agreed....There is no fear of death in Milton's verse but, on the contrary, the ripening of the soul to meet God, and Plato would here too have agreed.']

[In a short paper of generalized reflection, 'Le Thème de la Tentation dans le *Comus* de Milton' (*Revue d'Histoire et de Philosophie Religieuses*, 28–9, 1948–9, 43–8), J. Blondel seeks to define what he sees in *Comus* as Milton's youthful blend of Renaissance humanism and Christian faith. Sabrina, the goddess of the Severn, is the 'symbole d'un baptême qui confirme la pureté raisonnable de la jeune fille,' but he dwells chiefly on the Lady's and Milton's serene trust in reason, conscience, discipline, the dignity of individual responsibility—an attitude more moralistic than fundamentally Christian, but not grimly and unaesthetically Puritan. 'Nous assistons, en effet, à une synthèse entre cet individualisme, d'origine nettement puritaine, teintée déjà par l'humanisme, et un certain spiritualisme de nature platonicienne.' At the very heart of the problem of temptation, and its resolution, is a half-pagan, half-Christian conception of soul and body. 'La vertu crée l'équilibre, permet à l'homme de retrouver la félicité paradisiaque, la rupture n'étant pas définitivement consommée entre le monde et le créateur par une chute dont Milton ne mesure pas encore la profondeur. Pareille attitude relève de ce qu'un théologien appellerait le péché d'angélisme.' 'Cet angélisme constitue la tentation intellectuelle de l'humaniste qui veille toujours en Milton, et qui lui permet de lutter contre la tentation morale avec élégance, avec grâce.' Virtue 'est ordonnatrice,' but more than that: 'de cette fusion entre le culte de la vertu et l'angélisme, fondé sur le dualisme platonicien du corps et de l'âme, il apparaît que la leçon ultime en est une sagesse qui maintient Milton à l'intérieur du stoïcisme.' The optimistic voice of self-realization silences that of Calvinistic grace and makes possible a harmony between earth and heaven.]

Treating 'Milton's "Comus" as a Failure in Artistic Compromise' (*ELH* 16, 1949, 104–19; *The Harmonious Vision*, 1954, 24–40), D. C. Allen holds that Johnson was right in seeing *Comus* as an unsuccessful effort at drama and Warton wrong in his attempted rebuttal, and that Tillyard was right in detecting a variety of inconsistent styles (Allen adds that 'the pallium of classical tragedy covers the whole poem'), which indicates Milton's failure to achieve a satisfactory compromise. The same confusion appears in the variety of motifs on which the poet draws (for the Brothers, the Wandering Knight, Ulysses, Guyon, even Britomart; for Comus, Circe, Ariosto's Alcina, Tasso's Armida, Spenser's Acrasia; and for the 'satirically horrific' effects, Peele's *Old Wives' Tale*; while Milton departs at will from his different sources, e.g. in taking Sabrina from Geoffrey of Monmouth, Drayton's *Polyolbion*, etc., to act as *dea ex machina*): again no successful compromise is reached. And, finally, the 'intellectual texture...baffles readers on all levels.' Accepting Woodhouse's 'attempt to untangle its meaning' as generally correct, one still finds 'no effective compromise' and suspects that Milton failed to make his 'artistic emphasis' coincide with 'his intended moral emphasis.' The pagan and Christian elements are not clearly discriminated and hence cannot be clearly related. There is throughout a failure to reach a satisfactory compromise in and between content and style, and notably to ensure a unified effect under the conditions of dramatic form.

C. Clarke ('A Neglected Episode in *Comus*,' *The Wind and the Rain* 6, 1949, 103–7) pointed out the failure of Woodhouse's first article (as of other interpretations) to take into account the role of Sabrina. He argued that the transition from a negative and restrictive virtue to a positive and joyous one does not wait for expression in the Epilogue, but is already realized in the poetry of the Sabrina episode with its responsive emphasis on natural beauty. Of Sabrina and her release of the Lady as symbols of grace Clarke catches no hint; but his point about the poetry is valuable in clearing the objection that some have felt in the character of the surrounding imagery if Sabrina is indeed a symbol of grace.

Adopting Woodhouse's general line of interpretation, M. Macklem ('Love, Nature and Grace in Milton,' *Queen's Quarterly* 56, 1949–50, 534–47) proposed to read back into *Comus* the whole conception of love, and notably of marital love as a step toward heavenly love, as that is developed in *Paradise Lost*.

[M. Mack (*Milton*, 1950, 7–9) begins with the 'central metaphor...of pilgrimage. The forest through which the three children make their way home...is clearly in some sense an emblem of the perplexity and obscurity of mortal life, which constitutes God's trial of the soul (79, 328, 969–72).' Comus obviously 'stands for evil in its tempting disguises, as his train of brutish monsters stand for evil in its unmasked effects.' But, in a more complex way, Comus 'stands also for evil considered in its philosophical aspect as a perversion of the good: the misuse of the order of nature which makes the human being sink downward in the scale of being to the status of brute. For this reason, Milton allows him to express truths which in his mouth become distortions of truth'—as in his applying the harmonious dance of nature to the obscene rites of Cotytto, or the plenitude of nature's gifts to the abuse of such gifts.

'Set over against Comus...is the Attendant Spirit. Both present themselves to the mortal eye as shepherds (270, 492), preside over dances (144 ff., 957 ff.), celebrate the sensuous riches of nature (705 ff., 975 ff.), and use the tetrameter metre that Milton allots to no one else (93 ff., 866–1022). As the powers of Comus seduce men to sink to the level of brutes, the Attendant Spirit would persuade them to rise to the level of angels —"Higher than the sphery chime." But the Spirit is a guardian only; 'he exercises no supernatural powers. In the test that the wood presents, the victory of the Lady has to be won, by herself, and within; the Attendant Spirit, representing apparently a right use of nature in contrast to Comus's perversion, offers against the latter's arts simply a control derived from nature—"Haemony," or, as the Lady later puts it in her debate with Comus, the "holy dictate of spare Temperance." Though it is difficult to interpret the Spirit's final song, what it seems to say is that through temperate use of the natural order man may participate sinlessly in the life processes of nature (998–1001), and fuse them with grace (1002–10) in a union whose ultimate offspring will be eternal youth and joy.'

In spite of the general clarity of outline, *Comus* 'fails to elucidate how a doctrine of temperance such as the Lady proposes in her retort to Comus relates to a doctrine of virginity, or abstention, which she proposes in the same speech. Moreover, the Lady declares to Comus that the "high mystery" of virginity has a positive spiritual value, as in Christian philosophy it has; but the poem nowhere succeeds in "realizing" this value for us in poetic terms—that is to say, in terms which enable it to compete imaginatively with Comus's great lines on fruition. The Elder Brother, who comes closest to realizing virginity in poetic terms, seems no clearer than his sister whether the value that is to be balanced against "imbrutement" is temperate use or renunciation.' The various and ingenious explanations offered by critics suggest 'a fundamental irresolution in both...moral and artistic design.']

[J. E. Hardy begins his elaborate discussion (Brooks and Hardy, 1951,

187–237) by pronouncing 'a bit too obvious' the common view of *Comus* as 'a kind of allegory on the familiar theme of Virtue's conflict with Evil.' The work is dramatic, and 'the characters, and the symbolism which provides the basic pattern of Milton's imagery, are more *mythological* than allegorical. That is to say simply that the persons and objects here, as in myth, are conceived as having real, independent existence. They are not, as in allegory, more or less arbitrarily constructed vehicles, limited in their significant existence to the conceptual realities which they carry. The characters in *Comus* sometimes *speak* allegorically, in their own right; but they are not themselves allegorical. The pattern of significance in the action and imagery of this poem is, to a great extent, a pattern of complex association and suggestion which the abstract system of strict allegory cannot accommodate' (188). In the main lines of his commentary on the characters, action, and theme Hardy is often orthodox, and his close reading is active and provocative, but his emphasis on imagery and irony can lead to over-subtle aberrations and the blurring of Milton's ideas. For one random example, it is said (201), apropos of the last line of the Lady's song (and other items): 'In short, the Christian–pagan issue, the shock of the sudden juxtaposition of the seemingly disparate elements, becomes tonally a part of the Lady's confusion of mind itself'; the shock and confusion are entirely in the mind of the critic. His 'heaviest debt' is to Woodhouse's article of 1941 (the supplement of 1950, on Sabrina, may have appeared too late for use), 'the best study of the poem' he knows, although he is in 'frequent disagreement': e.g., Woodhouse 'has all but ignored the evidences of Milton's consciousness in the poem of the possibility of conflict between classical Virtue and Christian Grace' (235). To say this is to ignore the whole tradition of Christian humanism which Milton so strongly upheld in the *Apology for Smectymnuus* and elsewhere. Nor does it clarify the 'real conflict' Hardy sees to have Milton saying, in regard to haemony and 'wherever the Grace theme enters,...that Grace and Virtue are essentially the same' (212), and to be told that haemony is at once 'the supreme symbol' of Virtue and 'the special symbol of the element of Grace' (212–13).]

R. M. Adams ('Reading *Comus*,' *MP* 51, 1953–4, 18–32; *Ikon: John Milton and the Modern Critics*, Ithaca and London, 1955, 1–34) protests against what he takes to be the over-reading of *Comus*, exemplified especially by Brooks and Hardy (above, under 1951). *Comus* is not to be read as a metaphysical poem but as a masque, a form designed for public performance, whose functions are 'to voice a compliment, to present a moral allegory, and to provide occasion for spectacle,' and it is not likely to conceal a meaning 'not easily available to a single hearing by an informed, attentive listener.' The revisions do not at all alter the meaning: 'whatever main shape the masque had, it evidently had from the beginning.' 'The central episode...is clearly the temptation.' The sort of allurements offered to the Lady and the sort of energies which enable her to withstand them 'must determine the allegorical meaning,' and secondary elements—the destination of the journey, the debate of the brothers, the prologue and epilogue—can do no more than alter secondary emphases: 'the central dramatic conflict' is the key to the 'intellectual and emotional content.' The relation of Comus to Circe is important and is emphasized by Milton at 251 f., 635–6, as well as in the fate of Comus' victims, his equipment of cup and wand, his allurements, which culminate 'latently but climactically' with 'sexual enjoyment,' while 'Bacchus remains largely in the background.' Haemony does not, as Le Comte avers ⟨below, v, 637 n.⟩, stand for divine grace, but for temperance, exactly as moly does in the interpretation of most Renaissance mythographers (10–16). Nor does Sabrina. Plainly she and haemony cannot both stand for grace: in fact neither does, and Sabrina symbolizes chastity, not grace. Actually both are introduced in response to the demands of the action, and, taken literally, are white magic to offset the black magic of Comus. There is no intended criticism of the Elder Brother's reliance on virtue, without grace, as sufficient for its own protection. 'Thus three central elements...fit together on the earthly plane without notable inconsistency or incongruity. The spiritual energies of the Lady's virtue suffice to repel Comus without any divine back-stiffening. The brothers are able to approach Comus armed not with grace, but with temperance; and the doctrine that chastity or virginity possesses powers for its own defense is enunciated by the Elder Brother without any such backlash of ironic commentary as Brooks and Hardy have imputed to Milton. The machinery of magic is invoked to protect the Lady and her brothers,' and, though Milton may at this time have attributed magical powers to chastity itself (cf. Tillyard, under 1930 above), 'in the masque it serves moral ends which can be perfectly well understood on the secular plane' (22). That the masque moves on this level throughout is confirmed by the fact that the Attendant Spirit is not an angel nor has his dwelling in the highest heaven, but is a daemon as the MS. calls him ⟨below, v, initial stage direction, n.⟩; only at the end of his epilogue is heaven brought in, as an aspiration, and then no more is said than that if virtue were feeble (it has been shown not to be), heaven would 'stoop' to her. [Adams also (30–3) rejects the critical principles applied to *Comus* by D. C. Allen, principles which 'would make hash out of almost all the poetry written by John Milton, or for that matter by most English poets.']

[R. H. Bowers ('The Accent on Youth in *Comus*,' *SAMLA Studies*, 1953, 72–9) thinks that critics of *Comus* have not sufficiently appreciated the significance of youthfulness in its theme, its author, and its performers, and the pleasure an aristocratic audience would feel in this aspect of the presentation. *Comus* is concerned, like much Renaissance literature (pastoral, masque, prose romance), with 'the sensibilities and emotional experiences of the adolescent.' 'And the specific theme of seduction indignantly resisted by a spirited young lady' was a commonplace of the Jacobean and Caroline stage. Social convention accepted a girl of thirteen or fourteen as a woman 'Ripe for a husband.' In *Comus* the 'moral conflict is limned in black and white,' in the way 'unsubtle youth wants to regard the choices of life.' The language would not bruise the 'tender sensibilities and sense of social propriety of youth.' Finally, if one considers the performance in its social milieu, the high point is not the Lady's natural refusal of the enchanted cup but the Spirit's restoring the children, now seen as the Egerton children, to their parents. 'The happy ending of youth triumphant over the gross temptations of "sensual Folly, and Intemperance," then, provides a conventional, happy tone to a happy social gathering in a great hall of the great.' And Milton provided not only a courtly entertainment but 'an indirect outlet for his own restless struggling' with moral problems.]

[N. E. Enkvist ('The Functions of Magic in Milton's *Comus*,' *Neuphilologische Mitteilungen* 54, 1953, 310–18) concludes with this summary:

The function of magic is to make *Comus* consistent within its own framework, to suspend external interference and to bring the action under one set of immutable rules, and to rivet together the various elements, including nature and grace, into one philosophically (though not always artistically) perfect whole— in short, to give the masque unity of action and thought. Such pregnancy of meaning and also such an interweaving of many traditions into a consistent philosophy as we find in *Comus* is characteristic of the best literature of the English Renaissance, a period when [in Tillyard's words] 'theology included all philosophy and a great deal of natural science.'

Noting that Wales was a traditional 'haunt of magicians,' and that magic was a convenient device for dramatizing the victory of virtue over vice, Enkvist discusses both black and white magic, to whose exponents theological and secular tradition gave 'very definite places in the chain of being,' the degrees of potency in both kinds, and their partly ritualistic character. These things are related to the ethical and religious theme of nature and grace, to which black and white magic respectively belong. 'Obviously magic plays a more important part in *Comus* than in any other of Milton's poetical works....And the great skill with which the magic of *Comus* is integrated with the many other elements and rivets them seamlessly together suggests that to Milton, at the time of the composition and revision, magic was an intellectual rather than emotional issue.' In comparison with Spenser's Bower of Bliss, 'the magic of *Comus* is better integrated with the action and argument; everybody has to obey the same immutable rules.']

[J. Arthos' *On A Mask Presented at Ludlow-Castle* (Ann Arbor, 1954) and later studies are cited in the Notes below. He has expounded *Comus* in Platonic rather than Christian terms: 'Ultimately the poem's Christianity depends on the affirmation of Jove's grace, but the Platonic philosophy in itself is always sufficient to explain the means of the [Attendant] Spirit's action' (*Mask*, 37). More broadly, commenting on Woodhouse's two articles, Arthos says: 'To me Platonic and Neo-Platonic illustrations seem to provide a self-consistent and comprehensive interpretation of the thought of the *Mask*, and I can find no detail in the thought that requires a special theological interpretation and in particular no reference to an idea of grace to be explained only by seventeenth-century theology' (ibid. 71, n. 38).]

[The comments of F. T. Prince (*Italian Element*, 1954, 66–9) are purely literary and technical. He finds Italian influence (i.e. Tasso and Guarini) 'indirect and subordinate'; Milton owes more to Fletcher, Jonson, Shakespeare, and Spenser. '*Comus* is by virtue of its length and the variety of its verse one of the most important illustrations of Milton's art before his visit to Italy. In the blank verse dialogues there is much that remains apparent in his mature epic verse...': his 'feeling for the English language, the peculiar weight of his verse,...his skill in constructing elaborate and extended verse-paragraphs, and his delight in an overwhelming fullness of expression. Many passages convey a sense of discovery as well as achievement, a reaching out towards a new style,' as in lines 519–35. This passage 'has Shakespeare's plenitude and weight, invaluable in dramatic verse. But it has these qualities to excess, because Milton's prime purpose is not dramatic but literary, and he is working towards the creation of a style essentially unsuited to drama....Milton's special preoccupation here is clearly to extend the limits of the sentence, as he is to find means of doing, more appropriately, in his epic verse.

'Yet it is worth observing that the wonderful elaboration of this blank verse style in *Comus* is achieved without making use of many of the devices of *Paradise Lost*. Astonishing periods are constructed almost entirely without the " Miltonic inversions" to be derived later from Virgil and the Italian experiments in epic diction. Lines and sequences of lines may be found almost everywhere which could occur also in the later blank verse; there is no consistent difference in the prosodic basis, though certain "liberties" appear, both here and in the dialogues of *Samson Agonistes*, which suggest that Milton distinguishes between dramatic blank verse and blank verse in narrative poetry. It would be difficult to demonstrate that the blank verse of *Comus* is a different metre from that of the epics. But it is sung to a different tune, as it were; it has a different movement and pitch; it has behind it a different pattern. *Paradise Lost* has the movement and tone of Virgil, and it has the pattern of Italian *versi sciolti* of the sixteenth century. *Comus* observes the tone and movement of Shakespeare's blank verse, adapting also inflexions from lesser dramatists.

'The lyrics of *Comus*, like those of *Arcades*, are related primarily to Jonson and Fletcher....

'The importance of *Comus* for our study of the development of Milton's verse is that it illustrates copiously his relation to the Elizabethans and Jacobeans. It shows him consciously assimilating what he could of these native beauties. He had no Italian models in mind on this occasion; if he had had any idea of reproducing in English the special qualities of the Italian pastoral dramas, the result would assuredly have been very different from what we have.']

[Dick Taylor ('Grace as a Means of Poetry: Milton's Pattern for Salvation,' *Tulane Studies in English* 4, 1954, 57–90) sees all Milton's major poems, from *Comus* onward, as organized, flexibly, on one religious and structural principle that is central in his creed: 'trial of the protagonist, proof, and extension of grace accompanied by a miraculous event.' This principle, in its first operation in *Comus*, is of course subject to the demands of the genre, but Milton is at pains to build up both the seductive powers of Comus and the strength of the Lady. When she has given sufficient proof of her own virtue, Comus himself (799–804) feels the presence of a higher power, and there follows, in the manner of a masque, 'the miraculous event which signifies the extension of grace' (62), the coming of Sabrina. 'Heaven itself will stoop to hard-pressed virtue, but it must be virtue that has been proven; after the proof, heaven will reach down with a miracle. The brothers are not on trial,' and they, not the Lady, are protected by haemony. Yet she, however strong in virtue, can be deceived by Comus' magic dust, and she can be held physically captive, so that grace is needed to free her.

'God does not expect man to display divine strength; he has only to go so far along the road. The Lady and her brothers have done enough, and so should leave the danger zone as soon as possible [937–43]—the Lady must not make the mistake that Eve is to make in *Paradise Lost*' (64). Milton evidently wished 'to create a sense of tension and struggle in the Lady's trial,' and the lack of this may be attributed partly to the nature of the masque and the Lady's being Lady Alice Egerton, partly to Milton's own immaturity and inexperience. He 'spent too much time in establishing and explicating the issues, which were not complex enough to need such lengthy exposition' (66). Still, *Comus* already reveals 'his artistic strategy of careful preparation for the climactic miracle.']

[A. E. Dyson ('The Interpretation of *Comus*,' *Essays and Studies 1955*, 89–114) finds Woodhouse's analysis valuable but 'too elaborate and speculative' and 'intensively intellectual'; Woodhouse 'makes far too much of the closing section,' and 'maintains that the action of the poem is set in the realm of "Nature" until the closing pages, when the entry of "Sabrina fair" raises it to the realm of Grace.' Dyson also disagrees with Tillyard's idea that Comus and the Lady are both wrong (see above); and is in entire agreement with Maxwell (above). Dyson offers a simpler reading, the impression an educated seventeenth-century audience would have received: that is, a clear-cut encounter between good and evil. And 'the visions of life belonging to nature and Grace respectively are present side by side throughout the poem.' Like Maxwell, Dyson sees the Lady as standing not so much for Chastity as for Virtue; Chastity represents 'spiritual wholeness and the life of Grace,' the control of the passions by reason. The 'debate' between Comus and the Lady is between Passion and Reason—an argument thoroughly in accord with Renaissance tradition, with Milton's habitual contrasts between earth and heaven, anarchy and order, and with the rational and religious conviction of the age that good and evil are very distinct realities and enemies and that good must triumph in the end. The characters of *Comus* are all clearly placed in relation to that central issue, though the good ones differ in degrees of understanding. Quoting from the Attendant Spirit's first speech (lines 12–17), Dyson emphasizes the depth and prime importance of Milton's Platonic thinking: 'Virtue is Knowledge, and...an unclouded understanding is both the condition of Virtue, and its reward' (99). He runs through the masque, noting Milton's insistent contrasts between sensual pleasure, disorder, falsity, and purity, order, truth. Chastity, he repeats, 'is only one example (though the supreme one) of self-control, Reason, and the life of Grace. It is the entrance to that world of spiritual realities from which Comus and his crew are totally excluded' (106). The entire tenor of the masque is a demonstration of the falseness of Comus' argument from 'Nature,' and, though the Lady has suffered from much prejudice, 'Her verse has exactly the right qualities to offset that of Comus—short, decisive words, clear syntax, sharp diction, and firm structural control' (112). Dyson thinks that, at this stage in his life, Milton 'regarded Virginity as superior to Marriage,' and 'Virginity can be a shining and exalted ideal'; 'the Lady is an exponent of Virginity in its most absolute form.' Yet, in a larger way, 'it is certain that she stands for unswerving Virtue and for the life of Grace, and that her position is totally vindicated in the masque as a complete work of art' (114). 'The Lady's attitude is positive, and unified, and "right", and Comus's position is positive, and unified, and wrong,' and 'the masque consists of a straight battle between the two.']

[K. Muir (*J.M.*, 1955, 1960, 33–44) is more sympathetic toward *Comus* than he was in his earlier discussion (above, under 1945). Quoting both hostile and friendly critics, he sides with those who emphasize the Christian Platonism Milton outlined in his *Apology* (above, III. 11). Muir thinks (cf. Saurat and Tillyard) that for a time after the performance of *Comus* Milton was 'unduly obsessed with the question of virginity,' but his attitude in the masque is wholly sincere and 'much healthier' than that of Fletcher in *The Faithful Shepherdess*. In general, Muir goes along with Woodhouse, but he sees temperance, chastity, and virginity as 'merely particular examples' of a broader conception of virtue, and the doctrine of Christian liberty as 'implicit throughout the poem,' not enunciated only in the Epilogue. '*Comus* is a kind of Platonic dialogue in the guise of a masque,' and, like Milton's three late major works, it deals with a temptation. The central scene between Comus and the Lady may be regarded in some ways as 'a debate between two ways of life, the Cavalier and the Puritan, as seen through Puritan eyes.' Although Milton knows the fallacies of Renaissance libertinism, 'he gives the devil his due and puts into the mouth of his enchanter some of the best poetry in the whole masque'—not that that indicates the poet's unconscious sympathy with Comus. The Lady is not presented as a sour ascetic. 'In Jonson's *Pleasure Reconciled to Virtue* pleasure is merely a temporary interlude in a strenuous life....But Milton's reconciliation is more profound. Joy is not an interlude—it is the reward of virtue here on earth. "He repudiates false pleasures, but not joy", remarks Woodhouse. Among the rewards of the virtuous are "the very things that the adversary would declare to be taken away". The masque ends appropriately with music and dancing....There is nothing narrowly puritanical in the conclusion.'

'*Comus* in its way is a masterpiece, as it is certainly the greatest of all masques and pastoral plays.' Complaints by Johnson and others about its undramatic qualities are beside the mark; 'Milton was not writing a drama: he was writing a debate on opposing ways of life in a semi-dramatic form, a study of the rejection of temptation by innocence.' 'The blank verse of *Comus*, though it owes more to the verse of Shakespeare's middle period than to that of any other writer, is yet distinctly Miltonic. Milton felt, rightly, that the blank verse of his immediate contemporaries had become loose and flabby.' 'That Milton's avoidance of the style of contemporary dramatists was deliberate can be seen from an examination of the manuscript of *Comus*, which contains passages more akin to the work of the Jacobeans than anything in the printed text.']

[J. W. Saunders ('Milton, Diomede and Amaryllis,' *ELH* 22, 1955, 276–7), going on from *L'Allegro* and *Il Penseroso* (cf. Criticism of those poems), says: 'The conflict between Diomede and Amaryllis is sharper in *Comus*. Here the form and the occasion were wholly of the Renaissance and the Court; but the high seriousness and the dialectical didacticism struck a new note. It is a romance, a love story, dedicated to chastity, and Diomede and Amaryllis are dramatized in partial antithesis. The poem succeeds within the courtly medium, says what it has to say without outraging the courtly form, because Milton blurs the outlines of the antithesis. Comus is not wholly Amaryllis, in the mood of *L'Allegro*, nor is the Lady wholly Diomede, in the mood of *Il Penseroso*. True, "the light fantastick round" and the "Wood-Nymphs deckt with Daisies trim" are his allies, while the Lady relies on Temperance and the armour of Chastity. But Comus has melancholy associations, his own mystique in fealty bound to Cotytto and Hecate, and Night is his friend; and the Lady sings of the "violet imbroider'd Vale" and the "love-lorn Nightingale" in accents that owe nothing to "sowre Severity" and "strict Age." The Tempter is finally defeated, not because the Brothers charm him with their "divine Philosophy," nor because the Lady outwits him in dialectic, but because Milton pours into the defence of Chastity all his finest erotic imagery; the real victory in the drama belongs to Sabrina and to the epilogue which, like Shelley's fourth act in *Prometheus Unbound*, persuades with music and not with logic. It is the same kind of imagery that balances the dread voice of ecclesiastical polemics in *Lycidas*. Milton remained a Renaissance poet writing for courtly audiences and Amaryllis, however reformed, was still in her throne.'

Quoting from Milton's account of poetry in the *Reason of Church-Government* (*Works* 3, 237–42), Saunders says: 'This rationalizes the position he has been forced to adopt in poems like *Comus*; the emphasis on didacticism, on sweetening the pill of truth for courtly folk, is not to be found in his earlier verse....' From this somewhat dubious argument—which slights Milton's religious view of poetry and ignores his declaration that poetry is 'more simple, sensuous and passionate' than logic and rhetoric (*Educ, Works* 4, 286)—Saunders goes on to draw a still more dubious parallel with Dryden: 'Amaryllis is to be in chains, the prisoner of Diomede, and all his sensuousness in all its seductiveness is to serve as a palliative for those who cannot stomach the plain truth.']

[M. Van Doren (Preface to *The Masque of Comus...The Airs of Henry Lawes, with a Preface by Hubert Foss, illustrated...by Edmund Dulac*, New York, [1955]) praises the lyrics and the blank verse and emphasizes the dramatic character of the masque: it has persons, not abstractions, and 'the trial of each is real.' Of the theme he speaks thus: 'Milton has been accused of writing in *Comus* a parable of prudery; but to say such a thing is to miss the fact that it is truly a drama, and further-more to miss the signs in it that its author disapproves of prudery quite as much as he disapproves of sensuality. It is no longer the fashion, as it was in the seventeenth century, to conceive of chastity as the very type and symbol of human perfection, and therefore as realizable only in heaven. Those who thought they were perfect on earth committed the sin of pride; and those who thought they understood perfection, in others or in themselves, might well fall short of the truth, which in its fullest form was of mystical magnitude—a high doctrine which the ironies of drama might best elucidate. So Milton believed at any rate; and hence he proceeded to bury his vision deep among the particulars of a play none of whose characters ever speaks for him. The Elder Brother thinks he knows, and does not; he speaks like a prig, and Milton intends that we should note the fact. Even the Lady, who is not a prig, fails nevertheless to answer the arguments of Comus...; Comus has no comprehension of chastity at all, but neither does she have perfect comprehension; she identifies it, perhaps, with her own virtue; whereas it is a heavenly thing whose name is grace, and it is as much beyond her reach as salvation is beyond her power; in the end she is rescued by forces and persons that have nothing to do with this world. And Milton, together with the audience if its subtlety is sufficient, alone sees where truth lies. It lies before the starry threshold of Jove's court, or in the Garden of Adonis, or—if we prefer Christian to pagan symbols—in Heaven itself, whose solemn troops and sweet societies might sing it to us were our ears attuned and our intellects attentive.']

[W. B. C. Watkins (*An Anatomy of Milton's Verse*, Baton Rouge, 1955, 87–101) is more, and more successfully, concerned with aesthetic than with interpretative criticism (some comments are quoted in the notes below), although the former is weakened by failure to grasp Milton's theme and attitudes. '*Comus* and *Paradise Regained*, in the very course of demonstrating reason's triumph, show clearly that passion is always stronger in Milton than reason' (89). Watkins does not see the meta-physical poem of Brooks and Hardy. He agrees closely with Allen's main belief that *Comus* 'fails to reconcile its opposites,' though for him 'Basic contradictions, held temporarily in suspension by the magic of his verse, give an essentially static poem unpremeditated drama' (90–1). Woodhouse's 'seminal study' aggravates difficulties. 'In this doctrine of unassailable chastity what at once troubles us is sterility.' The issue is confused by Milton's giving to Comus 'all those time-honored pleas for plenitude' that he was to put forth in *Paradise Lost*. 'Whenever he is freed from his uncompromising elevation of the Elder Brother's faith and the Lady's impregnability, Milton elaborates with extraordinary zest the other symbolism of the poem, and by a series of instinctive choices reveals his own divided allegiance' (96–7). 'It is Comus, like Satan in *Paradise Lost*, who comes nearest to liberating Milton's imagination by providing a dramatic mouthpiece for arguing the other side with good conscience.']

[D. Daiches' account of *Comus* (*Milton*, 1957, 63–73), as a small part of a general survey, does not go into the issues of recent debate, but includes suggestive comments, e.g. on 'the occasional drunken lurch' in the rhythms of Comus' first speech, and on the dramatic irony with which he is presented (below, 709–35 n.). In *More Literary Essays* (1968), dealing with pastoral imagery, Daiches remarks that 'The counterpointing of classical and native here is more elaborately and more interestingly achieved than anywhere else in Milton.' 'The language of Comus himself is much more redolent of the actual English country-side...than that of any other character.' The younger Brother has something of this (e.g. 342–6); his elder's language has a more consistently classical tinge. Throughout the masque classical and native images rise and fall, and there are many pleasantly surprising juxtapositions, e.g. lines 670 and 674–5; Sabrina is enveloped in a mixture.]

Rosemond Tuve ('Image, Form, and Theme in *A Mask*,' *Images*, 1957, 112–61) attempts to keep the masque as actually performed before the mind's eye, since action and setting fortify and complete what the text presents. Thus 'If we have watched the motionless Lady as a "prison'd soul" ⟨813 f.⟩..., we are ready to see in these free dancing figures ⟨973–4⟩ an *image* of what "Heav'n it self" has stooped to protect ⟨1022⟩, the ordered Freedom ⟨1018⟩ conjoined with light of the many abstract statements concerning Virtue.' 'Masques, as a kind, are inescapably symbolical.' While dramatic, they 'do not have plots, but designs, "devices."' These devices 'are basically an extension...of some myth....They *start out* as great Images or speaking pictures and are by definition given "application."' A condition of the masque, as originally presented, is especially significant in *Comus*, namely, that the performers assume their symbolic roles without ceasing to be themselves: the Lady is all that her role implies and at the same time Alice Egerton; the wild Wood is the enchanted forest 'in which men meet Evil without ever ceasing to be the woods of Shropshire.' The pleasure taken 'in the double reality of scenes and of persons in a masque is simply a variant upon the usual pleasure in metaphor, where two ways of seeing things to be "true" are constantly and delightfully present, and yet seen as one' (118). We should not expect the suspense of dramatic action. Quite other expectations pertain to the genre and are fully realized in *Comus*: we expect allegory—'images allegorically read are the heart of the piece.' We expect 'some great simple contrast between Vice and Virtue' and 'some such expositor and guide of the action as the Attendant Spirit'; we expect pastoral imagery and 'mythological personages used to convey Christian ideas like that of grace....' (121–2). On these basic conformities of *Comus* to the masque the meaning and effect depend. 'The hinge upon which Milton's whole invention moves is the great and famous allegorical figure of Circe' (129–30), whose son and heir Comus is, and whose significance, as elaborated by Natalis Comes, Sandys, and others [see below, v, 635–6 n.], becomes 'a multiple metaphor,' not psychological only or moral, but involving a conception of man's nature and destiny with elements to be derived only from Christian thought (133): all of which was indeed traditional and was common ground for Milton and his readers. If adopted at all, the 'multiple metaphor' imposed its own meaning: it did not leave the poet (or his interpreters) free to depart radically therefrom. There is no room 'to manipulate the

Circe myth in order to show "that both the Lady and Comus were wrong: that there *was* another meaning" in her gift of feminine beauty and that "the meaning was marriage"' ⟨Tillyard, above, under 1943⟩, or for other additions and subtractions suggested by Adams, Saurat, or Brooks and Hardy ⟨above⟩. What Milton could and did do was to extend, not remake, the traditional meaning of chastity as inviolable 'fidelity to God,' so as to ally it with 'the sage And serious *doctrine* of Virginity.' If we ignore the implications which Christian commentary had bestowed upon chastity and assume the Elder Brother and the Lady to allude simply to a literal condition of the body or of body and soul, when they talk of chastity as a sure guard against every danger or a sure admission to communion with angels, the effect of this specious (to a reader familiar only with modern usage) but historically inaccurate assumption will be to infer (as has been done) that 'one brother is deluded, the other stupid, their sister self-righteous, and Milton's concern obsessive' (138). Properly understood, the Elder Brother's assertion is shown to be perfectly true: an angel (the Attendant Spirit) comes to drive off, in his own way, 'each thing of sin.' And 'the Lady perfectly typifies "Vertue...assail'd, but never hurt"'; Comus never manages to 'touch the freedom of [her] minde,' his real aim, in which he had succeeded with his followers, as their transformation shows. There are no intervals in the Lady's replies to him, whether in terms of temperance grounded in the rational order of nature, chastity, or virginity: they are ascending vindications of her basic possession of chastity in its full sense as opposed to the luxury advocated in its full sense by Comus, the former connoting freedom, the latter enslavement. 'The value of such a great traditional metaphor, as a hinge upon which the total invention can move, is that it can allow of a revelation of the nature of the opposition between good and evil. It is not a matter of "triumph over" after "conflict with," for the myth has become rather a way of looking at what the human moral predicament is' (142). 'The masque as a genre is peculiarly suited to this unveiling or discovery of the true nature of things through images....' '"Revelation" describes the functioning of the images from the very beginning of the poem.' It is fully illustrated in the scene of Comus' first entry with his rout—where beauty and gaiety predominate in the images, though licence lurks between the lines and the deformed crew are there to remind us of the essential affront to the natural order—so that the whole becomes a discovery of the insufficient conception of the natural which Comus entertains and is to set forth and whose insufficiency the Lady is not so much to demonstrate by argument as simply to reveal by her presence and the imagery she employs: we 'see that what is said is true.' Before we hear anything of reasonable temperance we see what its betrayal has done to Comus' followers: '"their human count'nance, Th'*express resemblance of the gods*, is chang'd Into som brutish form", some "*inglorious* likenes", "unmoulding *reasons mintage*".' Another way in which theme is conveyed through image is the pervasive play of light and darkness through the whole piece, whether in Comus' perverse ''Tis onely day-light that makes Sin' ⟨126⟩ or the Elder Brother's 'Unmuffle ye faint Stars,...Stoop...And disinherit *Chaos*, that raigns here In double night of *darkness*, and of *shades*' ⟨330–4⟩, or his confident 'Vertue could see to do what vertue would By her own radiant light, though Sun and Moon Were in the flat Sea sunk' ⟨372–4⟩—with various effects of symbolism and, on occasion, of dramatic irony. The wood is predominantly dark and the good can be temporarily baffled and deceived; but the inner light does not fail, and light, like the strength of goodness, triumphs in the end. 'That Heaven must stoop to the aid of strength is far from being nonsense. Two major images at least carry the burden of this idea, the Attendant Spirit and the Sabrina episode.... Not only is need shown in *Comus* for the greater *illumination* of grace, but the symbolic use of water suits with the demonstrated need for "a new infusion of divine grace" ⟨Woodhouse, above⟩ before the Lady can be freed (as no human creature can free another) from what Comus represents, and from every resulting bondage.' The masque indeed conveys its meaning primarily by image and symbol, as the play by subtleties of psychological motivation revealed in character; and to treat *Comus* as a play is to obscure its real nature and method, which are purely those of the masque.

[Geoffrey and Margaret Bullough, introducing a school and college text (*Milton's Dramatic Poems*, London and Fairlawn, N.J., 1958), deal mainly with conventions of the genre and Milton's sources and poetic qualities and give only a couple of pages to 'Governing Ideas.' These are described as 'a mixture of Platonism and Christian asceticism.' Along with his aspiring spirituality, 'Milton is inclined to worship Temperance, as if the act of self-denial were an end in itself and its result the Platonic vision of absolute joy; here repeating the confusion into which Spenser falls in *The Faerie Queene*. . . .' Such a view seems less close to current discussion than to the older anti-Puritan line. However, it is conceded that 'the glow and ardour generated in the attempted union of Christian renunciation and Platonic sublimation suffuse the poem with a warmth and light and joy which Milton never recaptured.']

Adopting Woodhouse's idea of the order of nature and the order of grace as a frame of reference within which action and argument are developed, W. G. Madsen (1958: see above, *Comus*: III. 10) simplifies the scheme by eliminating as a subject for distinct consideration an area of experience common to the two orders. This he can do because he does not regard the dialogue of the two Brothers, into which the Attendant Spirit breaks ⟨330–608⟩, as embodying any approach to specifically Christian doctrine or as laying a foundation for what is to follow in the Lady's encounter with Comus ⟨658–812⟩. The simplification does not perhaps otherwise alter the general conception of a progression from the order of nature to the order of grace. It does, however, entail or permit some shift in emphasis and a different evaluation of some conceptions and of the characters of the Elder Brother and the Attendant Spirit. The former is firmly relegated to the natural order: his 'doctrine of chastity, which culminates in the Platonic fancy that the body may be transmuted into soul's essence, symbolizes the highest reach of pagan thought (nature) unenlightened by Christian revelation (grace)' (215). And the Attendant Spirit is not (as in Woodhouse) a symbol of providential intervention in the natural order. His role 'is somewhat difficult of interpretation': 'he represents. . .the higher potentialities of human nature, as Comus represents the lower'; further, he 'represents the interpenetration of nature and grace from the point of view of nature; Sabrina from the point of view of grace.' He 'symbolizes the knowledge of right and wrong conferred by reason, she the power of doing right conferred by grace' (216). The reduction in status of the Attendant Spirit must result in a reduction of his gift of haemony to something approximating the natural virtue of temperance (symbolized for the moralizers of classical myth by moly). Sabrina is the only symbol of grace. Madsen attempts some fortifying of her religious character by examining the natural and mythological imagery which appears to dominate the Spirit's invocation to her, and by emphasizing the ritualistic character of that invocation. Finally, he is led by his examination of the place of 'virginity' in Christian thought (see III above) to a conclusion regarding two other controversial issues: virginity is not to be regarded as a mere symbol of Christian chastity but literally the highest state attainable, and the substitution of chastity for charity (at line 214) is not a rejection of the latter, since chastity and love are coupled in the passage in Milton's *Apology* (211–12).

G. W. Whiting ('*Comus*, Jonson, and the Critics,' *Milton and This Pendant World*, 1958, 3–28) does not dispute the relation of *Comus* to the masque, but brushes aside all comparison with Jonson's *Pleasure reconcild to Vertue*; he insists instead that *Comus* represents Milton's reaction against the ethics of Jonson's *Hymenaei*, which seems to Whiting to cloak under the guise of marriage the licence of Milton's enchanter. Whiting regards the whole effect of *Comus* as essentially and austerely moral, but not in any overt sense Christian: in other words, he finds virtually the whole meaning conveyed in the debate of the Lady and Comus (as was common with earlier critics) and accepts it as entirely satisfactory (which was much less common). Preferring argument to allegory and symbol, and in effect ignoring the Sabrina episode and the Epilogue, he sees no specifically Christian pattern in the poem, no progression from nature to grace, and no element of reconciliation on a higher level—and appears perfectly satisfied with this limited or (as some would feel) negative result.

Sears Jayne ('The Subject of Milton's Ludlow *Mask*,' *PMLA* 74,
1959, 533–43) proposes, as an approach most likely to yield a complete
interpretation, to see *Comus* from the point of view of Renaissance
Platonism (that is, of such a philosophy as Ficino's), in which 'Platonism,
mythology, and Christianity were already completely synthesized.' So
interpreted, the Jove of the opening lines (1, 20, 78) becomes the World
Soul and the Attendant Spirit (called a Daemon in the MS.) becomes 'a
Platonic airy spirit, carrying out the last stage in the process of emanation
from God to the outermost circle of the World Soul.' But a more important idea for Milton, as for Ficino, was the association of Jove with
divine providence, and for Milton, as for Petrus Calanna, the association
of natural providence with Neptune, in whose realm the whole action
takes place. Natural providence in subordination to divine providence
is the Platonic counterpart of the Christian order of nature and order
of grace. 'Comus, as one agent of natural providence, argues quite rightly
that his functions are natural..., but a soul's rejection of him is also
equally "natural." The alternative...put before the Lady is not a
choice between natural and unnatural, but between two equally natural
courses....Her choice is made with the sanction of divine providence,
but also, because she is still in the flesh, with the sanction of natural
providence.' That the action of the masque takes place in the dark is
explained by correspondence of the element 'water, in whose realm the
action occurs' and 'the night part of the daily cycle.' That the darkness
does not give way to light when the level of grace is reached is said to
have 'disturbed' those who think in terms of nature and grace ⟨no reference is given, and no account taken of the fact that all allusions to darkness cease with the flight of Comus⟩; this is explained by the fact
'that the whole...achievement of chastity takes place in the realm of
natural providence, that is, while the soul is still in the body.' Milton's
'chastity' is to be taken in the sense and context supplied by Renaissance
Platonism: souls not content with the presence of God but desirous of a
body are joined with body. But, even sunk in a gross body, the soul can
still escape the effects of the body. It can remember truer things,
recalling its proper nature and its natural seat; recognizing the baseness

of the body and loathing it, the soul finds its long-unused wings of goodness and wisdom and flies back to heaven again. To 'achieve chastity, or release from the bondage of the flesh...reason...must first conquer the passions, but this alone is not enough;...to escape its prison of the flesh the soul must..., through the *mens*, remember its own previous purely spiritual (chaste) state and so be led by the *mens* away from the flesh and back toward God.' 'Milton divides the narrative action of the masque into three scenes corresponding to the three motions of the soul, descending, stopped, and ascending.' *Descending* is where the Lady is wandering in the wood and is guided to his palace by Comus; *stopped* is where she is paralysed in his chair, at first still partially able to accept or reject his cup, 'as the unassisted reason is still subject to temptation. Only when Comus has been banished by the haemony, that is, when reason is fortified by philosophical knowledge, does the soul banish temptation entirely,' symbolized by the Lady's complete paralysis. *Ascending* is represented by Sabrina, symbolizing *mens*, as she restores the Lady to mobility, but *mens* is no external power, but a faculty of the soul and in the world of natural providence (as Sabrina is a water goddess, and of Neptune's, that is, of nature's, world), but its action, and the direction in which it points, are in accordance with divine providence (Jove). [This learned and acute exposition leaves us, even if we assume that the young poet was a thorough Ficinian, with two difficult alternatives: either that Milton was indulging himself in abstruse philosophic symbolism, regardless of his audience, or that he thought his audience could follow it. Jayne suggests that for the audience the masque would be focused 'on the glorification of the Earl and his family,' but that Milton was addressing rather 'the learned world in general.']

[Although it hardly comes under the heading of interpretation, one may mention here a highly romantic fancy put forth by the biographer of Milton, E. Saillens, 'Une Hypothèse à propos de *Comus*' (*Études Anglaises* 12, 1959, 100–11). The hypothesis is that, in the course of preparing for the production of *Comus*, the handsome and music-loving poet fell in love with one of the noble actresses, perhaps Lady Mary

Egerton. So, in terms of the Epilogue, 'Adonis-Milton, rendu à sa calme solitude, *waxes well of his deep wound*, et poursuit ses méditations sous le regard attristé de Vénus, mais tout là-haut, l'amour céleste accueille son âme lassée de sa longue quête. Un jour, Dieu voulant (et Dieu le veut: "so Jove hath sworn"), elle deviendra son épouse éternelle, de qui naîtront Jeunesse et Joie.']

[D. Wilkinson ('The Escape from Pollution: A Comment on *Comus*,' *Essays in Criticism* 10, 1960, 32–43) finds *Comus* satisfactory as, initially, 'the enactment of a family ritual,' but, as a public work, quite lacking in dramatic tension. The Lady is subject to no real threat or moral danger; she does not adequately answer Comus' arguments (which are also much finer poetry), and she merely rejects temptation. Milton's Platonic conception of virtue as knowledge does not supply a basis for dramatic conflict between virtue and evil. Chastity has no dramatic reality; moreover, it is not here a pure virtue, being marked by 'overweening self-righteousness' and 'a nasty assertiveness.' The best perhaps that can be said for the Lady is 'that she *escapes pollution*.'

These rather old-fashioned charges (cf. Greg et al., and Dr Johnson) were answered by G. Rans (ibid. 10, 364–9). Observing that Wilkinson exaggerates the family business, Rans insists that 'the primary interest must be moral, and that morality and religion illuminate the poetry.' Complaint about lack of drama is beside the point; it is idle to apply alien criteria to what does not attempt to be realistic. The Lady 'is an example of one strong in the whole armour of God,' and forthright rejection of evil belongs to her character and situation. 'Such drama as there is lies in the conflict of rhythm, image, tone, rhetoric, and moral idea.' To say that Comus has the poetry on his side is merely a perverse rejection of the poetry, lyricism, and eloquence on the other side, including the Lady's sound reply to Comus. W. Leahy also commented on Wilkinson (ibid. 11, 1961, 111).]

[J. B. Broadbent (*Milton: Comus and Samson Agonistes*, London, 1961: pp. 7–33 on *Comus*), along with information about the genre and the occasion of *Comus*, gives brief discussions of these topics: the plot, mythology, Comus, the Lady, music of the spheres, allegory, philosophy,

Platonism, chastity, the soul, Thyrsis, Comus and the Lady, Sabrina, the epilogue, the verse. He defines the action as 'a struggle between a discord which symbolises unregenerate nature and a harmony which is rational and of God' (14), and his account of Milton's Christian Platonism, so far as it goes, is mainly orthodox, 'within his prejudices' (as he says of the poet, p. 19). He makes an effort to capture young readers.]

[E. Sirluck ('Milton's Idle Right Hand,' *JEGP* 60, 1961, 749–85) is, among other things, intent upon showing that 'In 1637...we clearly are in the presence of some personal relation to celibacy' (766), that Milton made one of his many covenants and pledges in *Ad Patrem* (a poem Sirluck may be thought both to misdate and to misinterpret), and that 'the 1637 additions to *A Mask*, and "Lycidas," *Epitaphium Damonis*, and *An Apology* tell us what the covenant and pledge were. The covenant was the renewal yet again of his self-dedication as God's poet, and the pledge which made this self-dedication more convincing than its predecessors was sacrificial celibacy' (767). The complex argument may look in the right direction but seems to go beyond the evidence. In his effort to create and fix a crisis in 1637, Sirluck insists that the most significant additions to *Comus*—the second half of the Lady's reply (778–98) and the symbolic allusions of the Epilogue (996, 998–1010)—were made in that year; [cf. Shawcross in 1 above]. That is more than we know; they may have been made at any time from 1634 up to the printing of Lawes' edition. Moreover, in view of the total import of the *Comus* of 1634, Sirluck's stress on the additions may appear somewhat exaggerated.]

[T. Wheeler ('Magic and Morality in *Comus*,' *Studies in Honor of John C. Hodges and Alwin Thaler*, ed. R. B. Davis and J. L. Lievsay, Knoxville, Tenn., 1962, 43–7) comments on Allen, Adams, Woodhouse, and Jayne (see above). Although a masque was not expected to be dramatic, Milton failed to fuse diverse elements. The spell put upon the Lady is magic, and magic excludes morality; haemony is also magical, and grace is mysterious, and virtue is neither. Such generalities may seem rather to blur than to describe Milton's theme and method.]

[Roy Daniells (*Milton, Mannerism and Baroque*, 1963, 19–37) sees

4-2

Comus as a Mannerist work, a stage on Milton's way to the baroque *Paradise Lost*. He pronounces Woodhouse's exposition 'true and convincing,' but rehearses and enlarges old and new complaints against the masque as no less true and convincing: unreality and incongruity everywhere; lack of drama; lack of thematic and artistic coherence; 'the intolerable pride and self-sufficiency' of the Lady; the characters' 'extraordinary reluctance to communicate with one another'; and so on. 'The discrepancy between the pagan milieu, ideas, and language of Comus and those of the Lady, which are Platonic and Christian, is so great as to make real argument impossible' (29). About the stirring second half of the Lady's reply ('Shall I go on?') Daniells says that she 'had better not have continued.' But what appear as egregious faults may be seen as essential qualities of Mannerist art: 'firm reliance upon traditional stylistic elements'; 'changes of direction,...familiar effects rearranged'; a style 'elegant, precise, and refined'; 'the action...strangely limited and the situation static'; 'intense self-consciousness...in every character.'

Thus *Comus* is not the failure seen by Allen and some others, 'because the lapses and dislocations are such as to evoke an aesthetic response of a new and intensely gratifying kind, even as the Medici Chapel and the Laurentian Library, filled with violations of the rules, nevertheless ravish the beholder. Our senses are charmed, our emotions exalted, and our minds clarified' (33). The Lady, the counterpart of the young Milton, 'is pure aspiration without compromise.' Milton does not commit his character or himself 'to the Christian concept of martyrdom'—hence the 'backing and filling' that irks some critics. '*Comus* reveals the struggles of a soul both Puritan and proud...to free itself from the temptations of beauty and the snares of passion, to dedicate itself to God unreservedly...and without humility' (36). 'The Platonic mind dedicating itself to the service of the Christian God, but without humility (either natural or by grace or from experience) is trapped, for all its protestations, and has awkwardly to be saved by the intervention of divine grace through unexpectedly natural channels of beauty, magic, and incantation. Release and relief from the clash between the sensuous world and the world of straining idealism comes from unconscious sources, from underneath the waters, from the flowery banks, from music and poetry and memory, all the deep wells of nature's purity and innocence' (37).

Much of this account may seem only to put a Mannerist costume on the *Comus* of the anti-Puritan critics who were noticed in earlier pages.]

[Marjorie Nicolson (*John Milton*, 1963, 67–87) reacts both against critics who, like Allen, stress dramatic flaws or failure, and, especially, against the 'overweight' of philosophic and religious interpretation introduced by Woodhouse. Siding with Adams (above, under 1953–4), she chooses 'deliberately' to treat *Comus* as a charming 'fairy-tale' which (if sometimes endangered by the young author's unloading of moral commonplaces) is in the main a graceful and winning presentation of the traditional victory of Virtue over Vice.]

[Miss M.-S. Røstvig's discovery of occult numerology in the *Nativity* (*The Hidden Sense*, 1963) was noticed above under that poem (III: Criticism). The nature of her similar exposition of *Comus* may be indicated briefly. We are told (62–3) that Comus' first speech (93–144) has '52 lines—the number of weeks in a year. Comus, in other words, presents himself as a representative of the sphere of mutability, of the realm of matter subjected to the rule of time'; that the second part of the speech (145–69), 'where he prepares to cast his spell on the Lady, consists of 25 lines—the square of that number 5 which represents the world of sense' (63). The Lady's first speech (170–229) has 60 lines, and 60 represents chastity, the perfect fulfilment of the law (64–5). 'The fact that Comus begins his great speech with line 666—the notorious number of the beast in *Revelation*—is much too felicitous a circumstance to be the result of mere chance' (67). Along with portentous statistics (which do not fit the 1673 text), we have here numerologists' usual assumptions, which do not seem to bother them: either the poet was playing private games, or his early readers numbered the lines in their copies and, knowing the code (a very flexible code) of mystical mathematics, proceeded to brood and calculate. (Cf. similar comments on *Lycidas*, pp. 635–6 above.)]

[Jacques Blondel's short paper of 1948–9 (summarized above) might be called the conclusion or core of his 136-page monograph, *Le 'Comus' de John Milton: masque neptunien* (Paris, 1964). In this he deals more or less with all aspects of the masque: its place in the genre; Milton in 1632–8; some sources of the fable; pastoral elements; the Neptunian theme; art (figurative lyricism, style, prosody); mythology and religion. He gives also a French translation in blank verse, notes on the English text, and a bibliography which attests his up-to-date knowledge of modern criticism in English. His survey is comprehensive and suggestive, but we may skip what is largely familiar to English-speaking Miltonists and give our small space to his interpretation of the fable.

Comus is a product of the Renaissance and the Reformation; it presses traditional, secular motifs into the service of moral ideas. The central conflict is between two allegories of nature, one standing for purity, beauty, wisdom, order, the other for profusion, corruption, disorder (65). This sets black against white magic, and the force that thwarts black magic is virginity (63). However, the Lady's 'seule raison l'immobilise et sa chasteté n'est ainsi qu'une vertu négative, donc limitée, capable de déjouer Comus, mais non de transcender la nature' (65). Haemony represents moral insight, the power, like Guyon's, to see and abstain, but the brothers can offer only direct action; they cannot undo Comus' spell. Only the *dea ex machina*, Sabrina, can give the Lady full freedom. 'La place donnée ici à Neptune rapproche aussitôt le masque de Milton de la tradition baroque' (59). 'L'eau est salvatrice, comme celle du baptême, *opus operatum*' (87). Dramatic elements are subordinate to the lyrical: 'Les éléments dramatiques vont se trouver confondus avec le chant exaltant les forces bienveillantes, non pour rétablir la justice, comme dans une tragédie, mais pour faire triompher l'ordre, l'harmonie de l'âme et de la raison' (71). 'Mais cette victoire de la raison ne suppose pas une poésie raisonnable et froide: elle appelle le langage pastoral, langage de la sérénité arcadienne qui reflète celle de l'Olympe' (77). The references above to Sabrina might suggest agreement with Woodhouse about grace, but Blondel expressly dissents from any fully Christian interpretation and reverts to his argument (see above, under 1948–9) that Milton's *credo* here partakes 'd'un certain angélisme; la vertu semble se suffire à elle-même' (90). 'Milton en reste à ce qui demeure alors pour lui l'essentiel: l'être humain, s'il veut être digne de sa vocation divine, doit aimer ce qui le rend libre; alors, il pourra s'élever au-dessus du ciel platonicien' (91). 'Il apparaît donc que la mythologie domine ici la pensée sans l'étouffer; cette pensée est implicitement chrétienne et sans doute, la tradition anglicane à laquelle Milton restait alors attaché, quant au dogme tout au moins, s'y trouve réflétée. Mais plus encore compte pour le poète l'effet du discernement moral, héritage de l'éducation puritaine, qui permet aux figures païennes d'illustrer la victoire de la volonté sur le monde impur. Cette victoire s'achève avec grâce, sans qu'il soit pour autant nécessaire de voir ici en Milton un poète de la grâce dont l'effet, selon le christianisme paulinien, permet à la créature de parvenir à une stature humaine plus complète, et non pas, comme ici, de s'égaler aux dieux' (91–2). The beauty of virtue does not proceed from Christ, the suffering Saviour. 'Les figures neptuniennes sont incontestablement les allégories de valeurs morales qui s'ordonnent ici selon un rite original. Dès lors, c'est la poésie qui devient la grâce salvatrice ouvrant comme il est dit au vers 13 de *Comus*, le "palais de l'Eternité" à ceux-là seuls qui se laissent éclairer par la lumière intérieure descendue d'un ciel platonicien. Orphée triomphe' (92).

In 'The Function of Mythology in *Comus*' (*Durham University Journal* 58, 1966, 63–6) Blondel takes a similar line, with the focus indicated by his title. He sees the Christian strain in *Comus* obscured by pagan myth, magic, and pastoral, and by a conception of virtue that owes more to human self-sufficiency than to grace. 'The deeper meaning eventually matters less than the mythological garb'; that is why 'the struggle between vice and virtue appears so artificial, though not unreal.']

[T. A. Riese ('Die Theatralik der Tugend in Miltons *Comus*,' *Festschrift für Walter Hübner*, Berlin, 1964, 192–202), starting from modern critics' awareness of the conventions of the masque, focuses on the figure and action of Sabrina. She is a cogent example of the way in which Milton combines the demands of the masque (including formal compliment) with the expression of his own Christian humanism in a story of redemption. Divine grace is not an incomprehensible gift but is bestowed on those who strive to maintain virtuous freedom. In keeping with this harmonious central conception, heathen magic is turned to Christian use, and the Sabrina scene is enveloped in sensuous lyrical beauty.]

[J. I. Ades ('The Pattern of Temptation in *Comus*,' *Papers on English Language & Literature* 1, 1965, 265–71), following up a remark of Hanford's, sees *Comus* as 'the youthful first elaboration' of the 'grand scheme of redemption' developed in Milton's three late major works. In all four 'the debate...is presented as a three-part structure,' based on the traditional patterns of Satan's temptations of Adam and Eve and Christ. Ades seeks to show that the debates in *Comus* and *Paradise Regained* are closely parallel, both focused on the flesh, the world, and the Devil, and in that order. But, while treatments of temptation by a Christian poet are bound to have some general likeness, Ades's parallels in structure and motive may seem forced; he refers to no criticism of *Comus*.]

[Akira Arai ('Milton in *Comus*,' *Studies in English Literature* [Tokyo], 42, 1965, 19–31) thinks that Woodhouse overemphasizes the distinction between nature and grace. In his own view 'Milton tries...to demonstrate that beneath the duplicate appearance of these two qualities the Grace-motif remains consistent, and eventually refines and evolves the Nature-motif to a new whole on the soul's upward three-step journey from Sense, through Reason, to Faith' (19). The Elder Brother's confidence in unassisted rational virtue is good but inadequate. The invention of a new mystical herb is crucial, since more than human reason is needed; witness also the role of Sabrina. The Lady's conception of chastity goes beyond the Elder Brother's and is predominantly religious. The 'Sun-clad power of Chastity' is a key phrase which calls up such associations as 'the Sun of Righteousness.' For the Lady 'it is only Grace that guarantees the triumph of reason' (29).]

[C. L. Barber ('*A Mask Presented at Ludlow Castle*: The Masque as a Masque,' Summers, *Lyric Milton*, 1965, 35–63) asks two questions: 'How does Milton succeed...in making a happy work which centers, seemingly, on the denial of impulse, when typically in the Renaissance such works involve, in some fashion or other, release from restraint?

Second, what is the form of the piece? how does it relate to Renaissance comedy and allied traditions?' He begins with the second.

Barber removes Johnson's and later complaints about undramatic drama, and also Hardy's obsession with irony, by insisting that a masque is a masque. 'A masque was *presented*, not performed,' and, along with decorative compliment, 'the masquing could also be revelatory, exemplary, and persuasive, inviting nobility to realize an ideal in miming it' (38–9). In *Arcades* courtly compliment had been perfectly executed, but with severe restriction of the poet's sensibility. In *Comus* 'Milton did, astonishingly enough, convert the masque to his high purposes' by using 'the masque's altering and extending of situation with his own kind of seriousness' (42–5). He did not commit the indecorum of directly using 'Christian iconography in redefining the entertainment situation as a Christian situation.' To understand *Comus*, 'we must be aware of the kind of moral and spiritual meaning which Christian humanism had been finding in classical myth for more than a century. Spenser's mythopoeia was in the foreground for Milton and his audience; but Spenser was part of a wide and complex tradition.' Miss Tuve and Woodhouse have shown 'how positive a virtue Milton was celebrating in presenting Chastity as an obligation of the natural order which could find sublime fulfillment in the order of Grace' (47).

How were such meanings to be staged? Milton moves—somewhat like Eliot in *The Waste Land*—'through "secular" materials to mystery and spiritual discovery' (49). Critics looking for drama are put off by long speeches, but these speeches are *creating* the situation, not forwarding the event, and, read thus, yield 'high excitement and delight,' e.g. in lines 290–303, in which Comus tells the Lady he has seen her brothers, 'lines where the act of imaginative creation is emphasized by the whole thing's being a downright lie'; yet 'Comus' fabrication opens an exquisite vista, exactly in the manner of the masque.'

'To present a trial of chastity, the masque's way of moving by successive extensions of situation and awareness serves Milton perfectly. For preserving chastity involves keeping a relation with what is not present...,' and 'the young people's first resources are internal' (50–1).

The least satisfactory part of the masque is the Elder Brother's dogmatic and over-confident exposition of the strength of chastity, 'a youthful absolutism' we are intended to feel, even though 'he expresses convictions Milton himself held.' But even his lines can be felt 'as a reaching out for resources against the tensions of uncertain isolation' (52).

In the Lady's invocation of Echo, the pivotal gesture of the first scene, Milton makes dramatic use of a standard feature of masques; and nothing in *Comus* 'is more beautiful than the epiphany of the Lady's quality conveyed by the song and the descriptions of it.' The act of singing is an exercise of her integrity; 'she is internally related, beyond the darkness, to what she looks to and realizes in the song.' In it is 'exquisite maidenliness...along with a rich capacity for sensuous enjoyment and sympathy with passion,' along, too, with vulnerability and innocence. Chastity is presented 'as an intact disposition to love,' and 'The ultimate object of love, the masque repeatedly hints, is heavenly' (52–5).

'But on this side of heaven there is Thyrsis,' with his double role. As the Attendant Spirit he gives 'a background assurance' of Providence, but in a very limited degree; that assurance is embodied in the herb haemony. The plant is not Reason or Grace, though 'it looks *toward* both.' The second episode, Thyrsis' communication to the Brothers, 'is beautifully designed: it repeats the movement the Lady has been through from isolation in darkness to an encounter opening out the situation toward a world of pastoral generosity; but the succor offered the Brothers is real, not Comus' "glozing courtesy"' (57).

Barber's first question has already been virtually answered. No one but Milton would have elected so difficult a task as making 'a Masque of Chastity' with 'Revel in the role of villain.' He 'deliberately presented a figure of Revel who under the guise of refreshment tempts to dissolution from which there is no coming back. The whole historical development of English life, regret it though we may, was giving ground for Milton's new vantage toward the pleasures of Merry England' (59). But the satisfying beauty of the masque depends largely on the positive moral and religious conception of chastity that Milton held, however unpopular it was in his time or is in ours. In *Comus* 'he presents the possibility of destructive release, and meets it by another sort of release, the release of imagination carried by rhythm out and up to other objects of love' (60). In the character of Comus Milton faced a real artistic problem, since 'his whole design would not admit of Comus' capturing our imagination fully. His solution, so far as he does solve the difficulty, is to allow his god to revel, to begin each speech strongly, often beautifully, with appeals to the traditional sanctions, youth, feast, and nature's vital dance. Then he spoils it' (61). Milton's purpose required such a limitation, and it is one (if we think of Autolycus and Perdita); but that does not warrant the critical habit of seeing Comus as 'a more cultivated Autolycus.'

'The furthest reach of feeling, going out to the objects whose superior attraction defeats Comus, is in the Epilogue....' 'The end of Chastity is love fulfilled....' 'Closer to the Lady's actual condition, and crucial in her rescue, is the figure of Sabrina, perhaps the most remarkable inspiration or revelation of the whole masque.' 'In the story of Sabrina's coming back to life, and the poetry and song which create her, we encounter, along with suggestions of the healing and renewing powers of water, the innocent cherishing of femininity by femininity, waiting and yet not waiting for another destiny, which is the proper resource of the Lady's stage of life....Such is the power of the masque, in Milton's hands, to reach out and find, transformed, what, if embraced, is already there.']

[G. H. Carrithers ('Milton's Ludlow *Mask*: From Chaos to Community,' *ELH* 33, 1966, 23–42) sees *Comus* as 'a parable of society' 'animated by an ideal of community.' This ideal, 'explicitly stated nowhere but actuating speech and action everywhere, appears to be no less a conviction than that the true earthly fulfillment of man is free participation in loving, God-seeking society. Such loving concord, permitting orientation and aspiration towards "the Palace of Eternity," would seem to be the cosmos to "disinherit *Chaos*."' 'The bulk of the action involves the young people moving from threatened isolation and from relative passivity, to relative activity and charitable commitment, attending "their Father's state."' 'Their apparent community...shows itself to be centrifugal, idiosyncratic, extremist.' Comus himself is of course antisocial, opposed to 'the work of daylight, of nature, nurture, and the *polis*.' By the end the children are committed to all these things, but earlier they are the victims of their several kinds of innocent, egotistical illusion and fragmentation. 'The play moves ultimately by song, dance, and story to establish the stylistic, aesthetic, intellectual, moral primacy of something contrasting with pastoral and broader than "courtly," the superiority of—call it—the civic, or the communal.' The Attendant Spirit's vain efforts to rescue the Lady indicate that his gifts 'must work through the ties of human commitment and human relationship'; and even Sabrina has social implications.]

[Eric LaGuardia (*Nature Redeemed: The Imitation of Order in Three Renaissance Poems*, The Hague, 1966, 126–47) takes *Comus*, along with the *Faerie Queene* 3–4 and *All's Well That Ends Well*, to illustrate the effort of the English Renaissance to bring the world of nature, fallen yet redeemable, into accord with the divine world. In all three works the conflict between corrupted nature and pure nature is focused in a chaste heroine. Although Milton's Lady, unlike the other heroines, has no lover, the journey through the dark wood leads toward the perfection of the natural world and harmony with heaven; and the epilogue presents the marriage of Cupid and Psyche as an image of such harmony. For Milton, as for Spenser, chastity is not mere innocence or abstinence but the purification of the forces of life, the right use of nature. 'Like Malecasta and Busirane, Comus is rejected, but nature is not' (128). In its juxtaposing of the demonic and the divine, *Comus* is much narrower in range than the *Faerie Queene*, but Milton makes more consistent use of ironic parallels (as in Comus' false appearance and pretensions). 'The entire fictional world of *Comus* is devoted to indicating that a perfected natural world is a world which conforms morally and elementally to the eternal order of the divine, but is not itself divine.' Milton 'is less interested than Spenser in promoting the values of natural felicity through love'; in his vision of redeemed nature the emphasis falls more on the higher order than on nature itself (146).]

Comus

[Isabel G. MacCaffrey (*John Milton: Samson Agonistes and the Shorter Poems*, 1966, xxii–xxvii) notes the framework of both the masque and the morality play: the Attendant Spirit and Comus are 'versions of those heavenly and hellish powers that contend for man's soul'; the scene is 'the middle realm of earthly life, suspended between Heaven and Hell, where our moral decisions must be made'; and the three young travellers 'become versions of Everyman.' 'The children "play" themselves, but in doing so they also play out the destiny of the human soul.' Comus illustrates Milton's habit of presenting 'his evil characters as embodying good impulses in distorted form'; his 'revels imitate the pure pleasures of heaven,' but his '"Jollity" is not Joy. The Epilogue thus provides the true vision of which Comus's enchantments are a demonic parody.' In the myth of Circe the 'idea of metamorphosis expresses figuratively the choice offered to the soul in its journey through the wood of the world': witness the transformations of Comus' victims, those described by the Elder Brother (452–74), and the history of Sabrina (840–1), who is the Lady's fitting rescuer. 'Throughout the masque, images of freedom and bondage play against each other.... They are set in paradoxical relation in the central tableau,' in which the Lady, though captive in body, is the instrument of a power than makes Comus shudder with fear. In the fallen world innocent nature may be refined by reason and grace or corrupted by speciously 'natural' licence; the one course brings freedom and joy here and hereafter, the other slavery to sin.]

[R. B. Wilkenfeld ('The Seat at the Center: An Interpretation of *Comus*,' *ELH* 33, 1966, 170–97) sees as the 'hinge' of Milton's invention 'an *emblem*, the concrete, visual, dramatically viable emblem of the Lady paralyzed in the seat of Comus.... the whole verbal mechanism of *Comus* is geared to this emblem and *from* this emblem devolves the "turn" of Milton's "device."' The author's whole exposition elaborates this thesis, including the various ways in which imprisonment is contrasted with freedom. The analysis of the working and interworking of ideas, speech, and action is comprehensive, detailed, and precise: e.g. the introductory compliment to the Earl of Bridgewater has five functions; the story of

Sabrina climaxes eight 'transformations,' beginning with the 'mortal change' of the Attendant Spirit's opening speech. Wilkenfeld's running commentary brings out points of dramatic development and coherence, points which cannot be economically summarized; but his thesis—like that of Carrithers noticed just above—is in some danger of becoming a restrictive formula.

Wilkenfeld also gives a compendious summary of criticism, from Johnson to the present, on the question of drama or lack of drama in *Comus* (pp. 507–10 in his 'Miltonic Criticism and the "Dramatic Axiom,"' *PMLA* 82, 1967, 505–15).]

[R. Neuse ('Metamorphosis and Symbolic Action in *Comus*,' *ELH* 34, 1967, 49–64), deprecating emphasis on the debate, argues that the theme 'is close to "pleasure reconciled to virtue" and involves the poet's traditional concern with the life of the senses rather than the exaltation of an ideal like virginity as a vehicle to the divine' (51). The metamorphosis of haemony 'from bright golden *flower* to unsightly *root*,' a pastoral symbol of man's dual nature, is paralleled by the metamorphoses of the Attendant Spirit into the shepherd Thyrsis (54) and of Sabrina (who 'symbolizes a virtue or force in nature analogous to' haemony) into the goddess of the river. 'As river goddess she represents, not *mens*, but the "lower," unconscious life of nature—in a sacramental order' (56). 'The Lady's encounter with Comus must, then, be seen... as an encounter with the side of her nature below the threshold of rational consciousness' (57). 'In this view Sabrina becomes a symbolic expression of man's lower nature seen truly in a new light, transformed, namely as no longer in conflict with spirit and reason, but as harmoniously responsive to them' (58). 'This paradigm...is encompassed and reinforced by a seasonal pattern' of rural thanksgiving for the rebirth of vegetation. The Epilogue 'depicts a realm of perpetual youth that stands in direct contrast to the make-believe world of seasonless "waste fertility"' of Comus (60). 'The Spirit's timeless realm represents the completion of the seasonal cycle, in the manner of Spenser's Garden of Adonis, to which it is an extended allusion.' 'Thus there is a dual metamorphosis in the masque's "program" to restore the golden age or world: the metamorphosis of the Platonic forms into active participants in the realm of human trial and error, . . . ; and the metamorphosis of the social world, as represented by masquers and audience, when the two come together and mingle in the final dance' (63). Finally, 'In the pictured flight to the earthly paradises of the imagination, the Spirit becomes a dramatic image or projection of the human spirit realizing this condition of flight within itself.'

We may wonder if Milton thought and felt in these terms.]

[B. Rajan ('Comus: *The Inglorious Likeness*,' *UTQ* 37, 1967–8, 113–35; repr. in *The Lofty Rhyme*, 1970) endorses and elaborates Tillyard's view that 'the masque reflects man's central position on the Great Chain of Being, confronted with the way up into being or the way down into self-annihilation. This is perhaps the best way in which to look at *Comus*, both because it is universally accessible and because it couples and sets in motion a series of potent antitheses' (116). This is, in microcosm, the method of *Paradise Lost*. 'The alternatives set out by the Attendant Spirit in terms of the flesh and the spirit are also set out by the Elder Brother in terms of chastity and lust' (119). Milton criticism tends to regard 'nature–grace and reason–passion' as exclusive of each other. 'In fact their amalgamation is likely to be a primary objective in any poet determined to consummate the classical in the Christian,' and the language of each ethical and symbolic contrast 'involves and interpenetrates the language of the others' (121).

'Milton's first temptation scene' fully reveals Comus' perversion of the Christian doctrine of the plenitude of God's creation. 'The enormous triviality' of his conclusion—'But all to please and sate the curious taste'—'would have been all the more decisive because of the sense of order in abundance it violates' (122). 'As Comus proceeds, his rhetoric becomes more and more strangled in its waste fertility'; like Satan, 'the speaker judges himself in the very language he finds to express himself' (124). The Lady 'is rejecting Comus rather than arguing with him,' perhaps because Milton's art is as yet inadequate for a debate; but 'The point is that the dismissal has both dramatic and symbolic sanction and that the answer is not withheld but only postponed' (126).

Milton's conception of chastity 'is a consecration of the soul to the good that rejects the other than good and the disproportionate claims of lesser goods.' When he risks adverse reactions by substituting Chastity for Charity (line 214), he is suggesting that charity should govern man's dealings with others, not his dealings with himself: 'Eternal vigilance is the price of Christian liberty, and faith and hope can only be grounded in self-discipline' (126). 'While Sabrina may be an agent of grace she is also...a force of nature,' and her 'liberation of the Lady shows on which side the truth lies and also shows that grace and nature ultimately act in unison.' It is 'standard Miltonic thinking' that 'the world of the senses is included and not annulled by consecration to the world of the spirit and that discipline forms the basis for the liberation of creative energy rather than the means for its confinement' (128).

The Epilogue subtly and indirectly sums up all that has preceded. The symbolism of Spenser's Garden of Adonis is refined in the elevation of Cupid and Psyche above Venus and Adonis, and nature, in the form of 'Youth and Joy', is on the Lady's side (129–30). 'Within its chosen limits the language of the poem is philosophic rather than religious.' 'Religious significances press in upon the world of *Comus* particularly in its central confrontation; but they do not transgress its decorum since the purpose of that decorum is to suggest how an action shaped in terms of a classical fable invokes and opens out into a Christian meaning.' In the 'final tableau of aspiration and balance,' we have 'the upward effort of the individual soul, the downward reaching response of the divine and the meeting point of self-reliance and dependence where freedom is discovered in the total commitment to virtue. This is the highest of the three unions through which the Epilogue has climbed heavenwards, but the treatment of Cupid and Psyche has already told us the lower reality is not annulled in the acceptance of the higher. Rather it is restored and stabilized and given its due function in the shapeliness of things.']

[P. Brockbank ('The Measure of *Comus*,' *Essays and Studies 1968*, 46–61) would relate our simple but important first impressions to the sophisticated moral and religious interpretation, as Milton himself does through his poetry and devices appropriate to the masque. Thus in lines 46–53, on Bacchus and Circe, he creates remoteness, mystery, enchantment, and subtly adds a moral dimension by the repetition of 'fell' (50) in 'And downward fell into a groveling Swine' (53). So too there is enchantment in the Attendant Spirit's account of himself (82–8); he and Comus 'are in some sense rival enchanters,' good and bad. In the opening lines Milton accomplishes the essential feat of holding in perspective his vision of man's frail and feverish being; neither Comus nor the lady and her brothers 'can enjoy the comprehensive vision which is a prerogative of the Attendant Spirit and the audience.'

The wood is an actual wood, but it 'seems sometimes to signify the whole span of human life—the mortal state—and sometimes only a precarious phase of it.' The nature of the masque enables Milton 'to hover daintily between possibilities of meaning.' While the wood is an ordeal the travellers survive, we are left free to wonder if the triumph (973–4) is consummated 'in maturity or in death.'

The masque is a *presentation* of 'the perplexities of the waking adolescent imagination,' and that is blended with 'a neo-platonic allegory—about the survival of the spirit's purity in an alien sensual world.'

Another kind of first impression comes through rhythm, as in 'the sensual music of Comus' poetic dialect, and the moral music of the Elder Brother's'; the latter delights us less than it delighted the Younger Brother. But there is a third kind of 'verbal music, opening the masque and closing it, and heard from time to time within it'—the lines on the 'fair Hesperian Tree' (392–6), the lady's song and Comus' response to it, and above all the Epilogue, where 'a transfigured and sublimated sensuality' moves into intimations of 'the Divine Wedding, or ultimate ecstatic union of the soul with God.' And the final dance reminds us of 'the processes by which *grace* has come to mean both "charm, ease and refinement of movement" and "the divine influence which operates in men to regenerate and sanctify, to inspire virtuous impulses, and to impart strength to endure trial and to resist temptation"' (definitions adapted from *OED*).]

[J. G. Demaray (*Masque Tradition*, 1968) is much more concerned with formal elements than with interpretation, but in notes (175–80) he comments on Woodhouse and other critics. His comments on staging, etc., are cited *passim* in v below.]

[W. J. Grace (*Ideas in Milton*, 1968, 130–9) relates *Comus* to his general philosophic and religious exposition. 'In the union of lushness and restraint which Milton lyrically presents in the nature setting in *Comus*, we see a strong sense of humanistic order imposed on the fertile and the fecund.' Nature 'is pregnant with mysterious spiritual movements,' and Milton's imagery 'concentrates the psychological movement of drama in terse symbols of music and of the movement of sound.' 'The almost liturgical movement of sounds in nature sustains the tension of the drama even more than do the characters themselves. The characters are like a chorus putting into words a drama that is occurring elsewhere.' The central opposition between Comus and the Lady resembles a medieval debate, but 'a debate paradoxically maintained not so much by argumentation but by contrasting and most delicately attuned poetic images.' Milton's conception unites the Platonic and the Christian quest of the good, since grace fulfils nature; yet 'The success of *Comus* does not lie in its extended debate between excess and moderation, in its definition of ideas. It lies in its pattern of imagery which effectively dramatizes the human situation torn by the seductiveness of natural beauty and its responsibility to go beyond what is transitory and find "that Golden Key / That opes the Palace of Eternity" (13–14).']

[J. S. Lawry (*Shadow*, 1968, 64–95) sees the opening lines of *Comus* as registering a distinct change (apparent also in the *Solemn Musick*) from the serenity of Milton's earlier poems to a fuller awareness of sin as an enduring danger that must be met. But along with that awareness there is the assurance of heavenly aid for fallen man. This exposition is the first of what Lawry takes as 'Three great speeches, two indicating ultimate stances and choices and the other the unfailing human imperative and stance of choice' (72). The other two are the first speech of Comus, 'the antagonist of God and man,' and the first speech of the Lady, who, misled at first by trusting her ear (lines 169–70), 'all but returns to the Platonic and Christian realities most relevant to her,

Conscience and "visible" Chastity (not Charity—this drama is of the mind, not of society, and chastity is fidelity to both reason and God)' (77).

Then 'a series of three related calls…takes up the structural burden of the masque' (78). These are: the prayer that concludes the Lady's first speech; the prayer of the two Brothers, which calls in the Attendant Spirit; and the prayer to Sabrina, whose 'typic human role is that of Lycidas, Orpheus, or Christ.'

Around these stances, the principal matter of the poem shapes into a series of debates (choices, in a verbal mode) that probe or rebut or in the end triumphantly reassert the original proclamation of the Attendant Spirit. Each debate—the initial contest of the Lady with the revealed Comus, of the Brothers with one another, of the Brothers with the Attendant Spirit, of the Lady with Comus in a second encounter, and (in effect) of the Spirit with Sabrina—leads to the center: the choice between the stances of Comus and Jove, and to proper action upon it. The last in the series produces the act of redemption, conferred by Heaven and elective by men. (80)

In the debate between Comus and the Lady, her and Milton's argument 'is not a personal or doctrinal refusal of sexuality'; secondly, 'even a technical—that is, physical—virginity is correct for the Lady as she is represented on stage'; thirdly, 'a poem in either the Christian or classical tradition should be allowed to treat of virginity without rebuke,' in view of the spotless Christ and Mary, Athene and Artemis; finally, chastity is a 'Sun-clad power' supported by Heaven. Lawry had already (below, 618-40 n.) suggested that the 'Shepherd Lad' whose herbs included haemony is 'the redemptive Christ'; he now says: 'It seems to me that in the doctrine of Meliboeus and the figure of Sabrina, the Spirit intimates likenesses, even identification, with God and with Christ (as well as Spenser), just as Comus had quite surely united himself with Satan' (91). In the end, Ludlow is heaven; 'the home of the human father and the divine Father are one'; and the way to eternity, 'the ascent from lower to higher forms of love,' and Heaven's readiness to help aspiring man, are made joyously clear.]

[J. Reesing (*Milton's Poetic Art*, 1968, 3-18) meets complaints about the undramatic character of *Comus* by emphasizing both the ideal world represented in the normal masque and, especially, Milton's religious conception of Nature, 'the perfect physico-moral order that he looks back to as the pristine historical reality, the whole creation as God originally made it.' That ideal perfection remains a reality in the fallen world, and *Comus* depicts 'the relation of mortals to the world of the divine.' In keeping with this conception are two opposed kinds of metamorphosis, that of Comus' victims who become beasts and that of Sabrina who becomes a goddess. The upward metamorphosis, the way to heaven described in the Attendant Spirit's first and last lines, is open to all seekers of virtue. The masque tests and vindicates 'the Lady's right to membership in the divine order of timeless permanence.... The Lady and her brothers, ultimately the whole court, are presented as members of a Nature that is believed to be the ideal moral order' (7). Thus, following the Jonsonian tradition, Milton 'involves the whole court in an idealized vision of itself....' Comparing the acting and the printed versions, Reesing sees Milton's additions, above all the second part of the Lady's reply to Comus (779–98), as stressing Christian grace and removing any Pelagian taint. The plot allows for the exercise of the virtuous will, for the Lady's captivity, and for her brothers' being unable to rescue her; for her deliverance divine grace is needed. Although some allegorical details, such as haemony, are uncertain, the total scheme is coherent and clear.]

[J. Carey (*Milton*, 1969, 41–54), though he recognizes the nature of a masque, gives much space to questions of realistic logic and consistency. His account of the central debate between Comus and the Lady (as indeed of the whole masque) exemplifies a prejudice against Milton's moral and religious theme and vision which—to borrow his phrase about the Lady's reply—'bespeaks an almost metallic insensitivity' (51). His exposition of the Spirit's epilogue ends on this note: 'Virtue and, as the masque's constant emphasis implies, virginity, will teach you to soar up through the musical spheres (1019–21), and at the top you will find yourself in the *Book of Revelation*' (53–4). 'Comus,' he concludes, 'embodies the unifying charge of poetic language. He is a growth of the passionate life that Milton had tried to throttle in Elegy 6 and the *Nativity Ode*. His riotous sociability would clog the epic aspirant's wings, and Milton fiercely brutalises it, but his poetic fluency cannot be resisted.']

[What was said in *Lycidas* III (under 1969) of J. B. Leishman's lectures, *Milton's Minor Poems*, may, *mutatis mutandis*, be said of his long discussion of *Comus* (174–246), though here he does deal with Milton's theme ('Doctrine,' 209–29). He follows at length B. A. Wright's Platonic interpretation of the masque as a whole, though he recognizes Christian elements: 'Milton's last word [in the final couplet] is not the Platonic but the Christian λόγος, the Word made flesh' (228). And he insists on Milton's 'essentially poetic' presentation of both 'partly Platonic and partly Christian conceptions' (217). But Leishman cites no generally interpretative modern criticism except A. E. Dyson's [above, under 1955] and he does not seem to be aware of the issues that have so much occupied modern critics (and that occupied Dyson). The commentary is mainly concerned with *Comus* as masque and pastoral drama (though it is, he affirms, 'really *sui generis*') and with 'Style and Diction.' A rather old-fashioned approach does not of course preclude authentic insight, and Leishman here, as in his other books, was quite capable of that; but his account of *Comus* is in general better fare for the uninitiated—for whom the lectures were evidently designed—than for sophisticated readers.]

[D. M. Rosenberg's title, 'Milton's Masque: A Social Occasion for Philosophic Laughter' (*SP* 67, 1970, 245–53), indicates what may be thought a dubious theme. He seeks to show that 'comedy in *Comus* forms a significant part of the work as a whole.' Along with the homogeneous family and communal atmosphere of a happy ceremonial, the masque itself contains comic elements that range from orgiastic dancing to touches of high comedy that spring from the relations of man and nature and the opposed ideals of Comus and the Lady.]

[P. E. Boyette ('Milton's Abstracted Sublimities: The Structure of Meaning in *A Mask*,' *Tulane Studies in English* 18, 1970, 35–58) seeks to 'examine the way in which Milton creates a basic figurative structure and to amplify the meaning of that figure in relation to the didactic intent of the masque as a whole.' The immediate and the cosmic setting (this created by the imagery) create 'a hierarchy of figures' which depict a pilgrimage through the dark wood (the fallen world) to the 'light and order' represented by Ludlow Castle. In the course of their journey the children learn something about life and themselves that they did not know at the start. Along with the allegorical tradition of the pilgrimage goes that of 'the Choice of Life' (notably exemplified in the fable of Hercules), the choice of virtue and true life over vice and spiritual death. The choice involves the discovery of evil and can be perfected only through grace. The Lady's paralysis signifies 'the insufficiency of the natural man to triumph over the liabilities of his infected nature,' and Sabrina's mode of deliverance suggests the symbolic rite of baptism. Haemony is (as Steadman argued) the lesser power of protective knowledge. The author concludes, from his detailed analysis, that Milton dramatized his abstracted sublimities with a sound instinct for symbolic language and action and a high degree of artistic control.]

V. NOTES

The text followed is that of *Poems*, 1673, as reprinted in *Works* 1, 85–123. The other texts cited are (with abbreviations in brackets): (1) the separate edition, *A Maske presented At Ludlow Castle, 1634 : On Michaelmasse night...London...* *1637* (1637), reproduced in Fletcher, *Facs.* 1, 262–99; (2) that of *Poems*, 1645 (1645), in *Facs.* 189–215; (3) that of the Cambridge MS. (MS.), in *Facs.* 398–433; (4) that of the Bridgewater MS. (Br.), a fair copy of the acting text, in *Facs.* 300–39 [and in Diekhoff, *A Maske at Ludlow* (1968)]. The variants are listed in *Works* 1, 474–577. Here only variants of critical interest are noticed; the reader may, if he wishes, consider what Milton added, deleted, and altered in the process of composition and revision. Further details (e.g. the mode and position of the changes in MS.) will be found in the list of variants in *Works*. [It may be noted that, since the Columbia text is that of 1673, which omitted line 167 ('Whom thrift keeps up about his Country gear'), the Columbia and Variorum numbering of lines, from that point on, is one less than in most editions. This fact sometimes necessitates the silent changing of line numbers in quotations from commentators. Textual details and variants are also supplied

by Fletcher and by H. Darbishire (2, 336–61). These details and variants have
been especially studied by J. S. Diekhoff in several articles in *PMLA*: 51,
1936, 757–68; 52, 1937, 705–27 (repr. in Diekhoff's *A Maske at Ludlow*); 55,
1940, 748–72; and by J. T. Shawcross (cited in 1 above).]

The 1637 edition is anonymous but carries a dedication to 'John Lord Vicount
Bracly,' signed by Henry Lawes. It has on the title-page, as motto, *Eheu quid
volui misero mihi! floribus austrum / Perditus* (Virgil, *E.* 2. 58–9). This has been
taken to indicate that, though he preferred to remain anonymous, Milton had
consented, perhaps reluctantly, to publication (Verity, *Comus*, 1909 f.). [Parker
(143) questions the traditional view and says: 'but the quotation, in context,
means that the shepherd accuses himself of *neglecting his proper business.*' It may
be doubted if Milton would use the Virgilian tag in what would be, on this
interpretation, a private sense.] The final page lists 'The principall persons in
this Maske,' namely the three Egertons. The text in the *Poems* of 1645 has a new
title-page, which omits the Virgilian motto [the title-page of the volume has a
more assertive one from Virgil, *E.* 7. 27–8]; reprints Lawes' dedication; and
adds 'The Copy of a Letter Writt'n By Sir Henry Wootton, To the Author,
upon the following Poem' (text in *Works* 1, 476–7; *Facs.* 1, 191–2), and 'The
Persons': 'The attendant Spirit afterwards in the habit of *Thyrsis. / Comus* with
his crew. / The Lady. / 1. Brother. / 2. Brother. / *Sabrina* the Nymph. / *The
cheif* persons which presented, were / The Lord *Bracly*, / Mr. *Thomas Egerton*
his Brother, / The Lady *Alice Egerton.*'

[References in Wotton's letter raise problems, which are summarized by
Parker, 816–17, n. 96; cf. above, III: Sources and Analogues, sec. 9.]

⟨1st Direction⟩ *The first Scene discovers a wilde Wood. / The attendant Spirit
descends or enters.* MS.: *. . . A Guardian spirit, or Dæmon*; Br.: *. . . then a guardian
spiritt or demon descendes or enters* (*Facs.* 398, 303); in 1637 (ibid. 265) as in 1645,
1673, but not centred, suggesting that the alternative *Dæmon* may have been
deleted before *attendant Spirit.* Warton noted that the Platonic daemon, spirit,
and guardian angel appear as synonymous in Shakespeare, *Antony* 2. 3. 19–22.
Todd added that the terms had been discussed and differentiated in Tasso's
Messaggiero [*Prose*, ed. F. Flora, Milan, 1935, 11 f.]. In English *daemon* had as
one of its meanings (derived from Greek and classical Latin usage) 'An attendant, ministering, or indwelling spirit' (*OED*: demon 1 b). [M. Lloyd (*N&Q* 7,
1960, 421–3) quotes illustrative remarks on daemons from several essays of
Plutarch (*Morals*, tr. P. Holland, 1603, pp. 1181–2, 1219, 1222, 1327).] The
significance of the Attendant Spirit and the interpretation of his dwelling and

his role depend in part on the weight given to the alternative *Dæmon*. By 1637 Milton had decided to remove this ambiguous word, which, even when used in a good sense, is pagan. Verity supposes that *descends* implies as scenery a hill in the background down which the Spirit comes. It seems much more probable that, like many figures in the masques, he descends from the sky on a cloud, and that the alternative *or enters* provides for the possible lack of the requisite 'machinery.' [Cf. Demaray, *Masque Tradition*, 105; Parker, 793, n. 49.]

Br. has 20 lines before 1: with the exception of one added line (17), these are transferred with some necessary alterations from the Spirit's epilogue (975–82, 987–95, 997–8). The alteration was presumably made by Lawes to provide an opening song in the acting version, a common feature in Jonson's masques. In his transcript of Br., Fletcher (*Facs.* 303) notes line 17 as 'Present only here'; but it occurs in the first version of the epilogue in MS. (ibid. 431), whence it is here transferred, and in the second (ibid. 433).

1–92 ⟨The Spirit's Prologue⟩. Warton finds this expository prologue reminiscent of the manner of Euripides, e.g. *Hecuba, Hippolytus, Iphigenia in Tauris*. Todd is further reminded of the prologues to Tasso's *Aminta* and Guarini's *Pastor Fido*.

1–4 The Spirit describes the region from which he has descended (and to which he will return: 975–8). His *mansion* or dwelling place (*OED*: mansion 2) is not heaven—despite editors who quote 'In my Father's house are many mansions' (John 14. 2)—but *Before the starry threshold of Joves Court*. Wright (who emphasizes the Platonic elements in *Comus* throughout) cites John 14. 2 but reads *mansion* as an allusion to the 'mansions' of Plato's True Earth (*Phaedo* 109 f.); the *threshold* he takes to be Olympus, whose summit, rising above the clouds, was imagined to touch the sky. [Along with Wright's edition of Milton's *Shorter Poems* (1938), see his letters on line 5, and those of C. S. Lewis and R. Eisler, *TLS*, 1945, 14 July, 4 Aug., 22, 29 Sept., 27 Oct.] But *Jove* here stands for God (cf. *Lyc* 82) and his *Court* for heaven, since there is no overt use of Christian terminology till the final lines of the masque [but see the bracketed query in *Comus* III. 12 above]. The Attendant Spirit, like his fellow aerial Spirits, immortal creatures, dwells *insphear'd*, i.e. within one of the celestial spheres (*OED*: ensphere 1), and, if we are to take *starry* literally, within the eighth sphere, that of the fixed stars. The word *sphere* and its derivatives (as Verity notes) Milton habitually uses with some reference to the spheres of the Ptolemaic system (see *Nat* 125–32 and n.); and to the idea of the spheres he returns in the epilogue (1019–20 and n.). The word *aereal*, while retaining its connection with pure air (cf. 4–6, 979), appears here to describe an order of beneficent spirits, lower than the angels, with whom Milton never couples the adjective *aereal* (for 'Aereal Music,' *PL* 5. 548, refers merely to the fact that the 'Cherubic Songs' are borne on the air). Indeed, he never leaves us in doubt when he is referring to angels. The corresponding term for them is 'Ethereal' (cf. *PL* 1. 45, 2. 139, 311, 3. 7, 100), which describes the matter of heaven and its inhabitants. Marjorie Nicolson ('The Spirit World of Milton and More,' *SP* 22, 1925, 433–52) has shown that Milton adopts the threefold division of spirits, terrestrial, aerial, ethereal; the Attendant Spirit belongs to the second class. That he is *insphear'd* helps further to place him. Milton always distinguishes between the spheres (with their music) and the angelic orders (with theirs), the former typifying the perfection of the order of nature, the latter that of the order of grace (see *Nat* 125–32 n. and 1019–20 n.). The view taken of the Attendant Spirit and his significance will inevitably influence, and be influenced by, one's reading of the whole poem and will in turn colour one's interpretation of these and following lines, including the cancelled ones. Three main interpretations (advanced by critics cited in IV above) are: (1) that the doctrine is primarily Platonic throughout, and the Spirit a beneficent Platonic daemon; (2) that the doctrine throughout is Christian, though couched in classical images, and the Spirit, as it were, an angel in disguise; (3) that there is in fact an ascent in the poem from the order of nature (to which alone the classical is appropriate) to the order of grace, the specifically Christian, which both subsumes and transcends the values of natural ethics.

With line 1 Dunster compared Marino's *la stellata Corte*, for heaven, and *la dorata soglia*, in *L'Adone* (1623) 1, st. 17, 19: Dunster MS. [this is Woodhouse's label for MS. notes by Charles Dunster in a British Museum copy of Todd's separate edition of *Comus*, Canterbury, 1798].

3 *insphear'd*. Warton cited 'unsphear / The spirit of Plato' (*IlPen* 88–9); 'Whereas I will insphere her / In Regions high and starry' (*To the New Yeere* 35–6, Drayton, 2, 351). Todd compared: 'Like a lightning from the skie / . . . With that winged hast, come I, / Loosed from the Sphere of Jove' (*Fortunate Isles* 10–15, Ben Jonson 7, 708); the speaker is Johphiel, 'an aëry spirit. . . the Intelligence of Jupiters sphere.'

4 *serene*: Lat. *serenus*, clear, bright (contrasting with *smoak* and *dim* of 5). Newton (reported by Todd) compared Homer, *Od.* 6. 42–5, on the calm and clear air of Olympus, the dwelling of the gods. Hughes (1937) adds Lucretius 3. 18–22. [R. Eisler (*TLS*, 22 Sept. 1945) quoted St Ambrose, *De Bono Mortis*

12. 53 (Migne, *Pat. Lat.* 14, 564): 'There are no clouds nor thunderstorms, no darkness, no summer's heat or winter's cold, no hail or rain in this place where the just ones will dwell eternally'—which Eisler took as an imitation of Pindar, *Ol.* 2. 62–88 (quoted below, 975 n.); he also cited Josephus, *Jewish War* 2. 8. 11 (L.C.L. 1, 381–3).]

After 4, MS. (*Works* 1, 479; *Facs.* 398) adds, works over, and finally deletes 14 lines. The following are the lines in their last form (words originally written and later rejected are added in pointed brackets):

(5) amidst the Hesperian gardens, on whose bancks ⟨where the banks⟩
(6) bedew'd wth nectar, & celestiall songs
(7) aeternall roses grow ⟨yeeld, blow, blosme⟩ & hyacinth
     (6 and 7 in reverse order)
(8) & fruits of golden rind, on whose faire tree
(9) the scalie-harnest ⟨watchfull⟩ dragon ever keeps
(10) his uninchanted ⟨never charmed⟩ eye, & round the verge
(11) & sacred limits of this blisfull ⟨happie⟩ Isle
(12) the jealous ocean that old river winds
(13) his farre-extended armes till wth steepe fall
(14) halfe his wast flood ye wide Atlantique fills
(15) & halfe the slow unfadom'd Stygian poole ⟨poole of styx⟩
(16) but soft I was not sent to court y^or wonder
(17) wth distant worlds, & strange removed clim ⟨16 and 17 replacing 'I doubt me gentle mortalls these may seeme / strange distances to heare & unknowne climes'⟩
(18) yet thence I come and oft frō thence behold
(19) above the smoake & stirre... ⟨i.e. 5 of present text⟩.

For (5), (8)–(10), *Hesperian gardens, fruits of golden rind...uninchanted eye*, see below, 392–6 and n. Had Milton allowed the lines to stand, the references to the Hesperian fruit would have formed a pattern of three parts: (1) the dragon-guarded fruit here, in the ideal world of the Attendant Spirit; (2) the dragon-guarded fruit which is made the symbol of beauty and chastity in the actual and fallen world (392–6); and (3) the tree, no longer dragon-guarded, round which Hesperus and his daughters sing (in the Spirit's epilogue, 980–2). Presumably the first reference, (1), was cancelled because it introduced a note of austerity and menace into the account of the ideal world, and (2) and (3) were allowed to stand in simple contrast. For (10)–(15), *round the verge...Stygian poole*, Wright notes that among the early Greeks, for whom the known world was confined to the Mediterranean, the earth was thought of as a flat disk dividing the upper from the nether world, with the stream Ocean flowing around the earth and meeting the other two worlds, and in its western waters, where the sun set, the Gardens of the Hesperides. Later, as knowledge grew, the Atlantic replaced the stream Ocean, and Elysium, the islands of the blest, the Gardens of the Hesperides, etc., were pushed westward. Here Milton thinks of the stream Ocean as feeding at once the Atlantic and the waters of the nether world, a vague reminiscence perhaps of Plato, *Phaedo* 112–13. If the Attendant Spirit had been allowed to retain these lines, they would have been balanced (with an effect of irony) by Comus' words at 95–7.

[The contrast drawn in 1–11 of the present text between the two regions and their spiritual quality is the same (although here the Christian theme is kept implicit) as the contrast that is the theme of *On Time* and *At a solemn Musick* of 1632–3. Commenting on both the latter part of the Epilogue and the opening of the masque, C. S. Lewis (*RES* 8, 1932, 175: see above, *Comus* IV, under 1932) speaks of 'the contrast, beautifully emphasised by a change of metre (Celestial Cupid her fam'd son advanc't), between terrestrial and celestial love. The new passage, addressed to "mortals" only if their "ears be true" (like its counterpart in the *Apology for Smectymnuus* [*Works* 3, 303]), falls in naturally with the change at ll. 779 *et seq.*, and sums up the increasing gravity of the work in its progress towards the final text. It throws light, moreover, on the famous excised passage which *Trinity* gives us in the prologue.... In the present text we begin with six of the most impressive verses in English poetry: impressive because we pass in a single verse from the cold, tingling, almost unbreathable, region of the aerial spirits to the *smoak and stir of this dim spot*. Each level, by itself, is a masterly representation: in their juxtaposition ("Either other sweetly gracing") they are irresistible. The intrusion of an intermediate realm, as serene as the air and as warmly inviting as the earth, ruins this effect and therefore justly perished. But its erasure becomes all the more necessary when the poet, with his Platonic stair of earthly and heavenly love, has found the real philosophical intermediary and, with it, the real use for his Hesperean imagery. Having found the true reconciliation he knows that it must come at the end; we must begin with the contrast. Nothing that blurs the distinction between the region of the Spirit and the region of Comus must be admitted until we have passed the "hard assays"; then, and not till then, the more delicious imagery, which had been mere decoration in the opening speech, may be resumed and called into significant life.']

5   *smoak and stirr of this dim spot.* Verity compares *fumum et opes strepitumque*

Romae (Horace, *C.* 3. 29. 12); Hughes (1937) adds that Horace's Rome may have suggested to Milton London. [MS. originally read *this dim, narrow spot* (*Facs.* 398).]

6 *men call Earth*: in contrast, Wright thinks, to Plato's True Earth (*Phaedo* 109 f.). It is *low-thoughted* because confined to the body and material concerns.

7-8 MS. first had 7 and 8 in reverse order, interjecting the line *beyond the written date of mortall change* between them; then altered to present reading (*Works* 1, 480; *Facs.* 398).

7 *pester'd*: crowded or huddled (*OED* 3); but clogged, entangled, encumbered (*OED* 1), not by a multitude, but by *low-thoughted care*, to which the mind is *Confin'd*, seems more appropriate. *pin-fold*: pound (so defined in Shakespeare, *T.G.V.* 1. 1. 113) or enclosure for strayed animals—here figuratively for men who, forgetting the higher duties and rewards of virtue, live on the animal level. Warton quotes 'In such a pinfolde were his pleasures pent' (Gascoigne, *Works*, ed. Cunliffe, 1, 100).

8 *Strive...being.* Keightley's interpretation ('the love of life which is so strong in most men's bosoms') and Verity's elaboration (that men strive to live too long, instead of being glad when death releases them to a better life) seem curiously inept. Possibly Milton considered some such idea and rejected it; for MS. adds after 8, and then deletes, *beyond the written date of mortall change* (*Facs.* 398). The final meaning seems, rather, to be: directing their cares and affections to material things, men strive in vain for life and being, attaining only an existence *frail* (transient: *OED* 1 b) and *Feaverish* (restless: *OED* 2). Seeking a Platonic source, Wright finds it (not very convincingly) in *Rep.* 10. 613.

9-14 *Unmindfull of the crown...Palace of Eternity.* The epilogue (1017-22) returns to the idea of ascent to heaven by means of virtue, but there in recognizably Christian terms, for which this more general and classical formulation is preparatory. Masson's explanation, 'Christian doctrine in the language of classic mythology,' misses the element of progression. The *crown* (9) suggests to Verity the 'incorruptible' crown of 1 Cor. 9. 25; to Hughes (1937), the metaphorically crowned virtue of Wisd. of Sol. 4. 2. The *Sainted seats* suggest to Todd and modern editors: 'And round about the throne were four and twenty seats: and upon the seats...elders sitting...; and they had on their heads crowns of gold' (Rev. 4. 4); Todd also compares 'And ye glad Spirits, that now sainted sit / On your coelestiall thrones' (G. Fletcher, *C.T.* 1. 53). In deciding upon the general interpretation he will accept, the reader must balance with these suggestions of the Christian heaven the contrary indications (noticed above, 1–4 n.) of *starry threshold, aereal,* and *insphear'd.* Ignoring the latter, and placing the Attendant Spirit in heaven, Verity (on 3) places the souls of the virtuous dead there with him. But it seems clear that Milton thinks of the Spirit and of those souls in their intermediate state as inhabiting the same aerial region. Explanations of *After this mortal change* illustrate the vagaries of commentators: 'mortal life of change' (Rolfe); 'change from mortality' (Verity); 'this mortal state of life' (Masson); 'the change that comes to mortals—death' (Trent); the 'change to mortality...that befalls the soul when in the Cycle of Birth it is committed to this mortal body' (Wright, who traces the idea to Plato, *Rep.* 10. 611); 'change here has its old meaning of a figure in a dance' (Browne). But there seems no reason to reject the obvious meaning of *change,* the passing from life, or (in plain terms) death (*OED* 1 d), which does not even require the epithet *mortal;* cf. 'all the days of my appointed time...till my change come' (Job 14. 14).

13 *To lay...Key.* The epithet *just* means righteous (*OED* 1); cf. 'clean hands,' Ps. 24. 4 (Dunster MS.). With *Golden Key* cf. *Lyc* 110–11 and n.

14 *ope's.* MS. first read *shews* (*Works* 1, 481; *Facs.* 398).

15 *errand.* Todd compared *PL* 7. 572–3: 'Thither will send his winged Messengers / On errands of supernal Grace.' [Cf. Spenser, *F.Q.* 2. 8. 1–2. Rudrum (*Comus,* 31) wonders 'whether in writing *Comus* Milton paid any attention to the fact that it was to be presented on Michaelmas Day. Part of the Collect for that day reads "Mercifully grant, that as thy holy Angels always do thee service in heaven, so by thy appointment they may succour and defend us on earth."']

16–17 Verity is probably right in rejecting the common explanation of *rank vapours of this Sin-worn mould* as 'the noisom exhalations of this sin-corrupted earth' [Warton], which suits well enough with 5–6 but ignores the fact that for Milton '*mould* has the general sense "substance, material,"' as in 'mortal mixture of Earths mould' (below, 243) and (describing Adam) 'Heroic built, though of terrestrial mould' (*PL* 9. 485), the reference being to man created from the dust; and again, 'Creatures of other mould, earth-born..., / Not Spirits' (ibid. 4. 360–1). Thus *mould* refers to the fleshly body which the Attendant Spirit (as Verity supposes) has assumed—perhaps rather will assume at 488, for the phrasing at 16 suggests that he first appears in his true and original nature. This interpretation invites a second look at 16, where Verity adopts the common explanation of *Ambrosial weeds* as heavenly raiment, and this corresponds to the use of 'Weeds' at 84. But it is surely not his garb, which he will lay aside, that the Spirit feels to be soiled by his assuming a body of mortal clay; it is his immortal body of aerial substance, and *Ambrosial* (as Masson and Rolfe note) can retain its root meaning, immortal (*OED* 1), and *weed* can be used figuratively for the body (*OED*: *sb.*² 3 and *FInf* 58 and n.). The meaning, then, would be: 'I would not soil my pure immortal substance by a body of clay, the garb of sinful man and reeking of his sin.' In *rank*, having a strong and offensive smell (*OED* 12), a contrast is suggested with *Ambrosial*, which retains its secondary meaning, divinely fragrant (*OED* 1 c); cf. *PL* 9. 851–2: 'A bough of fairest fruit...ambrosial smell diffus'd.' Cf. also Shakespeare, *Antony* 5. 2. 211–13: 'In their thick breaths, / Rank of gross diet, shall we be enclouded, / And forc'd to drink their vapour.'

18   *But to my task*: MS. *buisnesse now*, deleted, and present reading substituted. The *task* is to refer to the occasion, pay a compliment to the Lord President, and furnish the necessary exposition. Warton (on 78) cites 'But, to my charge' (Fletcher, *F. Shep.* 3. 1. 181).

18–21   *Neptune...all the Sea-girt Iles*. Browne cites Homer, *Il.* 15. 187 f., where Poseidon (Neptune) asserts his equality with Zeus (Jove): 'For three brethren are we, begotten of Cronos,..., Zeus, and myself, and the third is Hades...lord of the dead below. And in threefold wise are all things divided, and unto each hath been apportioned his own domain. I verily, when the lots were shaken, won for my portion the grey sea to be my habitation for ever, and Hades won the murky darkness, while Zeus won the broad heaven..., but the earth and high Olympus remain yet common to us all' (L.C.L.). Masson notes that Homer (*Il.* 9. 457) calls Hades (Pluto) the 'underground Jove'; Virgil (*A.* 4. 638) calls Pluto *Jupiter Stygius*. Dunster (cited by Todd) compared 'Both upper Jove's and neather's diverse Thrones' (Sylvester, *Bethulians Rescue* 5. 348, Grosart, 2, 199).

19   *salt Flood*. Todd noted the phrase in Surrey: 'when the salt flood / Doth rise by rage of winde' (*Ladys Lament for her Lover Overseas, Poems*, ed. Padelford, 1928, 72).

21   *Sea-girt Iles*. Todd and Dunster MS. cite: 'Like to his island girt in with the ocean,' Shakespeare, *3 H. VI* 4. 8. 20; 'This sea-girt Isle' of Britain, *Ben Jonson* 8, 240; 'Beyond the Realm of Gaul, a Land there lies, / Sea-girt it lies,' Milton, *HistBr, Works* 10, 12.

22–3   *That like...the Deep*. Warton compared 'This precious stone set in the silver sea' (Shakespeare, *R. II* 2. 1. 46).

23 *unadorned*: without other (and inferior) ornaments.

24-7 *his tributary gods...little tridents*. These *tributary gods* stand in less intimate relation to Neptune than do his *blu-hair'd deities* (29); they pay him tribute, acknowledging his overlordship, and are suffered to rule in the areas committed to them. Hughes notices the list of subordinate deities that follow 'great Neptune' and 'First the Sea-gods' in Spenser, *F.Q.* 4. 11. 11 f., and those in Jonson's *Neptunes Triumph*. Osgood (*C.M.* 76) observes that, except for Nereus (Virgil, *A.* 2. 418), strictly only Neptune bears the trident. Todd evidently took *tributary* in the sense of contributary, since he compared only 'tributary rivers' (Shakespeare, *Cym.* 4. 2. 36) and 'tributary streams' and 'tributary brooks' as occurring repeatedly in Drayton's *Polyolbion*; but this cannot be the primary meaning here. *By course*: in due order (*OED*: course 33). *several*: separate (*OED* 1); [cf. *Nat* 234].

27-9 *but this Ile...blu-hair'd deities*. The *Ile* is Great Britain, which Neptune *quarters*, divides into parts (which may be fewer or more than four: *OED* 2), and assigns to his *blu-hair'd deities*, gods who rule in his behalf, as distinguished from the *tributary gods* (24). Commentators generally—with such exceptions as Bell and Trent—have assumed that the *deities* here mentioned are identified with (e.g. Rolfe) or included among (e.g. Masson) the *tributary gods* of 24, but the construction from 27, *but this Ile*, etc., as well as the exalting of these deities as different from those who are allowed to *weild their little tridents*, strongly suggests a contrast between two distinct classes. The deities are *blu-hair'd* because associated with the blue sea. [Cf. the description of six Tritons in the *Masque of Blacknesse*: 'their upper parts humane, save that their haires were blue, as partaking of the sea-colour' (*Ben Jonson* 7, 170)]; Verity noted that four Naiads with 'bluish tresses' appear in Francis Beaumont's *Masque of the Inner Temple* (Evans, *Masques*, 93; Spencer, *Masques*, 136). Warburton (reported by Warton and Todd) suggests that the King is here honoured with the name of Neptune (the antecedent of *he*), since from this British Neptune the *noble Peer of mickle trust* (31) derives his commission; [cf. Jonson, *Neptunes Triumph*]. Keightley notes that, while *quarters* need not signify a fourfold division, actually there was a fourfold government of Great Britain: from London, from Edinburgh, and in the Lord Presidencies of the North and (Bridgewater's) of Wales. If we accept Warburton's suggestion, and at the same time the distinction between two classes of gods, the compliment to the King becomes yet more magnificent, since it is implied that other maritime rulers acknowledge his supremacy and reign by his sufferance. Himes (*Enigmas* 12-13) offers a different interpretation, based on the heraldic meaning of *quarters* (*OED* 3b): Britain's importance is attested 'by its assignment to the armorial bearings, its *quartering* upon the escutcheon of all the great sea-powers...in token of their obligation to protect and defend the island....Rightly understood, Shakespeare has nothing so magnificently patriotic.'

28 *the main*: MS. *his empire*; present reading substituted (*Facs.* 398).

30–3 *And all this tract...proud in Arms.* This designates the region administered by the Council of Wales and the Marches under its Lord President, the Earl of Bridgewater, the *Peer of mickle trust*, of 'great fidelity' (Hughes, 1937; cf. *OED* 4), but rather, perhaps, having great confidence placed in him or great responsibility laid upon him (*OED* 5), and with it corresponding *power*, an interpretation supported by *new-entrusted Scepter* (36). 'Wales had been so efficiently annexed to England that the office had lost its warlike character. There were no longer fears of Welsh insurrections...' (Masson, *Life*, 1, 608). Thus the words *old, and haughty Nation* are retrospective; the President can rule with *temper'd awe*, i.e. by inspiring awe qualified with other and different feelings. The phrase *old...Arms* recalls Virgil's about the Romans, *populum...belloque superbum* (*A.* 1. 21: Warton), from whom through Aeneas the ancient inhabitants of Britain were traditionally descended (Hughes, 1937). [Cf. Milton, *Ps* 80. 35, 'Nations proud and haut' (Warton); Shakespeare, *R. III* 2. 3. 28, 'haught and proud' (Todd); Bacon, 'mighty and proud kingdoms in arms' (*New Atlantis, Works* 3, 142).]

30 *And all...Sun.* [H. Spencer (*MLN* 23, 1908, 30) compared Aeschylus, *Supp.* 254–5: 'Of all the region...on the side toward the setting sun, I am the lord.' Cf. Giles Fletcher the elder, *De Literis Antiquae Britanniae* (pr. 1633) 222: *Camber ad Occiduum spectantia littora Solem* (ed. L. E. Berry, *Anglia* 79, 1961–2, 351).]

34–7 After the elaborate compliment to the Earl, and the brief one to the people of Wales, Milton now compliments the chief masquers, the Earl's *fair off-spring nurs't in Princely lore*, before proceeding with his exposition. It is unnecessary to see in *Princely lore* (with Todd) an allusion to the Egertons' remote connection with the royal line, or to the fact noted by Warton (127–8), that the boys had taken part, early in 1634, in Carew's court masque *Coelum Britannicum*. What is said is that their education has been *Princely* (Masson), befitting the Earl's rank and position, to which the context pointedly alludes. In *attend their Fathers state*, the word *state* may mean pomp, solemnity (*OED* 17), but more probably chair of state, throne (ibid. 20), in keeping with *new-entrusted Scepter*.

Comus

On the legend that *Comus* found its starting point in an actual event, see the beginning of III above.

37 *perplex't paths*: Lat. *perplexus*, entangled. J. C. Maxwell (*N&Q* 6, 1959, 364) compares *perplexum iter... | fallacis silvae* (Virgil, *A.* 9. 391–2).

38 *nodding horror.* See above, *Nat* 172 n., and 'shag'd with horrid shades' (below, 428 and n.). [Hughes remarks: 'The *Wood* is symbolic like Spenser's wood of error (*F.Q.*, 1, i, 10, 8–9) and Dante's (*Inf.* 1, 2).'] Todd compared Tasso's description of an enchanted forest in *G.L.* 13. 2: *Sorge non lunge a le cristiane tende | tra solitarie valli alta foresta, | foltissima di piante antiche, orrende, | che spargon d'ogni intorno ombra funesta*; and Petrarch, *Rime*, 176: *Raro un silenzio, un solitario orrore | D'ombrosa selva mai tanto mi piacque.*

39 *forlorn* retains here a strong suggestion of its initial meaning, lost. *Passinger*: wayfarer, traveller (*OED* 1).

41 *quick command from Soveran Jove.* Verity compares *Arc* 44–5; but here Jove stands for God (see above, 1–4 n.). On *Soveran* see *Nat* 60 n.

43–5 *And listen...or Bowr.* Richardson (reported by Todd) compared: *favete linguis. carmina non prius | audita... | canto* (Horace, *C.* 3. 1. 2–4); cf. also *PL* 1. 16. That the epithet *modern*, here contrasted with *old* (antique), includes the medieval, the context plainly shows: *Bard* means minstrel; *Hall*, the chief room of a castle; *Bowr*, the ladies' apartment. The masque carries into 'modern' times something of the conventions and the tone of medieval chivalry; see above, II, and cf. *L'All* 119–30 and n. Warton noted that 'bower and hall' is a stock phrase in the metrical romances and cited Spenser, *Astrophel* 27–8; cf. *F.Q.* 1. 4. 43 and 8. 29, 4. 6. 39, etc.

46–9 *Bacchus...Tyrrhene shore.* In fabricating his own 'myth' of Comus' parentage, Milton starts from the story of Dionysus (Bacchus) and the pirates, made familiar by the *Homeric Hymn to Dionysus* (7) and Ovid (*M.* 3. 582–691). The former is probably Milton's principal source; for there the god is no longer a child, as in Ovid, but 'a stripling in the first flush of manhood' with 'his rich dark hair...waving about him' (cf. below, 54–5), and his captors are Tyrsenian pirates. 'Tyrsenian' was taken as Etruscan or Tuscan; cf. Apollodorus 3. 5. 3, Philostratus, *Imagines* 1. 19. Ovid placed the incident in the Aegean, Milton in the Tyrrhenian Sea, west of Italy (see below, 50–6 n.). In the *Homeric Hymn*, followed more or less closely by Ovid, the god bathes the ship in wine, festoons it with the vine and ivy, frightens his captors into the sea with apparitions of wild beasts, and transforms them to dolphins. These are the *Mariners transform'd.*

47 *sweet poyson*. The phrase occurs in Sidney, *Astrophel*, Song 5. 2. 2, and Shakespeare, *John* 1. 1. 213 (E. Le Comte, *PQ* 21, 1942, 296, n. 7) [and also in Campion, *Maske in honour of the Lord Hayes* (*Works* 67, line 30)].

48 *After the Tuscan Mariners transform'd*: a Latinism, like *post urbem conditam* (Verity).

49 *listed*: pleased (cf. John 3. 8).

50–6 *On Circes Iland...a Son*. The rhetorical question, a favourite device of Spenser (*S.C.*, *August* 141; *F.Q.*6. 10. 16, 7. 6. 36), here serves to emphasize the familiar. Circe furnishes a second point of contact with genuine myth. The two main sources are Homer, *Od*. 10. 135–574, and Ovid, *M*. 14. 248–440. For Milton's lines Bowle (reported by Warton and Todd) also cited Boethius, *Consol. Phil.* 4, met. 3. 4 f., and Warton added Virgil, *A*. 7. 11–17. Circe, *daughter of the Sun* (Helios) and the sea-nymph Perse, lived on the island of Aeaea in the Tyrrhenian Sea. Bacchus' imagined passage to her island might have been suggested by, but bears no resemblance to, that of Glaucus (Ovid, *M*. 14. 8 f.). The story of Circe and Odysseus was moralized summarily by Horace (*Ep*. 1. 2. 17–31) and elaborately by such Renaissance mythographers as N. Comes and George Sandys. It was utilized by Aurelian Townshend in his masque *Tempe Restord* and (without benefit of moralizing) by William Browne in his *Inner Temple Masque* (see II above). The Circe figure was adapted by Ariosto (in his Alcina), Tasso (Armida), Spenser (Acrasia), and G. Fletcher (*C.V.* 2. 47 f.). [Some references for the tradition are: M. Y. Hughes, 'Spenser's Acrasia and the Circe of the Renaissance' (*JHI* 4, 1943, 381–99); D. Bush, *Mythol*. (rev. ed., 1963), 279–80, and *Pagan Myth and Christian Tradition in English Poetry* (Philadelphia, 1968); D. P. Harding, *Milton and the Renaissance Ovid* (1946), 58–66; W. B. Stanford, *The Ulysses Theme: A Study in the Adaptability of a Traditional Hero* (Oxford, 1954; rev. ed., 1963); J. M. Steadman, 'Dalila, the Ulysses Myth, and Renaissance Allegorical Tradition,' *MLR* 57 (1962), 560–5; A. B. Giamatti, *The Earthly Paradise and the Renaissance Epic* (1966); and below, notes on 56–7, 635–6, 637.]

Milton freshens the convention by giving Circe's powers to her supposed son. His allusion to the *charmed Cup* and its transforming power is based on Homer and Ovid, where the victims are changed to *groveling Swine*, not, as in *Comus*, retaining their upright shape but with the heads of various animals; but Milton, curiously, does not allude to Circe's wand, which in both Homer and Ovid effected the transformation and is to play its part in *Comus* (652, 658, 814); all his emphasis falls on the cup (65, 524, 671–7, 810–12), which Milton later is to work into his Platonic account of true and false love: '...chastity and love, I meane that which is truly so, whose charming cup is only virtue...The rest are cheated with a thick intoxicating potion which a certaine Sorceresse the abuser of loves name carries about...' (*Apol*, *Works* 3, 305 [cf. *SA* 934]). It may be added that, though Milton could not exploit the idea in depicting Comus' victims, the *upright shape*, contrasted with *groveling*, is morally significant; cf. *PL* 4. 288–9, 8. 258–61, 441.

Although Bacchus' visit to Circe's island and Comus' parentage are Milton's own invention, he may have caught a hint from the tradition that Circe bore sons to Odysseus (Hesiod, *Theog.* 1011–14), a datum not mentioned by Homer or by Ovid in his story but glanced at in *Ex Ponto* 3. 1. 123; [cf. Milton, *Procan* 18 and n.]. Invented genealogies were not uncommon; among those involving Bacchus, Boccaccio (*Gen. Deor.* 5. 26; Arthos, *Mask*, 53) derives Hymen from him and Venus instead of the usual Apollo and a Muse, and there is Milton's own fancy in *L'All* (14–24 and n.). The Comus of Puteanus has also his imaginary parentage, from Mercury and Venus (R. H. Singleton, above, III. 7). For Bacchus' *blithe youth*, cf. *Homeric Hymn* 7. 3–5 (and above, 46–9 n.). With *clustring locks* Warton (1785) compared phrases in Apollon. Rhod. 2. 677, *PL* 4. 303, *SA* 568; none of these refers to Bacchus. The wreath of *Ivy berries*, unmentioned in the *Homeric Hymn*, is the traditional adornment of Bacchus; references are common from Pindar (*Ol.* 2. 27) onward. Warton cited Ovid, *F.* 1. 393, and Milton, *El* 6. 15; Osgood (*C.M.*), Euripides, *Phoen.* 649 f.; cf. *L'All* 16. [Concerning *On Circes Iland fell* (50), J. B. Broadbent (*Milton: Comus and Samson Agonistes*, 11) thinks that 'The verb hints at the fall of Adam'; cf. P. Brockbank's comment (IV above, under 1968).]

56–7 *a Son | ...his Mother more.* 'Comus typifies sensuality...and magical power. In the scene with the Lady (658–812) he represents sensual pleasure. To the Attendant Spirit he appears rather as "a sorcerer" (520), "that damned wizard" (570), "the foul enchanter" (644)....He owes the one character to his father the wine-god; the other to his mother the sorceress, skilled in magic drugs' (Verity). This is very well so far as it goes. Bacchus and Circe alike stand for incontinence, and Circe, in addition, for magic arts; hence Comus resembles Circe more than Bacchus. He does, however, resemble Bacchus, in the secondary rather than the primary association of the god, the venereal rather than the vinous. That aspect is noticed, e.g. in Diod. Sic. 1. 22. 6–7, 4. 4. 2–4, 4. 5. 6; N. Comes, *Mythol.* 5. 13 (Padua, 1616, p. 269), 10 (p. 541); Spenser, *F.Q.* 2. 1. 55, 2. 12. 61; Sandys, *Ovid* (1632), 107–9. Diod. Sic. also takes account of an elder Dionysus, born of Zeus and Persephone, with darker associations that fit well with Comus' worship of Cotytto and Hecate (see below, 128–37 and n.): for his rites 'are celebrated at night and in secret, because of the disgraceful conduct which is a consequence of the gatherings' (Diod. Sic. 4. 4. 1). The common ancient view of Circe was as the enchantress, 'sprung from Helius . . . and Perse, whom Oceanus begot,' and thus 'sister to Aeetes of baneful mind' (Homer, *Od.* 10. 136–9, 276), and versed in the lore of potent herbs and drugs (ibid. 236; Virgil, *A.* 7. 19; Ovid, *M.* 14. 14–22, 266–70). There is nothing in Milton's reference to her that goes beyond Homer (but cf. Diod. Sic. 4. 45. 1–5). If Circe is condemned by the ancients it is generally for dark magic and cruelty, not for sensuality, though Horace (*Ep.* 1. 2. 23–6) describes her as a harlot and praises Ulysses' temperance in not falling *sub domina meretrice*. But the allegorizers of myth fastened on this last idea. Following N. Comes (*Mythol.* 6. 6, p. 308), Sandys says: 'How Circe was said to bee the daughter of Sol and Persis, in that lust proceeds from heat and moisture, which naturally incites to luxury; and getting the dominion, deformes our soules with all bestiall vices; alluring some to inordinate Venus; others to anger, cruelty, and every excesse of passion: the Swines, the Lyons, and the Wolves, produced by her sensuall charms . . .' (*Ovid,* 1632, 480–1). For further extracts see below, 637 n., and Bush, *Mythol.*, 1963, 279–80.

58 *Comus nam'd.* On the literary history of the name before Milton and the character assigned to a being of that name by Philostratus, Puteanus, Jonson, and others, see above, III. 7.

59 *frolick*: sportive (*OED* 1) in the use to which he put his powers; cf. *L'All* 18–19.

60 *Celtick*: 'pertaining to the People of Gaul' (Thomas Blount, *Glossographia*, 1656: *OED* 1). *Celtae* was the name applied by Caesar to the inhabitants of middle Gaul or Gallia Celtica, though by other Roman writers to those of a larger region including Spain and upper Italy (*OED*: Celt 1). Milton evidently refers to France generally, as to Spain in the second epithet *Iberian*, the country of the *Iberi*, the name he uses for the Spaniards in *QNov* 103; in another context, as in *PR* 3. 318, *Iberian* might refer to the region between the Black Sea and the Caspian.

61 *ominous.* Warton (1785) explains as 'dangerous'; Verity as 'not so much "threatening", as "full of portents or magical appearances,"' and he cites 206 for subjective images thronging the Lady's mind. The meaning would seem rather to be 'Of doubtful or menacing aspect' (*OED* 3c, though the earliest example there given is of 1877), which is clearly supported by 37–9 (see 39 n.).

62 *black shades.* [Wright (*N&Q* 5, 1958, 206) remarks that, as often in Milton, 'In *Comus* "shades" always means trees, woods or foliage, whatever further particularity of meaning it carries.' Cf. below, 428 n.]

63 *Excells...Art.* See 56–7 and n.

65 *orient*: bright, lustrous (meaning derived from 'orient pearl,' supposed to be more lustrous than any other: *OED*: *a.* 2b; see also *Nat* 231 n.). Trent thinks it may refer to Eastern drugs which give the cup its potency.

66–7 *drouth of Phoebus*: thirst (*OED*: drought 4) caused by the heat of the sun, Phoebus being the sun-god. The periphrasis suggests that Milton did not choose to exploit the connection of Comus with the sun (Helios) through Circe (see 50–6 n.). Warton compared Ovid, *M.* 14. 276–7. The epithet *fond* (foolish, infatuated: *OED*: *a.* 2) is transferred to *thirst* from the *most* who seek thus to satisfy it.

68–77 *Soon as the Potion...sensual stie.* Editors note the general dependence of the passage on Homer's account (*Od.* 10. 235 f.) of Circe's treatment of Odysseus' followers. She mixed with their food 'baneful drugs, that they might utterly forget their native land. Now when she had given them the potion, and they had drunk it off, then she presently smote them with her wand, and penned them in the sties. And they had the heads, and voice, and bristles, and shape of swine, but their minds remained unchanged even as before. So they were penned there weeping, and before them Circe flung mast and acorns...to eat, such things as wallowing swine are wont to feed upon' (L.C.L.). But there are in Milton significant differences from Homer as from Ovid (*M.* 14. 273 f.), who follows Homer. (1) It is the potion, not the wand, that effects the fatal change. (2) Not the whole body but only the head is changed, the *human count'nance,* / *Th' express resemblance of the gods* (as in 'the express image of his person,' Heb. 1. 3: Verity), the phrase being intended to remind us of man created in God's image (Gen. 1. 27), and of the long tradition in commentary which held that man's reason reflected in his face was God's image in him and which culminates in *PL* 7. 506–11 (see n.). (3) The victims are not all transformed to swine, but to various animals (see next paragraph). (4) So complete is their subjugation that their forgetfulness continues while they wallow (metaphorically this time) in a sty of sensual pleasure, yet ignorant of their own state, as yet a more miserable condition, though they do not perceive it. (Verity contrasts the superior pathos of Homer's conscious victims repining at their lot, and Milton's emphasis on the completeness of Comus' power, the deadly pleasure he has to offer; Hughes suggests that the difference is that between folk-tale and allegory.) Perhaps it is in the sum of these differences that Comus is shown to excel his mother (63).

According to Virgil (*A.* 7. 15–20), Circe changed her victims into lions, boars, bears, and wolves; the idea was apparently common in antiquity, since it is recorded by Apollodorus—but in the *Epitome* (7. 13), unknown to Milton's age. It was very common in the Renaissance (doubtless derived from Virgil), e.g. in Sandys (above, 56–7 n.). [In Homer (*Od.* 10. 433), Eurylochus fears that Circe will change his comrades into swine or wolves or lions.] Hughes ('Acrasia,' *JHI* 4, 1943, 381–99) notes earlier examples, including—besides N. Comes' *Mythol.* 6. 6—Sir Thomas More's translation of Pico della Mirandola's 'life' by his nephew (*English Works*, ed. W. E. Campbell, 2 v., London, 1931, I, 10–11), Ascham's *Scholemaster* (*English Works*, 1904, 227), and W. Browne's *Inner Temple Masque*, where Circe's victims appear as harts, wolves, baboons, with the hog Grillus. Alcina's followers had animal heads on human bodies (Ariosto, *O.F.* 6. 61) [—a change more convenient for stage presentation (Newton; Todd; E. G. Ainsworth, *MLN* 46, 1931, 91–2). Cf. Demaray above, II, n. 4. Parker (129–30, 790, n. 34) suggests the use of 'animal heads left over from the recent *Cœlum Britanicum*,' in which the two Egerton boys had acted.] Todd found precedents for the victims' complete forgetfulness in Ariosto, *O.F.* 6. 47, and Spenser, *F.Q.* 2. 1. 54. Newton and Todd needlessly saw a source for the forgetfulness of friends and home in the effect of the lotus (Homer, *Od.* 9. 94–7), though Plato's application of it (*Rep.* 8. 560–1: Todd) is relevant to Milton's theme. For suggestions of the victims' contentment with their lot one may look back through Spenser's Grill (*F.Q.* 2. 12. 86–7) to its ultimate source in Plutarch's *Beasts Are Rational* (*Moralia*, L.C.L., 12, 496 f.), or to other works influenced by Plutarch, such as Machiavelli's *Asino d'Oro* or G. B. Gelli's *Circe* (Hughes).

70–1 *Woolf, or Bear, | …Goat.* Cf. 'Be it ounce or cat or bear, | Pard or boar with bristled hair' (Shakespeare, *Dream* 2. 2. 30–1). *Ounce*: a term then vaguely used for wild felines from the wildcat to the panther.

75–6 *But boast themselves more comely then before | And all their friends, and native home forget.* [Standard modern punctuation puts a comma after *before* and no comma after *friends*, and this pointing yields one clear meaning. But the earliest punctuation is not so clear. MS. has *then before | & all thire freinds &*

native home forget (*Facs.* 400); Br. has commas after *before* and *freinds* (ibid. 306); 1637 has nothing after *before* (Diekhoff, below, wrongly reports a comma) and a semicolon after *friends* (ibid. 267); 1645 is the same as 1673 above. J. S. Diekhoff (*PQ* 20, 1941, 603-4)—who does not take in Br.—showed the ambiguity: (1) are *friends* and *home* both objects of *forget* (as editors seem to commonly take them), or (2) is *friends* parallel to *themselves*, both being objects of *boast*? The punctuation of MS. and Br. is neutral or ambiguous; 1637 demands (2); 1645 and 1673 seem to favour (2). According to this reading, the *friends* would be Comus' transformed victims, not those left behind at home. Diekhoff sees support for (2) in the separation of the two objects by an intervening phrase, 'a typical Miltonic departure from the normal order,' and in the stronger antithesis between *native home* and *stie* than between *friends and native home* and *stie*. No doubt (1) makes the more obvious sense, although it goes against punctuation, but the more obvious sense was not necessarily Milton's intention.]

77   *roule with pleasure in a sensual stie.* The last word was no doubt used with a memory of Circe's confining her victims in a sty, but it was used figuratively for 'An abode of bestial lust' (*OED*: *sb.*[3] 2b) and so used by Milton, *Tetr*, *Works* 4, 89. MacKellar (*PR* 3. 86 n.) notes: 'To roll (*volutare*) in vice is an expression used by Cicero, in *Fam.* 9. 3; *Har. Res.* 20. 42; *Her.* 4. 13.' [Todd cited Jonson, *Pleasure* 102-3: 'in ye stye / of vice have wallow'd' (*Ben Jonson* 7, 483). Cf. *Epicuri de grege porcum* (Horace, *Ep.* 1. 4. 16); Browne, *Brit. Past.* 1. 2. 788: 'wallowing lie within a sensual sink.']

78-82   *Therefore...As now I do.* Cf. above, 40-2, 15 and n., and 3 n. (for a quotation from Jonson's *Fortunate Isles*). The Attendant Spirit is sent *from Heav'n*, i.e. from the heavens, from 'the starry threshold of Joves Court,' of which the references to *high Jove* and the *glancing Star* (78, 80) are intended to remind us. With the image of the shooting star Warton compared the descent of Michael, *stella cader*, etc., in Tasso, *G.L.* 9. 62; the departure of Adonis, 'Look how a bright star shooteth from the sky' (Shakespeare, *Venus* 815); and Milton's later 'Thither came Uriel...swift as a shooting Starr' (*PL* 4. 555-6) and *PR* 4. 619-20: all more relevant than Homer, *Il.* 4. 73-7, cited by earlier commentators, where, says Warton, 'The star to which Minerva is compared, emits sparkles, but is stationary.' Todd added: 'When, like the starres, the singing Angels shot / To earth' (G. Fletcher, *C.V.* 1. 78). [The traditional image may have started chiefly from Ovid's picture of Phaethon's fall (*M.* 2. 319-22).]

79 *adventrous*: hazardous, perilous (*OED* 2).

83 *skie robes*: dress worn in the Spirit's native habitat, the 'threshold of Joves Court.' *spun out of Iris Wooff*: woven from the colours of the rainbow, of which Iris was the goddess; cf. 991, *Nat* 143 (1645 reading), *PL* 11. 244. Dunster MS. compares 'Her Robe, Sky-colour'd' (Sylvester, *Bethulians Rescue* 4. 59, Grosart, 2, 191).

84 *Weeds*: here, garments. See 16–17 n.

84-8 *a Swain...waving Woods*. Warton noted these lines as a compliment to Henry Lawes (on whom see above, I, and notes on *Sonn* 13). He and Todd quoted verses by and to Lawes to show that the implied comparison with Orpheus was a commonplace. Hughes remarks that Milton's parallel 'is no bolder than Herrick's question...: "Tell me, canst thou be Less than Apollo?"' (*To Mr. Henry Lawes*).

87 *knows to*: knows how to (see *Lyc* 10–11 n.).

88 *nor of less faith*: 'not less trustworthy ⟨*OED* 10⟩ than he is skilled in music' (Masson).

89-91 *in this office...this occasion*: as a shepherd, viewing the scene from a mountain, seemingly best fitted (*OED*: like 3) and nearest placed to give aid in this present juncture (ibid. occasion 2) or need arising from circumstances (ibid. 5). At 90 MS. (*Facs.* 400) first had *give præsent aide*; it substituted *chance* for *aide*, then restored *aide* and substituted *the* for *give*, thus providing the present reading, which is that of Br. and 1637 (*Facs.* 307, 268). MS. deleted *of this occasion* (presumably when *chance* was introduced) but later restored it.

92 *viewles*: invisible (*OED* 1). Cf. *Passion* 50; *PL* 3. 518; Shakespeare, *Meas.* 3. 1. 124. [On *hatefull* see below, 145–68 n.]

Following **92** ⟨Direction⟩ *Comus enters*, etc. This signals the entry of the Antimasque (or the first Antimasque if the 'Countrey-Dancers' after 956 represent a second). The rout of monsters, with animal heads and human bodies, conform to the Spirit's description (68–72). *OED* (1 a, b, 4, 5) defines *rout* as a company, a pack of animals, a body of retainers, or a disorderly and tumultuous crowd, and all of these meanings are relevant here. Comus now bears Circe's wand, *a charming Rod*, as well as her cup, *his Glass*. For *their Apparel glistering... Torches in their hands*, MS. (*Facs.* 400) reads: *come on in* ⟨*begin* deleted⟩ *a wild & ⟨humorous* deleted⟩ *antick fashion*—a phrase which heightens the impression of antimasque. MS. also has *intrant* κωμάзοντες. For full variants see *Works* I, 488. Singleton (952–3) notes that the Comus of Puteanus bears a cup of wine (an addition to the description of Philostratus) and that his followers include dangerous beasts (though these conceal their faces behind masks); however, both these accompaniments of Milton's Comus find much closer parallels in the Circe myth. To Verity *glistering* (glittering) suggests that *their Apparel* was of tinsel; *glister* is the form in Shakespeare, *Merch.* 2. 7. 65, and below, 218.

93–144 No music for this entry has been preserved, though it seems almost certain that the lyric speech, if not sung, must have been spoken in recitative. [Pattison (*English Poets*, ed. T. H. Ward, 2, 298) called it 'a close imitation of the dithyrambic monody of Euripides.'] Trent remarks on the lyric character of both form and content and notes passages of similar effect in Tasso's *Aminta*, Fletcher's *F. Shep.*, Jonson's masques, etc. The beauty of the images, the (surface) innocence of their meaning, and the response to nature which they exhibit, have led Miss Welsford and others to argue the sympathy of Milton the poet with Comus, however much Milton the moralist may condemn him, and to declare the words indistinguishable from those of the Attendant Spirit. A closer reading shows that below the surface the images are by no means uniformly innocent, that Comus responds to natural beauty only to pervert it, and that the words could not possibly have been uttered by the Attendant Spirit, whose epilogue indeed will balance, and contrast with, them.

93–4 *The Star...doth hold.* Most editors have identified the *Star* as Hesperus, the evening star, the first to appear—which thus tells the shepherd it is time to shut up the sheep in the fold (*OED*: fold *v.*² 1)—and have supported the identification by reference to Spenser, *V. Gnat* 315–19 (based on Virgil, *Cul.* 203–4), where on the appearance of Vesper (i.e. Hesperus, in reality the planet Venus) the shepherd, 'Gathering his straying flocke, does homeward fare.' Todd compares *cogere donec ovis stabulis numerumque referre | iussit et invito processit Vesper Olympo* (Virgil, *E.* 6. 85–6). For the position of the evening star as it appears, first among the stars, editors cite Spenser, *F.Q.* 3. 4. 51: 'now the golden Hesperus | Was mounted high in top of heaven sheene, | And warnd his other brethren joyeous, | To light their blessed lamps.' O. F. Emerson (*Anglia* 39, 1916, 495–516) adds, e.g.: 'See where faire Venus shewes hir radiant face, | lets hence, and shut our sheepfolds in their coat' (Thomas Watson, *Poems*, ed. Arber, 175); 'Soon as the Shepheards Star abroad doth wend | (Nights harbinger) to shut in bright-some Day' (Davison, *Poetical Rhapsody*, ed. Rollins, 1, 29); 'Shepherds all, and maidens fair, | Fold your flocks up... | See the heavy clouds low falling, | And bright Hesperus down calling | The dead Night' (Fletcher, *F. Shep.* 2. 1. 1–2, 9–11); and lastly (in lines that find their main relevance in the connection of 93–4 with 97): 'Hesperus, yᵉ glory of yᵉ West, / the brightest star, yᵗ from his burning Crest / lights all on this side yᵉ Atlantick seas' (*Pleasure* 192–4, *Ben Jonson* 7, 486). [Cf. *PL* 4. 605 f.]

Keightley was inclined to attribute Milton's phrasing to a memory of 'Look, th' unfolding star calls up the shepherd' (Shakespeare, *Meas.* 4. 2. 219), which refers to the morning star (Phosphorus, or Lucifer, which is again the planet Venus and identical with Vesper, Hesperus, or the evening star; cf. Horace, *C.* 2. 9. 10–12, and see above, *Nat* 74 n.). But he recognized some difficulty in the position in the firmament that Milton assigns to the *Star*, since the evening star does not the *top of Heav'n...hold*, i.e. appear in the zenith. J. M. Hart, taking up this objection (N.Y. *Nation* 79, 1904, 9), inferred that Milton could not mean Hesperus. Emerson, noting the many literary precedents and also the exactness of Milton's knowledge, infers (507) that by the *top of Heav'n* he meant not the zenith but 'a fairly high place in the sky,' which may also be Spenser's meaning at *F.Q.* 3. 4. 51 (quoted above). He further cites (*MLN* 37, 1922, 119) 'At last faire Hesperus in highest skie / Had spent his lampe, and brought forth dawning light' (*F.Q.* 1. 2. 6), which of course refers to the planet's position at dawn, just before—as Lucifer, the morning star—it disappears. Hanford (*MLN* 37, 1922, 444–5) sides with Emerson but suggests that *the top of Heav'n* means, not 'a fairly high point in the sky,' but 'the upper half of the celestial sphere,' which would be 'astronomically accurate' and gives 'a better poetic sense': 'Hesperus holds the entire visible heavens as their sole lord.' J. A. Himes (*MLN* 35, 1920, 441–2; *Enigmas*, 13–14) suggests that Milton does not refer to Hesperus at all, but to the constellation Leo, with its representative star Regulus, which in early spring rises to the zenith as Aries sinks below the horizon—an explanation for which he claims symbolic value. In view of the poetic precedents for Hesperus as the star that signals the close of the shepherd's day, the weight of probability lies with the traditional identification, explained perhaps by the reasons urged by Emerson or Hanford. The problem cannot be isolated from that of *Lyc* 30–1 (see n.). [P. C. Ghosh (*TLS*, 19 Feb. 1931, 135) quoted Virgil, *E.* 6. 85–6, as clearly Milton's main source, although neglected because Todd cited only 'Cogere...stabulis, &c.,' leaving unquoted the decisive line 86 (quoted above); Ghosh also commented on Keightley, Verity, Emerson (see above).]

95–101 *And the gilded Car...Chamber in the East.* From the *Homeric Hymn to Helios* (31. 8–16) onward, classical poets and their imitators imagined the sun as rising in his chariot in the east, driving it across the sky, and sinking in the western (or Atlantic) Ocean, thence to make his way back to his starting point. Milton here has some of the traditional embellishments: the *gilded Car*, the *glowing Axle*, and perhaps the hissing when the sun *doth allay* (cool) it in the western waters; elsewhere he refers to the sun's setting forth (*L'All* 59–62), his 'burning Axletree' (*Nat* 84 and n.), his descent into the ocean (*El* 5. 81 f.; *PL* 4. 539–43), [and the hissing (*Naturam* 25–8)]; see Osgood, *C.M.* 11–12. Browne compares: 'The Sunne that measures heaven all day long, / At night doth baite his steedes the Ocean waves emong' (Spenser, *F.Q.* 1. 1. 32). Hughes traces the golden car with its fiery heat to Euripides, *Phoen.* 1–2, and notes Ovid's account of the last part of the sun's journey as so precipitous that Tethys, who will receive him in her waters, fears lest he fall headlong (*M.* 2. 59–69). Todd compared *Quando 'l sol bagna in mar l'aurato carro* (Petrarch, *Rime*, 223) and *Come 'l sol volge le 'nfiammate rote / Per dar luogo a la notte* (ibid. 50); and, for the hissing sound, *audiet Herculeo stridentem gurgite solem* (Juvenal 14. 280).

As applied to the *Atlantick stream*, *steep* (97) has puzzled commentators (the word *stream* of course recalls the ancient notion of the 'ocean stream' encircling the earth). Browne explains as 'deep,' comparing Lat. *altus* and the phrase 'high sea' (which, however, does not appear to support 'deep'); [cf. Prince: 'deep, i.e. far off from land']. Verity invokes the visual impression of the sea as sloping up to the horizon. [H. Belloc (*Milton*, 107) remarks: 'Look how "Steep" gives the whole landscape: the god dropping down the very wall of heaven into the waters, and the shaft of his last glory striking upwards to the roof of the skies....' Broadbent (*Comus and Samson Agonistes*, 15) sees a reminder of 'the steep roundness of the earth.'] *OED* (steep: 3e) quotes Milton under 'Of water...flowing precipitously,' which seems to catch exactly the meaning here; cf. the cancelled lines after 4 (quoted above), where the ocean with steep fall pours half his flood into the Atlantic. Otherwise (to add another conjecture), *steep* might be a transferred epithet whose real reference is to the swift descent of the sun's chariot; cf. Hughes above, and Ovid, *M.* 2. 67–9: *ultima prona via est...; / tunc etiam quae me subiectis excipit undis, / ne ferar in praeceps, Tethys solet ipsa vereri*, and *the slope Sun* (98). [The last suggestion might be supported by Milton, *El* 5. 79–80: *Ah quoties cum tu clivoso fessus Olympo / In vespertinas praecipitaris aquas.*]

MS. first read *Tartessian* for *Atlantick* [cf., in *V.C.* 1, *El* 3. 33 and n.]. *slope*: 'sloping, slanting' (*OED*); 'going down the slope of the horizon' (Elton); 'on an inclined course' (Wright). For *dusky Pole* MS. first read *northren pole* (*Facs.* 400). The reference is to the celestial (north) pole, about which the stars, in the northern hemisphere, seem to revolve; it is the point at which the earth's axis, being produced, meets the celestial sphere (*OED*: *sb.*² 1), i.e. *the top of Heav'n* (94), which becomes darkened (*dusky*) save for a last shaft, the *upward beam* shot by the declining sun (Elton). The *other gole* (goal) is the point of his rising, to which he makes his way on the ocean stream. His *chamber* is from Ps. 19. 5 (Newton); Spenser, necessarily shifting from Phoebus to Phoebe, refers to 'her chamber of the East' (*Epith.* 149).

102–4 *Joy...Jollity*. The ideas are 'half-personified' (cf. *L'All* 26–32), as Elton remarks. He compares 'Jollity in a flame-coloured suit, but tricked like a morice dancer, with scarfs....' (Shirley, *Triumph of Peace*, description of procession: Evans, *Masques*, 205; Spencer, *Masques*, 283).

105–6 Todd compares Horace, *C.* 2. 11. 13–17: *cur non...rosa | canos odorati capillos, | ...Assyriaque nardo | potamus uncti?* Hughes (1937) cites ibid. 3. 29. 1–5: *tibi | non ante verso lene merum cado | cum flore...rosarum et | pressa tuis balanus capillis....* Keightley notes 'Comus...riding in tryumph, his head crownd with roses, & other flowres' (*Pleasure* 6–8, *Ben Jonson* 7, 479). Philostratus describes Comus as wearing a crown of roses, and praises in the picture 'the dewy look of the roses,' which 'are painted fragrance and all' (*Imagines* 1. 2). Singleton (956) compares: *Licebit & venusto | Rorantium impedire | Serto caput rosarum* (Puteanus, *Comus*, 1608, 62; 1611, 57–8). Milton and Puteanus would seem to go back to Philostratus but to select different details. *Twine*: entwining of roses in the hair (Trent). [*Dropping odours*: dripping with perfumes. Cf. *Nat* 23 n., *Comus* 711 n.]

107 *Rigor now is gon to bed*. Warton compares, among other examples from Spenser, 'Delight is layd abedde' (*S.C.*, *December* 137). [Cf. Falstaff's query: 'What doth gravity out of his bed at midnight?' (*1 H. IV* 2. 4. 325–6).]

107–10 [Hughes (1937) cites *Nat* 136, 141, 144, and *L'All* 26–32, and remarks on the tradition of such personifications in morality plays, masques, and even in pastoral verse like Browne's *Brit. Past.*] Warton comments: 'Much in the strain of Sydney, *England's Helicon*': 'Night hath clos'd all in her cloke, | Twinkling starres Love-thoughts provoke; | Daunger hence good care dooth keepe | Jealousie it selfe doth sleepe' (ed. Rollins, 1, 7; *Poems*, ed. Ringler, 210).

108 MS., now partly illegible, first had what was earlier read as *quick Law* (Warburton, reported by Warton and Todd), but by W. Aldis Wright as *nice ⟨cus?⟩tom*. Wright's explanation is quoted by Fletcher, *Facs.* 400. The words *nice* and *scrupulous* do not sort well with *custom*, which also seems metrically

impossible. In any event *Advice* was added in the margin, and thus Br. and 1637 read. [Carey notes the personified Advice in Shakespeare, *Lucr.* 907.]
    scrupulous. Lockwood explains as 'cautious through fear of error,' but the context rather suggests 'filled with scruples of conscience' ('meticulous in matters of right and wrong': *OED* 1).

109 *Severity*: 'strictness or austerity' (*OED* 2). Rolfe notes that the epithet *sowre* (sour) occurs over thirty times in a figurative sense in Shakespeare.

110 *Saws*: sentential sayings (*OED*: *sb.*² 4). Newton (reported by Todd) cited 'all trivial fond records, / All saws of books' (Shakespeare, *Ham.* 1. 5. 99–100) and 'wise saws' (*A.Y.L.* 2. 7. 156). Rolfe compared 'Who fears a sentence or an old man's saw' (Shakespeare, *Lucr.* 244).

111 *We that are of purer fire.* J. S. Smart (reported by G. C. Moore Smith, *TLS*, 19 Jan. 1922, 44) saw a source for the phrase in 'But we, whose souls are made of purer fire, / Have other aims' (Thomas Randolph, *Eclogue to Master Jonson, Works* 2, 609). It was the common belief that man was composed of the four elements, of which the grossest was earth and the most refined fire; cf. 'he is pure air and fire; and the dull elements of earth and water never appear in him' (Shakespeare, *H. V* 3. 7. 22; 'I am fire and air; my other elements / I give to baser life' (*Antony* 5. 2. 292–3). It was also held that the heavens (above the moon) and their inhabitants were composed of celestial fire, the *purer fire* to which Comus lays claim. (Milton himself, in distinguishing elsewhere between the aerial and the ethereal, the latter connected with fire in its most refined form, adopted a more complicated scheme; cf. above, 1–4 n.)

112–14 *Imitate the Starry Quire*: in our song and dance imitate the movement and music of the spheres (to which Milton was later to liken the song and dance of the angels in heaven, *PL* 5. 618–27). With *in their nightly watchfull Sphears* cf. 'the Spherse of watchful fire' (*Vac* 40 and n.). Todd cites 'The starres shined in their watches' (Baruch 3. 34), and also Ecclus. 43. 10. The stars are, Comus would suggest, creatures of the night like himself and his followers. In their motion the stars *Lead in swift round the Months and Years*: cf. 'Let there be lights in the firmament...and let them be for signs, and for seasons, and for days, and years' (Gen. 1. 14); and 'they ⟨the constellations⟩ as they move / Thir starry dance in numbers that compute / Days, months, & years' (*PL* 3. 579–81). [Spaeth (*Music*, 45) and others cite Plato, *Timaeus* 40.] Thus Comus, the earthbound and evil spirit, impudently claims kindred with the starry regions whence comes the Attendant Spirit; lord of misrule as he is, he pretends to imitate the order and harmony of the spheres, likening his nightly orgies to their beneficent ministrations, and finally he seeks to integrate himself and his rout in the rhythm of the universe as seen in the procession of time and the seasons.

115–21 Passing from the theme of the heavens by night and their rhythmic motion, with its cosmic imagery, Comus proceeds, via the world of waters, with its rhythmic tides responsive to the moon, to the dance of elves and nymphs, that is, to folklore and myth in their more beautiful and seemingly innocent phases. The constant underlying subject is the dance of Comus and his rout, which is being implicitly likened to all these things.

115 *Sounds*: straits, arms of the sea or narrows between two bodies of land, as contrasted here with open *Seas*. The phrase *finny drove* may come from Spenser, *F.Q.* 3. 8. 29; [Le Comte (*N&Q* 184, 1943, 17) adds 'finny Heard,' Drayton, *Poly.* 2. 439.] Trent compared *pecus...piscium* (Horace, *C.* 1. 2. 7–9). [G. Tillotson (*On the Poetry of Pope*, Oxford, 1938, 76) suggested that a phrase which became a mere item in Augustan poetic diction is here functional, in making us see fins flashing in the moonlight.]

116 *wavering* suggests the visual effect of the moving water seen under moonlight (*OED*: *v.* 8). *Morrice*: the morris-dance (possibly derived from *morys*, Moorish), a fantastic costumed dance, popular, but frowned upon by the severe.

117 *Tawny*: brown, sometimes with a preponderance of yellow (*OED*). The deleted *yellow* of MS. was closer to 'Come unto these yellow sands' (Shakespeare, *Temp.* 1. 2. 377). *Shelves*: sandbanks or shallows, perhaps flats exposed by the receding tide; possibly reefs (Lockwood) or rock ledges, but not, it seems (as Verity imagined), river banks (*OED*: *sb.*²).

118 *Trip*: dance (*L'All* 33–4 and n.). The adjectives *pert* and *dapper* occur together in Skelton, *Image of Hypocrisy* (*OED*: dapper). As applied to appearance they seem to have been closer in meaning than now: *dapper* is defined as 'pretye' (Spenser, *S.C.*, Gloss on *October* 13), and *pert* occurs as a synonym for 'prettie, dapper' (Cotgrave's *Dict. of the French and English Tongues*, in *OED*: pert 2). Already in some contexts *pert* carried the suggestion of forward, saucy, but apparently not here, where *OED* (6) defines it as 'brisk, sprightly, cheerful,' as in 'Awake the pert and nimble spirit of mirth' (Shakespeare, *Dream* 1. 1. 13). *OED* (1, 1b) defines *dapper* as 'neat, trim,' applied especially to 'a little person... trim or smart in his ways and movements.' The *Fairies* and *Elves* (who are those of Shakespeare's, not Spenser's, imagining) are not distinguished, unless we are to think of the elves as masculine and the fairies as feminine (cf. 'the yellow-skirted Fayes,' *Nat* 235).

119–21 As in *Nat* (232–6 n.), Milton balances the figures of native and classic myth. With *dimpled Brook* Todd compared 'river with…dimpled cheek' (Browne, *Brit. Past.* 2. 5. 135–6); and with *Fountain brim* Warton compared 'Sporting with Hebe, by a Fountaine brim' (*Barons Warres* 6. 36, Drayton, 2, 112). *Wood-Nymphs*: dryads, but their location suggests rather naiads, fresh-water nymphs inhabiting rivers, brooks, and springs. They are sometimes linked (Ovid. *M.* 6. 453, 11. 49, 14. 326–8; Virgil, *Cul.* 116–17), and by Virgil (*E.* 10. 9–10) the groves of the dryads are assigned to the naiads; under the collective *Wood-Nymphs* Milton combines oread (mountain-nymph) and dryad (*PL* 9. 386–7). *wakes*: nocturnal revels, a sense derived, rather incongruously, from *wake*, the vigil of the feast of a patron saint (*OED* 4c).

122–42 'Comus celebrates the night time in his twofold character of magician and patron of license' (Verity). Here the note of evil, muted before, becomes emphatic.

123 *to prove*: i.e. by tasting, by experience (*OED* 2, 3).

124 *Venus*: here in her role as patroness of wanton love (see below, 998–1001 n.). Singleton notes that the Comus of Puteanus also invokes Venus in his ode.

125 The spelling *rights* for rites (also in MS., Br., 1637, 1645) occurs in Shakespeare (*Dream*, qto., 1600, 4. 1. 135, and elsewhere: *OED*: right *sb.*²), [and is said by H. Darbishire to be common in the 17th century]; but see 534 below. Trent, while noting precedents for the spelling, observes that *rights* is not impossible since Comus is asserting a claim.

126 Keightley regards the line as parenthetical since *Which* (127) refers to *rights* (125); but *Which* may refer to *Sin*, the meaning being 'which this darkness will never report them to be.' For the idea Warton cites: ''Tis no sinne, loves fruits to steale; / But the sweet thefts to reveale: / To be taken, to be seene, / These have crimes accounted beene' (Jonson, *Volpone* 3. 7. 180–3). Singleton notes a similar idea in Puteanus (Comus' description of the lover in his ode): *Nil turpe, nilque factu | Foedum putet: latere | Caliginis sub atrae | Velo potest opaco, | Quod turpe, quodque foedum* (*Comus*, 1608, 59–60; 1611, 55).

127 *dun shades*. Todd cited 'shadowes dunne' in Fairfax, *Jerusalem* 9. 62.

128–37 With the reference to *Cotytto*, coupled with *Hecat'* in 135, the note of licence and of the service of dark and evil ¦powers becomes strong. Allusions to Cotytto (or Cotys) are not very frequent. They are virtually lacking in the older Greek writers except for two lines from Aeschylus quoted by Strabo.

Cotys, according to Strabo (10. 3. 15–16), was first worshipped in the mountains of Thrace, with nocturnal rites and loud music, similar to what was used in the worship of Bendis and of the Phrygian Rhea (Cybele) and Dionysus. But it is chiefly to Roman writers that she owes her evil reputation, e.g. Juvenal, in lines whose setting adds much to the suggestion of depravity: *talia secreta coluerunt orgia taeda | Cecropiam soliti Baptae lassare Cotytton* (2. 91–2). Osgood (*C.M.* 25) quotes the scholium: *Baptae, titulus libri, quo impudici describuntur ab Epolide, qui inducit viros Athenienses ad imitationem foeminarum saltantes, lassare psaltriam. Baptae, ergo molles....* Horace glances ironically at 'Cotytian rites and the orgies of Cupid unrestrained' (*Epod.* 17. 56–7); and cf. Virgil, *Cat.* 13. 19–24. [Starnes–Talbert (247) cite Renaissance dictionaries.] It was with this general tradition in mind that Milton made Comus a worshipper of Cotytto and later bestowed the same stigma on Alexander More (*Defpro Se*, *Works* 9, 80 and 152).

129–30 *Dark vail'd Cotytto.* It is the rites that are veiled in darkness, lit only by *the secret flame | Of mid-night Torches*; cf. Juvenal, under 128–37 above. But the goddess herself is described as *mysterious*, probably in a double sense, as 'of obscure origin' (*OED* 1) and as worshipped with 'religious' rites or mysteries (*OED* 1c, and mystery 3).

131–2 Editors see in the word *Dragon* an allusion to the dragons that, in post-classical writers, drew the chariot of Night; see notes on *Eli* 57–8 (*V.C.* 1) and *IlPen* 59. Trent suggests that 'Milton either means to call "darkness" itself a dragon...or, better, that he means that the womb of darkness breeds monsters.' The darkness is *Stygian* (such as surrounds the river of hell, here standing for hell itself), that is, infernal, hellish; and this might suggest another association for *Dragon*, with 'the dragon, that old serpent, which is the Devil' (Rev. 20. 2). [The word *spet*, a variant of *spit*, is frequent in Sylvester.]

133 *one blot*: one has the force of 'universal,' 'entire' (Trent). [Cf. Shakespeare, *Macb.* 2. 2. 63: 'Making the green one red.'] Before reaching the final version, MS. (*Facs.* 402) shows several cancelled phrases: *and makes a blot of nature*; *and throws a blot*; *and makes one blot on all yᵉ aire* (*on* changed to *of*).

134–5 *thy cloudy Ebon chair*: chariot (*chair* is a variant of *char* meaning chariot: *OED*: *sb.*²), black like ebony, moving through the clouds. [In MS. *clowdie* replaced *polisht* (*Facs.* 402).] The chariot seems to be Hecate's rather than Cotytto's and spoken of as hers only because she rides in it with Hecate. In its context it recalls the dragon-drawn chariot of Medea (Ovid, *M.* 7. 218–23), which she mounts after prayer to Hecate, who comes to aid magicians' spells and arts (ibid. 194–5), and to all the gods of night (ibid. 198), by whose help, she declares, she controls the natural world (ibid. 199 f.). [Cf. *IlPen* 59–60 n. Cf. also Browne, *Brit. Past.* 2. 2. 236: 'Night's ascension to her eben throne.']

135 *Hecat'*: MS. *Hecate*, with final *e* deleted and apostrophe substituted, evidently in the interest of metre ('Hecate' at 534). Todd cited examples of dissyllabic pronunciation in Marlowe (*Faustus* 854), Shakespeare (*Dream*, below; *Macb.* 2. 1. 52, 3. 2. 41, 3. 5. 1; [*Ham.* 3. 2. 269]); Jonson, *Sad Shepherd* 2. 3. 42. In classical myth Hecate had a respectable origin. According to Hesiod (*Theog.* 411–52), she was the only daughter of Asteria and Perses, was greatly honoured by Zeus and the other gods, and, being both powerful and beneficent to men, was universally worshipped. She was also called the daughter of Night (Apollodorus, L.C.L., 1, 13, n. 8). By Pindar (*Paean* 2. 77–9) she was identified with Artemis, goddess of the moon, and this identification persists, with other elements, in Virgil (*A.* 4. 511) and Ovid (*M.* 7. 94, 194). They regard her as threefold, which may refer, says Servius (Osgood, *C.M.* 29), to the three phases of the moon or to the three forms, Luna, Diana, and Proserpina, as regents of heaven, earth, and hell, with each of whom Hecate was at times identified; [cf. Shakespeare, *Dream* 5. 391, 'triple Hecate's team']. Thus Virgil describes her as *caeloque Ereboque potentem* (*A.* 6. 247) and says that she made the Sibyl guardian of the groves of Avernus (ibid. 118, 564). Diod. Sic. (4. 45. 2–3) gives a modified account of her origin and career which brings Hecate and Circe into relation and emphasizes an element of evil and of magical power used for evil ends. Virgil, in the invocations and magical rites accompanying the death of Dido, coupled 'threefold Hecate' with Erebus and Chaos (*A.* 4. 509–16) and with the Furies (ibid. 609–10). Ovid developed these and similar associations in his accounts of Circe (*M.* 14. 44, 404–5) and Medea (ibid. 7. 194–5, 240–84); cf. Ovid, *H.* 12. 168. Although, to judge from Prudentius (*Apoth.* 460–502), Hecate remained in the first Christian centuries the recipient of public worship in the presence of the Emperor, her patronage of witches was already firmly established: witness Horace (*S.* 1. 8. 33–6) and Tibullus (1. 2. 52). Milton had no need to draw on medieval tradition or *Macbeth* (which he would certainly remember): all was ready to his hand in the classics. Comus the obscene sensualist worships Cotytto, while as sorcerer he worships Hecate, thus reinforcing his inheritance (above, 56–7 n.).

136 MS. (*Facs.* 402) first read *& favour our close revelrie* (deleted: *jocondrie* substituted). *Us thy vow'd Priests.* Cf. the Baptae, initiates, of Juvenal (above, 128–37 n.).

138 *blabbing*: telling or revealing indiscreetly (*OED*: *v.*¹ 2). Todd cites

'The...blabbing...day' (Shakespeare, *2 H. VI* 4. 1. 1) and a phrase from P. Fletcher quoted below, 141 n. *scout* combines two meanings: 'One sent out ahead of the main force to reconnoitre' (*OED: sb.*⁴ 2), and 'One who keeps watch upon the actions of another; ...Formerly often in opprobrious sense' (ibid. 4).

139 *nice*: 'over-fastidious, squeamish' (Moody; Lockwood); perhaps rather 'Precise or strict in matters of...conduct' (*OED* 7 d). *Indian steep*. Verity cited 'the farthest steep of India' (Shakespeare, *Dream* 2. 1. 69).

140 *cabin'd loop-hole*: ['tiny window: Comus envisages a tiny part of the rising sun peeping above the horizon. "Loophole" meant particularly "port-hole", thus there is a play on "cabined" (cramped or confined)' (Carey). But it is the *Morn* (Aurora) that peeps, not the sun.] *peep*. Todd collected more than enough examples of the verb applied to the sun (day, morning) to prove it a commonplace (Spenser, Drayton, Sylvester, Fairfax, P. Fletcher).

141 *tell-tale Sun*. Todd saw a possible allusion to Helios' having kept watch on, and betrayed to Hephaestus, the lovers Aphrodite and Ares (Homer, *Od.* 8. 270–1, 302), but found a closer parallel in P. Fletcher: 'The thicke-lockt bowes shut out the tell-tale Sunne, / (For Venus hated his all blabbing light,/ Since her knowne fault' (*Venus and Anchises* [*Brittain's Ida*] 2. 3); see above, 138 n. Rolfe cited 'Make me not object to the telltale Day' (Shakespeare, *Lucr.* 806). *discry*: descry: 'disclose,...betray' (*OED: v.*¹ 2c), as in Spenser, *F.Q.* 6. 7. 12 (Rolfe). *OED* (*v.*²) notes that *descry* occurs as a reduced variant of *describe* [cf. *PL* 4. 567].

142 *conceal'd Solemnity*: secret rites (cf. Lockwood). *OED* does not distinguish this meaning of *solemnity* but gives examples that confirm it. Cf. *Arc* 39 and n.

143–4 Singleton notes in Puteanus (Comus' ode): *Condiscat ille fracto / Terram gradu pavire* (*Comus*, 1608, 59; 1611, 55). Todd described a plate in A. T. d'Embry's *Les Images ou Tableaux...des...Philostrates* (Paris, 1629, 9) which 'represents part of *Comus's* crew with knit hands, dancing in a round. It is a midnight scene...Comus is in the front, with a torch in one hand, and a spear in the other; he appears to be intoxicated.' For Milton's phrasing Warton compared: 'And arm in arm / Tread we softly in a round, / Whilst the hollow neighbouring ground / Fills the music with her sound' (Fletcher, *F. Shep.* 1. 2. 32–5); and: 'And, since your hands are met, / Instruct your nimble feete, / In motions, swift, and meete, / The happy ground to beate' (*Hymenaei*

302–5, *Ben Jonson* 7, 220). Todd added *Nunc est bibendum, nunc pede libero /
pulsanda tellus* (Horace, *C.* 1. 37. 1–2); and 'With hand in hand dauncing an
endlesse round: / ... With equall foote they beate the flowry ground' (Sir John
Davies, *Orchestra*, st. 75: *Poems*, ed. C. Howard, New York, 1941). The *round*
was a dance in which the performers moved in a circle or ring (*OED: sb.*[1] 11).

fantastick. MS. (*Facs.* 402) first had *frolick*, deleted, and *fantastick* substituted.
The epithet carries the suggestion of 'eccentric, grotesque'; *OED* (6b) adds
that it is 'Arbitrarily used by Milton for: Making "fantastic" movements (in
the dance).' He in part repeats the imagery of the innocent dancing in *L'All*
33–4; here the suggestion is like that of the Witches in *Macb.* 4. 1. 127–30.

⟨Direction⟩ *The Measure.* Todd writes: 'A *measure* is said to have been a
court dance of a stately turn; but sometimes to have expressed *dances in general*';
Dunster supports the former by quoting Sylvester, *D.W.W.* 2. 4. 2. 878–80
(Grosart, 1, 234). *OED* 20 defines as 'a dance, especially a grave or stately
dance'; Lockwood as 'a grave and solemn dance,' citing only *PR* 1. 170; and
Hughes (1937) concludes that the dance here was 'probably rather formal.' But
the term was on occasion applied to dances that were far from formal: e.g. in
the rustic 'measure,' culminating in a 'round,' described by W. Browne (*Brit.
Past.* 1. 3. 409–20: Todd); and in this direction in F. Beaumont's *Masque of
the Inner Temple* (1613): 'The second Anti-masque rush in, dance their measure,
and as rudely depart.... The music was extremely well fitted, having such a
spirit of country jollity as can hardly be imagined' (Evans, *Masques*, 95; [Spen-
cer, *Masques*, 138–9; cf. Demaray, *Masque Tradition*, 110]). Indeed the MS.
direction seems conclusive, *the measure (in a wild rude & wanton antick)*, which
is repeated in Br., thus giving evidence of the actual performance, as well as of
Milton's intention that Comus and his rout should figure as antimasque.
Wright takes the direction as meaning that 'a slow and stately Court dance'
is here performed 'in a burlesque manner'; but the quotation from Beaumont,
and more emphatically the phrasing of 143–4 and of the MS. direction itself
negate this idea and confirm Verity's impression that *measure* 'came to be applied
to any sort of dance.' There seems to be no ground for supposing with Warton
that the measure is broken off 'almost as soon' as begun.

145–68 [Brooks and Hardy (193), R. Tuve (*Images*, 126), and V. Doyno
(*MiltonN* 2, 1968, 62–3) comment on the ironic parallel between the
announcements and actions of Comus and the Attendant Spirit (82–92). Doyno
cites J. S. Diekhoff (*PMLA* 52, 1937, 713–14) on the slip Milton made in line
92 in first writing *virgin* instead of *hatefull* (*Facs.* 400), a slip evidently due

to his thinking of 146–8—which Diekhoff took as evidence that the poet was transcribing, not composing.]

145–6 *different* because *chast*. After 146 MS. adds: *some virgin sure benighted in these woods*, followed by present 149; both deleted (*Facs.* 402).

147 *shrouds*: places of retreat or concealment (*OED*: *sb.*[1] 6). Todd quoted: 'But here must be no shelter, nor no shrowd / for such ⟨as Comus and his crew⟩: Sinck Grove, or vanish into clowd' (*Pleasure* 113–14, *Ben Jonson* 7, 483). See also *Nat* 218 n. [and Browne, *Brit. Past.* 1. 2. 383]. *Brakes*: clumps of bushes, thickets. MS. ⟨direction in margin⟩: *they all scatter*.

148 *sure*: [surely, for sure].

149 *Art*: i.e. Magic.

151 *wily trains*. MS. first had *mothers charmes*. *trains*: wiles, deceits (*OED*: *sb.*[2] 1 b), as in Spenser, *F.Q.* 1. 6. 3; but *trains* also meant traps or snares (*OED*: *sb.*[2] 2). Rolfe takes as 'allurements' and cites Shakespeare, *Macb.* 4. 3. 118; cf. lure, bait (*OED* 3), which would harmonize with the secondary suggestion of hunting game evident in the lines that follow.

151–3 *I shall...Circe.* See 50–6 n.

153–4 *Thus I hurl...spungy ayr*. Warton compared: 'I strew the herbs, to purge the air: / Let your odour drive hence / All mists that dazzle sense' (Fletcher, *F. Shep.* 3. 1. 322 f.). *dazling*: MS. *powder'd* (deleted); cf. 'this Magick dust' (165). Masson suggests that the actor here casts into the air some powder that produces a flash of blue light. [Demaray, 111, suggests 'a handful of gold or silver dust.'] The air is *spungy* as absorbing the charm. [Cf. W. Browne, *Brit. Past.* 1. 2. 339: 'The hand of Heaven his spongy clouds doth strain,' and 1. 5. 313.]

155 *blear*: 'Dim,...indistinct in outline' (*OED* 2), really transferred from the eye itself (ibid. 1; [Hunter, 'New Words,' and Carey note that this is the first recorded use of the word in a transferred sense]); 'deceptive, through blurring' (Trent). Todd cited 'blear'd thine eyne' (Shakespeare, *Shrew* 5. 1. 121) and 'bleard his eyes' (Sylvester, *D.W.W.* 2. 1. 1. 273, Grosart, 1, 101). [Cf. J. Hall, *Virgidemiarum*, Prol. 17: 'The worlds eye bleared with...lies' (*Poems*, ed. A. Davenport).]

156 *presentments*: appearances (*OED* 5c).

156–7 *the place...quaint habits*: my strange garb seen in such a place. *quaint*: strange, curious (*OED* 7), now obsolete, the meaning merging in that of ibid. 8, which adds, however, some suggestion of attractiveness, absent here, as in *Nat* 194 (see n.); cf. *Lyc* 139 n. *habits*: garments, clothes (*OED* 1c). Todd cites 'quaint habits' in Milton's *HistMosc* (*Works* 10, 327).

158 *suspicious*: indicative of suspicion (*OED* 2c) because caused thereby (cf. Lockwood).

159 *course*: manner of proceeding (Lockwood; cf. *OED* 21), perhaps with a secondary suggestion of hunting one's quarry (*OED* 7), as in 'Baited' (162) and 'snares' (164).

160 *ends*: purposes (*OED* 14).

161 *glozing*: flattering and deceiving, as in 'where the snares of glosing speech do lie to entangle them' (Hooker, *Eccles. Pol.* 5. 4. 2). Warton cited: 'With termes of love and lewdnesse dissolute; / For he could well his glozing speaches frame' (Spenser, *F.Q.* 3. 8. 14).

162 *Baited*: furnished with a bait, that is, figuratively, rendered alluring (*OED* 2c, which gives only later examples of figurative use). Todd compared 'He...bayted every word' (Spenser, *F.Q.* 3. 10. 6).

163 *Wind me into the easie-hearted man*: insinuate myself into the confidence of the man easily moved to belief. Initially the verb denotes motion (*OED: v.*[1] 1–3b); it came to denote a turning or writhing motion (ibid. 4), but apparently without the idea of serpentine movement which seems implicit here; finally, when coupled with *into* it came to mean insinuate oneself into (ibid. 13b), evidently the primary meaning here. [Hughes (1937) cites Shakespeare, *Cor.* 3. 3. 64–5: 'To wind / Yourself into a power tyrannical.'] The compound *easie-hearted* seems to be created on the analogy of such phrases as 'hard-hearted,' with *heart* as the seat of the understanding and the feelings (*OED: heart sb.* 5) and *easie* in the sense of easily moved to belief or action (*OED* 12).

164 *hug*: a word of unknown origin appearing in the second half of the 16th century: here meaning 'caress or court, in order to get favour or patronage' (*OED* 1c, citing this example). *snares*. MS. first had *nets*.

165 *vertue*: power or efficacy, often, as here, of an occult or magic quality (*OED* 9); cf. *vertuous* in 620 and *IlPen* 113. *this Magick dust*: the *powder'd spells* of original MS. reading of 154 (see n.).

166 *I shall appear some harmles Villager*. It would seem from this statement, following 153–6, that Comus, when he finally appears to the Lady (264), has not actually assumed a disguise, as the Attendant Spirit has when he accosts the

Brothers (after 488), but that in seeing a shepherd (270) she is imposed on by magic. It is to be inferred that the illusion is temporary, a device to gain her confidence, and that at 658 she sees Comus as he is.

166–9 After 166, the 1645 text, following MS., Br., and 1637 (*Facs.* 196, 402, 310, 271), has *Whom thrift keeps up about his Country gear*; they also transpose 167 and 168. [The quoted line, lacking in 1673, is omitted in Columbia *Works* (see 1, 495; and above, the first paragraph of v: Notes). *gear*: goods, movable property, etc. (*OED* III. 9, citing this example).]

167 *hearken, if I may her busines hear.* The 1645 text reads: *hearken, if I may, her busines here*; so also MS., Br. (but without commas), 1637, and 1673, but change made in 1673 Errata (*Works* 1, 495–6; *Facs.* 197, 402, 310, 271). The original reading, which makes *hearken* transitive, seems to have been intended, and that supplied by the Errata to have been introduced at the last minute as a new reading. [Hanford (*Handbook*, 394) thinks the change was made by a 'corrector' who did not understand the somewhat archaic use of *hearken* as a transitive verb. H. Darbishire suggests that the change was made 'to avoid the repetition of the word *here* in the next line' (which implies that the change was Milton's); but, as she says, '*hearken* and *hear* are tautological and the first version is preferable.' Carey thinks that the attention paid to the line in the Errata 'makes it unlikely that the differences between *1637* and *1645* on the one hand, and *1673* on the other, can at this point be attributed merely to the printer. Perhaps the rhyme of "gear" and "here" in *1637* and *1645* offended M.'s ear, and made him decide to change the passage.']

168 *fairly*: 'quietly, softly' (*OED* 5).

171 *Riot*: wanton festivity. *ill manag'd*: 'disorderly' (Verity).

173 *loose unletter'd Hinds*: rustics (*OED* 3), lewd and illiterate.

174 *granges*: granaries, barns (*OED* 1). [H. Darbishire quotes Warburton: 'Two rural scenes of festivity are alluded to, the Spring [*teeming Flocks*] and the Autumn [*granges full*], sheepshearing and harvest home.' *teeming*: 'breeding offspring' (Carey).]

175–6 *In wanton...the gods amiss. Pan* here stands for God, the giver of all increase, and only the character of the response is condemned. [The Lady, alone in the woods in the evening, is naturally apprehensive about rude merry-makers, but she is not an austere foe of dancing; cf. 937–64.]

177 *swill'd*: 'drunken' (the only example of *swilled* as adj. in *OED*); *swill*: 'drink...greedily, or to excess, like hogs devouring "swill"' (ibid. *v.* 3).

178 *late Wassailers*: revellers who have kept up their carousing till late (the first example of the word given by *OED*, though citations of vb. wassail, and of sb., for the liquor drunk, go back to *c.* 1300).

179 *inform*: 'direct, guide' (*OED* 4 d; cf. *SA* 335–6), but with a strong secondary suggestion of the commoner meaning, 'impart knowledge to,' reinforced by *unacquainted* and by the context (the necessity of accosting the revellers to gain information).

180 *blind.* The growth is so dense as not to be seen through, or as to admit no light (*OED* 10). Other meanings are perhaps suggested: enveloped in darkness (ibid. 6), deceptive (ibid. 5), having no egress, as in 'blind alley' (ibid. 11). *mazes*: MS. (*Facs.* 404) first had *alleys.* With *tangl'd* cf. *Nat* 188.

183 *spreading favour*: spreading boughs which offer kindly shade or shelter. Warton compared (perhaps rather remotely) *hospitiis teneat frondentibus arbos* (Virgil, *G.* 4. 24).

184 *se'd*: [said (cf. *Lyc* 129).]

186 *kind hospitable Woods.* The 'wilde Wood,' the first of the three settings, has a dual aspect, good and bad, beneficent and menacing, as these lines, along with 180, remind us; and the two aspects are reinforced by the presence of the Attendant Spirit and Comus. Warton observed: 'By laying the scene...in a wild forest, Milton secured...a perpetual fund of picturesque description...,' with 'opportunities of rural delineation, and that of the most romantic kind.' He compared in this respect Sophocles' *Phil.*, Shakespeare's *A.Y.L.*, and Fletcher's *F. Shep.*, noting Milton's advantage in having 'his forest...the residence of a magician,' and, like Fletcher's, 'exhibited under the gloom of midnight.'

187–9 Br. omits (*Works* 1, 498; *Facs.* 311). Despite the fact just cited from Warton, Milton seeks further sources of embellishment and romantic effect, and finds one in imagining Evening as a gray-hooded pilgrim journeying in fulfilment of her vow. Warton (1785: quoted by Todd) notes that Milton 'often dresses his imaginary beings in the habits of popery,' citing *IlPen* 31 and *PR* 4. 427. 'But poetry is of all religions: and popery is a very poetical one.' The combination here of medieval and classical imagery is bold, but pictorially effective in its suggestion of the gray figure coming into view as the bright receding chariot of the Sun disappears.

187 *Eev'n*: MS. *ev'n*; 1637, *Ev'n*; 1645, *Eev'n.* [H. Darbishire (1, xxvi–xxvii) notes that *eev'n* is the common monosyllabic form in *PL*, while *ev'ning* (in various forms) is always dissyllabic.]

188   *sad*: grave, serious, in appearance (*OED* 4b), but with secondary reference to the colour of the garb: dark, neutral-tinted, as in Spenser, *F.Q.* 1. 12. 5, 'sad habiliments' (*OED* 8b). *Votarist*: votary or votaress, one bound by a vow, Lat. *votum*. Milton's word is in Shakespeare, *Meas.* 1. 4. 5. *Palmers weed*: garb of a pilgrim, strictly one who has been to the Holy Land and on his return bears a palm branch or leaf as insignium. But *palmer* had long been more generally used to denote any pilgrim, as in Chaucer, *C.T.*, Prologue 13–14. Newton compared 'I wrapt my selfe in Palmers weed' (Spenser, *F.Q.* 2. 1. 52); Todd added 'a Palmer poore, in homely Russet clad' (Drayton, *Poly.* 12. 155).

189   *Phoebus wain*. Cf. 'Phoebus gan availe / His weary waine' (Spenser, *S.C., January* 73–4).   *wain*: wagon, but, in poetry, car or chariot (*OED* 1c). On the Sun's chariot see *Nat* 84 n. MS. first had *chaire*, i.e. chariot (*OED*: *sb.*², which quotes 'Phoebus in his chaire,' Drummond, 1, 33).

191   *labour of my thoughts*: question on which my mind is at work; perhaps with a secondary suggestion of being 'in labour' to bring an answer to birth (*OED* 6).

192   *ingag'd*: pledged, hence risked (*OED* 2). *wandring*: MS. first had *youthly*.

193   *envious*: malicious (*OED* 2), but with a secondary suggestion of envying the Lady her brothers. MS. first had *to the soone parting light*, deleted, and *and envious darknesse* substituted (*Facs.* 404).

193–9   Warton remarked that a period which notoriously tolerated 'monstrous and unnatural conceits' in its poetry accounts for such fancies as these lines contain, but added that, if *Comus* had been written in a later and more 'correct and rational' age, we should have lacked 'some of the greatest beauties of its wild and romantic imagery.' The whole series of images alludes 'to a robber with his dark-lantern' (Keightley). *Theevish Night* would then be a synonym for *envious darknes* and would be pictured as closing the shutter of the *dark Lantern* containing *the Stars*, which *nature hung in Heav'n* to burn perpetually and *give due light* to the *Traveller*, and as doing this in order to effect her *fellonious end*, the theft of the two brothers. [Raleigh (*Milton*, 182) pronounced this passage 'perhaps the nearest approach to a conceit of the metaphysical kind.' Demaray (*Masque Tradition*, 102) suggests that the dark lantern 'may have been one of a number of cylindrical canisters, open at both ends, which were lowered by cords over the burning candles or oil lamps to darken the stage.']

194 *stole.* MS., Br., and 1637 have *stolne* (*Facs.* 404, 311, 272); *stole* is presumably an uncorrected misprint from 1645. With *theevish Night* Warton compared: 'the theevish night / Steals on the world, and robs our eyes of sight' (P. Fletcher, *Pisc. Ecl.* 5. 20).

194–224 *els...Grove.* Not in Br. (*Works* 1, 498).

196 *dark Lantern:* dark-lantern, fitted with a shutter by which light can be concealed. The earliest example in *OED* is from Fuller, *A Pisgah-Sight of Palestine* (London, 1650), 4. 3. 9, p. 45. See above, 193–9 n.

198 *due.* MS. first had *thire*, replaced by *due* (*Works* 1, 499; *Facs.* 404).

202 *rife:* 'Strong, loud-sounding' (*OED* 4c, the only example given; related to 'abundant, large in quantity': ibid. 4). *perfet:* perfect, lacking nothing (*OED* 3), hence 'very distinct' (Lockwood).

203 *single:* 'unbroken, absolute' (*OED a.* 4 [which, Carey notes, finds the first example of this sense in Spenser, *F.Q.* 2. 10. 21]).

204 *fantasies:* mental images (*OED* 4b, whose earliest example is from Lamb, 1823, though much earlier examples occur: see below), or conceptions (hence *These thoughts,* 209) accompanied by images. Warton compared 'many legions of strange fantasies' (Shakespeare, *John* 5. 7. 18); see also 206–8 n. In non-technical uses of *fantasy* there is generally an implication of falsehood or fiction [cf. Spenser, *F.Q.* 2. 9. 49–51]. The word was also used as a synonym for phantom (*OED* 2), a secondary suggestion supported by the context (205–8).

[Rudrum (*Comus,* 44) remarks that this 'passage of Shakespearean intensity and power...establishes an extra dimension in the characterisation of the Lady, establishes a capacity for feeling and instinctive response so that we apprehend her more fully than as a mere cold blueprint for virtue.']

205 *into my memory.* In 'faculty psychology' memory was the storehouse of images: 'memorie supplieth none other office...than...to preserve the figures and fantasies of things' (Huarte's *Examination of Mens Wits,* tr. R. Carew, 1594, ed. C. Rogers, Gainesville, 1959, 155: quoted in *OED:* fantasy 1b). [Cf. Spenser, *F.Q.* 2. 9. 55–8.] Todd quoted: 'Methinks I hear, methinks I see, / Ghosts, goblins, fiends; my phantasy / Presents a thousand ugly shapes' (Burton, *Anatomy, The Author's Abstract of Melancholy*). In Burton 'phantasy' refers of course to the faculty, not the image.

206–8 Editors have adduced various more or less remote analogues of the *fantasies* here mentioned, which at least bear witness to widespread interest and a degree of credulity. Warton and Todd cite geographers from Marco Polo to Peter Heylyn. Todd further cites Burton's *Anatomy* (1. 2. 1. 2: 1, 195), where we read of spirits called '*ambulones*, that walk about midnight on great heaths and desert places, which (saith Lavater) "draw men out of the way, and lead them all night a by-way, or quite bar them of their way ". . . . In the deserts of Lop, in Asia, such illusions of walking spirits are often perceived, as you may read in M. Paulus the Venetian, his travels; if one lose his company by chance, these devils will call him by his name, and counterfeit voices of his companions to seduce him.' But with this tradition, wherever derived, Milton mingles (as Warton noted) memories of Fletcher's *Faithful Shepherdess*, where Clorin speaks of 'goblin,' 'fiend,' 'or other power that haunts these groves,' seeking 'by vain illusion' to 'Draw me to wander after idle fires; / Or voices calling me in dead of night / To make me follow' (1. 1 .114–19). Editors also cite the strange shapes, sounds, and voices of Shakespeare, *Temp.* 3. 2. 144–9 and 3. 18–39. But, as Elton remarks, Milton owes little to literary sources, drawing rather 'on a common fancy of folklore.'

207 *airy tongues*: heard in the air. *OED* 2 quotes 'ayrie moanes' from Quarles, *Sions Elegies* (1624), 1. 11 (ed. Grosart, 2, 106). [E. Seaton (*Essays and Studies* 31, 1946, 70) cites (after Keightley) 'airy tongue' (Echo's) in Shakespeare, *Romeo* 2. 2. 163.] *that...names.* MS. (*Facs.* 404) first had *that lure night wandring* (changed to *wanderers*), then substituted present reading. *syllable*: 'utter distinctly' (*OED* 2, which cites, as Warton does, P. Fletcher's 'syllabled in flesh-spell'd character' (*Asclepiads...translated* 3, 1633: *Works* 2, 248).

209 *These thoughts may startle well*: these mental images (204 n.) may very likely startle. Quoting this line, *OED* makes little distinction between *startle* (5) and *astound* (2), but Milton is clearly distinguishing momentary fright and one that bereaves of power (a figurative use of *astound*, to deprive of consciousness, stupefy: ibid. 1).

209–19 In the speech from Fletcher's *F. Shep.* cited above (206–8 n.) Clorin assures herself that the terrors named have no power to harm those who preserve their 'virgin flower uncropt, pure, chaste and fair' (1. 1. 113), and concludes: 'then, strong chastity, / Be thou my strongest guard' (ibid. 127–8). The same protective power of virtue, and especially chastity, is elaborated below at 417–36 (see n.). Singleton (954–5) notes some similarity in the words addressed by Puteanus to his companion Aderba, who fears the possible spectres in the dark approaches to Comus' palace: *noctis aura quid nigrae | Potest, quid umbris obsitae formidines; | Si liberam potente virtus asserit | Mentem manu, si Candor atque puritas, | Viraginisque dogmata Sapientiae?* (*Comus*, 1608, 26–7; 1611, 26).

211 *strong siding*: strongly supporting [the earliest example in *OED* of the word in this sense: Carey]. Cf. 'a stronger siding freind' (*Tetr, Works* 4, 185).

212–15 *O welcom...see ye visibly*. These 'thoughts' likewise give rise to images, but with a difference (see 215 n.). The untraditional epithets *pure-ey'd* and *white-handed* (connoting innocence, as remarked by writers in *N&Q*, Ser. 8, 7, 1895, 354, 472), applied to *Faith* and *Hope* respectively, are evidently designed to prepare for, and link them to, their new companion *Chastity* (214). While recognizing the appropriateness to the theme, readers have differed in their response to this deliberate substitution of *Chastity* for the Charity (love) of 1 Cor. 13. 13. Hughes and Wright explain that Chastity *is* Love in the Platonic sense of 'the love of the Supreme Good which chastens all inferior passions' (Hughes, 1937).

213 *hovering*: MS. *flittering* (*Facs.* 404), but in margin *hov'ring*, evidently a late correction after 1637, which has *flittering* (ibid. 272): i.e. flying low, fluttering (*OED*: flitter *v*. 1). *hovering Angel*. Todd cited (after Dunster): 'I surely know the Cherubins do hover | With flaming wings' (Sylvester, *D.W.W.* 2. 2. 1. 186–7, Grosart, 1, 134). [Cf. Marlowe, *Faustus* 1291: 'an Angell hovers ore thy head.'] Warton remarked on the propriety of *hovering* as applied to Hope, 'In sight, on the wing; and if not approaching, yet not flying away.' [H. Darbishire (*Essays and Studies 1957*, 39) suggests that Milton rejected *flittering* as 'thin-sounding' and perhaps 'too bat-like.'] The poets supplied various data for angels: 'golden wings,' Spenser, *Hymne of Heavenly Beautie* 93; 'Decked with diverse plumes, like painted Jayes,' *F.Q.* 2. 8. 5; 'Of silver wings...a shining paire, | Fringed with gold,' Fairfax, *Jerusalem* 1. 14. Milton strongly preferred *golden wings*; cf. *IlPen* 52, *FInf* 57.

214 *unblemish't*. MS. first had *unspotted*. Warton noted 'unblemish'd forme' in T. May's *Reigne Of King Henry the Second* (1633), sig. J 6. Verity takes *unblemish't* as unblemishable. The word *form* is rich in meaning and suggestion: here its primary meaning is image, representation (*OED* 2), but with a strong sense that the outward form reflects the inward meaning, the active and determining principle (ibid. 4).

215 *I see ye visibly*. Wright suggests a reflection of 'Plato ⟨who⟩ maintains that if we could *see* the Good we should be entranced by its beauty and pursue it with the devotion of lovers.' But Plato (*Phaedrus* 250) denies that the forms of the virtues can be seen ['denies' seems too strong for Plato's words in 249–51, where he speaks of the few who have not lost the memory of their primal vision]. Hughes quotes Bacon: 'And therefore as Plato said elegantly, *That virtue, if she could be seen, would move great love and affection*; so seeing that she cannot be shewed to the Sense by corporal shape, the next degree is to shew her to the Imagination in lively representation' (*Adv.*, *Works* 3, 410). [Cf. Sidney, *Defence of Poesie* (*Works* 3, 1923, 25): 'Who if the saying of Plato and Tully bee true, that who could see vertue, woulde bee woonderfullie ravished with the love of her bewtie.' Cf. Cicero, *Fin.* 2. 16. 52, *Offic.* 1. 5. 15.] But contrary to both Plato and Bacon, the Lady claims to *see* them *visibly*, i.e. as a vision of reality, not as mere 'fantasies' like those of 204–8. After *I see ye visibly*, MS. adds and then deletes: *& while I see yee | this dusky hollow is a paradise | & heaven gates ore my head* (*Facs.* 404).

216–17 *the Supreme good...of vengeance.* As Milton will later assert, evil occurs only as God permits it, and 'he causes evil by the infliction of judgments, which is called the evil of punishment' (*DocCh* 1. 8, *Works* 15, 67). This partial view of the problem of evil is supplemented at 592–8 below. [*Supreme*: 'here accented on the first syllable' (Darbishire).]

218 *Guardian.* MS. first had *cherub.*

218–19 The intervention of Providence in protection of the good is another recurrent theme, represented by the Attendant Spirit and Sabrina, and alluded to at 40–2, 328–9, 416–17, 1021–2. [Watkins (*Anatomy*, 94) quotes Ps. 91. 11, which is to be 'a pivot' of *PR*: 'For he shall give his angels charge over thee, to keep thee in all thy ways.' See 15 n. above.]

220–3 *Was I deceiv'd...silver lining on the night.* Hurd (reported by Warton) noted that the rhetorical structure resembles Ovid's *fallor, an arma sonant? non fallimur, arma sonabant* (*F.* 5. 549) [see, in *V.C.* 1, *El* 5. 5 and n.]. Keightley compared: 'raies of silver... / Which the darke foulds of nights blacke mantle linde' (Fairfax, *Jerusalem* 17. 57). [Cf. Spenser, *F.Q.* 3. 1. 43 (below, 331 n.).] It may be that Milton's lines gave rise to the proverbial phrase about clouds with a silver lining. [The repetition in 222–3 gives notice of the symbolic import of the image. Milton's *a sable cloud* appears in Sandys, *Ovid* (1626), 16.]

225 *I cannot hallow.* Warton noted the phrase in the semi-Shakespearian *Two N.K.* 3. 2. 9, where it is uttered by the Jailer's daughter, benighted and alone in a wood, in quest of Palamon.

226 *farthest.* [So in 1645, 1673. MS., Br., and 1637 (*Facs.* 404, 311, 273) had *fardest*, the form Milton generally preferred.]

227 *venter.* This appears to be the more usual spelling in the 16th and into the 17th century, though it gradually gave place to 'venture' (which is in Br.).

229–42 [Modern reproductions of the words and music of this and four other songs in *Comus* are noticed at the end of section 1 above.] A song invoking Echo is, as editors say, not without precedent in masques. Warton cited the song in Browne's *Inner Temple Masque* (267 f.), in which Echo caps each line, and the appearance of Echo in person in Jonson's play, *Cynthia's Revels* (1. 1), which burlesques her habit of answer but (as Elton observes) assigns to her an exquisite song. Milton's Echo returns no answer.

While the myth (Ovid, *M.* 3. 359–401) explains the allusion to Narcissus (236), other allusions are less clear. Echo's *airy shell* (230) has been generally explained since Warburton and Hurd (reported by Warton) as the 'hollow circumference of the heavens'; cf. 'Beneath the hollow round / Of Cynthia's seat, the Airy region' (*Nat* 102–3; see n.). This would be supported by *Daughter of the Sphear* (240): Echo is the daughter of, i.e. is native to, this sublunar hollow, and (if the Lady can have her wish) is to be *translated to the skies* (241), i.e. to the higher regions, there to give back *all Heav'ns Harmonies* (242), i.e. the music of all the spheres. But this interpretation corresponds to no literal or figurative meaning ever given to *shell*. The word was sometimes used for a hollow, spherical or hemispherical object (*OED* 12), but that fact in itself does not favour this interpretation beyond any other. MS. (*Facs.* 404) has in the margin *cell* (as an alternative, without cancelling *shell*, the reading of Br., 1637, 1645, 1673); and *cell*, always connoting a small confined space, would not of course admit this explanation, which must, on balance, be pronounced highly speculative. Todd observes that *cell* would be supported by 'And Eccho oft doth tell / Wondrous things from her Cell' (*Muses Elizium* 3. 209–10, Drayton, 3, 273); [he might have cited Ovid's *vivit in antris* (*M.* 3. 394)]. Keightley cites Juliet's reference to 'the cave where Echo lies' and to 'her airy tongue' (*Romeo* 2. 2. 162–3). Wright takes *shell* as a synonym for cell or cave. Verity gives either 'the vault of Heaven' or, more literally, '"a shell with air in it," lying by the river's side'; the latter would reflect the well-known phenomenon of such a shell's giving forth a sound, and might perhaps be supported by paraphrasing the context (229–34) thus: whether you dwell by the Maeander, echoing only the sound of the wind in the empty shells that strew its margin, or in the valley near Athens (if Hughes—see below—is right in this identification) famous for its violets and its nightingales, echoing the bird's sad song. But the syntax does not seem to confine the *airy shell* to the river's side or to present the two regions as alternative. Another possibility is that Milton, remembering Ovid's lines 396–9, thinks of the skeleton Echo became as her *airy shell*, while the alternative *cell* represents his hesitation whether to fix the association at this point or at the final stage when the bones have turned to stone. One could then abandon the effort to find a special significance in *Meander's margent*—with which, as Verity says, Echo has no known connection, though Hughes (1937) cites in the *Greek Anthology*, 9. 825, a glancing reference to her as a water nymph—and read 230–3, with Hughes, as referring simply to Echo's wandering by alluding to two distant points, the *Meander* in Phrygia, Asia Minor, and the *violet imbroider'd vale* where the *Nightingale* sings, which he identifies as near Athens. This identification, which no other editor seems to make, is attractive but far from certain. That there is no traditional association of Echo with Athens or with the nightingale is unimportant in this explanation and in view of Echo's lack of association with Maeander. Certainly the nightingale is associated with Athens, in the story of Philomela, an Athenian princess, in references in Sophocles and later poets, and notably for Milton, for whom the nightingale is 'the Attic bird' (*PR* 4. 245 and n.). The *violet imbroider'd vale* is more ambiguous, for, though Milton and Pindar are both alluding to the flower and not to the colour of the neighbouring hills, in Hughes's Pindaric citation, Frag. 76 (L.C.L., p. 556, n.), 'the violet-crowned' seems to allude, not to violets growing in or near Athens, but to the violet wreath as an offering to, and mark of, divinity [but here, according to Sandys' note, loc. cit., the city of Athens personified].

[Arthos (*Mask*, 75) remarks, in the course of a long note on music and magic: 'The invocations to Echo and Sabrina, and Sabrina's purification song, have some of the characteristics of incantations.' Hollander (319–23) has a good deal to say about several kinds of significance in the song, apart from its primary place in the action: 'It addresses itself to its own resonating effects (its echoes, here personified as the nymph Echo herself, not only a favorite pastoral figure but a favorite metaphor for the relationship of actual human music to the heavenly harmony), on the one hand; and on the other, it covertly refers to the Lady herself and her own predicament'; Hollander cites *love-lorn Nightingale* and lines 566–7. Secondly, from the Lady's opening reference to Comus' riotous dance 'to the final invocation of the "Spheary chime" (l. 1021) as the summit of a purely material world surmounted by the influences of Virtue, musical figures of several sorts are employed. But it is primarily the Lady's song that generates most of these intricacies.' 'The song is in some measure a hymn in praise of music itself,' and 'the transcendent power' of the song draws praise from both Comus and the Attendant Spirit.

Two more general comments on the song may be quoted. 'Perhaps nothing in a modern language comes nearer to giving the peculiar effect which is the glory of Pindar. Of course there is in it more of the fanciful, and more of the romantic, than there was in Pindar; and its style is tenderer, prettier and perhaps altogether smaller than his. But the elaborate and intricate perfection of its art and language, the way in which the intellect in it serves the imagination, is exactly Pindar.' (John Bailey, *Milton*, 117)

'The Lady's song...addresses Echo (notice Milton's fondness for *echoing* sounds),...the song itself remarkably suggesting a winding, labyrinthine move-ment that recalls the "winding bout", "sweetness long drawn out", "giddy cunning", and "mazes" of the dualism-resolving song in *L'Allegro*. The ex-press purpose of both is, indeed, to match labyrinthine distress with labyrin-thine harmony.' (G. Wilson Knight, *Burning Oracle*, 65)]

231 *slow Meander's margent green*: no doubt called *slow* on account of its winding course. *margent* (a variant of *margin*): here ground adjacent to a river (*OED*). *green*: because of its fertility, described by Strabo (Wright).

232 *violet imbroider'd vale*. See note on 229–42. Warton compared *PL* 4. 700–2. Todd added 'The Flow'r-embroydred earth' (Wither, *Emblemes*, 1635, 3. 25, p. 159) and 'they priz'd the broider'd vale' (Browne, *Brit. Past.* 2. 2. 547). Todd noted the association of Echo with valleys: 'Eccho voice of vallies, / Aierie Elfe, exempt from view' (Sylvester, *Wood-Mans Bear* 83, Grosart, 2, 312).

233–4 *the love-lorn Nightingale...mourneth well*. See note on 229–42. For Milton the nightingale's song is on occasion 'most Melancholy' (*IlPen* 62), but elsewhere in its association with love quite the reverse (*El* 5. 25; *Sonn* 1. 1–4). The word *mourneth* suggests the traditional mourning of Philomela or of the bird for her brood; Todd cites *philomela sub umbra* / *amissos queritur fetus*, etc. (Virgil, *G.* 4. 511–15). [Carey notes, from *OED*, that this is the first occur-rence of *love-lorn*.]

236 *thy Narcissus*. See note on 229–42.

240 *Daughter of the Sphear*. See note on 229–42. Warburton (reported by Todd) commented: 'Milton has given her [Echo] a much nobler and more poetical original than any of the ancient mythologists. He supposes her to owe her first existence to the reverberation of the musick of the spheres; in consequence of which he had just before called the horizon her *aery shell*. And from the gods (like other celestial beings of the classical order) she came down to men.' Todd compared 'Sphear-born harmonious Sisters, Voice, and Vers' (*SolMus* 2). [Hutton makes the same comparison, against the background of the musical tradition he describes; he is quoted in *SolMus* 1–2 n. With the whole line, cf. Ausonius, *Ep.* 32: *Aeris et Linguae filia* (L.C.L. 2, 174), which Sandys quotes and translates as 'Daughter of aire and tongue' (comment on Echo, *Ovid*, 1632, 104). Starnes–Talbert (249) quote an entry in C. Stephanus' *Dictionarium* which, they think, shows 'not only similarity of phrasing but almost exact correspondence in meaning': *Echo, Nympha, nullo oculo visa...physice coeli harmoniam significare dicitur, Solis amicam, tamquam domini, et moderatoris omnium corporum coelestium, ex quibus ipsa componitur atque temperatur....* Dunster cited 'Th'Aire's daughter Eccho' (Sylvester, *D.W.W.* 2. 1. 1. 132, Grosart, 1, 100).]

241–2 *So maist thou...all Heav'ns Harmonies*: 'and make the sphere-music resound or re-echo' (Elton); see above, 229–42 n. Taken by themselves, the lines might be thought to mean, not (as there suggested) translated from the sublunar region to the higher heavens so as to echo the music of all the spheres, but rather to heaven itself, there to echo the song of the angel choir. But, in this classical context, such an interpretation seems impossible; Milton always distinguishes clearly between the music of the spheres and the song of the angels, reserving the latter for use as a distinctively Christian symbol (see *Nat* 131–2 n., and below, 1017–22 n.). [Cf. Hollander later in this note. For the construction *So maist thou*, see *Lyc* 19 n.] *translated*: conveyed (used particularly of translation to heaven: *OED* 1 b). For *And give resounding grace* MS. (*Facs.* 406) first had *And hold a counterpoint* (the reading also of Br.), counterpoint being a melody added to another by way of accompaniment (*OED: sb.* 1 1). [This revision has been taken as one of a number of changes from technical to non-technical language (W. A. Wright, *Facsimile*, 5; L. E. Lockwood, *MLN* 25, 1910, 203; Diekhoff, *PMLA* 55, 1940, 749). Hollander (323) disagrees, remarking that '"grace" is, if anything, more "technical"...than is "counterpoint."' He thinks also that the revision (along with *translated*) was intended to give a Christian reference: '"Grace," of course, retains its musical meaning of "ornament" or "embellishment," which "resounds" because it is still that of Echo; the Christian implications of "grace" are secondary, but extremely strong.' On the other side, see the first part of this note, and cf. Hutton ('Music,' 48–9, quoted above in the note on *SolMus* 1–2). M. Emslie (see *Sonn* 13, 1, under 1968) sees a technical significance in Milton's revision, though not of the kind the other critics comment upon: 'Lawes' setting of the song...is not at all contrapuntal; it is a declamatory ayre.' Emslie takes *grace* to refer to the 'vocal ornaments' with which—as some manuscript song-books show—'able performers elaborated the voice-line.' 'Gracing was used especially at cadences— certainly at the final cadence of a song.' (101–2)

Line 242 is an alexandrine, the only one in *Comus* (Verity), suggesting (as Carey says) 'the lengthening of heaven's song by echo.' Cf. *Nat* 100.]

After **242**. MS. has direction, *Comus enters* (*enters* deleted), *looks in and speaks* (substituted). Probably he appears at the side of the stage but does not reveal himself to the Lady till 264 (Verity).

243 *mortal mixture of Earths mould*: mortal compound of earth's matter. Cf. above, 17 and n.

244 *ravishment*: rapture (*OED* 3, and 246 below, *raptures*).

245 *somthing holy lodges in that brest*: some heavenly spirit (Hughes, 1937, comparing *Leon* 1. 5–6), or (Verity) simply a pure soul, with 'reference to the idea, attributed to Pythagoras, that the soul *is* a harmony. Plato in the *Phaedo* (86 *et seq.*) compares it to a harmony.' Verity cites 'Such harmony is in immortal souls' (Shakespeare, *Merch.* 5. 1. 63) and: 'Touching musical harmony ...so pleasing effects it hath in that very part of man which is most divine, that some have been thereby induced to think that the soul itself by nature is or hath in it harmony' (Hooker, *Eccles. Pol.* 5. 38. 1). Browne compares *quod numen in isto | corpore sit, dubito; sed corpore numen in isto est* (Ovid, *M.* 3. 611–12).

246 *raptures*: the expression of ecstatic feeling in words or music (*OED* 6). Cf. 'they introduce / Thir sacred Song, and waken raptures high' (*PL* 3. 368–9).

247 *testifie*: bear witness to (*OED* 1).

248–51 *How sweetly...till it smil'd*. Verity called attention to Milton's power of suggestion through metaphor and compared *L'All* 6–7. The music floats upon the silence as if borne on wings through the empty vault of night; then, with a change of image, dark night is likened to a bird, a raven, whose ruffled plumes are smoothed by the caressing cadence (*fall*: *OED* 10) till the very darkness seems to smile. [For opposed opinions of the image one might quote Moody: 'A forced and rather tasteless figure, which has been nevertheless much admired'; and Watkins (*Anatomy*, 4–5): 'The quality of the Lady's song-notes as heard by Comus is made remarkable in terms of other senses....Here [in 248–51] the exquisite fusion of touch and motion and *plenitude* after emptiness is so intense that it trembles into sensuality, and this ecstasy, as frequently in Milton, culminates in involuntary *smile*, denoting complete gratification of the senses.' E. Seaton (*Essays and Studies* 31, 1946, 70) cites 248–51 as freshly woven from Shakespeare, *Romeo* 3. 2. 18–19.]

251–8 *I have oft heard . . . soft applause.* Ovid associates Circe's magical powers with song as well as with *potent hearbs, and balefull drugs*, in Glaucus' appeal to her (*M.* 14. 20–2; and cf. 34). In speaking of Circe's enchantments Virgil uses *potentibus herbis* (*A.* 7. 19). In Ovid, Glaucus has just confessed (17–18) his passion for relentless Scylla, which perhaps accounts for her inclusion in Milton's lines, although actually in Ovid Circe becomes the rival for Glaucus' love and, repulsed, transforms Scylla to a monster and later to the rock that bears her name, facing Charybdis (ibid. 25–74). It was after this final transformation that *Scylla wept,* | *And chid her barking waves into attention*; and the wrongs she suffered at Circe's hands, if they are remembered, intensify our sense of the charm of Circe's music. Homer speaks of Scylla as barking terribly (*Od.* 12. 85), and Virgil has the image of a rock (not Scylla) surrounded by barking waves, *multis circum latrantibus undis* (*A.* 7. 588). From Homer (*Od.* 12. 85–110, 234–59) onward, Charybdis is constantly named with Scylla in reference to the dangerous passage between the two rocks in the channel dividing Sicily from Italy: on the Italian side was the barking monster Scylla; on the Sicilian, Charybdis, whose whirlpool thrice daily swallowed and disgorged the surrounding sea (cf. Ovid, *M.* 7. 63–5). Sil. Ital., as Warton noted, used these words of the effect of music: *Scyllaei tacuere canes; stetit atra Charybdis* (14. 474). [Sandys quoted Sil. Ital. in his *Relation* (1615), 237; in quoting and translating a Latin epigram (ibid. 248; *Ovid*, 1632, 476), he used the phrase 'fell Charybdis.' Dunster and Todd cited it in Sylvester (*D.W.W.* 2. 1. 3. 710, Grosart, 1, 120).]

There seems to be no classical precedent for associating *the Sirens three* directly with Circe. They were like her in being skilled in song and in luring men to their doom; their rocky islands lay between Scylla and Circe's isle. (The number of Sirens is not fixed; Milton here specifies three and names two at 877–81.) The Sirens were passed by Odysseus on his way back toward Scylla (*Od.* 12. 166–200); Horace's reference, *Sirenum voces et Circae pocula nosti* (*Ep.* 1. 2. 23), perhaps accounts for Milton's linking them with Circe. Also, in W. Browne's *I. T. Masque* the Siren declares: 'Circe, bids me sing; | And till some greater power her hand can stay, | Whoe'er commands, I none but her obey' (48–50), and she is bidden by Circe: 'then away | To help the nymphs who now begin their lay' (95–6). Ovid describes Circe among her attendant nymphs: *pulchro sedet illa recessu | sollemni solio. . . | Nereides nymphaeque simul. . .: | gramina disponunt sparsosque sine ordine flores | secernunt calathis variasque coloribus herbas* (*M.* 14. 261–7). In the *Odyssey* (10. 348–51) Circe is served by four maidens, daughters of the wells, woods, and holy rivers. For *Nereides*, sea-nymphs, Milton substituted *Naiades*, nymphs of rivers and springs, with appropriate kirtles of flowers. So also Browne adds to Ovid's *Nereides* 'other Nymphs which do in every creek, / In woods, on plains, on mountains, simples seek' (*I.T.M.* 261–2). (Some of these references were given by Warton; others were added by Verity.)

253 *flowry-kirtl'd*: clad in a kirtle (literally, skirt: *OED*: *sb.*¹ 2) covered with, or perhaps made of, flowers. Keightley cited: 'A cap of flowers, and a kirtle, / Imbroydred all with leaves of Mirtle' (Marlowe, *Passionate Shepherd* 11–12).

255 *take*: combining the figurative senses of 'capture' and 'captivate, entrance.' See 557 below and *Nat* 98 n. *prison'd soul*: the soul imprisoned in the body.

256 *Elysium*: the abode of the blessed in Greek myth (see below, 975 n.), here used figuratively of complete bliss, as in 'all night / Sleeps in Elysium' (Shakespeare, *H. V* 4. 1. 291).

256–8 *Scylla. . .Charybdis.* See above, 251–8 n.

259–63 *in pleasing slumber lull'd the sense.* Todd compared 'My senses lulled are in slomber of delight' (Spenser, *F.Q.* 3, proem 4). If *slumber* is taken literally, then *sense* means consciousness (*OED* 6 b; *PL* 8. 289) and *rob'd it of it self* means induced unconsciousness (as Verity understands it). But *in sweet madnes* and the pointed contrast with *sober certainty of waking bliss* suggest that *slumber* and *waking* are figurative and that *sense* means reason (*OED* 10 b). [G. L. Finney (*Musical Backgrounds*, 168–9) comments: 'The singing of Circe and the sirens inspired false ecstasy, which robbed the soul of perceptive power.' This singing is distinguished from the Lady's, not by technical qualities, but by the character and motives of the singers.]

261 *home-felt*: felt intimately, heartfelt (*OED*: first example; probably of Milton's coinage).

264–7 *Hail forren wonder. . .Dwell'st here.* Warton and Todd trace the tradition of this courtly compliment from Homer (*Od.* 6. 149) and Virgil (*A.* 1. 326–33) onward. Their examples, which include Shakespeare, *Temp.* 1. 2. 421–7, Browne, *Brit. Past.* 1. 4. 272–6, and Fletcher, *F. Shep.* 5. 5. 41–3, are not very close to Milton in phrasing.

266 *Unless the Goddes*: unless you are the goddess.

267 Although he has assumed no disguise (see 270 n.), Comus has provided that the Lady shall take him for a humble rustic, and he speaks in this pastoral character in his reference to Pan, the Arcadian god of shepherds and flocks (Virgil, *E.* 10. 26, etc.), which carries neither the overtone of 175 above (see n.) nor any suggestion of Pan's sensuality. Similar is the reference to Silvan, Silvanus, the ancient Italian rural deity (Virgil, *G.* 2. 493-4, *A.* 8. 600-1) later identified with Pan. [In *E.* 10 and *G.* 2 Virgil mentions the two gods together.]

268-9 Cf. *Arc* 48-9. *prosperous*. MS. first had *prospering* (so also Br.): *Facs.* 406, 313.

270 *Nay gentle Shepherd.* Both from the absence of any direction such as marks the entrance of the Attendant Spirit 'habited like a Shepherd' at 489, and from the words of Comus himself at 153-6, 164-6, it is evident that he does not change his garb or assume any disguise. By his magic he obscures the Lady's vision, so that she may take him for 'some harmles Villager' or 'Shepherd,' an illusion supported by her very natural interpretation of the sound of revelry she has heard (170-6). The illusion intensifies the sense of the magician's power while leaving the parallel and contrast of Comus and the Attendant Spirit sufficiently plain to be recognized at 489 (see n.). *ill is lost*: a Latinism, *male perditur* (Keightley).

272 *boast of skill*: pride (*OED* 3c) in my own skill. *extreme shift*: last resource (*OED* 5d). Todd noted the phrase, with the same initial stress, in the *Mirror for Magistrates* [ed. L. B. Campbell, Cambridge, 1938, 294: *Lord Hastings* 689].

274-5 *awake the courteous Echo...mossie Couch.* Todd cited 'Wakes Eccho from her seate' (*Pans Anniversarie* 217, *Ben Jonson* 7, 536).

276-89 Commentators from Hurd onward have remarked on this example of *stichomythia* (dialogue in single lines), a common practice in Greek tragedy, which, as Hughes (1937) observes, 'often gave curious excitement to encounters between strangers, as...in Sophocles' *Oedipus at Colonus*.' [Milton seems to have made a deliberate (and successful) effort to catch the somewhat stiff and stilted manner of his Greek models.]

277 *Dim darknes.* Todd noted the phrase in Shakespeare, *Lucr.* 118. *Labyrinth*: maze (cf. 180), with a secondary suggestion of the original Labyrinth of Minos in Crete. Cf.: 'Thou mayst not wander in that labyrinth; / There Minotaurs and ugly treasons lurk' (Shakespeare, *1 H. VI* 5. 3. 188-9). Though the Lady does not yet guess it, treasons abound here, and Comus is the Minotaur.

278 *neer-ushering guides*: leading the way and close at hand like an usher (a male attendant on a lady: *OED* 2b). MS. first had *thire ushering hands* (*Facs.* 406).

284 *prevented*: forestalled (*OED* 5; [cf. *Nat* 24]), perhaps already merging with the modern meaning (*OED* 7 gives no example till after *Comus* but might have cited Shakespeare, *Caesar* 3. 1. 35).

286 *Imports their loss...need?*: is their loss of consequence (*OED* 6) apart from your present need?

288 *manly prime, or youthful bloom*. The alternative helps to fix the meaning of *prime*, which might connote the earliest period of manhood (*OED* 8), or, as it appears to do here, the period of greatest vigour before strength begins to decay (ibid. 9). Warton quoted 'prime / In Manhood where Youth ended' (*PL* 11. 245–6) and 'a stripling Cherube he appeers, / Not of the prime' (ibid. 3. 636–7). *bloom*: state of greatest beauty or perfection (*OED* 2 gives *prime* as one synonym and quotes Shakespeare, *Much* 5. 1. 76: 'His May of youth and bloom of lustihood'). Here *bloom* carries the secondary suggestion of the tint of the cheek, flush, glow (of which *OED* gives no example before 1752).

289 *Hebe's*: see *L'All* 29 n.

290 *what time*. [For English examples of the Latin idiom (*quo tempore*) see *Lyc* 28 n.]

290–1 Newton (reported by Todd) noted Homer's *boulutonde* (*Il.* 16. 779)—toward evening, literally the time for unyoking the oxen—and cited similar images in Virgil, *E.* 2. 66–7, and Horace, *C.* 3. 6. 42–3.

292 *swink't*: wearied with labour (*swink*, toil, as in Spenser, 'swinck and sweat,' *F.Q.* 2. 7. 8; cf. 6. 4. 32). ['This is the first occurrence of the word in *OED*; Milton has coined an archaistic past-participial adjective' (Carey).]

293 *mantling*: enveloping (*OED* 2). [Carey notes this as the first example in *OED* of the word 'in the sense "spreading and covering": previously it had been applied only to liquids, meaning "gathering a coating of scum." Cf. *PL* 4. 258, 5. 279, 7. 439.]

296–301 *Their port...I worshipt*. Warton suggested a reminiscence of Pylades and Orestes, taken by shepherds for divine beings and worthy of worship, in Euripides, *Iph. Taur.* 241 f. [Cf. the fishermen's thinking Pyrocles 'some God' (Sidney, *Arcadia*, *Works* 1, 10).]

296 *port*: bearing, mien (*OED*: sb.[4] 1).

297 *faëry*. An obsolete meaning of *fairy* is 'enchantment, magic,...an illusion, a dream' (*OED* 3, whose latest example is a century before *Comus*); with this meaning *faëry* here seems to be connected, as also in a measure does Spenser's use of the word. Sometimes the spelling *faerie, faery*, whether revived or invented by Spenser, connotes in his followers a conscious reminiscence of his invented world of romance [cf. C. L. Wrenn, 'Language,' 259], as in Keats's *Nightingale* 70, but nothing can be inferred from Milton's spelling (*faëry* here and at 435; *Faery, L'All* 102; *Faerie, PL* 1. 781; but *Fairies* above, 118, and *Fairy, PR* 2. 359).

298 *the element*: the sky (*OED* 10); cf. *PL* 2. 490.

300 *plighted*: interwoven (*OED*: *v.*² 2).

302-3 *It were a journey...find them*: 'Referring either to the difficulty of the way or (more probably) to the happiness of finding them' (Browne). Certainly the latter: 'the whole is a compliment to the Lady' (Verity). [Brooks and Hardy (204) see, as often, a positively religious allusion (here ironical) to the whole journey and theme of the masque.]

304 *that place*: i.e. where Comus saw them (293-4).

309 *sure guess of well-practiz'd feet*. The adjective counteracts the suggestion of uncertainty in nearly all the meanings of *guess*; the whole phrase combines the ideas of right conjecture and intuitive inference. For *guess* MS. first had *steerage* (*Facs.* 408).

310 *alley*: usually a tree-bordered walk or a walk under trees in a garden (*OED* 2), as at 989, but here qualified by *of this wilde Wood* (311).

311 *Dingle*: originally a deep valley between hills (as in 'Dingles deepe, and Mountaines hore,' *Muses Elizium* 2. 29, Drayton, 3, 258), but, in and after Milton's phrase, a densely wooded hollow (*OED*). [C. L. Wrenn ('Language,' 261) remarks that, apart from place-names, the word had not been used between *c.* 1200 and Drayton: 'One cannot say whether Milton was here following a dialect usage or imitating Drayton's revival.'] *wilde*: MS. *wide* (followed by Br.); changed in 1637, 1645, 1673 (*Works* 1, 508; *Facs.* 408, 315, 275, 200).

312 *bosky bourn*: small stream (*OED*: *sb.*¹) amid bushes (*bosk*, bush: *OED*: *a.*¹). [Warton cited, *inter alia*, 'My bosky acres' (Shakespeare, *Temp.* 4. 1. 81).]

313 *ancient*: long-accustomed (*OED* 5).

314 *stray attendance*: strayed attendants. Verity takes *lodg'd* to mean received into some dwelling (cf. 319, 338, 345) in contrast to *shroud* (315), sheltered under a tree or bank.

315 *shroud*: seek or take shelter (*OED*: *v.*¹ 2 c); see 147 n. *limits*: tract defined by boundaries (*OED* 3), here the Wood.

316 *morrow*: to-morrow; cf. *PL* 5. 33.

316–17 *the low roosted lark...rowse*. The lark's nest, built on the ground, relies for protection on being concealed amid long grass, hence *low roosted* and *thatch't pallat* (a humble couch, literally a straw bed, under a thatched roof); cf. *PR* 2. 279–81. [Muir (*J.M.*, 29), following Masson, remarks that '*roosted* merely means *rested*, and *thatched* refers to the composition of the nest: it does not imply a roof.'] Rolfe takes *rowse* to be intransitive; Masson thinks that *morrow* may be the subject and *lark* the object [Rolfe would seem to be supported by the MS., which had *ere the larke rowse* before *morrow* was introduced (*Facs.* 408)].

317 *if otherwise*: i.e. if I fail to find them.

318–19 *low | But loyal*: 'humble but reliable' (Verity).

320 *further*: [so also in 1637, 1645; MS. and Br. had *furder*. See above, 226 n.]

321–5 *And trust...most pretended*. Warton compared Ariosto, *O.F.* 14. 62, and Harington's summary translation (14.52): 'As curtesie ofttimes in simple bowres / Is found as great as in the stately towres.' Newton (reported by Todd) compared Spenser, *F.Q.* 6. 1. 1 ⟨where, however, courtesy is associated with courts and the contrast is not drawn⟩. Elton translates from Dante, *Convivio* 2. 11 (ed. M. Simonelli, 2. 10, p. 54; tr. Jackson, 100): 'Because virtues and fair manners were the custom in Courts anciently, as to-day the opposite is the custom, this word (*cortesia*) was taken from Courts.' [Hughes (1937) cites Aeschylus, *Agam.* 772–3 (which has 'smoke-begrimed dwellings'); and, for such a commonplace, one might add Horace (below, 323–4 n.); Marlowe, *H. and L.* 1. 393–4; Shakespeare, *2 H. IV* 3. 1. 9–14.] There is no reason to link these lines, as Verity does, with Milton's later republicanism; in its context the speech carries dramatic irony.

322 *sheds*: in poetry, cottages or humble dwellings. Cf. 'borne in lowly shed / Of parents base' (Fairfax, *Jerusalem* 2. 58).

323–4 *With*. MS. first had *&*. *tapstry Halls*. *Hall* may mean either the whole mansion (*OED* 1 and 3) or one of its large public rooms (ibid. 2), which would be the part actually hung with tapestries. Adopting the meaning 'state-apartments,' Warton emended *And* (324) to *In*, on the assumption that Milton had neglected to change the first word of 324 as he had changed that of 323; Todd followed Warton. But the emendation is quite unnecessary. *Halls* stand for the mansions of the nobility as grouped with *Courts of Princes* and contrasted with the *lowly sheds* of the peasantry. Finley (33, n. 3) notes a similar contrast in Horace, *C.* 3. 29. 14–16: *sub lare pauperum* | *...sine aulaeis et ostro....*

325 *pretended*: claimed (*OED* 5) or asserted (to exist), probably with the suggestion (much more common in later usage) of 'unfounded,' 'false' (ibid. 7). This suggestion is strengthened by *yet*, if taken as 'despite this fact,' less so if taken as 'still, to this day'; the latter was probably Milton's original intention, since MS. first had *& is praetended yet* (*Facs.* 408).

326 *warranted*: protected from danger (*OED v.* 1).

328 *Eie me*: 'keep your watch over me' (Verity); see 218–19 and n. It seems possible, though much less probable, that the meaning intended is 'furnish me with eyes (to see and avoid encompassing dangers)': neither meaning (nor any other that would fit this phrase) is given by *OED*.

328–9 *square my triall...strength*: adjust (*OED*: square *v.* 4b) to the strength allotted (ibid. proportion *v.* 5) to me. It is perhaps significant that the Lady, trusting in her own strength, does not pray for any accession, but simply that the trial may be such as she can meet successfully.

330 *Unmuffle*: remove the covering (of darkness) that envelops and conceals you. *Muffle*, however, is normally transitive, as in Shakespeare, *Romeo* 5. 3. 21, *Caesar* 3. 2. 192. [It would seem possible that *ye* (though probably parallel to *thou* in the same line) is the object of *Unmuffle*, since *ye* is often a direct or indirect object: e.g. *Arc* 81, 101, *Comus* 43 (1645 reading), 215, *PL* 4. 368, 5. 789, 10. 40, *PR* 2. 142.] Warton (supplemented by Dunster and Todd) was at pains to show, by citations from Drayton, W. Browne, Sylvester, and others, that the verb was common and not thought too prosaic. One citation was: 'If it chanc'd night's sable shrouds / Muffled Cynthia up in clouds' (Browne, *Shep. Pipe* 1. 765–6). [Demaray (*Masque Tradition*, 102, 113) suggests that *Unmuffle* may be an indirect request that the canisters that 'muffle' the burning tapers be lifted and the stage brightened (see above, 193–9 n.).]

331 *wontst*. See above, *Nat* 10 n. *benizon*: invoking a blessing (*OED* 2). [Newton (reported by Todd) cited Spenser's lines about the poor traveller's blessing the moon when she 'Breakes forth her silver beames' from a cloud (*F.Q.* 3. 1. 43).]

332 *Stoop...amber cloud.* Commentators cite the moon 'Stooping through a fleecy cloud' (*IlPen* 72). *amber.* See above, *L'All* 61 n. The word is 'exactly descriptive of the fringe of light round the moon when shining through a cloud' (Verity).

333–4 *disinherit Chaos...shades.* Behind this image is the ancient and varied association of primeval Chaos with Darkness (and Night): cf. 'the Reign of Chaos and old Night' (*PL* 1. 543; and 2. 894 f.), and Spenser, *F.Q.* 1. 5. 22, 4. 2. 47. *disinherit*: dispossess of his inheritance. *double night.* Cf. *duplicataque noctis imago est* (Ovid, *M.* 11. 550); and *PR* 1. 500 and n.

335 *influence.* See *Nat* 71 and n. The astrological image is used here, though what is actually *damm'd up* | *With black usurping mists* is the moon's light.

337 *rush Candle*: one made by dipping the pith of a rush in tallow.

337–8 *wicker hole* | *Of som clay habitation*: aperture in some wattle hut plastered with clay; perhaps a wickerwork shutter over that opening (Trent).

339 *rule*: (in poetry) 'A shaft or beam of light' (*OED* 18 c; but this and a palpable imitation by Warton are the only examples given). Perhaps a figurative use derived from the verb *rule*, 'mark out (a line) with or as with a ruler' (ibid. *v.* 11), or from *rule*, 'A bar (of gold)' (ibid. 18a). Warton cited 'the setting Sun...Leveld his eevning Rayes' (*PL* 4. 540–3). The sound of the line in *Comus* suggests the idea of both length (Hanford) and straightness.

340–1 *And thou...Cynosure.* The allusion is to the myth (Ovid, *M.* 2. 409–531, *F.* 2. 155–92) of Callisto, a princess of Arcadia and one of Diana's train, who was raped by Jove and gave birth to a son, Arcas; Juno transformed her to a bear, and Jove stellified her as the constellation Ursa Major (hence *our star o, Arcady*) and her son as Ursa Minor, otherwise known as Cynosura, 'the dog's tail' (cf. *L'All* 80 n.). 'Greek sailors steered by the Great Bear; the Phoenicians (or *Tyrians*) by the Lesser—hence "Tyrian Cynosure"' (Verity). Cf. *esse duas Arctos, quarum Cynosura petatur* | *Sidoniis, Helicen Graia carina notet* (Ovid, *F.* 3. 107–8).

343 *folded flocks...watled cotes.* Todd compared *claudensque textis cratibus laetum pecus* (Horace, *Epod.* 2. 45), and 'Shepherds pen thir Flocks at eeve | In hurdl'd Cotes' (*PL* 4. 185–6); [cf. *EpDam* 141]. On *folded* see above, 93 n.

watled cotes: shelters for animals (*OED*: cote sb.[1] 2), made of wattles, stakes interlaced with twigs or branches (ibid. wattle sb.[1] 1), sometimes used as a synonym for hurdles (ibid. 2).

344 *pastoral reed with oaten stops.* The shepherd's pipe in English pastoral poetry is usually thought of as made of oat straw, Virgil's *avena* (*E.* 1. 2; see above, *Lyc* 33 and n., and ibid. 88); *reed* could be applied to the stem of any plant made into a rustic musical pipe (*OED: sb.*[1] 7). A *stop* is 'The closing of a finger-hole or ventage in the tube of a wind instrument....Also, the hole or aperture thus closed' (*OED* 15). Cf. Shakespeare, *Ham.* 3. 2. 372–81, partly quoted in *Lyc* 188 n.

345 *the Lodge*: the dwelling of the gamekeeper or other guardian of the place (*OED* 3), coloured by *lodge* as applied to a house built in a forest or desert area (ibid. 2).

346 *Count the night watches*: mark (by crowing), so that they might be counted, the watches of the night (the equal periods into which the night was traditionally divided—three by the O.T. Hebrews, four or five by the Greeks, four by the Romans: *OED* 4).

348 *close*: confined, shut in. MS. had *lone*, deleted, then *sad*, deleted, then *close*; Br. *lone* (*Works* 1, 511; *Facs.* 408, 316). *innumerous*: innumerable (Lat. *innumerus*).

349–65 These lines are a good deal corrected in MS. A separate sheet was seen by Todd, who in an appendix (4, 183) printed 351–8 as he there found the lines (here cited as MS. Todd). Most of this sheet has been lost, but the margin supplies clues [see *Facs.* 408, and H. Darbishire, 2, 348].

350 *whether* (thus in MS., Br., 1637, 1645): old variant of *whither*, persisting after Milton; cf. Dryden, *Æneis*, 1697, 10. 514: 'Whether wou'd you run?'

351 *amongst...thistles*. MS. (*Facs.* 408) has *in this dead solitude*, deleted (but retained in MS. Todd); then, *surrounding wilde*, deleted; then, *perhapps some cold harde banke*, deleted; finally, the present reading (which is in Br.: *Facs.* 316).

354 *Leans*: MS. (*Facs.* 408) and MS. Todd, *she leans*. *unpillow'd*: MS. *thoughtfull*, deleted; *unpillow'd* substituted (*thoughtfull* in MS. Todd). *fraught with sad fears*. MS. has *musing at our unkindnesse*, deleted (but retained in MS. Todd), and present reading substituted; Br. (*Facs.* 316), present reading. See *Works* 1, 512–13.

355 *What if.* MS. has *or else*, deleted, *what if* substituted; Br., *or els*; MS. Todd, *Or lost* [Todd's misreading: Darbishire, 2, 348]. *amazement*: frenzy (*OED* 1). Here follow in MS. three lines: *so fares as did forsaken Proserpine* | *when the big wallowing* (deleted) *rowling* (deleted) *flakes of pitchie clowds* | *& darknesse* *wound her in. 1 Bro. Peace brother peace*: the whole deleted. MS. Todd and Br. preserve the whole with *rowling*. See *Facs.* 408, 316–17; *Works* 1, 513.

356–64 are absent in MS. and Br., but present in 1637 (*Works* 1, 513; *Facs.* 277). They seem to have been in MS. Todd, with two or three minor deviations.

357 *Of Savage…heat*: hunger of savage beasts or lust of savage men.

358–598 Milton uses the speeches of the Elder Brother to set forth an important part of the doctrine and praise of chastity, which is essential to the effect of the whole, but which the Lady does not elaborate in her debate with Comus, since he is incapable of comprehending and unworthy to hear such doctrine (782–8). Here, what dramatic propriety is necessary is afforded by the need to reassure the Younger Brother. But the succession of the ideas expressed by the Elder reveals the deeper purpose. He commences with the security given its possessor by virtue generally (358–84), and by chastity in particular (418–74), enforcing the doctrine by reference to *the old Schools of Greece* (438), that is, first, to classic myth (440–51), then to Platonic philosophy (452–74), and finally, after the entry of the Attendant Spirit (488), and as if to emphasize for the audience the Spirit's role as heaven-sent protector, he ascends to what Todd was acute enough to recognize as specifically Christian teaching on the Providence of God (583–98). [This was no doubt Todd's meaning: what he says (4, 128) is that the speech 'exhibits the sublimer sentiments of the Christian. Religion here gave energy to the poet's strains.']

358 *over-exquisite*: excessively precise (*OED* 2) in inquiring, and unduly sensitive to (ibid. 7).

359 *cast*: forecast (*OED* 41); as Warton (1785) explained, a metaphor from astrology—cast a nativity (*OED* 39).

360 *be so*: be indeed as you imagine them.

361 *forestall*: introduce before the proper time (*OED* 7).

364 ['This is one of the cases where the printer uses *?* for *!*' (Darbishire).]

365 *so to seek*: so at fault, so deficient (*OED* 20).

366 Warton compared 'souls so unprincipl'd in vertue' (*Educ, Works* 4, 279); Todd added 'the whole book of sanctity and vertu' (*RCG, Works* 3, 239). [This is the first example of *unprincipled* in *OED* (Hunter, 'New Words'; Carey).]

367 *boosoms*: carries in its bosom (*OED* 4). See *L'All* 78 n.

368 *single*: mere. *noise*: 'The aggregate of loud sounds arising in a busy community' (*OED* 3b). This meaning, which associates noise with human companionship (cf. 'the various bustle of resort,' 378), fits the Lady's lonely situation and leads on to the praise of solitude (374–9).

370 *stir*: trouble, disturb (*OED* 4). *constant*: MS. *steadie*, deleted, then *constant* (*Facs.* 408).

371 Put them into 'amazement' (above, 355 and n.).

372–3 *Vertue...radiant light.* Todd cited 'Vertue gives her selfe light' (Spenser, *F.Q.* 1. 1. 12) and ''tis she ⟨Virtue⟩ yᵗ still hir-self refines, / by hir owne light' (*Pleasure* 340–1, Ben Jonson 7, 491). [Verity (on *IlPen* 122) cited Shakespeare, *Romeo* 3. 2. 8–9: 'Lovers can see to do their amorous rites / By their own beauties' (where of course the image is closer than the idea). Following Todd et al., Verity cited probable or possible echoes of Juliet's speech in *Comus* 552–3 and *IlPen* 122 (see notes below and above); see also E. Seaton in *Comus* III. 5 above.]

374–9 [The image of wings may come from *Phaedrus*, e.g. 246 C, where Plato says of the soul: 'now when it is perfect and fully winged, it mounts upward and governs the whole world; but the soul which has lost its wings...settles down, taking upon itself an earthly body...' (L.C.L., p. 473; Wright, pp. 158–9).]

374 *flat Sea.* See above, *Lyc* 98 and n. and 167.

375 *seeks to*: resorts to (*OED* 13). Todd cited 'And all the earth sought to Solomon, to hear his wisdom' (1 Kings 10. 24), and Deut. 12. 5; cf. Isa. 11. 10.

sweet retired Solitude: MS. *solitarie sweet retire*, deleted, and changed to present reading (*Facs.* 410).

376 *Contemplation.* See above, *IlPen* 54 and n. Dunster (reported by Todd) quoted Sidney's *Arcadia* (*Works* 1, 56): 'my solitarines perchaunce is the nurse of these contemplations.'

377 *plumes*: prunes or preens. *lets grow her wings.* Cf. '*Quid agam vero?* πτεροφυῶ, & volare meditor' (*Epistol* 7, *Works* 12, 26). The phrase in *Comus*, repeated in the Greek word in this letter to Diodati three years later, confirms Mark Pattison's impression (*Milton*, 17–18: noted by Verity) that the whole passage (374–9) is a reflection on Milton's retirement. See 374–9 n.

379 *all to ruffl'd*: utterly ruffled; *to* is an intensive, and *all* gives the particle further emphasis (*OED*: all 14, 15; and to, *prefix*, 2, 3). The absence of a hyphen led Trent to ask if the meaning may not be 'much too ruffled.' [Cf. Sandys, *Ovid*, 1626, 257: 'all to hackt and torne' (*M.* 13. 118–19); Spenser, *F.Q.* 5. 8. 44. 2, 'all to brusd'; and numerous examples in Chaucer (ed. Robinson, Glossary, 'Toscatered,' etc.).]

380 *cleer.* [See *Lyc* 70 n.]

381 *center*: the centre of the earth. Cf. 'I will find / Where truth is hid, though it were hid indeed / Within the centre' (Shakespeare, *Ham.* 2. 2. 157–9: *OED* 2). [Since *center* can mean simply the earth (as in *PL* 1. 686 and probably 1. 74: *OED* 2b), it may here mean only inside, in the depths of, the earth.]

383–4 *Benighted walks...his own dungeon.* MS. and Br. have *walks in black vapours, though the noontyde brand | blaze in the summer solstice*; deleted in MS. (*Facs.* 410) and replaced by present reading. [To C. S. Lewis (*RES* 8, 1932, 172–3) both readings are excellent, but the first has natural syntax and a more highly coloured pictorial quality, while the second is a less dramatic product of the moral imagination.]

384 *Himself...dungeon.* Todd compared: 'Thou art become (O worst imprisonment!) / The Dungeon of thy self' (*SA* 155–6), and 'Heare plaints come forth from dungeon of my minde' (Sidney, *Arcadia, Works* 1, 130; Ringler, 18, line 133), and 'in himselfe nothing, but...a dungeon of sorrow' (*Works* 1, 161).

385–91 Praises of a simple life abound in poetry. Verity cites *IlPen* 167–74 and Shakespeare, *R. II* 3. 3. 147–50; [cf., e.g., *3 H. VI* 2. 5. 21–54].

385 *affects*: is drawn to, has an affection for (*OED* 2).

386 *desert cell.* The reference to the Hermit (389) fixes the meaning.

387 *haunt*: place of habitual resort, hence society (*OED* 3, 2b).

388 *Senat house*: a type of security, as at once a place of resort, the source of law, and guarded by its own 'privileges.' Editors' references to later violations of Parliament by Cromwell are irrelevant, but the idea perhaps reflects Milton's sympathy with the Puritans' desire for parliamentary government in the period of Charles' arbitrary rule (1629–40), while the image bears witness to the Roman senate as an influence on his and their thinking [cf. *Sonn* 17. 1–4].

389 *Weeds.* See 16–17 n. and 84 n. MS. (*Facs.* 410) has *beads*, deleted; then, *gowne*, deleted; then, *beads*, deleted; finally *weeds*. Br. has *weeds* (ibid. 318).

390 *Beads.* MS. has *hairie gowne* (cf. *IlPen* 169], deleted, *beads* substituted; Br. *beads.* *Maple Dish*: bowl of maple wood. This item carries a secondary suggestion of pastoral; cf. Spenser, *S.C., August* 26, and Gloss, which refers to Theocritus and Virgil. [The hermit's bowl, however, is not a prize for a singing match.]

392–6 The basic image [salvaged from the cancelled lines that originally followed 4: see above] is supplied by the myth of the golden apples of the

Hesperides, which differs in details in different accounts. The apples, given by Earth to Hera on her marriage to Zeus, were planted by her, and Hesperus and his daughters, the three (or more) Hesperides, were set to guard them [Apollodorus 2. 5. 11 and references, L.C.L.; Starnes–Talbert (308–16) cite Renaissance dictionaries]. Either Hera or Hesperus, aware of a prophecy that a son of Zeus would steal them, installed a dragon as guardian. Milton might have derived the idea of making *the fair Hesperian Tree* with its golden fruit stand for female beauty from Diod. Sic. (4. 27. 2, 4), who says that the Hesperides (or Atlantides) excelled in beauty and chastity, that Busiris, king of Egypt, wishing to get them into his power, sent pirates to capture them, but that Heracles rescued them. Hughes notes this interpretation in N. Comes, *Mythol.* 7. 7. Cf. also (however different the context): 'Before thee stands this fair Hesperides, / With golden fruit, but dangerous to be touch'd; / For death, like dragons, here affright the hoard' (Shakespeare, *Per.* 1. 1. 27–9). [Carey quotes Shakespeare, *A.Y.L.* (see below, 397–402 n.) and says that Milton 'was clearly recalling also' Jonson, *Every Man in His Humour* (1601), 3. 1. 16–23: 'Who will not judge him worthy to be robd, / That sets his doores wide open to a theefe, / And shewes the felon, where his treasure lyes? / Againe, what earthy spirit but will attempt / To taste the fruite of beauties golden tree, / When leaden sleepe seales up the dragons eyes? / Oh beauty is a Project of some power, / Chiefely when oportunitie attends her' (*Ben Jonson* 3, 233). The passage is shortened in the 1616 text (3. 3. 15–20: 3, 346). C. S. Lewis ('Variation in Shakespeare and Others,' *Rehabilitations and Other Essays*, London and New York, 1939, 167) had remarked: 'The whole passage [in Jonson] may very profitably be compared with Milton's imitation of it in *Comus*. The six lines beginning "Oh beauty is a project", which contain four distinct metaphorical expressions of precisely the same idea, he throws out altogether. He keeps the dragon idea, and the stores spread out in the sight of a thief, but reverses the order. The dragon comes first and is used for a different purpose. The marvellous line "Of dragon watch with unenchanted eye" is the central phrase, and the metaphor as a whole becomes less a rhetorical illustration of the theme than an escape into pure imagination. The hoard-and-thief idea is separated from it by the words "You may as well", and has the effect of summing up the previous argument. It is not simply one more point that has occurred to the speaker; it is a return to the person addressed, as if he had rounded on him.']

394 *uninchanted*: undeluded, unbeguiled (*OED*: enchant v. 2), a figurative use now obsolete. Warton and editors who follow him in explaining as 'which cannot be enchanted' miss this meaning. [But Warton's explanation may seem probable in view of Milton's common use of the past participle; cf. 'uncontrouled' (792), 'unreproved' (*L'All* 40), 'unremov'd' (*PL* 4. 987), etc.]

397–402 Warton compared: 'Alas, what danger will it be to us, / Maids as we are, to travel forth so far! / Beauty provoketh thieves sooner than gold' (Shakespeare, *A.Y.L.* 1. 3. 110–12).

397 *unsun'd*: unsunned, hidden away from the light of day. Todd noted that Spenser put Mammon 'in a delve [den or cave], / Sunning his threasure hore' (*F.Q.* 2. 7, arg.; cf. 2. 8. 4). Here the context shows that sunning must mean exposing to the light, not placing in the sun's rays. *OED* misses these meanings and examples.

399 *hope*: MS. *thinke*, deleted, *hope* substituted (*Facs.* 410).

400 This line has presented some difficulty. Verity found the personification of *Danger* strained and wished Milton had written Desire instead; he apparently did not understand that here *Danger* means 'power to do injury' (*OED* 1 b and Wright [who has a further note in *RES* 22, 1946, 225–6]). *OED* (wink 6 b) seems to have slipped in interpreting *wink on*, which means 'be blind to' (Verity). [Br. has *winke at* (*Facs.* 318).]

402 *wilde surrounding wast*: MS. *vast, & hideous wild*, replaced by *wide surrounding wast* (so also Br.; 1637, *wild*: *Works* 1, 517; *Facs.* 410, 318, 278). *wast*: waste; wild and desolate region.

403 *it recks me not*: I am not concerned (about). [Cf. *Lyc* 122.]

404 *events that dog them*: occurrences, dangers, that go along with night and loneliness.

405 *ill greeting touch*: a touch that greets with evil intent. Given the context, it is not irrelevant that *touch* was also a euphemism for sexual contact, as in Shakespeare, *Meas.* 5. 1. 141 (*OED* 1 b).

406 *unowned*: lost (cf. 349); literally, without an owner or protector (*OED* 1).

407 *Inferr, as if I thought*: argue or conclude that. After *doubt* (408), MS. reads *or question, no* and adds the following lines (which are omitted in 1637, 1645, 1673, but are included in their corrected form in Br. (*Works* 1, 517; *Facs.* 410, 318): *beshrew me but I would* (deleted) *I could be willing though now i'th darke to trie / a tough (passado, deleted) encounter wth the shaggiest ruffian / that lurks by hedge or lane of this dead circuit / to have her by my side, though I were sure / she might be free from perill where she is.* The phrase *dead circuit* is unusual: *circuit* evidently means a given area or region; *dead* has perhaps a now obsolete meaning, 'causing death, deadly, mortal' (*OED* 9). [C. S. Lewis (*RES* 8, 1932, 173) takes the omission of the lines as indicating Milton's lessening concern for good theatre and his final version as heightening the Elder Brother's purely didactic tone.]

409–11 *an equal poise…rather then fear.* For *arbitrate* here *OED* 2b adopts Johnson's 'judge of'; Verity prefers 'decide the issue (=Latin *eventus*)'; cf. *OED* 1. The image is that of a scale with an equal weight, *poise*, in each balance, where no decision is given and the observer is left to arbitrate between them. [Carey cites 'equal poise of sin and charity' in Shakespeare, *Meas.* 2. 4. 68.]

412 *squint*: figuratively, suspicious. With this (the first example given by *OED* 2b) Todd compared 'squint-ey'd Suspicion' (Quarles, *Feast for Wormes*, 1620, *Medit.* 11, sig. I2ᵛ: *Works*, ed. Grosart, 2, 22, line 1482). [Cf. 'squint-ey'd world' (ibid. 2, 17, line 855). Hughes (1937) cites 'I feare me, thou have a squint eye' (Spenser, *S.C.*, *August* 129).]

414–19 *she has a hidden strength…'Tis chastity.* The Second Brother takes the *strength* to be providential protection. The Elder Brother recognizes that, but explains that he referred to chastity, which is indeed the gift of Heaven but at the same time her own possession. To Saurat (*Milton*, 8–10, 16–20, etc.), followed by Tillyard, Milton appears at this period of his life to have ascribed mystical power to chastity; see these critics in IV above, under 1925 and 1930.

420 *clad in compleat steel.* Editors compare 'in complete steel' (Shakespeare, *Ham.* 1. 4. 52); but Warton argued that it was 'a common expression for "armed from head to foot."' This purely figurative arming of the Lady has led editors, quite groundlessly, to compare the descriptions of those other exemplars of chastity, Spenser's Belphoebe and P. Fletcher's Parthenia (*P.I.* 10. 27–32). [But are not the arms of Belphoebe and Parthenia symbolic as well as literal?]

421 In place of this line MS. first read: *& may (upon any needfull accident | be it not don in pride or in wilfull ⟨tempting,* deleted⟩ *præsumption*); the whole then deleted and replaced by present line; but the second of the cancelled lines is used at 430 (*Facs.* 410). *like a quiver'd Nymph*: like a nymph of Diana's train (see below, 440–51 n.); [cf. *pharetrata Camilla* (Virgil, *A.* 11. 649), *pharetratae Virginis* (Ovid, *Am.* 1. 1. 10)].

422 *trace*: range through, traverse (*OED* 4). Editors compare 'to trace the forests wild' (Shakespeare, *Dream* 2. 1. 25). MS. first had *walke through*.

unharbour'd: affording no shelter (*OED* 2: the only example given; cf. ibid. *harbour, sb.*¹ 1, 2).

423 *Infamous*: of ill fame. Newton and Todd cited *infames scopulos* (Horace, *C.* 1. 3. 20).

424–6 Warton compared: 'Sure there is a power / In that great name of virgin, that binds fast / All rude uncivil bloods, all appetites / That break their confines' (Fletcher, *F. Shep.* 1. 1. 124–7).

425 *Mountaneer*. Warton remarked that the word 'seems to have conveyed the idea of something very savage and ferocious.' This may well be, though it is not supported by *OED*; and only two of Warton's quotations ('Some villain mountainers' and 'Who call'd me traitor, mountaineer': Shakespeare, *Cym.* 4. 2. 71 and 120) carry the idea of crime or violence. Probably the word was suggested here by *Bandite*, since bandits were often referred to as infesting mountains; cf. quotations under *OED*, bandit.

427 *very*: adj. denoting 'truly entitled to the name or designation' (*OED* I. 1); and used to intensify the noun it modifies, as is common in the Bible and Shakespeare. Hence here 'utter' (Verity).

428 *grots*: caves or caverns, without the suggestion of agreeable picturesqueness associated with grottoes (*OED*: grot³ 1, and grotto 1). *shag'd*. Like *shaggy* (cf. *Lyc* 54 and n.), the word refers generally to the rough coats of animals, but was also applied, as here, to the rough, tangled growth of bushes and trees (*OED*: shagged 2b and shaggy 1 f). *horrid shades*: rough, bristling shrubs and bushes (Lat. *horridus*). Editors cite *PL* 9. 185 and *PR* 1. 296. [Wright (*Milton's 'Paradise Lost,'* London, 1962, 70–2) comments on Milton's idiosyncratic use of *shade*: 'The word occurs sixty times in his poetry, and two out of three times as a metonymy for tree, bush, woods or foliage.' See above, 62 n.]

After **428** MS. has: *& yawning dens where glaring monsters house*: later deleted in MS. but present in Br. (*Works* 1, 520; *Facs.* 410, 319).

429 *unblench't majesty*: stateliness of bearing or demeanour (*OED*: majesty 4), 'Not blenched or turned aside, undismayed, unflinching' (*OED* 1; ibid. blench *v.*¹ 5). But the senses of the verb *blench* are various and shade off into one another: it occurs as a variant, or at least as responding to the meaning, of *blanch* (ibid. blanch *v.*² 3), 'make pale with fear' (ibid. blanch *v.*¹ 4); also as a variant of *blemish* (ibid. blench *v.*³), 'impair...the beauty...or perfection of' (ibid. blemish 4).

430   See 421 n. for earlier and cancelled form of this line occurring there in MS.

431-2   *Som say*. MS. deleted, substituted *Nay more* (Br. *Naye more*), then restored. *evil thing*: i.e. evil spirit (as contrasted with savage beast and evil man referred to above), called a *thing* because it cannot be precisely described or because the speaker does not wish to be more specific, as in 'What, has this thing appear'd again to-night?' (Shakespeare, *Ham.* 1. 1. 21; *OED*: *sb.*¹ 7c).

walks: appears (*OED* 9). Warton compared: 'Some say...no spirit dare stir abroad' (*Ham.* 1. 1. 158-61), and Fletcher, *F. Shep.* 1. 1. 111-29: 'Yet I have heard—my mother told it me, / ...find my ruin.... / Sure there is a power / ...against fate and hell!'

432   *fire*. Verity, Wright, et al. interpret as the *ignis fatuus*, which appears over marshy ground and leads travellers astray. Cf. *L'All* 104 n., and *PL* 9. 634-42: 'a wandring Fire, / Compact of unctuous vapor, which the Night / Condenses, and the cold invirons round, / Kindl'd...to a Flame, / Which...some evil Spirit attends / Hovering and blazing with delusive Light, / Misleads th' amaz'd Night-wanderer from his way / To Boggs and Mires, and oft through Pond or Poole, / There swallow'd up and lost, from succour farr.' This passage explains the association of this *fire* with *fog*, *lake*, and *moorish fen*. Verity pointed out that witches—also called hags—in Jonson's *Masque of Queenes* come 'From the lakes, and from the fennes, / From the rockes, and from the dennes'; and that Jonson says in a note: 'These places, in theyr own nature dire, & dismall, are reckond up, as the fittest, from whence such persons should come' (*Ben Jonson* 7, 284). [The word *moorish* appears in Br., 1637, 1645, and 1673; in MS. it is *moorie* (*Facs.* 320, 279, 202, 412; Shawcross, *PBSA* 56, 1962, 318).]

433   *Blew*: blue, i.e. livid, cadaverous (*OED* 2; Hanford). Verity compares 'This blue-ey'd hag' ⟨the witch Sycorax⟩ (Shakespeare, *Temp.* 1. 2. 269), interpreting 'blue-ey'd' as referring to dark circles under the eyes. *meager*: emaciated (*OED* 1; 'That art so leane and meagre waxen late,' Spenser, *M. Hubberds Tale* 599). MS. first had *wrinckled*. *Hag*: 'An evil spirit...in female form,' 'Applied to...ghosts...and other terrors of the night' (*OED*: *sb.*¹ 1, 1b).

433-4   *stubborn unlaid ghost...at curfeu time*. *unlaid*: 'Not laid by exorcism' (*OED* 2); cf. 'Ghost unlaid forbear thee! / Nothing ill come near thee!' (Shakespeare, *Cym.* 4. 2. 278-9). *stubborn*: presumably because resisting all efforts to be rid of it. *magick chains*: the fetters (cf. *Nat* 234 n.) which restrain the ghost as if by magic (*OED*: magic *a.* 2, the closest among definitions offered, but not entirely satisfactory; it is rather as if the magic power required to raise a ghost were thought of as countering a magic power restraining it, but here the ghost of its own volition breaks through the restraining power). The reference to *curfeu time* (cf. *IlPen* 74 n.) was explained by Warton, who cited: 'He ⟨the foul fiend⟩ begins at curfew, and walks till the first cock' (Shakespeare, *Lear* 3. 4. 121),and:'Ye elves of hills, brooks, standing lakes, and groves, / ...that rejoice / To hear the solemn curfew' (Shakespeare, *Temp.* 5. 1. 33–40).

435 *Goblin*: a mischievous and ugly demon (*OED* 1). For Milton the word has sinister overtones; cf. 'the Goblin' (Death) in *PL* 2. 688. *swart Faëry of the mine.* Warton commented: 'In the Gothic system of pneumatology, mines were supposed to be inhabited by various sorts of spirits.' He cited, *inter alia*, Lavater's *Of ghostes and spirites walking by nyght* (1572, 73; ed. J. D. Wilson and M. Yardley, 1929, 73): 'Pioners or diggers for mettal, do affirme, that in many mines, there appeare straunge shapes and spirites, who are apparelled like unto other laborers in the pit'; and 'The spirits that haunt the Mynes' (Drayton, *Poly.* 26. 389). The epithet *swart* (dark, dusky) needs no explanation when applied to such beings, but one may note a figurative use as '"Black," wicked, iniquitous' or 'Baleful, malignant' (*OED* 3). On Milton's spelling of *fairy*, see above, 297 n.

437–9 *call...arms of Chastity.* Verity explains as 'appeal to the works of Greek philosophers for testimony to the power of purity,' interpreting *Schools* as schools or sects among philosophers. But in what follows the reference is rather to classical myth as it was or might be interpreted by later Neo-platonists. Todd cited St Jerome, *Ad Principiam Virginem* : *Ut autem scias semper virgini-tatem gladium habere pudicitiae....Gentilis quoque error Deas virgines finxit armatas* (Migne, *Pat. Lat.* 22, 629). Warton anticipated some modern critics in finding the whole dialogue of the Brothers 'an amicable contest between fact and philosophy,' with some contrast in the two characters but not enough for dramatic interest. 'The whole dialogue...is little more than a solitary declamation' and 'much resembles the manner of our author's Latin Prolusions...', where philosophy is inforced by pagan fable and poetical allusion.' The last statement overlooks the ascent of the Elder Brother's references, as the dialogue proceeds from the classical to the Christian (see Woodhouse, in iv above).

440–51 Artemis (Roman Diana) and Athene (Minerva) both chose maidenhood and were, some said, brought up together (Diod. Sic. 5. 3. 4). When Aphrodite asked Eros why among all the deities he spared only these two, he replied that Athene frightened him by her severe look and the Gorgon head worn on her breast, and Artemis, since she was always hunting, he could not catch (Lucian, *Dialogue of Aphrodite and Eros*, L.C.L. 7, 343–5, cited by Thyer, reported by

Todd). There is no need of assembling references to Diana as the virgin goddess and huntress (Callimachus, *Hymn* 3; Ovid, *passim*; etc.). The phrase *Fair silver-shafted Queen* (in a line, 441, added in margin of MS.) alludes probably both to her role as huntress and to her role as moon goddess, the shafts suggesting rays of light. Cf. Jonson's song, 'Queene, and Huntresse, chaste, and faire' (*Cynthia's Revels* 5. 6. 1 f.), where, however, she lays aside her 'cristall-shining quiver' before assuming her place as moon goddess. [In Milton's *El* 5. 45–8, when Phoebus brings day, his sister Cynthia, the moon, gives up her celestial office and returns to the woods.]

442 *brinded*: [brindled, streaked (Lockwood; *OED*).]

443–5 *set at nought | The frivolous bolt of Cupid* (and 429: *She may pass on with unblench't majesty*). [Cf. Shakespeare, *Dream* 2. 1. 161–5: 'young Cupid's fiery shaft / Quench'd in the chaste beams of the wat'ry moon, / And the imperial vot'ress passed on, / In maiden meditation, fancy-free. / Yet mark'd I where the bolt of Cupid fell.']

446–7 *that snaky-headed Gorgon sheild | That wise Minerva wore.* [Medusa, one of the three Gorgons, whose face turned beholders to stone, had her head cut off by Perseus, the rescuer of Andromeda. Because, in the chaste Minerva's temple, Medusa had been ravished by Neptune, the goddess had 'changed the Gorgon's locks to ugly snakes. And now to frighten her fear-numbed foes, she still wears that snaky head upon her breast,' i.e. on her shield (Ovid, *M.* 4. 798–803; cf. Homer, *Il.* 5. 738–42). Hughes remarks that N. Comes (*Mythol.* 4. 5) explains this as 'symbolizing the dread which she strikes into her lustful enemies.' Cf. Spenser's Belphoebe, whose 'wondrous bright' eyes 'quite bereav'd the rash beholders sight:...For with dredd Majestie, and awfull ire, / She broke his [Cupid's] wanton darts, and quenched base desire' (*F.Q.* 2. 3. 23). See below, 448 n.]

447 *unconquer'd.* MS. (*Facs.* 412) first had *aeternall*, then *unvanquisht.* [The first change was from a vague to an active and functional word; the second was perhaps made to avoid alliteration (Diekhoff, *PMLA* 55, 755). With *Minerva...unconquer'd Virgin* Le Comte (*Yet Once More*, 12) compares *Palladis invicta virtus* (*Prol* 1, *Works* 12, 124).]

448 *Wherwith...stone?* MS. (*Facs.* 412) first had *freezind*, deleted, followed by *wherwith she freez'd.* [Cf. the epilogue that follows *El* 7 (*Works* 1, 222), in which Milton apologizes for his early erotic pieces and uses the image of cold to describe the effect of his Platonic reading: *Protinus extinctis ex illo tempore* *flammis,* | *Cincta rigent multo pectora nostra gelu.* | *Unde suis frigus metuit puer ipse Sagittis,* | *Et Diomedeam vim timet ipsa Venus.* See the notes on the epilogue, *V.C.* 1, 141–2.]

450 *dash't*: confounded, put to shame, abashed (*OED* 7 b).

451 After *adoration* MS. (*Facs.* 412) first had *of her purenesse*, then *of bright rays*, finally *and blank aw.* [H. Darbishire hears in *rays* an echo of Spenser's description of Britomart, *F.Q.* 3. 1. 43. 8–9, and cites also 4. 6. 33. 5, on her face 'So goodly grave, and full of princely aw.' *blank*: rendering powerless (Lockwood).]

452 Browne observes that Spenser speaks of Heaven's 'voluntary grace, | And soveraine favour towards chastity' (*F.Q.* 3. 8. 29).

452–8 On the association of angels and chastity Todd cited St Ambrose: *Neque mirum si pro vobis angeli militant, quae angelorum moribus militatis. Meretur eorum praesidium castitas virginalis, quorum vitam meretur. Et quid pluribus exsequar laudem castitatis? Castitas enim angelos fecit.* (*De Virginibus* 1. 8. 51–2, Migne, *Pat. Lat.* 16, 202)

453 *sincerely*: [purely, entirely (Lat. *sincerus*).]

454 *liveried*: [wearing the uniform of servants, heavenly servants; cf. 83–5 above, *Nat* 244, *PL* 5. 276–85.] Warton remarked that the essential idea of *liveried Angels lacky her* is repeated, 'without the lowness of allusion and expression,' in 'About her, as a guard Angelic plac't' (*PL* 8. 559).

457 *Tell…no gross ear can hear.* [Cf. *Arc* 72–3, *Comus* 513, 996.]

458 *oft*: here an adjective, but, since the noun modified denotes action, something of the common adverbial sense is implied (*OED*: oft B); cf. 'warn'd by oft experience' (*SA* 382). *convers*: spiritual or mental intercourse, communion (*OED*: sb.¹ 4, whose earliest example is of 1668); the antithesis is perhaps sharpened by the fact that *converse* was also used for sexual intercourse (ibid. 1).

460 *temple of the mind.* The body is described as a temple in John 2. 21, 1 Cor. 3. 16–17, and Shakespeare, *Temp.* 1. 2. 457, *Lucr.* 719 (Todd). [Cf. *PL* 1. 17–18 and the personal passage in Milton's *Apol* quoted above in *Comus* III. 11.]

461 *turns…essence.* The early Warburton and the modern Hughes and Wright [and cf. Carey] see here Milton's 'fundamental idea' (cf. *PL* 5. 469–503) 'that body and spirit are not different kinds but only different degrees in the scale of existence' (Wright). But it is unlikely that his thought had as yet taken this direction; when it was taken, it implied a revision—if not indeed an abandonment—of the whole soul–body dichotomy, though Masson may be right in suggesting that here we have 'a hint of a peculiar doctrine' (see below, 761–73 n.). There seems to be nothing in the present context that is not readily explainable in terms of Renaissance Platonism. J. S. Harrison (*Platonism*, 55) points out that the 'conversion of body to soul' is not a tenet of Plato's own philosophy in any phase. What Milton implies is rather an extension of the doctrine expressed by Spenser: 'For of the soule the bodie forme doth take: / For soule is forme, and doth the bodie make' (*Hymne...of Beautie* 132–3: cited by Browne). This is true for Milton where the soul is dominant; he proceeds to develop the converse of the proposition where the body is dominant (462–74; cf. Verity n.).

462–74   Here, as Warton and later editors recognize, Milton is drawing on, and adapting to his purpose, part of Plato's account of the fortunes of souls after death: 'But...if when it ⟨the soul⟩ departs from the body it is defiled and impure, because it was always with the body and cared for it and loved it and was fascinated by it and its desires and pleasures, so that it thought nothing was true except the corporeal, which one can touch and see...—do you think a soul in this condition will depart pure and uncontaminated?...And...the corporeal is burdensome and heavy....And such a soul is weighed down by this and is dragged back into the visible world, through fear of the invisible and of the other world, and so...it flits about the monuments and the tombs, where shadowy shapes of souls have been seen, figures of those souls which were not set free in purity but retain something of the visible' (*Phaedo* 81 B–D, L.C.L.); '...each pleasure or pain nails it ⟨the soul⟩ as with a nail to the body and rivets it on and makes it corporeal....For because it has the same beliefs and pleasures as the body it is compelled to adopt also the same habits and mode of life...' (ibid. 83D). We must remember with J. S. Harrison (*Platonism*, 48, 50) that in the *Phaedo* Plato is not primarily concerned, as Milton is, with the degrading moral effect of sensuality, but with the soul's quest of pure knowledge and the tendency of all sense experience to impede this quest, confine the soul to the body, and debase its essence. Todd cited Horace's echo of Platonic doctrine: *quin corpus onustum | hesternis vitiis animum quoque praegravat una | atque adfigit humo divinae particulam aurae* (*S.* 2. 2. 77–9).

464   *lavish*: loose, licentious (*OED*: *a.* 1 b). For *leud and lavish* MS. first had *the lascivious* (*Works* 1, 523; *Facs.* 412).

465   *Lets in...inward parts*. [Hughes cites Ps. 51. 6: 'Thou desirest truth in the inward parts.']

467 *Imbodies*: takes on a corporeal and sensual character (a transitive verb, to impart, etc., here used intransitively with the force of a reflexive: *OED*: embody 2). [This is the first recorded occurrence of the word in this sense (Hunter, 'New Words'; Carey).] *imbrutes*: sinks to the level of a brute (*OED* 2; [the first example of the word: Carey]. For transitive use, cf. *PL* 9. 166.

471 *Lingering*. MS. [and Br., 1637], *hovering* (*Facs.* 412, 321, 281).

473 *sensuality*. [MS. and 1645 have *sensualtie* and *sensualty* (*Facs.* 412, 203), which the metre requires. Br. and 1637 (*Facs.* 321, 281) have *sensualitie*, the five syllables of 1673.]

475-9 A commonplace of the defence of poetry (to be used by Milton himself in *RCG*, *Works* 3, 239) was that, while philosophy furnished principles and precepts, poetry added delight to instruction. Here delight is claimed for philosophy itself. See further, 477 n. [The phrase *divine Philosophy* needs no source, but it might have come from *Phaedrus* 239 B. In the *Apol* (*Works* 3, 305–6) Milton was to speak of 'the divine volumes of Plato' and of the sufficiency of 'the noblest Philosophy' (i.e. the ethical philosophy of Plato and other ancient pagans) to keep him, even without Christian teaching, in the path of virtue.]

477 Warton [1785] cited Milton's later phrase applied to education, 'that the Harp of Orpheus was not more charming' (*Educ*, *Works* 4, 280), and 'as sweet and musical / As bright Apollo's lute' (Shakespeare, *L.L.L.* 4. 3. 342–3). Verity finds 'a certain humour in transferring the phrase ⟨from Berowne's description of love⟩ to philosophy.' But in the context the transfer is not hard to justify. The general contrast established is between a life dedicated to truth and virtue (in which, according to the Platonic doctrine adopted, philosophy is a principal agent) and a life given over to sensual indulgence and illusion; and it is here contended that the former (with its agent, philosophy) is superior to the latter even in delight. Now delight had been recognized as an attribute not of philosophy but of poetry; but Milton, as we have seen (475–9 n.), is speaking of philosophy in terms commonly reserved for poetry, as if he were intent on resolving what the Platonic Socrates calls the old quarrel between philosophy and poetry (*Rep.* 10. 607 B), a quarrel which Plato, on whom Milton relies so heavily at this point in *Comus* (see 462–74 n.), had carried on in words assigned to Socrates. In attributing delight to philosophy it is not, then, inappropriate to invoke Apollo, the god of poetry; for had not Socrates himself dedicated some of his last hours to honouring the god in an ode (*Phaedo* 60)?

478-9 *And a perpetual...surfet raigns*. Perhaps there is a glancing contrast

with the feast alluded to by Horace, *S.* 2. 2. 71–9 (see above, 462–74 n.).
crude: [indigestible (*OED* 3 b), with a suggestion of grossness.]

479 *List...hear.* MS. first had *list bro. list, me thought I heared* (*Facs.* 412).

480 MS. adds in margin what appears to be a stage direction: *hallow farre off.*

482 It is not easy to determine the exact meaning Milton attached to the participle *founder'd.* In 'night-founder'd Skiff' (*PL* 1. 204; see n.) *founder'd* certainly cannot mean sunk [Wright, *N&Q* 5, 1958, 203]. Here the meaning may be either engulfed in the darkness of night, like a ship sunk in the sea (Masson), or, conceivably, immobilized by the dark night, like a rider whose horse has fallen or is mired in a bog (*OED*: founder *v.* 2 and 4).

484 *roaving Robber.* MS. first had *curl'd man of ye swoord* (*Facs.* 412). This is deleted, but so is the present reading, added in the margin. Written above the line, and undeleted, is a word which Fletcher [and H. Darbishire] read *hedge,* to be inserted before *man*; but Todd (4, 184) read *hedger* as alternative to the phrase *curl'd...swoord.*

488–9 Before reaching the present reading, MS. had tried *a just Defence,* deleted, and the discarded idea, *he may chaunce scratch,* or *had best looke to his forehead. heere be brambles,* deleted. At this point MS. adds, as stage direction, *he hallows* (*hallo* deleted) *the guardian Dæmon hallows agen & enters in the habit of shepheard.* Br. has: *he hallows and is answered, the guardian dæmon comes in habited like a shepheard* (*Facs.* 412, 322).

490 *iron.* MS. first had *pointed,* deleted.   *stakes*: [i.e. their swords].

491 *Spir.* (MS. *Dæ.*: also at 500, 512 (*Shep.* deleted, though *Sheph.* left at 510), 608, 616.]

492 *father.* MS. and Br. (*Facs.* 412, 322) have the correct reading *fathers* (i.e. father's).

492–511 As we have noticed (above, II, III), various elements contributed to the tone of Milton's *Mask.* Here the chivalric (479–91) is immediately succeeded by the pastoral (492–511). The name *Thyrsis* at once converts *my father[s] Shepherd* into a figure of pastoral poetry, a shepherd singer (as in Theocritus I and Virgil, *E.* 7). Taking advantage, as Masson notes, of the etymology of *madrigal* (< Ital. *madrigale,* a shepherd's song < *mandra,* a flock) and its current use, for an elaborate composition in parts, Milton combines with pastoralism a compliment to Henry Lawes, who played the role of the Attendant Spirit and was a composer of madrigals. The rhymed pentameter couplets of this passage follow a practice common in pastoral dramas such as Jonson's *Sad Shepherd* (Todd) and Fletcher's *F. Shep.* (Warton).

493–4 Todd compared Horace's words about Orpheus, *rapidos morantem / fluminum lapsus* (*C.* 1. 12. 9–10). *hudling*: crowding together (*OED*: huddle 6); the reference, presumably, is to the piling up of the waters as they are delayed by the music.

495 *And sweetn'd every muskrose*: bestowed an added fragrance on this already fragrant flower. *dale*: replacing MS. *valley*.

496 *Swain*: MS. *shepheard*.

496–8 Dunster MS. quotes *The Sad Shepherd* 2. 4. 9 f.: 'Hath any Vermin broke into your Fold?' etc. (*Ben Jonson* 7, 31). [The question is a bit of traditional pastoralism. *Slipt from the fold*. So in Br. (*Facs.* 322). MS. first had *leapt ore the penne*, replaced by *slip't from his fold* (*Works* 1, 528; *Facs.* 414).]

498 *Weather*: wether.

500 *his next joy*: i.e. the second Brother, thought of as the next in succession to his father's title and estates. Trent would read *next* as 'closest,' 'dearest,' and apply to the Elder Brother.

501 *toy*: trifle.

505 *To this*: in comparison with this.

507 *How chance she is not*. The construction occurs in Shakespeare and other writers, e.g. 'How chance my daughter is not with you?' (*Per.* 4. 1. 23: cited by Todd). [As Verity remarked—and later J. F. Bense, *Englische Studien* 46, 1913, 333–5 (the latter is cited in Carey)—Thyrsis' question is unnecessary, since he already knew the Lady was in Comus' power (569–79); but, as Verity also says, 'the enquiry leads up to the explanation that follows.']

508 *sadly*: seriously, in earnest (*OED* 7). [*without blame*: without our being blameworthy (Hughes).]

512 *vain*: idle, devoid of significance (*OED* 1). *fabulous*: merely fictitious.

514 *sage Poets taught by th'heav'nly Muse*. Todd thinks that Milton here alludes particularly to Tasso, who refers to the heavenly Muse in *G.L.* 1. 2; but he does so with an apology: 'If fictions light I mix with truth divine, / And fill these lines with others praise than thine' (Fairfax). Verity sees an allusion to a series of poets from Homer to Tasso, but 'especially Spenser, who influenced Milton greatly.' [Cf. *IlPen* 117–20 and n., and 'our sage and serious Poet Spencer'

(*Areop, Works* 4, 311).] But the context (515–17) seems rather to support Keightley, who refers in general terms to passages in Homer and Virgil cited below, and Masson, who takes the allusion to be especially to these poets. In any case *heav'nly Muse* cannot be used here in the full Christian sense in which Milton himself claims her inspiration (*Nat* 15, *PL* 1. 6, 3. 19); rather the Muse is called heavenly because poetic 'abilities, wheresoever they be found, are the inspired guift of God' (*RCG, Works* 3, 238). [Milton's reference is in accord with the tradition of allegorical interpretation developed by Christian writers from their pagan predecessors, and exemplified in *Comus* itself by the use of Haemony and indeed the whole Circean myth. With 513 cf. 996.]

516 *Chimera's.* The fire-breathing monster, with a lion's head, goat's body, and dragon's tail, is referred to by Homer, *Il.* 6. 179–82, Virgil, *A.* 6. 288, Ovid, *M.* 9. 647, and Milton, *PL* 2. 628. *inchanted Iles.* Verity suggests the 'wandring Islands' of Spenser, *F.Q.* 2. 12. 11; Elton, such islands as that of Calypso (Homer, *Od.* 5. 1 f., 12. 447 f.); Wright, more appropriately to the context, 'such as the isle of Circe.'

517 *And rifted Rocks...to Hell.* Such a cavern gave Aeneas entrance to the nether world (Virgil, *A.* 6. 237 f.). Elton adds Taenarus in Laconia (Virgil, *G.* 4. 467). Todd compared 'Sent through the rifted rocks' (Drayton, *Poly.* 14. 312). Dunster MS. refers to the underworld journeys of Odysseus and Aeneas and to Sandys' *Relation* (1615, 279): 'This [Avernus] was supposed the entrance into hell by ignorant Antiquity: where they offered infernal sacrifice to Pluto, and the Manes, here said to give answers.' [Cf. also Spenser's cave of Mammon (*F.Q.* 2. 7. 20–1), which Milton referred to in *Areop* (*Works* 4, 311).

519–38 Having prepared his auditors for the sort of story he is about to tell, Thyrsis rapidly repeats the account of Comus' parentage and activities given in his prologue (46–77), to the notes on which the reader is referred.

519 *navil*: navel, centre of a country or district (*OED* 2), a usage paralleling the Greek *omphalos* (applied to Delphi as the centre of the earth) and Latin *umbilicus*. Todd cited 'Up tow'rds the Navell then, of England' (Drayton, *Poly.* 23. 147).

520 *cypress shades*. Verity remarks that the gloomy shade of the cypress, with its thick foliage, is appropriate to the scene of the 'abhorred rites' of Comus. The association of cypress with death and burial (above, *EpWin* 22 and n.) adds further to the appropriateness. [On the meaning Milton commonly attaches to *shades* see above, 62 n., 428 n.]

522 *Deep skill'd.* MS. tried *enur'd*, then *deepe learnt*, finally the present reading (*Works* 1, 530; *Facs.* 414).

525 *With many murmurs mixt*: the incantations that accompanied the mixing of the magic potion. Todd compared *cantusque sacros et conscia miscet | murmura* (Statius, *Theb.* 9. 733–4) and *nel cerchio accolto, | mormorò potentissime parole* (Tasso, *G.L.* 13. 6). For *murmurs* as beneficent incantations see *Arc* 60 and n.

526–9 *The visage. . . | Character'd in the face.* The metaphor is that of the alteration of a coin whereby the image originally stamped or engraved on it is destroyed and another substituted—a beast's head for the original human visage which betokened and expressed rationality.

528 *unmoulding*: destroying the mould or form. *mintage*: the stamp or impression put on a coin.

529 *Character'd.* Editors cite Shakespeare: 'the table wherein all my thoughts / Are visibly character'd and engrav'd' (*T.G.V.* 2. 7. 3–4), and 'character'd in my brow, / The story of sweet chastity's decay' (*Lucr.* 807–8).

530 *hilly crofts*: MS. *pastur'd lawns*, deleted, and replaced by present reading. *crofts*: pieces of 'enclosed ground used for tillage or pasture' (*OED* 1).

531 *brow*: be on the brow of, overlook (rare; this is the earliest example in *OED* 1). *bottom*: valley or dell (*OED* 4b), here used with the force of an adjective.

532 *monstrous*: composed of monsters; cf. *Lyc* 158 and n. The force of *monster* here implied is of something unnatural; the word was applied, *inter alia*, to imaginary creatures of different forms, animal and human (*OED* 3). *rout*: see above, note on Direction following 92. *heard to howl.* Todd recalled the action of Comus' mother Circe, *longis Hecaten ululatibus orat* (Ovid, *M.* 14. 405).

533 *stabl'd wolves*: (1) put or sheltered in a stable: which seems possible only if we think of the 'stable' as confining rather than sheltering the wolves and of their complaining like the lions at their bonds in Virgil's description of the sounds heard from Circe's island (*A.* 7. 15–20). (2) Browne compares *Triste lupus stabulis* (Virgil, *E.* 3. 80). This Verity accepts as possibly explaining *stabl'd*, i.e., having got into the sheepfold (Lat. *stabulum*); but he also notes (3) that in *PL* 11. 752 *stabl'd* means 'made their ⟨the Sea-monsters'⟩ lair.' This meaning [accepted by Trent], if dominant here, would make the phrase equivalent to 'wolves in their lairs' [favoured by Hughes, 1937]—not 'their haunts,' as Verity infers. But *OED* recognizes no such meaning for *stable*, and strictly speaking the context in *PL* suggests no more than a shelter. The next phrase, *tigers at their prey*, supports the second meaning above. [One may not think so; the tigers are introduced by *or*, as a different kind of idea. The second meaning may seem very strained; the first, involving a recollection of Virgil, quite probable, since Milton has just been describing Circean transformations.]

534 *Doing...rites*: Lat. *sacra facere* (Verity).

537 *sense.* MS. first had *spell*, deleted (*Facs.* 414).

538 *unweeting*: unwitting, not knowing (of the danger). See above, *FInf* 23 n.

539 *by then*: by the time that. *chewing* refers to the flocks as ruminant.

539–40 Warton found here a reminiscence of Spenser (*F.Q.* 1. 1. 23): 'As gentle Shepheard in sweete even-tide, / ...High on an hill, his flocke to vewen wide, / Markes which do byte their hasty supper best.'

541 *Knot-grass*: a term loosely applied to various plants with knotty stems (*OED* 2). *dew-besprent*: besprinkled with dew. Browne notes that *besprent* is Spenserian (e.g. *S.C., December* 135). Todd cited 'dewe besprent' from Drayton, *Poly.* 9. 100. [Cf. the same phrase in G. Fletcher (*C.T.* 2. 12), quoted in *Lyc* 168 n.]

543–4 *With Ivy canopied...Hony-suckle.* Warton compared 'Quite over-canopied with luscious woodbine' (Shakespeare, *Dream* 2. 1. 251). *flaunting*: waving gaily like a plume or banner (*OED* 1). [MS. first had *suckling*, replaced by *blowing*, by *flaunting*, by *blowing* again, finally *flaunting* (as in Br. and 1637: *Facs.* 324, 283) restored (*Works* 1, 532; *Facs.* 414).]

545 *Wrapt in...melancholy.* See *IlPen*.

546 *To meditate upon my rural minstrelsie.* MS., Br., 1637, and 1645 (*Works* 1, 532; *Facs.* 414, 324, 283, 205) all omit *upon*, which is evidently a misprint, since it gives the line six feet. *meditate* (Lat. *meditari*): practise (cf. *Lyc* 66 n.). Editors cite *silvestrem tenui musam meditaris avena* (Virgil, *E.* 1. 2); Browne, *Brit. Past.* 2. 2. 27: 'To meditate the songs they meant to play.' Warton found the phrase *rural minstrelsy* in Browne, *Brit. Past.* 1. 1. 15 and also in John Davies, *Shepherd's Pipe* (1614), sig. G6ᵛ (*Complete Works of John Davies of Hereford*, ed. Grosart, 1878, 2, Commendatory Poems, p. 21, line 228). Todd added *2 Return from Parnassus* 1. 2. 214, in reference to Spenser.

547 *fancy.* The context suggests the combination of two meanings: fancy as the inventive faculty exercised in poetry and music, and fancy as associated with desire. *close.* The primary meaning is conclusion, but in the context the word strongly suggests its technical sense in music, the conclusion of a phrase, theme, or movement, a cadence (*OED*: *sb.*² 2).

548 *was up*: had begun (cf. the common phrase, 'The hunt is up': Verity).

549 *barbarous dissonance*: in contrast with Thyrsis' *rural minstrelsie* (546). Since the reference is to the scene enacted by Comus and his rout (93–145), we must suppose that, despite the ordered lyric movement of the lines spoken, 'the Measure' was danced to the accompaniment of wild noise from the followers. [The phrase reappears in *PL* 7. 32, in the lines on the slaying of Orpheus by 'Bacchus and his revellers.']

550 *listen'd them*. [For the transitive use Todd cited 'List'ning their fear' (Shakespeare, *Macb*. 2. 2. 29).]

551 *stop*: cessation—that ordered by Comus at 145.

552 *frighted*: MS. *flighted*; Br., 1637, 1645, 1673, *frighted* (*Facs*. 414, 324, 283, 205). The MS. reading was first noticed by Peck (147). Newton restored *flighted* (printing *drowsy-flighted* as a compound), argued that *frighted* was 'an errour of the press' that escaped Milton's eye, and supported his reading by reference to the lines in Shakespeare's *2 H. VI* (quoted below under 552–3) which, he believed, had suggested Milton's image. Most editors have followed Newton. Warton, Todd, Keightley, and the Columbia editors are exceptions. The error (if error it was) evidently originated, not in 'the press,' but in Br. That the Cambridge MS. gives the reading Milton desired is strongly supported by the absence of any correction here in that much-corrected document. Verity argues that *drowsy-flighted* 'is in form an *essentially* Miltonic compound,' and compares 'flowry-kirtl'd' (253) and 'rushy-fringed' (889); *drowsie frighted* would of course have to be read as two separate and in some degree contrasting words. It is scarcely necessary to mention Bowle's emendation, *drowsy-freighted*. The choice lies between *frighted* and *flighted*.

[It seems best to let the above note stand (whether or not Woodhouse would have revised it), but some remarks need to be qualified. While one cannot take account of all the popular and school editions, it may be said that the majority of modern editors have not followed Newton in printing *flighted*. That reading is adopted by Masson, Verity, Elton, Moody, W. A. Wright (*Poetical Works*, Cambridge, 1903), Grierson, Hughes (1937), Mack, Hanford, G. and M. Bullough, M. Nicolson, I. G. MacCaffrey. As Woodhouse says, *frighted* is the reading of Todd, Keightley, and Columbia (Warton printed *flighted* but defended *frighted*), but they are hardly exceptions; *frighted* is read also by Rolfe,

923

Bell, Browne, Trent, Beeching (*Poetical Works*, Oxford, 1900), Patterson (*Student's Milton*), H. F. Fletcher, Brooks and Hardy, E. M. W. and P. B. Tillyard (*Comus*, etc., 1952), H. Darbishire, B. A. Wright (1938 and *Milton's Poems*, London, 1956), Hughes (1957), Shawcross, Bush, Prince, Carey. Lascelles Abercrombie had a cogent defence of the poetical, logical, and textual claims of *frighted* in *Proc. of the Leeds Philosophical ...Society* 2. 1 (1928), 1–5. Also, it seems dubious to hold by the Cambridge MS. as firm evidence of Milton's unaltered intention against the combined weight of Br. and the three editions. That MS. does not record all of Milton's changes: e.g. it has, without correction, *such tow* at 290 and *moorie* at 432 (*Facs.* 406, 412), while *Two such* and *moorish* are—like *frighted*—in Br., 1637, 1645, 1673. And some larger changes appeared first in 1645 (e.g. 607, 608, and notes). See the following note.]

552–3 *Gave respit...curtain'd sleep.* Newton (see beginning of 552 n.) compared: 'And now loud-howling wolves arouse the jades / That drag the tragic melancholy night, / Who with their drowsy, slow, and flagging wings...' (Shakespeare, 2 *H. VI* 4. 1. 3–5). Warton [who, as we saw, read *flighted* but defended *frighted*] paraphrased Milton thus: 'The *drowsy* steeds of Night, who were *affrighted* on this occasion, at the *barbarous dissonance*....' He added other passages on the car and steeds of Night (or Sleep): 'All-drowsy Night, who in a car of jet, / By steeds of iron-grey...drawn through the sky' (Browne, *Brit. Past.* 2. 1. 777–9); 'And, in a noys-less Coach all darkly dight, / Takes with him Silence, Drowsiness and Night' (Sylvester, *D.W.W.* 2. 3. 1. 598–9, Grosart, 1, 169). Warton further noticed that Milton had precedent for transferring the car and steeds of Night to Sleep in Claudian: *Umentes iam noctis equos...Somnus | frena regens* (15. 213–14: 1, 114); and Statius: *Sopor obvius illi | Noctis agebat equos* (*Theb.* 2. 59–60). *respit.* The word will serve whether it be from disturbance to their drowsiness in flight or to their feeling of fright.

litter. OED affords no support for Verity's gloss, 'chariot.' It explains as a 'vehicle...containing a couch shut in by curtains, and carried on men's shoulders or by beasts' (2a)—here evidently the latter. In transferring the equipage of Night to Sleep Milton appropriately substituted a litter for a chariot; but he thinks of it (Keightley noted) as drawn, not borne. *close curtain'd sleep.* Thyer compared 'The curtain'd sleep' (Shakespeare, *Macb.* 2. 1. 51); Todd, 'Spread thy close curtain...night' (*Romeo* 3. 2. 5).

554 *sound*: the Lady's song (229–42). *soft.* MS. shows hesitation between *soft*, *still*, and *sweet*; Br. *sweete.* *solemn breathing sound*: a sound breathing solemnity.

554–7 [Comparing these lines with Comus' praise of the Lady's singing (see 248–51 n.), Watkins (*Anatomy*, 5) comments: 'Sound, with its accompanying sensation of actual breathing, is conveyed' in the most seductive terms, yet images of smell are less sensual than those of touch, and 'there is subtle differentiation between the song's effect on Comus and on the Attendant Spirit.']

555 *Rose like a stream of rich distill'd perfumes.* MS. shows a good deal of revision (*Works* 1, 533; *Facs.* 414): *rose like* (*the softe*, deleted) *a steame of* (*slow*, deleted) *rich distill'd perfumes. stream*: MS., Br., 1637, *steame*; 1645, *steam* (*Facs.* 414, 324, 283, 205). Warton regarded the *stream* of 1673 as a manifest misprint, and Verity thought that it spoiled the metaphor. But the matter is not quite so easily settled. It is true that *steam* was used of 'an odorous exhalation or fume' (*OED* 1 b), which accounts for the earlier reading and perhaps for the original *slow distill'd*, Milton taking his image, as Warton suggested, from the actual process of making perfume; he used the word of Abel's sacrifice: flesh 'with Incense strew'd,' 'Consum'd with…grateful steame' (*PL* 11. 439, 442). But the other examples given under this and related meanings in *OED* suggest odours of varying degrees of unpleasantness; and a sense of the weight of connotation may have induced Milton to make the change to *stream* used figuratively, which does not really, when *slow* is changed to *rich*, spoil any metaphor. [Even if *stream* was Milton's own late change, which is extremely doubtful, it may be thought that the word changes an image that is both suggestive and logical to one that is commonplace and it seems a less accurate term for the process of distillation; the textual authority for *steam* is fourfold.] For the general comparison of sweet odours and musical sounds, Warton cited Shakespeare, *Twel.* 1. 1. 5–7; 'Yet let it like an odour rise / to all the Sences here, / And fall like sleep upon their eies, / or musick in their eare' (*Vision of Delight* 51–4, Ben Jonson 7, 465); and Bacon: '…the breath of flowers is far sweeter in the air (where it comes and goes like the warbling of music)' (*Of Gardens, Works* 6, 487).

556–9 *Silence…so displac't.* [Silence was so charmed (for *took* see *Nat* 98 n.) that she wished to give up her own essential nature or being if she might always be replaced by such melody.] In *PL* 4. 604 Milton reduced the conceit to 'Silence was pleas'd.'

559 *was all ear*: listened intently. *OED* (ear: *sb.*¹ 3 d) gives no example before 1786, and Warton's instances do not exactly parallel the phrase. [The figure is not uncommon. Newton (on *PL* 6. 350) quoted Pliny, *N.H.* 2. 5. 14: *quisquis est deus,… totus est sensus, totus visus, totus auditus, totus animae, totus animi,* *totus sui.* English examples are much closer: 'all eare to hear new utterance flow' (*PL* 4. 410); 'all Eare' in the quotation from Drummond in *IlPen* 57 n.; 'who now is growne all eye' (Donne, *Second Anniversary* 200); 'to growe all soule' (Habington, *To...I.C.* 28, *Poems*, ed. K. Allott, 96).]

564 *Amaz'd*: as Verity notes, stronger in its meaning than in later usage: 'stunned or stupified as by a blow' (*OED* 1). Cf. above, 355 n. and *Nat* 69 n.
    harrow'd...fear. Cf. 'It harrows me with fear' (Shakespeare, *Ham.* 1. 1. 44).

567 *Lawns*: open spaces between woods; glades (*OED*: *sb.*² 1). Cf. *Nat* 85, *L'All* 71.

570 *wisard*: not always used in pejorative sense (cf. *Nat* 23 and n.); hence *damn'd* added here.   *disguise*: Comus appearing as if 'some harmles Villager' (166) or 'Shepherd' (270).

573 *aidless.* MS. first had *helplesse*, deleted.

574 *such two*: the two Brothers (above, 283–90).

579 *further*: [*furder* in MS., Br., 1645; *farther*, 1637 (*Works* 1, 535; *Facs.* 416, 325, 205, 284). See above, 226 n., 320 n.]

582–3 *is this...me...?*: how does this compare with the assurance you gave me?

583–98 *Yes...on stubble.* Warton commented: 'This confidence of the Elder Brother in favour of the final efficacy of virtue, holds forth a very high strain of philosophy.' For Todd's comment on its religious import, see above, note on 358–598; and below, 586–7 n.

584 *period*: sentence (*OED* 10).

585 *for me*: ['for my part, by my judgement' (Hughes, 1937).]

586–7 *that power...Chance.* The Christian view of Providence rules out chance and transforms fate. Cf. God's words: 'Necessitie and Chance / Approach not mee, and what I will is Fate' (*PL* 7. 172–3). [See the note on *Time* 22.]

588 *Vertue...never hurt.* [A main theme of Socrates in Plato's *Apology*.]

590 *mischief*: evil intent.

590–1 The thought is related to another Christian conception, God's power to bring good out of evil [cf. *PL* 1. 162–5, etc.].

592–6 [Cf. *PL* 2. 137–42, 11. 50–3.]

593 *at last*: ['at the end of time, in the Last Judgment' (Prince).]

596–8 *if this fail...stubble.* If (as is clearly considered unthinkable) this belief proved deceptive or deficient on trial (*OED* 4), there would be no alternative but to regard evil as dominant and the whole terrestrial world from its foundations to the pillared firmament as rotten and utterly insecure. [For the rhetorical asseveration, if not the idea, cf. Shakespeare, *W. Tale* 2. 1. 100–3 (Steevens, in Todd).] *pillar'd firmament*: cf. 'the pillard frame of Heaven' (*PR* 4. 455); 'pillars of heaven' (Job 26. 11). The universe is imagined as a building with *earths base* as its foundation and the sky as a dome supported on pillars. [The phrase in *Comus* clearly refers to the sphere of fixed stars (Svendsen, *Science*, 55).]

built on stubble. This curious phrase, for which no precedent has been found, seems to have escaped the attention of editors. It may perhaps carry a threefold suggestion: as stubble would furnish a very insecure foundation (cf. the house built on sand, Matt. 7. 26–7); as it would rot away (cf. the firmament, 597); as it is worthless and fit only for burning (*OED* 2b quotes a sermon of 1596: 'But sinners are stubble, and their sentence is, Burne them'). [Biblical uses of stubble associate it with wickedness and the quick destruction of the wicked by wind or fire: e.g. Ps. 83. 13, Jer. 13. 24, Mal. 4. 1, and especially 1 Cor. 3. 12: 'Now if any man build upon this foundation gold, silver, precious stones, wood, hay, stubble....']

603 *the sooty flag of Acheron.* [Todd quoted P. Fletcher, *Apoll.* 2. 39: 'All hell run out, and sooty flagges display.']

604 *Harpyes*: described by Virgil as foul and ravenous bird-women (*A.* 3. 214–18) and placed, with other monsters, at the gate of the nether world (ibid. 6. 285–9). *Hydra's*: probably not the Lernean Hydra or huge serpent slain by Hercules and grouped with the Harpies by Virgil (6. 287), but the fifty-throated monster dwelling within the portals of Tartarus (ibid. 6. 576–7), or perhaps, since Milton uses the plural, its imagined brood. Cf. *PL* 2. 628. Warton noted the combination in Sylvester (*D.W.W.* 2. 1. 3. 260–1, Grosart, 1, 116): 'And th'ugly Gorgons, and the Sphinxes fel, / Hydraes and Harpies.' [*monstrous forms.* MS., Br., and 1637 (*Facs.* 416, 326, 285) had *monstrous bug(g)s*. C. S. Lewis (*RES* 8, 1932, 174), with a reminder of the old and strong sense of *bugs*, regrets the erasure of the 'more forcible, native word...in favour of the comparatively colourless loan word.']

605 *'Twixt Africa and Inde.* Verity explains as covering (west to east) virtually the whole world [within ancient limits]. The phrase may suggest something of this kind (like Dr Johnson's 'Survey mankind, from China to Peru'); but Warton cited Fairfax, *Jerusalem* 15. 51: 'All monsters which hot Affricke doth forth send.' [Dunster cited T. Hudson's *Judith*: 'From Araby, from Ynde, to Affrik shore' (Sylvester, *D.W.W.*, 1621, 705); and Sylvester, *Bethulians Rescue*: 'som Monster / New brought from Africk, or from Inde' (4. 351–2, Grosart, 2, 194).]

606 *restore his purchase back*: MS. *release his new got prey*, deleted, and present reading substituted. *purchase*: something attained by effort, sometimes, as here, with the implication of seizure or theft, as in the original *prey* (*OED* 8; Spenser, *F.Q.* 1. 3. 16).

607 *curls*. Verity notes that the (otherwise very different) Comus of Jonson's *Pleasure* (8) has 'his haire curld.' *to a foul death*: MS. *& cleave his scalpe*. Br. and 1637 follow MS. (*Facs.* 416, 326, 285); change made in 1645.

608 *Curs'd as his life*: MS. *downe to the lowest hipps* (*lowest* deleted). Br. and 1637 follow final MS. reading; change made in 1645. [C. S. Lewis (*RES* 8, 1932, 174) remarks that both readings in 607 (see note) and 608 'are full of energy; but the one is physical energy, demonstrable by the actor, the other is moral. Again Milton moves away from the theatre.']

609 *yet*: despite the fact that against Comus it is of no avail. *Emprise*: undertaking, or perhaps (abstract) enterprise (*OED* 1 and 2), of frequent use in *F.Q.* in first sense and occasional use in second (e.g. 5. 4. 2, 6. 4. 33); cf. 'bould emprise' in *PL* 11. 642.

610 *sword*: MS. *steele*, deleted, replaced by *swoord* (*Facs.* 416). *do thee little stead*: be of little use (*OED* 13 b). [Cf. the famous drinking song in *Gammer Gurton's Needle*: 'A little bread shall do me stead.'] MS. substituted *small availe* for *little stead*, then restored the original phrase.

611 *Far other arms*: i.e. spiritual, not physical. [With this use of *other* cf. *Lyc* 174 and n.]

612 *hellish charms*. Warton noted the phrase in Shakespeare, *R. III* 3. 4. 61. Todd added P. Fletcher (*P.I.* 11. 26) and R.A., *The Valiant Welshman* (1615), in a passage immediately following the reference to moly in the same play which is quoted below, 635–6 n.

613 *bare*: mere, without any addition (*OED* 11). *unthred*: MS. *unquilt*, deleted, replaced by *unthred*.

613–14 *unthred...sinews*. Warton compared: 'Go, charge my goblins that they grind their joints / ...shorten up their sinews' (Shakespeare, *Temp.* 4. 1. 259–60). Verity's explanations of *unthred* (dislocate) and *crumble* (cause to shrivel up) seem less than satisfactory. Rather, this is a single image: the magician can as it were draw out the sinews (threads) that control the joints and scatter them in fragments.

618-40 *a certain Shepherd Lad...furies apparition.* Some editors [e.g. Newton, Masson, Bell, Verity, Moody, Fletcher, Bullough, Blondel] see here a veiled reference to Charles Diodati and the intimate companionship to be recorded in *EpDam* (especially 147–52), although we need not take literally (as Masson appears to do and Verity does) the allusion to 'Diodati's botanical knowledge, and his habit of regaling Milton with the same' (Masson, *P.W.* 3, 229): this is the pastoral poet's way of recording Diodati's talk of his medical interests (*EpDam* 150–2) and—if indeed Diodati is meant—his ethical ideals (*Comus*). Hanford (*TLS*, 3 Nov. 1932, 815; *Handbook*; *Poems*, 1953) identifies the *Shepherd Lad* with Milton himself and sees in the lines a record of his friendship with Lawes, who as Thyrsis spoke the words. In this view it is Milton who would *hearken even to extasie* (624; cf. *IlPen* 165) to Lawes' singing (for other compliments to Lawes see 86–8 and 493–5). Wright supports this view: *Of small regard to see to* (619) is 'characteristic ⟨of Milton⟩ in its proud modesty, corresponding to the "uncouth swain" of *Lycidas* ⟨186⟩'; and *vertuous plant and healing herb* (620) are Milton's 'knowledge and skill,' especially 'the platonic philosophy' represented by Haemony (see 637 n.). [Prince follows Hanford and Wright. N. Frye also sees a reference to Milton himself, but takes Haemony as representing poetry. Some far-fetched notions may be mentioned. B. G. Hall (*TLS*, 12 Oct. 1933, 691) proposed Nathaniel Weld, who died young in 1633 and was mourned by his friend William Lathum in an elegy which included a reference to a 'Thessalian herb' (cf. *Lyc* 142–51 n.).] J. A. Himes (*Miltonic Enigmas*, 1921, 11–19) makes the *Shepherd Lad* no other than St Paul, a man of undistinguished presence (2 Cor. 10. 10), 'a shepherd over the churches,' the champion of purity against Corinthian licentiousness, who feels *extasie* in contemplating the truth of Christ; haemony, from the Greek *haima*, blood, 'is the blood-stained cross of Christ,' unknown and despised by the worldly (633; cf. 1 Cor. 1. 21–5); its prickly leaf symbolizes earthly tribulation, its golden flower heavenly glory. [J. S. Lawry (*Shadow*, 85–6) finds it 'difficult to avoid the suggestion' that the *Shepherd Lad* 'is the redemptive Christ whose "dim," earthly cross and crown of thorns darkly image a heavenly golden flower.']

619 *Of small regard to see to*: of small account in appearance (*OED*: regard 5), to look at.

620 *vertuous*: potent (to produce effects): *OED* 5 and above, 165 n.

624 *extasie*: ecstasy, rapture (*IlPen* 165 n.).

625 *scrip*: small leather bag such as was carried by shepherds. Cf. Fletcher, *F. Shep.* 1. 1. 21: 'hanging scrip of finest cordevan.'

626 *simples*: herbs with medicinal properties (from simples, medicines made of simple, not compounded, ingredients, the name being transferred to the herbs: *OED* B 6). *names*: replacing MS. *hews*, deleted.

627 *faculties*: efficient properties (*OED* 2).

628 *small unsightly root*. Epithets and context suggest that *root* here means the whole plant (*OED* 2). Homer (*Od.* 10. 302–6) mentions the root of moly but also says that the gift of Hermes was the whole plant; see below, 635–6 n.

628–40 See especially 635–6 n., 637 n.

629 *of divine effect*. The force attached to *divine* will depend on the interpretation adopted of the whole passage. It could mean either given by God or merely of surpassing excellence (*OED* 2 and 5 b). The adjective *divine* was applied to moly itself by Sir John Davies: 'Moly the gods most soveraigne herbe divine' (*Of Tabacco* 2, *Poems*, ed. C. Howard, 50; ed. Grosart, 1876, 2, 226) and by Milton (*El* 1. 88).

632–3 *but not in this soyl:* | *...like esteem'd*. This is the reading of 1637, 1645, 1673; MS. (*Facs.* 420) has no punctuation after *soile*; Br. omits 631–6. A supposed difficulty in interpretation, coupled with the extra syllable in 632, led early commentators (reported by Warton and Todd) to infer corruption or confusion. Fenton printed 'little esteem'd,' but later reverted to the original reading. Newton was prepared to read either '*but* in this soil, | Unknown and like esteem'd' (i.e. unknown and unesteemed) or '*not* in this soil: | Unknown, and like esteem'd.' Hurd went further: '*not* in this soil | Unknown, *though light esteem'd*'; and Seward suggested '*but* in this soil | Unknown and *light* esteem'd.' Warburton also adopted '*light* esteem'd.' Warton, keeping the original reading, remarked [1785]: 'Milton, notwithstanding his singular skill in music, appears to have had a very bad ear; and it is hard to say, on what principle he modulated his lines.' Todd, also keeping the original reading, sprang to Milton's defence. Modern editors retain the original reading. For interpretation, see below, 635–6 n. S. Elledge (*MLN* 58, 1943, 552–3) noted an interesting parallel in a fragment preserved in Demetrius' *De Elocutione* (106) and now attributed to Sappho: 'Like the hyacinth-flower, that shepherd folk 'mid the mountains tread | Underfoot, and low on the earth her bloom dark-splendid is shed' (tr. A. S. Way, in *Demetrius on Style*, ed. W. R. Roberts, 1902, 121). As Elledge further notes, Milton refers to or apparently echoes Demetrius' treatise in *Educ* (*Works* 4, 286), *Apol* (ibid. 3, 300), and *DDD* (ibid. 3, 491).

634 *clouted shoon.* The phrase occurs in Shakespeare, 2 *H. VI* 4. 2. 195, and Drayton, *Poly.* 23. 249. It means boots with iron plates (clouts) nailed to the soles (Warton), or, possibly, patched boots (Verity); cf. *OED*: clouted, *ppl. a.*¹ 2 and 1.

635–6 *that Moly | ...Ulysses gave.* For *Moly* MS. (*Facs.* 420) first had *ancient Moly, ancient* deleted; and for *Hermes, Mercury,* changed to *Hermes once.* Odysseus tells (*Od.* 10. 302–6) how Hermes plucked up and gave him, against the charms of Circe, a potent herb, hard for man to dig, and by the gods called moly, black at the root but with a milk-white flower. Ovid (*M.* 14. 291–2) refers briefly to Mercury's gift and to the black root and white flower. G. W. Whiting (*Milieu*, 87) notes that Pliny (*N.H.* 25. 8. 26–7) gives moly a golden-yellow flower (*florem luteum*), perhaps significant as suggesting Milton's *bright golden flowre* (632). From Homer and Ovid came the later references to the power of moly against the charms of witchcraft. Warton cited: 'Heere is my Moly of much fame, / In Magicks often used' (*Muses Elizium* 5. 205–6, Drayton, 3, 290; [cf. S. R. Watson, *N&Q* 176, 1939, 243–4]); and noted that in W. Browne's *Inner Temple Masque* (128–9) Circe herself uses moly as a charm (this is quite characteristic of the piece—see II above—which altogether eschews the moralized meanings that commentators found in Homer and Ovid). Todd quoted R. A., *The Valiant Welshman* (1615), 4. 2 (Tudor Facsimile Texts, 1913):

> No force of sword can conquer hellish fiends,
> By blacke inchantments made to take thy life...
> About thee take this precious soveraigne herbe,
> That Mercury to wise Ulisses gave,
> To keepe him from the rage of Cyrces charmes.
> This precious herbe, maugre the force of hell,
> From blackest sorcery keepes sound and well.

Various attempts have been made to connect Homer's moly with actual plants. Todd, in his 1798 edition of *Comus* but not in his Variorum, quoted Joannes Wierus, *De Praestigiis Daemonum* (Basle, 1583, 579) to the effect that moly was later known as *fuga daemonum* (Le Comte, 637 n. below). Warton suggested that 'Milton, through the whole of the context, had his eye on Fletcher,' in whose *F. Shep.* (2. 2. 15–18) the magic properties of moly are attributed to rhamnus (misprinted as *ramuus* and *ramuns* in the editions available to Milton: Le Comte, 291). This fact led Le Comte (637 n. below) to ask if Milton might have identified moly with rhamnus.

Moly of course attracted a long line of allegorical commentators. The Homeric scholiast, Eustathius (*Commentarii in Odysseam*, ed. J. G. Stallbaum, Leipzig, 1825, 1, 381), reported a myth to account for the plant's name, root, and flower, and suggested that Hermes represented reason (*logos*) and moly education (*paideia*), beginning with the black root of ignorance and culminating in the white flower of knowledge (Le Comte, 286–7). Arthur Golding is one exemplar of the ethical tradition: 'And what is else herbe Moly than the gift of stayednesse / And temperance...' (*Ovid's Metamorphosis*, 1567, Epist. Ded., 278–9). Roger Ascham (*English Works*, 227–8) took moly as 'the study of vertue, hard and irksome in the beginnyng, but in the end, easie and pleasant' (these qualities being symbolized by the black root and white flower); and he declares, on the basis of the gift's coming from Hermes, that this study 'is not found out by man, but given and taught by God.' [An earlier humanist, Budé, distinguished between Homeric and Christian moly as a contrast between pagan and Christian treatment of the effects of sensual vices (J. M. Steadman, *History of Ideas News Letter*, 4, 1958, 59–60). Milton was in accord with this long tradition when in 1626 he alluded to the help of divine moly (*El* 1. 87–8). For *Comus* no allegorical interpreter is more useful than George Sandys (*Ovid*, 1632, 480–1):

Yet Ulysses could not loose his shape with the rest, who being fortifyed by an immortall power, was not subject to mutation. For the divine & cœlestiall soule, subsisting through the bounty of the Creator, can by no assault of nature be violated, nor can that bee converted into a beast, which so highly participates of reason:...her sensuall charms...are not to bee resisted, but by the divine assistance, Moly, the guift of Mercury, which signifies temperance.

Sandys goes on to speak of

their head strong appetites, which revolt from the soveraignty of reason (by which wee are onely like unto God, and armed against our depraved affections) nor ever returne into their Country (from whence the soule deriveth her cœlestiall originall) unlesse disinchanted, and cleansed from their former impurity.

Sandys' ideas and language are obviously in the tradition of Christian Platonism. Many allegorical interpretations of moly are concisely listed by R. M. Adams, *Ikon*, 14. A long account, running from the ancients through Boethius to Ascham, is given by Hugo Rahner, *Greek Myths and Christian Mystery* (tr., London, 1963), 179–222.]

637 *Haemony.* Most editors have accepted Keightley's suggestion that, since Milton 'assigns it a kind of magic power, he probably derived its name from Haemonia or Thessaly, the land of magic.' Ovid (*M.*) often uses Haemonia for Thessaly; and Spenser, in imitation, uses Haemony as a place name (*Astrophel* 3; [S. R. Watson (*N&Q* 178, 1940, 260–1; and 321, 339) adds the herb described, ibid. 181–98]. The association of Thessaly with magic is amply attested: e.g. Plato, *Gorg.* 513A; Horace, *C.* 1. 27. 21–2, *Epod.* 5. 45, *Ep.* 2. 2. 208–9; Ovid, *M.* 7. 222–31 (where Medea gathers baleful plants from places in Thessaly); and Lucan 6. 434–506. Such references, however, are to malevolent witchcraft and not to counter-charms against it. [J. Arthos, who will not allow any allegorical meaning for the herb, and takes the name as only signifying Thessaly (*Mask*, 44–5, 48), adduces another parallel (*N&Q* 8, 1961, 172; *Anglia* 79, 1962, 204–13), namely, the flower *amellus* in Virgil, *G.* 4. 271–8, in the episode of Aristaeus which is set beside the river Peneus in Thessaly.]

OED tentatively suggests two quite different derivations for the name (and by implication different meanings) as tenable: (1) Greek *haimon*, skilful (which could suggest no more than that the plant possesses or confers a skill in magic superior to that of the charms it counteracts); or (2) Greek *haimonios*, blood-red (which, as Le Comte remarks, seems inconsistent with Milton's description of the plant).

[In commenting on *Haemony* a number of scholars have more or less followed the traditional ethical (and Platonic) interpretation of the Homeric moly (see 635–6 n.); some have taken a more positively religious line. Hughes (1937) sees in the name a suggestion of Socrates' story (Plato, *Charmides* 157) 'of the charm of a Thracian physician who wrought magical cures because he understood that the body's health depends upon the soul'; in 1957 Hughes is more non-committal, though he seems to incline toward ethical Platonism.] Wright (1938) says: '*Haemony* is the platonic philosophy expressed in "Comus," a symbol of that "sage and serious doctrine" which will protect its owner against sensual enchantments and deceits.' Hanford (*Poems*, 1953) sees Haemony as 'obviously a symbol of some saving moral principle (probably of the Platonic philosophy). In Milton's own age and nation, the doctrine symbolized is unbeautified and of low esteem: "but in another country" (i.e., in Greece), it "bore a bright golden flower."' He adds, in reference to views we are coming to: 'If Milton is thinking specifically of Christian grace, as some critics maintain, then the earlier and purer days of reformed religion would be the soil on which it bore a flower.' [Broadbent (*Comus and Samson Agonistes*, 26) remarks: 'Allegorically haemony stands for the virtue of temperance; dramatically, it is the talisman of white magic.' J. M. Steadman ('Milton's *Haemony*: Etymology and Allegory,' *PMLA* 77, 1962, 200–7) argues for Haemony as signifying Christian knowledge and wisdom. Going on from Steadman et al., S. Bercovitch ('Milton's "Haemony": Knowledge and Belief,' *HLQ* 33, 1969–70, 351–9) suggests that Milton intended an association with 'the Hebrew word-root *aman*,' which in its various forms denotes 'both "knowledge" and "belief."' 'The double meaning of *amon*, as "skill" and holy "truth," exactly parallels that of *haimon*.' The primary meanings of Greek and Hebrew words would provide a bridge between the two levels of knowledge and revelation.]

[The more positively religious interpreters have a progenitor in Coleridge. In a letter of 10 Sept. 1802 to Sotheby (*Collected Letters*, ed. E. L. Griggs, Oxford, 2, 1956, 866–7; also in *Coleridge*, ed. Brinkley, 553–5) Coleridge complained of notes on Haemony by botanizing commentators who missed 'Milton's platonizing Spirit.' He himself discerned here 'an Allegory of Christianity, or...more precisely of the Redemption by the Cross—every syllable is full of Light!' The dark root and prickly leaf symbolize the misery of this life, the golden flower 'the exceeding weight of Glory prepared for us hereafter.' Lines 633–4 ('Unknown...shoon') refer to the promises of redemption daily offered and not accepted. 'Now what is Haemony? Αἷμα-οἶνος—Blood-wine...This is my Blood— / the great Symbol of the Death on the Cross.']

Himes, who took moly to represent 'labor, physical or mental, Nature's corrective for idleness and vice' (*Enigmas*, 15), reached independently an interpretation of Haemony 'nearly identical' with Coleridge's (above, 618–40 n.): 'Had Coleridge recognized the *shepherd lad* [as St Paul], he would have settled the meaning for all time' (16).

Agreeing with Coleridge (and with Himes) that *Haemony* refers to the blood of Christ, E. S. Le Comte (*PQ* 21, 1942, 283–98) adds various supports. He cites the mythical account of moly given by Eustathius (above, 635–6 n.): how one of the giants defeated by Zeus fled to Circe's island and there assaulted her, how the Sun came to his daughter's rescue and slew the giant, how from his blood sprang the plant named moly in memory of the struggle, the flower milk-white because of the Sun, the root black like the giant's blood or because of Circe's terror. The origin thus supplied for moly might suggest the name Haemony for Milton's plant. But the deeper meaning that he proposes, Le Comte seeks through an examination of rhamnus, the plant with properties to counter-act witchcraft mentioned by Fletcher (above, 635–6 n.). It should be noticed that nowhere are moly and rhamnus identified. If, however, Milton's interest was aroused by Fletcher's reference (so runs the argument), he would find in John Gerard's *Herball* (2nd ed., revised, 1633), among different kinds of rham, 'Christs Thorn or Ram of Lybia' described: 'a...bush...having very long and sharpe pricklie branches: but the thornes that grow about the leaves are lesser...The leaves are...first of a dark greene colour, and then somewhat reddish. The floures grow in clusters at the top of the stalks of a yellow colour...'

(p. 1335; Le Comte, 293). The name refers to the tradition that from this plant was woven Christ's crown of thorns. Le Comte argues that Haemony is this plant, that Milton coined the name in order to suggest Christ's blood, and that he modified classical descriptions of the inferior moly so as to incorporate suggestions from Gerard: the darkish leaf (630), the *prickles* (ibid.), the *bright golden flowre* (ibid.), and the statement (631–2) that it bloomed *in another Countrey* (in Gerard, literally Libya, but in Milton, heaven). Le Comte also finds a connection between the rhamnus and *the dull swain...with clouted shoon* (633–4) in Theocritus 4. 57–8, where Battus is warned not to go shoeless because rhamnus and prickly shrubs abound in the mountains; and finally confirmation for Fletcher's assertion that rhamnus had power against charms, and hence for Milton's transferring this power to his Haemony (638–9), in the work of Wierus quoted by Todd (above, 635–6 n.). T. P. Harrison (*PQ* 22, 1943, 251–4) suggested Henry Lyte's *New Herball* (1619, p. 500) rather than Gerard as a source, since it mentions the efficacy of the shrub against witch-craft and states of one kind that it is 'not knowne in this country' and of another that it 'is called in Italie, Christs thorne.'

In opposition to Hanford, Le Comte (288) maintains that the allegory is not Platonic but is what Coleridge had made it (see above). *This soyl* is man's life on earth and 'the plant the favor from on high which only a virtuous few are willing and able to maintain amid trial and suffering until "haemony" blossoms for them in heaven' (Le Comte, 288). This reading accords with the Attendant Spirit's prologue (9–14) and the last couplets of the epilogue. 'When the same heaven-sent emissary comes to tell of haemony, he has changed his metaphors, but not his theme. This humble, unsightly plant does not itself signify Virtue, but rather the grace given those who are virtuous'; and this he supports by quoting lines 937–8. (The couplet, as noted below, underlines a difficulty Le Comte's interpretation ignores, that of accommodating haemony as a symbol of grace with another symbol of grace in the poem.) Le Comte continues: '...the ultimate implication must be that haemony would never bloom for men, were it not for the Saviour's blood. Thus again αἷμων puts forward its etymological claim,' and *But of divine effect* (629) 'takes on a new significance' (289–90).

Brooks and Hardy in their commentary on *Comus* (especially pp. 212 f.) adopt Le Comte's view although they discount his distinction between virtue and grace (see IV above, under 1951). [Svendsen (*Science*, 132), citing Le Comte and Brooks and Hardy, thinks that the 'blood-red haemony, symbol of God's grace,...blends both the pagan connotations of magical moly and the Christian legend of the Redeemer's blood.'] Rosemond Tuve (*Images*, 152) so far agrees with Le Comte as to observe that, since 'haemony, carefully distinguished from the moly of temperance, protects the brothers from one aspect of the enchantment...a relation between haemony and grace seems probable, though another symbol bears...the burden of completing Milton's Christian argument...—the symbol of water' (i.e. in Sabrina's release of the Lady, 907 f.). This seems to be the minimum reservation necessary if one is to avoid the difficulty of having to recognize two quite different symbols for the same power—a difficulty noticed by R. M. Adams (*Ikon*, 1955, 17), who himself recognizes neither symbol. Another, related difficulty is the severe limitation set upon the power of Haemony in the action: if it can protect the Brothers against the enchantments of Comus—against their falling into the same predicament as the Lady— it can do nothing to reverse the spell and rescue her; hence the necessity of invoking Sabrina's aid. This aspect of the action Le Comte altogether overlooks, and with it the awkward fact that such limitation sorts ill with the exalted claim for Haemony of symbolizing saving grace through the blood of Christ. Yet unless one is to adopt (with Adams) a purely sceptical attitude on the whole subject of symbols, some explanation of Haemony, compatible at once with Milton's description and the herb's place and effect in the action, must be found. For—quite apart from Le Comte's argument—it can hardly signify merely temperance, the meaning commonly assigned to moly, on whose inferiority to Haemony Milton is emphatic. Nor can we suppose that the Lady, though she does not bear Haemony with her, is deficient in temperance. To do so would be to reduce the action of the piece to nonsense. It is not temperance, then, that can protect one against the spells of Comus, though it can enable one to resist, as the Lady does, his solicitations. Haemony, it would seem if one follows this line of argument, represents some sort of divine intervention (it is of *divine effect*), but different from, and inferior to, saving grace. If theology recognized some divine fortifying of natural virtue to meet an occasion of special temptation, and distinguished it clearly from the grace that effects salvation, this would meet the requirements of Haemony in the total context: its relation to moly, which signifies temperance, its divine effect, helping to win the reward of virtue in heaven, symbolized by the *bright golden flowre* in *another Countrey*, and yet preserving its limited efficacy as compared with that other symbol of grace, the fully resolving intervention of Sabrina.

[Woodhouse's papers included a digest of part of an unpublished thesis by Rev. F. X. Reitzel, on a distinction clearly recognized in Roman Catholic theology between 'actual grace' (aid extended in a particular instance) and 'habitual' or 'saving grace.' Reitzel found that the distinction (without the terms) was made or assumed in St Augustine and other Fathers, and in English theologians of Milton's period, notably Richard Baxter (*Directions to the Converted*, 1665, in *Practical Works*, 1830, 8, 272).]

It must be confessed that each of the explanations here reported or suggested presents some difficulty. Naturally, the less the meaning read in the lines the less the difficulty; but even a critic who rejects all symbolic meaning is left with the problem of the name Haemony, not quite satisfactorily solved (as noted above) by Keightley's suggestion about Thessaly. The evidence, however, for symbolic meanings in *Comus* is cumulatively very strong, although in attempting to read the symbolism of this passage difficulties multiply. The two alternative explanations of the Shepherd Lad (618 and n.) will fit only an interpretation which equates Haemony with some sort of moral doctrine communicated by the Shepherd Lad; but it is difficult to see how moral doctrine can itself protect; and if for doctrine one substitutes the moral quality or saving influence which the doctrine enjoins or describes, it is not in the power of a second person to bestow it—whether one interprets the quality as temperance (which leaves unexplained the clear differentiation of Haemony from Moly) or the influence as grace (which raises the new difficulties of the evident limitation upon the power of Haemony and the whole relation to the Sabrina episode). Finally, the explanation last offered above, while it meets the other difficulties, leaves the name Haemony unexplained and obviates none of the difficulty respecting the Shepherd Lad. The reader may perhaps conclude that the crux has not been completely resolved and be content to await further light.

[One may perhaps briefly supplement or qualify some of the remarks in this acute and candid editorial summary. While the complete text of *Comus*, addressed to readers, cannot be limited in symbolic suggestion to the immediate comprehension of hearers, symbolism can lead to oversubtle explication; and some apparent difficulties may be due merely to the exigencies of the plot. The Platonic and Christian ideas and tone of George Sandys (above, end of note on 635–6), for example, suggest the kind of difference Milton might have had in mind between the Homeric moly and his own Haemony, that is, the difference between the pagan, natural, and rational concept of temperance and that virtue as refined and elevated by Christian teaching; the Lady combines the two when she speaks of the 'holy dictate of spare Temperance' (766). We may recall too Milton's saying that, even without the final illumination of Christianity, he would have been kept free from vice by his own reservedness of natural disposition and by 'morall discipline learnt out of the noblest Philosophy,' i.e. Plato and other pagans (*Apol, Works* 3, 305–6). And either kind of doctrine may or must be learned from others, since it is not wholly intuitive. For the probably religious overtone in the phrase *in another Countrey...but not in this soyl*, we might compare Sandys' Platonic–Christian phrase about souls returning 'into their Country.' As for the Lady's being temperate without Haemony, she is presented as more mature and complete in virtue and illumination (even if she does need to be rescued by grace) than her brothers, of whom the younger represents natural innocence and the elder, while sincerely accepting religion, emphasizes reason. Perhaps the most satisfactory interpretation of Haemony, which includes some earlier ones, is that of Steadman, cited in the third paragraph of this note: accepting one *OED* derivation, from *haimon* (informed, wise), a word traditionally related to *daimon*, which Milton first used for the Attendant Spirit, he takes the allegorical meaning of the herb to be Christian knowledge and wisdom.]

639 *mildew blast*: infection caused by mildew (*OED* 6). Todd compared 'urchin blasts' (844) and 'like a mildew'd ear / Blasting his wholesome brother' (Shakespeare, *Ham.* 3. 4. 64–5). For mildew as the effect of malign influence Verity cited: 'This is the foul fiend....He...mildews the white wheat' (*Lear* 3. 4. 120–4). [Cf. *Arc* 48 f.] *damp*: a noxious vapour (*OED* 1).

640 *gastly furies apparition.* Warton (1785) explained as 'any frightful appearance raised by magic,' and cited the apparitions raised by Satan: 'Infernal Ghosts, and Hellish Furies, round / Environ'd thee' (*PR* 4. 422–3). Todd noted the phrase 'ghastly Furies' in Sylvester (*D.W.W.* 2. 1. 3, Arg., Grosart, 1, 114).

641 *purs't it up*: [put it away in a purse (Hanford).]

645 *lime-twigs of his spells*: trap of his enchantments, from the practice of smearing branches with bird-lime. Cf. 'Somtime I wold betraye the Byrds, / that lyght on lymed tree' (B. Googe, *Eglogs*, etc., ed. Arber, 54).

646–55 Whatever its deeper significance (637 n.) and its relation to moly, Haemony is here represented, according to Warton (who emphasizes Milton's blending of the romantic with the classical), as the talisman, often a herb, which in the romances ensured its bearer victory in combat (1785 ed.). In *assault the necromancers hall* (648), Milton, he continues, 'thought of a magician's castle which has an inchanted Hall invaded by christian knights,' as in 'the adventure of the Black Castle in the *Seven Champions of Christendom*....' In *with...brandish't blade rush on him* (649–50) Milton is following Odysseus' approach to Circe, according to Hermes' counsel (*Od.* 10. 294, 321; Ovid, *M.* 14. 293–6: Warton, corrected); but *break his glass, | And shed the lushious liquor on the ground* recalls Guyon's treatment of the cups of the porter and Excesse (*F.Q.* 2. 12. 49, 57). Comus' glass and wand derive ultimately from Circe's cup and wand; but Headley (reported by Todd) noted that the rose-crowned Panglory of G. Fletcher bears 'a Silver wande' and 'A hollowe globe of glasse' (*C.V.* 2. 58). For *But sease his wand* (652) Warton found no immediate precedent but compared Caliban's 'Remember | First to possess his books' (*Temp.* 3. 2. 99–100). The expression *curst crew* is applied to Alcina's monsters (Ariosto, *O.F.*, tr. Harington, 6. 61: cited by Todd); [it was cited by Dunster in Sylvester (*D.W.W.* 1. 1. 628, Grosart, 1, 24)]. With *like the Sons of Vulcan vomit smoak* Milton returns to a classical source: *ille* ⟨Cacus, a son of Vulcan⟩... *| faucibus ingentem fumum... | evomit involvitque domum caligine caeca* (Virgil, *A.* 8. 251–3: Todd); cf. Ovid, *F.* 1. 571–2, 577.

647 *when we go*: MS. *as wee goe*, deleted, followed by *when on the way*, deleted, and finally the present reading (*Facs.* 420).

648 *the necromancers.* MS. first had *his necromantik.*

649 *dauntless hardihood.* MS. first had *suddaine violence* (*Facs.* 420).

651 *shed...liquor.* MS. first had *powre...potion* (*Facs.* 420).

657 *And som good angel...before us.* MS. (*Facs.* 420) first had *& good heaven cast his best regard upon us Ex* ⟨Exeunt?⟩. Dunster (reported by Todd) cited Tasso's Raimondo shielded by his guardian angel: 'The sacred Angell tooke his target sheene | And by the Christian champion stood unseene' (Fairfax, *Jerusalem* 7. 82; cf. 8. 84).

After **657** ⟨Direction⟩ *The Scene changes*, etc. The scene would appear to be before the Palace; on the place and duration of the scene see below, 944 n. Singleton notes that, in Puteanus, Comus and his crew have two habitats: a dense wood and the stately palace (*tectum augustum*) of the god, wherein are all sensual delights; before entering upon them one must drink of the wine offered (but not by the god). Puteanus depicts Comus for the first time not as reveller merely but as seducer; his appeal is to youth, and he urges the life of sensual pleasure with specious arguments. Warton (1785) comments on the banquet as 'common in the magic of romance,' suggesting an ultimate source in Virgil, *A.* 6. 603–5; he compares Shakespeare, *Temp.* 3. 3. 19 (s.d.), and notes Milton's own later use of the device (*PR* 2. 337–405). [Demaray (*Masque Tradition*, 114) conceives thus of a rapid change of scene: 'Few people probably note that a back flat has been pulled or a back curtain dropped to reveal the palace painted on another curtain or flat. Tables with all "dainties"...are either painted on the scenery or carried on the stage as Comus now appears with his rabble. "An enchanted chair" bearing the Lady may have been rolled or carried on stage and set at an angle to stage right or left. In this position the chair and Lady would not obscure the view of Sabrina, who could then rise in her chariot from the rear-center of the stage.']

658–61 ['Here the swift changes from intensely physical *nerves*, conceived of as chained bundles, to the smooth deadness of alabaster (with its rich sub-suggestion of flesh) and thence to the perfectly appropriate myth, all in less than four lines, contain all the essential elements, though none of the trimmings, of seventeenth century wit' (Tillyard, *Poetry Direct and Oblique*, 1934, 82).]

658–9 Warton compared Prospero's threat to disarm Ferdinand with his 'stick' (wand) and reduce his 'nerves' (sinews) to an infant's impotence (*Temp.* 1. 2. 472, 484–5). Browne quoted 'monumental alablaster' (Shakespeare, *Oth.* 5. 2. 5). Verity added: 'Why should a man... / Sit like his grandsire cut in alablaster?' (*Merch.* 1. 1. 83–4).

660 MS. first had *statue, fixt, as Daphne was*, then *fixt* deleted and *or* substituted (*Facs.* 420).

660–1 *Daphne.* Ovid (*M.* 1. 452–567) tells of Apollo's passion for Daphne, her resolve to remain a virgin like Diana, Apollo's pursuit and her flight, and her transformation, in answer to her own prayer, into the laurel (548–52): *vix prece finita torpor gravis occupat artus, | mollia cinguntur tenui praecordia libro, | in frondem crines, in ramos bracchia crescunt, | pes modo tam velox pigris radicibus haeret....*Remembering this bit, and perhaps also the lines from *The Merchant of Venice* (658–9 n.), Milton would not fail to see that Comus' magic really made against his aim and served rather to fortify the Lady's resolve: to be rooted like Daphne, and as passionless as a statue, would be to thwart her seducer.

661–4 MS. completes 661 with *why doe ye frowne*, deleted. Lines 662–4 first appeared with others (671–7, and a passage standing for 692–702) in a passage after 754 which was there deleted; lines 662–5 are here copied in the margin (*Facs.* 420). The Columbia editors designate the passage as it occurs after 754 as MS. 2 (*Works* 1, 543, 545, 553). For *Fool do not boast* (661) MS. 2 (*Facs.* 422) had *stand back false traitor*; MS., *foole thou art over proud*, deleted, and present reading substituted.

662–4 Todd compared: *recte invictus, cuius etiamsi corpus constringatur, animo tamen vincula inici nulla possint* (Cicero, *Fin.* 3. 22. 75). Here the lines build on the idea of inner security emphasized by the Elder Brother (365–81), add the note of freedom, and in turn are completed by the Attendant Spirit's 'Love vertue, she alone is free' (1018). [*this corporal rinde*: the body thought of as the husk of the soul (Hughes, 1937). Hunter ('New Words,' 255) lists *immanacle* as a Miltonic coinage. *OED* lists only this and an example of 1810. *while Heav'n sees good*: while Providence permits.]

667–70 Warton detected echoes of Fletcher's *F. Shep.*: 'Here be all new delights' (1. 3. 21) and 'whose virtues do refine / The blood of man, making it free and fair / As the first hour it breathed' (2. 2. 30–2). Thyer (reported by Todd) quoted Shakespeare: 'Such comfort as do lusty young men feel / When well-apparell'd April on the heel / Of limping Winter treads' (*Romeo* 1. 2. 26–8). Verity saw a kind of parody of 'they shall obtain joy and gladness, and sorrow and sighing shall flee away' (Isa. 35. 10).

668 For *fancy* MS. first had *youth & fancie*; and for *beget* it substituted *invent*, then deleted and restored *beget* (*Facs.* 420). *fancy*: [in a broad sense, but especially 'Amorous inclination, love' (*OED* 8b, citing Shakespeare, *Merchant* 3. 2. 63: 'Tell me, where is fancy bred...').]

669 *fresh*: replacing MS. *briske*, deleted.

671–704 appear in MS. on a smaller inserted leaf to which a direction is given in the margin; its readings are here designated MS. For what in the following notes is called MS. 2, see above, 661–4 [and *Facs.* 418–22, H. Darbishire, 2, 355].

671 For *And first behold* MS. 2 had *& looke upon* (*Works* 1, 545; *Facs.* 422). *cordial Julep*. *Julep*: a sweet drink, used figuratively of something to cool or assuage the heat of passion (*OED*), which is clearly the secondary suggestion here. *OED* lends no support to Verity's 'any bright drink.' *cordial*: stimulating or 'comforting' to the heart (*OED* 2).

673 *balm*: used figuratively with the sense of aromatic fragrance (*OED* 4).

674–7 *Nepenthes*: the drug mingled with the wine by Helen, daughter of Zeus and wife of Menelaus, 'to quiet all pain and strife, and bring forgetfulness of every ill,' a drug given her by 'Polydamna, the wife of Thon,...a woman of Egypt,' where the 'earth...bears greatest store of drugs, many that are healing ...and many that are baneful' (Homer, *Od.* 4. 219–32, L.C.L.). Although the action is there beneficent (as in Spenser, *F.Q.* 4. 3. 42–5) and Helen, who gives it to Menelaus and Telemachus, is a reformed character, her name and the evil associations of Egypt are quite enough, with Comus' praise, to convey the required sinister effect. Cf. 'Where is...that herbe Nepenthes that procureth all delights?' (Lyly, *Euphues*, ed. Arber, 425). Burton supplies a useful gloss on Comus' meaning: '*Amor, voluptas, Venus, gaudium, | Jocus, ludus, sermo suavis, suaviatio* [cf. Plautus, *Bacch.* 1. 1. 115–16] are the true nepenthes' (*Anat.* 2. 2. 6. 4, 2, 119). After 677 MS. has an additional line, *poore ladie thou hast need of some refreshing*, deleted; retained in Br. (*Facs.* 418, 422, 329).

677 *To life so friendly.* [The phrase is closer to G. Sandys than to Homer. Homer's words are *pharmaka metioenta, esthla*, which Sandys (*Relation*, 1615, 126) quotes in Latin as *pharmaca utilia | Bona* and translates very freely as 'a friend to life' (Bush, *Mythol.*, ed. 1963, 272, n. 24).]

678–86 In MS. (*Facs.* 418) written, without lining, in margin of inserted leaf (see above, 671–704 n.); not in Br. (*Works* 1, 546).

678 Todd compared: 'Thyself thy foe, to thy sweet self too cruel' (Shakespeare, *Sonn.* 1. 8).

678–80 Singleton (953) quotes the words given by Puteanus to his Comus (1608, 22): *Quae mortalium sine voluptate vita? poena est...quem in finem benigna te Natura produxerit cogita : non ut miserum dura virtute crucies animum, & è felicitatis contubernio proturbes; sed ut mollitie bees, ut suavitatibus lubentiisque omnibus irriges....*

679 *dainty limms.* Todd cites Spenser, *F.Q.* 1. 11. 32, but indicates that the phrase was a commonplace. *which nature lent.* Steevens (reported by Todd) quoted Shakespeare, *Sonn.* 4. 3–6: 'Nature's bequest gives nothing, but doth lend, / And, being frank, she lends to those are free. / Then, beauteous niggard, why dost thou abuse / The bounteous largess given thee to give?' Not only does this parallel the basic image and some of the words, but its purport points the direction of Comus' argument and the significance of the cup he offers.

681 *the cov'nants of her trust*: the particular clauses of the agreements (*OED* 3b) governing nature's loan.

684–5 *the unexempt...must subsist*: the condition of life from which no frail mortal is exempt.

686 Perhaps, as Elton suggests, a distant echo of another tempter, Despair (Spenser, *F.Q.* 1. 9. 40).

687 *That.* [The antecedent is *you* in 683 (Hanford).]

688   *but*: replacing MS. *heere*, deleted (*Works* 1, 546; *Facs.* 418).

692–702   MS. 2 (i.e. the passage following 754) placed a form of these lines, later much altered, after 664, the whole passage subsequently deleted. It is scarcely possible to determine the order of the various trials made, but some of the more important can be indicated. For *oughly-headed Monsters* (694) MS. 2 (*Facs.* 422) tried *amoung'st these musl'd monsters*. After 694 it added *O my simplicity ⟨what sights are these?*, apparently replaced by⟩ *how have I bin betrai'd wth darke disguises | whether deluded and soothing ⟨lies*, apparently replaced by⟩ *flatteries*. For *brew'd inchantments* (695) it first tried *treacherous kindnesse*, then *bru'd sorcerie*. For *foul deceiver* (695) it tried *thou man of lies & ⟨falshood*, then *fraud*, and finally⟩ *falshood*. It then proceeded: *if thou give me it | I throw it on the ground*, *were it a draft for Juno | I ⟨hate*, replaced by⟩ *should reject it from thy ⟨hands*, possibly replaced by⟩ *treasonous offer*. It appears to indicate after *sorcerie* an insertion (to replace *thou man of lies...a draft*): hence *wth thy hel bru'd liquor lest I | throw it against ye ground were it a draft* &c. (In Cambridge MS., as reproduced in *Facs.* 423, the wavering line seems to indicate insertion at this point, as do the words *were it a draft* &c., which link up with *were it a draft for Juno*; and so the Columbia editors take it (*Works* 1, 547), while the line in Fletcher's explanatory transcription (422) would seem to indicate earlier insertion at a point where the connection is not evident.) It omits, as Br. does, 696–9. At 700 MS. 2 omits *when she banquets* and omits 703–4.

692–3   *Was this...told'st me of?* Above, 318–19.

693   *grim aspects.* The phrase *grim aspect* is in Spenser, *F.Q.* 5. 9. 48, Drayton, *Poly.* 27. 296 (Warton), and Shakespeare, *1 H. VI* 2. 3. 20 (Todd), and seems to be a commonplace. But here *aspect* is used in its now obsolete sense as a concrete appearance, thing seen (*OED* 13); and *grim* has its older and stronger sense of fierce, savage (*OED* 1).

694   *oughly*: thus in MS. (*Works* 1, 547). Among various spellings of ugly, *oug-* was fairly common (as in Br. and in P. Fletcher, *P.I.* 1. 40), but the addition of *h* seems to have been very unusual.

695   *brew'd inchantments*: 'his baneful cup, / With many murmurs mixt' (524–5 and n.).

696   *innocence*: ignorance (*OED* 3).

697   *visor'd*: concealed, figuratively, with a mask (*OED* 1). *forgery*: deceit (*OED* 2).

699 *lickerish*: tempting to the palate (*OED* 1); this of the contents of the cup, but, with reference to what the cup stands for, lustful (ibid. 3).

700 *Juno*. Although Hebe the cup-bearer is usually depicted as bringing 'Immortal Nectar to her Kingly Sire' (*Vac* 38-9), she may with equal propriety be thought of as presenting it to her mother at celestial banquets. [It is logical for a female speaker to shift from Jove to Juno. Lines 700-1 might be an oblique echo of Jonson's *Drinke to me*: 'But might I of Jove's Nectar sup, / I would not change for thine' (*Ben Jonson* 8, 106).]

701-2 *none | . . .good things*. Newton (reported by Todd) traced the sentiment to Euripides, *Medea* 618: 'No profit is there in a villain's gifts' (L.C.L.).

706-7 The reference is to two ancient schools of philosophy which contemned pleasure and luxury: the Stoics, whose ethics became increasingly ascetic (the *Doctors* might be Seneca, Epictetus, Marcus Aurelius, or more probably their modern academic exponents), and the Cynics, whose leader, Diogenes, won notoriety by making a tub his dwelling. The only problem is *budge*. Warton referred to budge, a fur (originally from the skin of lamb or goat) used to trim garments, including academic robes (*OED*: *sb.*[1] 1). Thus *budge* would be a noun used adjectivally, as later in *OAP*: 'part freely with their own budge gownes from off their backs' (*Works* 6, 261). Todd concludes: 'After all, *budge* is probably here used. . .in the sense of *stiff* or *surly*' (cf. *OED*: *a.*, obsolete, and etymology unknown, 1: solemn in demeanour, stiff, formal). Todd quotes the *History of the Life* of Milton's later friend, Thomas Ellwood: 'The Warden was a budge old Man' (ed. 1714, 65)—which may be an echo of this passage. Todd also quotes: 'Poore Budgeface, bowcase sleeve, but let him passe, / Once fur and beard shall priviledge an Asse' (Marston, *Scourge of Villanie*, 1598, 3. 10. 25-6: ed. Davenport, 164); 'bowcase' here stands for the academic gown or for its wearer (*OED*: sleeve 1 d). Todd notes that one of the antimasquers in Shirley's *Triumph of Peace* [Evans, *Masques*, 206; Spencer, *Masques*, 283] is 'a grim Philosophical-faced fellow, in his gown, furred' (but this is a 'projector,' a student of natural, not moral, philosophy). Whiting (*Milieu*, 247) cites John Wilson's translation (1668) of Erasmus' *Moriae Encomium*: 'our Philosophers, so much reverenc'd for their Fur'd Gowns.' C. W. Brodribb (*TLS*, 8 May 1937, 364) suggested that Milton was thinking of the well-known portrait of Erasmus in his furs, or of Holbein's illustrations of the *Encomium*, where two Stoic philosophers are depicted thus clad. Hughes infers that the academic garb implied 'stodginess or pomposity.' [Cf.: '. . .line't within / With Presbyterian budge, that drowsie trance, / The Synods sable, foggy ignorance' (*The*

Kings Disguise 18–20, *Poems of John Cleveland*, ed. B. Morris and E. Withington, 6 and 88.] We may best take *budge* as an adjective of unknown etymology, meaning stiff, formal, and *Stoick Furr* as Milton's deliberate play on the meaning of the substantive, the whole indicating Comus' contempt for academic moralizers as representing 'Rigor,' 'Advice,' 'Strict Age, and sowre Severity, / With their grave Saws,' already dismissed (107–10).

709–35 The primary and ostensible argument of these lines is that nature's abundance should be joyfully accepted and used. The secondary and subtler argument is that (as Renan was to observe) nature knows nothing of chastity; this is conveyed in the emphasis on nature's prolificness, her *waste fertility*, and its full import becomes apparent only in 736 f. For further comment on the ideas see 'Sources and Analogues,' III. 9, above. [F. R. Leavis (above, IV: Criticism, under 1936) has emphasized and analysed the extraordinary tactual and visual vitality and immediacy of these lines, their actively sensuous rendering of natural life and process. But he totally ignores the thematic and dramatic significance of the speech: the artistic qualities he rightly praises reflect the libertine excess, the anarchic moral disorder, of the speaker. Some general remarks of D. Daiches may be quoted here: 'For a man of Milton's temperament, and his strongly held personal views, it is remarkable how he is able to get inside Comus' character (as later he was to get inside Satan's) and put some of his most persuasive verse into Comus' mouth. This is—perhaps it need hardly be said—a deliberate dramatic device. . . . It was Milton's study of rhetoric that enabled him to voice persuasively views that he detested. With Comus as with Satan he builds up character. . . by devising occasions which call from his characters their most persuasive statements of their position' (*Milton*, 1957, 71).]

710 *unwithdrawing*: bounteous, holding back nothing (Verity).

711 *odours*: sweet-smelling objects (usually perfumes or spices), here flowers; cf. *Nat* 23 n., *Comus* 105–6 n.

712 *Thronging*. MS. first had *cramming*. *spawn*: the eggs of fish or the young brood hatched therefrom (*OED* 2). MS. deletes a line, *the feilds w*th *cattell & the aire w*th *fowle*, replacing it in the margin with 713 (*Facs.* 420).

713 *curious*: fastidious (*OED* quotes the Elizabethan Henry Smith: 'he [Christ] was not curious in his diet': *Twelve Sermons*, 1632, sig. P4^r; London, 1866, 2, 329), but, in the context, with a secondary suggestion of a desire for experience and knowledge.

715 *green shops*: the mulberry trees, their workshops (Verity).

716 *To deck.* MS. substituted *to adorne*, then restored *deck* (*Works* 1, 550; *Facs.* 420).

717–18 *in her own loyns* | *She hutch't*: laid up as in a hutch or coffer (*OED* 1). Warton so explains, but, recognizing that the emphasis is on nature's prolific-ness, observes that 'Some perhaps may read *hatch'd*, for it was "in her own loyns."'

720–1 *in a pet of temperance feed on Pulse,* | *Drink the clear stream.* Cf. Dan. 1. 8, 11–13, 15, 17: 'But Daniel purposed in his heart that he would not defile himself with the portion of the king's meat, nor with the wine which he drank....Then said Daniel...let them give us ⟨himself and his companions⟩ pulse to eat, and water to drink. Then let our countenances be looked upon....And... their countenances appeared fairer and fatter...than all the children which did eat the portion of the king's meat....As for these four children, God gave them knowledge and...wisdom; and Daniel had understanding in all visions and dreams.' To speak with Masson of Daniel's 'pet of temperance' is to talk the language of Comus; to cite with Verity only 1. 12 is likewise to miss the point of the allusion and, with Comus himself, its irony; for Daniel and his companions are not the worse but the better for this abstinence (which refutes Comus' assumption) and their virtue is supported by God, who gives them wisdom and knowledge of a higher order (which confirms the Elder Brother's belief—above, 414–19, 456–7, 587–91). *pet.* The word, of obscure origin and without demon-strable connection either with *pet* as applied to an indulged child or with *petulance*, came into use in the 16th century. Its meaning was offence, or a fit of peevishness, at some slight (*OED: sb.*[2] 1). To this Milton's phrase must be related; its precise connotation is determined by the context: Comus is sug-gesting that temperance, with its wilful rejection of nature's gifts, is the effect of, or manifests, ill-humour or peevishness. *Pulse.* MS. substituted *fetches* (i.e. vetches, any kind of bean), then restored *pulse.*

721 *Freize*: frieze, a coarse woollen cloth (connected with Fr. *friser*, to curl: *OED: sb.*[1]).

726 *live like...sons*: ['like those who have no legitimate claim to inherit Nature's wealth' (Hanford).] Newton (reported by Todd) cited: 'But if ye be without chastisement...then are ye bastards, and not sons' (Heb. 12. 8). Comus can quote Scripture—out of context: Nature (as he understands it) is his ever-indulgent god. [E. Seaton (*Essays and Studies* 31, 77) cites 'nature's bastards' (Shakespeare, *W. Tale* 4. 4. 83).]

727-35 The secondary theme of the speech, Nature's *waste fertility*, now receives full emphasis as Comus approaches the actual temptation. Warburton and Newton complained of childish logic, but, as Todd said, sophistry belongs to the speaker's character; and the force of the whole lies in its imagery and the steadily mounting suggestion it conveys as Comus completes the rhetorical pattern by running again through the elements and ending with the gems *hutch't* in Nature's *loyns*.

727 *Who*: i.e. Nature.   *surcharg'd*: overloaded (*OED* 3). Cf. 'O fair Plant,... with fruit surcharg'd, / Deigns none to ease thy load and taste thy sweet...?' (*PL* 5. 58-9).

728 *strangl'd*: suffocated (*OED* 2), as in Shakespeare, *Romeo* 4. 3. 34-6: 'Shall I not then be stifled in the vault, / ...And there die strangled...?' *waste*: superfluous (*OED* 6).

729 *cumber'd*: encumbered (*OED* 2).   *wing'd*: filled with wings (*OED* 1c, where this is the only example).   *dark't*: made dark (*OED*: v. 2: obsolete).

730 *over-multitude*: surpass in multitude; perhaps with some suggestion of the 'many' (*OED*: multitude 4) overwhelming 'their Lords.'

731-5 *& th' unsought diamonds...shameles brows.* At 732 MS. had *would so be studde the center wth thire starrelight / were they not taken thence*; deleted and approximately the present reading substituted (*Facs.* 422). Br. has *would soe emblaze with starrs, that they belowe* (ibid. 331). Some editors, e.g. Verity, have taken *the Deep* (732) to be the sea. Later ones—Hughes, Wright, Hanford, et al.—have recognized that *Deep* means the interior of the earth (cf. *center* in the MS. reading cited above). The *forhead of the Deep* is the roof of that underground space; it sparkles with *unsought diamonds* as if lighted by *Stars*; *they below* would be 'ghosts and spirits of the underworld' (Wright), typified by the 'swart Faëry of the mine' (435 above) or the fiends that labour for Mammon underground (Spenser, *F.Q.* 2. 7. 35). Since in classic myth all precious ore and gems below the earth's surface are the property of Hades, *they below* might be the shades of his kingdom; in either case they would normally avoid the light of the *Sun*. Milton would be well aware of the theory that attributed the gems themselves to the operation of the sun's rays (cf. *PL* 3. 608-12, and see Hughes' note and H. F. Robins, *MLQ* 12, 1951, 422-8), which would add a touch of unconscious irony to Comus' words. Commenting on the theory of the generation and growth of diamonds current in Milton's day, D. C. Allen (*MLN* 64, 1949, 179-80) cites Anselm Boetius' statement that 'small diamonds are usually found in the head of the pits, but after they have been all taken out and the pit closed for two years, other diamonds will be found to have grown in their place' (*Gemmarum et Lapidum Historia*, Leyden, 1636, 121).

731 *o'refraught*: filled to excess (with fish; cf. 712). *swel*: MS. *heave her waters up | above the shoare*, deleted, and *swell* substituted (*Facs.* 422).

732 *emblaze*. [The word seems to combine the sense of 'light up' with that of the heraldic *emblazon* (Oras, 'Notes,' 33–4). Hunter ('New Words,' 255) lists the former meaning as Milton's coinage.]

733 *And so bestudd with Stars*. For MS. reading see note on 731–5. Warton cites 'her Starre-bestudded Crowne' (*King John to Matilda* 124, Drayton, 2, 150) and Sylvester's description of the stars as 'the gilt studs of the Firmament' (*D.W.W.* 1. 7. 476, Grosart, 1, 87). [Cf. Sandys, *Ovid*, 1626, 135: 'Studded with stars.']

734 *light*: MS. *day* deleted, replaced by *light*.

736–54 These lines are not in Br., the script used for performance (*Works* 1, 552). [Some references for these conventional libertine arguments are given above in III. 9.]

736 *coy*: shy or reserved (*OED* 2).—[*cosen'd*: cozened, cheated.]

736–7 Verity remarks on 'the contemptuous effect of the alliteration' in Comus' lines. Among many parallels commentators cite: 'This idoll which you terme Virginitie' (Marlowe, *H. and L.* 1. 269; 'Vertue it selfe is but an idle name' (Fairfax, *Jerusalem* 14. 63; 'Prize not this word (*Virginitie*) so deere' (*Matilda* 787, Drayton, 1, 236); [Shakespeare, *Sonnets* and *Romeo* 1. 1. 222 f.].

738–41 [Cf. 'Base boullion for the stampes sake we allow, / Even so for mens impression do we you,' and 'Nor staine thy youthfull years with avarice' (Marlowe, *H. and L.* 1. 265–6, 325).] Verity noted the image of money lent at interest, used on a similar theme, in Shakespeare, *Sonn.* 4, etc. Todd cited Drayton's *Legend of Matilda* 232: 'Hoord not thy Beautie, when thou hast such store' (Drayton, 2, 417).

740 *mutual*. The common meaning is perhaps coloured by a meaning now obsolete, 'intimate,' as in 'The stealth of our most mutual entertainment / With character too gross is writ on Juliet' (Shakespeare, *Meas.* 1. 2. 158–9; cf. *OED* 3).

742–3 Warton cited: 'But earthlier happy is the rose distill'd / Than that which, withering on the virgin thorn, / Grows, lives, and dies in single blessedness' (Shakespeare, *Dream* 1. 1. 76–8). Todd added: *Corrò la fresca e matutina rosa, | che, tardando, stagion perder potria* (Ariosto, *O.F.* 1. 58). [The theme of *carpe diem* and the neglected rose was exploited in countless amatory poems of the Renaissance; many English examples are familiar. See above, III. 9.]

743 *with languish't head.* MS. *& fades away*, deleted, replaced by present reading (*Facs.* 422).

744-6 In describing the Lady's beauty as *natures brag*—that which Nature boasts of and which is not to be hidden from sight—Milton had, as in all of 736–54, ample precedent: Marlowe, *H. and L.* 1. 199 f.; Spenser, *F.Q.* 2. 3. 39; Daniel, *Complaint of Rosamond* 505 f.; *King John to Matilda* 51–9 (Drayton, 2, 148); Shakespeare, *Per.* 2. 2. 6–7.

745 *solemnities*: festal and ceremonial occasions (*OED* 2). Cf. 142 n.

747 Newton (reported by Todd) cited 'Home-keeping youth have ever homely wits' (Shakespeare, *T.G.V.* 1. 1. 2). Milton's phrase in its context defines the meaning of *homely*: not beautiful, plain (*OED* 5), one of the meanings current, though not dominant, in Milton's day, and now virtually obsolete (except as dialectal) in Britain, though persistent and dominant in North America.

748 *course*: coarse. *complexions*: replacing MS. *beetle brows*, deleted.

749 *sorry*: mean or poor (*OED* 5). *grain*. Verity and others are probably right (with Warton) in taking the word to mean, not texture (as *OED* 14 says), already suggested by *course complexions* (748), but hue, used of the cochineal insect and of the scarlet dyes made therefrom, and thence of the hue itself and colour in general. Warton noted this use in *IlPen* 33, *PL* 5. 285, 11. 242. [Cf. Sidney's Pamela, 'whose cheeks were died in the beautifullest graine of vertuous anger' (*Arcadia, Works* 1, 407).]

749-50 *ply...wooll*: typical occupations of the girl kept at home. *sampler*: a beginner's exercise in embroidery. *teize*: tease, i.e., comb or card (*OED*: *v.*[1]).

752 *Love-darting eyes.* Warton cited 'her sweet, love-darting Eyn' (Sylvester, *D.W.W.* 2. 3. 4. 849, Grosart, 1, 205).

754 *be adviz'd, you are but young yet.* MS. *looke upon this cordiall julep*, deleted, followed by 672–7 (for this is the point at which occurs the long passage, much altered and finally wholly deleted, embodying a draft of lines which now appear at earlier points; see above, 661–4 n.). These are followed by: *poore Ladie thou hast need of some refreshing | that hast bin tir'd all day w*[th]*out repast | & timely rest hast wanted heere sweet Ladie* ⟨*sweet Ladie* deleted, replaced by *fairest*, changed to⟩ *faire virgin | this will restore all soone La stand back false traitor*; followed by 662–4 and a passage much altered which stands for 692–702 (*Works* 1, 553; *Facs.* 422; H. Darbishire, 2, 357).

755–60 Some editors suggest that these lines are spoken aside.

756 *Jugler*: magician, sorcerer (*OED* 2), in conformity with the basic character of Comus on the literal level, but with a strong suggestion also of trickster (*OED* 3), and some perhaps of the obsolete meaning, entertainer, jester, often used contemptuously (*OED* 1).

757 *charm*: put a spell upon (*OED* 1), with secondary suggestions corresponding to those noticed in 756 n.

758 *Obtruding*: thrusting forward, forcing upon my attention. *rules*: principles or maxims of conduct, as in 'The rule of not too much, by temperance taught' (*PL* 11. 531). *pranckt*: dressed up, figuratively, as in 'they do prank them in authority' (Shakespeare, *Cor.* 3. 1. 23). Todd quoted 'pranks her selfe in the weeds of Popish Masse' (Milton, *Animad, Works* 3, 129). Dunster cited Sylvester, *D.W.W.* 2. 2. 2. 487–8 (Grosart, 1, 142).

759 *bolt*. There is little to be said for the meaning 'blurt out' as against 'sift,' 'pass through a bolting cloth' (*OED*: *v.*¹), hence 'refine.' The metaphor 'is a reflection on Comus' fine-spun sophistry' (Hughes). Editors cite many examples: Chaucer, *Nun's Priest's Tale* 4430–1; Spenser, *F.Q.* 2. 4. 24; Shakespeare, *Cor.* 3. 1. 321–3; Milton (*Animad, Works* 3, 129): 'to sift Masse into no Masse and Popish into not Popish; yet saving this passing fine sophisticall boulting hutch.'

761–73 Comus has argued from the character and analogy of nature. It is to be noticed that in her answer the Lady does not deny the truth of Comus' picture of prolific nature, but only its completeness and the inference he draws from it. Nature is a rational as well as a vital scale of being; if nature the vital and prolific furnishes the provisions among which one must choose, nature the rational furnishes the principle of choice. These two aspects of nature will receive due recognition in Milton's account of creation in *PL* 7, and his doctrine of temperance, when more fully developed, will turn on this question of rational choice, as in *Areop* (*Works* 4, 319–20): 'Wherefore did he creat passions within us, pleasures round about us, but that these rightly temper'd are the very ingredients of vertu?... This justifies the high providence of God, who though he command us temperance, justice, continence, yet powrs out before us ev'n to a profusenes all desirable things, and gives us minds that can wander beyond all limit and satiety.' In the Lady's reply, then, are some embryo elements of Milton's mature thought, although they have not yet led to that thorough reappraisal which (in *DocCh* 1. 7 and *PL*) substituted for a dualistic a monistic (often erroneously called materialist) theory, of which there is no adumbration in *Comus* (see 461 n. above). [See W. G. Madsen, 'The Idea of Nature' (above, *Comus* III. 10), 195 f.]

765 *her*: i.e. Nature's.

766 *holy*: of high and reverend excellence, not necessarily implying a religious character or sanction (*OED* 3c). [It may be thought that, while the Lady has so far opposed Comus on his own rational level, the word *holy* does very positively bring the rational pagan virtue into Christian teaching, a strain continued in 774–8, on God the creator and *giver*. So, in books 1 and 2 of the *F.Q.*, Spenser at once distinguishes and unites Holiness and Temperance.] *spare*: moderate, not profuse (*OED* 5); cf. 'Spare Fast' (*IlPen* 46).

767–72 Todd and later editors quote *Lear* 4. 1. 67–72:

> Heavens, deal so still!
> Let the superfluous and lust-dieted man,
> That slaves your ordinance, that will not see
> Because he does not feel, feel your pow'r quickly;
> So distribution should undo excess,
> And each man have enough.

768 *beseeming*: fitting, seemly.

769 *lewdly-pamper'd Luxury*. Although in Milton's day *lewd* had long acquired (cf. above, 464 and n., and *OED* 7), and *luxury* still retained, the suggestion of lasciviousness, the context here excludes the idea (as it would not if Comus' main drift were under discussion). *Luxury* here is habitual indulgence in the choice and costly; *OED* 3 cites 'I never knew or want or luxurie' (P. Fletcher, *Elisa* 1. 25). *pamper'd*: overindulged, with here a strong suggestion of the obsolete meaning, overfed (*OED*); cf. *Cramms* (778). The contemptuous *lewdly* bears a sense related to *lewd* as base, unprincipled (*OED*: lewd 5).

773–8 Having developed Shakespeare's proposition (767–72 n. above), the Lady turns it to account in her reply to Comus' point (727–35). [Carey quotes Plato, *Rep.* 586A on 'those who have no experience of wisdom and virtue... but with eyes ever bent upon the earth and heads bowed down over their tables they feast like cattle, grazing and copulating....' (L.C.L., 2, 391). Shorey, the L.C.L. translator, cites *Comus* 776 in connection with the first clause quoted above.]

777 *besotted*: intellectually or morally stupefied (*OED* 2). MS. had *sottish*, changed to *besotted* (*Facs.* 424).

778 *blasphemes his feeder*: by in effect denying that it is God who feeds the hungry; Comus has attributed all to Nature. Todd quotes Martial 4. 21: *Nullos esse deos, inane caelum | adfirmat Segius: probatque, quod se | factum, dum negat haec, videt beatum.*

778–805 *Shall I go on?...yet more strongly.* These lines are not in MS. (and thus not part of Milton's original text) or in Br. (thus not added before performance): *Works* 1, 555. They first appeared in the 1637 edition (*Facs.* 291) and were repeated, with only one significant change (780 n.), in 1645 and 1673. [We do not know when this and other added passages were composed; orthographical and other arguments for 1637 have been given by Shawcross (*Comus* 1, above) and Sirluck (ibid. IV, under 1961).]

778–86 Having countered Comus' argument from nature and vindicated the idea of temperance and continence, the Lady excuses herself from moving up to a higher level, to the dynamic virtues of chastity and virginity. She can do this because the Elder Brother had partly dealt with this subject (413–74, 583–98). [But she does, with ardent and suggestive vehemence, move up to the religious level even while refusing to do so.]

779 *anow*: [*enough*, 1637; *anough*, 1645 (*Facs.* 291, 210).

780 *contemptuous*: 1645, 1673; 1637, *reproachfull*.

781 *Sun-clad power of Chastity*. Todd cited 'a woman clothed with the sun' (Rev. 12. 1) and Petrarch's *canzone* to the Virgin Mary, *Vergine bella, che di sol vestita* (*Rime* 366). Milton has already referred to 'the sacred rayes of Chastity' (424). [The positive and powerful epithet in 781 distils the traditional half-religious conception of the grand source of light and life, which Milton held with special fervour; cf. *PL* 3. 1 f., 571 f.]

784–6 Milton speaks of himself as having been instructed in 'the doctrine of holy Scripture unfolding those chaste and high mysteries...*that the body is for the Lord and the Lord for the body*...Nor did I slumber over that place ⟨Rev. 14. 1–4⟩ expressing such high rewards of ever accompanying the Lambe, with those celestiall songs to others inapprehensible, but not to those who were not defil'd with women...' (*Apol, Works* 3, 306). The passage in Rev. contains the phrase 'for they are virgins,' omitted by Milton in his summary, in favour of an exception made for marriage, but significant in relation to *the sage | And serious doctrine of Virginity* in *Comus*. [Cf. Haller, *ELH* 13, 1946,86.] *sublime*:

belonging to the highest regions of thought and reality (*OED* 4). *notion*: idea or concept; a philosophical term (*OED* 4) here used rather loosely. *mystery*: doctrine or truth transcending ordinary human reason (*OED* 2). [Cf. the quotation from *Apol* just above and the fuller extract in III. 12 above. The word 'implies both St. Paul's "mystery of godliness, God was manifest in the flesh" (I Tim. iii, 16) and a mystery such as Socrates was taught about love by Diotima in Plato's *Symposium*, 201 d–212 b. . .' (Hughes).] *sage | And serious*: the epithets Milton is to apply to Spenser in *Areop* (*Works* 4, 311).

787 *worthy. . .not*: here deserving not by merit but the reverse (*OED* 9).

788 Just as the Lady does not deny Comus' picture of nature, but only its completeness and the soundness of his inferences (761–73 and n.), so she does not deny that he enjoys a kind of happiness but only that it is a high kind.

789 *Wit*: cleverness, mental agility (*OED* 5). *dear*: which is so prized by you (*OED*: *a.*¹ 5). *gay*: specious, plausible, of reasoning (obsolete: *OED* 5).
   Rhetorick: skill in using eloquent and persuasive language (*OED* 3), with, here, emphasis on argument (cf. *fence*, 790 and n.). The word often carries the suggestion of falsity, as in *PR* 4. 4 and Sylvester's 'glozing Rhetorick' (*D.W.W.* 2. 1. 3. 765, Grosart, 1, 121), cited by Todd. [Carey cites Marlowe, *H. and L.* 1. 338: 'Who taught thee Rhethoricke to deceive a maid?'] Probably *gay Rhetorick* is intended to suggest irresponsible use of rhetorical flourishes. [Cf. 'gay Religions full of Pomp and Gold,' *PL* 1. 372.]

790 *fence*: the art of fencing, here of course with words (*OED* 2 b). The image is of sword-play: the rhetoric dazzles like a flashing sword. This seems preferable to Verity's associating the noun with one specialized meaning of the verb, to fence with or parry, that is, to evade the question (*OED*: *v.* 1 d).

791 *convinc't*: confuted (*OED* 2). Cf. 'For he mightily convinced the Jews, and that publickly. . .' (Acts 18. 28); Job 32. 12; *PR* 3. 3–4: 'confuted and convinc't / Of his weak arguing, and fallacious drift.'

792 *uncontrouled*: undisputed, indisputable (obsolete: *OED* 3).

793 *rap't*: transported, enraptured (cf. *IlPen* 40 and n.). *spirits*: virtually a synonym for mind (*OED* 17).

794 *sacred vehemence*: ardour (expressing itself in words: *OED* 3) in this sacred cause.

795 *dumb things*: the lower creation without the power of speech (in contrast to the *vehemence* of 794).

796 *brute Earth*: the (usually) inert earth. Warton cited *bruta tellus* (Horace, C. 1. 34. 9). [In Milton's mind the recollection may have been more than verbal: Hughes (1937) notes that Horace is describing 'the earth as shaken by a thunderbolt so marvellous that it shook his scepticism about the gods.'] *nerves*: sinews (*OED* 1) regarded as the seat of strength (cf. 659 above).

797 *thy magick structures*: Comus' 'stately Palace, set out with all manner of deliciousness' (Direction before 658).

799–805 *She fables...more strongly*. Obviously an aside.

799 *fables*: speaks falsely, as in 'To say verity and not to fable' (Shakespeare, *Two N.K.* 3. 5. 105: *OED* 3) and 'He fables not; I hear the enemy' (*1 H. VI* 4. 2. 42) (Warton and Masson). *I feel that I do fear.* Explained by 801–2; though he is not a mortal and cannot be destroyed, he has all the sensations of fear.

800 *set off*. If the phrase is a metaphor from the setting of a jewel (*OED: v.* 147e; Verity; Elton; *Lyc* 80 and n.), it lacks the usual idea of contrast (e.g. Shakespeare, *1 H.IV* 1.2. 237–9). *OED* (147 f) recognizes 'enhance,' 'embellish,' without the idea of contrast, as in Shakespeare, *Cym.* 1. 6. 170–1: 'He hath a kind of honour sets him off / More than a mortal seeming,' where the idea would seem to be 'distinguishes from what is inferior'; and this appears to come closest to Milton's meaning, that the Lady's words are distinguished *by som superior power* they possess. Possibly, however, the superior power is a power, i.e. a superhuman being, superior to himself. [This last suggestion may be thought the best; the words may mean simply 'supported by' (Hanford), 'inspired by.']

801–2 Dunster MS. cites 'From all his body a cold deaw doth drop' (Sylvester, *D.W.W.* 2. 3. 2. 108, Grosart, 1, 179).

802–4 *as when...Saturns crew*. The reference is to the war of Zeus (*Jove*) and the Olympians against the Titans, sons of Earth and Heaven and brethren and supporters (*crew*) of Cronos (*Saturn*), whom Zeus defeated by the thunderbolt and with the aid of Briareos and his two brothers, whom Zeus had released from *Erebus* (the underworld), where in turn the rebellious Titans were confined in *chains* (Hesiod, *Theog.* 617–721).

803 *Speaks*: [used, as Verity and Hughes note, in two senses, with *thunder* and with *chains*.]

805 *no more*. MS. *y'are too morall*, deleted, and present reading substituted.

806–9 MS. had *this is* ⟨*meere*, deleted and replaced by⟩ *your morall stuffe*

the very ⟨tilted added⟩ *lees | & setlings of a melancholy blood*: the whole deleted
and the present 806-9 written in the margin (*Works* 1, 556; *Facs.* 424).

807 *Against the canon laws of our foundation.* Warton took this as ridicule (by
Milton) of ecclesiastical establishments and the Canon Law and cited contemptuous allusions in Milton's prose of 1641-4; but, as Masson said, 'Milton
had not yet figured as a church-reformer and satirist of ecclesiastical laws and
law-courts.' Keightley, countering Warton, saw 'a humorous application of the
language of universities and other foundations.' Todd, Verity, Wright, and
Hanford follow Warton; Masson follows Keightley, as Elton does with a happy
phrase, Comus' 'College of Pleasure.' It seems impossible that Milton should
here use such words without intending a reference to the laws of the church, as
if Comus were to say: 'The rules of our foundation are as binding as the Canon
Law itself.' If Comus is referring ironically to his 'foundation' as a college, then
the *meer moral babble* (806) perhaps glances at the ethical instruction of other
foundations (cf. 706 and n.). [Here, as in some other places, Comus seems—with
a glint of ironical humour—to be twisting 'good' words and ideas to suit his
own warped character (as the young and witty Donne sometimes turned
accepted terms and values upside down). Comus' posing as a sort of priest
of misrule is, in a small way, a foretaste of the dramatic presentation of Satan,
who can also pervert 'merit,' 'courage,' 'faithful,' 'amity,' etc. Milton is not
here necessarily judging Canon Law and foundations, but only having Comus
take them as representing orthodox tradition and authority.]

808-9 *melancholy blood.* On traditional medical and psychological ideas see the
introduction to *L'All* and *IlPen*. Dunster cited 'Sunk down in Lees, Earths
Melancholy showes' (Sylvester, *D.W.W.* 1. 2. 90, Grosart, 1, 28). [Todd cited
Nashe on the kind of melancholy that 'sinketh downe to the bottome like the
lees of the wine, and that corrupteth all the blood, and is the causer of lunacie'
(*Terrors of the night, Works* 1, 357).]

810-12 *one sip…bliss of dreams.* Warton cited 'One suppe thereof the drinkers
hart doth bring | To sudden joy' (Fairfax, *Jerusalem* 14. 74) and 'it passeth
dreams' (Fletcher, *F. Shep.* 4. 3. 35). The alliterative phrase 'bathe in bliss'
was common from Chaucer onward (Todd), but Milton incorporates it in a more
complex alliterative scheme, with *d* and *s* as well as *b*. The context may recall
Burton's best recipe for curing melancholy, 'a cup of strong drink, mirth,
music, and merry company' (*Anat.* 2. 2. 6. 3: 2, 115).

812 *Be wise, and taste*: [the exact text, as Hanford observes, of Satan's exhortation to Eve, *PL* 9. 679-732.]

After **812**: ⟨Direction⟩. Here, as elsewhere, MS. has *Dæmon* for *attendant Spirit*. In *F.Q*. 2. 12. 49, as editors note, Guyon 'overthrew' the 'bowle of wine' offered by the false Genius of the Bower of Bliss, 'And broke his staffe, with which he charmed semblants sly.' The Brothers, under direction (651–2), spill Comus' 'lushious liquor' but fail to 'sease his wand.' The rout, as there predicted, 'Fierce signe of battail make' (653) but 'soon retire' (655).

814–17 *O ye mistook…free the Lady*. Warton cited Ovid's account of Circe's restoring of her victims to human form: *percutimurque caput conversae verbere virgae, / verbaque dicuntur dictis contraria verbis* (*M*. 14. 300–1); he noted that Sandys translated *conversae virgae* as 'her wand reverst.' [Sandys (*Ovid*, 1632, 481) thus moralized the process of restoration: 'For as Circes rod, waved over their heads from the right side to the left: presents those false and sinister perswasions of pleasure, which so much deformes them: so the reversion thereof, by discipline, and a view of their owne deformity, restores them to their former beauties.'] Warton further compared Busyrane's release of Amoret (under Britomart's compulsion) by the reversing of his charms (*F.Q*. 3. 12. 36). [Hanford, slighting Ovid, appeals to this Spenserian incident ('Youth,' 141; *Handbook*, 162–3). G. W. Knight (*Burning Oracle*, 68) gives an over-subtle Freudian reading: 'Mental inhibition is shadowed by the frozen paralysis during resistance imposed by Comus. The reversal of Comus's rod…is needed to unbind the spell: which suggests a *redirection of the same instinct*. But the rod is lost; instinct sunk in repression. Therefore assistance is invoked from Sabrina,' who symbolizes, 'it seems, some mastery of passions.']

817 *sits here*. MS. had *remaines*, deleted, and *heere sits* substituted.

820 *Som other means I have*: MS. *there is another way*, deleted, and present reading substituted (*Facs*. 424).

821 *Meliboeus*. Meliboeus and Tityrus are the two shepherds in Virgil, *E*. 1; the former figures in *E*. 7 and is mentioned in 3 and 5. The name recurs in Renaissance pastorals; [and Meliboe is the sage old man in Spenser's pastoral episode, *F.Q*. 6. 9–11]. Since it here introduces Milton's account of Sabrina, it has been supposed to allude to the author from whom he derived the story. Masson inclined to the original source, Geoffrey of Monmouth's *History of the Kings of Britain* (tr. S. Evans, rev. by C. W. Dunn, London, 1963), which Milton followed in his own *HistBrit*, and suggested that *The soothest Shepherd* (822) 'has a sly significance' because of Geoffrey's reputation as an unblushing romancer; but slyness is very unlikely in this sober context.

J. F. Bense (*Neophilologus* 1, 1915, 62–4), Hanford ('Youth,' 142), and most modern editors confidently identify Meliboeus as Spenser, who told the story of Sabrina in *F.Q.* 2. 10. 17–19. This identification seems to have several kinds of support: in Spenser's description of Sabrina as 'the sad virgin innocent of all'; in Milton's well-known admiration for the sage and serious Spenser as a moral teacher (*Areop, Works* 4, 311), whose poetical son, as he told Dryden, he felt himself to be (Dryden, *Essays*, ed. W. P. Ker, Oxford, 1900, 2, 247); in the phrase *The soothest Shepherd that ere pip't on plains*, applicable without irony to the great poet-teacher who loved to picture himself as Colin, the simple shepherd; and in the model afforded by Spenser himself, who referred to Chaucer as his poetical father, as Milton recognized (Dryden, loc. cit.), under the pastoral name of Tityrus (*S.C., February* 91–2 and Gloss [cf. *June* 81–8 and Gloss]). Thus as Spenser used one name from Virgil's *E.* 1 for Chaucer, Milton used the name of the other speaker for Spenser. But, as the Gloss noted, the 'tale of truth' told by Spenser was not Chaucerian but 'cleane in another kind'; and Milton's treatment of Sabrina is quite different from Spenser's, so that the parallel between the two references to an earlier poet becomes still closer than at first appears. Finally, it should be noted that in strictness what the Attendant Spirit says he learned from Meliboeus old is not the story of Sabrina, or not that story alone, but the remedy that will effect the Lady's release; and this in turn opens the possibility of a second and deeper level of meaning in the allusion to Spenser, who also (*F.Q.* 1. 11. 29–30, 34, and 2. 11. 46) utilizes water as the symbol of grace. [See Woodhouse in IV above, under 1941–2, and critiques subsequent to his article of 1950. One of the latest commentators, P. Brockbank (IV above, under 1968), finds Sabrina's 'principal significance' in 'the returning flow of natural life' that she 'represents when the girl is released from the seducer's spell'; 'but her associations with the River Severn, with Shropshire and the line of sovereignty from ancient Troy (Locrine and Anchises) are quite as telling in the masque's political and regional aspects' (60 and n.).]

822 *soothest*: most truthful (*OED* 3, citing this example); perhaps here, rather, one speaking the profoundest truths, the superlative being as it were transferred to the truths uttered.

823–31 Warton noted, without discrimination, the following versions of the legend: 'Sabrine' (*Mirror for Magistrates*); Drayton, *Poly.*, Song 6; Warner, *Albion's England*; Hardyng's *Chronicle*, and 'an old English Ballad on the subject': these in addition to Spenser, *F.Q.* 2. 10. 17–19; Geoffrey of Monmouth he strangely omits. In Geoffrey (2. 4–5) Locrine, Brutus' eldest son, having defeated Humber and his Huns, took among other spoils the princess Estrildis, with whom he fell in love. Being already betrothed to Gwendolen, daughter of Corineus, Locrine was compelled by her father to marry her, but he kept Estrildis in his palace and had by her a beautiful daughter Sabrina. When Corineus died, Locrine divorced Gwendolen and acknowledged Estrildis as his wife; Gwendolen, withdrawing to her native Cornwall, raised an army and defeated and slew her husband. She thereupon commanded that Estrildis¦ and Sabrina should be cast into the river now called the Severn and that the river should bear the daughter's name and thus perpetuate the memory of her husband's infamy.

The version of Sabrina's story added to the *Mirror for Magistrates* in 1574 (*Parts Added to The Mirror for Magistrates*, ed. Lily B. Campbell, Cambridge, 1946, 102–10), with that of her mother (ibid. 87–101), makes Sabrine a child, emphasizes her innocence, and heightens the pathos by her pleading to be allowed to die in her mother's stead; it also refers (30) to Guendoline as her 'gelous stepdame' (cf. *enraged stepdam*, *Comus* 829). William Warner (*Albion's England*, 1586, 3. 14) gives a brief summary which adds nothing. Spenser's version, likewise brief, has Sabrina alone perish in the Severn, and, while severely reprobating the love of Locrine and Estrild, emphasizes Sabrina's innocence and mentions her virgin state. The tragedy *Locrine* (1595) makes Sabren (who has survived Estrild, dead by her own hand beside Locrine) try to slay herself with her father's sword; then call on the 'Driades,' 'Satiri,' and 'gracious Faries' to join her mourning; and finally forestall Guendoline by drowning herself, whereupon the Queen names the river in recognition of how 'little Sabren resolutely died' (Malone Society Reprints, 1908, 2133–254). Drayton (*Poly.* 6. 153–78) returns to the original version and has mother and daughter cast together into the stream. Drayton adds nothing of significance here, but in 5. 1–24 he describes Sabrine as the enthroned goddess of the river (cf. 841) clad in 'a watchet weed,' the gift of Amphitrite, taught by Nereus, and the object of Thetis' 'speciall care.'

[The story of Sabrina was told briefly by Giles Fletcher the elder in *De Literis Antiquae Britanniae* 236–44. This poem, much altered when published by Phineas Fletcher in 1633, was edited from the MS., with several others, by L. E. Berry (*Anglia* 79, 1961–2, 345–63). L. Bradner (*Musae Anglicanae*, New York, 1940, 39) remarks that 'Milton could not have taken his Sabrina story... from Spenser,... since Spenser does not tell of her transformation into a goddess,' as Fletcher does. It is quite possible that Milton knew this poem (see the account of Fletcher's Latin elegy above, in *Lycidas*: 11), although he was at least as capable of inventing an Ovidian metamorphosis; and Drayton, as we just saw, had made Sabrina goddess of the river.

J. Arthos (*Anglia* 79, 1962, 204–13) observes that in *Comus* and in the episode of the nymph Cyrene in Virgil (*G.* 4. 315 f.) there are 'nymphs who live beneath the waters of a river, and who rise on the supplication of someone in distress'; and he cites some particulars (e.g. note below, on 836–9, including the reference to Spenser's Marinell). For the release of the Lady from imprisonment in the world of matter he finds suggestions of Platonic purification in Porphyry, *De antro Nympharum*.

M. T. Jones-Davies ('Note sur la légende de Sabrina dans le *Comus* de Milton,' *Études Anglaises* 20, 1967, 416–19) cites Thomas Lodge's *Tragicall Complaint of Elstred*, which recounts the misfortunes of Locrine, Elstred and Sabrina, stressing Sabrina's innocence, and she notes some slight incidental parallels on common motifs.]

To conclude, requiring a personage to effect by superior magic the Lady's release, and wishing to use water as the instrument of that magic, Milton chose Sabrina, the goddess of the Severn, as affording a local association for his story. But he had to divest her of all suggestion of her adulterous birth and stress her virgin innocence. [See Hughes's note and R. Blenner-Hassett's discussions of Geoffrey of Monmouth and *Comus* in *Studia Neophilologica* 21 (1949), 216–21, and *MLN* 64 (1949), 315–18. See also above, 821 n.]

823 *Nymph*: see note on 823–31.

824 *sways*: controls (*OED* 9 b). The image is from the driving of horses, as is indicated by *curb* (already used of the curb attached to the bit; cf. Spenser, *F.Q.* 1. 1. 1).

825 *Virgin pure*: MS. *virgin goddesse chast*, changed to present reading.

828 *The*: [*She* in MS., Br., 1637, 1645 (*Works* 1, 559; *Facs.* 424, 332, 292, 211).]

830 *flood*: MS. *floud*, deleted, then *streame*, deleted, and *floud* restored (*Facs.* 424).

832 *water Nymphs*: here evidently Naiads, since river-dwellers, and distinguished from the Nereids (836).

833 *pearled wrists*: MS. *white*, deleted, and *pearled* substituted. Warton noted that Drayton speaks of pearls in connection with the Severn and says of Sabrine as goddess of the river: 'where she meant to goe, / The path was strew'd with Pearle' (*Poly.* 5. 16–17). Verity referred to the masquers in Jonson's *Masque of Blacknesse*: 'twelve Nymphs' who wore 'jewells interlaced with ropes of pearle.

And, for the front, eare, neck, and wrists, the ornament was of the most choise and orient pearle'; and Niger has 'wrists adorned with pearle' (*Ben Jonson* 7, 170–1). Elton suggested *pearled* 'with the dripping water.' *took*: MS. had *receave*, deleted, then *carie*, deleted, then *take*, deleted, finally *took* (*Facs.* 424).

834 *Bearing*. MS. had *and bore*, deleted in favour of *Bearing*. *aged Nereus*: *grandaevus Nereus* (Virgil, *G.* 4. 392); cf. Homer, *Il.* 18. 35 f.; Hesiod, *Theog.* 233–6, 240–64.

835 *lank*: [drooping (*OED a.* 3).]

836–9 Hughes compares the tending of Marinell by the Nereids, who pour into his wounds 'soveraine balme, and Nectar good' (Spenser, *F.Q.* 3. 4. 40). Warton saw the original of *Ambrosial Oils* in Aphrodite's anointing of the dead body of Hector (not Patroclus, as he mistakenly says) in *Il.* 23. 187. Todd added the infusing of nectar and ambrosia into Patroclus' nostrils by Thetis (*Il.* 19. 38). With *through the porch and inlet of each sense* Newton (reported by Todd) compared 'And in the porches of my ears did pour' (Shakespeare, *Ham.* 1. 5. 63). [Arthos (*Anglia* 79, 1962, 206) cites Virgil, *G.* 4. 376–7: *manibus liquidos dant ordine fontis | germanae, tonsisque ferunt mantelia villis*; also 415–18. Watkins (*Anatomy*, 6–7) remarks: 'But surprisingly it is the pure Attendant Spirit who voices the most arresting sensuousness in his account of Sabrina's revival.... This healing spell is counterpart of evil magic, working so much in the same way as Comus' proffered transformation that there is pleasure on the surface of the whole body (*imbathe*), in the smell and taste, in the very feel of the soothing oils penetrating each inlet.']

837 *Asphodil*: [asphodel, the immortal flower of the Elysian fields (Homer, *Od.* 11. 539, 24. 13).]

841 *Made Goddess of the River*. See Drayton, cited under 823–31.

843–6 Warton noted that Clorin in Fletcher's *F. Shep.* (1. 1. 30–40) knows how to cure wounds in men and cattle and counteract the charms put upon them by 'powerful words of wicked art': 'such secret virtue lies / In herbs applied by a virgin's hand.'

844–56 Sabrina's beneficent magical powers and her special care of virgins are Milton's additions to the legend.

844 *Helping*: relieving or curing (*OED* 10), or possibly, in view of the second object, counteracting. Warton took *urchin* in its original sense of hedgehog (*OED* 1), but with a series of quotations from Shakespeare, some of them connecting the urchin with magic and witchcraft (e.g. *Temp.* 2. 2. 4–7); he noted that 'its shape was sometimes supposed to be assumed by mischievous elves.' Cf. *OED* 1 c. *blasts*: probably not the mildewing of crops (as in 639) but more generally infections destructive of animal life (*OED* 6); hence the gratitude of the *Shepherds* (847–8). *ill luck signes*: possibly ill omens, as in 'The owl shriek'd at thy birth, an evil sign' (Shakespeare, *3 H. VI* 5. 6. 44; cf. *OED* 9); but in view of the more acceptable meaning of *Helping*, and the repetition of the idea in *heals* (846), *signes* should perhaps be interpreted as tokens or intentions (*OED* 7) of ill fortune already suffered.

845 *shrewd*: 'evil-disposed, malignant. Passing into a weaker sense: Malicious, mischievous' (*OED* 1, which quotes 'that shrewd and knavish sprite / Call'd Robin Goodfellow,' Shakespeare, *Dream* 2. 1. 33–4). *make*: MS. *leave*, deleted, *make* substituted. After 845 MS. has *and often takes our cattell wth strange pinches* (*Facs.* 424).

846 *pretious viold liquors*: precious liquid (*OED* 1; undifferentiated and hence strictly applicable to water) kept in a vial (*OED*); doubtless the same as the 'Drops that from my fountain pure, / I have kept of pretious cure' (911–12). Whatever symbolic value is attached to the pure and beneficent water in Sabrina's vial, it is clearly contrasted with the 'liquor' in Comus' glass.

847–50 Verity refers the reader back to the Lady's description of shepherd festivals (170–6), but the relation is, like that observed in 846 n., clearly one of contrast. Warton compared Spenser, *Proth.* 73–7: 'Then forth they all out of their baskets drew / Great store of Flowers, the honour of the field / . . .And all the Waves did strew.' Verity added: 'how oft hath Thyrsil crown'd / With songs and garlands thy ⟨Cam's⟩ obscurer head?' (P. Fletcher, *Pisc. Ecl.* 2. 8).

848 *rustick*: MS. *lovely*, deleted, *rustick* substituted.

850 *pinks, and gaudy*: MS. *& of bonnie*, deleted, replaced by present reading.

851 *the old Swain*: Meliboeus. [By a conventional kind of fiction, his authority is claimed, although what follows was not said by Spenser (or Geoffrey of Monmouth). See above, 821 n.]

852 *The*: MS. *each*, deleted, *the* substituted. *clasping*: encircling. *thaw the numming spell*. MS. (*Facs.* 424) first had *secret holding spell*, deleted, then *melt each numming spell*, changed to *thaw the*. Todd cited 'benumming Charmes' (*Barons Warres* 2, st. 11, Drayton, 2, 30).

855–6 Milton emphasizes the care of the virgin Sabrina for virgins and virginity in a plea that Thyer (in Todd) related to that of the Danaides to Artemis in Aeschylus, *Supp.* 144 f.: 'And may Zeus' pure daughter. . .look upon me;

and, grieved at our pursuit, come with all her might, a virgin to a virgin's aid, to deliver me' (L.C.L.).

856 *In hard besetting need.* MS. had *in honourd vertues cause*, deleted, and *in hard distressed need* substituted (*Facs.* 424).

857 MS. had *power*, deleted, and *call* substituted, but deleted and *power* restored; *strong*, deleted, replaced by *adjuring* (*Works* 1, 562; *Facs.* 424).

858–65 On the music for the Attendant Spirit's (i.e. Lawes') song see above, the end of *Comus* 1 and the beginning of 229–42 n.

859 *Listen*: MS. *Listen virgin*, but *virgin* deleted (*Facs.* 426).

860 *glassie...wave* translates Virgil's *vitrea unda* (*A.* 7. 759: Todd). *translucent*: the earliest example of the word in *OED* 2, but Warton noted it in R. Brathwait's *Loves Labyrinth* (1615), 29; and Dunster noted 'tra-lucent' in Sylvester, *Sonn.* 14 (Grosart, 2, 39); [this appears also in Sylvester's *Ode to Astraea* (Grosart, 2, 50) and in Drayton's *Idea* 17 (Drayton, 2, 319). Todd cites other examples.]

861 *knitting*: tying as with a knot (*OED* 1).

862 *train*: apparently a figurative use derived from the train of a robe (not recorded in *OED*). *amber-dropping*. The explanation depends of course on the sense in which *amber* is taken. (1) According to *OED* (*sb.*[1]), it originally meant what soon came to be called (but without displacing in Milton's day the earlier and less specific term) ambergris, a product of the whale used for its perfume. If that is the meaning of *amber* here, *amber-dropping* means shedding perfume (of ambergris), and the marine association makes it probable. Todd quoted: 'Their haire they ware loose..., whose dangling amber trammells...seemed to drop baulme on their delicious bodies' (Nashe, *Works* 1, 380). Cf. Milton's 'Amber sent of odorous perfume' (*SA* 720). (2) Amber had also, and perhaps more commonly, its modern meaning, a yellowish translucent fossil resin (*OED*: *sb.*[1] 3), and was used for colour; cf. 'an amber cloud' (332 above) and 'Amber light' (*L'All* 61). (3) Amber was used, less commonly, for *liquidamber*, the resinous gum exuded from the bark of the tree (*OED*: *sb.* 1). Warton, in his rather confused note, seems to favour (2). Dunster cited 'Locks like streames of liquid Amber' (Sylvester, *Wood-Mans Bear*, st. 42, Grosart, 2, 309). Verity, adopting (2), explains *amber-dropping* as 'wet with the amber-coloured water of the river'; [likewise Hanford, who allows for a suggestion of perfume]. Elton also adopts (2) but explains: 'Sabrina has amber-hued hair through which the water drips'; he summarily dismisses (1) as a needless complication (as though poetry had no use for secondary suggestions). Todd's extract from Nashe seems to make amber refer to the colour of the hair (2) and to the perfume, not of ambergris but of the scented gum (3), since 'balm' was used of this natural product (*OED*: balm 1). Wright adopts (1), as the present editor would, at least for the primary meaning, since it furnishes a marine association without contradicting the suggestion conveyed in *silver lake* (864), avoiding indeed all the difficulties attendant on the idea of colour whether of the water or the hair. But *OED* (amber: *sb.*[1] 7) notices the tendency of the poets to confuse sense (3) with (1) and (2) in such phrases as *amber-dropping*, which it does not seek to explain with any precision. [It seems likely that Milton would not forget the mythological and watery origin of amber given in Ovid, *M.* 2. 364–6. To quote Sandys' translation (1626, 31): 'From these cleere dropping trees, tears yearly flow: / They, hardned by the Sunne, to Amber grow; / Which, on the moysture-giving River spent, / To Roman Ladies, as his gift, is sent.' This perhaps favours the idea of drops of water falling from Sabrina's hair (cf. 'The dropping amber' in a tree-list in Browne, *Brit. Past.* 1. 4. 668); but probably (1) is the most satisfactory explanation. Blondel (135) remarks that *Amber* suggests at once 'la transparence et le parfum....Ne pas confondre avec l'ambregris (*grisamber*)....L'ambre s'applique ici à la chevelure blonde (couleur classique) de la nymphe....' He cites (after Todd) Drayton's nereids, who perfume their lips with 'costly Ambergris' (*Poly.* 20. 112).]

863 *dear honours sake*: i.e. chastity's sake (*OED* 3).

864 *silver lake*. Todd compared 'Severn's silver waves' (*A Mirour for Magistrates*, 1610, 730; ed. J. Haslewood, 1815, 2, 2, 760. [*Silver* was a common epithet for rivers, especially in Drayton, e.g. 'silver Severne' (2, 283), and Browne.] Verity noted that Virgil used *lacus* of a river (the Tiber) in *A.* 8. 74; cf. ibid. 66.

866–88 After 865 MS. adds direction for the following lines: *to be said*; Br.: *The verse to singe or not* (*Facs.* 426, 334). There is no music extant for this passage. While Milton evidently intended the whole passage (866–88) to be uttered by the Attendant Spirit (MS. and printed texts), at the performance, according to directions in Br., 870–1, 874–5, 878–81 were assigned to the Elder Brother, the intervening couplets to the Second Brother, the Attendant Spirit (*De*:) resuming at 882 and completing the passage (*Facs.* 334–5).

Lines 866–88 are the 'adjuring verse' promised at 857. In MS., 868–73 are inserted in margin; 878–81 are marked for deletion (but restored in printed text); and 882–3 are inserted in margin (*Facs.* 426). Warton noticed a similar form of invocation in Fletcher's *F. Shep.* 5. 3. 91–101. Milton had placed 'this

Ile' under the sway of Neptune and his 'blu-hair'd deities' (18–29); hence, except Sabrina herself, the deities named are classical, not local, and are given more or less classical epithets and attributes.

867 *great Oceanus.* For the Ocean stream that surrounds the earth and is the source of all rivers, editors cite Homer, *Il.* 14. 245, 21. 195–7, Hesiod, *Theog.* 20; and 'Fayre Niger, sonne to great Oceanus' (*Masque of Blacknesse* 99, Ben Jonson 7, 172); Drayton, *Poly.* 17. 14.

868 *earth-shaking Neptune's mace*: the stock Homeric epithet for Poseidon.
mace: trident, as in 'First came great Neptune with his threeforkt mace' (Spenser, *F.Q.* 4. 11. 11; cf. *Muiopotmos* 313–15).

869 *Tethys grave majestick pace*: wife of Oceanus, mother of rivers and of the Oceanids (Hesiod, *Theog.* 337); the epithets are perhaps suggested by the Greek *potnia* (ibid. 368).

870 *hoary Nereus wrincled look*: an obvious inference from Nereus' old age (above, 834 and n.). Servius (on Virgil, *G.* 4. 402) says that all the sea gods are old and are presented as white-headed because of the foam of the waves (Newton).

871 *Carpathian wisards hook.* Virgil (*G.* 4. 387–95) describes Proteus as living in Carpathian waters (Carpathos, an island between Rhodes and Crete: see Osgood, *C.M.* 77); as *vates*, hence *wisard*; and as the shepherd of Neptune's herds, hence his *hook*; cf. Homer, *Od.* 4. 411–13. Todd cited Ovid's label, *Carpathius vates* (*M.* 11. 249); [also in Statius, *Ach.* 1. 136].

872 *scaly Tritons winding shell.* Triton was Neptune's trumpeter ('the Herald of the Sea,' *Lyc* 89), and *scaly*, like the sea deities described by Pliny, *squamis modo hispido corpore* (*N.H.* 9. 4. 9; cf. Osgood, *C.M.* 77). His *winding* [twisted, curling] *shell* is the *cava bucina...tortilis* of Ovid, *M.* 1. 335–6. [Although the appearance of Triton was familiar enough, one might quote Sandys' commentary (*Ovid*, 1632, 32): 'a body covered with small and hard scales...winding a shell.' Sandys' translation (p. 8) has 'his lowd sounding shell' and 'his wreathed trumpet.']

873 *old sooth-saying Glaucus spell.* Glaucus, a Euboean fisherman, was transformed into a sea god by his chance eating of a magical herb and endowed with prophetic power (Ovid, *M.* 13. 904–68; Euripides, *Orest.* 363–4; Spenser, *F.Q.* 4. 11. 13: 'Glaucus, that wise southsayes understood').

874 *Leucothea's lovely hands.* Ino, daughter of Cadmus and sister to Semele, the mother of Bacchus, became his foster-mother; by proclaiming Bacchus' powers and by marrying Ino, Athamas, son of Aeolus, incurred Juno's wrath; driven to madness by Juno, he killed one of his infant sons, while Ino escaped with the other, Melicertes; pursued by Athamas, she leaped with the child into the sea; at Venus' entreaty, Neptune transformed her into a marine deity under the Greek name Leucothea ('the white goddess'). She was identified with the Roman Matuta, goddess of the dawn, and Melicertes became Palaemon, identified with the Roman Portunus, guardian of harbours (Ovid, *M.* 4. 416–542, *F.* 6. 485–550). Homer (*Od.* 5. 332) refers to her as Ino of the fair ankles and mentions her hands (462) but with no descriptive epithet. It is perhaps less the beauty of her hands than her beneficence to mortals that explains Milton's *lovely*, which means either loving, kind (*OED* 1) or worthy of being loved (ibid. 2). Hughes (1937) suggests that, because of her identification with Matuta, Milton was adapting the Homeric 'rosy-fingered Dawn.'

875 *her son*: Melicertes (Palaemon, Portunus); see 874 n. and *Lyc* 164 n.

876 *Thetis tinsel-slipper'd feet.* Thetis, one of the Nereids (Hesiod, *Theog.* 244), bears in Homer the epithet 'silver-footed,' which, as Todd noted, was carried on by the English poets, e.g. Chapman, *Il.* 18. 124; Browne, *Brit. Past.* 2. 1. 817; Jonson, *Pans Anniversarie* 208, *Neptunes Triumph* 397 (*Ben Jonson* 7, 536, 694). *Tinsel*, probably in the obsolete sense of glittering, did not always carry a suggestion of disparagement (*OED*: *sb.* 3 and *a.* 6).

877 *Songs of Sirens sweet.* The names so far invoked have been appropriate as belonging not only to marine deities but to deities more or less beneficent to man. Some have a further appropriateness: Nereus for his compassionate aid of Sabrina, Thetis as one of the Nereids to whom he committed her, and Leucothea as having a fate partly parallel to Sabrina's. But the Sirens, though sea nymphs, are malevolent destroyers of men (Homer, *Od.* 12. 39–54, 165–200; Virgil, *A.* 5. 864–6; etc.). There is little use in urging the beneficence of the Sirens in seeking for Proserpina, whose companions they were (Ovid, *M.* 5. 552–63), since Milton alludes only to their song. Nor can these lines be linked with the Platonic Sirens of the eight celestial spheres (Plato, *Rep.* 10. 617; cf. *Arc* 63–9 n.), since this would break the connection with the sea and since the following names (878–9) belong to the Homeric Sirens. All one can say is that Milton here concentrates our attention on the beauty of the song and throws over it a mantle of innocence in contrast with the singing of Circe and the 'Sirens three' described by Comus (251–60 and n.). [Cf. the linking of Leonora Baroni with Parthenope (*Leon* 3. 1 f.); and in the *Shep. Garl.* 3. 93 (Drayton, 1, 57) 'The Syrens sing sweete layes' in praise of Beta.]

878 *dead Parthenope's dear tomb.* The Siren Parthenope was supposed to have her tomb near Naples, which was therefore called Parthenope (Virgil, *G.* 4. 564; Ovid, *M.* 14. 101); see note on *Leon* 3. 1 f. (*V.C.* 1, 151).

879–81 Ligea is named among a group of river nymphs by Virgil (*G.* 4. 336; cf. Drayton, *Poly.* 20. 127). That Milton had the passage in mind is probable, since he goes on to speak of *all the Nymphs* (882). [He would know the tradition, starting from the commentator Eustathius, that Ligea was the name of one of Homer's Sirens: Hughes.] Verity notes Virgil's reference to the hair of his nymphs, *caesariem effusae nitidam per candida colla* (*G.* 4. 337). While Ovid describes the nymph Salmacis as combing her tresses with a boxwood comb, *saepe Cytoriaco deducit pectine crines* (*M.* 4. 311), Milton's fiction is 'heightened with the brilliancy of romance' (Warton); the suggestion is of the mermaids of Northern mythology (Masson) or of the Lorelei, later pictured by Heine as combing her hair *mit goldener Kamme* (Elton). From the Middle Ages onward the classical Sirens were often equated with mermaids (*OED*: siren 2; [W. P. Mustard, *MLN* 23, 1908, 21–4; Shakespeare, *Dream* 2. 1. 149–54. Mustard cites Lyly's *Loves Metamorphosis* 4. 2 (*Works*, ed. Bond, 3, 322), where the 'Syren' speaks of her 'golden lockes' and a stage direction is 'Sing with a Glasse in her hand and a Combe.'] Osgood (*C.M.* 78) notes that, whereas Homer (*Od.* 12. 45) has the Sirens seated in a meadow singing, Virgil (*A.* 5. 864–6) places them on cliffs above drumming surf. While the *golden comb* is literal, *diamond rocks* is perhaps figurative for wet rocks shining with diamond brightness (*OED*: diamond 3b, though examples are from 19th century only). Warton compared 'Such light as from maine rocks of diamound' (G. Fletcher, *C.V.* 1. 61). Todd added: 'Christall lights that shone / Against the Sunne like Rockes of Diamond' (H. Peacham, *Period of Mourning*, 1613, *Vis.* vi, sig. C2).

882–3 *all the Nymphs...wily glance.* Drayton describes, with very different effect, a dance of the Nymphs 'her reed when Syrinx sounds' (*Poly.* 20. 145–8).

wily glance. It is not easy to attach a precise and appropriate meaning to *wily* (which seems, however, to have troubled no editor), unless it refers to the secrecy of the dance, though this would seem to fit native fairies rather than classical Nymphs. [Might the word mean 'seductive' in an innocent sense? Or frolicsome (cf. 'Quips and Cranks, and wanton Wiles,' *L'All* 27)?]

884 *heave thy rosie head:* heave, lift (*OED* 1; cf. *L'All* 145; *SA* 197). *rosie:* probably sweet-smelling, fragrant as a rose (*OED* 2); possibly rose-encircled (ibid. 3), which would afford another contrast with Comus (105–6).

885 *coral-pav'n.* Warton found a parallel in Drayton's 'cleare pearle-paved

Irt' (*Poly.* 30. 121) and an association of Sabrina with coral in his description of her robe (ibid. 5. 15). Todd reported the actual epithet, differently applied, in Anthony Stafford's *Staffords Niobe* (1611), p. 9 [apparently it is not in *The first Part*; presumably it is in the second]. Cf. *PL* 7. 405.

886 *bridle in thy headlong wave*: a return to the image of 824 (see n.).

After **888** ⟨Direction⟩. This, like the direction on Comus' palace (after 657) is less detailed than was common in the printed versions of many masques, which were often written in the past tense and constituted a fairly elaborate description of the performance. While at Ludlow the intricate machinery used at Whitehall would not be available, we may safely imagine Sabrina's slowly rising from the centre of the stage in her chariot, surrounded by the Nymphs, all adorned in ways suggested in preceding lines. The time occupied by this slow-moving tableau and the action that followed would give the audience an opportunity to apprehend whatever symbolic significance the poet intended and they were capable of grasping. [Demaray (*Masque Tradition*, 101–2, 104, 116–17) suggests that Sabrina's sliding chariot could, like other properties, have been borrowed from 'Sir Henry Herbert's revels storeroom' in London, and that the chariot 'may have slid, not back and forth, but up and down.' He sees Sabrina rising under multi-coloured lights; he also (116) refers to 'the Nymph of Severn' in Daniel's *Tethys Festival* (1610). Brooks and Hardy (225) remark that Sabrina's '"sliding Chariot" is simply the water, and "stayes," waits for her, beside the bank, only in the paradoxical sense that there is always the flowing water there. The jewels that adorn it are only the names of gems applied to the colors of the water....' They do not explain how this idea would be dramatically rendered.]

889–900 Music for Sabrina's song is not preserved [*Facs.* 342–3; Diekhoff, *Maske*, 241–50: see Parker, 794–5, n. 58]. Nor is there any indication as to the person, perhaps a professional, who played the role. [M. Nicolson (*John Milton*, 69) suggests Lady Alice's 'older married sister, Lady Penelope, who had had masquing experience.' Demaray (*Masque Tradition*, 77, etc.) repeats the nomination (without reference to Miss Nicolson). The idea is questioned by Diekhoff (*Maske*, 5) because Lady Penelope would have been listed with other members of the family. Parker (791, n. 36) suggests: 'Since *Comus* was in so many ways a family entertainment, perhaps Henry Lawes's wife played the part.']

889–90 Warton compared: 'I am this fountain's god: below, / My waters to a river grow, / And 'twixt two banks with osiers set, / That only prosper in the wet, / Through the meadows do they glide' (Fletcher, *F. Shep.* 3. 1. 404–7).

891 *sliding*: gliding. *stayes*: halts (*OED*: *v.*¹ 1).

892–4 The lines may be explained by this paraphrase: the chariot is set with agate and blue turquoise and green emerald, of which the lustre seems to take on a wayward motion when reflected in the flowing water. [Coleridge (Brinkley, 567) took 894 to refer to 'the wandering flitting tints and hues of the Water.' Trent in a full note remarked that '"Strays," being singular, need not keep us from making it agree with the stones, for it might agree with its nearest subject,' though he questioned the use of the word. Cf. above, 'After 888 ⟨Direction⟩,' n.]

892 *azurn*. Todd (followed by Browne) suggested that Milton coined the form from the Italian *azzurino*, as *cedar'n* (989) from *cedrino*. [Br. has *Azur'd*.]

    sheen: lustre (*OED*: *sb.*[1] 1).

893 *Turkis*: turquoise, sometimes called Turkey or Turkish stone because, though originating in Persia, it was imported through Turkey (Masson).

894 *That in the channel strayes*. MS. had *that my rich wheeles inlayes*, deleted, and replaced by present reading, which is also in Br. (*Works* 1, 565; *Facs*. 426, 335).

896–8 Ideas and phrases echo or parallel earlier poets. Warton cited 'on the sands with printless foot' (Shakespeare, *Temp*. 5. 1. 34): 'when she dooth walke? / Scarce she dooth the Primrose head depresse, / or tender stalke / Of blew-vein'd Violets, / Whereon her foote she sets' (W. H., *England's Helicon*, ed. Rollins, 1, 67). Todd compared: 'See the dew-drops how they kiss / Every little flower..., / Hanging on their velvet heads' (Fletcher, *F. Shep*. 2. 1. 5–7); (of Camilla): *cursuque pedum praevertere ventos. / illa vel intactae segetis per summa volaret / gramina nec teneras cursu laesisset aristas* (Virgil, *A*. 7. 807–9); (of Venus): 'The grass stoops not, she treads on it so light' (Shakespeare, *Venus* 1028); 'Her treading would not bend a blade of grasse' (Jonson, *Sad Shepherd* 1. 1. 5). We may add: 'Or, like a nymph,... / Dance on the sands, and yet no footing seen' (Shakespeare, *Venus* 147–8); 'And thence did Venus learne to lead / Th' Idalian Braules, and so ⟨to⟩ tread / As if the wind, not she did walke; / Nor prest a flower, nor bow'd a stalke' (*Vision of Delight* 228–31, *Ben Jonson* 7, 470).

899 *request*. In MS. Milton first wrote *behe* (evidently starting *behest*), then substituted *request* (*Facs*. 426).

903 *charmed band*: bonds (*OED*: *sb.*[1] 1) imposed by magic (see 51 n., 852 n.). MS. has *mag*, deleted, followed by *charmed*.

906 *unblest*: unhallowed, evil (*OED* 3; cf. *PL* 1. 238).

907 *best*: apparently an adverb modifying *To help* rather than an adjective modifying *office*.

909 *Brightest Lady*: MS. *vertuous*, deleted, and *Brightest* substituted (*Works* 1, 566; *Facs.* 426).

912 *of pretious cure*: of great value as a remedy (*OED*: cure *sb.*[1] 7).

913 *Thrice*. 'All this ceremony...is from the ancient practice of lustration by drops of water,' as in Virgil, *A.* 6. 229–30: *idem ter socios pura circumtulit unda,* / *spargens rore levi*; and Ovid, *M.* 4. 479–80 (Warton). For the symbolic significance and the possible influence of Spenser see above, 821 n. Warton, who probably exaggerated the influence of Fletcher's *F. Shep.* on *Comus*, cited a number of passages therefrom illustrating magic or purifying rituals with water, one of them involving a thrice-repeated act.

914 *rubied lip*. Todd cited 'The melting rubies on her cherry lip' (Browne, *Brit. Past.* 2. 3. 1045) and 'Wanton Eye, or Lip of Ruby' (Wither, *Faire-Virtue*, *Juvenilia*, Part 3, Spenser Society, 1871, 815). Browne added 'Diana's lip / Is not more smooth and rubious' (Shakespeare, *Twel.* 1. 4. 31–2); *rubied*, referring to colour, occurs also in Shakespeare, *Per.* 5, prol. 8, and *PL* 5. 633.

915–16 *this marble...glutenous heat*: the 'inchanted Chair' of the Direction after 657; the gum is kept glutinous by magically induced heat.

917–18 Warton added further, and still more remote, parallels from Fletcher's *F. Shep.*

920 *Amphitrite's bowr*. Amphitrite, who with her sisters calms the waves, was the daughter of Nereus and Doris (Hesiod, *Theog.* 243, 254) and wife of Poseidon (Neptune). Her *bowr* stands for Neptune's court.

After **920** ⟨Direction⟩ *Sabrina descends*, etc. MS. (*Facs.* 426) adds this direction after 918 (i.e. the Lady rises as Sabrina pronounces the spell broken, and Sabrina's two final lines are spoken as she descends).

921–36 There is no indication in the printed texts that these lines were sung (other songs are clearly indicated and printed in italics); nor is there music for these lines. But at 936 MS. has (in margin) *Song ends*; so also Br. (*Works* 1, 568; *Facs.* 428, 337).

921–2 According to the legend, as established by Geoffrey of Monmouth (1. 3 f.) and rehearsed by Milton (*HistBrit, Works* 10, 6–16), Brutus, who led the Trojan settlement of Britain and was the father of Locrine and grandfather of

Sabrina, was himself the son of Silvius, son of Ascanius, son of Aeneas, whose father Anchises died on the voyage to Italy (Virgil, *A*. 3. 708–11). [For references to the whole tradition of 'New Troy,' see Bush, *Mythol.*, 1963, 37–40. The fullest account is Sir T. D. Kendrick's *British Antiquity* (London, 1950); a recent short one is in Patrides, *Milton*, 252–6.]

923–36 Warton quotes at length votive addresses of gratitude to river gods from Fletcher's *F. Shep.* (3. 1. 463–74) and Browne's *Brit. Past.* (1. 2. 272–90). To illustrate the more homely pastoral tone of these passages, we might take some lines from Fletcher: 'For thy kindness to me shown, / Never from thy banks be blown / Any tree, with windy force, / Cross thy streams, to stop thy course; / May no beast that comes to drink, / With his horns cast down thy brink; / May none that for thy fish do look, / Cut thy banks to dam thy brook' (3. 1. 463–70). It seems idle to suppose with Masson and Verity that Milton is by his references tracing the course of the Severn—especially when we come to *Groves of myrrhe, and cinnamon* (936). The Attendant Spirit is uttering a prayer that would heap every blessing upon Sabrina and her river. The goddess is central (as she is to the action of the masque); the local references are secondary and a concession to the occasion. If this is kept firmly in mind, most of the difficulties in interpreting the passage disappear.

923 *brimmed*: filled to the brim, with waves standing perhaps for the river (not merely for the water within the banks, in which case we should expect 'brimming' as in *PL* 4. 336, although we should note that Milton does not always distinguish clearly between the force of present and perfect participles, and that *brimmed* may here have in intention an active force (cf. *singed*, 927 and n.). MS. had *crystall*, deleted, and *brimmed* substituted (*Facs.* 428).

924–6 Warton remarked on the accuracy of this reference to the effect on the Severn of flood waters from the Welsh mountains. Todd cited: 'To whom the Rivers tribute pay, / Downe the high mountaines sliding' (Campion, *Hymne in praise of Neptune*, in Davison's *Poetical Rhapsody*, ed. Rollins, 1, 213). *the snowy hills*: MS. *from*, deleted, replaced by *the*.

927 *singed*. The participle has the active force of singeing, scorching (Verity).

928 *tresses*: 'the foliage along the banks' (Masson; Hanford); more probably the tresses of Sabrina herself.

929–30 Dunster compared 'muds / Defil'd the crystall of smooth-sliding floods' (Sylvester, *D.W.W.* 2. 1. 1. 116–17, Grosart, 1, 100); and cited *Lyc* 86 ('Smooth-sliding'). Todd added: 'As long as…Rivers… / Their moulten

Crystall poure... / Into the Maine' (W. L'isle, *To the Prince*, st. 35, prefixed to his *Saxon Treatise*, 1623). This parallels Milton's use of *molten* to mean liquified without the usual implication of heat.

931-2 Todd cited Spenser's description of a shore 'bestrowed all with rich aray / Of pearles and pretious stones of great assay, / And all the gravell mixt with golden owre' (*F.Q*. 3. 4. 18). *Beryl* is a class of precious or semi-precious stones, including the aquamarine (*OED* 1); beryl and gold occur together in Exod. 28. 20. If one could accept Masson's prosaic suggestion that the purport of the blessings invoked for the Severn was 'solid commercial prosperity,' and if a realistic reading had to be conjured up for these lines, they might be taken as referring to ships laden with wealth and brought on the billows from foreign shores to the port of Bristol.

933-4 Carrying on the suggestion from 931-2 n., one might interpret *many a tower and terras* as referring to cities or to mansions; and *lofty head* (according to Masson and to Verity, who shares Masson's preoccupation with literal readings) to the river's sources in the Welsh mountains, or perhaps to the top of the cliffs in the Gorge of the Severn at Bristol, since in the figurative use *head* need not necessarily mean the source of a river (*OED* 16), although the context would suggest it.

935-6 Editors have puzzled over the grammar and sense. Masson, following an explanation reported by Todd, suggests that Milton is influenced by two Greek verbs meaning to put a crown around and to put a crown upon, so that the sense would be: 'May thy lofty head be *crowned round* with many a tower and terrace, and thy banks here and there be *crowned upon* with groves.' [Trent sees this as 'a rather stiff and mechanical explanation.' Bell's paraphrase is: 'May thy lofty head be crowned round with many a tower and terrace, and here and there (may thy lofty head be crowned) with groves of myrrh and cinnamon (growing) upon thy banks.'] Verity and Elton in effect adopt the first paraphrase without reference to the Greek (or to Todd or Masson); but Verity adds a comparison with the 'crown of towers' (Sophocles, *Antig.* 120, referring to the towers around Thebes), and Elton the more fruitful idea that Milton is adding to the literal meaning a suggestion that the river goddess is 'a kind of *turrita Cybele* [cf. Ovid, *M.* 10. 696, *turrita Mater*, and Milton, *El* 1. 74, *Turrigerum late conspicienda caput*] with a tiara of towers. But we are hardly meant to stop and think the matter out distinctly'—or, in other words, consult a Variorum Commentary. Ovid gives an explanation of Cybele's crown: *at cur turrifera caput est onerata corona? / an primis turres urbibus illa dedit?* (*F.* 4. 219-20). The scents of myrrh and cinnamon were prized in Old Testament times (Prov. 7. 17, etc.). Even Masson and Verity are at a loss for a local reference here.

After **936**: MS. *Song ends* (see 921–36 n.); Br., same note; 1637 and 1645, a space after 936, indicating a separation and pause.

937–56 Br. divides the passage between the Attendant Spirit and the Elder Brother: 937–42, 955–6 go to the latter, with the direction *El bro:* at 937; *De:* (i.e. Demon, Attendant Spirit) at 943; and *el br:* at 955 (*Facs.* 337–8). At 937 Br. has *lady*, deleted, and *sister* substituted. These variants are not in MS.; and 1637, 1645, 1673 return to what was evidently Milton's intention, to give the whole speech (or song and speech) 921–56 to the Attendant Spirit.

937 *Com Lady while Heaven lends us grace.* [Editors seem to have been unanimous in ignoring this line, since religious symbolism has been largely a concern of recent criticism. Woodhouse (*UTQ* 19, 1949–50, 223) sees the line as a signal 'lest we should fail to realize the significance of Sabrina's intervention [as the symbol or channel of grace], and the limitation of his [the Attendant Spirit's] own role.' Brooks and Hardy (226–7) dwell on the line, along with other evidence for the theme of grace. The theme comes up in the critical interpretations of Woodhouse and some others (above, IV).]

941 *waste*: superfluous (see 728 n.).

944 *this gloomy covert wide.* Assuming that the 'stately Palace' (Direction after 657) is an interior, Elton bids us imagine that the Spirit points out of a window of the palace into the wild wood. Verity hesitates between an interior, from which the wild wood is visible, and 'some change of scenery so as to represent the original wood again instead of the interior of the palace.' Both ideas are patently absurd. There is no direction for such a change. Nor can one conceive when it is supposed to have occurred unless at some point the 'inchanted Chair' with the Lady in it were transported to the wood, which would surely call for some notice in the text. But the rising of Sabrina from the water cannot have been *in* Comus' palace. The only solution that avoids all difficulties is to suppose—as the phrasing of the Direction after 657 readily permits—that the whole scene is *before* the palace. [Cf. M. Nicolson, *John Milton*, 72–3; Demaray, *Masque Tradition*, 116 f.]

948 *gratulate*: welcome, greet (*OED* 1). [Verity cites: 'And gratulate his safe return to Rome' (Shakespeare, *Tit.* 1. 1. 221).]

955–6 No editor seems to find an explanation requisite—or perhaps available. The meaning must be that the first light of dawn is appearing from beyond the horizon, but above their heads darkness prevails and the stars are visible. [With 956 cf. Virgil, *A.* 3. 512, 5. 721, 738, 835. Madsen ('Idea of Nature,' 217) interprets thus: 'The imagery of light...continues to reinforce the main theme.... It may seem surprising that after the intervention of Divine Grace "night sits monarch yet in the mid sky." But this is the human condition: perfect illumination will be found only in our heavenly home. But the light of nature shines bright ("the Stars grow high") for those under the influence of grace.' Some readers may take the lines as literal and scenic rather than allegorical.]

956 *sits*: MS. *raignes*, deleted, replaced by *sitts* (*Facs.* 428).

After **956** ⟨Direction⟩ *The Scene changes*, etc. Here the scene is before the Castle (cf. 944 n.). The *Countrey-Dancers* present what is 'technically...the second Anti-masque' (Verity). MS. has *countrie dances & such like gambols &c.*; then, just below, *After* (deleted, replaced by) *at those sports the Dæmon wᵗʰ yᵉ 2 bro. & the Ladie enter the Dæmon sings* (*Facs.* 428). Br. has *towards the end of these sports....* (ibid. 338). ['The country dancers clearly do not join in—indeed they are explicitly excluded from—the final dance of the masque.... Though country dances were occasionally danced by courtiers, I suspect that the "country dancers" of *Comus* were actually rustics of Ludlow, called upon, most appropriately, to join in the entertainment honouring their new Lord President.' (Parker, 790, n. 34)]

957-74 [The music for these two songs is given in *Facs.* 343-4 and Diekhoff, *Maske*, 248-9.]

958 Cf. *L'All* 98.

959 *without duck or nod.* Warton compared 'Duck with French nods and apish courtesy' (Shakespeare, *R. III* 1. 3. 49), but the suggestion here is quite different: there is nothing of *Court guise* in the ungainly gestures, the jerking bows (*OED*: duck *sb.*² 2), of the *Countrey-Dancers*.

960-1 *Other trippings...lighter toes.* Cf. *L'All* 33-4. *trippings*: dances (*OED* 1; cf. *Arc* 96-9). *trod*: Todd illustrates the related and 'customary' phrase to 'tread a measure' from Shakespeare, *L.L.L.* 5. 2. 185 and *A.Y.L.* 5. 4. 45. *Of lighter toes*: MS. *of speedier toeing*, changed to *of nimbler toe*, and finally to present reading. [*lighter*: more accomplished and graceful (than the *Countrey-Dancers*).]

Court guise: courtly deportment (*OED*: guise 3). Verity takes the announcement to signify other dances in which unnamed characters, as well as the Lady, her Brothers, and the Attendant Spirit, will take part; see 'After 974 ⟨Direction⟩' n.

962-4 *As Mercury...on the Leas.* There seems to be no classical source for Mercury as inventor of the dance as well as the lyre, but Osgood (*C.M.* 42) notes a reference to the dance of the nymphs among the immortals and the association with them of the Sileni and Hermes (*Homeric Hymn to Aphrodite* 257-66). [Cf. *IlPen* 136-7 n.] Milton may be thinking less of classical precedents than of masques, and specifically, as Bush suggests (*SP* 28, 1931, 264; *Mythol.*, 1963, 275, n. 34), of *Pans Anniversarie* 176-8 (*Ben Jonson* 7, 535): 'Pan, / That leads the Naiad's, and the Dryad's forth; / And to their daunces more then Hermes can'; and he might be contrasting the more sophisticated Hermes with the rural Pan, whose followers are the *Countrey-Dancers.* *mincing.* The *OED* explanation is not satisfactory because it is derogatory, emphasizing affectedness instead of a conscious (but in the context desirable) daintiness, which is plainly its force here. This was apparently not unusual when *mince* and its derivatives were applied to dancing: cf. 'Ye Mayds, the Horne-pipe then, so minsingly that tread' (Drayton, *Poly.* 27. 125), and 'Now, Shepheards... / in neate Jackets minsen on the Playnes' (*Egl.* 7. 13-14, Drayton, 2, 552), both cited by Warton. [Demaray (119), citing James Arnold, says that *mincing* 'was a dancing term that meant doubling the time to make twice as many steps to a musical measure.' He also remarks that Mercury 'very often presented the main masque dancers in court masques, a task the Daemon next performs.']

964 *Lawns*: see above, 567 n. The *Dryades* are woodland nymphs. *Leas*: tracts of open ground; in poetic use, meadows (*OED*: *sb.*[1]).

969 *timely*: early (*OED*: *adv.* 1).

970 *patience.* MS. deleted *patience*, substituted *temperance*, then restored *patience* (*Facs.* 428). [The word has the original Latin sense of 'endurance, capacity to suffer.'] *truth*: fidelity, constancy, to principle (*OED* 1).

971 *assays*: testings (*OED* 1; cf. *PL* 4. 932), but with a strong secondary suggestion of tribulation (*OED* 2; cf. *PR* 1. 264).

972 *Praise.* MS. had *bays*, deleted, replaced by *praise*.

973-4 These words give significance to the dance by connecting it with the main action.

After **974** ⟨Direction⟩ *The dances ended*, etc. MS. (*Facs.* 430) adds *all* after *dances*. This, and indeed the plural, support Verity's suggestion (above, 960-1 n.) that there were dances in which others besides the Egerton children and Lawes took part—in other words, that the formal dance bulked larger in *Comus* than critics often assume. *the Spirit Epiloguizes*: MS. *the Dæmon sings.* or

974

sayes. The British Museum MS. that preserves the music provides as first song music for the lines transferred in Br. to Prologue (*Facs.* 341); but *Epiloguizes* suggests rather recitation, which would of course permit a greater concentration upon content.

975–1022 MS. had a first draft of these lines (34 in all), deleted, designated in *Works* 1, 572, and here, as MS. 1; and the expanded [and corrected] version (47 lines) designated as MS. 2; the additions in MS. 2 are 983–6 and 998–1010. MS. 1 had two lines, after 978 (deleted before final deletion of the whole) which were restored in MS. 2 and printed texts as 1013–14. For these lines and for the principal changes in phrasing, see *Facs.* 430, 432, *Works* 1, 572 f., and notes below. Br. omits 975–98, having transferred them with the necessary changes to the opening of the Prologue; Br. follows MS. 1 and 999–1010, which occur only in MS. 2, were apparently not yet written. [See C. S. Lewis' comment quoted under line 4 above.]

[Woodhouse's early and full interpretation of *Comus* is summarized in IV above under 1941. His later analysis of the Epilogue may be quoted here (from *The Poet and his Faith*, 1965, 98–100): 'I have said that the whole theme assumes the traditional framework of nature and grace, that is, the progression from nature to grace; and it is from the standing ground of grace that the Attendant Spirit utters his Epilogue: the key to the whole deeper meaning of the masque. For in a series of symbolic images—the crown of all the superb poetry which has gone before—he retraces the ascent through the natural order up to the point where it is transcended in the Christian vision of freedom through virtue achieved by the grace of God. From the standing ground of grace the whole natural order is transfigured: everything falls into place, and (as when God looked upon it in the Creation) it is seen to be good. First come symbols of natural beauty, and with them the note of freedom and joy (the golden fruit of the Hesperides is no longer dragon-guarded); next, the generative principle, figured in the love of Venus and Adonis (as in Spenser's allegory of the Garden of Adonis); then, far above them, the intellectual or heavenly love, figured by the celestial Cupid and Psyche his betrothed, whose destined offspring is not Pleasure (as in the old legend) but a twin birth whose names are Youth and Joy, and these (if we know our Milton) we shall recognize as the Platonic twins, offspring of love in its higher manifestation—namely, Knowledge and Virtue— now transformed in the light of grace to Youth eternal and Joy ineffable. And finally, in the last six lines we come to the light of grace itself—the light that has illuminated all the preceding images. By grace, virtue is free and not constrained (this is the doctrine of Christian liberty); by grace, it can ascend beyond the music of the spheres (that favorite symbol of ordered harmony) and reach the heaven of heavens (and the higher harmony of the angelic choir); and if Virtue feeble were, there is still the grace of God which Virtue can invoke—that grace symbolized by Sabrina's intervention.... This is surely not the merely negative and ascetic doctrine that too many of the critics have found in *Comus*. Rather, it betokens the realization of a genuine religious experience by the poet—a sense of dependence on the grace of God, of the liberating effect of grace bestowed, and of nature transfigured when viewed from the vantage ground of this experience. And the experience was realized, and could be realized, only through the poem, only by the fusion of aesthetic and religious experience which the poem effects.']

975–80 Warburton (reported by Todd) noticed the reminiscence of Ariel's song ('Where the bee sucks,' *Temp.* 5. 1. 88–94), which is put beyond doubt by the clear echo at 979, but otherwise is a matter only of metre and the run of *i* rhymes.

975 *To the Ocean.* Warton found a starting point for this phrase, and the description that follows, in the idea of the Islands of the Blest, lying to the west of the stream Ocean, at the world's end where the Sun dwells. He cites Homer, *Od.* 4. 562–8, and Pindar, *Ol.* 2. 61–77, and we may add Hesiod, *W. and D.* 169–73: (1) Homer (L.C.L.): '...to the Elysian plain and the bounds of the earth will the immortals convey thee, where dwells fair-haired Rhadamanthus, and where life is easiest for men. No snow is there, nor heavy storm, nor ever rain, but ever does Ocean send up blasts of the shrill-blowing West Wind that they may give cooling to men....' (2) Hesiod (L.C.L.): 'But to the others [the more virtuous heroes] ...Zeus...gave...an abode apart from men, and made them dwell at the ends of the earth. And they live untouched by sorrow in the islands of the blessed along the shore of deep swirling Ocean, happy heroes for whom the grain-giving earth bears honey-sweet fruit flourishing thrice a year....' (3) Pindar (L.C.L.): '...the good, having the sun shining for evermore... receive the boon of a life of lightened toil...; ...in the presence of the honoured gods, all who were wont to rejoice in keeping their oaths, share a life that knoweth no tears...[And] whosoever...have thrice been courageous in keeping their souls pure from all deeds of wrong, pass by the highway of Zeus unto the tower of Cronus, where the ocean-breezes blow around the Islands of the Blest, and flowers of gold are blazing, some on the shore from radiant trees, while others the water fostereth; and with chaplets thereof they entwine their hands, and with crowns....' 'This luxuriant imagery Milton has dressed anew,' says Warton, adding further sources on which he supposes the poet to have drawn, including Spenser's garden of Adonis (*F.Q.* 3. 6. 29–51) and Marino's (*L'Adone*, c. 6), Ariosto's garden of Paradise (*O.F.* 34. 49–51), and Tasso's garden of Armida (*G.L.* 15. 53–4).

To the classical sources noticed above, Wright (146–9) adds (4) Plato's account of the True Earth, the abode of the immortal soul (*Phaedo* 107–14). This 'is a celestial, a more spiritual version of the older view of an earthly paradise; and Plato's aerial islands are an attempt to fit the Isles of the Blest into his mythical landscape.' We must here resort to brief summary, with extracts from the *Phaedo* (L.C.L.). The 'earth itself is pure and is situated in the pure heaven' high above us. The whole of that true earth has various colours, but 'they are much brighter and purer than ours.' The very 'hollows of the earth...present an appearance of colour as they glisten amid the variety of the other colours, so that the whole produces one continuous effect of variety. And in this fair earth the things that grow, the trees, and flowers and fruits, are correspondingly beautiful; and so too the mountains and the stones are smoother, and more transparent and more lovely in colour than ours....And there are many animals upon it, and men also, some dwelling inland, others on the coasts of the air, as we dwell about the sea, and others on islands, which the air flows around...; and in short, what water and the sea are in our lives, air is in theirs, and what the air is to us, ether is to them....And they have sacred groves and temples of the gods, in which the gods really dwell, and they have intercourse with the gods by speech and prophecies and visions, and they see the sun and moon and stars as they really are, and in all other ways their blessedness is in accord with this' (110–11). There are rivers, 'the greatest and outermost of which is that called Oceanus, which flows round in a circle' (112E). Provision is made for the punishment and for the purification of those who have sinned, but 'those who are found to have excelled in holy living are freed from these regions within the earth and are released as from prisons; they mount upward into their pure abode and dwell upon the earth' (113–14). It is natural to suppose that the Attendant Spirit returns whence he came, and there are indications that this is the case, particularly in echoes of the cancelled lines after 4 (see 4 n.), with their references to Ocean, to the golden apples of the Hesperides (980–2), to hyacinth and roses (997), and also in the allusion to the atmosphere (979). [On the whole tradition see A. B. Giamatti, *The Earthly Paradise*, etc., cited in *Nat* 133–48 n. With particular reference to 975–8 and 1016, Carey cites Plutarch, 'The Face of the Moon,' 942 F (L.C.L., 12, 195), where the moon is said to be, except at times of eclipse, beyond the range of the earth's shadow. Plutarch quoted Homer, *Od.* 4. 563.]

976–7   See the extract from Pindar in 975 n.

978   *broad fields of the sky.* Warton compared *aëris in campis latis* (Virgil, *A.* 6. 887), though *aëris* should probably be rendered 'misty' (L.C.L.). Todd cited 'Ore the broad fields of heav'ns bright wildernesse' (Fairfax, *Jerusalem* 8. 57). MS. 1 has *plaine*, deleted, and *broad* substituted. It adds thereafter: *farre beyond yᵉ earths end | where the welkin ⟨cleere*, deleted, replaced by⟩ *low doth bend* (the whole deleted here, but see 1013–14) (*Facs.* 430).

979   Editors cite Shakespeare, *Temp.* (see 975–80 n.). Warton cited 'And there in liquid aire my selfe disport' (Fairfax, *Jerusalem* 14. 43); cf. Spenser, 'liquid ayre' (*F.Q.* 1. 1. 45). *liquid:* figuratively for clear, bright (*OED* 2), but see Plato above (975 n.): 'what water and the sea are in our lives, air is in theirs.' [While Milton's phrase may here have this Platonic overtone, *liquidus*, applied to air, sky, etc., is a Latin commonplace, e.g. Virgil, *G.* 1. 404, Ovid, *M.* 1. 23, 67, 2. 532; Milton, *El* 3. 23, 5. 15.]

980–2   See above, cancelled lines after 4 and n., and 392–6 and n. At 981 MS. 1 has *Atlas*, deleted, and *Hesperus* substituted; *daughters*, deleted, *neeces* substituted, then *daughters* restored (*Facs.* 430). This is not a mistake corrected but a variant rejected and another chosen. In Ovid, *M.* 4. 637–48, it is Atlas who, far in the west where the ocean receives the descending sun, guards the tree with 'leaves...of gleaming gold, concealing golden branches and golden fruits,' and who had 'enclosed his orchard with massive walls and had put a huge dragon there to watch it' (L.C.L.). Here, as Warton noted, not the fruit only but the tree itself is golden; hence there is no need to assume with Verity that Milton transfers the epithet from the fruit to the tree. Ovid does not here mention the Hesperides, though at 11. 114 he ascribes to them possession of the golden fruit; this common ascription goes back to Hesiod, who, however, makes them the daughters of Night (*Theog.* 215). Milton adopts, first, the version of the myth that makes them daughters of Atlas and Hesperis (deriving their name through their mother), then the version that makes Hesperus, the evening star, brother of Atlas, their father and derives their name from him (here following Servius on *A.* 4. 484: Osgood, *C.M.* 43). Their number was variously given as three, four, and seven; Milton follows Servius, loc. cit., and Apollon. Rhod. 4. 1427, in adopting three (Osgood: [Servius cites Hesiod as naming four]). Almost all the various versions of the myth place the golden apples far in the west, either in the realm of Atlas bordering the stream of Ocean or on islands in the stream. From this it was an easy step to identify the garden of the Hesperides with the Islands of the Blest, as Milton in effect does here. Cf. Pindar above, 975 n., for the Islands' having trees with golden flowers. Osgood notes Hesiod's epithet for the sisters as 'clear-voiced' (*Theog.* 275, 518), and that the idea of their singing was widely current is supported by Euripides' allusions (*Herc. Fur.* 394, *Hipp.* 743), cited by Todd. The context in Apollon. Rhod. indicates that the sisters are singing no joyful song but a dirge for the dragon Ladon, slain by Heracles. The absence here of the dragon, which is central in Milton's two earlier references, is significant; the whole suggestion is of joy, not sorrow. At 982 MS. 2 (*Facs.* 432) has *where grows the right-borne gold upon his native tree*, deleted, and replaced by *that sing about the golden tree* (the reading of MS. 1, Br., ibid. 303, and the printed texts). Thus Milton adopts Ovid's idea of a golden tree, rejects it, and finally restores it. Starnes–Talbert (308–13) find most of Milton's details in C. Stephanus' *Dict.* or N. Comes' *Mythol.*: in Stephanus, the Hesperides described as daughters of Hesperus, and three in number, and a rather tentative identification of the Gardens with the Islands of the Blest. In Comes (3. 19, 7. 7) they find these Miltonic details: that the air sustains life (so they interpret 979); that the Hesperides sing (Apollon. Rhod. cited); that it is always spring there, with Zephyr blowing, and a variety of sweet smells, including cassia, and of flowers, including the rose and hyacinth (cf. 993, 997); and finally, an association of Venus (but not Adonis) with Elysium (cf. 998–1001), based on Tibullus 1. 3. 57–64.

983–6 Lacking in MS. 1 and Br. (*Works* 1, 573).

983 *crisped shades and bowres. crisped*: 'Applied to trees: sense uncertain' (*OED* 4). As Warton noted, the epithet is most often applied to water (cf. *PL* 4. 237, 'crisped Brooks'), and editors gloss the word here in terms that fit both foliage and water: 'curled,' 'rippled,' 'ruffled' (by the wind). *shades*: objects (here evidently leafy boughs) that afford shade (*OED* 8). [See Wright above, 62 n., 428 n., on Milton's use of *shade*. Taking *crisped* as 'closely curled or crimped,' Wright says that '"crisped shades" presents the tracery both of leaf and its sharp sunlit shadow.'] *bowres*: shady recesses overarched with boughs. Cf. 'where th' Etrurian shades / High overarch't imbowr' (*PL* 1. 303–4).

984 *Revels*. Cf. 'Love... / Reigns here and revels' (*PL* 4. 763–5). *spruce*: brisk, lively (*OED* 1); trim (Elton); prettily adorned (Verity); gay, both in manner and appearance (Wright). Only Elton receives support from *OED* (2). *jocond*: gay (*OED*).

985 *The Graces*. See *L'All* 12–16 n. The Graces appear in a number of Stuart masques, e.g. Samuel Daniel's *Vision of the Twelve Goddesses* and Jonson's *Haddington Masque* and *Love Freed*. Osgood (*C.M.* 39) notes that, though not otherwise specially connected with spring, they are often joined with the Hours (*Homeric Hymn to the Pythian Apollo* 194; Pausanias 2. 17. 4, 5. 11. 7). They are associated in Ovid's account of Flora and her garden (already referred to in *L'All* 17–24 n.), which Osgood (44) finds suggestive of this passage in *Comus*: 'Chloris I was, a nymph of the happy fields where...dwelt fortunate men of old ⟨i.e. Elysium⟩...I enjoy perpetual spring...In the fields that are my dower, I have a fruitful garden, fanned by the breeze...Soon as...the varied foliage is warmed by the sunbeams, the Hours assemble...and cull my gifts.... Straightway the Graces draw near, and twine garlands and wreaths to bind their heavenly hair' (*F.* 5. 197–220: L.C.L.). They are likewise associated, and again with perpetual spring, in *PL* 4. 266–8. [Milton's brief allusions seem to be unrelated to Calidore's vision, *F.Q.* 6. 10. 9 f.]

rosie-boosom'd Howres. [*OED* strangely takes this as its earliest reference to the classical Hours. See above, *Sonn* 1. 4 n.] As Osgood explains, the Hours were the daughters of Zeus and Themis (Hesiod, *Theog.* 901) and they presided over the seasons of the revolving year (Homer, *Od.* 10. 469). Milton associates them especially with spring and flowers: cf. Pindar, *Frag.* 75. 13–16; Callimachus, *Hymn to Apollo* 81 f.; Ovid, quoted under the *Graces*, just above. Philostratus (*Imagines* 2. 34) associates the Hours of springtime with the hyacinth and the rose, and Theocritus (15. 102–5) couples the Hours with the return of Adonis (cf. 997–8 below). Milton's epithet may have been suggested by another function of the Hours, their bringing in of dawn, the idea of a rosy light being transferred from the stock descriptions of dawn (cf. *PL* 6. 2–4 and n.), or, as Osgood remarks, the association may be with the roses of spring and the meaning be that their bosoms are adorned with roses.

986 *their bounties*: gifts freely bestowed in kindness (*OED* 4 and 4b). [Cf. Comus' account of Nature's 'bounties' in 709 f.]

987 *That*. The word is omitted in MS. 1 (*Facs.* 430) and in Br., where the passage is transferred to the beginning of the masque (ibid. 303). The 1673 Errata say 'leave out *that*.' The Columbia editors failed to correct this error in their text; it first appeared in 1637 and was repeated in 1645 and 1673. [It is a question if *That* can be called simply an error, since it appears not only in the printed texts but in MS. 2, the expanded and corrected version of this passage (*Facs.* 432; see above, 975–1022 n.), and since the 1673 Errata are not necessarily all Milton's or infallible (see 167 n.). Editors are divided: *That* is printed

Comus

by Browne, Beeching, Patterson (*Works* and *Student's Milton*), Hanford, Hughes, C. Williams (Beeching text), Brooks and Hardy, M. Nicolson, Shawcross, Bush, I. G. MacCaffrey, Carey; it is omitted by Masson, Rolfe, Bell, Elton, Trent, Verity, Moody, W. A. Wright, Grierson, B. A. Wright, H. Fletcher, Mack, Tillyard, H. Darbishire, Bullough, Prince.]

987 *eternal Summer*: [A common feature of the golden age and earthly paradises; or eternal spring may be preferred, as in the prototypical Ovid, *M.* 1. 107, or *PL* 4. 268.] Editors cite Spenser, *F.Q.* 3. 6. 42: 'There is continuall spring, and harvest there, / Continuall'; R. Niccols, *The Cuckow*, 1607, p. 10: 'For there eternall spring doth ever dwell'; Fletcher, *F. Shep.* 4. 2. 148-9: 'On this bower may ever dwell / Spring and Summer.'

988 *West winds, with musky wing*: 'the "Zephyrs" of classical poetry; traditionally the fragrance-laden winds' (Verity). Cf. *El* 5. 69, and 'Where sweet Myrrh-breathing Zephire in the Spring, / Gently distills his Nectar-dropping showres' (*Idea* 53, Drayton, 2, 337). *musky*: perfumed as with musk. Todd cited 'musked Zephires' (*Shadow of the Judgment* 153, Drummond, 2, 54); 'Zephyr fils with Musk and Amber smels' (Sylvester, *D.W.W.* 2. 1. 1. 81, Grosart, 1, 100), and 'Zephyr did sweet musky sighes afford' (ibid. line 146).

989 *cedar'n*: composed of cedars (*OED*); see the note on *azurn*, 892 above. MS. 1 has *myrtle*, deleted, replaced by *cedar'ne*. *alleys*: see 310 n. *fling*. Warton cited 'And every where your odours fling' (H. Peacham, *Period of Mourning*, 1613, *Nuptiall Hymnes* 1, st. 3).

990 *Nard*. MS. 1 (*Facs.* 430) has *balme*, deleted, and *nard* substituted. Nard, otherwise spikenard, the term used in the 1611 Bible (e.g. Song of Sol. 1. 12, 4. 14): a root employed in the preparation of an aromatic ointment, and the scent derived from the root. The term *spikenard* was also applied to English lavender (*OED*: nard 2 and spikenard 3a), but that the suggestion here is biblical is evident from the grouping with *Cassia's balmy smels*, i.e. the cinnamon-like odour derived from the bark of the cassia tree (*OED* 1 and Exod. 30. 24). The word cassia was also used in poetry for a small aromatic shrub. This is explained as due to a rhetorical combination of Ps. 45. 8 ('All thy garments smell of myrrh, and aloes, and cassia') with the *casia* of Virgil, *E.* 2. 49, *casia atque aliis intexens suavibus herbis* (cf. *G.* 2. 213, 4. 30, 182; but in *G.* 2. 466 *casia* is used of the tree). Cf. *OED* 3, which quotes *PL* 5. 292-3, 'through Groves of Myrrhe, / And flouring Odours, Cassia, Nard, and Balme'—the same combination as in this line in *Comus* and equally ambiguous. The epithet *balmy* (substituted in MS. 1 for *fragrant*) does nothing to remove the ambiguity; its primary meaning is aromatic (*OED*: balm 4, and above, 673 n.). But *PL* 5. 293 suggests that Milton may be thinking of balm-yielding trees (*OED*: balm 8) or fragrant herbs (ibid. 9). Todd compares: 'Makes spring the Casia, Narde, and fragrant Balmes' (Drummond, 2, 63).

991 *Iris.* Osgood gives most of the references [see also Heninger, *Meteorology*, 140–4]. Iris, daughter of Thaumas (Hesiod, *Theog.* 780), messenger of the gods (ibid. and Homer, *Il.* 15. 158) and especially of Juno (Ovid, *M.* 1. 270, 11. 585, etc.), wears a cloak of a thousand hues and moves through the sky in a rainbow curve (Virgil, *A.* 4. 701; Ovid, *M.* 11. 589–90, 14. 838). Cf. Milton, *El* 3. 41–2. She is the source of showers (Ovid, *M.* 1. 270–1), of which the rainbow is the agent or sign; in Tibullus 1. 4. 44, Seneca, *Oed.* 315–17, Statius, *Theb.* 9. 405, it bears the epithet *imbrifer*, rainy or rain-bringing, perhaps a source of *with humid bow*. [Cf. Claudian's *umida* (35. 100: 2, 324).] MS. 1 has *garnish't*, corrected in margin to *garish*, both deleted and replaced by *humid*. Cf. 'Iris: "...the queen o' th' sky, / Whose wat'ry arch and messenger am I"' (Shakespeare, *Temp.* 4. 1. 70–1).

992 *blow.* Warton took the verb as transitive with *Flowers* (993) as object, citing 'Favonius here shall blow / New flowers, which you shall see to grow' (*Entertainment at Highgate* 152–3, Ben Jonson 7, 140); i.e. *the odorous banks engender the flowers, cause them to bloom.* Though later editors concur, the interpretation depends only on the lack of punctuation after *blow*; otherwise it would be more satisfactory to take *blow* as intransitive and *Flowers* in apposition to *banks*. [But this seems forced; no text has punctuation, which such a reading demands; the words *banks* and *Flowers* are not, in apposition, very logical; the transitive use of the verb is—along with the Jonsonian example—found in the period (*OED*: *v.*² 3).]

994 *purfl'd* (substituted in MS. 1 for *watchet*). Todd explains as 'fringed, or, embroidered' (*OED*: *ppl. a.*¹ 1), as in Chaucer, *C.T.*, Prol. 193, and Spenser, *F.Q.* 1. 2. 13, 2. 3. 26. Editors concur, but the context supports only 'variegated' (*OED*: *ppl. a.*¹ 4), and this is further supported by the line here added in MS. 1, *yellow, watchet, greene, & blew*, retained in Br. (*Facs.* 430, 303) but deleted in MS. 2 [cf. Browne: 'The blue with watchet, green and red with yellow' (*Brit. Past.* 2. 3. 399). Blondel cites *Endimion and Phoebe* 111: 'An Azur'd Mantle purfled with a vaile' (Drayton 1, 132).]

995–1010 were evidently written (as Hurd, reported by Warton and Todd, seems to have been the first to notice) with Spenser's Garden of Adonis in mind

(*F.Q.* 3. 6. 43–50); and it would appear that Milton intended the reader to recall Spenser. See the notes following.

995 *Elysian*: MS. 1, Br., *manna*; MS. 2, *Sabaean*, deleted, and *Elysian* substituted (*Facs.* 430, 303, 432). *manna dew*: presumably dew coming like manna as a gift from above. Manna is of course associated with dew in the O.T.; it was gathered where the dew lay after the dew disappeared (Exod. 16. 14–15; Num. 11. 6–9). *OED* gives no example of the phrase except Keats's (*La Belle Dame*); [the phrase 'Manna dew' occurs in the *Mirror for Magistrates* (*Lord Hastings* 665), ed. L. B. Campbell, 1938, 293]. This and Milton's figurative use of manna (*PL* 2. 113) would seem to throw no light on this phrase unless manna here connotes merely delectation, as indeed the emphasis on sweet odours in 988 f. and the substituted *Sabaean* might suggest. *Sabaean*: of Saba, the biblical Sheba, in S.W. Arabia, famous for its spices (*PL* 4. 162–3; *OED*: Sabaean A.). Among the features of Spenser's Garden of Adonis are 'most dainty odours' and 'precious deaw' (*F.Q.* 3. 6. 43). *Elysian* brings the lines back into direct relation with the idea on which the Epilogue begins, namely, that the abode of the Attendant Spirit is Elysium, identified with the Islands of the Blest. [This identification, however clearly made in the text (see also 980–2 n.), seems hard to reconcile with 1–4, where the Attendant Spirit's home is among the spheres, 'Before the starry threshold of Joves Court.' When Milton first wrote the whole opening passage, including the lines cancelled after 4, he treated the celestial scene among the spheres as 'Hesperian gardens,' apparently feeling no contradiction; and the scene described in the epilogue is obviously of the same Hesperidean quality. Such a fusion may have seemed warranted by Plato's account of the 'true earth' emphasized by Wright in relation to *Comus*; see notes on 1–4 and 975.]

996 (*List mortals...true*) MS. 1 and Br. lack this line; MS. 2 adds it in margin (*Works* 1, 575). *true*: of the right kind, as they should be (*OED* 4b): i.e. uncorrupted and so attuned to a higher meaning; approximately this meaning is found in 'True appetite' (*PL* 5. 305), 'true Love' (ibid. 8. 589), 'true tasts' (*PR* 4. 347), but not in 'if mine ear be true' (above, 169). There is, as Warton suggests, an implied contrast with Comus, who has 'nor Ear, nor Soul to apprehend' such higher truth (783). The line directs how the ensuing lines are to be read. [Cf. 'let rude eares be absent' (*Apol, Works* 2, 303), cited by C. S. Lewis (*RES* 8, 1932, 175); *Comus* 457; *Arc* 71–3.]

997 *Beds of Hyacinth, and Roses*. Todd cited 'And I will make thee beds of Roses' (Marlowe, *Passionate Shepherd* 9).

998 *young Adonis oft.* MS. 1, *many a cherub soft* (so also Br.); MS. 2, present reading (*Facs.* 430, 303, 432).

999–1010 Wanting in MS. 1 and Br.; present in MS. 2 and 1637 (*Facs.* 432, 298). Reverting to 995, we observe that Milton first wrote: *and drenches oft wᵗʰ manna dew | beds of Hyacinth, & roses | where many a cherub soft reposes*; later, presumably after the performance (which used Br.) and at some time before Lawes' edition of 1637, he produced by revision and addition the present text, 995–1010. So far as we can judge from MS. 2, he introduced the whole idea of the Garden of Adonis (see 995–1010 n., and below), and then linked it with the initial conception of the Islands of the Blest by changing *Sabaean* to *Elysian* (995) and, in order to ensure a proper reading of the new passage, inserted (*list mortals if yoʳ eares be true*).

Behind the passage in Spenser, which Milton has chiefly in mind, is the story of Venus' love for the youthful Adonis, the hunter slain by the wild boar (Bion 1; Ovid, *M.* 10. 519–59, 708–39; and Renaissance poets). It is against confusion with the type of treatment exemplified by Shakespeare's *Venus and Adonis* [though] some recent critics have found philosophical symbolism in it] that Milton seeks to guard by the added line 996. Behind this story again lie a seasonal or fertility myth and ritual of oriental origin; see note on *Nat* 204. The traditional symbolism is described by G. Sandys, *Ovid* (1632), 366–7. There seems to be no classical authority for associating the Garden of the Hesperides and the Garden of Adonis, though Pliny speaks of them together, along with the garden of Alcinous (*N.H.* 19. 19. 49: Osgood). Osgood notes the allusion in *PL* 9. 439–41 to the gardens of Alcinous and 'reviv'd Adonis.'

1001 *th'Assyrian Queen*: alluding to the oriental origin of the Adonis myth; see preceding note and notes on *Nat* 200–4. Osgood (*C.M.* 4) explains the phrase by 'the statement of Pausanias (1. 14. 6) that the Assyrians were "the first of men to pay reverence to Celestial Aphrodite."' The value set upon the explanation will depend upon one's reading of the whole passage. Venus (and on each level it is easy to infer a corresponding role for Cupid) was conceived as the goddess of wanton love (which is plainly ruled out by the whole purport of *Comus* and specifically by 996), as the great mother, the patroness of love and the generative principle (her role in Spenser, *F.Q.* 3. 6. 43–9), and as the celestial Venus, patroness of intellectual or heavenly love. This third, assumed to be hers by Osgood and Hughes, seems to be denied by the distinction in levels introduced in 1002–3 (see 1002–10 n.). 'In those happy regions of the air to which the Spirit is ascending there are not only...all those physical delights he has been describing [980–94]...; there is also, in a higher way than can be conceived on Earth, the full experience of that passion of Love...on the recognition of which, though in its most ignoble form, even Comus might be said to have based his action. It was just because Comus had misapprehended Love...that he had been outwitted and defeated. But there *is* true Love, and it is to be found in Heaven' (Masson). Except for the last sentence, this seems entirely acceptable. If one recognizes any principle of ascent within the Epilogue itself, a reference to the Christian heaven is not reached until 1017–22; and indeed there is nothing in the text to suggest that the Garden of Adonis is equated with the Christian heaven, for Milton proceeds immediately to what is *far above* the Garden.

1002–10 Milton, like Spenser (*F.Q.* 3. 6. 49–50), links the Garden of Adonis with the story of Cupid and Psyche (Apuleius, *Met.* 4. 28–6. 24) at the point where Psyche, after her betrayal of Cupid's secret and consequent wanderings and labours (1005), is restored to Cupid by a council of the gods and Jove's decree. In Apuleius she becomes, by Cupid, the mother of Voluptas, and in Spenser of Pleasure. From this conclusion Milton departs by making her prospectively the mother of *Two blissful twins...* / *Youth and Joy* (1009–10). This is Milton's second departure from Spenser, not his first. In *F.Q.* 3. 6. 49–50 Cupid and Psyche are in the Garden of Adonis; Milton deliberately places them *far above* (1002) and says that he is speaking of *Celestial Cupid*. If we are to apprehend Milton's meaning we must be clear first about Spenser's. The Variorum Spenser (3, 261) gives this interpretation:

> ...the allegorical meaning...is clearly developed by Boccaccio and fits Spenser's intention. Boccaccio says: 'Psyche is the soul...and there is joined with her that which preserves the rational element, that is, pure Love.' Psyche passes through trials and purgations. 'At length ...she attains to the consummation of divine joy and contemplation, and is joined to her lover forever, and, with mortal things sloughed off, is born into eternal glory; and from this love is born Pleasure which is eternal joy and gladness.' Pleasure, so interpreted, is very similar to Plato's 'Eudaimonia....'

But this interpretation appears to receive no support either from Spenser's phrasing or from the context, which plainly points to his eclectic application of the myth to represent the principle of love and generation as it is operative in human life. [Recent commentators, whatever their differences, seem to agree that the Garden of Adonis, whatever its overtones, is a myth of earthly, physical generation. Thus R. Ellrodt, discounting Platonism, sees 'an actual garden of generation and growth' and Cupid and Psyche as apparently representing 'wedded love' (*Neoplatonism in the Poetry of Spenser*, Geneva, 1960, 84–5). Cf., e.g., C. S. Lewis' review of Ellrodt (*Études Anglaises* 14, 1961, 107–16, repr. in Lewis' *Studies in Medieval and Renaissance Literature*, Cambridge, 1966); W. Nelson, *The Poetry of Edmund Spenser* (New York, 1963), 204–15; R. L. Colie, *Paradoxia Epidemica* (Princeton, 1966), 335–41; A. B. Giamatti, *The Earthly Paradise* (1966), 284–90.] The principle of love and generation Milton incorporated in his allusion to Venus and Adonis; but, paradoxically, the interpretation quoted from the Variorum Spenser is a fairly adequate reading of Milton's lines on Cupid and Psyche, though the precise meaning needs to be explained. After the remarks quoted above on 1001, Masson continues: 'Much more is there realised there ⟨in heaven⟩ the highly spiritual or pre-eminently celestial love set forth perhaps in the...myth of Cupid and Psyche.' Though recognizing a measure of ascent from Venus and Adonis to Cupid and Psyche, Masson places the whole in heaven, confidently compares *Lyc* 172–7, *EpDam* 212–19, and *PL* 8. 612–29, and obscures at once his very distinction and the difference between Milton's and Spenser's treatments by remarking that in *F.Q.* 3. 6. 46–52 the two myths are 'similarly lifted up into heaven.' Verity follows Masson. Elton is content to note: 'Above Astarte, the Phenician Venus, sits Cupid with Psyche; the celestial above the earthly love'; but, like Masson, he finds 'a similar glorification' of the two myths in *F.Q.* 3. 6. 46 f. Hanford takes the same position as Elton, but adds: 'The obvious Christian parallel is the mystic marriage of the soul with Christ. It would be inappropriate here to allude to it explicitly...' (*Poems*). Wright (who insists throughout on the dominant Platonism of *Comus*) in effect excludes Christian doctrine and overtone by finding in the first two of Spenser's *Fowre Hymnes* 'the best commentary on this whole passage.' [Arthos (*MLN* 76, 1961, 321–4) quotes Wright on Plato's 'True Earth' and Ficino, who names the Garden of the Hesperides as one of two different Elysian fields; he concludes that Venus and Adonis represent a love the Platonists thought divine, and that that of Cupid and Psyche is in some sense more divine.] Masson and Browne had called attention to the important statement in *Apol*, written in 1642: 'Where ⟨i.e. in Plato and Xenophon⟩ if I should tell ye what I learnt, of chastity and love, I meane that which is truly so, whose charming cup is only vertue which she bears in her hand to those who are worthy. The rest are cheated with a thick intoxicating potion which a certaine Sorceresse the abuser of loves name carries about; and how the first and chiefest office of love, begins and ends in the soule, producing those happy twins of her divine generation knowledge and vertue, with such abstracted sublimities as these, it might be worth your listning...' (*Works* 3, 305). They observe that in *Comus* (1009–10) Milton had bestowed upon Psyche the twins Youth and Joy, in place of Voluptas or Pleasure. Three additional facts should be noticed: the image of the cups indicates that Milton is recalling Circe and hence Comus; that the change in name of the twins, while no doubt significant, is not a complete reversal since they are still 'happy twins'; and thirdly, and most important, the passage in *Apol* represents the Platonic phase of Milton's development, which precedes the account of the Christian, 'Last of all not in time, but as perfection is last.' The parallel would seem to confirm the reading of 1002–10 in a Platonic sense but at the same time to suggest that a Christian reference would in due course follow (see 1017–22 and n.).

1002 *spangled sheen*. See 892 n. [and *Ps* 136. 27 n.]. Todd cited 'spangled starlight sheen' (Shakespeare, *Dream* 2. 1. 29).

1003 *advanc't*: raised or high, as in 'To see the Redcrosse thus advaunced hye' (Spenser, *F.Q.* 2. 1. 23; *OED* 4); 'perhaps with a sense of promotion,' as in *PL* 4. 359 (Elton).

1011 For *task* MS. 1 had *message*, deleted, *buisnesse* substituted, then deleted, and finally *taske*; for *is smoothly*, first *well is*, then *is smoothly* (*Works* 1, 576; *Facs.* 430).

1012–16 Warton traced hints for movement, phrase, or image to: 'I must go, I must run / Swifter than the fiery sun' (Fletcher, *F. Shep.* 1. 1. 100–1); 'We the globe can compass soon, / Swifter than the wand'ring moon' (Shakespeare, *Dream* 4. 1. 100–1); 'Whence lyes a way up to the Moone, / And thence the Fayrie can as soone / Passe to the earth below it' (*Nimphidia* 38–40, Drayton, 3, 126). Cf. also Ariel: 'be't to fly, / To swim,...to ride / On the curl'd clouds' (*Temp.* 1. 2. 190–2), and 'To run' (ibid. 254).

1013–14 *green earths end, | ...welkin*. The first phrase means the utmost western bound of the earth, washed by the Ocean stream. Sympson (reported by Todd) suggested a more precise reference, to the Cape Verde Islands off the most westerly point of Africa. The lines are transferred from MS. 1 after 978; see 978 n. and *Facs.* 430. Here *green* is an addition; Milton seems first to have written *earths greene end* (MS. 1 before correction and Br.), then changed it to *greene earths end*; further, *low* is here exchanged for the more figurative *slow*, suggesting the vast sweep of the arch (bow) of the firmament. [Hughes defines *welkin* as 'the sky, bending to the horizon.' Le Comte (*Yet Once More*, 106–7) quotes *QNov* 166: *longo flectens curvamine coelos*.]

1016 *the corners of the Moon*. [Editors cite Shakespeare, *Macb.* 3. 5. 23, 'the corner of the moon.' *OED* (corner: 8) defines as 'An extremity or end of the earth; a region, quarter,' but seems to miss the moon. The idea is similar to that of 'horn' (the pointed extremity of the moon in its first and last quarter: *OED* 17; and each tip of a bow: ibid. 17b). Cf. the classical image of the horns of the bow of Diana, goddess of the moon. Cf. 'horned moon' in Milton's *Ps* 136. 26 and n.]

1017–22　There is precedent in Jonson's masques for ending thus on a didactic note in praise of virtue. Verity cites the last song of *Pleasure* (quoted above, near the end of II). Elton adds the somewhat less relevant final song of the *Masque of Queenes*: 'Who, Virtue, can thy power forget...?' (*Ben Jonson* 7, 316). But, for all Jonson's reference to heaven, the conclusions of *Pleasure* and of *Comus*, like the masques as wholes, move on different levels. Critics who recognize a principle of ascent operative throughout Milton's epilogue will recognize here its overtly Christian culmination. Those who do not will seek another explanation. The debate goes back further than might be supposed. Thyer (reported by Todd) found a source for 1021–2 in 'the *Table of Cebes*, where Patience and Perseverance are represented stooping and stretching out their hands to help up those, who are endeavouring to climb the craggy hill of Virtue, and yet are too feeble to ascend of themselves.' Todd then quotes a long note (for which he is 'indebted...to Mr. Egerton [late Earl of Bridgewater]'), whose purport is the insufficiency of such a source, the tendency indeed of Thyer's suggestion to stifle 'the sublime effect so happily produced,' and the reduction of Milton's belief to the point of making 'the religion of Socrates and Cebes (or that of Nature) supersede the religion of Christ.' The lines point to salvation in Christ, and his power 'to strengthen feeble Virtue by the influence of his Grace.' Wright, returning to the position, though not to the specific suggestion, of Thyer, says: 'The meaning is that the virtuous soul will escape from this mortal world and pass beyond the music of the spheres to the heaven of heavens. The idea is probably inspired by the myth of the "Phaedrus"..., where Plato describes how the souls who have been lovers of the beauty of truth and goodness follow Zeus and the gods in their journeys beyond the outermost sphere of this universe and behold all things as they really are; and those who have once attained to this vision of eternal truth are free spirits, safe for ever from the bonds of the mortal world. Thus Milton closes on the Platonic theme with which he opened— the free immortal life awaiting the virtuous soul, the lover of wisdom.' The reference here is evidently to *Phaedrus* 246–56, though the paraphrase is at once selective and free [cf. extracts from *Phaedo* above, 975 n.]. But to place this comment beside interpretations of *Comus* summarized in IV above is to see that debate is by no means closed. Verity finds these lines 'particularly notable as summing up the whole teaching of the poem...chastity (the Lady) has triumphed over the temptations of intemperance (Comus), through its own "hidden strength" (417), and through supernatural aid (the Attendant Spirit and Sabrina), such as the Elder Brother spoke of (454–5) and the last line of the Masque promises.'

1018 *she alone is free.* See the quotation from Wright in 1017–22 n. But on its positive side Christian liberty involves the equation of liberty with virtue, for (as Milton is to write): *quemadmodum esse liberum idem plane est atque esse pium, esse sapientem, esse justum ac temperantem, sui providum, alieni abstinentem, atque exinde demum magnanimum ac fortem, ita his contrarium esse, idem esse atque esse servum* (*Def* 2, *Works* 8, 248–50). [One might quote Sandys' translation of Seneca, *Herc. Oet.* 1983–4 (*Ovid*, 1632, 329): 'High vertue never sinks to Hell. / Be valiant mortalls, and live well.']

1020 *Higher then the Spheary chime*: higher than the spheres enclosing the Ptolemaic universe and the music that accompanies their motion (see *Nat* 125–32 and n.). The idea of the music of the spheres, initially Pythagorean, was taken over by Plato. To this level Wright (above, 1017–22 n.) and some others would confine it. But it may be thought that Milton gives to this favourite idea its place in his total conception of reality, which is of course Christian and embraces not only the order of nature but the order of grace. For him the music of the spheres would appear to symbolize the highest perfection of the natural order and to parallel on this lower level the song of the angels (cf. *PL* 5. 618–27). To ascend *Higher then the Spheary chime* would be, then, to reach the heavenly order and hear instead the angelic choir. Dunster quoted 'O Grace (whereby men climbe the heavenly stair)' from Sylvester, *Sonn.* 3 (Grosart, 2, 37).

1021–2 The idea of God's condescension to human frailty and the intervention of divine grace is in itself one of the most distinctive marks of Christianity, and the idea is underlined by the fact that for *stoop* MS. 1 first had *bow*, deleted, and *stoope* substituted. The interpretation given to these two lines will condition, and be conditioned by, one's interpretation of the whole masque. If the lines are taken as specifically Christian, it will be held that they are supported by an allusion to Christian liberty (1018 and n.) and to the order of grace as above the order of nature (1020 and n.). And it will appear that the epilogue, beginning with images and ideas of natural beauty, proceeds by steady ascent through the principle of love and generation on the natural, including the human, level (995–1001) to intellectual or heavenly love in the Platonic sense (1002–10), and comes at last, 'as perfection is last,' to the Christian outlook at 1017; or premonitions of it may be read, as by Hanford, at an earlier point (1002–10 and n.). In the broadest terms, what is matter of debate is whether the poet, as Wright asserts, 'closes on the Platonic theme with which he opened' (above, 1017–22 n.), or whether there is not a steady ascent in the epilogue, whether it does not then extend as a principle to the argument of the whole work. [See Woodhouse's comment on the whole epilogue, quoted above in 975–1022 n.]

1022 *Heav'n it self would stoop to her.* [Milton's change from *bow* to *stoop* is noticed in 1021–2 n. Hughes quotes Spenser: 'See how the heavens of voluntary grace, / And soveraine favour towards chastity, / Doe succour send to her distressed cace: / So much high God doth innocence embrace' (*F.Q.* 3. 8. 29). And one might add the great opening of *F.Q.* 2. 8: 'And is there care in heaven?'] H. Schaus (University of Texas *Studies in English*, 25, 1945–6, 136) cites Marlowe, *H. and L.* 1. 365–6: 'And hands so pure, so innocent, nay such, / As might have made heaven stoope to have a touch.' [Whether or not Milton remembered Marlowe's 'stoope,' the contrast is rich in significance.]

Psalms I–VIII,
LXXX–LXXXVIII

I. DATES, CIRCUMSTANCES, AND CHARACTER [D.B.]

The translation of Psalms 80–8 Milton dated April 1648. His title was *Nine of the Psalms done into Metre, wherein all but what is in a different Character* [i.e. italics], *are the very words of the Text, translated from the Original.* They were first printed in the *Poems* of 1673. The headnote to Milton's boyish version of two Psalms (above) briefly indicated the general motives that inspired so much versification of the Psalms. For an official statement of the main one there is the Ordinance of 4 January 1645, which abolished the *Book of Common Prayer* and established the *Directory for Public Worship*: 'It is the duty of Christians to praise God publiquely by singing of Psalmes together in the Congregation, and also privately in the Family' (Firth and Rait, *Acts and Ordinances of the Interregnum*, 1, 607). As even our sparse collection of comments makes clear, scholars have differed in regard to the nature and relative weight of Milton's public or private motives, both in his general impulse to translate and in his choice of Psalms. On this last point partly similar suggestions were made by M. H. Studley ('Milton and his Paraphrases of the Psalms,' *PQ* 4, 1925, 364–72) and P. von Rohr-Sauer (*English Metrical Psalms*, 1938, 39–43). Miss Studley saw a possible reason 'in the arguments preceding them [Psalms 80–8] in both the Authorized and the Douay Versions....They express the need of the Church for God's guidance. To the mind of Milton, the church was passing through the most critical period of her history. These psalms, then, parallel his controversial pamphlets. They are his poetic protest and appeal on behalf of the church.' Thinking of 1648 as one of the 'deciding' years for Puritanism [the outbreak of the second civil war early in the year?], Rohr-Sauer (42) suggests that Milton felt drawn to 'the so-called "judgment psalms" 81, 82, and 83 in each of which God is spoken of as a judge above the judges of earth.... The rest of the psalms in this group are substantially psalms of confidence in God, showing faith that help will come.' (Rohr-Sauer mistakenly speaks of these Psalms as immediately published for the sake of public encouragement.)

The background of the second civil war has been stressed by Michael Fixler (*Milton and the Kingdoms of God*, 1964, 143). He cites George Wither (who was to produce one of the best-known versions of the Psalms) as saying that the best Protestant commentators interpreted Psalms 81–7 as handling 'the estate of the Church, and Commonwealth of the Messias, distinguishing it into her Politicall, Ecclesiasticall, and Oeconomicke Orders' (*A Preparation to the Psalter*, 1619: repr. Spenser Society, no. 37, 1884, p. 50). Fixler remarks: 'Milton's choice had some significance. As a group the psalms deal with kindred themes: God's displeasure with his chosen people, praise of Zion, prayers for renewal of grace and divine guidance for a nation racked by conspiracies and surrounded by its enemies, assurance that deliverance will follow and the saints triumph, and that the Kingdom of God will be established. One paraphrase [*Ps* 82], differing in emphasis from the Authorized Version, is suggestively relevant in view of the demand on the left for the execution of divinely authorized justice against King and Parliament both.' While it would be natural for a lifelong devotee of the Psalms to turn to them in a time of national crisis, it might be said, by way of partial qualification, that there had been more dangerous crises in previous years, and also that the quoted summaries of the themes of Psalms 80–8 would apply to other Psalms as well.

At any rate the idea of the public situation is not at all incompatible with another motive. Masson (*P.W.* 1, 241–5) supplied a different and cogent reason, not for Milton's choice of these Psalms, but for his embarking on translation, by recounting briefly the controversy of the 1640s concerning the adoption of a national psalter. The story has been amplified by W. B. Hunter ('Milton Translates the Psalms,' *PQ* 40, 1961,

485–94), and his account may be summarized here. When the Westminster Assembly met in 1643 to reorganize the Church of England on Presbyterian lines, one question before it was the preparation of a psalter. The version of Francis Rous (a member of the Assembly as well as of Parliament), which had been printed in 1638 and again in 1641, was revised by three committees and accepted by the Assembly (November 1645). But a psalter (1644) by William Barton was preferred by the House of Lords, which did not approve Rous's version, while the Commons, rejecting Barton, in April 1646 ordered the printing of Rous for use in all churches. 'It was poorly received by the people in both England and Scotland, and the General Assembly of the Church of Scotland flatly refused it' (Hunter, 491). In July 1647 the Assembly recommended a revised psalter and in August appointed four men to revise the Rous or Westminster text. In April 1648—the month of Milton's translations— these four submitted their work, but it was apparently unsatisfactory, for later in April a new committee of revision was set up; and in August still another. The new Scottish Psalter did appear in 1650. A relation between Milton's private activity and that of the Assembly seems a clear inference. Hunter notes Milton's use of common metre (lines of 8 and 6 syllables), the metre enjoined upon the Assembly's committees.

M. Boddy ('Milton's Translation of Psalms 80–88,' *MP* 64, 1966–7, 1–9) puts forward an interesting though inevitably inconclusive theory. She notes that Milton dated *Sonnet* 13 (to Lawes) precisely as of 9 February 1646, and *Psalms* 80–8 as of April 1648; that, although the sonnet was written for Lawes' *Ayres and Dialogues*, it did not appear in that book (1653), which contained commendatory verses from Edward and John Phillips; and that Du Moulin, in his *Regii Sanguinis Clamor* (1652), said [to quote Milton, *C.P.W.* 4, 1966, 1051, instead of Masson, *Life*, 4, 456]: 'Thus when the sentence on the king's life was being considered by the conspirators and many were frightened at such a horrible crime, this hellish gallows-bird wrote to those who were wavering and persuaded them to the side of evil, urging this in particular concerning the execution: that either they or the king had to die.' [Du Moulin cited *Eikonoklastes* of 1649 (*C.P.W.*, loc. cit.).]

Miss Boddy suggests that Lawes' dedication of *Choice Psalmes* (1648) to the king was 'clearly a move in the propaganda war' now being waged by the Royalists and that Milton must have been upset by the presence of his sonnet in such a book as giving apparent approval. She further suggests (3) that Milton's *Psalms* were 'chosen possibly to answer the Royalist points made in the Lawes volume and perhaps initially attempted specifically in answer to it.' Possibly, too, 'Milton saw an immediate use' for his *Psalms* in 'the famous prayer meeting of the army, largely Independent, at Windsor, which took place apparently on three days ending on the first of May.' She quotes the full report of the meeting from Adjutant General Allen (Carlyle, *Cromwell*, ed. S. C. Lomas, London, 1904, 1, 308–10). There may be a relation between the themes of the meeting and 'psalms...that exalt obedience to the will of God, even though surrounded by hosts of oppressors.' Some items in *Psalms* 88, 86, and 83, original or added by Milton, have 'a definitely contemporary sound' (*Ps* 88, lines 29–36; 86. 49–52; 83. 9–14). 'Psalms 80, 81, and 85 are principally on the theme that God will turn aside his wrath and show his mercy to his saints when they turn to him. The last three [i.e. 87, 84, 82] turn with confidence to the future' (87. 9–12; 82. 1–4, 21–4; 84. 11–16, 29–32). 'Here the emphasis is on the temporal king as sometimes wicked and as subordinate to God's rule, so that God may even decree his overthrow.' 'If a copy of Milton's Nine Psalms...had fallen into Royalist hands, would the Royalist reader not have assumed that the translator was inciting to regicide? Also, would a prayer meeting that used these psalms in the order I have suggested not produce the effects described in the account of Adjutant General Allen?'

Miss Boddy quotes Bishop Henry King's letter to Ussher, printed at the beginning of his translation of the psalms and dated 30 October 1651, in which he says that George Sandys 'and lately one of our praetended Reformers' had both failed, Sandys in being 'too elegant for the vulgar use,' 'The Other as flat and poor, as lamely worded and unhandsomly rhimed as the Old; which, with much confidence, he undertook to amend' [quoted in Ronald Berman, *Henry King & The Seventeenth Century*, London, 1964, 90]. Miss Boddy thinks that neither

Barton (1644) nor Rous (1641: [cf. Berman, 149, n. 21]) 'seems to be quite late enough' to be the unnamed translator, and that Milton fits, especially as she finds that 'King's translation contains lines, phrases, and rhymes identical with Milton's and not matched elsewhere in metrical translations current in the century, that is, not in such translations as those of Sternhold and Hopkins, Rous, Barton, Boyd, Withers, or the metrical translation called King James's'; and 'many of the rhyming words which Milton and King alone share are those that Milton has italicized because they were not the exact words of the text.'

'If the Royalists had some knowledge of the use of these psalms at the Windsor prayer meeting, this would explain Pierre du Moulin's accusation against Milton' (see above). 'We can assume, I think, that Milton could feel that his translation was not an attack on the king but a rejection of the misinterpretation of the psalms to defend him against all attacks' (see his remarks in *Eikon, Works* 5, 83). Miss Boddy sees possible gibes at Milton in John Phillips' *Satyr against Hypocrites* (1655).

As Miss Boddy says, it cannot 'be proved that Milton's translation of the psalms had a specific political application,' but her theory 'has at least the merit of suggesting an explanation of a number of minor oddities.' The theory is ingenious; it involves, however, a number of suppositions.

We may turn from motives to methods.

E. C. Baldwin ('Milton and the Psalms,' *MP* 17, 1919–20, 457–63) had argued, to quote M. H. Studley's summary, 'that Milton relies upon the Vulgate rather than upon the Hebrew both for error and strength, that he weakens the original by unwise expansion, being at times less concrete than the original; he notes allusions not in the original and the expression of opinions that turn the thought of the text; and all these are evidences of Hebrew scholarship or the lack of it' (*PQ* 4, 1925, 367–8). On the contrary, Miss Studley found ample warrant for Milton's alterations and additions in the common aims and practice of the English translators. While Milton indicated by italics his additions to the original, in claiming to work closely from the Hebrew he followed the tradition inaugurated by Sternhold and Hopkins. Like his predecessors, 'he deliberately used words and phrases that did not render the text literally, because he evidently considered acceptable religious interpretation of more importance than accurate translation. In addition, he again and again used expressions already made dear by familiar use, preferring them to the more scholarly term and more exact meaning. In his translations Milton is doing the customary and popular thing....' The traditional purpose 'required the sacrifice of literalness for the sake of dogma, and of lyricism for the sake of form. The psalms must be written in accordance with accepted theological belief, and in the popular service metre so that they could be sung to the long-used tunes' (Studley, 365–6). This general explanation and defence of Milton's method Miss Studley supports by comparing a number of particular items with some of the popular translators from Sternhold to Sandys. She concludes that the basis of Milton's work 'is not only the Hebrew, but all available texts.'

H. F. Fletcher (*Milton's Semitic Studies*, Chicago, 1926, 97–110) allows for the influence of current efforts to make a new version of the Psalms suitable for public worship, although, he thinks, such influence may have been rather cumulative than specific and conscious. Fletcher's comparison of Psalm 82 with other versions is noticed below. He finds, in Milton's whole group of Psalms, that deviations and expansions nowhere indicate misunderstanding of the text; Milton evidently read the Hebrew with ease. But he 'failed dismally' to make effective use of the common service metre.

W. B. Hunter (*PQ* 40, 1961, 485–94: partly summarized above), going on from Miss Studley's examples of similarity of idea between Milton and other translators, showed that 'the phraseology also is frequently similar if not identical.' The numerous Puritan writers borrowed so freely from their predecessors that 'it is now very difficult to determine with certainty who first composed a line which had met with popular success' (485). Thus versions of Ps. 83. 4 in Sternhold and Hopkins, Henry Ainsworth (1612), H. Dod (1620), the *Bay Psalm Book* (1640), Barton (1645), and Rous (1646 revision) reveal such shuffling of identical or similar phrases that—especially when set beside George

Sandys' 'independent version' (1636)—they appear 'almost indistinguishable' (486–7). The Psalms become 'traditional, almost communal,
poetry.' Milton followed the usual procedure; he 'could have composed
his lines without any reference to the Bible at all, though his marginal
notes show that he consulted it,' and 'perhaps half' of his work 'may
be matched more or less exactly from other psalters.' One 'interesting
probability' is that Milton 'used the first book published in America,'
the *Bay Psalm Book*, 'reprinted in England in 1647.' In his borrowings
Milton worked in the same way as the other translators, and 'he was
especially likely to follow the phraseology of those from the Puritan wing
of the church.' This is all natural enough, in view of the purpose he
apparently shared with other versifiers.

In 'The Sources of Milton's Prosody' (*PQ* 28, 1949, 125–44) Hunter
commented on the metrics of Milton's Psalms. In those of 1648 he
handled the common metre in much the same way as other translators,
using common contractions, etc. He 'expands the *-ion* suffix to two
syllables, a frequent practice of the psalters but not found in *PL*'
[this is fairly common in Milton's early English poetry]. The 'complete
absence of feminine endings' suggests Ainsworth as a model. Hunter
concludes 'that Milton was not especially interested in the prosody of
these psalms but was merely practicing well-known, traditional principles' (142). Hunter's remarks on the Psalms of 1653 are summarized
below.

What interest Milton's versions have is mainly in their relation to
contemporary activity in the genre and in the more speculative question
of the degree to which they reflected personal emotions. On their poetic
quality not much has been or needs to be said, though even relative
silence must take account of the popular aims and character of psalmody.
One critic at least has found larger implications. M. Jarrett-Kerr
('Milton, Poet and Paraphrast,' *Essays in Criticism* 10, 1960, 373–89),
in the course of demolishing the claims made for 'Milton, that supreme
craftsman,' glances briefly at the Psalms of 1648, not 'to make easy game
of them,' but 'because both the reverence for Scriptural literalism, and
the technique for easing Biblical language into poetry, both have had

their effect upon Milton's verse.' By way of evidence he quotes such 'doggerel' as *PL* 9. 655 f., etc.

'In spite of the relatively poor poetry in these psalms they have had an influence on the tradition that they were intended for. From the 1648 group in C[ommon] M[etre] no less than five hymns have come into common use, and even the 136th Psalm of Milton's youthful effort has gone into the hymnal tradition. From his translation of Ps. 85 two centos, still in use as hymns, have been taken. One is "Cause us to see Thy goodness, Lord" from stanza 7; the other is "The Lord will come and not be slow" from stanza 13. Ps. 82; "God in the great assembly stands," is used with some variations as a hymn and "Defend the poor and desolate" is also fashioned from stanzas of that psalm. From Ps. 84 beginning with stanza 6 the hymn "They pass refreshed the thirsty vale" has been taken. Most of these hymns, having been used by non-conformists at various times, are now found in Unitarian collections, some being in extensive use' (Rohr-Sauer, 43, citing John Julian, *Dictionary of Hymnology*, London, ed. 1925, 'Milton'). Parker (937–8, n. 66), referring to *Songs of Praise* (Oxford, 1925; enlar. 1931), says: 'One hymn, No. 12, is part of his translation of Psalm 136, adapted: another, No. 525, is twenty lines drawn from his Psalm 84; a third, No. 634, consists of three stanzas from the *Nativity Ode*; and the fourth, No. 658, is five stanzas from his Psalms 82, 85, and 86.'

Parker (322–5) discounts the motive derived from current concern with psalmody. Being convinced that *Samson Agonistes* was largely written in 1647, he sees Milton laying aside the uncompleted drama to compose this group of translations. 'The spirit of *Samson Agonistes* is everywhere in these psalms (as the spirit of the Psalms is everywhere in *Samson Agonistes*).' 'The consolation and relief which Milton found in this exercise are easily guessed, for his choices are an eloquent suggestion of a troubled and despairing soul. The first, Psalm 80, is the lament of a desolated country, tired of strife and tears, praying God to return His divine favour. Israel, of course, becomes England in the translator's mind, although in a few lines [25–8] he can hardly avoid thinking of his personal unhappiness.' While most of these Psalms have to do with national sins and thoughts of divine punishment or mercy, Psalm 88, the last of the series, is, like the first, 'an elegy, a lyric lament of tribulation; but unlike the first, and like *Samson Agonistes*, it is an expression of deep personal woe. The psalmist fears a lifelong severance from human intercourse as the result of some incurable affliction. Beyond doubt Milton was attracted to this poem by his own dread of approaching blindness, for it was not even necessary to modify the wording of the original to make it apply to himself.' 'In April of 1648, when Milton translated these nine psalms, his left eye had grown "dim and dead", and his health was wretched, probably as a result of the medicines which he was frantically taking to preserve his sight. It was some comfort perhaps, for a man in such personal misery, to realize that another poet had walked through the same shadows. It was some comfort, for a man who saw in his country's troubles the rebuke of an angry God, to reflect that it had happened before. In making his translations he allowed himself but little freedom, for the original was more pertinent than a paraphrase.' Parker recognizes that, while the Psalms might do for singing, they are 'tinkling and monotonous' in reading; they must, however, 'be regarded as exercises in *morale* as well as in linguistics. They compensated for unaccountable stoppages in direct personal expression. The suggestion sometimes made, that Milton hoped to produce a new hymnal, ignores both the nature of the psalms chosen and the state of the poet's mind in 1648, to say nothing of the fact of a hymnal not produced.'

A. Oras (*Blank Verse and Chronology in Milton*, Gainesville, 1966, 4–5), opposing Parker's argument for an early date for *Samson* and his relating of the drama to the Psalms, remarks: 'The spirit of the psalms translated by Milton in 1648 and 1653 is of the kind that may have recurred to him during any part of his later years, which especially after the Restoration for a man of Milton's temper and persuasion must have seemed years of grievous humiliation, no matter how bravely he may have endured them. The rhythm of the translations of 1653 prepares us not only for what we find in *SA* but also for the rhythmical boldness of *PL*....I see a marked difference between the perfection with which he makes Samson utter his extreme despondency and the somewhat hectic, at times indeed anarchic, fashion in which he in places translated Psalms 1–8 in 1653. It is these pieces that seem to me to have been done under the stress of an agony which did not permit full artistic control even in translations: the feeling here seems "raw."'

We may turn to this second group of Psalms. Psalm 1 Milton dated only 1653; Psalms 2–8 he dated on successive days, August 8–14, 1653. The question of public and private motives and implications comes up here again. On April 20 Cromwell had angrily dissolved the Rump and the new Nominated Parliament met on July 4. Fixler remarks (182): 'About a month after the members began sitting, and before their discord became very evident, Milton paraphrased the first eight Psalms of the Psalter, which in general dwell upon God's vindication of the just cause. And indeed the first Psalm's phrase, "th'assembly of just men", could have summed up Milton's view of the Nominated Parliament. For their programme was concerned with the enactment of righteousness in the kind of reforms long demanded by the sects and which the Rump had failed to provide, that is to say, the simplification of the laws and the administration of justice, and the abolition of tithes—precisely the programme Milton commended to Cromwell in the *Second Defence* (*Works* 8, 235–39).' Cf. Parker, 1025, n. 50.

Milton's view of the state of the nation must have been considerably more cheerful than it had been in 1648. He himself had routed the great Salmasius in his first *Defence* (1651), and, though he had now been blind for at least a year and a half, he was working on the second *Defence*, which was to manifest heroic pride in the achievements of Cromwell and the Commonwealth. Psalms 1–8—like many others—proclaim God's wrath against the unrighteous and his favour toward the just.

Since Milton had a lifelong devotion to the Psalms—they 'were in esteem with him above all Poetry' (Darbishire, *Early Lives*, 33)—we may assume that they came home to him personally with special force. But the Psalms have come home to many readers of diverse temperaments and circumstances, and their main themes are everywhere recurrent, so that we cannot feel quite certain what elements in these particular Psalms especially appealed to Milton. M. H. Studley (371) puts the matter thus: 'The 1653 group of Psalms reveals Milton's struggle and suffering in the early days of his blindness. Excepting the 8th, which is a song of praise, these Psalms voice the conflict of the godly and the ungodly....As Milton uses them, they become a reflection of his deplorable condition, a cry from his wounded, thwarted spirit.' Miss Studley quotes *Psalm* 6. 13–15: 'mine Eie / Through grief consumes, is waxen old and dark / Ith' mid'st of all mine enemies that mark.' 'Of all the versifiers of this Psalm, he alone uses the word *dark* as if to express a total want of sight'; he seems to intensify the Psalmist's mood. 'Another personal note unvoiced by Scripture or the other paraphrasers sounds from the word *mark*. Milton is acutely conscious that his enemies are on the alert to find cause to criticize' (cf. 5. 22–3). Eleanor G. Brown (*Milton's Blindness*, 84), Rohr-Sauer (43), and Parker (430) have also emphasized these lines in *Psalm* 6 in discussing reflections of personal feeling. Other lines too 'are the cry of human trouble' and express 'the sense of God's protection' against slanderous foes (Parker, 430–1).

On the literary side, one thing is manifest, that Milton has abandoned the common metre of psalmody for metrical experimentation. Rohr-Sauer (42), noting, like others, that 'no two of the eight psalms have the same form,' thus sums up technical facts: 'In these stanzas there is a great deal of the overlapping of lines that is characteristic of Milton's later style, so that rhymed pentameter reads almost like blank verse. The lines are no longer bound by italics where they are unliteral, and the effect is freedom and considerably smoother rhythms. There are, however, inversions, abrupt cesuras near the ends or beginnings of lines, clipped syllables made for the sake of rhythm and many prosaic expressions. In general, therefore, this group of psalms is only a degree better than the earlier one.' But devices that Rohr-Sauer sees as liabilities also point toward Milton's later style, the style he had been developing in his occasional sonnets. Laurence Binyon, the poet and translator of Dante, sees Milton (in *Ps* 2) bending Dante's *terza rima* into his own pattern: 'The special character of the metre is quite spoilt. In the *Divina Commedia* each tercet is a stanza complete in itself, and almost always closed by a full stop. It is the interwoven rhymes that give the necessary continuity to the metre and the narrative. Milton, with his instinct for moving on in a continuous motion and making his pauses without reference to the stanza, largely annuls the value of the rhymes, so that one feels a kind of dislocation in the verse' (*Seventeenth Century Studies Presented to Sir Herbert Grierson*, 1938, 185).

In the Psalms of 1653 Milton 'was surely more concerned with the prosody than with exactness of translation. Each is in a different meter, but only the decasyllabic couplets of the first had been employed in the psalters. Indeed, the impetus for such metrical experiments suggests a direct interest in the original variety of Calvin's Geneva psalter' (Hunter, *PQ* 28, 142). Milton 'uses all of the common speech contractions: *th'upright*' (1.15), etc. He has several unusual elisions, indicated by apostrophes, such as *holi' hill* (2. 13; cf. 5. 16, 7. 22). 'There are still very few feminine endings....But the proportion of run-on lines is perhaps higher than that of any other riming poetry before the 19th century....Regardless of the stanza form, every one of the eight [Psalms] contains this feature in some degree.' 'Likewise the caesura tends to fall near the beginning or end of the line. But most important of all is the extended use of reversed feet....' Hunter thinks 'that it is in these last psalms that Milton first reaches his mature prosody, combining principles taken from Sylvester and from the psalters: and their syllabic nature is the same as that of *PL*' (143). Considering the very wide range of Milton's models and artistic originality, one may question such a narrowing of focus; see G. A. Kellog, *PMLA* 68 (1953), 272, n. 10.

II. NOTES [D.B.]

Bits quoted from other paraphrases are only sample parallels, cited chiefly by Miss Studley and Hunter, who judiciously shrink from attempting a full list. These are not to be taken as necessarily pointing to Milton's preferred models; and natural coincidence must be allowed for. Such parallels are mostly given as modernized by the commentators (and are corrected in a few places). The *Bay Psalm Book* (1640; reprinted in England 1647) is cited as *Bay*; 'Rous' means the revised edition of 1646. In the notes the first numbers (after the numbers of the Psalms) are those of the verses in the Authorized Version (cited as A.V.); numbers in parentheses are the line numbers in Milton. Since phrases quoted from Milton for annotation are, as usual, italicized, his additions to *Ps* 80–8, which he italicized, are here put in roman type.

2. 6 (11–13) *but I saith hee | Anointed have my King (though ye rebell) | On Sion my holi' hill.* A.V.: 'Yet have I set my king upon my holy hill of Zion.' Milton's parenthesis, his own interpolation, is of interest. Verses 6–7 become of structural significance in *PL* 5. 603–15.

6. 10 (21–2) *Mine enemies shall all be blank and dash't | With much confusion.* Warton cited *Comus* 450–1: 'And noble grace that dash't brute violence | With ...blank aw.'

7 For the metre Todd cited Song Eleven in Sidney's *Astrophel and Stella* (Ringler, 233) and Sylvester's *Ode to Astraea* (Grosart, 2, 47).

8. 8 (21–2) *Fish that through the wet | Sea-paths in shoals do slide.* A.V.: 'the fish of the sea, and whatsoever passeth through the paths of the seas.' Todd cited Sandys' version: 'Or through the rowling Ocean slide'; and *PL* 7. 400 f.

80. 1 (5–6) *the Cherubs* bright | Between their wings out-spread. 'Milton's insertion alludes to the ark of the covenant, which had two golden cherubs kneeling, with their wings meeting above (*Exod.* xxv 18–22)' (Carey).

80. 5 (21) *Thou feed'st them with the bread of tears.* From A.V. (Hunter).

80. 5 (22) *Their bread with tears they eat.* The same in Sternhold and Hopkins (Hunter).

80. 8 (35) *Nations* proud and haut. See *Comus* 30–3 n.

80. 13 (56) tender Shoots. Warton cited the phrase in *Comus* 295.

80. 17 (69–72) *Upon the man of thy right hand | Let thy good hand be laid, | Upon the Son of Man, whom thou | Strong for thy self hast made.* Hunter (489) quotes *Bay* as the version nearest Milton: 'Upon the man of thy right hand | let thine hand present be: | Upon the son of man whom thou | hast made so strong for thee.'

81. 5 (17) *Testimony ordain'd.* Hunter (*PQ* 28, 142) notes this as 'one elision somewhat in his later manner, ... with elision of the open vowels between words and a light fourth foot.'

81. 10 (43–4) *Ask large enough, and I...demand.* M. H. Studley (369) quoted Wither: 'And, will thy largest askings give.'

81. 12 (49–50) *Then did I leave them to their will | And to their wandring mind.* A.V.: 'So I gave them up unto their own hearts' lust: and they walked in their own counsels.' Miss Studley (369–70) sees Milton, like other translators, altering the original to emphasize 'his conception of the cause of sin, an act of the will resulting in disobedience toward God.' Here, 'departing widely from Scripture,' Milton gives a more precise definition, as in Sternhold ('Then did I leave them to their will, / In hardnesse of their heart') and Sandys ('Whom I unto their lusts resign'd, / And errors of their wandring minde'). But the departures from Scripture do not seem very wide.

82. 1 (1–2) *God in the great assembly stands* | Of Kings and lordly states. Fletcher (*Milton's Semitic Studies*, 99–107) compares Psalm 82, as a specimen, with Hebrew, Latin, Italian, and versions in several English Bibles. Milton's second line, rather a deviation than an interpolation, seems to confuse 'the assembly of gods with an assembly of gods and kings or potentates.' But there were strong hints for this in Tremellius' use of *magistratus*, in George Buchanan's repeated *Reges*, and in the 'congregation of the mighty' (A.V.); Sternhold and Hopkins dispensed 'entirely with the divine aspect of the assembly' ('Amid the presse with men of might...with Judges of the land'). As in *PL* 2. 387, Milton uses *States* for 'estates of parliament,' statesmen; cf. Shakespeare, *John* 2. 1. 395.

82. 5 (17) *They know not nor will understand.* Identical in H. Dod (1620), *Bay*, Z. Boyd (1646), Rous (1646) (Hunter, 487). All are very close to A.V.: 'They know not, neither will they understand.'

82. 5 (18) *In darkness they walk on.* Identical with *Bay*, Boyd, Rous (Hunter, 487). A.V. has: 'they walk on in darkness.'

82. 5 (19) *The Earths foundations all are mov'd.* A.V.: 'all the foundations of the earth are out of course.' Dod, *Bay*, and Boyd read: 'All the foundations of the earth'; Rous: 'Ev'n the foundations of the earth' (Hunter, 487).

82. 5 (20) *And out of order gon.* Hunter (487) cites, e.g. *Bay*: 'quite out of course are gone'; Boyd: 'out of their course are gone'; Rous: 'all out of course are gone.' Cf. A.V., quoted under 82. 5 (19).

82. 6 (21) *I said that ye were Gods, yea all.* Hunter (488) cites *Bay*: 'I said that ye are gods, and sons'; Boyd: 'I thus have said that ye are gods'; Rous: 'I said that you are gods, and are.' A.V.: 'I have said, Ye are gods.'

82. 6 (22) *The Sons of God most high.* The same in Wither (Hunter, 488). A.V.: 'and all of you are children of the most High.'

82. 7 (23) *But ye shall die like men, and fall.* Hunter (488) cites Dod (identical);

Bay and Boyd: 'But ye shall die like men, and like'; Rous: 'But die ye shall like men, and like'; etc. Milton's line is identical with A.V.

82. 7 (24) *As other Princes* die. Hunter (488) cites Wither: 'and, like such Princes die'; Ainsworth, *Bay*, Boyd, Rous: 'one of the Princes fall'; etc. A.V.: 'and fall like one of the princes.' Fletcher (106–7: see 82. 1 above) notes that the Hebrew says: 'But like man ye shall die and like one of the princes ye shall fall'; that Milton would seem to have mistaken the word for 'one' for the closely similar word for 'other'; but that the same mistake or change had appeared in Tremellius, G. Diodati, and the Geneva and Bishops' Bibles.

83. 4 (13–16) *Come let us cut them off say they,* | *Till they no Nation be* | *That Israels name for ever may* | *Be lost in memory.* Hunter (486–7) finds Ainsworth (1612) especially close: 'They said, Come, let us cut them off / that they no nation be: / That name of Isr'el may no more / be had in memory.' A.V.: 'They have said, Come, and let us cut them off from being a nation; that the name of Israel may be no more in remembrance.'

83. 16 (59) *honour due*: a stock phrase, as Todd's citations show.

83. 17 (62, 64) Remarking on 'the complete absence of feminine endings' in the Psalms of 1648, Hunter (*PQ* 28, 142) presumes that here 'contraction of *ever* and *never* avoids them'; but they are not printed as contractions. He cites a similar avoidance in the *flowr* and *bowr* of 85. 11 (45, 47).

83. 18 (65–8) Baldwin (*MP* 17, 461) saw here an expression of 'Arian opinions,' but Miss Studley (370) takes Milton's words as an echo of Barton: 'In all the earth the onely one / art highest over all'; and notes 'thou art alone' in Coverdale and Geneva texts.

84. 6 (21) thirstie *Vale*: in Sandys' version (Todd).

86 In Psalms 86 and 88, which express 'a sense of personal estrangement from God,' Miss Studley (370) sees Milton as less successful than some other translators because his religious sensibility is less given to direct, emotional representation of guilt and sorrow; for him 'The fact of repentance is enough.'

86. 11 (39) *To fear thy name my heart unite.* A.V.: 'unite my heart to fear thy name.' Ainsworth, Dod, *Bay*, and Barton, like Milton, rearrange the words of A.V., some with *mine* for *my* (Hunter, 487).

86. 16 (57–60) *O turn to me* thy face at length, | *And me have mercy on,* | *Unto thy servant give thy strength,* | *And save thy hand-maids Son.* Hunter (489) notes that, while *Bay* does not use Milton's common metre, its language is similar:

'O turn thou unto me, / and mercy on me have: / unto thy servant give thy strength; / thine handmaid's son do save.' But both are close to A.V.

87. 1 (1, 3) Hunter (*PQ* 28, 142) notes that '*Sanctuary* rimes with *high* and must be trisyllabic, contracting *ua* as the psalters regularly do.'

87. 6 (21–3) *The Lord shall write it in a Scrowle / . . . When he the Nations doth enrowle.* Todd quoted Sandys: 'The Lord, in his eternall Scroll, / Shall these, as Citizens, inroll.'

88. 3 (11–12) *My life* at deaths uncherful dore / *Unto the grave draws nigh.* A.V.: 'my life draweth nigh unto the grave.' Todd quoted Sackville's *Induction* 334: 'His withered fist still knocking at deathes dore'; and the phrase 'at Death's door' from 'the old translation of the Psalms. *Ps.* cvii. 18.' If he meant Sternhold and Hopkins, I do not find it there, but the phrase does appear in their version in Ps. 23. 4 and 119. 107.

STUDIES OF VERSE FORM
IN THE MINOR ENGLISH POEMS
by
EDWARD R. WEISMILLER

The study of prosody consists in the determination and examination of the rules or laws in accordance with which particular kinds or specimens of verse were written. The prosody of a line or of a poem is, then, its embodiment of meter in actual sound, in language. No meter subjects (or could, or would, subject) to law all of the sounds of a spoken language in their complex and subtle interrelationships. The skilled writer of verse is nonetheless at all times concerned with the effective management of sound, and not merely of such sounds or relationships of sound as are governed by the meter he has chosen. He is concerned with rhythm and with verbal music.

Of course these are qualified by meter in fundamental, if limited, ways; some meters are more restrictive than others. In any line or group of lines, however, in any meter, there is much a writer may do to vary the movement of his verse, the patterning of sound in it. If his meter does not forbid he may at times, and in differing ways, set grammatical unit (phrase, clause, sentence) at odds with verse unit (line, stanza). He may —is, indeed, all but certain to—choose words in part for the grace or awkwardness with which they enter into the specific flow of sound that is to convey his meaning. The study of rhythm and of the patterning of sound *insofar as these are not metrically determined* is the study of versification. Effects of versification are as much formal as are those that are a consequence of basic prosody; an alliteration not required by the meter, a non-metrical pause, are effects we hear as formal. Either prosody or versification, then, or both together, we may think of as verse form.

It is important to insist on these discriminations because many critics of verse—including critics of Milton's verse—have thought of themselves, and spoken of themselves, as writing about prosody when they were in fact writing about versification. Confusion is not easy to avoid: the student of verse form is likely to be at least as interested in versification as he is in strict prosody; and if he is interested in versification as nearly as may be to the exclusion of prosody and its technicalities, what nonetheless can he call himself, without tiresome circumlocution, but 'prosodist'? Yet if he is not writing, in part at least, about basic rule, about the *meter* of the verse under discussion, the name should be reserved. The versification of a line is not its prosody. Any study or criticism may be of interest and value, of course, provided its nature is understood. Certainly the reader must understand the distinctions to which attention has been called here if he is to make full sense of the best available criticisms of verse form—or if he is to salvage worthwhile observations and insights, about prosody *or* versification, from the confusing contexts in which they are sometimes to be found.

More has been written about form in Milton's verse than about form in the verse of any other poet writing in English. One reason for this is the unusual variety of the forms which Milton employed successfully; another is the originality and the complexity of his use of them. Not surprisingly, very much the most extended and searching study has been made of the blank verse of *PL*; and since all of Milton's verse in English is written in the meter called accentual-syllabic—a meter of counted syllables, generally understood as having been written on an iambic base (though the degree to which the base is actually present in the line, the way in which it is *heard*, remain subjects of controversy among prosodists)—it is doubtless to be expected that a given critic may, if only by implication, ask us to understand the basic structure of a line of (say) *Vac* in relation to what he has told us of the line in *PL*. Rhyme will constitute the sole *metrical* difference; and the difference is an obvious one, or at any rate easily analyzable. Indeed, Milton's use of the decasyllable rhymed, in the late sonnets, may seem closer to his management of the unrhymed line in *PL* than does his use of the dramatic blank verse line in *Comus*; and in the complex stanza of the 'Hymn' in *Nat* we have no difficulty in proportioning and relating lines of six, eight and twelve syllables to what we may somehow feel to be the *basic* ten-syllable line. Short or long, rhymed or unrhymed, Milton's lines do, in fact, obey for the most part the same prosodic laws. It may still be profitable to discuss the versification of the minor poems, or certain ones among them, separately, but if we learn that, in general, prosodists interested in Milton's verse have devoted most of their attention to *PL* —or to *PL, PR*, and the blank verse portions of *Comus* and *SA*—we cannot be much surprised. There is matter of great interest beyond these limits, and it has been taken up: but often incidentally, often more briefly, or less searchingly, than we might wish.

When we look for analysis and criticism of form in Milton's shorter English poems, we find the following materials: (1) histories of English prosody, which customarily devote a great deal of space to Milton (though not necessarily to the shorter poems); (2) collected or separate editions of Milton's poems, which may include introductory essays—or briefer remarks in headnotes or notes to individual poems—on verse form; (3) general studies of Milton's prosody, which may or may not deal systematically with all the poems; (4) studies, usually of essay or monograph length, of the form of, or of particular formal effects in, individual poems; and (5) scattered commentary which, though it may be most insightful, is incidental to analysis, or criticism, of other kinds.

Commentary of this last sort is extraordinarily voluminous, and poses problems of treatment. Where it is clearly derivative (however useful it may be in its own context), notice of it may be omitted here, especially where the work from which it derives is to be noticed. Commentary too general, abstract, or impressionistic, commentary intended principally to express modulations of approval or disapproval, may likewise be omitted, except where a particular fresh judgment may find appropriate place in the detailed, line-by-line notes on form in individual poems in my volume on *The Prosody of the English Poems* (to be published last in this series). Useful observations from all sources on minor details of form will in general be reserved for that volume. The criteria for notice here must be (*a*) a relatively sustained attention to verse form in any or all of Milton's minor poems, and/or (*b*) importance, or consequence, or broad applicability in formal analysis less sustained.

Since early criticism of the verse is, on the whole, recorded adequately in Warton and Todd, this essay will concern itself more particularly with nineteenth- and twentieth-century analyses of the form of Milton's shorter English poems. And first it will be necessary to describe the general prosodic background against which such criticism must be viewed.

Readers of verse are not ordinarily prosodists, and the student of Milton today is unlikely to be aware that in Regions far from milde, but well over his head all the same, the New Grammarians are hammering out theories of prosody some one of which may radically affect the way in which his children, or their children, will one day read the verse he now reads as heir to vastly different presuppositions. He may not, indeed, be aware that alternative ways of reading poetry exist, have existed, and will—not necessarily wrongly—continue to come into existence. If he had been alive a hundred years ago he would not have read Milton quite as (perhaps) he reads him now. He reads now from texts which probably would not have been printed as they are, accompanied by prosodic commentary which would certainly not have been written as it is, if the earlier twentieth century had not seen at least a partial acceptance of the conclusions embodied in a series of studies by the British poet Robert Bridges, culminating in the revised and final edition of his *Milton's Prosody*.[1]

Bridges is concerned primarily with the *theoretical* structure of the blank verse line in *PL*; it is his position that that line consists of ten metrical syllables, and that lines which appear to have more than ten syllables may in our understanding, at least, be reduced to the appropriate number by means of 'elisions' the greater number of which he takes

---

[1] Robert Bridges, *Milton's Prosody* (Oxford: Clarendon Press, 1921). Hereafter, as here, full bibliographical information will be given in the first footnote mention of every work cited, even where the result is a partial duplication of material already supplied; the reader will thus be enabled conveniently to use the footnotes to amplify far briefer later references to the same work(s), which will be given in the text only.

Page numbers in bold figures in the footnotes indicate the precise pages of articles or books dealing with the point at issue.

care to designate as 'optional.' He does not mean merely that the poet may use a given form contracted or not, as the meter requires:

$$\text{With Tur|tle wing | the ám} \phi \text{|rous clouds | divid(ing}$$
(*Nat* 50)
$$\text{And sweet | reluc|tant ám|orous | delay (} PL \text{ 4. 311)—}$$

he means that 'elisions,' unless they are what he calls 'vowel-elisions of common speech' (19), need not—as, indeed, certain ones of them cannot fully—be performed. 'Milton came to scan his verses in one way,' he says, 'and to read them in another' (35). And earlier, 'There is some indication that Dryden and his school...in their own verse intended the "elided" vowels—which they represented by apostrophs—to be omitted from pronunciation: but if so, the absurdity perished' (18). On the other hand, Bridges says that 'When two vowel-sounds come together, then if the first of the two has a tail-glide...the sounds may be glided together so as to make a sound which can be reckoned as one syllable in the disyllabic verse' (23); this is clearly a direction which has something to do with performance.

But even though the line between the theoretical and the actual is in the end blurred, Bridges details the circumstances in which 'elision' may take place with care, with thoroughness, and with a basic accuracy which now seems all but revolutionary (8–10, 19–37). More recent scholarship suggests that a greater proportion of the 'elisions' or metrical compressions in sixteenth- and seventeenth-century English verse were in some way performed than Bridges appears to have believed; but this reduces the value of his work by very little. For he is himself the father of the theories that revise him. And it seems certain, now, that—almost in spite of himself, in some ways—he rescued early modern English accentual-syllabic verse from serious nineteenth- and early twentieth-century misreading.

We cannot be altogether certain how Edwin Guest, the chief English prosodist of the first half of the nineteenth century,[2] read the verse he discusses, for his notation and terminology are idiosyncratic, and attempts

[2] Edwin Guest, *History of English Rhythms*, ed. W. W. Skeat (London, 1882). First ed., 1838.

to translate them into language we would use must have results in some degree arbitrary. That Guest had a strong, if uneven, historic sense, however, is evident again and again in his work. He understood very well that *actual* metrical compressions of various kinds accounted for many apparent cases of extra syllable in Milton and his predecessors; and though he was not a phonetician, he understood something of the mechanism whereby those compressions took place. Guest has relatively little to say about Milton's minor poems. But the general student of English prosody must find his work of real importance.

Well before Guest wrote, however, the Romantic poets had begun mingling duple and triple rhythms; not infrequently they introduced trisyllabic feet into lines which would once have consisted of dissyllabic feet only:

> Dust as we are, the immortal spirit grows
> Like harmony in music; there is a dark
> Inscrutable workmanship that reconciles
> Discordant elements, makes them cling together
> In one society...(Wordsworth, *Prelude*, 1. 340–4).

The extra syllable in the first of these lines would once have been easily elidable ('the immortal'). In the second we might invoke the principle of the extrametrical syllable at the caesura, though in English this has been a device restricted to the verse drama, and in 1799–1805, when *The Prelude* was written (still more in 1850, when it was published), the device was centuries out of date. In the third line—was Wordsworth thinking, perhaps, of lines like Shylock's

> A pound of man's flesh taken from a man
> Is not | so es|timable, | profit|able nei(ther
> As flesh of muttons...(*Merch.* 1. 3. 166–8)?

But again, the understanding that made the second line in this passage a recognized (hen)decasyllable did not survive the early years of the seventeenth century. The sense must grow in us that in lines 341 and 342 of the Wordsworth there are trisyllabic feet; and if there are, why 'elide' in 340 and 343? If, later, in *Fra Lippo Lippi*, Browning wrote not merely this line, in which obviously the sound is suited to the sense,

> Like the skip|ping of rab|bits by moon|light, — three | slim shapes—(59)

but numbers of lines such as these,

> The world and life's too big to pass | for a dream (251)
> Then steps a sweet angelic slip | of a thing (370),

why should we try to 'regularize' lines like

> There came | a hur|ry of feet | and lit|tle feet (51)
>
> Trash, such | as these | poor devils | of Me|dici
> Have given | their hearts | to...(100–1)
> To the breath|less fel|low at | the al|tar-foot (149)
>
> Signing | himself | with the other | because | of Christ (155)
> And yet | the old school|ing sticks, | the old | grave eyes (231)—

in accordance with principles followed by poets two to three centuries previously?

It would appear that prosodists of the later nineteenth century asked themselves these questions; and answered as we should answer. But they asked one question more: if these lines contain trisyllabic feet, why is it not reasonable to hear the verse of the sixteenth and seventeenth centuries as also containing trisyllabic feet?

> Without | other limmes | of men | unbu|rièd (Browne, *Brit. Past.* 1. 5. 552)
> To th' touch | of golden wires, while *Hebe* brings (*Vac* 38)
>
> This was a Stat|ute giv'n | of old (*Ps* 81. 13)
> And wake for me, their fu|ri' asswage (*Ps* 7. 22)
> Purification in | the old Law | did save (*Sonn* 23. 6)
>
> Both Good | and Evil, | Good lost, | and E|vil got (*PL* 9. 1072)

Relaxation of the metrical compressions traditionally read in such lines had already suggested itself to a few prosodists who scanned English verse quantitatively, or in terms of complex combinations of quantity and accent.[3] More and more, nonetheless, it had come to be felt that however important 'fit' quantity might be in the production of harmonious verses, it was accent that governed English verse law. Into the prosodic criticism of Milton's verse thus understood—and into English prosodic criticism generally—relaxation of the old metrical compressions entered as a principle with the publication of David Masson's three-volume edition of Milton's poems in 1874.[4] Masson announced (1, cxv) that he could accept the reality of such printed contractions as 'flam'd' and 'Heav'n' in the early texts of Milton's poems; but he could not accept 'th'*Aonian*,' 'th'imbattelld.' He could not accept them 'for these reasons—

(1) Because the strict utterances *thAonian* and *thimbattelld* are comicalities now, which I cannot conceive ever to have been serious;

(2) because such contracted utterances are quite unnecessary for the metre, inasmuch as the lines are perfectly good to the ear even if the word *the* is fully, but softly, uttered, according to prose custom; and

(3) because I find the same elision mark used in the old texts in cases where it is utterly impossible that the total suppression of the *e* can have been meant. No doubt the reading of English poetry in Milton's time or Shakespeare's differed in some respects from ours. The differences, however, must have been in details of pronunciation rather than in metrical instinct.'

Masson goes on to recognize the option between, e.g., 'inflam'd' and 'inflamèd,' and 'the old liberty of lengthening words by resolution of single syllables of custom into two at will: e.g. *ocèan* (*Od. Nat.* 66), *contemplatiön* (*Il Pens.* 54)....' But 'On the whole...it is best to assume that strictly metrical effects are pretty permanent, that what was agreeable to the English metrical sense in former generations is agreeable now, and that, even in verse so old as Chaucer's, one of the tests of the right metrical reading of any line is that it shall satisfy the present ear' (loc. cit.). It satisfied Masson's ear to read trisyllabic feet

[3] See, e.g., John Foster, *An Essay on the Different Nature of Accent and Quantity* (Eton, 1762), and William Mitford, *An Essay upon the Harmony of Language* (London, 1774).

[4] David Masson, ed., *The Poetical Works of John Milton*, 3 vols. (London, 1874).

in lines like those of Milton quoted above—and in the thousands upon thousands of accentual-syllabic lines fashioned similarly in the sixteenth and seventeenth centuries. And though in 1887, little more than a decade after Masson's edition was published, there appeared an edition of *PL* 1 prepared by the Rev. H. C. Beeching[5]—an edition in which was printed (anonymously) Robert Bridges' first essay into the field in which he was to contribute so conscientiously, and so fruitfully, over the next thirty to thirty-five years—the idea of the existence of trisyllabic feet in Milton's verse (anapests, dactyls, amphibrachs, tribrachs, and others more complex) was an idea whose time had come. Most of the principal English prosodists for the next half-century and more argued hotly for recognition of the existence of such feet in sixteenth- and seventeenth-century English verse.

One of the strongest proponents of the idea—and Bridges' most determined opponent—was George Saintsbury, the erudite and prolific British scholar in whose three-volume *History of English Prosody*[6] perhaps the greater part of Book 6, chapter 1 (vol. 2), the chapter on Milton, constitutes a scathing attack on Bridges. In vain had Bridges insisted that he was talking about *theoretical prosody*, not *actual rhythm*. Discussing *Sonn* 10, Saintsbury says, 'In [line 7 of] the "Lady Margaret" I believe the persons just referred to ['the people who believe in elision, and especially in Miltonic elision'] scan "fa|tal to lib|erty" "fat'l to"; but as this is a collocation of sounds which my tongue cannot express, and my ear rejects with horror, I prefer the fact to the non-fact' (2, 216). As a controversialist witty, deft, and often grossly unfair, Saintsbury would seem, again and again, to have overwhelmed his less dazzling opponent. But however reasonable his exasperation over a system which divorces meter and rhythm so nearly incomprehensibly, the metrical structures Bridges had perceived in sixteenth- and seventeenth-century verse *were* fact. And as has been noted, the later twentieth century was to accept, not the eloquent arguments of Saintsbury and Masson,

---

[5] The Rev. H. C. Beeching, ed., *Paradise Lost, Bk. I* (Oxford, 1887).
[6] George Saintsbury, *A History of English Prosody*, 3 vols. (London: Macmillan, 1923). First ed., 1908–10.

but differing versions of Bridges' theory, a number of them at once more consistent and more exacting than the one in which Bridges himself believed.

The prosody of English accentual-syllabic verse involves other problems, of course, than the problem of syllable-counting, the problem of 'elision' theoretical or actual. There is the question of whether the individual line in that verse is simply a line of counted syllables, or whether it is divided into feet. If it does consist of feet, are those feet equal-timed, or are they characterized only by accent and number? What limitations are there, if any, upon the way in which accent is disposed in the line? Do accentual pyrrhics and spondees exist, or must we think of the line as made up all but entirely of accentual iambs, varied only by an occasional trochaic 'substitution'?

In my essay on 'The Prosody of *Paradise Lost*,' to be published in Volume III of the *Variorum Commentary*, I shall attempt to give a full summary account of the history of prosodic inquiry into all these questions, as it has affected our understanding of Milton's verse: of his blank verse in particular, of course, but by extension, of all his verse in accentual-syllabic meters. Here, and for the present, we must content ourselves with recognizing the main outlines of prosodic belief against the background of which the work of nineteenth- and twentieth-century critics of verse form in Milton must be viewed. Four major prosodists have addressed themselves to an examination of Milton's verse (including his early verse) since the publication of the revised *Milton's Prosody* in 1921: John S. Diekhoff, in a series of articles which will be noticed separately below; Ants Oras, also in articles and monographs; and S. Ernest Sprott[7] and F. T. Prince,[8] in full book-length studies with very different designs and purposes.

One article of Diekhoff's[9] has the avowed purpose of extending Bridges' principles, in detail, to Milton's shorter English poems (with which Bridges scarcely deals). And though S. E. Sprott does not agree

[7] S. Ernest Sprott, *Milton's Art of Prosody* (Oxford: Blackwell, 1953).
[8] F. T. Prince, *The Italian Element in Milton's Verse* (Oxford: Clarendon Press, 1954).
[9] John S. Diekhoff, 'Milton's Prosody in the Poems of the Trinity Manuscript,' *PMLA* 54 (1939), 153–83.

with Bridges in everything, it is fair to say that his work, which has the intent of analyzing fully the prosody of all of Milton's verse in English, assumes Bridges as a background. Much of the work of Oras, too, assumes Bridges (doubtless with qualifications), though Oras concerns himself for the most part with matters which do not bear directly on the demonstrations central to Bridges. Prince is the most recent, articulate and (perhaps) thorough of a series of prosodists (including Oras) who have explored Italian verse forms in the belief that they, rather than English forms, supply the most important background for Milton's prosodic practices. Prince voices strong disagreement with Bridges in *Italian Element*; his chapter 8, 'Milton's Blank Verse: the Prosody,' is an attempt to demonstrate that Milton's decasyllable obeys no other rules than those which underlie the Italian hendecasyllable, that is, that 'the tenth syllable must always have, or be capable of being given, a stress,' and that 'one other stress must fall, in any one line, on either the fourth or the sixth syllable' (143). M. Whiteley, however, has questioned this position so cogently[10] that Prince has returned to a position which, though not yet formulated in detail, seems far less distant than it was from Bridges' position.[11]

Bridges' studies have not, then, been superseded; they remain of central importance, though they have been supplemented and modified by the work of many scholars. And though numbers of these, as is natural, continue to be more interested in *PL*, *PR* and *SA* than in the shorter English poems, it is true also that the shorter poems have, in this century especially, come in for an increased share of attention. Perhaps it will be best now to take up these poems singly or (where it is appropriate to do so) in groups; and in the discussion of each poem or group of poems we may note briefly the prosodic problems involved, and the important or interesting discussions of those problems (or others apposite) which have been published in the last two centuries. The following grouping suggests itself: (*a*) *Nat*; *FInf*; *Passion*; (*b*) *Hor*; (*c*) *L'All*, *IlPen*; *EpWin*; (*d*) *Vac*; *Shak*; *Carrier* 1 and 2; *Arc*; *May*; (*e*) *Comus*; (*f*) *Time*; *Circum*; *SolMus*;

[10] M. Whiteley, 'Verse and Its Feet,' *RES*, n.s. 9 (1958), 268–78.
[11] Prince's reply to Mrs Whiteley follows her article, *RES*, n.s. 9 (1958), 278–9.

(g) *Lyc*; (h) Sonnets; (i) Psalms. It will be noted that the poems are grouped on the basis of prosodic comparability, and that while a very rough chronology has been preserved in the ordering of the groups, discussion of the poems in (f) comes later than might have been expected. This is so that the poems written under direct and strong Italian influence may be discussed in sequence.

Regrettably indeed, limitations of space, and the number of titles to be noticed, make it impossible to give a sufficient account of much of the critical work we are to consider. Studies devoted to the amassing of particulars can seldom be summarized; mention of them cannot always make clear how much they contain. Studies which can be summarized, in part or in whole, and studies which concern perplexing or controversial subjects, make possible or at times require notice at greater length than may be devoted to studies more comprehensive and basically of greater significance; problems of balance result. Published discussion of the verse of certain poems or groups of poems is very full, that of others, disappointingly scant; this imbalance too will be reflected in the pages that follow, and the form of not a few poems must await substantial discussion in *The Prosody of the English Poems*. It must be the simple purpose of this essay to provide an introduction and something of a guide to available criticism of verse form in the minor poems. Seldom indeed will a reading of these pages prove an adequate substitute for a reading of the materials discussed.

(a) Nat; FInf; Passion

Only a few stanza patterns are so unusual as to make it strongly unlikely that two poets, able technicians, could or would have devised them independently of one another. The stanza of *FInf*, of *Passion*, and of the opening section of *Nat* is a seven-line stanza the design of which is $ababbc_5c_6$; that is, it is basically rhyme royal (Chaucer's *Troilus* stanza) with an Alexandrine replacing the final decasyllable. Guest remarks (669) that Phineas Fletcher had used this stanza 'thirty years before' Milton used it; but though Fletcher was born in 1582, his poems were printed in 1627, 1628, and 1633, the last date being the publication date of the poems written in the stanza in question. Hanford identifies these poems, and says that they were 'doubtless known to Milton in MS.'[12]

Perhaps they were. But the stanza in Fletcher differs far more markedly from the rhyme royal with which our ears are familiar than does the stanza in Milton, since in Fletcher at least one of the rhymes—usually *b* —is double, or feminine, rhyme; often two are feminine (*a* and *b*, or *b* and *c*; rarely *a* and *c*); and in three of the hundred stanzas of *Elisa*, all three rhymes are feminine. To compare with this plenitude we have in Milton only *FInf* 1–3 and *Nat* 8–10—both *a* rhymes. Jakob Schipper compares the *FInf* stanza with that of Donne's 'The Good Morrow,' the pattern of which is $ababcc_5c_6$; he also cites theoretically similar stanzas of Giles and Phineas Fletcher.[13] But a glance at 'The Good Morrow' will show how much is involved in our sense of a stanza besides line length and rhyme scheme—among other important things, the relationship of grammar to line. In the end, Fletcher sounds like Fletcher, Donne like Donne, Milton like Milton. And after Spenser's impressive example (of ending stanza and strophe with variously divided Alexandrines), the six-foot line as appropriate to round out stanza could not be far from any poet's thought.

Indeed, prosodists have long agreed that the final Alexandrine in the 'Hymn' stanza of *Nat* gives it, too, a 'Spenserian' quality (see, e.g., Prince, 60). Bridges, however, points out how individually Milton handles the twelve-syllable line from the beginning—in *Nat*, that is, as well as in the choruses of *SA*. In most earlier verse, Bridges notes, the break in the Alexandrine came after the sixth syllable. 'The characteristic of Milton's twelve-syllable line is his neglect of this break, and he makes a verse which has a strong unity in itself, and no tendency to break up. In fact, though he allows himself the same liberty of caesura in this as he does in his ten-syllable verse…yet his "Alexandrine" is sometimes almost more coherent, as if it was composed expressly to counteract its tendency to divide into two' (60). Sprott feels rather that the Alexandrines in *SA* differ substantially from those in *Nat*, principally because

---

[12] J. H. Hanford, *A Milton Handbook*, 4th ed. (New York: Crofts, 1946), **139 and n. 8**.
[13] Jakob Schipper, *A History of English Versification* (Oxford: Clarendon Press, 1910), **359**.

of 'the sense variously drawn into and out of' the lines written later, and a greater variety in them of midverse breaks (132).

Enid Hamer takes the 'Hymn' stanza (patterned $aa_3b_5cc_3b_5d_4d_6$) to be the superior result of a representative seventeenth-century attempt to devise an effective strophe for the ode in English. 'The commonest method...was the evolution of a fairly elaborate stanza, distinguished by its greater amplitude and complexity from the lyric metres, and from the narrative stanzas by being composed of lines of varying length....'[14] The 'Hymn' stanza is presumed to be Milton's own invention. Nonetheless prosodists have searched diligently for possible antecedents, general or specific. While he admits that the concluding Alexandrine and the octosyllable preceding it 'would be impossible in any strict adherence to the methods of the Italian *canzone*,' Prince feels sure that 'the pattern and movement of the stanza, and the very notion of employing such a stanza for a solemn ode of this sort, could only derive from the tradition of the *canzone*' (60). In his edition of selected shorter poems of Milton, Prince notes additionally that the first six lines of the 'Hymn' stanza (called by Carol Maddison 'a romance six'[15]) may have been suggested by the openings of many of Tasso's lyrics (e.g. *Parafrasi dell'inno Stabat Mater*).[16]

Robert Shafer points out that 'the rime-scheme a a b c c b was a favourite one...with both Ronsard and Drayton';[17] John Carey notes that Drummond's madrigal 'To the delightful green' begins with the verse pattern $aa_3b_5cc_3b_5$.[18] Saintsbury (2, 210, n. 1) finds something 'partly like' Milton's stanza, but inferior to it, in a stanza of Drummond's from the *Divine Poems* (patterned $ab_3a_5cb_3c_5$), and suggests that we compare also Sir John Beaumont's 'Ode of the Blessed Trinity.' Of this last George N. Shuster says that it 'seems to enshrine the prosodic germ of

[14] Enid Hamer, *The Metres of English Poetry* (London: Methuen, 1930), **221–2**.
[15] Carol Maddison, *Apollo and the Nine* (Baltimore: Johns Hopkins University Press, 1960), **321**.
[16] F. T. Prince, ed., *Comus and Other Poems* (Oxford: Clarendon Press, 1968), **107**.
[17] Robert Shafer, *The English Ode to 1660* (New York: Gordian Press, 1966), **93**. First published, 1918.
[18] John Carey and Alastair Fowler, eds., *The Poems of John Milton* (London: Longmans, Green, 1968), **98–9**.

Milton's poem'; yet he finds the 'Hymn' stanza specifically Jonsonian: 'Above all the resemblance lies in the shifting line length and the swift movement achieved by the introduction of trimeter lines.'[19] Carol Maddison is content to characterize the music of the poem as 'Elizabethan' (321). Oras also reminds us of the Elizabethan effect of the early poems (through *Comus*), but he is speaking in precise terms of Milton's frequent use, in those poems, of devices of versification typical of poets who had written a generation or two before: especially, use of the syllabized -*ed* ending (see, e.g., 'hookèd,' *Nat* 56, 'armèd,' 58), and of other terminations—normally contracted—resolved into two syllables (see 'O-ce-an,' 66, 'ses-si-on,' 163).[20] Harris Francis Fletcher, nevertheless, hears as early as in *Nat* the 'double rhythm' which, to his ear, characterizes Milton's mature verse, and which 'derived from his writing of verse in languages other than English, and then transferring the rhythms he so discovered to his English verse.'[21] The idea is genuinely interesting, though perhaps in the end somewhat elusive.

Saintsbury thinks that the feminine rhymes in *Nat*—except, perhaps, for the last one—'were better away.' (It may be mentioned here parenthetically that the last line of the poem is the only six-foot line with a feminine ending in all of Milton's verse; such lines are uncommon also in Spenser—see, however, e.g., *F.Q.*7.8.1.9—but as has been mentioned, they are fairly common in the poems of Phineas Fletcher.) Noting many excellences in *Nat*, prosodic and other, Saintsbury calls attention to the fact that 'almost without exception...the two opening lines in each stanza end with a monosyllable'; he notes also 'the proportion of the rise in line length from 6, 10 to 8, 12' (2, 210). Shafer (93) commends Milton's 'singular skill in so constructing his stanza as to lead up gradually but inevitably to the final Alexandrine, thus gaining a cumulatively impressive effect in which, nevertheless, there is considerable variety

---

[19] George N. Shuster, *The English Ode from Milton to Keats* (New York: Columbia University Press, 1940), **68–9**.

[20] Ants Oras, *Blank Verse and Chronology in Milton*, University of Florida Monographs, Humanities—No. 20 (Gainesville: University of Florida Press, 1966), **12–14**, 37.

[21] Harris Francis Fletcher, 'A Possible Origin of Milton's "Counterpoint" or Double Rhythm,' *JEGP* 54 (1955), 521–5, **525**.

for the ear.' Cleanth Brooks and John Edward Hardy point out the appropriateness of a stanza thus constructed to the use Milton wished to make of it: 'This stanza, with its intricate, interlaced rhyme scheme and with its long final line, sets up resistance to any rapid narrative drive. It tends to break up a narrative into separate segments, each relatively complete in itself. In the Hymn, however, Milton does not want either a sense of a rapid narrative drive or a sense of dramatic urgency.'[22]

The overall form of a poem—its divisions of thought and movement; the total number of its lines and stanzas—may be thought to lie outside the province of prosody. But of course the small harmonies and proportions of line and stanza affect, and are affected by, the largest harmonies and proportions we are able to apprehend. Arthur Barker surely touches on matters of deep interest to the student of verse form when he points out that stanzas 1–8 of the 'Hymn' of *Nat* 'describe the setting of the Nativity, the next nine the angelic choir, the next nine the flight of the heathen gods. The conclusion, the last stanza, presents the scene in the stable'[23]—and, it might seem, completes the nine-stanza group begun in 1–8, thus dividing the 'Hymn' into three sets of nine verses. The formal balance, the essential *meaningfulness*, of such an arrangement must be evident, whether or not we go on to ascribe symbolic significance to the numbers involved, as does Maren-Sophie Røstvig. Miss Røstvig reminds us of the 'ninefold harmony' of the spheres (*Nat* 131); she finds the number of lines per stanza and the number of stanzas in both the introduction and the 'Hymn' of symbolic force, and discloses further arithmetical-intellectual harmonies of extraordinary complexity in the poem, based on a system of occult numerology which she is persuaded Milton knew, and intended to embody (in part) in the numbers governing the proportions of the ode.[24] Finding Miss Røstvig's argument at once 'loose and Procrustean,' Douglas Bush objects.[25]

[22] Cleanth Brooks and John Edward Hardy, eds., *Poems of Mr. John Milton: the 1645 Edition with Essays in Analysis* (New York: Harcourt, Brace, 1951), **104**.
[23] Arthur Barker, 'The Pattern of Milton's *Nativity Ode*,' *UTQ* 10 (1940–1), 167–81, **173**.
[24] Maren-Sophie Røstvig, 'The Hidden Sense,' *The Hidden Sense and Other Essays*, Norwegian Studies in English No. 9 (Oslo: Universitetsverlaget, 1963), **55–8**.
[25] Douglas Bush, 'Calculus Racked Him,' *SEL* 6 (1966), 1–6, **4**.

(b) *Hor*

With *Hor* we reach the first of the true metrical problems posed by Milton's verse. This exquisite translation Milton claims to have 'Rendred almost word for word without Rhyme according to the Latin Measure, as near as the Language will permit.' The question is, of course—what will the language permit, or what did Milton conclude that it would permit? Was he for once, and briefly, writing what he considered to be quantitative verse in English (that he was sensitive to quantity in his own language we know from his prefatory remarks on 'The Verse' of *PL*), or was his attempt rather to devise an English form as closely comparable *in effect* to the Latin form as he thought possible?

The question is complicated by the fact that in English, quantity and accent are related (accent is the degree or intensity of effort expended in the articulation of a syllable, quantity is the duration of the effort), and the two have often been confused; the student of prosodic criticism finds much of which the intelligibility, and usefulness, is vitiated by such confusion. No one who thought quantity and accent in English *precisely* interchangeable could, of course, suppose that Milton had illustrated the same belief in his translation of *Hor*. Many eighteenth- and nineteenth-century critics with extensive backgrounds in the classical literatures seem, however, to have had personal systems (or senses) of equivalence between Latin and English syllables, Latin and English meters, which they did not feel the need to explain in careful detail. Whether, at all events, the form of Milton's translation has seemed too obvious to require explanation, or too perplexing to allow of it, many critics have commended *Hor*, but few have written on its prosody.

This may seem especially surprising since the extraordinary and prosodically fascinating choruses of *SA* have themselves, as Sprott says (25–6), not seldom been taken to be 'English renderings of Greek (or Latin) measures as near as the language will permit; and this translation [i.e., *Hor*] affords the only data from which we may discover Milton's practice in converting a measure from one language into another.' Sprott devotes two pages to an assessment of the form of the translation. His central conclusion is that 'the classical quantitative system is in English completely abandoned in favour of strict syllabic English verse.'[26] The original measure of the ode, then, the fourth Asclepiad, which he gives —slightly inaccurately[27]—as

$$
\begin{array}{ll}
-- \;|\; -\cup\cup \;|\; -, & |\; -\cup\cup \;|\; -\cup\underline{\cup}\;| \\
-- \;|\; -\cup\cup \;|\; -, & |\; -\cup\cup \;|\; -\cup\underline{\cup}\;| \\
-- \;|\; -\cup\cup \;|\; -- & \\
-- \;|\; -\cup\cup \;|\; -\cup\underline{\cup}\;|, &
\end{array}
$$

becomes in English

$$
\begin{array}{ll}
\overline{\cup}\,\underline{\cup} \;|\; \cup - \;|\; (\overline{\cup\cup}) \; | \; \cup - \;|\; \cup - \;|\; (\cup) \\
\overline{\cup}\,\underline{\cup} \;|\; \cup - \;|\; \cup - \;|\; \cup - \;|\; \cup - \; | \\
\overline{\cup}\,\underline{\cup} \;|\; \cup - \;|\; \cup - \\
\overline{\cup}\,\underline{\cup} \;|\; \cup - \;|\; \cup - \;|.
\end{array}
$$

It will be noted that Sprott retains the macron (properly the symbol for long quantity) as the symbol of the accented syllable, and the breve (properly the symbol for short quantity) as the symbol of the unaccented syllable. He does not believe in the accentual pyrrhic or the accentual spondee, and so the spondees of the Latin measure (and the dactyls, which are quantitatively though of course not rhythmically equivalent to spondees) become iambs in English, with occasional trochaic substitution in accordance with English convention. Sprott interprets in detail the relationship between the two metrical forms, and concludes, 'This is...a most radical and free "Englishing" of the foreign measure'

---

26 All of Milton's early poems, says Sprott (15), are 'composed in a mixture of syllabic and accentual verse.' He is indebted to Bridges for the ambiguous phrasing; '...Nowadays all readers of English verse are accustomed to find syllabic and accentual verses alternating in a poem,' Bridges says (18). What both appear to feel is that a line in which natural full stresses occur on all even-numbered syllables is accentual; a line the stress patterning of which is not thus regular, but which contains nonetheless an expected number of syllables— whether or not that number is achieved through 'elision'—is syllabic. The formulation is very doubtful. In real stress verse the intervals between stresses are isochronous; real syllabic verse is not written exclusively in duple rhythms. Here, at all events, all Sprott would seem to mean is that each line of *Hor* contains a fixed number of syllables, but not all lines in the poem are perfectly regular in accent.

27 It appears that in lines 1, 2 and 4 of the stanza the final foot as Sprott gives it should be divided into a trochee ($-\cup$) and a catalectic foot ($\underline{\cup}_\wedge$).

(26). Many readers would agree—and would also conclude that the lines of Milton's translation are basically accentual-syllabic, though in some of them accent is handled unconventionally.

John T. Shawcross, however, does not agree; it is his belief that syllabic prosody for *Hor* is 'inadequate' (why, he does not explain), and so he concludes that Milton was, after all, writing quantitative verse according to the general rules that governed the writing of verse in Latin.[28] He proceeds, then, to scan *Hor* quantitatively, 'according to the Latin measure.' That he runs into difficulties is not surprising; though why the second syllable of 'Pyrrha' should be short in Latin but long in (Shawcross's) English is not made clear, nor does the mysterious second foot in the Shawcross scansion of line 14, | 'thē sacrēd' |, seem adequately covered by the explanation 'Milton often elided *the* to *th*', and one long replaces two shorts' (85). Milton did not elide the vowel of 'the' before a consonant except in the traditional combinations 'i' th',' 'o' th',' 'by th',' and 'to th'.' As for one long replacing two shorts, this equivalence is permitted in some Latin verse, but not automatically in all; Horace does not use the allowance in the original of the ode in question—clearly he wants the rhythm of the dactyls as dactyls—and that Milton would have to be recognized as fairly systematically replacing dactyls in the scheme with (sometimes doubtful) spondees may seem a difficulty. Shawcross objects (83) to Sprott's 'specious conclusion' that 'the space of the pause at the *caesura* is filled by an articulated syllable in the English translation. This is a strong argument against monosyllabic feet in Miltonic blank verse' (Sprott, 26); but why the claim that Milton, in an alternative quantitative rendering, 'frequently reduced a trochee to a stressed monosyllable' (Shawcross, 86) should seem more plausible is hard to say. Like Sprott, Shawcross proceeds finally to a glancing consideration of the choral verse of *SA*; as might be expected, the conclusions the two reach are, once again, widely divergent.

Shuster would seem to be in accord with Sprott in finding that Milton 'achieved almost perfectly the substitution of stresses for the long Latin

[28] John T. Shawcross, 'The Prosody of Milton's Translation of Horace's Fifth Ode,' *Tennessee Studies in Literature* 13 (1968), 81–9, **82, 81**.

syllables, though the rhythm is of course not the same' (76). Shuster gives us a sensitive appreciation of the verse of *Hor* (which he calls 'the version of the forty triumphs'): 'The unrhymed lines that lap over like waves of music; the delicate beauty of the half-revealed assonance that takes the place of rhyme; the inverted stresses that afford a faint but perceptible trace of antique choriambic rhythm; the admirable spondees of

> and Seas
> Rough with black winds and storms;

the stanza itself, Horatian and yet seemingly native English;...these are some of the treasures of this little poem' (loc. cit.).

Saintsbury, regrettably, devotes only two footnotes to *Hor*. The first (2, 212) is designed principally to sidestep the difficulties posed by the fact that he reads trisyllabic feet in Milton's verse generally—but they do not appear (or can scarcely be made to appear) in *Hor*, though they are so important to the poem's original. 'I think Milton's ear would always have protected him,' Saintsbury says, 'against the attempt to combine dactyls with iambs or spondees in English.' As though to exemplify the foredoomed nature of the attempt, Saintsbury remarks later (2, 255 n.), 'I do not know whether anyone has noticed that it is easy enough to English *Pyrrha* exactly—

> What boy elegant with many a rose now thee
> Courts, while perfumes around everywhere drop from him?
>   For whom bind'st thou thy golden locks,
>   Pyrrha, cool in a grotto?

But it is very ugly, like all its kind.'

(c) *L'All, IlPen; EpWin*

If for the present we leave out of account the translations of *Ps* 136 and *Ps* 7, and the songs in *Arc*, Milton's sustained tetrameter verse consists of *EpWin, L'All, IlPen*, and all but a few lines of *Comus* 93–144, 866–87 and 902–1022. There are as well scattered or isolated tetrameters in others of Milton's minor poems. We recall, for example, *SolMus* 15–16, *May* 5–8, and the seventh line of the 'Hymn' stanza of *Nat*, in form twenty-seven times repeated; and the odd-numbered lines of *Ps* 80–8 (in so-called 'common measure') are of course tetrameters. The sustained tetrameter verse is a center also of prosodic controversy, though the point at issue may seem so technical—so nearly, in one sense, academic—that even experienced readers, if they are aware of it at all, may be inclined to dismiss it as unimportant. If at times such readers sense an ambiguity or difficulty in the construction of Milton's tetrameter verse, or of verse like it, they may not distinguish between deliberate (or permitted) disturbances of rhythm and uncertainties built into the basic meter. *L'All* 11–24 will provide us with materials for illustration.

> But com thou Goddess fair and free,
> In Heav'n ycleap'd *Euphrosyne,*
> And by men, heart-easing Mirth,
> Whom lovely *Venus* at a birth
> With two sister Graces more
> To Ivy-crowned *Bacchus* bore;
> Or whether (as som Sager sing)
> The frolick Wind that breathes the Spring,
> *Zephir* with *Aurora* playing,
> As he met her once a Maying,
> There on Beds of Violets blew,
> And fresh-blown Roses washt in dew,
> Fill'd her with thee a daughter fair,
> So bucksom, blith, and debonair.

First we may note the *variety* of lines in the passage quoted: eight- and seven-syllable lines are freely intermingled, and in a later couplet (45–6),

> Then to com in spight of sorrow,
> And at my window bid good morrow,

the second line is actually of nine syllables. The final syllable of this line constitutes a (familiar enough) feminine ending; it is extrametrical; and we do not need to know before we reach it whether or not it will be there, since its existence or non-existence scarcely affects the reading of the rest of the line. But not to know whether a tetrameter is to be of seven or of eight metrical syllables until we are well into it—this may cause a greater uncertainty in our reading, in the way in which we dispose the rhythms of the line, than we might at first imagine.

Line 13 above,

> And by men, heart-easing Mirth,

we may compare with *L'All* 104,

> And by the Friars Lanthorn led.

How are we to know until we reach the 'the' of the second line that that line is to be of a full eight syllables? How can we know until we reach 'thee' in line 23 that the line will not read 'Fill'd her with a daughter fair'? Alternatively, how can we know until we reach 'Beds' in line 21 that that line will not read 'There on a Bed of Violets blew'? About the reading of such lines as 11, 12, 14, 16, 17, 18, 22 and 24 above there is no ambiguity; but about all full tetrameters which begin with accentual pyrrhics or trochees, and about all heptasyllables, there must be, in a meter of mixed octosyllables and heptasyllables (8's and 7's), at least an initial uncertainty. And in a few oddly constructed tetrameters, such as *Comus* 139,

> The nice Morn on th' *Indian* steep,

and *EpWin* 15,

> Her high birth, and her graces sweet,

uncertainty of rhythmic phrasing is continued past the middle of the line. *EpWin* 15 *could* read

> Her high birth, and graces sweet;

the line quoted from *Comus does* read, in the Bridgewater MS.,

> The nice morne on the Indian steepe,

and some editors today would wish us to adopt that reading, though the odder and more awkward version of the line occurs in the Trinity MS. (in Milton's holograph) and in all three editions of the poem printed during Milton's lifetime. Readers very properly find Milton's tetrameter verse enchanting, and delightful to read; but it would be preposterous to claim that tetrameters which consist of mixed octosyllables and heptasyllables are as secure in rhythm as unvaried octosyllables, or as (say) Milton's decasyllables, however complex in movement these may be. Uncertainty, its swift or slightly delayed resolution, uncertainty again—these may, in fact, be a large part of what we come to value most in the rhythm of mixed 8's and 7's. The rhythm is often called dance-like, and so it is: the poet leads, and we follow, conscious as we move of every rhythmic clue that will help us to decide correctly what the next step, the next movement, will be.

Most prosodists describe the rhythm of lines like 'There on Beds of Violets blew' as trochaic; speaking of the 'fairy verses,' 8's and 7's, at the beginning of Act 2 of Shakespeare's *Dream*, Saintsbury commends the 'tripping measure—which pirouettes on either foot, iamb or trochee, with equal ease, and "twinkles interchange" of the two with almost bewildering but never-failing accuracy and intricacy combined' (2, 213), and he means the commendation to apply to Milton's 8's and 7's as well: 'The famous "light fantastic toe"' he equates (2, 214) with 'the metre itself.' Enid Hamer is equally admiring: 'The charm of Milton's four-foot technique is its continuous variety, the lightness and rapidity with which the iambic movement glides into trochaic, or hovers bewitchingly between the two...' (30). In a particularly sensitive discussion of the meter, E. N. S. Thompson, though he too speaks of 'the subtle shifting from rising to falling rhythm,' contrives to make a useful discrimination between heptasyllables variously constructed: '"Sober, steadfast, and demure" [*IlPen* 32] and "Tow'red Cities please us then" [*L'All* 117] seem like trochaic lines mainly because the phrasing is in falling rhythm. Quite different is the line "Black, but such as in esteem" [*IlPen* 17]. The pause after the first word and the iambic phrasing of the remainder of the line leave the reader conscious of the first lost syllable and the line is iambic in effect.'[29]

With this the nature of the prosodic controversy over the meter of mixed octosyllables and heptasyllables becomes clear. Are the hepta-syllables trochaic in rhythm only (many, perhaps most of them, are at first trochaic in rhythm), or are they actually, metrically, trochaic lines,

---

[29] Elbert N. S. Thompson, 'The Octosyllabic Couplet,' *PQ* 18 (1939), 257–68, **266**.

mixed with iambic lines? Mixtures of meter are not common; but that is not to say that they cannot exist. It was said above that the point at issue may seem academic. Let us explore its consequences a little further. As trochaic lines, *L'All* 21 and 117 would be scanned

> There on | Beds of | Violets | blew (x)
> Towred | Cities | please us | then (x);

as iambic lines, they would be scanned

> (x) There | on Beds | of Vio|lets blew
> (x) Tow|red Cit|ies please | us then.

In lines so definite in rhythm it may seem to make little difference, though we should note, in the lines scanned as trochaic, an assumption that an unstressed syllable would normally complete and close the fourth foot (as in the verse of Longfellow's *Hiawatha*), but is here missing. Still, the relationship of accent to accent in the lines as alternatively scanned seems unvaried.

Can the same be said of

> (x) The | nice Morn | on th' *In*|*dian* steep,
> The nice | Morn on | the *In*|*dian* steep

and

> The nice | Morn on | th' *Indian* | steep (x)?

of

> Her high | birth, and | her gra|ces sweet

and

> (x) Her | high birth, | and gra|ces sweet...?

Clearly it cannot. For a variety of reasons which, to the degree that they are not self-evident, cannot be attended to here (but have to do with our management of accent), we are sensitive to the position of particular syllables in the foot in particular meters.

> (x) And | by men, | heart-eas|ing Mirth

may not differ much from

> And by | men, heart-|easing | Mirth (x)—

that it does not, indeed, is the chief reason why the problem we are posing does not, to many readers, seem to be a problem, once it is certain that the line does not read (say)

x   x́
And by | mankind, | heart-eas|ing Mirth.

Yet it is not clear that trochaic meters in English do not enforce a more singsong reading than their iambic counterparts; and when to this we add the difficulties posed by such revealing lines as *EpWin* 15 and *Comus* 139 (above), we may come to feel that the problem is not academic, after all.

Thompson's mention of 'the first lost syllable' of *IlPen* 17 makes it apparent that he believes all lines in the meter of mixed octosyllables and heptasyllables to be, metrically, iambic, and this is the explanation we find in Jakob Schipper's historical treatment of the subject. Though as a prosodist Schipper is at times too rigid, here his discussion is helpful. He distinguishes between a strict version of tetrameter verse and a freer variety to which, he feels, 'a greater interest attaches.' 'The characteristic feature in this treatment of the four-foot verse is the frequent suppression of the anacrusis,' he says (188).[30] Schipper quotes *L'All* 11–16, and continues, 'The structure of the verse is essentially iambic, though the iambic metre frequently, by suppression of the initial theses, as in the thirteenth and fifteenth lines of this passage, falls into a trochaic cadence.' Thus he distinguishes, usefully, between meter and rhythm. In a review of the 1888–9 *Neuenglische Metrik*, however, the German original of that part of Schipper's *Englische Metrik* which contains the above analysis, Francis B. Gummere takes issue with Schipper on the point in question: 'Schipper reasons that while "L'Allegro" and "Il Penseroso" have many trochaic lines [this phrasing, it will be seen, is Gummere's own], the majority are iambic; and hence we must assume the poem to be written in iambic verse. This is political scansion. Majority rules, and of

---

[30] W. P. Ker, in *Form and Style in Poetry* (New York: Russell and Russell, 1966), **300**, uses much the same language. With the verse of *L'All* and *IlPen* Ker compares the Spanish verse of *arte mayor*: 'It is a form of verse in which the *anacrusis* is frequently dropped, and to speak of this licence as a fault is to mistake the character of the rhythm.' *Form and Style in Poetry* was first published in 1928; it is made up of two series of lectures, the first delivered in 1912, the second in 1914–15.

course a Pennsylvania democrat is a republican.'[31] The analogy is amusing but wrong-headed; a poem is no more a democracy for Gummere's purposes than he implies it to be for Schipper's.

And so the argument continues, with some analysts of verse coming down on one side, some on the other. Speaking in particular of *EpWin*, Walter Savage Landor says regretfully that Milton 'has often much injured this beautiful metre by the prefix of a syllable which distorts every foot....The flow of the poem...is trochaic: he turns it into the iambic, which is exactly its opposite.'[32] Masson speaks perhaps with greater precision of the 'trochaic *effect* [italics mine] of a line in which the initial unaccented syllable is missing' (1, cix); A. W. Verity, however, speaks instead of there being, in such a line, 'an extra syllable, stressed, at the end,' and he thus scans *Comus* 94

$$\text{Now the} \mid \text{top of} \mid \text{heav'n doth} \mid \text{hold.}^{33}$$

All this is confusing enough. But perhaps more critics still, avoiding recognition of the problem or decision on it, waver between the two positions. Sprott's consideration of the issues seems sufficiently insightful to be taken here as conclusive. Speaking of Milton's heptasyllables, he says: 'As in practice these lines are in falling rhythm, especially where there is a long block of them (*Comus* 903–17), they raise the question of whether Milton regarded them as consisting theoretically of four inverted feet with the final syllable missing, or whether he merely dropped the initial syllable and thought of them as iambic....I think the evidence is against their being regarded as catalectic trochaic lines, for this reason, if for nothing else, that in over six hundred lines, only seven (five in "L'Allegro" and two in *Comus*) have four complete feet in falling rhythm.[34]

---

[31] *Englische Metrik* von Dr. J. Schipper. Zweiter Theil: Neuenglische Metrik (Bonn, 1888–9), reviewed by Francis B. Gummere, *MLN* 4 (1889), 145–7, **147**.

[32] *The Works and Life of Walter Savage Landor*, 8 vols. (London, 1874–6); vol. 4, *Imaginary Conversations*, Third Series, Conversation 18 (between Southey and Landor), part 2, 476–528, **516**. The *Imaginary Conversations of Literary Men and Statesmen* were first published, in 5 vols., 1824–9.

[33] A. W. Verity, ed., *Comus* (Cambridge: Cambridge University Press, 1921), **xliv**.

[34] In fact, twelve lines in Milton's minor poems answer Sprott's description: *May* 7–8; *L'All* 19–20, 45, 69–70; *IlPen* 12; *Comus* 997; *Ps* 3. 15; and *Ps* 7. 2 and 25.

There is more needed to account for this than the difficulty of dissyllabic rhyme. If at the time of writing Milton had thought of the complete lines as inverted, surely he would have made freer use of inverted second and third feet in iambic lines. It is best to assume that he thought of the line as ending with the strong syllable, so that the seven-syllable lines with four full feet in falling rhythm [see, e.g., *L'All* 19–20, quoted above] will likewise be initially catalectic, and have also final extrametrical syllables' (18). In all meters we know, the end of the line is of very great importance to our sense of the *nature* of the line, and so of the meter. That metrically trochaic lines should almost never end in trochees may seem, at last, a notion too unlikely to be accepted.

Another suggestion of Sprott's regarding Milton's tetrameter verse is less convincing. Noting that the percentage of headless lines in *EpWin* is 45·9, in *L'All* 11–100, 50, in *L'All* 101–52, 15·4, and in *IlPen* 11–176, 16·9, Sprott conjectures (18–19) that *L'All* may have been begun before *EpWin* (perhaps at Cambridge), laid aside, then later—conceivably at Horton—taken up again and completed, with the writing of *IlPen* following immediately. The statistics Sprott offers relating to trochaic openings in full octosyllables, and feminine endings to headless lines (he finds these only in the first part of *L'All*) support, he feels, the same conclusion. Oras objects, pointing out that 'if we divide not only *L'All.* but also *Il P.* into two parts (11–100 and 101–174 [*sic*; 176]), we notice a remarkable parallelism between the two pieces, for *Il P.*, like *L'All.*, has considerably more trochaic lines before line 100 (20 = 22·2%) than after this point (10 = 13·2%), and all its double rhymes occur in lines 11–100 (ten, i.e., more than in the corresponding part of *L'All.*). The contrast within the latter is sharper, but in both poems the movement is from metrical variety and relative irregularity towards statelier and more regular, almost epic measures, in close correspondence with changes of tone, mood and style.'[35] The disunity which Sprott claims to feel between the earlier and the later part of *L'All* is, in Oras' judgment, 'suggested by an excessively statistical approach disregarding problems of "Gestalt"' (333).

---

[35] Ants Oras, 'Metre and Chronology in Milton's "Epitaph on the Marchioness of Winchester," "L'Allegro" and "Il Penseroso,"' *N&Q* 198 (1953), 332–3.

To Oras, 'both *L'All.* and *Il P.* show clear indications of a careful metrical unity (not uniformity!) of structure of a kind scarcely observable in the "Epitaph," which looks rather like an experiment in an as yet incompletely mastered form' (loc. cit.). Saintsbury too dismisses *EpWin* as 'a less perfect study' for the meter of the admirable twin poems (2, 211). Speaking more strongly, Albert Cook scores *EpWin* for 'inept prosiness,' for 'a rhythm uncertain to the point of brokenness, without even the spontaneity of doggerel.'[36] Soon, Cook feels, 'Milton was to achieve a kind of abstract musical balance in the tetrameters of *L'Allegro* and *Il Penseroso*, whose indeterminate mingling of light and dark as a sort of abstract antinomic image...is matched by a syllabic indeterminacy between iamb and trochee, and by the nearly Spenserian tuning-up rhythms of each poem's opening lines' (379). Michael F. Moloney, however, comes to the defense of *EpWin*. Accepting suggestions of R. D. Havens and E. M. W. Tillyard that the verse of the earlier poem ought to be distinguished from that of *L'All* and *IlPen* because it derives from a different tradition, the 'funerary art' of Jonson and Browne, Moloney analyzes the qualities which give 'stateliness' to Jonson's verse, and finds the same qualities in *EpWin*.[37] Lines 47–59 of that poem he thinks 'not unworthy to be set beside Jonson's best' (176); with them he compares *L'All* 69–80, and says, 'Whereas the thirteen lines from the *Epitaph* are shackled by the weighted caesura and a diction that admits an average of only one polysyllable [i.e., word of more than one syllable] per line, the twelve lines from *L'Allegro* contain twenty polysyllables. Moreover, the caesura virtually disappears, the rhymes are all on front vowels and there is a deliberate marshalling of liquid and sibilant consonants to accelerate movement' (177). Moloney admits that at times, in *EpWin*, 'Milton mingled octosyllables and heptasyllables with uncertain results' (176). Nonetheless his defense of the formal virtues of that poem is specific and detailed, and in it he stands, it would appear, almost alone.

[36] Albert Cook, 'Milton's Abstract Music,' *UTQ* 29 (1959–60), 370–85, **378, 379.**
[37] Michael F. Moloney, 'The Prosody of Milton's *Epitaph, L'Allegro* and *Il Penseroso*,' *MLN* 72 (1957), 174–8, **174–6.**

Comments in general appreciation of the versification of *L'All* and *IlPen* are to be found in the work of many writers, including most of those already mentioned as discussing the poems. Of *L'All* 139–40,

> In notes, with many a winding bout
> Of lincked sweetness long drawn out,

Hazlitt says, 'Milton has himself given us the theory of his versification.'[38] D. R. Roberts, quoting the same couplet and the four lines following, says rather, 'No better epitome could be conceived of the character of the madrigal—its delicacy, subtlety, artifice, and gentle movement.'[39] Roberts is particularly interested in the relationship between the rhythms of music and the rhythms of Milton's verse, early and late. More specifically concerned with allusions to music in *L'All* and *IlPen*, Nan Cooke Carpenter, having discussed these, differentiates between the rhythms of the two poems: '*L'Allegro*...does indeed live up to its musical name. After the initial verses on Melancholy, purposely lumbering and awkward, the busy lines of the poem sweep along with a brisk rocking motion.... The tone of *Il Penseroso* is much soberer and the prevailing rhythm of the piece far different, not only in the smoother verse lines but in a different pattern of content.'[40] To Saintsbury it seems that 'the graver effect in *Il Penseroso* is attained by the use of feet which are practically spondees....[Milton]...scarcely ever...clogs the trochaically cadenced lines with these feet, but keeps them for double-shotting the pure iambics' (2, 214–15).

It may have been noticed that both Cook and Miss Carpenter, in the paragraphs above, make serious, if not sustained, comments on the opening ten-line sections of *L'All* and *IlPen*. In his edition of *Comus and Other Poems*, Prince says, 'The slower rhythm and somewhat exaggerated rhetoric of these introductions contrast with what follows; they are like solemn chords arresting the attention at the beginning of a musical

[38] William Hazlitt, 'On Milton's Versification,' *The Round Table* (London, 1817), 102–10, **110**.
[39] Donald Ramsay Roberts, 'The Music of Milton,' *PQ* 26 (1947), 328–44, **337**.
[40] Nan Cooke Carpenter, 'The Place of Music in *L'Allegro* and *Il Penseroso*,' *UTQ* 22 (1952–3), 354–67, **365**.

composition' (119). The effect of such comments is hardly consonant with Tillyard's characterization of the introductions as deliberate bombast, burlesque in intent.[41] Critics of the verse of the twin poems do not, it appears, hear in the elaborately orchestrated introductions what Tillyard hears in them: are the music and the meaning of the verse at odds, or is Tillyard's interpretation of the introductions being silently revised? This reader has never been comfortable with it, for reasons having to do, as much as anything, with verse technique. Formally, the introductions are masterpieces; and they are not overdone. That they are highly *artificial*, and that this is a part of their tone, is of course true.

The tetrameter verse in *Comus*, surely no less admired than the verse of the twin poems, is seldom analyzed independently. Diekhoff, however, in 'Prosody in the MS.,' 174–7, gives a detailed formal analysis of *Comus* 93–144, and Thompson (267) analyzes *Comus* 975–1022 more briefly. Sprott (17) gives us statistics on the number of heptasyllables among the tetrameters of *Comus*, and on the number of octosyllables in the poem that begin with trochees, but his figures seem wildly divergent from those of Oras (332); of the two, Oras' figures seem the more nearly correct. Oras counts 189 tetrameters in *Comus*, excluding the songs, and says that of these 111, or 58·7%, are headless; of 78 octosyllables he finds that 18, or 21·8%, begin with trochees. The proportion of heptasyllables is, without question, particularly high. 'It is conceivable that the poet may here have emphasized the falling rhythms in deliberate contrast to the rising rhythms of the blank verse' (333).

English tetrameters, including the meter of mixed 8's and 7's, go back to Chaucer and beyond. Historical discussions of the meter and surveys of the verse written in it (including verse supposed to have influenced Milton) will be found in the work of Mrs Hamer, Saintsbury, Schipper, and Thompson. Mrs Hamer is particularly interesting on the subject of the heptasyllable in which 'a weak or light monosyllable take[s] the place of the first foot' (30); *L'All* 13, quoted toward the beginning of this account, is such a line.

[41] E. M. W. Tillyard, *The Miltonic Setting* (London: Chatto and Windus, 1961), **8**. First published, 1938.

(*d*) *Vac; Shak; Carrier* 1 and 2; *Arc; May*

Of the form of Milton's verse in pentameter couplets there is little criticism sufficiently full or detailed to be useful. Sprott (15–16) notes the general paucity in the verse of feminine endings, inversions other than initial, enjambed lines, etc.; pauses occur generally, he says, around mid-line. In short, the verse is handled conventionally, though 'with competence.' In Sprott's chapter 4, 'The Vexation of Rhyming' (28–37), the pentameter couplets divide attention with Milton's other rhymed verse; the investigation of Milton's rhyming practice is conscientious, but in many ways insensitive. Thus Sprott suggests that wide separation of rhymes, as in the opening sections of *L'All* and *IlPen*, may be 'an attempt to bind together the paragraph,' but 'manifestly makes for ease of composition' (31). One can only marvel at the sheer courage it must have taken for Milton to turn so promptly to the writing of the tetrameter couplets. Sprott takes over-seriously the phrase that provides his chapter title. That 'rhyme is the natural enemy of enjambment' (32) is, however, in one sense at least, true; and Sprott's estimate that the percentage of run-on lines in all of Milton's rhymed pentameters is only half that in *PL* is of interest.

Masson too discusses rhyme in Milton, especially imperfect rhyme (1, cxxx-cxxxii); he finds that even after we have made allowance for later changes in pronunciation, 'the proof is positive that Milton made free and large use of imperfect rhymes' (1, cxxxii). He calculates that of the approximately 2,700 rhymed lines in Milton, 'every eighth or tenth rhyme is more or less imperfect. Nor is it only in his least elaborate poems and passages that such rhymes occur. They occur in passages the most finished and dainty, the most lyrical and musical.' He instances the Echo Song in *Comus*.

To return to the couplet verse, Brooks and Hardy note that 'the sudden opening of the couplets in lines 9–12' of *Shak* 'is beautifully adapted to the idea of the "flow" of Shakespeare's "easie numbers"' (127). They print a fairly detailed discussion of the verse of *May* (124). Saintsbury commends briefly the verse of *Vac*, *Shak* and *May*, but characterizes the mirth of 'the Hobson pieces' as 'rather dismal, prosodically and otherwise' (2, 209). Tillyard defends the verse of *Carrier* 1, essentially on grounds of decorum: 'It is a humorous but kindly epitaph on a homely person; and for it Milton uses the language, word-order, and broken rhythm of common speech, because he thought that style to be appropriate....Here indeed Milton is "keeping English up", writing in a pure northern language and indulging in not a single Latin inversion or drawn-out sentence' (*M. Set.*, 121).

The couplet verse of *Arc*, Saintsbury says, 'makes one sorry that we have not more couplet from him' (2, 212). Sprott too admires *Arc*, concluding that it 'exhibits a new and lovely smoothness of flow and "breadth," a foretaste of Miltonic paragraphing' (16). Discussing characteristic or interesting revisions in the MS., Diekhoff points out one or two revisions in *Arc* designed to improve the musical effectiveness of the verse.[42] For Prince, 'Jonson is the presiding influence' in *Arc* (*Italian Element*, 66); 'the songs show Milton outdoing Ben Jonson and other Elizabethans in writing verse of concentrated beauty for musical settings' (*Comus*, 130). Saintsbury finds the songs 'quite Peelian-Shakespearian' (2, 212). Oras analyzes the first song in *Arc* as showing, like certain of Tasso's madrigals, 'gradation' of stanza pattern, though he finds the song 'hardly Italian in other respects'; Milton's handling of rhyme in it looks forward, he feels, to the management of rhyme in *Lyc*.[43]

(e) Comus

Because it is the longest, most varied and most sustained of the early poems, because it is in a puzzling version of an otherwise moderately familiar form, and because its blank verse offers clear and valuable opportunities for comparison with the much later and stylistically very different blank verse of *PL* and *PR*, as well as with the decasyllabic unrhymed verse of *SA*, *Comus* has received a great deal of attention from prosodists. Their studies cannot be treated here in full detail, but an

---

[42] John S. Diekhoff, 'Critical Activity of the Poetic Mind: John Milton,' *PMLA* 55 (1940), 748–72, **757, 765**.
[43] Ants Oras, 'Milton's Early Rhyme Schemes and the Structure of *Lycidas*,' *MP* 52 (1954–5), 12–22, **14**.

attempt will be made to indicate the general nature of what has been done, and to comment on a few particulars of special interest.

No fewer than five important articles by John S. Diekhoff are concerned entirely or in large part with the verse of *Comus*, particularly as it is illuminated by a study of the Trinity MS. The first of these articles points out that there is in the MS. of *Comus* 'almost literally no punctuation at the end of lines—not even at the ends of sentences and speeches'; from this Diekhoff argues that Milton considered the line end itself— even where there is enjambment—sufficient to mark a pause, and proceeds to the conclusion that 'Milton considered the line the fundamental unit of his verse,' 'a more or less isolated unit...to be indicated as such by some sort of breath pause or lingering at the end.'[44] Diekhoff's second article concerns the punctuation of the poem generally; he points out that internal punctuation in the MS., like terminal punctuation, is relatively light, and after study of many passages, concludes that the use of punctuation in the poem is principally 'elocutionary' or 'rhythmic'[45]—designed, that is, to help the reader or speaker achieve the verse movement desired. Sprott (117–20) differs. Diekhoff accepts, of course, that some of the pointing has a simple grammatical function. Here and there in *Comus* he finds in addition marks of punctuation which he takes to have a prosodic function only: thus the midline commas in lines 399, 411 and 673 are there, he thinks, 'to mark the caesura' (767).

Diekhoff's third article argues that the version of *Comus* we have in the MS. is a transcription, which in a few places Milton reworked as he transcribed.[46] In some of the details of revision noted there are, of course, implications for prosody, or at least for versification. In his fifth article —to pass over his fourth for a moment—Diekhoff takes up at even greater length the nature of the revisions in *Comus* in the MS., and discusses with some particularity the improvements in sound and rhythm that result from a number of them ('Critical Activity,' 753–6, 762, 765–71). An earlier article by Laura Lockwood discusses, more briefly, the same

[44] John S. Diekhoff, 'Terminal Pause in Milton's Verse,' *SP* 32 (1935), 235–9, **238, 235**.

[45] John S. Diekhoff, 'The Punctuation of *Comus*,' *PMLA* 51 (1936), 757–68, **761–2, 764**.

[46] John S. Diekhoff, 'The Text of *Comus*, 1634 to 1645,' *PMLA* 52 (1937), 705–27.

general materials;[47] both articles are worth reading, since the conclusions reached depend so largely upon the precise materials noticed. Diekhoff ends with interesting speculations about Milton's working habits ('Critical Activity,' 771–2).

It has been mentioned that 'Milton's Prosody in the Poems of the Trinity Manuscript,' the fourth and longest of Diekhoff's articles in this series, extends the principles of Bridges' *Milton's Prosody* to a number of the important early poems which Bridges did not examine in detail. Diekhoff accepts Bridges' conclusion that Milton's 'elisions' (except for 'vowel-elisions of common speech') are 'optional,' that 'Milton came to scan his verses in one way, and to read them in another'; in his treatment of metrical compression in *Comus* (154–60), then, he must again and again repeat that it is scansion he is talking about, not the actual rhythms of the poem. This apart, his work is excellent; it is thorough, and on the whole consistent and accurate, though he does not always recognize the persistence, in Milton's early poems, of character-istic contractions of Elizabethan verse (and probably of speech) not all of which fit Bridges' 'categories.' After amassing, presenting and discussing the greater part of his evidence, Diekhoff concludes that '*Comus* is just as truly decasyllabic as *Paradise Lost*.' However, 'the verse of *Comus* is much less varied than that of the later poems and gives a greater im-pression of regularity—in part because there are many fewer elisions involving sounds in different words.... In *Comus* almost all the elisions take place within words and hence are much nearer to the contractions of ordinary speech' (158).

Diekhoff does not accept Bridges' theory of 'failure of stress' (Bridges, 37–40, concludes in effect that one may find accentual pyrrhics in Mil-ton's verse, but not accentual spondees, in the existence of which he does not believe—also on theoretical grounds); thus Diekhoff (166) scans *Comus* 90

neerest & likliest tó the praesent aíde.

He would merely characterize the stress on 'to' as not being a 'full stress,' and he cites the MS. corrections in, e.g., lines 464, 711 and 850

---

[47] Laura E. Lockwood, 'Milton's Corrections to the *Minor Poems*,' *MLN* 25 (1910), 201–5.

(Fletcher, *Facs.*, 1, 413, 421 and 425) as showing that Milton tried to eliminate 'weak stresses' when he could. Diekhoff's observations on the prosodic consequences of other MS. revisions (162–3) are of equal interest, as is his treatment of the final extrametrical syllable or feminine ending (161, 164) and the extrametrical syllable at the caesura (161).

Since the midverse extrametrical syllable occurs only in *Comus*, of all Milton's poems, it is a prosodic phenomenon of some uncertainty and importance, much discussed, and we must pause on it here. Guest (218) mentions what he calls the 'supernumerary syllable between the sections' as occurring in *Macb.* 2. 2. 53 and 66, and in *Comus* 604,

> *Harpyes* and *Hydra*'s, or all the monstrous forms;

Diekhoff ('Prosody in the MS.,' 162) points out that 'all' in this line was inserted in MS., as a deliberate addition to the finished decasyllable as first written. Masson, who believed, it will be recalled, in the existence of trisyllabic feet in Milton's verse, had of course another explanation for the structure of lines which would later be explained as showing the midverse extrametrical syllable; in 1, cxx–cxxi he quotes seventy lines from Milton, the first eight from *Comus* (66, 90, 281, 445, 601, 778, 808 and 841), and says, 'All these lines might be rectified into Decasyllabics by supposing elisions, slurs, or contracted utterances; and there are some who seem to favour such a practice. There could be no more absurd error. Will anyone venture to say that the word "*Phoebus*" in No. 1 is to be pronounced "*Phoebs*," the words "feeder" and "river" in Nos. 6 and 8 "feed'" and "riv'" ...?'

Masson does not presume to guess what horrifying treatment his opponents would accord to *Comus* 808, which also shows the midverse extrametrical syllable, but we may guess how he would have scanned the line from the alternative scansions offered (86) by a later believer in the trisyllabic foot, Enid Hamer:

> I must | not suf|fer this, | yet 'tis but | the lees

or

> I must | not suffer | this, yet | 'tis but | the lees.

Saintsbury too, as would be expected, reads trisyllabic feet in such lines; in 66, 778, and 661—a line not mentioned by Masson—he reads a final anapest, and in 601 (as well as in 598 and 604, the line noted by Guest) 'invite[s] attention to the presence of the trisyllable at a caesura' (2, 231). Why he does not read a final anapest in 601, which he gives as

> But for that damned Magi|cian, let him | be girt,

must remain a mystery, but, as with Mrs Hamer's scansion above, that there should seem the alternative may cast doubt on the intelligibility, the *necessity*, of either explanation of the line's structure.

As early as the 1901 edition of *Milton's Prosody*, Robert Bridges listed *Comus* 66, 301, 598, 601, 661 and 778 as displaying the midverse extra-metrical syllable. In 1907, in the second of three articles chiefly concerned with *PL* and *PR*,[48] Walter Thomas notes that in those two poems Milton 'discards many so-called licences familiar to his predecessors. Perhaps the best-known of these is the extra syllable before the caesura allowed in early French heroics, though not counted in the measure' (*MLR* 3, 18). He cites *Comus* 614 and 661. In the first of the articles Thomas illustrates (in the French decasyllable, which, he says, underlies the Italian hendecasyllable) 'what [Friedrich Christian] Diez aptly termed the epic caesura' (*MLR* 2, 290). Bridges, in the 1921 edition of *Milton's Prosody*, gives an expanded historical account of the midverse extra-metrical syllable (6–8), with examples of its use in French twelve-syllable and ten-syllable verse and in Shakespeare (*Antony* and *Temp.*). Verity adds as examples in *Comus*, correctly, 841, plausibly, 406, and doubtfully, 414 and 616 (xlii–xliii); the last of these is perhaps better explained by Masson (1, cxxvi) and Diekhoff ('Prosody in the MS.,' 161) as an Alexandrine, 414 becomes a decasyllable if we read the familiar metrical compression 'she has,' and in reading also (though of course not in an acted version, in which the two halves of the line would be delivered by different speakers), 406 becomes a normal hendecasyllable if we read

[48] Walter Thomas, 'Milton's Heroic Line Viewed from an Historical Standpoint,' *MLR* 2 (1906–7), 289–315; *MLR* 3 (1907–8), 16–39, 232–56.

'sister. I' as of two syllables. See also 485, and compare George Gascoigne, *The Steele Glas* 59 (Cunliffe, 2, 144),

> My sistr' and I into this world were sent.

The list thus far compiled includes *Comus* 66, 301, (406), 598, 601, 604, 614, 661, (778), and 841. Line 778, first cited by Bridges as displaying the extrametrical syllable at the caesura, is parenthesized because by his own rules (though apparently he overlooked the fact) the line *could* be regularized as a decasyllable by the reading—or counting—of 'go on' as a single syllable. Diekhoff (loc. cit.) reviews this list, pointing out that 661 (and 414) come from Alexandrines in the MS., and adds (485), [742], 801 and 808. The latter two are unquestionable; 485 is comparable to 406, discussed above. Line 742 Diekhoff himself calls the 'most troublesome in the list' ('Prosody in the MS.,' 162), and it is perhaps the most puzzling line, metrically, in *Comus*:

> If you let slip time, like a neglected rose.

As Diekhoff notes, in the MS. the article, there for some reason 'an,' is circled, and a large, uneven *X* stands against the line in the left-hand margin (Fletcher, *Facs.*, 1, 423); this is profoundly interesting, but it actually tells us no more than we already know—that there is something odd about the line. If it is considered as having a midverse extrametrical syllable, that syllable is—perfectly exceptionally—stressed; Diekhoff therefore compares the line with *Comus* 632,

> Bore a bright golden flowre, but not in thís (sóyl,

in which a *final* extrametrical syllable appears to be at least somewhat stressed, even though emphasis may require greater stress in the syllable preceding (loc. cit.). In 742, however, no such explanation is possible, and the line remains unexplained.

Sprott too (61–2) lists 742 with lines containing an extrametrical syllable at the caesura, and adds to the list 582. The final version of the list of lines in *Comus certainly* explained as containing a midverse extrametrical syllable reads, then, 66, 301, 582, 598, 601, 604, 614, 661, 801, 808 and 841, with 406, 485, 742 and 778 possible or probable. Jacques

Blondel points out that in 808 the extrametrical syllable occurs *after* the caesura;[49] less plausibly, he says the same of 801, and implausibly, of 778. Sprott, like Diekhoff, accepts *Comus* 616 as a hexameter (62); he points out as even more exceptional *Comus* 596,

> Self-fed, and self-consum'd, if this fail.

It is, says Sprott, the only line in 'some fifteen thousand' in Milton's verse 'with a certain monosyllabic foot' (48). Furthermore, it reads identically in the MS., in 1645 and in 1673, and so is no accident—if 'self-consum'd' were 'self-consumèd' the line would return to the decasyllabic norm—but must be reckoned as 'an exception, the only one, to Milton's otherwise completely consistent practice.'

Sprott's chapter 5, 'The Iambic Pentameter and Its Scansion,' is devoted in part to theory, in larger part to the late poems; during the course of it, however, Sprott gives us much incidental intelligence about metrical compressions in *Comus* (75–97); about inversions (101); about pause (126–7). James Whaler remarks that only about a third of the lines in *Comus* are enjambed.[50] In another study devoted principally to the later poems[51] Robert O. Evans tells us that 'Milton had not fully developed his system of elision when he wrote *Comus*. Quantitatively he used only 182 elisions per 1000 [decasyllabic] lines' (46): the figure contrasts with 351 per 1000 in *PL* 1–6, 279 per 1000 in *PL* 7–12, 288 per 1000 in *PR*, and 245 per 1000 in *SA* (47). And 'qualitatively,' Evans says, Milton was 'freer' in *Comus*, 'sticking less rigidly to the categories he later adopted, than elsewhere' (46). Evans gives us a further breakdown of statistics in tabular form (66).

Bridges (19–20) discusses Milton's use in *Comus* of such 'old-fashioned and out of date' extended forms as 'Consci-ence,' 211, 'visi-on,' 297, 'contemplati-on,' 376, 'legi-ons,' 602, 'conditi-on,' 684, and 'com-

49 Jacques Blondel, *Le 'Comus' de John Milton* (Paris: Presses Universitaires de France, 1964), **82**.
50 James Whaler, *Counterpoint and Symbol*, *Anglistica* 6 (Copenhagen: Rosenkilde and Bagger, 1956), **50**.
51 Robert O. Evans, *Milton's Elisions*, University of Florida Monographs, Humanities—No. 21 (Gainesville: University of Florida Press, 1966).

plexi-ons,' 748; he points out further that 'there is no example of the old pronunciations of such words' in *PL*. Dealing with the same materials in commenting on pyrrhic endings in *Comus*, *PL*, *PR* and *SA*, Oras says, 'In *Comus*, the words appearing in such endings, the general tone of the passages in question, and the archaic pronunciations employed to obtain the extra syllable needed for them (apparitión [640], self-delusión [364]) suggest a harking back to Elizabethan times when this device was often used to achieve lyrical mellifluousness or sonorous oratorical effects' (*Blank Verse and Chronology*, 37).

Other devices of style and versification that 'hark back,' or are, at any rate, according to Oras, characteristic rather of Milton's early than of his late writing of verse, are the relatively frequent use in *Comus* of forms ending in syllabized -*ed* (Oras counts 66 such forms in the minor poems, 17 of them in *Comus*, as against 47 in *PL* 1–6 and 15 in *PL* 7–12, *PR* and *SA* together) (14–15), and (2) phrases showing recession of accent ('sérene Air,' 4, 'énthron'd gods,' 11, plus others in 37, 217, 274, 421, 430, 434, 449, 464, 469, 590, 732 and 785) (20); Oras finds (20–1) that Milton preferred in his later poems to reverse the position of adjective and noun (as in 'Front seréne,' *PL* 7. 509, 'look seréne,' *PL* 10. 1094), thus achieving at once normal accent and—Prince would say—a heightening of style derived from interference with normal word order. Bridges (67–75) also discusses recession of accent, in Shakespeare, in *Comus*, and in Milton's later poems; he notes that certain dissyllabic prepositions accented on the second syllable, as well as certain adjectives so accented, are subject to stress shift when followed by an accented monosyllable or by a longer word accented on the first syllable, and cites (74) 'Here be without duck or nod,' *Comus* 959. Oras compares the placement of words of more than one syllable in the line in *Comus* and in the later poems; in *Comus* such words 'strongly tend towards the end of the line' (34), whereas in, e.g., *PL*, they tend to concentrate rather in the first half of the line. Finally, Oras presents elaborately marshaled arguments (24–31) and pages of charts (45–52) and tables (59–69) on the use of what he calls 'metrical pauses' in *Comus*, *PL*, *PR* and *SA*. These materials are hard to make simple sense of; but Oras contends that they support his belief in the traditionally accepted chronological ordering of the major poems.[52]

Saintsbury too is interested in pause in *Comus*; he says that Milton 'makes great use' in the poem 'of the full stop in middle line. But his use of the pause has not yet thoroughly perfected itself; and what is more remarkable, he has not yet made any fast grip of the instrument which afterwards he was to employ with such astonishing effect—the development of the verse-paragraph. He has fine periods, but his working up of them into paragraphs is very uncertain: it might almost seem as if he did not attempt it much' (2, 234). Evidently long speeches—those speeches which Samuel Johnson found 'too long,'[53] and which Saintsbury calls (without, he insists, pejorative intent) 'tirades' (2, 233 and n.)—are not, *ipso facto*, verse paragraphs.

Prince appears to disagree on the absence from *Comus* of verse paragraphs, but the final effect of his analysis is much the same as that of Saintsbury's. 'Milton's feeling for the English language, the peculiar weight of his verse, these are of course fully present' in *Comus*, Prince says (*Italian Element*, 67). 'We find his skill in constructing elaborate and extended verse-paragraphs, and his delight in an overwhelming fullness of expression.' All the same, 'the diction and the versification of the blank verse of *Comus* are not in fact identical with those of the great epics.' The verse of *Comus* 'is sung to a different tune, as it were; it has

---

[52] See Ants Oras, 'Milton's Blank Verse and the Chronology of His Major Poems,' *SAMLA Studies in Milton*, ed. J. Max Patrick (Gainesville: University of Florida Press, 1953), 128–97. The conclusions embodied in this essay were challenged by John T. Shawcross in his article 'The Chronology of Milton's Major Poems,' *PMLA* 76 (1961), 345–58; and Oras' *Blank Verse and Chronology in Milton*, a revised version of his original essay in *SAMLA Studies in Milton*, is expanded in order to reply to Shawcross. Oras' treatment of the minor poems, which alone concerns us at the moment, is substantially the same in both versions of his article, though materials in the second version are slightly fuller. Shawcross tends generally to deny that Oras makes valid use of his materials; otherwise, the controversy between the two scholars has relatively little to do with the early poems, and need not be further considered here.

[53] James Thorpe reprints the last third of Samuel Johnson's essay on Milton from the 1779 *Lives of the English Poets* in his *Milton Criticism* (New York: Rinehart, 1950), 65–88; the essay contains remarks on the verse of *Lyc* (66–7), *L'All* and *IlPen* (67–9), *Comus* (69–71), the Sonnets (71), *PL* (71–84), *PR* (84–5), and *SA* (85). The judgment quoted above is to be found on **70**.

a different movement and pitch; it has behind it a different pattern. *Paradise Lost* has the movement and tone of Virgil....*Comus* observes the tone and movement of Shakespeare's blank verse, adapting also inflexions from lesser dramatists' (68–9).

We may go to John Addington Symonds for a discriminating commentary on the verse of *Comus* as it relates to English verse of the period immediately preceding. 'Comus, as might have been expected from the time of its composition and its form, is the one of Milton's masterpieces in which he has adhered most closely to the traditions of the Elizabethan drama. His style, it is true, is already more complex and peculiarly harmonious, more characteristically Miltonic, than that of any of the dramatists. Yet there are passages in Comus which may remind us forcibly of Fletcher. Others, like...[lines 248–51] might have been written by Shakspere. Alliteration is used freely, but more after the manner of Fletcher or of Spenser, not with the sustained elaboration of Milton's maturity. The truly Miltonic licences are rare: we find fewer inverted sentences, less lengthy systems of concatenated periods,—in a word, a more fluent and simpler versification. Both in the imagery and the melody of Comus there is a youthful freshness, an almost wanton display of vernal bloom and beauty.'[54]

Ker finds 'the rhythms of Fletcher both in the blank verse and in the lyrical parts of *Comus*' (142). To Saintsbury, 'Peele and Shakespeare, Marlowe and Euripides' appear, 'however "confusedly",' to be before Milton's eyes 'as the inspirers of his *mimesis*'; prosodically, 'it is clear that the writer has immediately before him such things of Shakespeare's as *A Midsummer Night's Dream* and *The Tempest*, but that he is also paying special attention to the University Wits, and has not exactly cleared his prosodic mind of the mixed impressions derived from these studies' (2, 225). Later, Saintsbury finds 'the overture of the Spirit... naturally enough...somewhat Senecan and declamatory' (2, 228); Tillyard finds it Euripidean (*Milton*, 68). For Saintsbury, Euripides

[54] John Addington Symonds, 'The Blank Verse of Milton,' *Fortnightly Review* 22 (1874), 767–81, **780**. The article is reprinted as a part of Symonds' expanded study *Blank Verse* (New York, 1895).

perhaps disappears into the pomp of lines 264-9 and the brief *stichomythia* of 276-89. Lines 330-6 'are quite early Shakespeare, if not even Marlowe —*Titus Andronicus,* if not *Tamburlaine...*' (2, 229). In comparing Milton with Shakespeare Saintsbury intends neither compliment nor derogation to Milton: 'That marvellous, billowy flow of verse on which Shakespeare floats us, with an occasional break or ripple, but mostly "too full for noise or foam," is not what Milton aims at. His verses do not float: they march, and march magnificently, quickening and slacken-ing, altering formation slightly, but always with more touch of *mechanism* in them than we find in Shakespeare...' (2, 234).

F. R. Leavis speaks of 'the Shakespearian life' of *Comus* 714-15,

> And set to work millions of spinning Worms,
> That in their green shops weave the smooth-hair'd silk,

and pays tribute, indeed, to the whole passage from which the lines come—he quotes and in part analyzes 709-35—in order to make it clear that he finds little else in *Comus,* or in all the rest of Milton, to admire.[55] Robert Graves' ability to resist the charms of Milton's verse is equally well known: 'Milton fell from grace because he allowed his rhetorical skill...to dull his poetic sense. While reading his "minor poems" one becomes aware of poetry still struggling against the serpent coils. It is the unhappy flutterings of its wings in *Comus* and the Nativity Ode—I am thinking particularly of *Sabrina Fair* and "the yellow-skirted fays"— that give these poems their poignant and, on the whole, distasteful character.'[56] We may recall the equally positive dictum of Dr Johnson's: 'The songs are vigorous, and full of imagery; but they are harsh in their diction, and not very musical in their numbers' (Thorpe, 71).

It is a curious experience to turn from these comments to an anony-mous review of Coleridge published in 1834: 'Spenser's Hymns, and Shakespeare's "Venus and Adonis," and "Rape of Lucrece," are striking instances of the overbalance of mere sweetness of sound. Even "Comus" is what we should, in this sense, call luxurious; and all four

[55] F. R. Leavis, *Revaluation* (London: Chatto & Windus, 1959), **48, 47-9**. First published, 1936.
[56] Robert Graves, *The Crowning Privilege* (New York: Doubleday, 1956), **108**.

gratify the outward ear much more than that inner and severer sense
which is associated with the reason, and requires a meaning even in the
very music for its full satisfaction. Compare the versification of the
youthful pieces mentioned above with that of the maturer works of those
great poets, and you will recognize how possible it is for verses to be
exquisitely melodious, and yet to fall far short of that exalted excellence
of numbers of which language is in itself capable.'[57] Every critic, apparently, has his own *Comus*. Or perhaps the difficulty lies in generalization, about a poem in fact so various. Tillyard finds that 'not a little
of *Comus* is deliberately and successfully dramatic' (*Milton*, 66); Saintsbury says that 'there is not much in *Comus*, outside the lyrics, which calls
for a stamp of verse not equally available for pure narrative, and for the
actual speeches with which narrative is usually diversified...' (2, 234).
Both critics at least find various styles in the poem—what Tillyard calls
a 'mixture of styles' (*Milton*, 67)—and since both admire a considerable
part of what they find, and appear to discriminate with accuracy and
genuine interest, their responses seem preferable to generalized approval
or disapproval, on whatever grounds.

At least two critics perceive patterns in the stylistic and musical variety
of the poem. Jacques Blondel writes very interestingly of the contrasting
uses of the decasyllabic and octosyllabic verse, and in particular of the
way in which Comus is 'dispossessed,' as it were, of the latter: 'L'or-
donnance du poème fait apparaître une symétrie concertée. Le pentamètre
expose le thème, se prête à l'affirmation morale, à l'expression de
l'incertitude dans ce cadre pastoral. Le vers plus court dispose les deux
forces en présence: Comus intervient au vers 93 sur le rythme de l'*Allegro*,
une fois que la Providence a parlé et, une fois le conflit exposé entre la
Dame et lui sur le mode plus digne du pentamètre, la libération est
chantée sur le même rythme qui avait accompagné les paroles du magicien.
Ainsi l'ordre est rétabli sur le rythme même qui l'avait menacé' (81).
For the establishment of final order, more important still, obviously, is
the Attendant Spirit's use of octosyllabics in the closing lines of the
masque: 'La montée vers le monde où s'entend la musique des sphères

---

[57] Review of *The Poetical Works of S. T. Coleridge, Quarterly Review* 52 (1834), 1–38, 7.

d'où descend l'Esprit protecteur...[est] chantée sur le rythme même dont d'abord avait usé l'usurpateur magicien' (84). Blondel concludes, 'Tour à tour grave et léger, le vers de Milton tend déjà vers le sublime.'

Philip Brockbank finds in *Comus* three distinguishable strains: the 'sensual music' of Comus himself, which 'is made out of dance and turns back into dance,' the 'moral music' which is 'most fully orchestrated' in the speeches of the Elder Brother, and what Brockbank calls 'the Hesperian music' of the poem's opening and close and of, e.g., the Lady's song: 'This is the "Divine inchanting ravishment", a Miltonic song quite distinct from the sensual music and the moral music, and yet related to both: a transfigured and sublimated sensuality.'[58] Perhaps 'the Hesperian music' and 'the moral music' ('Milton spent a good part of his life looking for ways of making "divine philosophy" as "musical as is Apollo's lute,"' 57) are not quite '*rival* verbal musics' (60; italics mine). And one could wish for specific analyses, however brief, of the three kinds of verse. The analyses of others will not serve Brockbank's turn: Albert Cook, for example, gives us (379) a sensitive and somewhat detailed analysis of a six-line passage from the 'moral music,' *Comus* 440-5, but Cook has his own interesting purposes, and they are not (exactly) Brockbank's. Nor are Leavis's when he admires Comus' great seduction speech, or says of the Lady's song, 'The exquisite achievement has been sufficiently praised' (57). But Brockbank's discussion is nonetheless stimulating, and his analysis, and that of Blondel, are valuable antidotes to the chaotic impressions left by some criticisms of the verse of *Comus*, and the over-generalized and over-consistent sense imparted by others.

Of the overall form of *Comus* little need be said here. Prince divides the masque into five sections: lines 1-92; 93-329; 330-657; 658-956; and 957-1022 (*Comus*, 133). Once again, Maren-Sophie Røstvig sees a numerological 'hidden' form in at least the 'key speeches' of *Comus*; the symbolisms involved she discusses at some length (59-69). Douglas Bush remarks 'how infinitely adaptable numbers are' (5).

[58] Philip Brockbank, 'The Measure of "Comus",' *Essays and Studies*, n.s. 21 (1968), 46-61, **55-8**.

Fuller notice must be given to Gretchen Finney's attempt to demonstrate the similarity of the form of *Comus* to that of the Italian *dramma per musica*, especially to Tronsarelli's *La Catena d'Adone* (together with Marino's 'L'Adone,' the poem on which Tronsarelli's work was based).[59] Musical drama in Italy was, says Mrs Finney, 'apparently unlike *Comus*...completely sung—the narrative or explanatory passages in recitative, the lyrics, both solos and choruses, in a more melodic style. But metrically they resemble *Comus*, for they are written with variety of verse form' (486). In *Comus* 'the blank verse suggests recitative; the shorter lines are better adapted to aria.' The opening section of Comus' first speech or song, Mrs Finney says, 'suits choral style and could, intelligibly have been sung by the chorus....The introduction of a longer line such as is found beginning with line 115 would indicate, to judge by the style of the Italian works, the entrance of a solo part. The inserted songs in *Comus* are, of course, definitely lyrical and for solo voice; and Lawes' settings for them are clearly in the Italian style of the time, for they represent a departure from strict recitative...toward a semi-recitative which is more tuneful and more lyrical' (loc. cit.). John G. Demaray, however, without denying that Italian musical drama may somewhat have influenced the form of *Comus*—without even denying the existence of the specific parallels Mrs Finney believes she sees— makes it clear that *Comus* is after all solidly in the English court masque tradition.[60] Prince argues, similarly, that the relationship between *Comus* and Italian pastoral drama—Tasso's *Aminta* and Guarini's *Il Pastor Fido*—'is indirect and subordinate' (*Italian Element*, 66).

Doubtless it is true that the overall form of *Comus*, like its prosody, is in some respects traditional, even conventional, in others as odd as anything in the canon of Milton's verse; as its language is now plain, now rich, its music now sweet, now harsh. 'The blank verse of *Comus*,' Saintsbury says (2, 226), 'is obviously and multifariously experimental.' But in general, as students of that verse have come increasingly to under-

[59] Gretchen Ludke Finney, '*Comus, Dramma per Musica*,' SP 37 (1940), 482–500.
[60] John G. Demaray, *Milton and the Masque Tradition* (Cambridge, Mass.: Harvard University Press, 1968); see esp. the Appendix, '*Comus* and the Italian *Dramma per Musica*,' 145–6.

stand, the formal oddities of *Comus* look homeward, to Elizabethan and Jacobean masque and drama; whereas the most unusual formal qualities of the later verse look away from England, toward Italy.

(f) Time; Circum; SolMus

In the MS. *SolMus* appears on 4–5, in a series of four drafts, the first three much revised and finally crossed out; *Time* and *Circum*, by contrast, are merely copied in on 8, with no more correction than a last-minute decision or indecision may have made necessary. In 1645 and 1673 the three poems are grouped together, with *Time* printed first, then *Circum*, then *SolMus*. In theme, of course, *Circum* relates to *Nat* and *Passion*; critics, however, have all but invariably discussed it in relation to the poems with which it is grouped in the printed editions. And perhaps little more than the simple fact of the grouping (together with the fact that in 1645 and 1673 the poem is printed without a break between the two stanzas) is responsible for the curious notion still, apparently, held by some scholars, that *Circum* is irregular in form, as *Time* and *SolMus* undoubtedly are. There is reason, however, to discuss the three poems together, since as both Oras and Prince have pointed out, their formal antecedents are closely related.

The most useful and interesting criticism of all three poems is relatively recent. Masson calls *Time* and *SolMus* 'single bursts' of 22 and 28 lines respectively, 'of combined 3xa, 4xa, 5xa, and 6xa [i.e., 3, 4, 5 and 6 iambic feet], rhyming irregularly in pairs' (1, cix); the characterization is at once exact and uninformative. Saintsbury suggests that *Time, Circum* and *SolMus* 'are chiefly interesting to compare with the choruses of *Samson*' (2, 212), but never so compares them. Schipper makes a serious attempt to search out the antecedents of the English irregular ode; he looks back, reasonably enough in one sense, to the irregular odes of Pindar. These were, he says, 'possibly modeled on certain non-strophical poems or hymns, consisting of anisometrical verses throughout, with an entirely irregular system of rhymes. We have an example of them already in...[Donne's] poem *The Dissolution*...consisting of twenty-two [*sic*; twenty-four] rhyming verses of two to seven measures....A similar form is found in Milton's poems *On Time*...and *At a Solemn Music*...' (366).

Tillyard attempts to define the uses of innovation in form in the three grouped poems. 'Technically,' he says, 'they mark a new departure in...[Milton's] metrical paragraphing: he is deliberately aiming at and achieving a new kind of sustained music' (*Milton*, 61). Of *Time* and *SolMus* Tillyard remarks, 'Metrically they would seem to be the fruit of Milton's Italian studies and to be modelled on the canzone, but he may have got the idea of the long metrical paragraph from Spenser's *Epithalamium* [*sic*]. Even if he was indebted to Spenser for the idea, the slow concentrated stateliness of his verse is utterly different from the ample swell of his model's' (62). Tillyard points out that *Time* is 'divided into two paragraphs: lines 1–8 and 9–22....The rhythm of the first is slow, and dwindles grudgingly till the short last lines. The second paragraph, in superbly simple contrast, swells, after cunning little temporary ebbings, to the magnificent final Alexandrine' (63). Brooks and Hardy provide a similar analysis of the movement of the poem, and point out how alliteration accentuates the deliberate pace of the first three lines, how the short lines 6, 7 and 8 'slow the reader for meditation,' and how 'the periodic structure of the last five lines' works with the length of the final Alexandrine to bring the poem 'to a triumphant close' (114).

In devising the structure of *Time*, George N. Shuster suggests, 'Milton may have been following Dante's precept that lyric stanzas might be varied by the introduction of irregular lines, or he may have had before him the pattern of an Italian ode. One is inclined to think, however, that the poem was fashioned after some piece of academic verse based directly on Greek practice' (66). Oras doubts that Milton was following an Italian *pattern*, pointing out that the drafts of the comparable *SolMus* show formal experimentation. Oras suggests rather that *Time* and *SolMus* resemble *canzoni*—one-stanza *canzoni*, 'like Milton's own "Ridonsi donne"'; he points out a number of elements in the construction of the poems (their bipartite form; occasional wide separation of rhymes) which go back to the *canzone* tradition, or for which precedent can be found in it.[61]

[61] Ants Oras, 'Milton's "Upon the Circumcision" and Tasso,' *N&Q* 197 (1952), 314–15, 315.

But it is F. T. Prince who provides us with the most detailed, convincing and illuminating information on the form of *Time* and of the poems grouped with it. *Time* and *SolMus*, he says, resemble in structure the Italian madrigal (*Italian Element*, 63), 'used to reproduce the Greek epigram' (64). In origin 'the madrigal…was as it were merely one stanza of a *canzone*—a stanza which was not repeated; and it shared with the *canzone* the metrical basis of hendecasyllables and heptasyllables which had proved useful in English verse' (loc. cit.). Prince accepts that variation in line length in *Time* and *SolMus* may owe something to the precedent provided by Spenser in adapting the Italian model to English in his *Epithalamion* and *Prothalamion* (*Comus*, 116–17). Further, 'Spenser had not observed the strict Italian interweaving of rhymes [see *Italian Element*, 84], Milton disregards it altogether. He concentrates instead on running his sentences over from one line to another, and building up a sustained logical statement; this is another method of making the poem a single verse-paragraph, like a madrigal. The effect, in each poem, is of a fervent burst of feeling, rising to a solemn climax; the conclusions have an almost epigrammatic brilliance, recalling the argument to its starting-point' (*Comus*, 117).

P. L. Heyworth examines the MS. drafts of *SolMus* for the 'evidence' they afford of 'Milton's method of composition'; he is interested especially in alterations made 'in the interest of euphony,' and in the poet's struggle to achieve the final structure of the poem.[62] Shuster wonders whether *SolMus* may not be 'an experiment in classical metrics'; he attempts the quantitative scansion of line 3, then suggests as an alternative explanation of the poem's form that it is 'almost a variant of one of the less regular stanzas in *Lycidas*' (67). Brooks and Hardy look on the poem as 'another experiment in verse-paragraph construction' (119); they analyze its form briefly, and conclude that 'Milton's touch is not yet quite sure—not so sure as in "Lycidas".' Prince finds in the poem instead evidences of a 'disciplined improvisation' which has enabled Milton to develop, successfully, a 'long and elaborate sentence' (*Italian*

[62] P. L. Heyworth, 'The Composition of Milton's *At a Solemn Musick*,' *BNYPL* 70 (1966), 450–8.

Element, 65). This is doubtless much what Leavis means—however differently he feels about it—when he speaks of the verse of *SolMus* as 'a weightier kind of music' than the songs of *Comus*, 'a more impressive and less delicate instrument' (57). Prince quotes *SolMus* 17–24, and says, 'The poet who can draw upon such a syntax and rhythm as this has little need of intricate rhyme or stanzaic form....The importance of *On Time* and *At a Solemn Musick* is that they point forward to *Lycidas* and the choruses of *Samson Agonistes*, and foreshadow Milton's exploitation of syntax as a structural element both in those later lyrics and in his blank verse' (*Italian Element*, 65–6).

It will have been noted that Masson does not speak of *Circum* as a 'single burst.' Nor does Schipper derive it from the irregular Pindaric ode; he derives it, instead, from the *Epithalamion* stanza (365). Tillyard finds it, of the grouped poems, 'the least good' (though 'it reaches considerable grandeur and has hardly received due credit'); but he does not find it irregular. Quite to the contrary, 'there is,' he says, 'something very unsatisfactory in a poem consisting of two stanzas of equal length. A third stanza seems needed; or if there are to be two divisions only they should be of unequal length, as in...*At a Solemn Musick*' (*Milton*, 62).

As has been mentioned, however, there is an alternative tradition in respect to the form of *Circum*. Shuster says that 'irregularity is...dominant' in it, as in *Time* (67); Harris Francis Fletcher too feels that 'metrically,' *Circum* 'belongs with' *Time* and *SolMus*, 'all three employing an irregular rhyme scheme and varying length of line. These three poems are the only surviving experiments with this type of metrical structure, which culminated in the metrics of *Lycidas*.'[63] Brooks and Hardy take much the same position: 'The two verse paragraphs are approximately equal in length, but the pattern of variation in length of lines is not precisely the same in both. The absence of strict stanzaic form here is interesting in view of the loose verse paragraph construction of "Lycidas." One is tempted to see in "Upon the Circumcision" an early experiment in the metrical form which, in "Lycidas," was to be brought to per-

---

[63] H. F. Fletcher, ed., *The Complete Poetical Works of John Milton* (Boston: Houghton, Mifflin, 1941), **65**.

fection' (116). As recently as 1960 Carol Maddison speaks of *Circum* as a 'baroque piece in one long irregular stanza' (328). It seems unlikely that the beclouded view will here have end.

In a brief note published in 1943, W. R. Parker, reacting in particular to Fletcher, criticizes the continuing assumption that *Circum* is irregular.[64] 'The poem is divided into two fourteen-line stanzas exactly alike in both meter and rime scheme (which resembles the rime scheme of the Italian sonnet in reverse). One may be reminded of the sonnet-like final chorus of "Samson Agonistes".' Parker ends by pointing out that *Circum* is closer to *FInf, Nat, Passion,* the opening lines of *L'All* and *IlPen,* and the Italian *canzone* than to the truly irregular *Time* and *SolMus.*

Responding principally to Shuster and to Brooks and Hardy, Oras, writing on the question in 1952, also sees exact form in *Circum;* 'Apart from his Latin poems, it is. . .his most elaborate exercise in strict metrical regularity' ('Milton's *Circum,*' 315). Oras shows the near-identity of the stanza with Tasso's *canzone Alla Beatissima Vergine in Loreto,* from which it differs only (*a*) in rhyme order, (*b*) in that virtually all lines in Italian end with final unaccented syllables, and (*c*) in that Tasso prints as one line what become the two final lines of Milton's stanza. The likelihood of Milton's having known the 'Loreto' *canzone* is increased, Oras feels, by the fact that in editions of Tasso it is followed immediately by the ode *Pel Presepio di Nostro Signore nella Capella di Sisto V,* the list of heathen deities in the fifth stanza of which, he says, 'has been referred to as having perhaps influenced the "Nativity Ode".'

Prince points out (*Italian Element,* 62 n.) that the last two lines of the *Circum* stanza are written as one in the MS., and he finds (61–2) an exact model for Milton's stanza in that of Petrarch's *canzone* to the Virgin, 366 of the *Rime Sparse. Circum* is, says Prince, 'Milton's only attempt to follow an Italian model in exactly this manner: that is to say, copying a complex stanza which must be repeated throughout the poem' (63). It is true, Prince points out, that Milton does not divide his first stanza, as Petrarch divides all his in accordance with the traditional pattern devised for the poem, into a six-line *fronte* linked by rhyme to a following

---

[64] W. R. Parker, 'Milton's Meter: A Note,' *Seventeenth Century News Letter* 2 (1943), 3.

(slightly longer) *sirima* or *coda*. Prince comments, interestingly, 'Petrarch's *canzone* is 137 lines long; the fact that Milton, taking a stanza designed for a poem of this length, repeats it only once, may be a mere accident. There is nothing to indicate that his poem was intended to be longer than it is. But the brevity of the poem, and its unique fidelity to such a stanza-form, may well suggest that Milton's talent did not function easily on such a basis. The only stanza-form he continued to use was that of the sonnet, and then only in a manner which very considerably modified its stanzaic character' (loc. cit.).

Writing at very nearly the same time on 'Milton's Early Rhyme Schemes and the Structure of *Lycidas*,' Oras repeats his own claim, in a footnote picking up Prince's identification and pointing out that Milton was likely to have known both the Petrarch and the Tasso poems. Oras too finds *Circum* to be the only one of Milton's poems in which he 'exactly and conscientiously' follows an Italian model, 'if, besides his sonnets, we disregard such familiar forms as *terza rima* in his version of Psalm II and *ottava rima* in parts of *Lycidas*' (13).

(g) *Lyc*

Samuel Johnson thought it clear that Milton had overvalued the 'little pieces' of his earlier years, and set about to redress the balance, it would seem, by undervaluing them. The student of verse form in *Lyc* finds standing across his path, as he begins, Johnson's dispraise of that poem: '...*Lycidas*, of which the diction is harsh, the rhymes uncertain, and the numbers unpleasing' (Thorpe, 66). It is a reassurance, of course, to note the near-unanimity with which succeeding critics have rejected Johnson's estimate. Curiously enough, however, the student today finds two more recent statements also standing in his path, somewhat farther along, and these two are less easy to come to terms with precisely because they are not flat dicta; their meaning depends far more on context than does that of Johnson's remark, and adequate context is seldom supplied for them, or even considered by their critics. They are Saintsbury's remark that *Lyc* 'is in effect a piece of blank verse carefully equipped with rhyme' (2, 222), and John Crowe Ransom's conjecture that the poem 'was written smooth and rewritten rough.'[65] Both statements— which have called forth almost as much indignation as has Johnson's— may be used to help us characterize the verse of *Lyc* and understand, at length, the nature of its irregularities.

The *fact* of irregularity is clear enough, though not all the facts about it are clear. Faced with the fact, critics have taken one of three courses: they have condemned, or praised, or merely accepted, without really analyzing; or they have tried to find precedents for the irregularity, distant or close, vague or exact; or they have tried to demonstrate the effects of irregularity and its function in the poem. The second and third courses described are not necessarily, of course, inconsistent with one another, and some critics have attempted both.

English poems suggested as having perhaps supplied at least a part of the model for Milton's practice are Lodowick Bryskett's *The Mourning Muse of Thestylis* ('From it Milton borrowed his irregular rimes'— Guest, 265); Spenser's *Prothalamion* and, especially, *Epithalamion* (Saintsbury, 2, 219; Ransom, 68–9); two elegies of Josuah Sylvester's (Shuster, 73–4); and—as a general form—English madrigal (Donald R. Roberts, 338, and Joseph A. Wittreich, Jr.[66]). Saintsbury says further, 'That Milton had the actual choruses of Greek tragedy in his mind there can be no doubt' (loc. cit.); and it will be seen in a moment that Shuster parallels and elaborates the suggestion. In a footnote, Saintsbury makes a third ascription of influence: 'Of course, Milton had the *canzone* in mind more or less directly. I need hardly keep the warning bell of "Italian" constantly ringing in regard to him. But the *canzone* is regular' (2, 219 n.). Far more specifically, Landor says of *Lyc*, in the second Imaginary Conversation with Southey (4, 499), 'No poetry so harmonious had ever been written in our language; but in the same free metre both Tasso and Guarini had captivated the ear of Italy.'

---

[65] John Crowe Ransom, 'A Poem Nearly Anonymous,' *American Review* I (1933), 179–203, 444–67. Reprinted in *The World's Body* (New York: Scribner's, 1938), 1–28; also in C. A. Patrides, ed., *Milton's* Lycidas: *The Tradition and the Poem* (New York: Holt, Rinehart and Winston, 1961), 64–81. The phrase quoted may be found in Patrides, **71**.

[66] Joseph Anthony Wittreich, Jr., 'Milton's "Destin'd Urn": the Art of *Lycidas*,' *PMLA* 84 (1969), 60–70, **61–2**.

Milton's familiarity with Italian poetry was a commonplace of early criticism; but that criticism tends to be at least as general on the subject as Saintsbury's. Landor's remark in the *Imaginary Conversations*, and another in *The Poems of Catullus*, 'There is no verse whatsoever in any of...[Milton's] poems for the metre of which he has not an Italian prototype' (quoted in Prince, *Italian Element*, 138 n.), must be among the earliest examples of criticism specifically relating verse form in Milton to Italian verse form. The twentieth century has seen the growth of such criticism in volume and specificity. W. P. Ker speaks again and again of particulars of Italian versification—especially 'the right proportion between the heptasyllable and the heroic line' (325)—which give the *canzone* its characteristic qualities, and impart those qualities to English verse written (as, Ker reiterates, *Lyc* is written) in the *canzone* tradition (162). More recently the work of Oras and Prince—as was made clear in the discussion of *Time*, *Circum* and *SolMus*—has very greatly expanded our understanding of the detailed formal relationship between certain of Milton's poems and Italian verse form, particularly the *canzone* and the short lyric, and Gretchen Finney's writings have brought to our attention the possible influence upon Milton also of the Italian musical drama.

Mrs Finney feels that 'in structure, poetic style, mood, and subject' *Lyc* suggests Alessandro Striggio's *La favola d'Orfeo* and Stefano Landi's *La morte d'Orfeo*, 'musical productions that Milton surely knew, and with which he would have been in sympathy.'[67] Without denying the possibility of this, Oras finds Italian madrigal behind Milton's management of the rhyme structures in *Lyc*; he notes, indeed, a variety of resemblances between *Lyc* and the lyrical speeches of Tasso's pastoral drama *Il Rogo di Corinna*, speeches which are 'in effect a sequence of madrigals joined into a more extensive and intricate lyric whole' ('Early Rhyme Schemes,' 20). Both Oras and Prince, like Landor, call attention to irregular rhyming in the choruses of Tasso's *Aminta* and Guarini's *Pastor F*. But Prince adduces as formal background for *Lyc* rather 'the

[67] Gretchen Finney, 'A Musical Background for "Lycidas",' *HLQ* 15 (1951–2), 325–50, **349**.

discipline of the *canzone*, as it was modified and adapted in lyrics and eclogues of the *Cinquecento*' (*Italian Element*, 72) than any specific model or models.

Both Oras and Prince have much more of interest to say, and will be commented on at greater length below. It remains, in this discussion of the antecedents that have been proposed for the verse of *Lyc*, to quote Shuster: 'Prosodically the poem reaches almost every goal toward which the Pindaric ode would later on tend. Nowhere outside of Greece could Milton have found authority for the very great license he permits himself in his building and arranging stanzas which are not verse paragraphs (they are too definitely variants of one underlying pattern for that) but which are still too individual to owe their origin to Italian practice, though the influence of that practice is manifest in the rich pastoral coloring and in the rhythmic texture of certain passages. Saintsbury has suggested a relationship between the poem and the choruses of Greek tragedy; and it is equally possible that the irregular measure was based on humanistic models at least indirectly derived from Pindar' (71). Shuster seems not to distinguish between the irregular odes of Pindar himself, and what English might make of them, or might think it was making of them. Here, then, it might be worth while to quote a passage in Ker just cited: 'The so-called "Pindaric Odes" of the seventeenth century, of Cowley and his imitators, professed to be related to Pindar, but in so far as they were good they were imitated from a kind of lyric...going back to the Middle Ages, when Pindar was unknown. *Lycidas*, the *Ode to Mrs. Anne Killigrew*, *Alexander's Feast*, the *Odes* of Gray and Keats, and, before them all, Spenser's *Prothalamion* and *Epithalamion*, all belong to the order of the Italian *canzone*' (162).

F. T. Prince's chapter on *Lyc* in *Italian Element* (5; 71–88) is in the main devoted to a discussion of formal experimentation in the verse of sixteenth-century Italian pastoral and pastoral drama, and to a brief demonstration of the variety of technical effects of which this body of writing gave Milton examples to be heard, pondered, and in some way adapted to English verse. Prince has an impressive store of information; his mind is flexible and subtle, and he has (what we must be most grateful for) a poet's ear. He writes temperately and lucidly, with a combination of incisiveness and grace. No student of Milton's verse can afford not to read *Italian Element*. There is the less need here to attempt to 'cover' the complex suggestions which Prince weaves into so persuasive and illuminating an argument during the course of the chapter. Prince is not, perhaps, so fully and dazzlingly a *discoverer* as his gifts have made him appear. The broad outlines of much that he says (though by no means all) have been sketched out before; other prosodists (notably Oras), working independently on some of the same materials, have substantially helped to promote knowledge in us, and deserve recognition. Prince's virtue is clearest when he goes beyond outlines; his real discoveries lie among the details that are the life of form. And he helps the reader to discover rather than merely to register information. Prince's work on the minor poems is probably his best work; and of this the chapter on *Lyc* may well be finest of all.

Prince's subject, then, is the way in which the regular repetition of form traditional in the *canzone* could be converted to a progressive modulation of form so carefully controlled that each stanza, or section, or verse paragraph would have an independent identity—and thus 'irregularity'— suitable to its individual content, and yet retain a profound relationship with the paragraphs preceding and following in the flow of the poem. Prince's most interesting demonstration is that Milton uses (or begins with) the 'principle of articulation' of the *canzone* as conventionally employed—the *stanza divisa*, its parts linked by rhyme in exactly placed key lines—but simplifies the structure, and frees the rhyme so that it may be used to organize the verse paragraph even more closely than had been customary (84–6). 'The divisions in both sonnet and *canzone* made possible a kind of rhetoric of rhyme: lines which rhymed had differing weight and emphasis according to their position and function. It is impossible to follow Milton's methods in *Lycidas* without perceiving that he makes use of such a rhetoric of rhyme, combining it and contrasting it with the more usual rhetoric of sentence structure' (85). Prince discusses, revealingly, the overriding of sentence division by rhyme, the placing and rhyming of the short lines, the use of true and false couplets, etc. (86–7). 'The poem is built upon movements of thought and emotion; Milton is able to use the methods of repeated transitions, of a continuous unfolding and developing, because his mind and emotions naturally moved with power and confidence, with a sustained strength' (88). Prince provides an excellent summary discussion of the form of *Lyc* in his edition of *Comus and Other Poems* (146–7).

Whatever the source of the verse of *Lyc*, whatever the nature of its irregularity, 'There did not at the time anywhere exist in English,' says Ransom, 'among the poems done by competent technical poets, another poem so wilful and illegal in form as this one' (Patrides, 71). 'The eleven stanzas of *Lycidas* occupy 193 lines, but are grossly unequal and unlike. Such stanzas are not in strictness stanzas at all; Milton has all but scrapped the stanza in its proper sense as a formal and binding element. But there is perhaps an even more startling lapse. Within the poem are ten lines which do not rhyme at all, and which technically do not belong therefore in any stanza, nor in the poem' (69).

Ransom is not, of course, the first critic to have noted the presence in *Lyc* of 'unrhymed' lines. But from their presence he draws far-reaching conclusions. The lines are not, he feels, especially felicitous, or especially important. Therefore 'they are defiances' (70); 'at this critical stage in the poet's career...he is uneasy, sceptical, about the whole foundation of poetry as an art. He has a lordly contempt for its tedious formalities, and is determined to show what he can do with only half trying to attend to them. Or he thinks they are definitely bad, and proposes to see if it is not better to shove them aside' (70–1). It is from this series of interpretations, or imaginations, that Ransom moves to the position which so offends his critics: it is easy, he says, for a skilled technician to write smoothly; in some circumstances, however, smoothness seems to reflect on the sincerity of the ideas and emotions presented; a 'modern' poet is capable of going over a poem written too smoothly and roughening it. 'I venture to think that just such a practice, *speaking very broadly* [italics mine], obtained in the composition of *Lycidas*' (71).

An entire generation, apparently, was able to read Ransom's essay as the grand What If it is; could see that in it a poet is talking about timeless problems of writing poetry; could understand that to say 'or....Or' is not really to claim certainty of fact; could turn from reading, imaginatively refreshed, to a more responsive re-reading of the poem. Undoubtedly Ransom actually says some things that actually are not so; and of the truth of some of them he may have convinced himself. Yet there may continue to be readers able to read the essay undeceived; and with profit, and delight.

Martin C. Battestin, however, cannot refrain from castigating Ransom for 'an approach to literature too nearly autonomous, too little governed by sound historical inference and too much dependent on intuition.'[68] He doubts that Ransom could have examined the MS. when he alleged a 'deliberate, *ex post facto* roughening of an originally smooth and perfectly conventional composition' (223). He must conclude the version of *Lyc* in the MS. to be a first draft, in spite of the long passages in it which show almost no revision; he can then assert that the ten 'rhymeless' lines were a part of the poem *from the beginning*—as, indeed, they may have been. 'If the aim of the great majority of the revisions were to be briefly stated,' Battestin says, 'it would be to polish and perfect, rather than to roughen, the poem' (226). Finally, Battestin adopts Prince's idea that the form of *Lyc* is achieved through 'disciplined improvisation' (*Italian Element*, 72): 'The irregularities of the poem result from a...controlled improvisation of rhyme and stanzaic patterns, tending— appropriately enough for one whose greatest successes were to be made with the blank verse paragraph—toward a reconciliation of form and freedom' (227).

Responding to Battestin, though not particularly in defense of Ransom, Charles Hinnant reminds us of the uncouthness of the 'uncouth Swain' and of the rudeness of his 'forc'd fingers': polished the poem may be, but there is reason for roughness.[69] First, intense grief is 'obviously antithetical to the rigid patterns of verse measures' (323). Second, 'the

---

[68] Martin C. Battestin, 'John Crowe Ransom and *Lycidas*: A Reappraisal,' *CE* 17 (1955–6), 223–8, **228**.

[69] Charles H. Hinnant, 'Freedom and Form in Milton's *Lycidas*,' *Papers of the Michigan Academy of Science, Arts, and Letters* 53 (1968), 321–8.

persona of pastoral was conceived of as an actual shepherd, half-civilized, half-barbarian' (324). In *Lyc*, says Hinnant, Milton 'seems to balance, or perhaps reconcile, conflicting qualities: while the language is magnificently adjusted to a "higher mood," the complicated stanza patterns are expressive of the rustic shepherd's grief, a grief which, if it existed alone, would lead to a base style. Beyond doubt, Milton experimented with Italian literary and musical forms.... But these experiments appear to be exercised with the artistic intention of reflecting the anguish of the un-learned shepherd, which was regarded by many in the 16th and 17th centuries as the essential element of the pastoral elegy' (328).

Is the irregularity of *Lyc* 'uncouth'? To twentieth-century ears, attuned to irregularities of form far greater than anything the seventeenth century could have accepted, it does not seem so. To Robert Graves, indeed, *Lyc* is 'a poem strangled by art' (305). But let us remind ourselves of the observations on the poem which Newton attributes to Thyer: '...What gives the greatest grace to the whole is that natural and agreeable wildness and irregularity which runs quite through it, than which nothing could be better suited to express the warm affection which Milton had for his friend and the extreme grief he was in for the loss of him. Grief is eloquent, but not formal.'[70] Richard Hurd comments, 'I see no extraordinary "wildness" and "irregularity"...in the conduct of this little poem. It is true there is a very original air in it... but this I think is owing, not to any disorder in the plan...but, in a good degree, to the looseness and variety of the meter. Milton's ear was a good second to his imagination.'[71] Guest returns to Newton's point: 'It may be questioned, if the peculiarity in the metre can fairly be considered as a blemish. Like endings, recurring at uncertain distances, impart a wildness and an appearance of negligence to the verse, which suits well with the character of elegy' (265). Doubtless one cannot, and should not, forget that even for Newton, the 'wildness' ends in 'grace.'

[70] From Bishop Thomas Newton's ed. of *PR*, *SA* and *Poems upon Several Occasions* (London, 1752), **501**; quoted in Scott Elledge, ed., *Milton's 'Lycidas'* (New York: Harper and Row, 1966), **227**.
[71] Richard Hurd, in Thomas Warton, ed., *Poems upon Several Occasions...by John Milton*, 2nd ed. (London, 1791), **34-5**; quoted in Elledge, **227-8**.

But perhaps there is a sophisticated, and an unsophisticated, reader in us all; and the unsophisticated reader may be permitted, or helped, to feel an extempore quality in verse which, to have its desired effect, must be controlled with the most exquisite care, but must seem not to be. Saintsbury speaks of *Lyc* as 'one of the very masterpieces of English prosody, displaying a virtuosity at once in diction, numbers, and rhyme hardly paralleled elsewhere, and yet converting this from *mere* virtuosity—from pretentious and elaborate art—into something more like actual nature...' (2, 218–19). And Albert Cook feels that while 'as music...[*Lyc*] is tuned perhaps too high for its theme,' 'its achievement is carrying this off successfully...' (380).

To one strand of the argument brought up by Ransom (ultimately, by Johnson) we should return for a moment, and that is to the significance, or the function, or the reason for the existence of, the 'unrhymed' lines. Sprott simply remarks that 'omission of rhymes is even easier than spacing' (32). Saintsbury gives us a brilliant alternative explanation: 'With stanzas of regular length, and regularly rhymed, the individual stanza is what chiefly takes the attention; and when it is mastered, there is mere repetition. Here the attention, aroused at first by the failure of the rhyme—it was probably for this reason that Milton left *both* the opening lines of the first two stanzas blank—is reassured by the prompt appearance of it, and yet warned by the irregularity of that appearance that it must not go to sleep....Never till the end—when the regular octave is probably intended to have something like the effect of the Shakespearian end-couplet to a blank-verse *tirade*—is the interest of uncertainty and chance allowed to drop; seldom is expectation defrauded by blank lines; and yet the evident possibility of these heightens the pleasure of the ear when the rhyme comes. Besides this, the recurrence has a *knitting* effect within the paragraph, while its disappearance marks the paragraph close' (2, 221). Prince remarks that Milton 'appears to have decided that his rhymes must not generally be separated' in *Lyc* 'by more than two lines' (*Italian Element*, 87). The reason seems clear; Milton wanted the reader to be aware of failure of rhyme as well as of its occurrence: and if rhymed lines were often widely separated, unrhymed lines might well not be recognized as such. If they were not recognized, the effects of which Saintsbury speaks would not communicate themselves; as they must.

I do not know how many dozens or hundreds of times I had read *Lyc* before I noticed that it is not quite correct to say that the first line of the poem is unrhymed. There is of course slant rhyme between 'more' and 'sear' in line 2; one cannot help hearing it, and one cannot help wondering about it, since obviously Milton heard it too. But that is not what I am talking about. In the first line of the poem our ears are possessed by the powerful and incantatory 'once more...and once more....' In line 131, the last line of what is often thought of as the second section of the poem, the phrase modulates into 'once, and...no more.' And in line 165, the first line of the tenth paragraph, it becomes 'no more...no more,' to echo a final time, in line 182, 'no more.' Clearly this is an intended repetition and sound progression; it aids very powerfully in organizing the poem into a single and coherent structure. 'More' when it occurs at line-end in 131, 165 and 182 completes or initiates close local rhyme patterns. Between line 1 and line 131 the sound is kept alive by the rhyme between 'roar' and 'shore' in lines 61-3, the second of which ends a verse paragraph. In what sense is it meaningful to say that *Lyc* 1 is unrhymed?

The lines in the poem traditionally counted as unrhymed are 1, 13, 15, 22, 39, 51, 82, 91, 92, and 161. Now Joseph Wittreich has reduced this number to three, one in each of the poem's three sections. 'Lycidas' in 51 remains unrhymed; 'winds' in 91 Wittreich counts as unrhymed, though it is merely the plural of 'wind' in 13, which is rhymed (with 'mind' and 'find') in 71-3; 'Mount' in 161 is more properly taken as unrhymed, though it assonates with 'shroud' in 22 and slant rhymes with 'lament'-'sent' in 60-2. Wittreich takes 'shroud' as rhyming with 'crude' and 'rude' in 3-4; he takes 'well' in 15 as rhyming with 'wheel'-'heel' in 31-4, and argues that the 'dissonances' thus created—'deliberately sounded in the early lines of the poem—are in keeping with Milton's "uncouth" persona. Thereafter, the rhymes become increasingly more exact and thus contribute significantly to the poem's final harmony' (63). Wittreich discovers that 'Caves' in 39 rhymes with 'waves' and 'laves' in 173–5; that 'swain' in 92 merely anticipates the 'swain' in 113 which is prepared for by 'twain' and 'amain' in 110–11; and that 'Jove' in 82 equates well enough in seventeenth-century rhyming practice with the 'love'–'above'–'move' sequence in 177–78–80. Finally, he points out that the rhymes in the concluding octave of the poem combine with images and other allusions paired across the poem to return us to the beginning, thus making of the monody a circle: 'rills,' 'Quills' and 'hills' in 186–88–90 go back to 'rill' and 'hill' in 23–4, 'gray,' 'lay' and 'bay' in 187–89–91 go back to 'lays' and 'graze' in 44–6, and 'blue'–'new' in 192–3 rhyme with 'due'–'knew' in 7–10. Whatever interpretation we are to put upon it, most of the factual basis of Wittreich's argument—most of what he has discovered, or observed—seems undeniably true. *Lyc* will never be the same. Of course, it never was.

For of course what Wittreich has discovered exists, and existed, therefore, from the beginning. And readers not deafened by the expectation of something else have, it would seem, responded increasingly to the poem's extraordinary patterning of sound. Can one *hear* rhymes separated as, say, 'Caves' and 'waves'–'laves' are separated? Not usually; not consciously. But rhyme is one of a constellation of effects which appeal only secondarily to the identifying intellect; we respond in many ways to many kinds and degrees of form which we do not consciously identify as form. The rhymes to which Wittreich calls our attention could not be accidental; too many possible rhymes exist of which the poem does not make use. And what we must now recognize is that rhyme is used in *Lyc* in (at least) two ways: to bind together verse paragraphs; and to bind into a unity the whole poem.

Wittreich's article has a purpose much broader than simply to redefine the rhyme pattern of the poem; it was noted above that he believes the English madrigal to provide a model for its patterning. Here we need detail and demonstration. Wittreich appears further to be convinced, or half-convinced, or ready to be convinced, of the symbolic significance of numerological structure in *Lyc*. Quite apart from the fact that it really has not so far proved demonstrable that Milton played this game—or went in it, at any rate, beyond the first simple moves, in which 'the hidden sense' is not deeply hidden—I should honestly think that too eager an interest in the possibilities of arithmology must impair, or threaten, our indispensable *non*-intellectual response to form, especially to the larger and more distant harmonies and proportions, those which most of us read too narrowly to receive in any appreciable way as it is. But what Wittreich gives us—it includes copious and usually just reference to the relevant preceding work, so that his article is in little a Variorum Commentary—is at its best truly impressive.

The revelation that there is a rhyme structure in *Lyc* presumably intended to make a unity of the whole poem must increase rather than decrease our interest in the way in which rhyme is managed in the individual paragraphs. We may resume consideration of that subject with a generalization that may seem distant enough in its applicability— Eliot's remark that 'the peculiar feeling, almost a physical sensation of a breathless leap, communicated by Milton's long periods, and by his alone, is impossible to procure from rhymed verse.'[72] Robert Adams replies, '...These judgments are dubious; "Lycidas," lines 56–63, will suffice to show that Milton's gift for massive impetus was not dependent on blank verse.'[73] And now perhaps we are in a position to understand Saintsbury's much-criticized earlier judgment that the poem 'is in effect a piece of blank verse carefully equipped with rhyme, for the purpose, technically speaking, of providing it with a lyric vehicle' (2, 222). The next sentence and a half should concern us equally: 'The pause-arrangement is quite that of blank verse, modified a little by the fact of the rhyme, which relieves pause of some of the duties that fall upon it in pure blanks. His system, moreover, has freed the poet, almost automatically, from the tendency to adopt the stopped Marlowesque line-form which...is so frequent in *Comus*....'

What 'freed the poet' was doubtless by no means automatic. But the results of the liberation may be what Eliot and Adams are talking about, somewhat at cross purposes. The 'breathless leap' is not perhaps im-

---

[72] T. S. Eliot, *Milton*, *Proceedings of the British Academy* 33 (London: Geoffrey Cumberlege, 1947), **13**.
[73] Robert Martin Adams, *Ikon: John Milton and the Modern Critics* (Ithaca: Cornell University Press, 1955), **190**.

possible even within *fixed* rhyme patterns, but it is assuredly difficult, as the freest of Milton's sonnets will attest; when we encounter, and identify, a minor element of an expectable, major rhyme structure, there is no doubt that our movement is checked somewhat, even if the individual rhyme we hear does not coincide with a sense break. With unexpected rhyme, rhyme which has no predetermined arrangement, it is different: we have no way of relating what we recognize to larger, anticipated structures, and so we yield ourselves with the less constraint to the flow of sense.

Saintsbury is talking about irregular rhyme as it relates to sense: to structures of meaning, and therefore to pause and enjambment. These are his first concern in the sentences quoted. Critics principally interested in the rhyme itself have supposed Saintsbury to imply that rhyme in the poem is (however beautiful) mere decoration, a separable external, a device, somehow of secondary interest. But Saintsbury understood blank verse to be an inappropriate vehicle for lyric; he understood that Milton wished nonetheless, in *Lyc*, to write lyric that could have the powerful and varied *movement* of blank verse. Earlier quotation has made clear his strong sense of the value of rhyme in the poem. Whether or not we agree with every detail of his commentary, he helps us to understand precisely that rhyme is not *merely* rhyme; that its effect depends in great part upon its relationship to the underlying metrical *and syntactical* structure.

The nature and the effects of freedom in the rhyme scheme of *Lyc* are of principal concern to Diekhoff also. He devotes the last seven pages of 'Prosody in the MS.' to a careful discussion of the poem, speaking especially interestingly of the disposition and rhyming of the short lines (180–1). But it is 'the great flexibility of Milton's plan' which Diekhoff emphasizes particularly, 'the ease with which the verse pattern could be changed.' In proof of this he discusses the MS. revisions of the fifth and ninth paragraphs of the poem (see Fletcher, *Facs.*, 1, 437, 435 and 441), noting that lines 142–50 are 'an insertion in a finished stanza-paragraph' (181–2). Nonetheless 'flexibility' is not to be taken to mean carelessness, or indifference to the final result. The paragraph in *Lyc* 'is really,' he says, 'as Saintsbury points out, a sort of stanza, with the rhetorical and musical advantages that adhere to the stanzaic form, but without the sacrifice of freedom that a stanza pattern usually involves. This is not to say that Milton felt free to do the easiest thing;...rather... [he] hedges himself in with quite as many restrictions as a preconceived stanza pattern could place about him, but deprives himself of the support he might have gotten from such a pattern' (182–3).

What are these restrictions? Diekhoff comments on them only generally, as evolving during the course of construction of the individual paragraph, and his own earlier comments on 'the ease with which the verse pattern could be changed' may not seem quite consonant with his conclusions. Perhaps specific analysis of the 'building' of 'the lofty rhyme' is needed here; and fortunately, a number of excellent critics have undertaken such analysis. It has been spurred, almost certainly, by the recognition in the nineteenth century of all-but-buried elements of traditional form in the poem. In 1855 Thomas Keightley said, 'It has not, we believe, been observed by any critic that the last eight lines of "Lycidas" form a perfect stanza in *ottava rima*. As they stand detached, such was probably the poet's design; but we meet with eight other lines (124–131) which, though they terminate a paragraph, are united with what precedes more closely than is ever the case in the Italian poets. Whether this was accidental or not, we are unable to determine. He had, it is true, the authority of Fairfax (see *Godfrey of Bullogne*, XIX, 3, 4) for such a structure; but we are inclined to think it casual, as in another place (165–172) by merely transposing two lines we should have a perfect stanza, and a third (111–118), by altering a single line.'[74]

What Keightley is 'inclined to think...casual,' more recent critics have interpreted as being very carefully designed. Writing almost a century after Keightley, Ants Oras undertakes 'to show that the effect of effortless spontaneity and force achieved by Milton depends very largely on his care in devising the complex formal pattern of the elegy and on his deliberate attempts to veil the regularity underlying its seemingly

---

[74] Thomas Keightley, *An Account of the Life, Opinions, and Writings of John Milton* (London, 1859), 293–4; quoted in Elledge, 237. Keightley's *Account* was first published in 1855.

unpremeditated rhyme scheme' ('Early Rhyme Schemes,' 15). Oras discusses Tasso's madrigal *Mentre per farvi onore*, and shows in it a pattern of rhyme evolving through successive groups of lines: *abba, cdeedc, affa, ghiihg, ajja, akka* (14). He then points out comparable, perhaps even more complex modulations of form in the first song of *Arc* (see discussion of that poem above) and in *Comus* 890–911 (14–15), and is ready to take up consideration of 'the essential features' of *Lyc*: '(1) the way the length of the verse paragraphs is arranged; (2) the division of the paragraphs into subordinate rhyme patterns; (3) the varying complexity of the patterns; (4) the calculated experimentation with certain basic rhyme schemes throughout the poem; and, significantly, (5) the methods of creating effects of irregularity, the "blurring" of design' (15).

First Oras breaks down the rhyme patterns of the eleven paragraphs into subpatterns; the reader should be warned that these generally run counter to syntactical patterns, so that they tend to be more persuasive as abstract schemes on Oras's page than recognizable as subpatterns on Milton's. Prince, in his discussion of the overriding of sentence divisions in *Lyc* by rhyme (*Italian Element*, 85–7), is talking about a linking device, a device of organization and articulation, which must, precisely, obscure the subpatterns to which Oras would call our attention. Oras has already spoken, it is true, of Milton's 'deliberate attempts to veil the regularity' underlying the poem's 'seemingly unpremeditated rhyme scheme,' so that presumably the objection has been forestalled. Still, a hidden form may be thought comparable to a hidden sense; and perhaps at least the criterion for our acceptance of the actuality of its existence ought to be that, once revealed, it remains visible (or audible), instead of disappearing the moment one turns away from the analyst's diagram. At all events, 'the number of principal subpatterns' listed paragraph by paragraph 'is 2, 1, 2, 2, 2, 3, 3, 4, 4, 4, and 1. It varies less than the length of the paragraphs but is in general accord with it, increasing until just before the end, and then declining.' The complexity of the rhyme patterns follows a similar curve. The opening paragraph is complex; the second simple; thereafter, complexity 'rises with notable regularity, reaching a culmination in paragraphs 8 and 9, whereupon it falls off' (15–16).

As for the patterns themselves, 'The first subpattern of paragraph 3 is slightly extended and varied to produce the initial pattern of paragraph 4, as the second subpattern of the latter is elaborated to form its positional counterpart in paragraph 5. In each case the change is worked by adding one unit to the design (*ababcc* > *ab–abcc*, *dedfef* > *dedfefe*). Later in the poem further variants of the *ababcc* pattern reveal the same method of gradual increase in length and intricacy. The beginning of paragraph 7 has *ababcc*; that of paragraph 9, *ababbcc*; and that of paragraph 10, *ababbacc*: again, a single component has been added each time. In the next, and final, paragraph the inversion of two components changes the previous pattern to *abababcc* (i.e., *ottava rima*).' Since the final pattern defines a complete paragraph, and the three preceding are paragraph openings, all four 'were doubtless meant to be viewed in relation to one another, each growing out of its predecessor with something of the inevitability and logic of a mathematical progression' (16). And of the at least partly defined, and therefore apprehensible, patterns to which Oras calls attention, including the last, this must be so. Whether, however, an interlacing of two or three rhymes not syntactically isolated, its identity further blurred by interruptions and interpolations of extraneous rhyme sounds, may be regarded as having *a* structural function, is doubtful; probably the effect is simply that of the individual rhymes.

The tendency of contemporary criticism, at all events, is to look upon *Lyc* as a poem relatively indeterminate in form at the beginning, as it were seeking a form, gradually achieving one, and ending in the repose of perfect traditional pattern. Thus nine of the ten 'unrhymed' lines occur in the first half of the poem; thus, as Shuster points out (71), the last short line is 145, almost precisely three-quarters of the way through. The general movement is 'from drift to discipline,' says George W. Nitchie: 'Clearly, the abortive *ottava rima* at line 124 is not accident but strategy; it gives us something attempting to emerge, something potentially present but not fully realized, that will not quite surface until the end of the poem. And the analogy between the prosodic situation and the psychological situation of the speaker is self-evident.'[75]

[75] George W. Nitchie, '*Lycidas*: A Footnote,' *N&Q*, n.s. 13 (1966), 377–8, **378**.

There remain to be mentioned a handful of interesting treatments or discussions of passages within *Lyc*. Keith Rinehart characterizes the first fourteen-line paragraph of the poem as a 'broken sonnet';[76] in the 'extravagantly artful interlacing of alliteration' through the first six of these lines Graves sees an adaptation 'to English metrical use' of 'the device of *cynghanedd*, or recurrent consonantal sequences, used by the Welsh bards whom ...[Milton] mentions appreciatively early in the poem' (305). Donald R. Roberts hears in *Lyc* 76 'a striking quasi-musical effect' illustrative of the quality of madrigal which, as has been mentioned, he finds in the poem as a whole: 'The words, "But not the praise...," to my ear produce not only an effect of hasty interruption, but of a new musical voice, perhaps in another register, interposed to maintain the rhythmic flow' (338).

In the first of his two essays on Milton's verse Eliot remarks the poet's use of proper names 'to obtain the same effect of magnificence with them as does Marlowe—nowhere perhaps better than in' *Lyc* 156–62— 'than which, for the single effect of grandeur of sound, there is nothing finer in poetry....'[77] Saintsbury (2, 222) admires the lines as much, and without Eliot's reservations. But F. R. Leavis compares the same passage with Donne's *Satyre* 3. 79–84, and says that though Milton's words 'are doing so much less work' than those in Donne, 'they seem to value themselves more highly—they seem, comparatively, to be occupied with valuing themselves rather than with doing anything....The consummate art of *Lycidas*...exhibits a use of language in the spirit of Spenser— incantatory, remote from speech....What predominates in the handling of...[the words] is...a concern for mellifluousness—for liquid sequences and a pleasing opening and closing of the vowels' (56–7). G. S. Fraser examines these opinions, and many others, in a very readable, useful and wide-ranging essay contributed to *The Living Milton*.[78]

Finally, Prince reminds us (*Italian Element*, 72–3) that the regular

---

[76] Keith Rinehart, 'A Note on the First Fourteen Lines of Milton's "Lycidas,"' *N&Q* 198 (1953), 103.
[77] T. S. Eliot, 'A Note on the Verse of John Milton,' *Essays and Studies* 21 (1936), 32–40, **39**.
[78] G. S. Fraser, 'Approaches to "Lycidas,"' *The Living Milton*, ed. Frank Kermode (London: Routledge & Kegan Paul, 1960), 32–54.

Italian *canzone* 'consisted of a complex, fully rhymed stanza of some length, repeated several times and followed by a shorter concluding stanza, the *commiato*. . . . The last verse-paragraph . . . [of *Lyc*] undoubtedly corresponds in its own way to a *commiato*.'

(*h*) The Sonnets

Accurate and illuminating explanations of the form of Milton's sonnets are to be found in two works: John S. Smart's 1921 edition of the sonnets[79] (Introduction, 11–33), and Prince's *Italian Element* (chapters 2, 'Della Casa and the Heroic Sonnet,' 14–33, and 6, 'Milton's Sonnets,' 89–107). What these works explain, and illustrate, is—once again—Milton's dependence on specific Italian models. Worthwhile analyses of the versification of a few of the individual sonnets exist as well; but complex and innovative as many of the sonnets are, little sustained examination of their form has, it would seem, been undertaken.

Criticism has never lost sight of the fact that the sonnet is in its very origins an Italian form. And that the sonnet in English nonetheless developed early a characteristic form of its own is a matter equally of general knowledge, or acceptance. Briefly, the sonnet is of fourteen lines (hendecasyllables in Italian, decasyllables in English); the traditional Petrarchan scheme divides the sonnet into two quatrains, rhymed (usually) *abba abba*, and two tercets, rhymed variously *cde cde*, or *cdc dcd*, or *cde dce* or *dec* or *edc*—other combinations still are possible, and as Smart says (13), there are few that have not been employed. Among combinations which were tried by Petrarch's successors, though rarely, were forms ending with a final *ee*. Interlaced rhyme in the four lines preceding might then have the pattern *cdd c*. . or *cdc d*. . . Introducing the sonnet into English, Wyatt settled on the first alternative, Surrey on the second. To both writers, the logic of the rhyme arrangement suggested a division of the last six lines into quatrain and couplet rather than into two tercets. Wyatt's favored sonnet form thus became *abba abba cddc ee*: it was to be Sidney's and Donne's as well. Surrey extended the logic of

---

[79] John S. Smart, ed., *The Sonnets of Milton* (Oxford: Clarendon Press, 1966). First published, 1921.

the *cdcd* quatrain patterning back into the octave (which had in any event, in Italy, sometimes been rhymed *abab abab*); the resulting form was *abab cdcd efef gg*. This became Shakespeare's form, the form known as the English sonnet.

That Milton, with his direct and extensive knowledge of Italian poetry, should have gone back to primary Italian models occasions no surprise. *Sonn* 7 he himself speaks of as having been written in 'a Petrarchian stanza' (*LetFr*, MS., 6). The rhyme patterning of the later sonnets continues to be 'Petrarchian'; but the way in which, increasingly often, sentence structure is set at odds with rhyme structure in those sonnets has seemed to critics by no means traditional. Masson says briskly that *Sonns* 8 through 23 'are all after the Italian form of the Sonnet in its authorized varieties' (1, cx); but considering how little Masson seems to have known about the Italian sources of others of Milton's poems, it is difficult not to wonder what he thought he meant by the statement. In the prefatory essay to the section of his edition devoted to the sonnets, 2, 276–81, he speaks of rhyme arrangement only, passing over such phenomena as the strong enjambment of the octave in *Sonns* 17, 18, 19, 22 and 23, the strong midline breaks in, e.g., *Sonns* 9. 11, 15. 13, 16. 9 and 10, 18. 8 and 10, 19. 8 and 12, and 22. 6 and 9.

Early twentieth-century criticism deals with the unusual or 'irregular' features just noted principally by describing their nature and/or their effects. Thus Saintsbury says that to Milton 'the sonnet is not much more than a form of verse-paragraph'; and he adds, 'this peculiarity, in which he is followed by Wordsworth, seems to me to put him, as a sonnetteer, not merely below Shakespeare but below Keats and Rossetti' (2, 217). Saintsbury does understand that the couplet close of the English sonnet is incisive, and that the more extended tercet close of the Italian sonnet is softer, and better suited to the treatment of certain kinds of themes (2, 215). Schipper, however, remarks that Milton 'imitated the Italian sonnet only in its form, and paid no regard to the relationship of its single parts or to the distribution of its contents through the quatrains and terzets.' He then proceeds to obscure the implications of his statement: 'In this respect he kept to the monostrophic structure of the specifically English form of the sonnet, consisting, as a rule, of one continuous train of thought' (376). All one can say by way of comment is that the continuities of Shakespeare and of Milton are, in the end, very different. Enid Hamer seems both more willing and more able to respond with an impersonal exactitude when she says, 'Except for the presence of rhyme, Milton constructs a sonnet as he does a blank-verse paragraph, a woven harmony of long and short phrases, crossing the line limit designedly, with a few intermediate or secondary pauses, with ample modulation, and the final resolution to the normal movement for the close' (203).

The balance of Mrs Hamer's view may result in part from the fact that she was writing some years after the publication of Smart's edition of Milton's sonnets, and that her understanding had been deepened by her reading of Smart's work. The passages in that work that concern us are three. In the first (11–22) Smart elucidates in careful detail the form, or forms, of the (traditional) Italian sonnet, and discusses the history of the English sonnet up to the time of Milton. In the second (22–9) Smart defines and inquires into the 'irregularities' in Milton's late sonnets numbered 16, 17, 18, 19, 20 and 23: 'In these poems the divisions of the metre and those required by the thought are not brought into strict agreement; pauses occur in any part of the line; and a sentence is sometimes continued, in rapid and unbroken flow, from the second quatrain into the first tercet, the definite pause usually placed after the quatrains being disregarded' (23). Smart perceives the relationship of these facts to Milton's development as an English poet: 'As examples of his treatment of verse the sonnets stand midway between the simpler style of *Comus* and that of *Paradise Lost*, with its sentences "variously drawn out from one verse into another"....In his epic style he gains both beauty of sound and effective emphasis by an unexpected ending at an unusual part of the line, metre and meaning being separated or opposed, instead of being combined with monotonous uniformity' (24). Smart cannot, then, accept the irregularities of form in certain of the late sonnets as accidental or careless; where they occur they have, he insists, 'metrical and poetic purpose' (23).

They also have precedent: in a momentous demonstration, Smart shows that the sixteenth-century Italian poet Giovanni della Casa had deliberately broken with 'the Petrarchian tradition of regularity and smoothness, which had been carried to excess by minor sonneteers' (26), in exactly the ways in which Milton was to break with the conventions of the sonnet in English a century later. Smart acknowledges (28) that his attention had been drawn to the similarity between Milton's sonnets and Della Casa's by James Glassford, writing in the preceding century.[80] Glassford, collecting, translating and commenting on certain Italian lyrics, quotes Della Casa's *O Sonno, o della queta umida ombrosa* (120). His remarks on Della Casa and Milton may be quoted here:

It is...[Della Casa's] custom to carry on the sense from the close of one line to the beginning or middle of that which follows, thus suspending the attention of the reader, and avoiding the monotony which is produced by a uniform termination of the sentence at the close of the line or couplet. The advantage is not merely to give a relief by the varieties of the pause, but often to add much force and grandeur to the sentiment itself, by arresting the reader at a place and time unexpected, and forcing him, as it were, to halt for a moment and consider. In this manner his compositions possess, as to their style, both the beauty of rhyme and the solemnity and varied cadence of blank verse. It is evident how much Milton profited in the formation of his style by his acquaintance with the Italian poets, and his familiar knowledge of their lyrical writers; and to none, it may be presumed, more than to Della Casa, who may fairly be looked upon as his prototype (587–8).

As Smart points out (28–9), it is demonstrable that Milton owned, and knew, Della Casa's sonnets.

Smart's third point which concerns us is an argument against the critical theory of the *volta*, the theory, or dictum, that there must be a 'suspense or turn' after the octave of the sonnet. Smart argues (29–33) that no such rule governs the writing of the Italian sonnet, and that English critics who have insisted upon it *as* a rule (and have charged, therefore, that Milton often broke that rule) are simply mistaken.

The critics who have followed Smart have expanded upon his excellent

[80] James Glassford, ed., *Lyrical Compositions from the Italian Poets* (Edinburgh, 1846).

work rather than seriously revising it; if in any way the weight of his argument has been shifted, it has been in respect to his final point, the contention that the 'Italian principle of the *volta*' in the sonnet is non-existent. It is not argued that there *is* a firm law requiring a 'suspense or turn' in the sonnet. But Prince points out that 'the internal divisions and the scheme of rhymes of the Italian sonnet impose a certain parallelism or balance on the whole poem. The movement of quatrains or tercets may be affected or determined by this parallelism; but so are individual words and phrases, and the unfolding of whole sentences and trains of thought. This parallelism or duplex structure dominates the whole shape of the poem and all its parts...' (*Italian Element*, 92). Phrases like 'lucid symmetry,' 'the structural principle of parallelism,' 'antithesis and balance' stud Prince's following pages; and he demonstrates (96) that Milton was aware of the principle, and applied it.

Clearly a 'duplex structure' does not require *a* turn; but it may indeed invite one. W. P. Ker says, 'The sonnet is not a mere stanza; it is at least a double thing, with position in it and contradiction. It is a true argument. In the Italian sonnet there is obviously a form provided for a position in the first eight lines, and a contradiction or variation or conclusion in the last six. And that is a very common form of the argument— protasis and apodosis' (173). E. A. J. Honigmann, in a recent re-edition of the sonnets, reminds us gently that the ends of many of the sonnets do look back to their beginnings. Whether we use the word '*volta*,' or some other, 'the frequency with which Milton placed a turn at the very commencement of the sestet proves that he understood the intentions of earlier poets (cf. VII, X, XIII, XV and XX). A sharp turn, less exactly co-inciding with the start of the sestet, is also found elsewhere, in the eighth, ninth or tenth lines (XI, XVI, XVII, XIX and XXII), and confirms that a structural principle is involved—though not, be it added, one to which Milton felt invariably committed.'[81] Perhaps we should speak, not of a law or laws, but, as Prince does, of 'the necessities and opportunities of the Italian sonnet-form' (*Italian Element*, 92).

[81] E. A. J. Honigmann, ed., *Milton's Sonnets* (London: Macmillan, 1966), **43.**

Prince supports and extends Smart's demonstrations and suggestions in a number of useful ways. Smart, for example, devotes only three pages to Della Casa and his sonnets; in Prince a twenty-page chapter is taken up with a minute examination of Della Casa's work and of the rationale behind it, as well as of the *Heroic Sonnets* of Della Casa's 'chief advocate and imitator' Tasso (19), as all these affected Milton's mature style. The technical characteristics of verse sought for by Della Casa, Prince tells us, were (*a*) artificiality and complexity of word order, (*b*) a 'breaking up of the verses' by unusual and difficult enjambments and by the placing of major sense breaks within the line, and (*c*) 'the deliberate accumulation of elisions' (27). The rhythms achieved by these devices have the quality Tasso calls '*asprezza*, "roughness" or "difficulty"' (loc. cit.); Oras tells us that a use of words which show heavy concentrations of post-vocalic consonant clusters will also help in the achievement of *asprezza*.[82] Guest, in the early nineteenth century, seems to have known something about experimentation in style in Italian sonnet writing during the *Cinquecento*; but when we have been reading Smart and Prince his remarks fall oddly upon our ears: 'In the sixteenth century, many of the Italians ventured to alter the structure of the sonnet, and were of course followed by their imitators in this country. The object of all these changes was greater facility' (655).

In his edition of *Comus and Other Poems* Prince once again provides an excellent summation of the materials presented in *Italian Element*. On the sonnets this reads in part: 'The technical changes...[Milton] takes over from the Renaissance Italians make what is necessarily a short poem into one that seems weighty and sustained...' (158). Prince reminds us also, 'The rhymes...may be partly submerged by the flow of the sense, but remain in our consciousness, since they are generally full-sounding and sometimes obtrusive.... The sonnet becomes a single verse-paragraph flowing through a sound-pattern made up of the four divisions marked by the rhymes...' (158-9).

---

[82] Ants Oras, 'Spenser and Milton: Some Parallels and Contrasts in the Handling of Sound,' *Sound and Poetry*, ed. Northrop Frye, English Institute Essays 1956 (New York: Columbia University Press, 1957), 109-33, **115**.

Philip M. Withim, undertaking an analysis of the verse of *Sonn* 7, bases his discussion on a scansion so full of errors—several of them consequential, and at least one catastrophic—that the value of his work is seriously impaired.[83] David V. Harrington, feeling that 'the careful reader of Milton's sonnets, or of any other poetry, should be guided by the form of the poem to a comprehension of significant controlled feeling,' briefly analyzes *Sonns* 11, 14, 15, 16, 17, 18, 22 and 23 from this point of view; he finds that the 'conventional prosody' of *Sonn* 15 makes it little more than 'rhyming, metrical prose,' otherwise seems able to approve most of the sonnets he discusses.[84] The level of the performance is not remarkably high; an occasional comment on the verse is of interest, but on the whole Harrington's responses seem predictable.

Taylor Stoehr's detailed analyses of *Sonns* 7, 16, 18, 19 and 23—7 for its regularity, its control and containment of a threatened rebellion, the others for their various irregularities—are another matter.[85] Stoehr writes from the point of view of structural linguistics, and uses its vocabulary, though unobtrusively; but if his analyses seem exact, even 'scientific,' it is simply because he is an excellent reader of poetry, and because he writes as well as he reads. For the individual analyses the student should go to the article itself. Here a few sentences may be quoted from Stoehr's conclusion:

Whether...[Milton's] focus is painfully intimate or consciously public, whether the movement of feeling is from anger to determined faith, or from uneasy wonder to pathos and despair, in every case the artistic strength is apparent in the manipulation of form and syntax in complex tensions and balances, giving the thought and feeling its poetic discipline and display....Even in those lines which might be described as confused or desperate, the poet is perhaps most in control, shaping an artistic emotion. The point is not that syntax betrays hidden or unconscious feeling in the author; rather, that Milton plays the conventional elements of linguistic structure off against the less flexible con-

[83] Philip M. Withim, 'A Prosodic Analysis of Milton's Seventh Sonnet,' *Bucknell Review* 6 (1956–7), 29–34.

[84] David V. Harrington, 'Feeling and Form in Milton's Sonnets,' *Western Humanities Review* 20 (1966), 317–28, **325**.

[85] Taylor Stoehr, 'Syntax and Poetic Form in Milton's Sonnets,' *English Studies* 45 (1964), 289–301.

ventions of the sonnet form itself, to produce a compelling expression of poetic feeling, beyond the reach of less self-conscious art.... In large part, meaning depends on the denotations and connotations of the words used—in any poetry, good or bad. But there is also such a thing as *structural* meaning, and the particularly moving quality of Milton's sonnets ultimately results from his ability to control *both* kinds of meaning, to match sound and sense, to adjust syntactic and poetic form in a delicate interaction which itself deepens the significance of the bare words (301).

What Stoehr says here finds application and illustration again and again, of course, in some of the greatest verse effects in Milton's greatest poems; and those effects could hardly be more sensitively and exactly described.

The Italian *sonetto caudato* or tailed sonnet, represented in Milton by *NewF*, is discussed in some detail by Smart (112). Prince gives the following brief account of it: 'The form of the sonnet is one often used by the Italians for humorous or satirical subjects; it has a coda or tail, consisting of a half-line (rhyming with the previous line) and a couplet; the coda could be extended indefinitely by adding such units of three lines' (*Comus*, 170). Of *NewF* Saintsbury remarks, interestingly, 'The thing is obviously close to the old long stanzas with "bob and wheel"— things so thoroughly English that they deserved resuscitation' (2, 217).

Prince comments on certain others of Milton's sonnets: 'Certainly, if the majority... are on religious or political themes, the proper field of heroic verse, a few may be distinguished as verging upon the mock-heroic: the more intimate, and particularly the convivial invitations to his young pupils, have the Horatian quality of something approaching self-parody. The controversial sonnets also turn the stiff difficulty of the verse, the *asprezza* of the "magnificent" style, to a mocking purpose' (*Italian Element*, 103). Brief individual comments, of varying interest, on the verse of most of the sonnets will be found here and there in the editions and criticisms so far discussed.

(*i*) The Psalms

The most extensive consideration of Milton's psalm translations available is to be found in a long essay by William Bridges Hunter, Jr., the major contentions of which must, unhappily, be set aside as ill-founded and ill-argued.[86] Hunter would like to convince us that Milton's mature prosody is based not on Chaucer's, as Bridges claimed, but on Josuah Sylvester's, and on the prosody of the metrical psalters. Both are indeed a part of the tradition upon which Milton draws; Hunter's crippling error results from his failure to understand what a prosodic tradition is, and how individual poets relate to it. But Hunter's method and the conclusions to which it leads him have been sufficiently criticized,[87] and the intention here is not to cite his study merely so that it may be dismissed. The second half of the essay in question, though flawed wherever basic prosody and prosodic influences are concerned, has nonetheless much of interest to say about the syllabic nature of English psalmody, and about the form of Milton's psalm translations.

Of the verse of the early paraphrases there is little notice except in Hunter. Milton's *Ps* 114, Hunter points out, 'is in the same decasyllabic couplet as the *Divine Weeks* [of Josuah Sylvester], a form used occasionally in psalmody' (141); the style of Milton's paraphrase suggests that in this one instance he may very well be principally indebted to Sylvester, and other critics have seen the matter so.[88] Of *Ps* 136 Hunter speaks with greater particularity: the lines, he says, 'are normally iambic tetrameter, but they frequently show truncation; that is, they often lose their first syllable. Now while this became Milton's regular practice in *L'Allegro* and *Il Penseroso*, it could never do for a psalm meant to be sung, since the melody would be broken by omission of the syllable for its first note. There are no comparable examples in the psalters, and I am thus forced to conclude either that the young Milton was writing this psalm as a literary exercise or that if it were meant to be sung its music would have been of quite an individual kind which cannot be matched elsewhere' (loc. cit.). Brooks and Hardy feel that 'the meter in both Psalms is poorly managed, and that used in Psalm 136 noticeably so. The four-

---

[86] William Bridges Hunter, Jr., 'The Sources of Milton's Prosody,' *PQ* 28 (1949), 125–44.

[87] See, e.g., George A. Kellog, 'Bridges' *Milton's Prosody* and Renaissance Metrical Theory,' *PMLA* 68 (1953), 268–85, **272, n. 10**.

[88] See, e.g., Merritt Y. Hughes, ed., *John Milton, Complete Poems and Major Prose* (New York: Odyssey Press, 1957), **3**.

stress lines in this paraphrase seem even less appropriate to the Psalmist's verses than Psalm 114, where the basic line is five-stress and the greater length helps conceal the awkward insistence on the rhymes' (105).

In a separate article on Milton's translations of *Ps* 80–8, Hunter points out that the General Assembly of the Church of Scotland passed an act in 1647 authorizing a revision of the Westminster version of the psalms, dividing them, for the purposes of retranslation, 40/40/40/30.[89] The Assembly, says Hunter, recommended to the translators the use of a measure 'which may agree to the common tunes; that is, having the first line of eight syllabs, and the second line of six.' This is 'an accurate description of common meter, a form which Milton used here in his translation but never elsewhere in his poetry, including his versions of other psalms,' Hunter notes (493). He feels that this fact, plus the date of Milton's translations (April 1648) and the numbers of the psalms chosen, suggest the possibility that Milton may have wished to be appointed by the Church of Scotland official translator of the third group of psalms, and that he may have prepared and submitted *Ps* 80–8 as samples of what he could do.

Maren-Sophie Røstvig, as would be expected, offers a very different reason for the choice. *Ps* 80–8, 1–8—'We observe the decided preference for the number eight, a preference which suggests a desire to offer up a perfect octave, or diapason in honour of God. The Psalms were traditionally believed to be arranged in sequence so that the number of a Psalm serves as its title, as it were....Thus the first Psalm praises the man who is one with God, the great Monad; the second denounces the sinful plots and rebellions of men, the fourth their inordinate love of the things of this earth, while the eighth praises the perfection of the created universe....Psalm LXXX has been given 80 lines, and...two of the Psalms where the subject-matter is Justice and Judgment, have respectively 16 and 64 lines—numbers that symbolize Justice because they divide into equal halves until the Monad is reached' (53–4).

Milton's 1653 translations of *Ps* 1–8 are prosodically of the greatest interest. 'Each is in a different meter,' Hunter notes ('Sources,' 142),

---

[89] William B. Hunter, Jr., 'Milton Translated the Psalms,' *PQ* 40 (1961), 485–94, **491**.

'but only the decasyllabic couplets of the first had been employed in the psalters. Indeed, the impetus for such metrical experiments suggests a direct interest in the original variety of Calvin's Geneva psalter.' Milton employs in these translations, not only 'the common speech contractions,' but also relatively less common metrical compressions between words: 'holi' hill' in *Ps* 2. 13, 'bloodi' and' in *Ps* 5. 16, 'furi' asswage' in *Ps* 7. 22 (loc. cit.). 'There are...very few feminine endings. ...But the proportion of run-on lines is perhaps higher than that of any other riming poetry before the 19th century....Likewise the caesura tends to fall near the beginning or end of the line. But most important of all is the extended use of reversed feet...' (143).

Speaking of Milton's handling of stanza forms at various times during his life, Sprott says that 'the terrible Terzetti' of *Ps* 2 'expose his long-confined genius, raging in its mature strength, and ramping to break loose' (23). But it is *Ps* 3, of course, which is strangest in effect, and most experimental in form, of all the 1653 psalm translations. Shuster speaks of its 'curious rhyme scheme...set against the background of a stanzaic pattern more irregular than any...[Milton] otherwise employed...' (75). Shuster adds in a footnote, 'This appears to be an essay in the mono-strophic ode form of Aeschylus and is governed by a subtle speech principle difficult to fathom or expound. Observe the effect of the trochaic and spondaic submeter in the opening lines. And the effect of combining short lines with feminine rhymes in...[14–18] is most unusual....'

Sprott, speaking of the late psalm translations as a group, feels that they 'exhibit almost for the first time in Milton's verse several features which became prominent only in his major poems. Indeed, it might not be an exaggeration to say that they sometimes appear like full-dress rehearsals for the lyric choruses of *Samson Agonistes*.' Sprott instances 'the typical elision (I, 14, 15), disposition of breaks (II, 14–22), stress-syllable openings and appearances of falling rhythm (VII, 1–6), multiple inversions (VI, 9, 17) and tortured idiom (VI)....' The psalm translations, of course, retain rhyme, retain stanzaic forms—'but they are abrupt, masculine, even cruel verses, far removed from the gentle cadences of the early Hymn' (27).

The association of the 1653 psalm translations with the writing of the choruses of *SA* is made also by W. R. Parker; in his argument for the early dating of *SA* he comments on the 'great variety of rime and metrical patterns, and strangely anarchic rhythms' of *Ps* 1–8.[90] Trying to counter this argument, Oras says, 'The spirit of the psalms translated by Milton in 1648 and 1653 is of the kind that may have recurred to him during any part of his later years. . . . The rhythm of the translations of 1653 prepares us not only for what we find in *SA* but also for the rhythmic boldness of *PL*, which, closely considered, abounds in rhythms whose unusualness and strangeness we do not realize because we have come to take the Miltonic style for granted, and also because the poet's control of them is so perfect' (*Blank Verse and Chronology*, 4–5). Whatever the relationship of the 1653 translations to the verse of specific later—or earlier—poems, many critics would agree with Hunter, as Sprott does, that 'it is in these last psalms that Milton first reaches his mature prosody. . . .' ('Sources,' 143).

There remain to be mentioned one or two points of general interest and importance. The Introduction to Miss Helen Darbishire's edition of the MS. of *PL* 1 contains, among other things, carefully phrased conclusions about the spelling and punctuation of the MS., as against those of eds. 1 and 2 of *PL*; Miss Darbishire feels that by the time *PL* 1 was ready for the press Milton had certain clear spelling preferences a number of which had the function of indicating the sounds the poet heard and wished the reader to hear, especially in words or phrases where accent, or pronunciation otherwise, might be uncertain.[91] Miss Darbishire's studies, and the convictions she came to hold as a result of them, led her eventually to publish an edition of *PL* (again with a detailed Introduction) the spelling and punctuation of which are revised from those of the early editions to produce a text as close as possible to that which Miss Darbishire believes Milton would have produced if he had been able to

---

[90] William R. Parker, 'The Date of *Samson Agonistes*,' *PQ* 28 (1949), 145–66, **161**.
[91] Helen Darbishire, ed., *The Manuscript of Milton's Paradise Lost Book I* (Oxford: Clarendon Press, 1931); Introduction, esp. xvii–xlvii.

supervise the printing of the poem in meticulous detail.[92] B. A. Wright
follows Miss Darbishire in at least some of her conclusions, and the
Textual Introduction to his edition of Milton likewise discusses spelling
and punctuation in considerable detail.[93]

But if some editors and critics have, at least in part, accepted Miss
Darbishire's conclusions about Milton's spelling preferences, others have
been skeptical.[94] The matter would not at first seem much to affect the
early poems: but certain of the spellings most argued over begin to
appear in the Trinity MS. (compare, e.g., 'this this is shee,' *Arc* 5, with
'this this is she alone,' *Arc* 17, Fletcher, *Facs.*, 1, 384–5; and see 'thir'
in *Sonn* 12, 1 and 9, *Facs.*, 1, 444–5—all in Milton's handwriting). Whatever the significance of these spellings, clearly it does behoove us to
know that, e.g., 'unshak'n' and 'brok'n' in *Sonn* 15, lines 5 and 8 (also
in Milton's handwriting; *Facs.*, 1, 452–3) are not contracted forms, but
display syllabic *'n*. See also the comparable forms 'rip'n'd' (*Sonn* 14. 2;
Facs., 1, 446–7), 'new enlightn'd' (*Nat* 82; 1645 and 1673), etc.: as often
as these forms have been explained,[95] there are critics who do not understand their function, and who suppose the forms to be contractions, or
the spellings to be misprints. Few of Milton's spellings are specifically
'poetic'; forms that occur in his verse occur in his prose as well. But
that some of them have implications for meter when used in verse is
obvious.

Probably we should recognize that the effective study of Milton's
spelling, in its relationship to sixteenth- and seventeenth-century spelling generally, is only beginning. The MSS., the printed texts, and the
connections between them are not easy to understand and interpret.
A number of studies of the Trinity MS. have been noted above: clearly
there must be more studies, of all available MS. and printed material

---

[92] Helen Darbishire, ed., *The Poetical Works of John Milton*, Volume I, *Paradise Lost* (Oxford: Clarendon Press, 1952); Introduction, ix–xxxv.

[93] B. A. Wright, ed., *Milton's Poems*, Everyman's Library (London: Dent; New York: Dutton, 1956); Textual Introduction, v–xxxii.

[94] See, e.g., Robert Martin Adams, *Ikon*, 61–76; also John T. Shawcross, 'One Aspect of Milton's Spelling: Idle Final "E",' *PMLA* 78 (1963), 501–10.

[95] In addition to the careful accounts given by Miss Darbishire, see, e.g., H. C. Wyld, 'The Significance of -'*n* and -*en* in Milton's Spelling,' *Englische Studien* 70 (1935), 138–48.

that may tell us anything about what Milton expected, or wanted, his readers to hear.[96] John T. Shawcross has published a number of articles on the texts of various of the early poems,[97] and on Milton's spelling:[98] even though the present writer differs with some of Shawcross's interpretations and conclusions, he can only be glad of the existence of the articles, and wish that other scholars would undertake equally thorough, parallel and independent studies. What is at stake is by no means trifling. We may never know exactly how Milton read or heard his poems—or what he understood to be the laws governing the meters in which he wrote. But the two are related. And it is certain that a great deal more can be found out than we have found out so far.

For the very bases of Milton's prosody, of sixteenth- and seventeenth-century accentual-syllabic prosody generally, remain in question. It has been shown how Bridges differs from Masson, and Saintsbury from Bridges; it has been suggested more briefly how Diekhoff and Sprott follow Bridges, but sometimes into contradiction and confusion. It has been remarked that Prince broke away—to return how far? to what position? What is the student today to think? Must he hope that the New Grammarians will serve him better than the prosodists who were essentially literary historians have done?

Without implying that contemporary investigations of the structure of English will prove to be without relevance—they may prove rather to be of central importance—it may be said that the literary historians have by no means exhausted the evidence available to them. Let the studies of verse form, and of everything that may help us to understand verse form, continue. What has been done is of great use. More is needed.

[96] A basic study of unusual interest is Professor E. J. Dobson's 'Milton's Pronunciation,' *Language and Style in Milton*, ed. Ronald David Emma and John T. Shawcross (New York: Frederick Ungar, 1967), 154–92.

[97] John T. Shawcross, 'The Manuscript of *Arcades*,' *N&Q*, n.s. 6 (1959), 359–64; 'Speculations on the Dating of the Trinity MS. of Milton's Poems,' *MLN* 75 (1960), 11–17; 'Establishment of a Text of Milton's Poems Through a Study of *Lycidas*,' *PBSA* 56 (1962), 317–31; and 'Henry Lawes's Settings of Songs for Milton's "Comus,"' *JRUL* 28 (1964), 22–8.

[98] John T. Shawcross, 'What We Can Learn from Milton's Spelling,' *HLQ* 26 (1963), 351–61.

Bibliographical Index

To keep the index from swelling into another volume, some restrictions have been necessary. It records only the first or the first major reference to authors and works cited in illustration of the substance or language of the poems. To this compiler it would seem meaningless to pile up rows of titles and page numbers for first (not to think of all) references to, say, fifty books of the Bible or thirty plays of Shakespeare or twenty masques of Jonson, and so on. But rigid consistency is impossible, and various writings of some authors are recorded. The first mention in the text indicates the edition used. Greek and Roman authors, while continually referred to in the commentary, are not indexed, since they are cited from the volumes in the Loeb Classical Library and since again names and titles and rows of page numbers would have little meaning in regard to classical influence.

For modern scholarly and critical books, articles, and essays, which may be cited more than once, bibliographical data are given with the first reference; the first major citation, if different, may also be noted. The index may give only a brief identification. For modern books that have been quoted the names of publishers are given ('U. P.' and 'U. ... P.' stand for University Press). The titles of many short articles and notes are not recorded in either text or index but their subjects are indicated. The index includes a few items not cited; most of these were seen too late for use.

Abbreviated Miltonic titles and numbers in square brackets, at the end of individual items, indicate the section or note in which the first or first major reference occurs. These are followed by page numbers in parentheses, which make consultation easier. Page numbers between 1007 and 1087 indicate new or repeated references by Edward Weismiller. The paging of the three volumes may be noted here: Part One, v–xvii, 1–338; Part Two, v–xi, 339–734; Part Three, v–xi, 735–1087.

For the reader's convenience and the further saving of space the index includes five special groups of entries: (1) under Milton, (a) the individual poems and the commentaries on them, and (b) editions of his works (complete, selected, and individual) that have been cited, in the alphabetical order of their editors' names; (2) and (3), under 'Lark' and 'tale, tells his,' commentators on the small problems raised by lines 45–6 and 67–8 of *L'Allegro*; (4) under 'engine,' participants in the endless debate over the crux in *Lycidas* 130–1; (5) under Psalms, English translators cited in the headnote and notes to *Psalms* 1–8, 80–8. Items listed in these groups are not recorded elsewhere in the index, apart from a few cited in other connections as well.

Stevens, David H. *Reference Guide to Milton from 1800 to the Present Day.* U. of Chicago P., 1930.

Fletcher, Harris F. *Contributions to a Milton Bibliography 1800–1930 Being a List of Addenda to Stevens's Reference Guide to Milton.* University of Illinois Studies in Language and Literature 16 (1931), 5–166; repr., New York: Russell, 1967.

Bateson, F. W., ed. *The Cambridge Bibliography of English Literature.* 4 v. Cambridge: U. P., 1940; New York: Macmillan, 1941. 'Milton': 1, 463–73. Rev. ed. of whole work in progress.

Hanford, James Holly, and C. W. Crupi. *Milton.* Goldentree Bibliographies. New York: Appleton-Century-Crofts, 1966.

Patrides, C. A. 'An Annotated Reading List.' *Milton's Epic Poetry* (Penguin, 1967), 381–428.

Huckabay, Calvin. *John Milton: An Annotated Bibliography 1929–1968.* Rev. ed. Pittsburgh: Duquesne U. P.; Louvain: Editions E. Nauwelaerts, 1969.

Bush, Douglas. 'Milton.' *English Poetry: Select Bibliographical Guides,* ed. A. E. Dyson. Oxford U.P., 1971.

A., R. *The Valiant Welshman.* [*L'All* 5] (272).

Abbott, Wilbur C. *The Writings and Speeches of Oliver Cromwell.* Harvard U. P.; Oxford U. P., v. 2, 1939 [*Sonn* 15. 10–13] (414).

Abercrombie, L. 'Drowsy Frighted Steeds' [*Comus* 552] (924); [*Sonn* 20. 13–14] (475).

Abrams, M. H. *Lycidas* (609).

Adams, H. H. 'The Development of the Flower Passage in "Lycidas" ' [*Lyc* 142–51] (713).

Adams, Robert M. 'Reading *Comus.*' *Ikon: John Milton and the Modern Critics.* Cornell U. P., 1955; Oxford U. P., 1956 (814, 1068); 'Bounding *Lycidas.*' *Hudson Review* 23 (1970), 293–304.

Adams, Robert P. *Lycidas* (583).

Bibliographical Index

Arthos, John. *On A Mask Presented at Ludlow-Castle by John Milton*, U. of Michigan P.; Oxford U. P., 1954 (759); 'Milton, Ficino, and the *Charmides*' [*Comus*] (781); 'Milton's Haemony and Virgil's Amellus,' *N&Q* 8 (1961), 172 [*Comus* 637] (933); 'The Realms of Being in the Epilogue of *Comus*,' *MLN* 76 (1961), 321–4 [*Comus* 1002–10] (986); 'Milton's Sabrina, Virgil and Porphyry,' *Anglia* 79 (1961–2), 204–13 [*Comus* 637] (933).

Ascham, Roger. *English Works*, ed. Wright [*Sonn* 9. 2–4] (381).

Athanasius, St. *Expositio in Psalmum 67. 34* [*Lyc* 167–73] (725).

Aubrey, John. *Brief Lives*, ed. Clark [*Sonn* 21] (477).

Auffret, J. *Lycidas* (632).

Augustine, St. *City of God* (Migne; L.C.L.; tr. J. Healey, rev., 2 v., London, 1945) [*Nat* 53–60] (74); *Confessions* [*Lyc* 130–1: I. b. 8] (692); *Enarratio in Psalmum 103, Sermo 3. 21* [*Lyc* 167–73] (725).

Austin, W. B. 'Milton's *Lycidas* and Two Latin Elegies by Giles Fletcher, the Elder' (561).

Axon, W. E. A. 'Milton's "Comus" and Fletcher's "Faithful Shepherdess" Compared' (759).

Babb, Lawrence. 'The Background of "Il Penseroso" ' (235); *The Elizabethan Malady: A Study of Melancholia in English Literature from 1580 to 1642*. East Lansing: Michigan State U. P.; Oxford: Blackwell, 1951 (235); *Sanity in Bedlam: A Study of Robert Burton's Anatomy of Melancholy*. East Lansing, 1959 (235).

Bacon, Francis. *Works*, ed. Spedding et al. [*Nat* 28] (68–9).

Badt, B. 'Miltons "Comus" und Peeles "Old wifes tale" ' (755).

Bagehot, Walter. 'John Milton' [*Comus*] (787–8).

Baïf, Antoine de. *E. 2* [*Lyc* 50–5] (653–4); *Euvres*, ed. Marty-Laveaux [*Lyc* 91] (668).

Bailey, John. *Milton*. London: Williams & Norgate; New York: Holt, 1915 [*Ps* 114, 136] (112).

Baillie, Robert. *A Dissuasive from the Errours Of the Time* [*NewF* 8, 9–12] (514–15).

Baines, A. H. J. 'The Topography of "L'Allegro" ' (227).

Baldwin, E. C. [*IlPen* 88–96] (325); 'Milton and *Ezekiel*' [*Lyc* 108–31] (676); 'Milton and the Psalms' (995).

Balter, C. A. [*Nat* 130] (87).

Banks, T. H. 'A Source for *Lycidas*: 154–158' [*Lyc* 157] (719–20).

Banquet Of Jests, A [*Carrier*] (214).

Barber, C. L. *Comus* (838).

Barclay, Alexander. *Eclogues*, ed. B. White [*Nat* 195] (100).

Barker, Arthur. *Nativity* (43, 1022); *Milton and the Puritan Dilemma 1641–1660.* U. of Toronto P.; London: Oxford U. P., 1942. [*NewF*] (508); ed. *Milton: Modern Essays in Criticism.* New York and London: Oxford U. P., 1965 (48).

Barnes, Barnabe. *Sonnets* [*Sonn* 19. 3] (465).

Barrett, J. A. S. *Lyc* 22 (646).

Bartlett's Familiar Quotations [*Sonn* 17. 8] (429).

Basil, St. *Hexaemeron* [*Nat* 68] (75).

Baskervill, C. R. 'Two Parallels to *Lycidas*' [*Lyc* 89–131] (667).

Basse, William [*Shak*] (208).

Bateson, F. W. *English Poetry: A Critical Introduction.* London and New York: Longmans, Green, 1950; 2nd ed., 1966 [*L'All* and *IlPen*] (253).

Battestin, M. C. 'John Crowe Ransom and *Lycidas*: A Reappraisal' (574, 1063).

Baumgartner, P. R. 'Milton and Patience' [*Sonn* 19] (456).

Baxter, Richard. *Directions to the Converted* [*Comus* 637] (937); *Reliquiae Baxterianae* [*Sonn* 17. 13–14] (430).

Beaumont, Francis. *Masque of the Inner Temple* [*Comus* 27–9] (861); *Poems* [*Lyc* 11] (643).

Beaumont, Francis and John Fletcher. *Comedies and Tragedies*; *Works*, ed. Dyce [*L'All* 119–24] (300); *Beaumont and Fletcher* [four plays], ed. Schelling. New York: American Book Co., 1912 [*Nat* 19–20] (66).

Beaumont, G. *Lyc* 68–9 (661).

Beaumont, Sir John. *Bosworth-field*; *Poems*, ed. Grosart [*Sonn* 20. 6] (474).

Becon, Thomas. *Catechism*, etc. [*Lyc* 116–17] (681).

Belloc, Hilaire. *Milton.* London: Cassell; Philadelphia: Lippincott, 1935 [*Comus*] (797).

Benlowes, Edward. *Theophila* [*Lyc* 130–1: I. b. 13] (694).

Bennett, A. L. 'The Principal Rhetorical Conventions in the Renaissance Personal Elegy' [*Lyc*] (550, n. 1).

Bennett, J. A. W. 'Milton's "Cato"' [*Sonn* 20. 13–14] (476).

Benoit de Sainte-Maure. *Le Roman de Troie*, ed. Constans [*IlPen* 17–18] (312).

Bense, J. F. 'The Conduct of the "Attendant Spirit" in *Comus*.' *Englische Studien* 46 (1912–13), 333–5 [*Comus* 507] (919); ' "Meliboeus old" in Milton's *Comus*.' *Neophilologus* 1 (1915), 62–4 [*Comus* 821] (957).

Bentley, Gerald E. *The Jacobean and Caroline Stage* [*Comus*] (740, n. 1).

Bercovitch, S. 'Milton's "Haemony"' [*Comus* 637] (933–4).

Berkeley, D. S. *Sonn* 18. 3–4 (439); 'The Revision of the Orpheus Passage in "Lycidas"' [*Lyc* 58–63] (658); *Lyc* 1 (639).

Berman, Ronald. *Henry King & The Seventeenth Century*. London: Chatto & Windus, 1964 [*Psalms*] (994).

Bernard of Morlais. *De Contemptu Mundi* [*Lyc* 108–31] (677).

Berni, Francesco. *Orlando Innamorato*. [*IlPen* 116–20] (329).

Berry, Francis. *Poetry and the Physical Voice*. London: Routledge, 1962 [*Nat* 197–220] (100).

Berry, L. E., ed. 'Five Latin Poems by Giles Fletcher, the Elder' [*Lyc*] (561).

Beum, R. *Lycidas* (612).

Bible: Translated according to the Ebrew and Greeke, The [Geneva Bible]. Ed. London, 1614 [*Lyc* 130–1: I. b. 12] (693).

Bible 1611, The Authorised Version of the English, ed. W. A. Wright. 5 v. Cambridge U. P., 1909 [*Nat* 21] (66).

Binyon, Laurence. 'A Note on Milton's Imagery and Rhythm.' *Seventeenth Century Studies Presented to Sir Herbert Grierson*. Clarendon Press, 1938 [*Ps* 2] (1001).

Blau, S. D. *Arcades* (529).

Blenner-Hassett, R. 'Geoffrey of Monmouth and Milton's *Comus*.' [*Comus* 823–31] (959); 'Geoffrey of Monmouth and Milton's *Comus*: A Problem in Composition' [*Comus* 823–31] (959).

Blondel, Jacques. 'Le Thème de la Tentation dans le *Comus* de Milton' (809); 'The Function of Mythology in *Comus*' (837). See also Milton, editions.

Blount, Thomas. *Glossographia* [*Comus* 60] (866).

Boas, George. *Sonn* 23 (492–3).

Boccaccio, Giovanni. *Filocolo* [*L'All* 122–4] (300); *Genealogie Deorum Gentilium*, ed. Romano [*IlPen* 103–8] (327); *Olympia* [*Lyc*] (556).

Boddy, Margaret. 'Milton's Translation of Psalms 80–88' (993).

Boethius, *Consolation of Philosophy* [*Lyc* 71] (663).

Boetius, Anselm. *Gemmarum et Lapidum Historia* [*Comus* 731–5] (947–8).

Bolton, Edmund [*Nat* 93–4] (81).

Boswell's Life of Johnson, ed. Hill and Powell [*Sonnets*] (344).

Bowers, F. T. *Textual and Literary Criticism* [*Lyc*] (574).

Bowers, R. H. *Comus* (815).

Boyette, P. E. *Comus* (851–2).

Bradford, John. *Writings*, ed. Townsend [*Sonn* 18. 3–4)] (439).

Carew, Thomas. *Poems*, ed. Dunlap. Clarendon Press, 1949 [*Nat* 146] (92); *Coelum Britannicum* [*Comus*] (762).

Carey, John. 'The Date of Milton's Italian Poems' (20); 'Milton's *Ad Patrem*, 35–37' [*Vac* 29–52] (143); *Milton*. London: Evans, 1969 [*Nat*] (62). See also Milton, editions.

Carlyle, Thomas. *Letters and Speeches of Oliver Cromwell*, ed. Lomas [*Psalms*] (994).

Carpenter, Nan C. Music in *L'All* and *IlPen* (256, 1035); *L'All* and *IlPen* and Spenser's *Epithalamion* (231).

Carpenter, Richard. *Experience, Historie, and Divinitie* [*Nat* 115] (83).

Carrithers, G. H. *Comus* (841).

Cartari, Vi[n]cenzo. *Le Vere e Nove Imagini de gli Dei delli Antichi*. Ed. Padua, 1615 [*FInf* 53–4] (133).

Cartwright, William. *Plays and Poems*, ed. Evans [*Sonn* 13. 11] (404).

Casa, Giovanni della [*Sonnets*] (343).

Caspari, Fritz. *Humanism...in Tudor England* [*Sonn* 11. 12–14] (392).

Cassirer, E., et al. *The Renaissance Philosophy of Man*. London: Cambridge U. P.; U. of Chicago P., 1948 [*IlPen* 45–54] (318).

Castiglione, B. *Alcon* [*Lyc*] (558).

Catonis Disticha De Moribus [*Sonn* 20. 13–14] (476).

Cavendish, George. *Cardinal Wolsey* [*Passion* 19] (157).

Cebes, Table of. Cebetis...Tabula, ed. J. Caselius (Leyden, 1618), etc.; tr. R. T. Clark, *The Characters of Theophrastos*, etc. London and New York, 1909 [*Comus* 1017–22] (988).

Chalmers, Alexander, ed. *Works of the English Poets*. 21 v. London, 1810 [*IlPen* 23–30] (314).

Chamberlain, The Letters of John, ed. N. E. McClure. 2 v. Philadelphia: American Philosophical Society, 1939 [*Ps* 114] (112, n. 1).

Chambers, Sir Edmund K., ed. *English Pastorals*. London: Blackie, 1895 [*Lyc*] (550): 'The Mask.' *The Elizabethan Stage*. 4 v. Clarendon Press, 1923 [*Comus*] (740, n. 1); *William Shakespeare: A Study of Facts and Problems*. 2 v. Clarendon Press, 1930 [*Shak*] (208).

Chapman, George. *Chapman's Homer*, ed. Nicoll. 2 v. New York: Pantheon Books, 1956; London: Routledge, 1957 [*Shak* 11] (210); *Plays and Poems: The Tragedies*, ed. Parrott. London: Routledge; New York: Dutton, 1910 [*Nat* 84] (78); *Poems*, ed. P. B. Bartlett. New York: Modern Language Association; London: Oxford U. P., 1941 [*Nat* 229–31] (107).

son; New York: Rinehart, 1957 [*Nat*] (53); 'Some Aspects of Milton's Pastoral Imagery.' *More Literary Essays*. Edinburgh and London: Oliver & Boyd, 1968 [*Nat* 32–44] (69–70).

Damon, S. F. 'Milton and Marston' [*L'All* 1–10] (270).

Daniel, Samuel. *Complete Works in Verse and Prose*, ed. Grosart [*Lyc* 161–2] (722); *Poems and A Defence of Ryme*, ed. Sprague [*Sonn* 9. 2–4] (381).

Daniells, Roy. *Milton, Mannerism and Baroque*. U. of Toronto P.; London: Oxford U. P., 1963 [*Lyc*] (619).

Daniels, Earl. *The Art of Reading Poetry*. New York: Farrar and Rinehart, 1941 [*Sonn* 19] (453).

Daniels, Edgar F. *Lyc* 29 (648); 'Climactic Rhythms in "Lycidas"' [*Lyc* 170] (727).

Dante. *Il Convivio*, ed. M. Simonelli; tr. Jackson [*Nat* 53–60] (74); *La Divina Commedia*, ed. Vandelli [*Nat* 46–52] (72); *The Divine Comedy*, tr. C. E. Norton. 3 v. Boston: Houghton Mifflin, 1902 [*Nat* 125–32] (86); *Rime*, ed. Contini [*Sonn* 10. 14] (386).

Darbishire, Helen, ed. *The Early Lives of Milton*. London: Constable, 1932; New York: Barnes & Noble, 1965 [*FInf*] (119); 'Milton's Poetic Language.' *Essays and Studies 1957*. London: John Murray [*Ps* 136] (115). See also Milton, editions.

Das Gupta, R. K. 'Milton on Shakespeare' (207).

Davenant, Sir William. *The Witts* [*Shak* 13–14] (212); *Dramatic Works* [*Arc* 14–19] (532).

David, W. H. 'Penseroso' [*IlPen*, Title] (309).

Davidson, Audrey. 'Milton on the Music of Henry Lawes' [*Sonn* 13] (402).

Davies, Sir John. *Poems*, ed. Howard. New York: Columbia U. P.; London: Oxford U. P., 1941 [*Comus* 143–4] (881).

Davies of Hereford, John. *Complete Works*, ed. Grosart [*Comus* 546] (922).

Davies, W. 'Milton's Sonnets' [*Sonn* 14] (407).

Davison, Francis, ed. *A Poetical Rhapsody*, ed. H. E. Rollins. 2 v. Harvard U. P.; Oxford U. P., 1931 [*Nat* 128] (87).

Day, Mabel. *IlPen* 17–18 (312); 'Milton and Lydgate' [*IlPen* 17–18] (312).

De Beer, E. S. 'St. Peter in "Lycidas"' [*Lyc* 128–9] (686); 'Milton's Old Damaetas' [*Lyc* 23–36] (647).

Dekker, Thomas. *Dramatic Works*, ed. Bowers [*Nat* 136] (89); *The Gull's Hornbook*, ed. McKerrow. London: De la More Press, 1904 [*Comus*] (772); *The Guls Hornbook and The Belman of London*. London: Dent,

Doyno, V. [*Comus* 145–68] (881).

Drayton, Michael. *Complete Works*, ed. Hebel et al. Oxford: Blackwell [*Nat*] (39); *Poly-Olbion*: v. 4 of *Works* [cited as *Poly.*] [*Vac* 91–100] (148).

Drummond, William. *Poetical Works*, ed. Kastner. Edinburgh and London: Blackwood, 1913 [*Nat* 1] (64); *Teares...Moeliades* [*Lyc*] (562–3).

Drury, William. *Alvredus sive Alfredus: Tragicocomoedia*. Douay, 1620 [*Comus*] (758).

Dryden, John. *Poems*, ed. J. Kinsley. 4 v. Clarendon Press, 1958 [*L'All* 67–8] (287); *Essays*, ed. Ker [*Comus* 821] (957).

Du Moulin, Peter [*Psalms*] (993).

Duncan-Jones, E. E. ' "Lycidas" and Lucan' [*Lyc*, Title] (637).

Dunster, Charles. *Considerations on Milton's Early Reading*, etc. [*Nat* 14] (65); 'Dunster MS.' [*Comus* 1–4] (855).

Dyson, A. E. *Comus. Essays and Studies 1955*. London: John Murray (819).

Earle, John. *Micro-cosmographie*, ed. G. Murphy. London: Golden Cockerel Press, 1928 [*Hobsons Epitaph* 2–6] (222).

Edwards, Thomas. *Antapologia* [*NewF*] (511); *The Casting Down of the last and strongest hold of Satan* [*NewF*] (511); *Gangraena* [*Sonn* 12. 8–12] (389).

Eisler, R. [*Comus* 1–4] *TLS*, 22 Sept. 1945, 451 (854).

ELH. Critical Essays on Milton from. Baltimore and London: Johns Hopkins Press, 1969 [includes essays on *Comus* by Carrithers, Neuse, Wilkenfeld (q. v.)].

Eliot, T. S. 'A Note on the Verse of John Milton.' *Essays and Studies* 21. London: Oxford U. P., 1936 [*L'All* and *IlPen*] (245–6); [*Lyc* 152–62] (717, 1073); 'Milton.' *Proc. Brit. Academy* 33. London: Oxford U. P., 1947 (1068). Both pieces repr. in *On Poetry and Poets*. London: Faber; New York: Farrar, Straus and Cudahy, 1957; *The Waste Land. Collected Poems*. London: Faber; New York: Harcourt, Brace, 1936 [*L'All* 35–6] (279).

Elledge, Scott. 'Milton, Sappho (?), and Demetrius' [*Sonn* 1. 6] (360). See also Milton, editions.

Ellmann, Richard. *The Identity of Yeats* [*Lyc* 164] (725).

Ellrodt, Robert. *Neoplatonism in the Poetry of Spenser*. Geneva: E. Droz, 1960 [*Comus* 1002–10] (985).

Ellwood, The History of the Life of Thomas [*Comus* 706–7] (944).

Elmen, Paul. 'Shakespeare's Gentle Hours' [*Sonn* 1. 4] (360).

Elton, Oliver. *The English Muse* [*Lyc*] (571). See also Milton, editions.

Elton, W. 'Two Milton Notes' [*L'All* 1–10; *Lyc* 119] (271, 682).

d'Embry, A. T. *Les Images ou Tableaux...des...Philostrates* [*Comus* 143–4] (880).

Emerson, F. W. 'Cambuscan' and 'Camball' [*IlPen* 109–15] (328).

Emerson, O. F. 'The Shepherd's Star in English Poetry' [*Comus* 93–4] (871); 'Milton's *Comus*, 93–94' (872).

Emma, R. D. and J. T. Shawcross, eds. *Language and Style in Milton* (1087).

Empson, William. *Some Versions of Pastoral*. London: Chatto & Windus, 1935, 1950; Norfolk, Conn.: New Directions, 1950 [*Nat* 74] (77); review of C. Brooks' *Well Wrought Urn*, *Sewanee Review* 55, 1947 [*L'All* and *IlPen*] (252).

Emslie, M. 'Milton on Lawes: The Trinity MS Revisions' [*Sonn* 13] (402).

'engine, that two-handed' (*Lyc* 130–1). The fullest lists of interpretations hitherto printed are those of Patrides (*Milton's Lycidas*, 1961, 241) and Elledge (*Milton's "Lycidas,"* 1966, 293–7); cf. Carey, 238–9. The present list is presumably not complete, 'but 'tis enough, 'twill serve.' Parenthetical symbols at the end of each item indicate the place in the long note on lines 130–1 where the commentator's view is recorded. Names with dates but without bibliographical references are those of editors, whose works may be identified from the list of editions indexed below under 'Milton.' Page references for the various sections are: I. a (688); I. b (689); I. c (696); I. d (697); I. e (699); II (702).

J. Auffret, *Anglia* 87, 1969, 34 (I. e. 8); E. C. Baldwin, *MLN* 33, 1918, 211–15 (I. b. 3); H. Beckett, *TLS*, 3 July 1943, 319 (I. a. 3); William Bell, 1889 f. (I. a. 2); C. W. Brodribb, *TLS*, 12 June 1930, 496; ibid. 5 June 1943, 271 (I. d. 3); E. L. Brooks, *N&Q* 3, 1956, 67–8 (I. e. 7); R. C. Browne, 1870, 1894 (I. a. 2); A. H. T. Clarke, *TLS*, 11 April 1929, 295 (I. b. 7); K. N. Colvile, *TLS*, 22 Nov. 1928, 909–10 (II. 2); L. W. Coolidge, *PQ* 29, 1950, 444–5 (I. d. 3); M.D., *Athenaeum*, 28 April 1906, 515 (I. d. 4); R. Daniells, *Milton*, 1963, 40–1 (I. b. 5); E. S. de Beer, *RES* 23, 1947, 60–3 (I. b. 4); D. C. Dorian, *PMLA* 45, 1930, 204–15 (I. c. 3); W. R. Dunstan, *TLS*, 12 June 1943, 283 (I. b. 1); O. Elton, 1893 (I. c. 2); K. A. Esdaile, *TLS*, 19 June 1943, 295 (I. d. 4); M. Fixler, *Milton*, 1964, 60–1 (I. b. 14); H. F. Fletcher, 1941 (I. b. 2); J. M. French, *MLN* 68, 1953, 229–31 (I. e. 1); N. Frye, 1951 (I. e. 6); E. S. Fussell, *N&Q* 193, 1948, 338–9 (I.e. 8); W. J. Grace, *SP* 52, 1955, 583–9 (II. 4); J. W. Hales, 1872 (I. a. 2); J. H. Hanford, 1936, 1953 (I. b. 5); G. M. Harper, *TLS*, 16 June 1927, 424 (II. 1); N. W. Hill, *TLS*, 28 July 1927, 520 (I. e. 8);

L. Howard, *HLQ* 15, 1951–2, 173–84 (I. b. 12); M. Y. Hughes, 1937, 1957 (I. c. 2); R. E. Hughes, *N&Q* 2, 1955, 58–9 (I. b. 8); M. Hussey, *N&Q* 193, 1948, 503 (I. b. 11); C.M.I., *N&Q*, Ser. 6, 12, 1885, 351 (I. b. 5); C. S. Jerram, 1874, 1881 (I. a. 2); T. Keightley, 1859 (I. a. 2, I. b. 1, I. c. 1); M. Kelley, *N&Q* 181, 1941, 273 (I. b. 5); H.L., *Athenaeum*, 30 June 1900, 815 (I. b. 1); E. S. Le Comte, *SP* 47, 1950, 589–606; ibid. 49, 1952, 548–50 (I. b. 5 and 6, I. e. 1); J. B. Leishman, *Minor Poems*, 1969, 276 (I. b. 4); G. G. Loane, *TLS*, 25 April 1929, 338; *N&Q* 181, 1941, 320 (I. a. 3); I. G. MacCaffrey, 1966 (I. b. 5); M. Mack, 1950 (I. b. 2); E. L. Marilla, *PMLA* 67, 1952, 1181–4 (I. e. 4); D. Masson, 1874 f., 1890 (I. c. 2); J. Mitford, 1834–5 (I. a. 3); W. V. Moody, 1899 (I. a. 2); H. Mutschmann, *TLS*, 25 April 1936, 356; ibid. 15 Aug., 664; *N&Q* 2, 1955, 515 (I. b. 7); T. Newton, 1761–2 (I. a. 1); M. H. Nicolson, *John Milton*, 1963, 99–100 (I. b. 5); C. G. Osgood, *RES* 1, 1925, 339–41 (I. d. 1); F. A. Patterson, 1933 (I. c. 3); M. Pattison, 1883 (I. b. 9); A. F. Pollard, *TLS*, 29 Aug. 1936, 697 (I. b. 7); G. H. Powell, *Athenaeum*, 5 May 1906, 547 (I. a. 3); F. T. Prince, 1968 (I. b. 3); J. Reesing, *Milton's Poetic Art*, 1968, 31–49 (I. d. 3); B. R. Rhodes, *N&Q* 13, 1966, 24 (I. b. 14); H. F. Robins, *RES* 5, 1954, 25–36 (*Lyc* 108–31 n. and I. e. 5); W. J. Rolfe, 1887 (I. a. 2, I. c. 1); M. M. Ross, *HLQ* 14, 1950–1, 146 (I. c. 3); E. Saillens, *Milton*, 1964, 62 (I. b. 2, I. c. 2); R. J. Schoeck, *N&Q* 2, 1955, 235–7 (I. b. 8); J. T. Shawcross, 1963 (I. b. 5); G. N. Shuster, *English Ode*, 1940, 74 (II. 3); Nowell Smith, *TLS*, 6 Dec. 1928, 965 (II. 5); D. A. Stauffer, *MLR* 31, 1936, 57–60 (I. b. 7, I. c. 2); J. M. Steadman, *N&Q* 3, 1956, 249–50 (I. b. 13); ibid. 335 (I. d. 1); ibid. 7, 1960, 237 (I. b. 13); D. Stempel, *ELN* 3, 1965–6, 259–63 (I. b. 15); T. B. Stroup, *N&Q* 6, 1959, 366–7 (I. e. 3); M. H. Studley, *English Journal* 26, 1937, 148–51 (I. d. 3); K. M. Swaim, *Milton Studies II*, 1970, 119–29 (I. e. 9); C. A. Thompson, *SP* 59, 1962, 184–200 (I. e. 8); E. M. W. Tillyard, *Milton*, 1930, 387, and E. M. W. and P. B. Tillyard, 1952 (I. d. 2); H. J. Todd, 5th ed., 1852 (I. a. 2); K. C. Tomlinson, *TLS*, 12 June 1943, 283 (I. d. 4); M. C. Treip, *N&Q* 6, 1959, 364–6 (I. b. 5); W. P. Trent, 1897 (I. a. 2); G. M. Trevelyan, *TLS*, 25 April 1929, 338 (I. b. 7, I. c. 2); W. Tuckwell, "*Lycidas*", 1911 (I. a. 3); W. A. Turner, *JEGP* 49, 1950, 562–5 (I. e. 2); R. Tuve, *Images*, 1957, 78 (I. e. 5); E. Tuveson, *JHI* 27, 1966, 447–58 (*Lyc* 108–31 n. and I. b. 16); H. van Tromp, *TLS*, 25 April 1929, 338 (I. b. 9); A. W. Verity, 1891, 1898 f. (I. b. 2); E. H. Visiak, [1938] (I. a. 2); W. Warburton (in Warton) (I. b. 1); C. A. Ward, *N&Q*, Ser. 6,

Gilbert, Allan H. *A Geographical Dictionary of Milton.* Yale U. P., 1919 [*Vac* 91–100] (148); *The Symbolic Persons in the Masques of Ben Jonson* [*L'All* 17–14] (275); 'Is *Samson Agonistes* Unfinished?' *PQ* 28 (1949), 98–106 (31); *Lyc* 11 (643).

Gill, Alexander [*Lyc* 130–1] (692).

Gilles, Peter [*Sonn* 18] (431).

Giraldus (Gyraldus), Lilius G. *Historiae Deorum. Opera.* Basle, 1580 [*Comus*] (770); *Syntagma deorum. Opera.* Leyden, 1696 [*FInf* 53–4] (133).

Glassford, James, ed. *Lyrical Compositions from the Italian Poets* [*Sonnets*] (343, 1077).

Godolphin, F. R. B. *Lyc* and Propertius 3. 7 (554, n. 9).

Godolphin, Sidney. *Poems*, ed. Dighton [*Nat* 92] (81).

Godwin, Thomas. *Moses and Aaron* [*NewF* 15–17] (516).

Golding, Arthur, tr. *Shakespeare's Ovid...the Metamorphoses*, ed. W. H. D. Rouse. London, 1904 [*Comus* 635–6] (932).

Golding, Sanford. 'The Sources of the *Theatrum Poetarum*' [by Edward Phillips] [*L'All* 131–4] (303).

Goodman, Paul. *The Structure of Literature.* U. of Chicago P.; Cambridge U. P., 1954 [*Sonn* 19] (454).

Goodwin, Thomas, et al. *An Apologeticall Narration* [*NewF*] (510–11).

Googe, Barnabe. *Eglogs, Epytaphes, & Sonettes*, ed. Arber [*IlPen* 4] (310).

Gorboduc. In *Early English Classical Tragedies*, ed. J. W. Cunliffe. Oxford, 1912 [*Lyc* 75] (664).

Gossman, Ann, and G. W. Whiting. '*Comus*, Once More, 1761' (754–5); *Sonn* 19 (456).

Gottfried, R. B. 'Milton and Poliziano' [*Lyc* 58–63] (658).

Grace, William J. 'Notes on Robert Burton and John Milton' [*L'All* and *IlPen*] (234); *Ideas in Milton.* Notre Dame and London: U. of Notre Dame P., 1968 [*Nat* 133–48] (89).

Grant, W. Leonard. *Neo-Latin Literature and the Pastoral* [*Lyc* II] (550, n. 1).

Graves, Robert. 'The Ghost of Milton.' *The Common Asphodel.* London: Hamish Hamilton, 1949; repr. in *The Crowning Privilege.* New York: Doubleday, 1956 [*Lycidas*] (578); *The Clark Lectures, 1954–1955*, in *The Crowning Privilege* (1048); 'Legitimate Criticism of Poetry.' *5 Pens in Hand.* Doubleday, 1958 [*L'All* and *IlPen*] (261).

Greene, D. *Lyc* 68–9 (661).

Greene, Robert. *Plays and Poems*, ed. Collins [*Lyc* 89–131] (667).

Greene, Thomas. *The Descent from Heaven: A Study in Epic Continuity.* New Haven and London: Yale U. P., 1963 (33, n. 4).

Greene, William C. *Moira: Fate, Good, and Evil in Greek Thought* [*Lyc* 75] (664).

Greg, Sir Walter W. *Pastoral Poetry and Pastoral Drama.* London: A. H. Bullen, 1906 [*Comus*] (791); *A Bibliography of the English Printed Drama to the Restoration* [*Shak*] (203).

Gregory, E. R. *L'All* and *IlPen* (269).

Grierson, Sir Herbert J. C. *The First Half of the Seventeenth Century.* Edinburgh: Blackwood; New York: Scribner, 1906 [*Nat*] (36); ed. *Metaphysical Lyrics & Poems of The Seventeenth Century.* Clarendon Press, 1921 [*Nat*] (36); *Sonn* 14. 12 (409); *Cross Currents in English Literature of the XVIIth Century.* London: Chatto & Windus, 1929; New York: Harper, 1958 [*Nat* 37–44] (70); with J. C. Smith, *A Critical History of English Poetry.* London, 1944 [*Lyc*] (571). See also Milton, editions.

Grierson, Seventeenth Century Studies Presented to Sir Herbert. Clarendon Press, 1938 [*Vac*] (139).

Griffin, Bartholomew. *Fidessa* [*Sonn* 23] (491).

Grillo, Angelo. *Lettere* [*Lyc* 71] (663).

Grim the Collier of Croydon [*L'All* 107–9] (297).

Gros Louis, K. R. R. 'The Triumph and Death of Orpheus in the English Renaissance' [*IlPen* 103–8] (327).

Grove's Dictionary of Music and Musicians, ed. Eric Bloom. 5th ed. 10 v. London and New York, 1954–61 [*L'All* 94] (293).

Grundy, Joan. 'Brave Translunary Things.' *MLR* 59 (1964), 501–10 [*Lyc* 70] (663).

Guarini, G. B. *Pastor Fido* [*Comus*] (775).

Guest, Edwin. *History of English Rhythms,* ed. Skeat (1011).

Guido de Columnis. *Historia Destructionis Troiae,* ed. Griffin [*IlPen* 17–18] (312).

Guilpin, Everard. *Skialetheia,* ed. Harrison [*L'All* and *IlPen*] (231).

Gummere, F. B. Review of J. Schipper, *Englische Metrik* (1031).

Guss, D. L. *John Donne, Petrarchist.* Wayne State U. P., 1966 [*Circum* 8–9] (173).

Gyraldus. See Giraldus.

H., C. E. et al. 'The Pansy Freaked with Jet' [*Lyc* 144] (715).

Habington, William. *Castara,* ed. Arber; *Poems,* ed. Allott [*L'All* and *IlPen*] (229).

(305); 'Spenser's Acrasia and the Circe of the Renaissance' [*Comus*] (755); 'The Arthurs of *The Faerie Queene.*' *Études Anglaises* 6 (1953), 193–213 [*Nat* 227–8] (106); '"Devils to Adore for Deities"' [*Nat* 173] (97). See also Milton, editions.

Humphreys-Edwards, Julia. *IlPen* 93–4 [*IlPen* 88–96] (326).

Hunt, R. W. See below, W. R. Parker, *TLS*, 13 Sept. 1957.

Hunter, W. B. 'The Sources of Milton's Prosody' [*Ps* 136] (113, 1081–2); *Lyc* 127 (685); 'New Words in Milton's English Poems' [cited as 'New Words'] [*Nat* 42] (71); 'Milton Translates the Psalms' (992–3, 1083); 'Milton and the Waldensians.' *SEL* 11 (1971), 153–64.

Huntley, F. L. *Lyc* 113–31 and folklore. *MiltonN* 1 (1967), 53–5 [*Lyc* 108–31] (678).

Huntley, J. F. *Sonn* 19 (458); 'Milton's 23rd Sonnet' (498).

Hurd, Richard [*IlPen* 45–54] (318); [*Lyc*] (1064).

Hurt, J. R. '*Lycidas*: Toward a Variorum Edition.' Thesis, University of Kentucky, 1957 [*Lyc* 130–1] (686).

Hussey, R. *Shak* 13–14 (212).

Hutton, James. 'Some English Poems in Praise of Music' [*Nat* 125–32] (85–6).

Hyginus [*IlPen* 19–21] (312).

Hyman, L. *Sonn* 18 (437); 'Christ's Nativity and the Pagan Deities' [*Nat* 173] (97).

Jackson, Elizabeth. *Sonn* 20. 13–14 (475).

Jackson, J. L. and W. E. Weese. *Sonn* 19. 14 (468).

Jacobs, J. 'Childe Rowland' [*Comus*] (758).

Jarrett-Kerr, M. 'Milton, Poet and Paraphrast' [*Psalms*] (997).

Jayne, Sears. *Comus* (781, 830–1).

Jerome, St. *Ad Principiam Virginem* [*Comus* 437–9] (913); *Commentarius in Ecclesiasten* [*Lyc* 167–73] (725); *In Isaiam Prophetam* [*Nat* 53–60] (73–4).

John of Salisbury. *Entheticus* and *Policraticus* [*Lyc* 71] (663).

Johnson, Robert. *The Travellers Breviat.* 1601 [*L'All* 119–24] (300).

Johnson, Samuel. *Lives of the English Poets*, ed. Hill. 3 v. Clarendon Press, 1905 [*L'All* and *IlPen*] (241–2, 1046).

Jones, E. B. C. *L'All* 28 (277).

Jones, Katherine. *Lycidas* (615).

Jones, W. M. [*FInf*] *Myth and Symbol*, ed. B. Slote. U. of Nebraska P., 1963 (124).

Jones-Davies, M. T. Sabrina [*Comus* 823–31] (959).

Ben Jonson, ed. C. H. Herford and P. and E. Simpson. 11 v. Clarendon Press, 1925–52 [*Nat* 46–52] (72); *Pleasure reconcild to Vertue* [*Comus*] (752–3).

Jordan, Thomas. *The Muses Melody* [*IlPen* 163] (336).

Jordan, Wilbur K. *The Development of Religious Toleration in England...* *1640–1660* [*NewF*] (508).

Josephus. *The Jewish War* [*Comus* 4] (856).

Julian, John. *Dictionary of Hymnology*. London, 1925 (first pub. 1892) [*Psalms*] (998).

Kane, R. J. *Lyc* 119 (682).

Kastor, F. S. *Nativity* (60).

Keats, John. *Letters*, ed. Rollins [*L'All* 138] (306); *Ode to a Nightingale* [*Lyc*] (573).

Keightley, Thomas. *The Fairy Mythology* [*L'All* 104] (296); *An Account of the Life, Opinions, and Writings of John Milton* [*Lyc*] (1070). See also Milton, editions.

Kelley, Maurice. 'Milton and Machiavelli's *Discorsi*' [*Sonn* 17. 8] (429); *Sonn* 19 (444); 'Milton's Later Sonnets and the Cambridge Manuscript' (340). See also below, W. R. Parker, *TLS*, 13 Sept. 1957.

Kellog, G. A. 'Bridges' *Milton's Prosody* and Renaissance Metrical Theory' [*Psalms*] (1002, 1082, n. 87).

Kelly, L. G. *Lycidas* (564).

Kemp, L. *Sonn* 19 (453).

Kendall, L. H. *Lyc* 163 (723); *Sonn* 19 and Wither (463).

Kendrick, Sir Thomas D. *British Antiquity* [*Comus* 921–2] (970).

Ker, W. P. *Form and Style in Poetry*, ed. R. W. Chambers. London: Macmillan, 1928; New York: Russell, 1966 [*Lyc*] (570); [*L'All* and *IlPen*] (1031, n. 30).

Kermode, Frank, ed. *English Pastoral Poetry From the Beginnings to Marvell*. London and New York, 1952 [*Lyc*] (551, n. 3); ed. *The Living Milton: Essays by Various Hands*. London: Routledge, 1960; New York: Macmillan, 1961; Barnes and Noble, 1968 [*Nat*] (54).

Killeen, J. F. *Lyc* 144 (715).

King, Edward [*Lyc*] (544).

King, Henry. *Obsequies...Edward King* [*Lyc* 97–102] (669).

King, Henry (bishop). Elegy on Donne [*Lyc* 151] (717); *The Exequy* [*Sonn* 23. 1] (499).

Lathum, William [*Lyc* 142–51] (713).

Laud, William [*Lyc* 108–31] (673).

Lavater, Lewes. *Of ghostes and spirites walking by nyght* [*Nat* 89] (80).

Lawes, Henry. [*Sonn* 13] (399–405); *Ayres and Dialogues* [*L'All* 136] (305).

Lawes, Henry and William. *Choice Psalmes put into Musick*. [*Sonn* 13] (399–400).

Lawrence, Edward [*Sonn* 20] (470–6).

Lawrence, Henry [*Sonn* 20] (470).

Lawry, Jon S. *Lycidas* (615); *The Shadow of Heaven: Matter and Stance in Milton's Poetry*. Cornell U. P., 1968 [*Nat*] (60).

Leach, A. F. 'Milton as Schoolboy and Schoolmaster' [*Nat*] (35).

Leahy, W. 'Pollution and *Comus*' (832).

Leavis, F. R. 'Milton's Verse.' *Scrutiny* 2 (1933–4), 123–36; repr. in *Revaluation: Transition and Development in English Poetry*. London: Chatto & Windus, 1936; New York: G. W. Stewart, 1947; Norton, 1963 [*Lyc* 152–62] (717, 1073).

Le Comte, Edward S. 'New Light on the "Haemony" Passage in *Comus*' [*Comus* 637] (934); 'Milton: Two Verbal Parallels' [*Comus* 115] (876); *Yet Once More: Verbal and Psychological Pattern in Milton*. New York: Liberal Arts Press, 1953 [*L'All* and *IlPen*] (226); 'The Veiled Face of Milton's Wife' [*Sonn* 23. 9–10] (500); '*Lycidas*, Petrarch, and the Plague' [*Lyc* 127] (685); *A Milton Dictionary*. New York: Philosophical Library, 1961 [*Sonnets*] (339); 'Milton as Satirist and Wit' [*Ps* 114] (112, n. 1); *Lyc* 68–9 (661).

Lee, Sir Sidney, ed. *Elizabethan Sonnets* [*Sonn* 23] (491).

Lefkowitz, M. *William Lawes*. London: Routledge, 1960 [*Sonn* 13] (401).

Legouis, Emile and L. Cazamian. *Histoire de la littérature anglaise*. Paris: Hachette, 1924 [*Lyc*] (571).

Leishman, J. B. '*L'Allegro* and *Il Penseroso* in Their Relation to Seventeenth-Century Poetry.' *Essays and Studies 1951*. London: John Murray: repr. in Leishman's *Milton's Minor Poems* (below) (226); *Translating Horace: Thirty Odes translated into the original metres with the Latin text and an Introductory and Critical Essay*. Oxford: B. Cassirer, 1956 [*Hor*] (506); *Milton's Minor Poems*, ed. G. Tillotson. London: Hutchinson, 1969; U. of Pittsburgh P., 1971 [*L'All* and *IlPen*] (226).

Lendrum, W. T. 'Milton and Pindar' [*Sonn* 7. 10–12] (371).

Levin, Harry. 'The Golden Age and the Renaissance'; *The Myth of the Golden Age in the Renaissance* [*Nat* 133–48] (89).

Lewis, C. S. 'A Note on *Comus*'; repr. in his *Studies* (below) (796–7); 'Variation in Shakespeare and Others.' *Rehabilitations and Other Essays*. London and New York: Oxford U. P., 1939 [*Comus* 392–6] (908); [*Comus* 1–4] *TLS*, 14 July 1945, 331; 29 Sept., 463 (854); review of Ellrodt (q.v.) [*Comus* 1002–10] (985–6); *Studies in Medieval and Renaissance Literature*, ed. W. Hooper. London and New York: Cambridge U. P., 1966 [*Comus*] (796).

Lewis, Wyndham. *The Lion and the Fox*. London: Grant Richards, 1927; Methuen, 1955; New York: Harper 1927; Barnes & Noble, 1966 [*Comus*] (794).

Ley, Lady Margaret [*Sonn* 10] (383).

Lhuyd, Humphrey. [*Lyc* 52–3] (655).

Lievsay, J. L. 'Milton among the Nightingales' [*Sonn* 1] (357).

Linche, Richard. *Diella* [*Sonn* 23] (491); *The Fountaine of Ancient Fiction* [*Comus*] (770).

L'isle, William. *A Saxon Treatise concerning the Old and New Testament* [*Nat* 47–8] (72).

Lloyd, Michael. '*Justa Edouardo King*.' *N&Q* 5 (1958), 432–4 (546); ' "Comus" and Plutarch's Daemons' [*Comus*, 1st Direction] (853); 'The Fatal Bark' [*Lyc* 75] (664); 'The Two Worlds of "Lycidas" ' (612).

Loane, G. G. *L'All* 2–3 (271); *L'All* 48 (285); *Lyc* 100–1 (670).

Lockwood, Laura E. *Lexicon to the English Poetical Works of John Milton*. New York and London: Macmillan, 1907 [*Nat* 52] (73); 'Milton's Corrections to the *Minor Poems*' [*SolMus* 3] (185); [*Comus*] (1040).

Locrine, The Tragedy of, ed. McKerrow [*L'All* 8–9] (273).

Lodge, Thomas. *The Tragicall Complaint of Elstred* [*Comus* 823–31] (959).

Lok, Henry, *Poems*, ed. Grosart [*Sonn* 19] (459).

Lovejoy, Arthur O., and G. Boas. *Primitivism and Related Ideas in Antiquity* [*Nat* 133–48] (89).

Lovelace, Richard. *Poems*, ed. Wilkinson. Clarendon Press, 1930 [*Passion* 48–9] (161).

Lowes, J. L. ' "L'Allegro" and "The Passionate Shepheard" ' (230).

Lumiansky, R. M. 'Milton's English Again' [*L'All* and *IlPen*] (248).

Lydgate, John. *Lydgate's Troy Book*, ed. Bergen. E.E.T.S., 1906–35 [*IlPen* 17–18] (312).

Lyly, John. *Euphues*, ed. Arber [*Nat* 53–60] (74); *Works*, ed. Bond. 3 v. Clarendon Press, 1902 [*L'All* 27] (277).

Lynskey, W. J. C. Ransom on *Lycidas* (574).

Lyte, Henry. *A New Herball* [*Lyc* 143] (714–15).

Markham, Gervase. *The Dumb Knight* [*Nat* 128] (87).

Marks, E. R. *Lycidas* (591, n. 1).

Marlowe, Christopher. *Works*, ed. Brooke. Clarendon Press, 1910 [*Nat* 59] (74).

Marot, Clément [*Lyc* 1–2] (640).

Marshall, G. O. [*Lyc* 20] (646).

Marshall, L. B. 'William Lathum' [*Lyc* 142–51] (713).

Marston. John. *Poems*, ed. Davenport. Liverpool U. P., 1961 [*Nat* 14] (65); *Plays*, ed. Wood [*Lyc* 19] (646); *The...Lord & Lady of Huntingdons Entertainment of Alice: Countesse Dowager of Darby* [*Arc*] (522).

Martin, L. C. 'Thomas Warton and the Early Poems of Milton' (xi, n. 1).

Martz, Louis L. *The Poetry of Meditation*. Yale U. P.; Oxford U. P., 1954; Yale U. P., 1962 [*Nat*] (50–1); 'The Rising Poet, 1645' [*Nat*] (57).

Marvell, Andrew. *Poems*, ed. Macdonald. Routledge; Harvard U. P., 1952 [*Sonn* 15. 6–8] (412).

Massinger, Philip. *Plays*, ed. Cunningham [*Shak* 7–14] (210).

Masson, David. *The Life of John Milton*. 6 v. London and New York: Macmillan, 1859–80, wth rev. edns. of vols. 1–3 and an Index, 1881–96 (16, n. 2). See also Milton, editions.

Masterman, J. H. B. *The Age of Milton* [*Lyc*] (569).

Maxwell, J. C. 'The Pseudo-Problem of *Comus*' (807); *Comus* 37 (863); 'Milton's "Cato" ' [*Sonn* 20. 13–14] (476).

May, Thomas, tr. Lucan [*IlPen* 142–6] (332); *The Reigne Of King Henry the Second* [*Comus* 214] (889).

Mayerson, Caroline W. 'The Orpheus Image in *Lycidas*' (584).

Mead (Mede), Joseph [*Lyc* 23–36] (647).

Meagher, John C. *Method and Meaning in Jonson's Masques* [*Comus*] (740, n. 1).

Mercator, Gerhard. *Atlas* [*Lyc* 161–2] (722).

Merivale, Patricia. *Pan the Goat-God: His Myth in Modern Times* [*Nat* 89] (80).

Michael, P. *Lyc* 186–93 (731).

Middleton, Thomas. *A Game at Chesse*, ed. Bald [*Lyc* 26] (648).

Migne, Jacques P., ed. *Patrologia Graeca*. 162 v. Paris, 1857–66, with Index, 1912 [*Nat* 68] (75); *Patrologia Latina*. 221 v. Paris, 1844–64 [*Nat* 53–60] (73).

Miles, Josephine. 'The Primary Language of *Lycidas*' (581).

Miller, David M. "From Delusion to Illumination: A Larger Structure for *L'Allegro-Il Penseroso*." *PMLA* 86 (1971), 32–9.

Miller, Milton. 'Milton's Imagination and the Idyllic Solution' [*Comus*] (808).

b. Editions

The following list, beginning with the editions of Milton's lifetime, records all editions of the complete, selected, and individual poems that are cited in the commentary above (first reference only), in the alphabetical order of their editors' names.

A Maske Presented At Ludlow Castle, 1634 [With a dedicatory epistle from Henry Lawes to 'John Lord Vicount Bracly, Son and heire apparent to the Earle of Bridgewater'] London, 1637 (853).

Justa Edouardo King naufrago, ab Amicis moerentibus...[English section headed: *Obsequies to the memorie of Mr Edward King*]. Cambridge, 1638 (546). See Mossner below.

Poems of Mr. John Milton, both English and Latin, Compos'd at several times. London: Humphrey Moseley, 1645. (30) [Reproduced in 'type-facsimile' (Clarendon Press, 1924); in facsimile by Noel Douglas (1926), without the Latin and Greek poems; by H. F. Fletcher (see below); and by the Scolar Press (1968; and a 1970 edition including the 1638 *Lycidas*)].

Poems, &c. upon Several Occasions. By Mr. John Milton: Both English and Latin, &c. Composed at several times. With a small Tractate of Education To Mr. Hartlib. London, 1673 (11).

Beeching, H. C. *Paradise Lost, Book I.* Oxford, 1887 (1015).
— *Poetical Works.* Clarendon Press, 1900 [*Comus* 552] (924).
Bell, William. *Nativity Ode, Lycidas, Sonnets, &c.* London: Macmillan, 1929 (first pub. 1889). [*Nat* 140] (91).
— *Comus.* London: Macmillan, 1921 (first pub. 1890). [*Comus* 27–9] (861).
Blondel, Jacques. *Le "Comus" de John Milton: masque neptunien* [French translation, with introduction (pp. 11–92) and notes]. Paris: Presses Universitaires, 1964 (835–7, 1044).
Brooks, Cleanth and J. E. Hardy. *Poems of Mr. John Milton: The 1645 Edition with Essays in Analysis.* New York: Harcourt, Brace, 1951 [*Nat*] (48, 1022).
Browne, R. C. *English Poems by John Milton.* 2 v. Clarendon Press, 1870; rev. 1894 [*Nat* 75] (77).
Bullough, Geoffrey and Margaret. *Milton's Dramatic Poems* [*Arc, Comus, SA*]. London: U. of London P.; Fair Lawn, N.J.: Essential Books, 1958 [*Comus*] (828).
Burden, D. H. *The Shorter Poems of John Milton.* London and New York, 1970.
Bush, Douglas. *Complete Poetical Works.* Boston: Houghton Mifflin, 1965; London: Oxford U. P., 1966, 1969 [*Vac*] (136–7).
— *A Variorum Commentary on The Poems* [without a text]: *The Latin and Greek Poems*: D. Bush; *The Italian Poems*: J. E. Shaw and A. B. Giamatti. London: Routledge; New York: Columbia U. P., 1970. [Cited as *V.C.* 1] (15).
Carey, John and Alastair Fowler. *Poems.* London: Longmans, Green; New York: Atheneum 1968 [Minor poems and *SA* edited by Carey] [*Nat*] (36, 1020).
Darbishire, Helen. *The Manuscript of Milton's Paradise Lost Book I.* Clarendon Press, 1931 (1085).
— *Poetical Works.* 2 v. Clarendon Press, 1952–5 (14).
Diekhoff, J. S. *A Maske at Ludlow...With the Bridgewater Version of Comus* [see Diekhoff in the index above].
Elledge, Scott. *Milton's "Lycidas" edited to serve as An Introduction to Criticism.* New York and London: Harper & Row, 1966 (550, n. 1).

Elton, Oliver. *Comus*. Clarendon Press, 1894; repr. 1928 [*Comus*] (773).
— *L'Allegro*. Clarendon Press, 1893 [*L'All* 45–6] (282).
— *Lycidas*. Clarendon Press, 1893; repr. 1929 (569).
Fenton, Elijah. *Paradise Lost*. London, 1725 [*Sonn* 23] (486).
Fletcher, Harris F. *Complete Poetical Works*. Boston: Houghton Mifflin, 1941 [*Lyc* 130–1: I. b. 2] (690, 1055).
— *Complete Poetical Works Reproduced in Photographic Facsimile*. 4 v. Urbana: U. of Illinois P., 1943–8. [Vol. 1 cited as *Facs*.] (21–2).
Frye, Northrop. *Paradise Lost and Selected Poetry and Prose*. New York: Rinehart, 1951 [*L'All* 45–6] (283).
Garrod, H. W. *Poemata* (in H. Darbishire, v. 2, 1955) (14).
Grierson, H. J. C. *Poems...in English Latin Greek & Italian Arranged in Chronological Order*. 2 v. London: Chatto & Windus, 1925 (12).
Hales, John W. *Longer English Poems*. London: Macmillan, 1880 [first pub. 1872]. [General anthology, incl. *Nativity, L'Allegro, Il Penseroso, Lycidas*] [*L'All* 35–6] (278).
Hanford, James Holly. *Poems*. New York: Nelson, 1936; rev. and enlar., New York: Ronald Press, 1953 (17).
Hawkins, Edward. *Poetical Works*. 4 v. Oxford, 1824 [*L'All* 67–8] (287).
Honigmann, E. A. J. *Milton's Sonnets*. London: Macmillan; New York: St Martin's Press, 1966 (350, 1078).
Hughes, Merritt Y. *Paradise Regained, the Minor Poems, and Samson Agonistes*. New York: Odyssey Press, 1937 [cited as Hughes, 1937] [*Ps* 114. 1] (115).
— *Complete Poems and Major Prose*. New York: Odyssey Press, 1957 [cited as Hughes] (16, n. 2).
Jerram, C. S. *The Lycidas and Epitaphium Damonis of Milton*. London, 1874; rev. 1881 [*Lyc* 1–2] (640).
Keightley, Thomas. *Poems*. 2 v. London, 1859 [*Nat* 56] (74).
Le Comte, E. *Paradise Lost and other poems*. New York: New American Library; London: New English Library, 1961 [*Lyc* 68–9] (661).
MacCaffrey, Isabel G. *Samson Agonistes and the Shorter Poems*. New York: New American Library; London: New English Library, 1966 [*Nat*] (58).
Mack, Maynard. *Milton* [selections]. New York: Prentice-Hall, 1950 [*Nat*] (47).
MacKellar, Walter. *Variorum Commentary on Paradise Regained*. London: Routledge; New York: Columbia U. P. Forthcoming. [*Nat* 173] (96).
Madsen, William G. *Milton* [selections]. New York: Dell, 1964 [*Lyc*] (621).

Masson, David. *Poetical Works.* 3 v. London: Macmillan, 1874 (1014);
Poetical Works. 3 v. London and New York: Macmillan, 1890 [cited as
P.W.] (12).

Mitford, John. *Poetical Works.* 3 v. London, 1834–5 [*Lyc* 130–1 : I. a. 3] (689).

Moody, William Vaughn. *Complete Poetical Works.* Boston: Houghton
Mifflin, 1899; partly rev. by E. K. Rand, 1924 [*L'All* and *IlPen*] (243).

Mossner, Ernest C. *Justa Edouardo King: Reproduced from the Original
Edition, 1638.* New York: Facsimile Text Society, 1939 [*Lyc*] (545).

Newton, Thomas. *Paradise Regain'd,...Samson Agonistes: and Poems upon
Several Occasions.* London, 1752 [*Lyc*] (1064, n. 70).

— *Poetical Works.* 3 v. London, 1761–2 [*FInf* 53–4] (132).

Nicolson, Marjorie H. *Poems and Selected Prose.* New York: Bantam Books,
1962 [*L'All* 67–8] (287).

Patrides, C. A. *Milton's Lycidas: The Tradition and the Poem.* New York:
Holt, Rinehart and Winston, 1961 [*Lyc*] (566).

Patterson, Frank A. et al. *Works.* 20 v. New York: Columbia U. P., 1931–40
[cited as *Works*] (xi).

Patterson, F. A. *The Student's Milton...complete poems...with the greater
part of his prose works.* New York: Crofts, 1930; rev. 1933 [*L'All* 35–6]
(278–9).

Pattison, Mark. [Selections] *The English Poets,* ed. T. Humphry Ward.
London and New York: Macmillan, 2, 1880, 293–379 [*Shak*] (204).

— *The Sonnets of Milton.* London and New York, 1883 [*Sonn* 1. 4] (359).

Phillips, Edward. *Letters of State, Written by Mr. John Milton...To which
is added, An Account of his Life. Together with several of his Poems.* London,
1694 [*FInf*] (119).

Prince, F. T. *Comus and other Poems.* London: Oxford U. P., 1968 [cited as
Comus] [*Nat*] (69, 1020).

Rolfe, W. J. *The Minor Poems of John Milton.* New York: Harper, 1887
[*Nat* 41] (71).

Shawcross, J. T. *Complete English Poetry of John Milton.* New York: New
York U. P. and Doubleday, 1963 [cited as *C.E.P.*] (17).

Smart, J. S. *The Sonnets of Milton.* Glasgow: Maclehose, 1921; repr.,
Clarendon Press, 1966 (342, 1074).

Tillyard, E. M. W. and P. B. *Milton: Private Correspondence and Academic
Exercises.* Cambridge U. P.; New York: Macmillan, 1932 (16, n. 2).

— *Comus and Some Shorter Poems of Milton.* London: Harrap, 1952 [*Lyc*
130–1 : I. d. 2] (698).

Todd, Henry J. *Comus...With Notes Critical and Explanatory by Various Commentators.* Canterbury, 1798 (773).

— *Poetical Works...With the Principal Notes of Various Commentators.* 6 v. London, 1801; 5th ed., 4 v. London, 1852 [the edition cited here] [*Nat* 14] (65).

Trent, William P. *John Milton's L'Allegro, Il Penseroso, Comus, and Lycidas.* New York: Longmans, Green, 1897 [*L'All* 45-6] (281).

Van Doren, Mark and H. Foss. *The Masque of Comus.* New York: Heritage Press, [1955]. [See Visiak below] (822-3).

Verity, A. W. *Milton's Arcades and Comus.* Cambridge U. P., 1891 [*Arc*] (531).

— *Milton's Ode on the Morning of Christ's Nativity, L'Allegro, Il Penseroso and Lycidas.* Cambridge U. P., 1924 (first pub. 1891) [*Nat* 7] (64).

— *Comus & Lycidas.* Cambridge U. P., 1919 (first pub. 1898) [*Lyc* 1-2] (640).

— *Comus.* Cambridge U. P., 1921 (first pub. 1909) (853, 1032).

— *Milton's Sonnets.* Cambridge U. P., 1916 (first pub. 1895; rev. 1898f.) (359).

Visiak, E. H. and H. Foss. *The Mask of Comus.* London: Nonesuch Press, 1937 (739).

Visiak, E. H. *Milton: Complete Poetry and Selected Prose.* London: Nonesuch Press; New York: Random House, [1938] [*IlPen* 156] (334).

Warton, Thomas. *Poems upon Several Occasions...by John Milton.* London, 1785; rev. and enlar., 1791 [*Nat* 52] (73).

Williams, Charles. *The English Poems of John Milton.* London and New York: Oxford U. P., 1940 [*Comus*] (800).

Wolfe, Don M. et al. *Complete Prose Works.* 8 v., in progress. Vols. 1-2, New Haven: Yale U. P.; London: Oxford U. P., 1953-9; vols. 3-5, New Haven and London: Yale U. P., 1962-71 [cited as *C.P.W.*] (16, n. 2).

Wright, B. A. *Shorter Poems of John Milton.* London: Macmillan; New York: St. Martin's Press, 1961 (first pub. 1938) [*Nat* 180] (98).

— *Milton's Poems.* London: Dent; New York: Dutton, 1956 [*Comus* 552] (924, 1086).

Wright, William A. *Facsimile of the Manuscript of Milton's Minor Poems Preserved in the Library of Trinity College Cambridge.* Cambridge U. P., 1899 (reproduced by Scolar Press, 1970) (21).

— *Poetical Works.* Cambridge U. P., 1903 [*Comus* 552] (923).

Minsheu, John. *Ductor in Linguas, The Guide into Tongues* [*Lyc* 186] (731).

Mirour For Magistrates, A, ed. R. Niccols. London, 1610 [*Comus* 864] (963).

Myhr, I. L. [*Nat* 89] (80).
Mylius, Hermann (447).

Nabbes, Thomas. *Microcosmus. A Morall Maske* [*Comus*] (750).
Nashe, Thomas. *Works*, ed. R. B. McKerrow. 5 v. London: Sidgwick and Jackson, 1904–10 [*Nat* 124] (85).
Neilson, William A. *The Origins and Sources of the Court of Love* [*L'All* 122–4] (301).
Neiman, F. *Sonn* 20. 13–14 (475).
Nelson, James G. *The Sublime Puritan: Milton and the Victorians*. U. of Wisconsin P., 1963 [*Lyc*] (567–8).
Nelson, Lowry, *Nativity* (51); *Baroque Lyric Poetry*. New Haven and London: Yale U. P., 1961 (51).
Nelson, William. *The Poetry of Edmund Spenser* [*Comus* 1002–10] (986).
Nemesian [*Lyc*] (554).
Nemser, Ruby. *Lyc* 176 (729).
Nethercot, A. H. 'Milton, Jonson, and the Young Cowley' [*Sonn* 7. 4–8] (371).
Neuse, R. *Comus* (844).
Niccols, Richard. *The Cuckow* [*May* 1–2] (202).
Nicholson, B. *Sonn* 22. 1 (482).
Nicoll, Allardyce. *Stuart Masques and the Renaissance Stage*. London: Harrap, 1937; New York: Harcourt, Brace, 1938 [*Comus*] (740, n. 1).
Nicolson, M. H. 'Milton's "Old Damoetas"' [*Lyc* 23–36] (647); 'The Spirit World of Milton and More' [*Comus* 1–4] (855); *John Milton: A reader's guide to his poetry*. New York: Farrar, Straus, 1963 [*L'All* and *IlPen*] (265). See also Milton, editions.
Nitchie, G. W. *Lyc* 124–31 (684, 1072).
Norlin, George. 'The Conventions of the Pastoral Elegy' [*Lyc*] (550, n. 1).

Oakley, J. H. I. *Sonn* 22. 1 (482).
O'Brien, Gordon W. *Renaissance Poetics and the Problem of Power*. Chicago: Institute of Elizabethan Studies, 1956 [*Lyc* 70] (663).
Ogden, H. V. S. 'The Principles of Variety and Contrast in Seventeenth Century Aesthetics and Milton's Poetry' [*L'All* 71–82] (289).
Oldenburg, Henry (471).
Oman, Sir Charles. 'Of Poor Mr. King, John Milton, and Certain Friends.' *Cornhill Magazine* 156 (1937), 377–87 [*Lyc*] (546).

Saillens, Emile. *Comus* (831); 'The Dating of Milton's Sonnet XIX' [*Sonn* 19. 2] (464); *John Milton: Man—Poet—Polemist* [tr. *John Milton, poète combattant*, Paris, 1959]. Oxford: Blackwell; New York: Barnes & Noble, 1964 [*Shak*] (203).

Saintsbury, George. *A Short History of English Literature*. London, 1919 (first pub. 1898) [*Lyc*] (569); ed. *Minor Poets of the Caroline Period*. 3 v. Clarendon Press, 1905–21 [*Nat* 10–11] (65); *A History of English Prosody*. 3 v. London: Macmillan, 1923 (first pub. 1908–10) (1015); 'Milton and the Grand Style' [*Lyc*] (569); 'Milton.' *Cambridge Hist. Eng. Lit.*, v. 7, 1911 [*Nat*] (40).

Saltonstall, Wye. *Picturae Loquentes*, ed. Wilkinson [*L'All* and *IlPen*] (240).

SAMLA Studies in Milton, ed. J. M. Patrick. U. of Florida P., 1953 [*Comus*] (765).

Sampson, Alden. *Studies in Milton* [*Sonn* 1] (357).

Samuel, Irene. *Plato and Milton*. Cornell U. P.; Oxford U. P., 1947 [*Comus*] (780); 'The Brood of Folly' [*L'All* and *IlPen*] (238).

Sandys, Edwin. *Sermons* [*Sonn* 7. 8] (371).

Sandys, George. *A Relation of a Journey begun An: Dom: 1610* [*Nat* 205–10] (102); *Ovid's Metamorphosis Englished*. London, 1626 [cited as *Ovid*] [*Nat* 8] (65); *Ovid's Metamorphosis English'd, Mythologiz'd*, etc. Oxford, 1632 (repr., U. of Nebraska P., 1970) [*Nat* 197] (101).

Sandys, Sir John E. 'The Literary Sources of Milton's "Lycidas" ' (550, n. 1).

Sannazaro, J. *De Partu Virginis. Poemata*, ed. Vulpius. Padua, 1731 [*Nat* 72–3] (76); Pastoral elegies [*Lyc*] (557); *Jacopo Sannazaro: Arcadia & Piscatorial Eclogues*, tr. Ralph Nash [*Lyc*] (557).

Sarpi, Paolo [*NewF* 13–14] (515–16).

Saunders, J. W. 'Milton, Diomede and Amaryllis' [*L'All* and *IlPen*] (259).

Saurat, Denis. *Milton: Man and Thinker*. London: Cape; New York: Dial Press, 1925; rev. 1944 [*Comus*] (794).

Schaus, H. *Comus, Hero and Leander*, and *Venus and Adonis* [*Comus*] (775).

Schipper, Jakob. *A History of English Versification*. Clarendon Press, 1910 (1019).

Schlüter, Kurt. *Die englische Ode: Studien zu ihrer Entwicklung unter dem Einfluss der antiken Hymne*. Bonn: Bouvier, 1964 [*Nat*] (40).

Schoeck, R. J. *Lyc* 68–9 (661); *Lyc* 71 (663).

Scholderer, V. 'Milton's "Cato" ' [*Sonn* 20. 13–14] (476).

Scholes, Percy A. *The Oxford Companion to Music*. London: Oxford U. P., ed. 1950 [*Nat* 130] (87).

Schultz, H. *Sonn* 11. 12–14 (392).
Schweitzer, E. C. *Lyc* 164 (724).
Scot, Reginald. *The discoverie of witchcraft* [*Nat* 173] (97).
Scott, Sir Walter. *A Legend of Montrose* [*Sonn* 11. 8–11] (391); *Marmion* [*L'All* 104] (296).
Scott-Craig, T. S. K. 'Milton's Song' [*SolMus*]. *Dartmouth College Library Bulletin* 11, n.s. (1970–1), 19–24.
Seaton, Ethel. '*Comus* and Shakespeare' (807).
Secundus, Joannes. *Opera*. 2 v. Leyden, 1821 [*Lyc* 68–9] (661).
Selden, John. *De Dis Syris* [*Nat* 197] (101); Illustrations of *Poly-Olbion* [*Lyc* 52–3] (655).
Sellar, W. Y. *The Roman Poets of the Augustan Age* [*Lyc*] (551).
Sensabaugh, G. F. 'The Milieu of *Comus*' (780).
Servii Grammatici...in Virgilii Carmina Commentarii, ed. G. Thilo and H. Hagen. 3 v. Leipzig, 1881–1902 [*FInf* 22–8] (130).
Shafer, Robert. *The English Ode to 1660*. Princeton U. P., 1918 [*Nat*] (39, 1020).
Shakespeare. *Complete Works*, ed. G. L. Kittredge. Boston: Ginn, 1936 [*Nat* 7] (64), [*Comus*] (765); Folios and *Poems*, 1640 [*Shak*] (203–4).
Shattuck, C. H. 'Macready's *Comus*: A Prompt-Book Study' (755).
Shaw, J. E., and A. B. Giamatti. *V.C.* 1 [*Sonn* 1] (355).
Shawcross, John T. *Sonn* 15. 6–8 (412); *Sonn* 23 (487); *Sonn* 19 (445); 'The Manuscript of "Arcades"' [*Time*] (163), [*Arc*] (520); (1087, n. 97); 'Certain Relationships of the Manuscripts of *Comus*' (737); 'Speculations on the Dating of the Trinity MS. of Milton's Poems' (22), [*Time*] (163), [*Arc*] (520); (1087, n. 97); 'Division of Labor in *Justa Edouardo King*' [*Lyc*] (546, n. 1); 'Two Milton Notes: "Clio" and Sonnet 11.' *N&Q* 8, (1961), 178–80 (393); 'The Chronology of Milton's Major Poems' (1046, n. 52); 'Establishment of a Text of Milton's Poems Through a Study of *Lycidas*' (548; 1087, n. 97); 'What We Can Learn from Milton's Spelling' (1087, n. 98); 'One Aspect of Milton's Spelling: Idle Final "E"' (1086, n. 94); 'Of Chronology and the Dates of Milton's Translation from Horace and the *New Forcers of Conscience*.' *SEL* 3 (1963), 77–84 (12–13); 'Milton's Decision to Become a Poet' (26); 'Henry Lawes's Settings of Songs for Milton's "Comus"' (740, n. 1; 1087, n. 97); 'The Dating of Certain Poems, Letters, and Prolusions Written by Milton' (16, n. 2); 'The Date of the Separate Edition of Milton's "Epitaphium Damonis."' *SB* 18 (1965), 262–5 (23, n. 3); 'Milton's *Nectar*: Symbol of Immortality' [*FInf*] (126); 'A Note on Milton's Hobson Poems' (214); 'The Prosody

Smith, William. *Chloris* [*Sonn* 23] (491).

Soden, G. I. *Godfrey Goodman* [*Lyc* 128–9] (686).

Songs of Praise, ed. P. Dearmer et al. London: Oxford U. P., 1925; enlar. 1931 [*Psalms*] (998).

Spaeth, S. G. *Milton's Knowledge of Music* [cited as *Music*]. Princeton University Library, 1913; ed. W. G. Rice, U. of Michigan P., 1963 [*Nat*] (40).

Spencer, H. 'A Greek Source for *Comus* 30' (862).

Spencer, Lois. 'The Professional and Literary Connexions of George Thomason'; 'The Politics of George Thomason' [*Sonn* 14] (406).

Spencer, T. J. B., et al., eds. *A Book of Masques in Honour of Allardyce Nicoll*. Cambridge U. P., 1967 [*L'All* 26–36] (277).

Spencer, Theodore. 'Shakespeare and Milton' [*Shak*] (208).

Spengel, L., ed. *Rhetores Graeci* [*Lyc*] (637).

Spenser, Edmund. *Works: A Variorum Edition*, ed. E. Greenlaw et al. 10 v. Johns Hopkins Press, 1932–57 [*Nat* 1] (64): *Poetical Works*, ed. Smith and De Selincourt [*Vac* 100] (150); *Amoretti* [*Time* 21] (169); *Colin Clouts Come Home Againe* [*IlPen* 35] (316); *Epithalamion* [*Nat* 21] (66); *Faerie Queene* [*Nat* 1] (64), [*Comus* III. 4] (762–5); *Fowre Hymnes* [*Nat*] (39); *Hymne of Heavenly Beautie* [*FInf* 57] (134); *Hymne of Heavenly Love* [*Nat* 8–14] (64); *M. Hubberds Tale* [*FInf* 48] (132); *Ruines of Time* [*Nat* 96–7] (81); *Shepheardes Calender* [cited as *S.C.*] [*Nat* 10] (65).

Spevack-Husmann, Helga. *The Mighty Pan: Miltons Mythologische Vergleiche* [*Nat* 89] (80).

Spingarn, J. E., ed. *Critical Essays of the Seventeenth Century*. 3 v. Clarendon Press, 1908–9 [*IlPen* 116–29] (329).

Spitzer, Leo. *Classical and Christian Ideas of World Harmony*, ed. A. G. Hatcher. Baltimore: Johns Hopkins Press, 1963 [*Nat* 125–32] (85); 'Understanding Milton.' *Essays on English and American Literature*, ed. A. Hatcher. Princeton U. P., 1962 [*Sonn* 23] (492).

Sprott, S. Ernest. *Milton's Art of Prosody*. Oxford: Blackwell, 1953 (1016).

Stafford, Anthony. *Niobe: or His Age of teares* [*Comus* 885] (967).

Stanford, W. B. *The Ulysses Theme: A Study in the Adaptability of a Traditional Hero* [*Comus* 50–6] (864).

Stanley, Arthur P. *Historical Memorials of Westminster Abbey* [*Lyc* 151] (717).

Stanyhurst, Richard, tr. *The first Four Books of the Æneis*, ed. Arber. London, 1880 [*Nat* 64–5] (75).

Stapleton, Laurence. 'Milton and the New Music' [*Nativity*] (48).

Starnes, DeWitt T., and E. W. Talbert. *Classical Myth and Legend in Renaissance Dictionaries.* U. of North Carolina P., 1955 [cited as Starnes-Talbert] [*L'All* 11–16] (274).

Starnes, D. T. 'The Figure Genius in the Renaissance' [*Arc*, 'After 25'] (535).

Steadman, John M. ' "Haemony" and Christian Moly.' *History of Ideas Newsletter* 4 (1958), 59–60 [*Comus* 635–6] (932); 'St. Peter and Ecclesiastical Satire' [*Lyc* 108–31] (677); 'Milton's "Walls of Glass" (Psalm 136)' [*Ps* 136. 38–9] (117); 'Milton's *Haemony*: Etymology and Allegory' [*Comus* 637] (933); 'Dalila, the Ulysses Myth, and Renaissance Allegorical Tradition' [*Comus* 50–6] (864).

Stebbins, Eunice B. *The Dolphin in the Literature and Art of Greece and Rome* [*Lyc* 164] (724).

Stephanus, Carolus (Charles Estienne). *Dictionarium Historicum, Geographicum, Poeticum.* Ed. Geneva, 1621 [*L'All* 2–3] (271).

Stephanus, Robertus (Robert Estienne). *Thesaurus Linguae Latinae.* Lyons, 1573 [*Sonn* 10. 6–8] (385).

Steuart (Stewart), Adam [*NewF* 8] (514).

Stevens, D. H. 'The Order of Milton's Sonnets' (19, 340); 'The Bridgewater MS. of Comus.' *MP* 24 (1926–7), 315–20.

Stoehr, T. 'Syntax and Poetic Form in Milton's Sonnets' (350, 1080).

Stoll, E. E. *Poets and Playwrights.* U. of Minnesota P., 1930 [*L'All* 99] (294).

Stone, C. F. *Lycidas* (630).

Storrs, Sir Ronald, ed. *Ad Pyrrham: A Polyglot Collection of Translations.* London and New York: Oxford U. P., 1959 [*Hor*] (506).

Stradling, Sir John. *Divine Poemes* [*Nat* 23] (67).

Strathmann, E. A. '*Lycidas* and the Translation of "May" ' [*Lyc*, Title] (637).

Striggio, A., and C. Monteverdi. *La favola d'Orfeo* [*Lyc*] (565).

Stringer, G. 'The Unity of "L'Allegro" and "Il Penseroso." ' *TSLL* 12 (1970), 221–9.

Strode, William. *Poetical Works*, ed. Dobell [*L'All* and *IlPen*] (241).

Strong, Eugenie. *Apotheosis and After Life* [*Lyc* 164] (724).

Stroup, Thomas B. 'Implications of the Theory of Climatic Influence in Milton' [*Arc* 24] (534); '*Lycidas and the Marinell Story*' (560, n. 12); 'Aeneas' Vision of Creusa and Milton's Twenty-third Sonnet' (491); *Religious Rite & Ceremony in Milton's Poetry.* U. of Kentucky P., 1968 [*Lyc*] (631).

Studley, Marian H. 'Milton and his Paraphrases of the Psalms' (991).

Sullivan, Mary. *Court Masques of James I* [*Comus*] (740, n. 1).

Summers, Joseph H., ed. *The Lyric and Dramatic Milton.* New York and London: Columbia U. P., 1965 [*Nat*] (57).

Surrey, Henry Howard, Earl of [*Sonnets*] (1074–5); *Poems*, ed. F. M. Padelford, U. of Washington P., 1928 [*Sonn* 15. 1–4] (411).

Svendsen, Kester. *Sonn* 18 (435); *Sonn* 7. 13–14 (372); *L'All* and *IlPen* (252); *Milton and Science.* Harvard U. P.; Oxford U. P., 1956 [*FInf* 16] (130).

Sylvester, Josuah, tr. *Du Bartas His Divine Weekes and Workes*, etc. London, 1621 [cited as *D. W. W.*] (xi); *Complete Works*, ed. Grosart (xi–xii).

Symonds, John Addington. 'The Blank Verse of Milton' (1047).

Sypher, Wylie. *Four Stages of Renaissance Style.* New York: Doubleday, 1955 [*Lyc*] (600).

Taaffe, J. G. 'Michaelmas, the "Lawless Hour," and the Occasion of Milton's *Comus*' (736).

'tale, tells his' [*L'All* 67–8 n.] (287–9). On the meaning of this phrase the note cites 20 editors and these commentators: A. Ainger, T. I. Bennett, S. Beauchamp, 'Pelagius,' *OED*, and J. M. Hart.

Tasso, Torquato. *Aminta* [*Comus*] (766–7); *Opere*, ed. G. Rosini. 33 v. Pisa, 1821–32 [*Nat*] (36); *Opere*, ed. G. Gherardini. 5 v. Milan, 1823–5 [*Nat*] (36); *Poesie*, ed. F. Flora. Milan, 1952 [*Nat* 55] (74); *Prose*, ed. Flora. Milan, 1935 [*Comus*, 1st Direction] (853).

Tate, Eleanor. *L'All* and *IlPen* (264).

Taylor, Dick. 'Grace as a Means of Poetry: Milton's Pattern for Salvation' [*Comus*] (818).

Taylor, G. C. 'Milton's English' [*Lyc*] (576).

Taylor, Jeremy. *Holy Dying* [*Comus*] (776).

Taylor, Thomas. *A Commentarie upon the Epistle of S. Paul to Titus* [*Nat* 136] (89).

Tennyson, Hallam, Lord. *Alfred Lord Tennyson: A Memoir.* 2 v. London, 1897 [*Lyc*] (569).

Tertullian. *Apologeticus* [*Sonn* 18. 10–14] (440).

Thaler, Alwin, 'The Shaksperian Element in Milton' [*Comus*] (765); 'Milton in the Theatre' [*Comus*] (754).

Theocritus, Bion and Moschus, tr. Andrew Lang. London: Macmillan, 1913 (first pub. 1880) [*Lyc*] (552, n. 5).

Thomas, Walter. 'Milton's Heroic Line Viewed from an Historical Standpoint' (1042).

Thomason, Catherine and George [*Sonn* 14] (406).

Thompson, Sir D'Arcy W. *A Glossary of Greek Birds* [*L'All* 7] (272).

Thompson, E. N. S. 'The Octosyllabic Couplet' (1029).

Thompson, W. L. 'The Source of the Flower Passage in "Lycidas" ' [*Lyc* 142–51] (714).

Thorpe, James, ed. *Milton Criticism*. New York: Rinehart, 1950 (1046).

Tillotson, Geoffrey. *On the Poetry of Pope*. Clarendon Press, 1938 [*Comus* 115] (876).

Tillyard, E. M. W. *Milton*. London: Chatto & Windus; New York: Dial Press, 1930 [*Nat*] (42); 'Milton: *L'Allegro* and *Il Penseroso*' (225, 1036); *Poetry Direct and Oblique*. London: Chatto & Windus, 1934 [*Lyc*] (573); 'Milton and the English Epic Tradition' [*Vac*] (139); *The Miltonic Setting Past & Present*. Cambridge U. P.; New York: Macmillan, 1938; Chatto & Windus, 1947; New York: Barnes & Noble, 1961 [cited as *M. Set.*] [*Vac*] (139); 'Milton and Keats' [*Lyc*] (573); 'The Action of *Comus*' (805–6); *Studies in Milton*. London: Chatto & Windus; New York: Macmillan, 1951; Barnes & Noble, 1963 [*Circum*] (171); *The Metaphysicals and Milton*. Chatto & Windus, 1956 [*Sonn* 23] (494). See also Milton, editions.

Tillyard, P. B. *L'All* 28 (277).

'MS. Todd.' *Comus* 349–65 n. (904).

Todd, W. B. 'The Issues and States of the Second Folio and Milton's Epitaph on Shakespeare' (203).

Toland, John [*Comus*] (736).

Tomkis, Thomas. *Albumazar* [*Shak* 7–14] (210).

Torquemada, Antonio de. *The Spanish Mandevile of Myracles* [*IlPen* 88–96] (324).

Tottel's Miscellany, ed. Arber; ed. Rollins [*L'All* and *IlPen*] (230).

Tovey, Sir Donald. 'Words and Music' [*Sonn* 13] (402).

Townshend's Poems and Masks, Aurelian, ed. E. K. Chambers. Clarendon Press, 1912 [*Comus*] (751).

Toynbee, Paget. *Dante in English Literature*. 2 v. London: Methuen; New York: Macmillan, 1909 [*Lyc* 108–31] (676).

Trapp, J. B. 'The Owl's Ivy and the Poet's Bays: An Enquiry into Poetic Garlands' [*Lyc* 1–2] (640).

Traver, Hope. *The Four Daughters of God* [*Nat* 141–6] (91).

Treip, Mindele. *Milton's Punctuation and Changing English Usage 1582–1676*. London: Methuen; New York: Barnes & Noble, 1970.

Trench, R. C. *IlPen* 17–18 (312).

Tronsarelli, Ottavio. *La Catena d'Adone* [*Comus*] (767).

Tuckwell, W. *"Lycidas": A Monograph* (570).

Warner, Rex. *John Milton*. London: Parrish, 1949; New York: Chanticleer Press, 1950 [*Nat*] (47).

Warner, William. *Albion's England* [*IlPen* 23–30] (314).

Watkins, W. B. C. *An Anatomy of Milton's Verse*. Louisiana State U. P., 1955 [*Comus*] (823).

Watson, Sara R. ' "Moly" in Drayton and Milton' [*Comus* 635–6] (931); Haemony [*Comus* 637] (932); *Lyc* 193 (734); 'Milton's Ideal Day: Its Development as a Pastoral Theme' [*L'All* and *IlPen*] (228).

Watson, Thomas. *Poems*, ed. Arber [*Lyc*] (561–2).

Webb, C. C. J. *John of Salisbury* [*Lyc* 71] (663).

Weitzman, A. J. *Sonn* 18. 10–14 (440).

Welsford, Enid. *The Court Masque: A Study in the Relationship of Poetry and the Revels*. Cambridge U. P., 1927 [*Comus*] (742).

West, H. F. *L'All* [on R. Graves] (261).

West, Robert H. *Milton and the Angels* [*SolMus* 10–11] (187).

Whaler, James. *Counterpoint and Symbol: An Inquiry into the Rhythm of Milton's Epic Style* (1044).

Wheeler, Thomas. *Sonn* 23 (495); 'Magic and Morality in *Comus*' (833).

Whichcote, Benjamin [*Sonn* 20. 13–14] (475).

Whiteley, M. 'Verse and Its Feet' (1017).

Whiting, G. W. *Milton's Literary Milieu*. U. of North Carolina P., 1939 [*L'All* and *IlPen*] (234); 'Milton and Cockeram's "Dictionarie" ' [*L'All* 24] (276); *Milton and This Pendant World*. U. of Texas P., 1958 [*Lyc* 110–11] (680).

Whittick, Arnold. *Symbols, Signs and their meaning*. London: L. Hill, 1960 [*Lyc* 192] (733).

Wierus, Joannes. *De Praestigiis Daemonum* [*Comus* 635–6] (931).

Wilde, H.-O. *Sonn* 19 (452).

Wilkenfeld, R. B. *Comus* (843); 'Miltonic Criticism and the "Dramatic Axiom" ' [*Comus*] (844).

Wilkinson, D. 'The Escape from Pollution: A Comment on *Comus*' (832).

Wilkinson, L. P. *Ovid Recalled*. Cambridge U. P., 1955 [*Lyc* 58–63] (657).

Willcock, John. *Life of Sir Henry Vane the Younger* [*Sonn* 17] (426).

Willetts, Pamela J. *The Henry Lawes Manuscript*. London: British Museum, 1969.

William of Worcester. *Itinerarium* [*Lyc* 161–2] (721).

Williams, Charles. 'Milton.' *The English Poetic Mind* [*Lyc*] (576). See also Milton, editions.

Williams, R. F., ed. *The Court and Times of Charles the First* [*EpWin*] (192).

Williams, Roger. *Queries of Highest Consideration* [*NewF*] (511); *The Bloudy Tenent, of Persecution, for cause of Conscience* [*Sonn* 16] (417); *The Hireling Ministry None of Christs* [*Sonn* 16] (419).

Williamson, George. 'The Obsequies for Edward King.' *Seventeenth Century Contexts*. London: Faber, 1960; U. of Chicago P., 1961 [cited as *S.C.C.*] [*Lyc*] (547); 'The Context of *Comus*.' *Milton and Others*. London: Faber; U. of Chicago P., 1965 (783).

Wilson, F. A. C. *W. B. Yeats and Tradition* [*Lyc* 164] (725).

Winchester, Jane Paulet, Marchioness of [*EpWin*] (192).

Wind, Edgar. *Bellini's Feast of the Gods: A Study in Venetian Humanism*. Harvard U. P., 1948 [*Comus*] (770); *Pagan Mysteries in the Renaissance*. London: Faber; New Haven: Yale U. P., 1958 [*Lyc* 175] (728).

Winter, Keith. *Lycidas* (632).

Wit Restor'd [*Carrier* 1] (214).

Wither, George. *Emblemes* [*Comus* 232] (893); *Faire-Virtue* [*L'All* 67–8] (288); *A Preparation to the Psalter* [*Psalms*] (992); *Prince Henries Obsequies* [*Sonn* 11. 4] (390); *The Shepheards Hunting* [*L'All* 67–8] (288).

Withim, P. M. *Sonn* 7 (368, 1080).

Wittreich, J. A. *Lycidas* (635, 1066); *Lyc* 192 (732).

Wood, Anthony. *Athenae Oxonienses*. 2 v. London, 1691–2 [*Sonn* 21] (477); *Life and Times of Anthony à Wood*, ed. L. Powys [*L'All* and *IlPen*] (238).

Woodcock, Katherine [*Sonn* 23] (486).

Woodhouse, A. S. P. 'Imitations of the "Ode to Evening"' [*Hor*] (507); *Puritanism and Liberty: Being the Army Debates (1647–9)*. London: Dent; U. of Chicago P., 1938; repr. 1950 [*Sonn* 15] (410–11); 'The Argument of Milton's *Comus*' (802); '*Comus* Once More' (802); 'Notes on Milton's Early Development' [cited as 'Notes'] (11, n. 1); 'Milton's Pastoral Monodies' [*Lycidas*] (593); *Milton the Poet*. Toronto and Vancouver: Dent, 1955 [*Sonn* 23] (494); *The Poet and his Faith*. Chicago and London: U. of Chicago P., 1965 [*Comus* 975–1022] (975); *A Preface to Milton*, ed. Hugh MacCallum. U. of Toronto P., 1972.

Wordsworth, William. *The Early Letters of William and Dorothy Wordsworth (1787–1805)*, ed. E. de Selincourt. Clarendon Press, 1935 [*Sonnets*] (344); *The Letters of William and Dorothy Wordsworth: The Later Years (1821–1850)*, ed. E. de Selincourt. 3 v. Clarendon Press, 1939 [*Sonnets*] (345); *Poetical Works*, ed. E. de Selincourt and H. Darbishire. 5 v. Clarendon Press, 1940–9 [*Sonnets*] (345, 1012).

Wotton, Sir Henry. *Reliquiae Wottonianae* [*Lyc* 71] (663); *Comus* (741, 760).

Wrenn, C. L. 'The Language of Milton' [*IlPen* 81–4] (323).

Wright, B. A. [*Comus* 1–4]. *TLS*, 4 August, 27 October, 1945, 367, 511 (854); 'Note on Milton's Use of the Word "Danger" ' [*Comus* 400] (909); 'Note on Milton's "Night-founder'd" ' [*Comus* 482] (918); ' "Shade" for "Tree" in Milton's Poetry' [*L'All* 8] (272); *Milton's 'Paradise Lost'*. London: Methuen; New York: Barnes & Noble, 1962 [*Comus* 428] (911). See also Milton, editions.

Wyatt, Sir Thomas [*Sonnets*] (1074).

Wyld, H. C. 'The Significance of -'*n* and -*en* in Milton's Spelling' (1086, n. 95).

Yates, Frances A. *The French Academies of the Sixteenth Century* [*SolMus* 1–2] (185); *Giordano Bruno and the Hermetic Tradition*. London: Routledge; U. of Chicago P., 1964 [*IlPen* 88] (324).

Young, Richard B., W. T. Furniss, and W. G. Madsen. *Three Studies in the Renaissance: Sidney, Jonson, Milton*. New Haven: Yale U. P., 1958 [*Comus*] (776–7).